Frommer's®

Walt Disney World® & Orlando

2007

by Laura Miller

Wiley Publishing, Inc.

About the Author

Laura Miller is a freelance writer based in Orchard Park, New York, though she's spent countless hours scouring Central Florida's theme parks, hotels, resorts, and restaurants over the years—both with and without her five children. A family-travel expert who religiously makes an annual pilgrimage (or two or three or more) to the Land the Mouse Built, she's currently writing a guide and operating a website filled with information on Central Florida just for families.

Published by:

Wiley Publishing, Inc.

111 River St.
Hoboken, NJ 07030

ISBN-13: 978-0-471-92291-9
ISBN-10: 0-471-92291-9

Editor: Naomi Kraus
Production Editor: Heather Wilcox
Cartographer: Elizabeth Puhl
Photo Editor: Richard Fox
Production by Wiley Indianapolis Composition Services

Front cover photo: Spaceship Earth and Monorail™ at Epcot, Walt Disney World Resort.
Back cover photo: Jurassic Park T-Rex at Universal Orlando.

For information on our other products and services or to obtain technical support, please contact our Customer Care Department within the U.S. at 800/762-2974, outside the U.S. at 317/572-3993 or fax 317/572-4002.

Wiley also publishes its books in a variety of electronic formats. Some content that appears in print may not be available in electronic formats.

Manufactured in the United States of America

5   4   3   2   1

Contents

4 Where to Stay   79

5 Where to Dine   125

6 Exploring Walt Disney World   178

List of Maps

Acknowledgments

I'd like to thank Amy Voss at the Orlando/Orange County Convention & Visitors Bureau; Gary Buchanan and Dave Herbst at Walt Disney World; Taryn Hari at Universal Orlando; and Jacquelyn Wilson at SeaWorld, not to mention all of the marketing and P.R. reps at the countless hotels and resorts, for all of their research assistance, not to mention their continued support during the many trips I made to the Orlando area while writing this book.

Thanks to my family, including my five kids—Ryan, Austin, Nicolas, Hailey, and Davis—my sister Cindy; my agent, Julie Hill; and last but not least, my parents. They all in some way, shape, or form played a part in this endeavor, whether it was spending endless hours touring the parks, hunting through the many hotels, helping to review the various restaurants, or simply making sure I was free to travel whenever necessary. I would also like to recognize a very special group of authors who over the past few years have been willing to share their insight and expertise—I thank you Herb, Tom, Bruce, Tim, Lee, and Allan for your continued support and encouragement.

And a special thanks to Naomi Kraus, my editor, not only for the time and effort she put into helping me with this project, but for the helpful advice and guidance she offered along the way—all of which I so greatly appreciate.

—Laura Miller

An Invitation to the Reader

In researching this book, we discovered many wonderful places—hotels, restaurants, shops, and more. We're sure you'll find others. Please tell us about them, so we can share the information with your fellow travelers in upcoming editions. If you were disappointed with a recommendation, we'd love to know that, too. Please write to:

Frommer's Walt Disney World® & Orlando 2007
Wiley Publishing, Inc. • 111 River St. • Hoboken, NJ 07030-5774

An Additional Note

Please be advised that travel information is subject to change at any time—and this is especially true of prices. We therefore suggest that you write or call ahead for confirmation when making your travel plans. The authors, editors, and publisher cannot be held responsible for the experiences of readers while traveling. Your safety is important to us, however, so we encourage you to stay alert and be aware of your surroundings. Keep a close eye on cameras, purses, and wallets, all favorite targets of thieves and pickpockets.

Other Great Guides for Your Trip:

Frommer's Florida
Walt Disney World® & Orlando For Dummies
Frommer's Irreverent Guide to Walt Disney World®
Frommer's Walt Disney World® with Kids
The Unofficial Guide to Walt Disney World®
Mini Mickey: The Pocket Sized Unofficial Guide to Walt Disney World®
Beyond Disney: The Unofficial Guide
Frommer's Florida's Best-Loved Driving Tours

Frommer's Star Ratings, Icons & Abbreviations

Every hotel, restaurant, and attraction listing in this guide has been ranked for quality, value, service, amenities, and special features using a **star-rating system**. In country, state, and regional guides, we also rate towns and regions to help you narrow down your choices and budget your time accordingly. Hotels and restaurants are rated on a scale of zero (recommended) to three stars (exceptional). Attractions, shopping, nightlife, towns, and regions are rated according to the following scale: zero stars (recommended), one star (highly recommended), two stars (very highly recommended), and three stars (must-see).

In addition to the star-rating system, we also use **seven feature icons** that point you to the great deals, in-the-know advice, and unique experiences that separate travelers from tourists. Throughout the book, look for:

Finds	Special finds—those places only insiders know about
Fun Fact	Fun facts—details that make travelers more informed and their trips more fun
Kids	Best bets for kids and advice for the whole family
Moments	Special moments—those experiences that memories are made of
Overrated	Places or experiences not worth your time or money
Tips	Insider tips—great ways to save time and money
Value	Great values—where to get the best deals

The following **abbreviations** are used for credit cards:

AE	American Express	DISC	Discover	V	Visa
DC	Diners Club	MC	MasterCard		

Frommers.com

Now that you have the guidebook to a great trip, visit our website at **www.frommers.com** for travel information on more than 3,000 destinations. With features updated regularly, we give you instant access to the most current trip-planning information available. At Frommers.com, you'll also find the best prices on airfares, accommodations, and car rentals—and you can even book travel online through our travel booking partners. At Frommers.com, you'll also find the following:

- Online updates to our most popular guidebooks
- Vacation sweepstakes and contest giveaways
- Newsletter highlighting the hottest travel trends
- Online travel message boards with featured travel discussions

What's New in Walt Disney World & Orlando

In keeping with its culture of "whatever you can do, I can do better," Orlando's theme parks try their darnedest to best each other, adding new attractions both big and small, and tweaking old ones to make them new and exciting again. Restaurants come and go in what seems like the blink of an eye, though fierce competition ensures a constant infusion of chic and trendy entries—the best of which remain year after year. And resorts continue to spring up at every turn, each bigger and better than the last. After the nightmare hurricane season of 2004, Orlando is once again growing rapidly, and 2006 was a particularly active year.

Downed trees alongside Walt Disney World's roadways are, for the most part, the only visual reminders of Charley, Ivan, and Jeanne, three of the most unwelcome visitors ever to land in the area, not to mention the most devastating hurricanes to make their way through Central Florida in decades. Face-lifts and renovations at the resorts (and other area businesses) still continue, but instead of repair work, construction crews are busy making enhancements in an effort to entice visitors. New rides, redesigned attractions, and accommodations in almost every category are being added to bring travelers back for more—often at a pace that's faster than I can write.

Here's a summary of just some of the things that have changed in the year since this Frommer's guide was last revised:

PLANNING YOUR TRIP The **Orlando Convention & Visitors Bureau** (or the Orlando CVB) not only offers information through its official website (**www.orlandoinfo.com**) and tourist center (8723 International Dr.) but now offers the services of official travel counselors (📞 **800/551-0181** or 407/363-5872) to help plan your Orlando vacation. Counselors are available from 8am to 7pm daily (except Christmas Day) to answer questions and assist visitors with everything from planning vacations to purchasing packages, attraction tickets, and more.

Disney World has added a fourth tier to their Magic Your Way vacation packages. The nearly all-inclusive Platinum Package offers personalized itinerary planning before your vacation, accommodations at select deluxe resorts, park tickets with all the frills, three meals a day at *any* of Disney's restaurants, and tons of additional perks—practically everything but the kitchen sink.

For tips on planning your vacation to Mickeyville, see chapter 2, "Planning Your Trip to Walt Disney World & Orlando."

WHERE TO STAY The Shingle Creek Resort (📞 866/996-9939) debuts in September 2006 near the Orlando Orange County Convention Center. The 1,500-room full-service convention resort will feature luxurious well-appointed accommodations along with extensive recreational facilities, including a rock climbing wall, several pools, and an 18-hole golf course. The world-renowned **Four Seasons** group will open its newest resort (and its fourth in Florida) in the picture-perfect town of Celebration in 2007. Expect lavish accommodations, indulgent amenities, and a first-class 18-hole golf course.

Veteran Orlando properties aren't resting on their laurels. **Disney's Contemporary Resort** (© 407/939-6244) has once again become . . . well . . . contemporary. Rooms have been completely redecorated to reflect a chic Asian flair that's far more upscale and sophisticated—finally worthy of the Disney name. **Disney's Polynesian Resort** (© 407/939-6244) has completely redecorated its rooms (and renovated its great ceremonial house) as well. Accommodations still have an island feel, but now have upgraded furnishings, including flatscreen TVs.

The **Renaissance Orlando Resort at SeaWorld** (© 800/327-6677 or 407/351-5555) recently gave its pool and outdoor recreational area a major face-lift and outfitted rooms with luxurious bedding. Now it's undergoing a $20-million makeover that includes the addition of an 8,000-square-foot full-service spa.

The **Hotel Royal Plaza** (© 407/828-2828), an old favorite, recently underwent extensive renovations and upgrades, adding new carpeting, furnishings, beds, and in-room media packages. And Universal's **Portofino Bay Hotel** (© 407/503-1000) has also redecorated. Rooms now feature a more sophisticated decor and added amenities.

For complete details on these and other lodging options in and around Orlando, see chapter 4, "Where to Stay."

WHERE TO DINE   Making a return to the Orlando dining scene is the **Chef's Table** at the Hyatt Regency Grand Cypress (© 407/239-1234). Offered Thursday through Sunday evenings, this experience allows guests to dine in an intimate private room with an exhibition kitchen that affords them the opportunity to watch and talk to the chef as their five-course dinner is prepared. Even at $85 per person (or $135 with wine pairing) it's well worth the splurge, and the price includes a personalized menu signed by the chef and a Grand Cypress apron.

The **Bubba Gump Shrimp Co.** (www.bubbagump.com or www.universalorlando.com) is the latest addition to Universal's CityWalk restaurant lineup. It takes the place of Decades Café near the CityWalk entrance (across from the Cineplex). This family-friendly eatery, based on the blockbuster hit *Forrest Gump*, brims with movie memorabilia, and offers a diverse menu that's not just for seafood lovers.

See chapter 5, "Where to Dine," for a complete menu of Orlando restaurants.

EXPLORING WALT DISNEY WORLD
WDW has announced that it will keep its convenient **Disney's Magical Express** program, which provides complimentary shuttle service between Orlando International Airport and any Disney-owned resort, running through 2011. Not only does the shuttle service get Disney resort guests to their hotels, but it also delivers their baggage straight from the plane to their room, allowing them to bypass luggage claim! The innovative service saves both time and money, not to mention a few of your back muscles. As an added bonus, guests can check their luggage and print out boarding passes for their return trip before leaving their Disney resort, allowing them to skip the long lines at the airport. Currently only select airlines participate in the program.

In the pricing department, Disney raised its prices at the beginning of 2006 to budget-busting levels. Stay only a day at a single park and you'll now pay a whopping $63 (not including tax!) for an adult and $52 for kids ages 3 to 9. Disney's **Magic Your Way** park ticket system does, however, reward vacationers who stay and play at the House of Mouse a bit longer than they may have before. Stay 4 days or longer and your price per day can drop significantly under the normal single-day ticket price, even if you tack on an extra option, such as park-hopping privileges. For complete details on the new pricing scheme, see p. 181.

The big news at Disney's theme parks (© **407/824-4321;** www.disneyworld. com) is the debut of **Expedition Everest** at Disney's Animal Kingdom. Set in the Himalayan Mountains, this thrill ride features some of the most impressive scenery and surroundings that Disney has ever created. You'll ride a speedy steam train that twists, turns, and spirals both forward and backward through the darkness of a mountain, before finally plummeting an incredible 80 feet to escape the formidable Yeti. All in all, it's a very impressive addition to a park that's been legitimately criticized for not featuring enough action.

At **MGM Studios** guests can walk through a gigantic wardrobe and onto a wintry set similar to that seen in *The Chronicles of Narnia: The Lion, The Witch, and the Wardrobe.* Props, costumes, and creatures straight from the movie fill the gallery at the end of the attraction.

The release of *Pirates of the Caribbean: The Curse of the Black Pearl* and its more-recent second installment, *Dead Man's Chest,* has revitalized not only the popularity of the Magic Kingdom's **Pirates of the Caribbean** attraction, but has inspired recent renovations that added Jack Sparrow and Barbossa to the set of swashbucklers. A tweak in the storyline and updated special effects have also been added to better mirror the movies.

At Downtown Disney, little girls will be transformed into enchanting little princesses at the **Bibbiddi Bobbiddi Boutique,** located within Downtown Disney's

World of Disney (© **407/939-7895** for appointments). The salon, debuting this past spring, offers makeovers and salon services for kids ages 3 and up—all performed by fairy-godmothers-in-training. Shimmering makeup, nail polish, and hairstyling services start at $35 but can run upwards of $175 for the royal treatment (which includes a Disney princess costume, accessories, and a photo package).

At press time Disney announced that it would kick off its "Year of a Million Dreams" celebration on October 1, 2006. The yearlong celebration will see the opening of several new attractions at Disney World, including an all-new *Finding Nemo*–themed musical at Animal Kingdom, and a *Monsters, Inc.*–themed comedy club in the Magic Kingdom. The year will also see Disney cast members giving away special treats in the parks to select visitors, including a 1-night stay in that holy of holies—Cinderella Castle.

See chapter 6, "Exploring Walt Disney World," and chapter 8, "Shopping," for complete details on all of Disney's latest improvements, events, shops, and rides.

EXPLORING UNIVERSAL ORLANDO & SEAWORLD Universal Studios Florida most recent addition is **Fear Factor Live** (© **800/837-2273** or 407/363-8000; www.universalorlando.com), the first-ever reality show turned into a theme-park attraction. Audience members become the stars of the show, performing stunts that test their courage, strength, and at times their stomach—similar to the stuff seen on the hit TV show, but live in Orlando.

Other news out of Universal Orlando includes higher single-day ticket prices ($63 adult, $52 kids ages 3–9). But the company is currently running *online* promotions that include some rather impressive options such as 3 days free (for a total of 5 days at the parks) for the price of a

2-day/two-park ticket; one free children's ticket for every purchase of a 2-day/two-park adult ticket; or a no-expiration option on purchased tickets. Even buying a single-day ticket online will save you a few dollars.

Other good news for Universal park-goers: In an attempt to better apprise visitors of the wait times at the rides, Universal has installed electronic messaging boards at the entrance to and throughout their parks that post real-time estimates for the length of the lines at its most popular attractions.

SeaWorld (© **800/327-2424** or 407/351-3600; www.seaworld.com) has announced the addition of an innovative eco-themed water park to its lineup. Scheduled to open in 2008, the yet unnamed park is set to feature an array of interactive experiences that combine the ecological themes of SeaWorld, the naturalistic setting of Discovery Cove, and the fun and excitement of a water park. Back at **SeaWorld,** two new shows have been added to the lineup. *Believe* is a killer whale show combining spectacular choreography, a three-story high set design, and an exciting musical score. *Blue Horizons* mixes elements of the sea and sky with a Broadway-style dolphin spectacular. Additionally, three new kid-friendly rides have sprung up at **Shamu's Happy Harbor,** including the **Shamu Express,** a kid-friendly coaster.

Discovery Cove (© **877/434-7268;** www.discoverycove.com) recently announced that guests will now get breakfast, lunch, and unlimited snacks and beverages as part of their regular admission.

For more on Universal Orlando and SeaWorld, check out Chapter 7, "Exploring Beyond Disney."

ORLANDO AFTER DARK Incredibly high ceilings, rich woodwork, leaded glass, and marble accents run throughout the inviting **Raglan Road,** in Downtown Disney's Pleasure Island (© **407/938-0300**), which opened in late 2005. The lively atmosphere, where singing, dancing, and clapping are all encouraged, is enhanced by the nightly entertainment. And the food's pretty good, too, thanks to the culinary wizardry of Kevin Dundon, one of Ireland's most celebrated chefs.

For more information on Orlando's nightlife, see chapter 9, "Walt Disney World & Orlando After Dark."

1

The Best of Walt Disney World & Orlando

In the beginning, Orlando may have been a sleepy little southern town filled with farmland as far as the eye could see, orange groves galore, and only two attractions to its name (a water-ski show and some great big gators). Then came the Mouse. More specifically, a mouse named Mickey and his creator, a man of fantastic imagination and vision named Walt Disney. Life in Orlando would never be the same. Since the opening of Walt Disney World back in 1971, Orlando has grown to become one of the world's top vacation destinations. Almost 48 million people from all parts of the world make their way to this city each year to sample its unending array of exciting, unique, and diverse activities. Those of us who continue to return year after year can count on each new visit to provide a host of new experiences and magical memories.

When Disney World first opened its gates to the public, I doubt if anyone but Walt Disney, the original Imagineer, could have predicted what lay ahead. Disney, searching for an East Coast location for his second theme park, decided Orlando was just the place he was looking for. In 1964, in a covert operation that would have made James Bond proud, Walt Disney began quietly purchasing large quantities of land in and around the Orlando area, and within months he had acquired property nearly twice the size of Manhattan. In 1965, Walt announced to the public his plans to bring to Orlando the world's most spectacular theme park. Fashioned after Disneyland in California, construction soon began on Disney's Magic Kingdom. Unfortunately, Walt Disney was never able to see his dream come to life, as he passed away in 1966, just 5 years shy of the opening of what, to this day, is still the world's most spectacular theme park—Walt Disney World.

Disney's legacy, while commercialized over the years, has practically become a right of passage, not to mention a national shrine to which visitors flock by the millions. And if you have kids, a visit here is almost a requirement. The opening of Walt Disney World's Magic Kingdom started a tourist boom in Central Florida the likes of which has never been seen elsewhere. Today, The Kingdom That Walt Built entices visitors with four theme parks, a dozen smaller attractions, two nightclub districts, tens of thousands of hotel rooms, a vacation club (otherwise known as timeshares), scores of restaurants, and even two cruise ships. Universal Orlando adds to the dizzying array with two theme parks, three luxury resorts, and an entertainment complex that's home to several unique restaurants, clubs, shops, and entertainment venues. SeaWorld tosses in two (soon to be three) theme parks and an entertainment, dining, and shopping district of its own. And those are just the major players. All in all, there are over 95 attractions, both large and small, that will keep you coming back for more. There are also plenty of restaurants, ranging from fine dining to on-the-fly fast food;

Fun Fact **By the Numbers**

Orlando's theme parks are beginning to reap the benefits of a stronger economy as they see increasing attendance levels—accompanied by predictions that these levels will continue to rise steadily over the next few years. Parks are also enticing visitors to return and to stay longer by offering special deals, and adding wild and wonderfully new attractions. Here are the 2005 attendance estimates (and their national rankings) for all of the major Orlando parks according to *Amusement Business* magazine:

- No. 1: Magic Kingdom, 16.1 million
- No. 3: Epcot, 9.9 million
- No. 4: Disney–MGM Studios, 8.6 million
- No. 5: Disney's Animal Kingdom, 8.2 million
- No. 6: Universal Studios Florida, 6.1 million
- No. 8: Islands of Adventure, 5.8 million
- No. 9: Sea World Orlando, 5.6 million

many of the more casual restaurants are as themed as the parks themselves. And the city doesn't lack for hotels and resorts either, with more than 114,000 rooms, villas, and suites to go around (and even more on the way). If you can believe it, the landscape is still changing, evolving, growing, and expanding to ensure your experiences will do the same each and every time you stay and play in Orlando.

Beyond the fast-paced excitement, glitz, and glitter of Orlando's theme parks you'll find Central Florida's more natural side, with hidden treasures just waiting to be discovered. Over 300 lakes, springs, and rivers are waiting to be explored and enjoyed. There are numerous parks and gardens, many with trails for walking and hiking, and the area's wildlife sanctuaries and zoos showcase Florida's animal inhabitants. The number of recreational opportunities—picnics in parks, boating along waterways, fishing, biking, and hiking, to name a few—is almost limitless. And Orlando's rich history and culture come to life through its many museums, galleries, and theaters.

Where to go, what to do, when to do it . . . with so many decisions to make you may very well find your head spinning. Because of the vast quantity of offerings, a vacation to Orlando requires a reasonable amount of planning, not to mention budgeting. The sheer number of attractions and available activities requires that you narrow down your choices to fit both your schedule and budget properly. Entrance fees can be daunting (a 1-day ticket to one of the major parks averages around $63 for adults and $52 for kids 3–9), and when you add in the costs of dining, accommodations, and souvenirs, sticker shock at the high price tag is not out of the question. A typical family of four could easily end up spending several hundred dollars a day! Some parks have begun offering deals to bring down the average daily price of your ticket if you buy multiday passes, but don't give them too much credit—the parks are wagering they'll generate additional revenues with all of the money you'll spend on extra hotel nights and meals. But even if you do have deep pockets, there is so much to experience in Orlando that to take it all in properly would require far more time than the average vacation would allow. I doubt if even two or three vacations could do the trick.

That's exactly why this book was written: to make available to you the most up-to-date and detailed information on what Orlando has to offer. A mix of options that take into account every budget and taste are included in each chapter so you can make the most informed decisions possible. With this book, you'll have the tools to plan ahead and ensure that your family has the best vacation possible. I have traveled to Central Florida more times than I can count over the past 18 years. Single, married, with kids, and without, I've stood in all the lines, ridden the rides, and dined in the restaurants—even during the height of summer and spring break. In other words, I've done all of the hard work, so you don't have to, and I give realistic and practical travel tips throughout this book in order to help you enjoy a more magical vacation. At the same time, I also give you options to help make your vacation more affordable and to keep expenses to a minimum while still having the maximum amount of fun. The Orlando tourism gurus will ensure your family has a steady stream of new things to see and do. (If you have any doubts about that, check out the "What's New in Walt Disney World & Orlando" chapter for a look at all the debuts made this past year alone.)

1 The Best Orlando Experiences

- **Explore Disney's Animal Kingdom.** Explore Disney's most spectacular and wildest Imagineering to date. Trek through the jungles of Africa along the Pangani Forest Exploration Trail or set out on Safari across the savanna with Kilimanjaro Safaris. Journey through the exotic lands of Asia and embark on an expedition to the peaks of Expedition Everest, then explore the mysteries of Anandapur wandering the Maharajah Jungle Trek. Be sure not to miss The Festival of the Lion King, absolutely the best show in all of WDW. See p. 240.

- **Go globe-trotting at Epcot.** You can travel around the world in only an afternoon at the World Showcase pavilions, rocket through space on a thrilling mission to Mars at Mission: Space, travel back in time to the age of the dinosaurs at the Universe of Energy, and dive deep below the sea to explore the ocean's inhabitants at The Living Seas. And there's no better way to cap your day off than watching Epcot's IllumiNations, a spectacular fireworks, laser lights, and fountain show! See p. 212.

- **Take Center Stage at Disney–MGM Studios.** Though it is more grown-up than the Magic Kingdom, it has plenty of great shows to entertain the kids and attractions to thrill movie buffs. Don't miss the Tower of Terror, Rock 'n' Roller Coaster, and Fantasmic!—the innovative, after-dark mix of live action, waterworks, fireworks, and laser lights that rivals IllumiNations. See p. 229.

- Escape to the **Magic Kingdom,** even if you've been here many times before. It may seem an obvious choice, but Disney's oldest is still the most magical of Orlando's theme parks. Speed through the universe on Space Mountain, watch Donald's antics at Mickey's PhilharMagic, or wave hello to the ghouls of the Haunted Mansion. Cap your day with the impressive Wishes fireworks display. There's plenty here to entertain all ages. See p. 191.

- **Experience Universal Orlando.** Universal Studios Florida and its sister, Islands of Adventure, are both chock-full of thrilling rides and spectacular shows that combine cutting-edge technology, high-tech special effects, and incredible imagination and creativity. The attention to detail throughout the parks is amazing—check out the street

Orlando Theme Parks

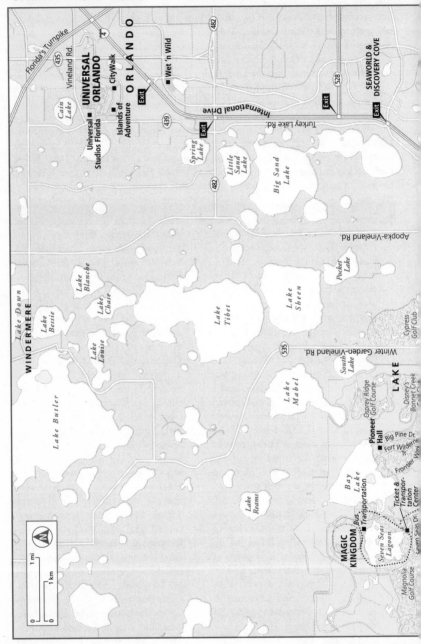

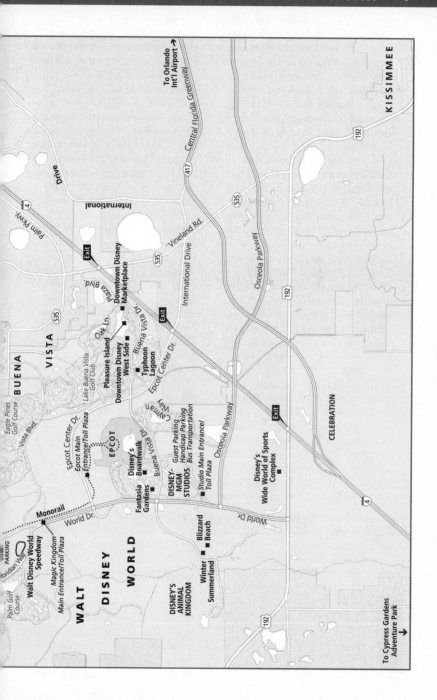

sets at USF and the wildly unique landscapes of IOA and you'll see what I mean. For thrill seekers, not-to-be-missed attractions include The Revenge of the Mummy, Back to the Future . . . The Ride, Men in Black Alien Attack, Dueling Dragons, the Incredible Hulk Coaster, The Amazing Adventures of Spider-Man, and Dudley Do-Right's Ripsaw Falls. See p. 257 and p. 271.

- **Dive into the Eco-Edutainment of SeaWorld and Discovery Cove.** Cleverly disguised as a theme park, your kids may never realize just how much they're learning as they explore, watch, and touch their way through both parks' eco-exhibits and shows. With the addition of Journey to Atlantis and Kraken, **SeaWorld** (p. 284) added a bit of zip and zing to the lineup, ensuring those in need of an adrenalin rush aren't left out in the cold (or over at the other parks). But it's still the hands-on encounters such as touching silky rays as they glide by you in droves, and up-close views of the animals, ranging from polar bears and penguins to killer whales, that draw the crowds. **Discovery Cove** (p. 293) is more of an island retreat than theme park. Rest and relax on the beach, or swim right along with the fishes. The big draw here is the chance to take a dip with the dolphins.

- **Go Wild at Gatorland.** Located between Orlando and Kissimmee, this throwback park is a great way to spend a half-day (an especially good choice for that extra time on your day of arrival), and costs less than a third of the price of some of the major theme parks. In addition to the animal exhibits, Gator Jumparoo, a signature show since the park opened in 1949, and Gator Wrestlin are worth a look. Other options include a train ride, children's water playground, and aviary. If you have some extra spending money, consider becoming a Trainer for a Day for a once-in-a-lifetime experience. See p. 295.

- **Pamper Yourself with a Spa Treatment.** Rest, relax, and rejuvenate— you may very well need to if you intend on surviving all of the fast-paced activities you've planned. After a few days at the parks it should almost be a requirement. **Disney's Grand Floridian Resort & Spa** (© **407/934-7639** or 407/824-3000); the **Mandara Spa at Universal's Portofino Bay Hotel** (© **888/322-5541** or 407/503-1000), and at the **WDW Dolphin** (© **407/-934-4000**); the **Canyon Ranch SpaClub at the Gaylord Palms** (© **877/677-9352** or 407/586-2051); and the **Ritz-Carlton Spa at the Grande Lakes Resort** (© **407/206-2400**) all offer an array of fabulous treatments, some with salon services to boot.

2 The Best Thrill Rides

Orlando lays claim to some of the biggest and baddest thrill rides and roller coasters anywhere—certainly one of the largest collections of them in any one locale. So if your idea of fun is to twist and turn at speeds only a jet should reach, dive uncontrollably from dizzying heights to below ground level and back, or see just how far up into your throat your stomach can go—this is the place for you. Here are the city's top stomach churners and G-force generators.

- **Incredible Hulk Coaster** (Islands of Adventure): It's the smoothest ride in town, but you'll still blast from 0 to 40 mph in 2 seconds flat (on your way up to 60 mph), spin upside down more than 100 feet above the ground, dive straight back down only to spin your way through seven

(Tips Orlando's Best Online Sites

Considering that Orlando welcomes over 48 million visitors each year, it should come as no surprise that literally hundreds of websites are devoted to vacationing here. These include information on just about everything, from the history of Walt Disney World to getting around town.

There are several sites written by Disney fans, employees, and self-proclaimed experts. A favorite (**www.hiddenmickeys.org**) is all about **Hidden Mickeys,** a park tradition (see chapter 6, "Exploring Walt Disney World"). These subtle Disney images can be found scattered throughout the realm, though they sometimes are in the eye, or imagination, of the beholder. **Deb's Unofficial Walt Disney World Information Guide** (**www.allearsnet.com**) is the best around, loaded with great tips and information on everything Disney from the parks and resorts to the restaurants, nightlife, and much more.

Definitely take a look at Disney's official site, **www.disneyworld.com**, if you're planning a pilgrimage to the House of Mouse. It recently got a top-to-bottom overhaul, making it easier to navigate and much more informative. It's loaded with some excellent photos and 360-degree views of Disney's resorts, rooms, parks, and more. **Magical Gatherings,** available on the Disney site as well, is a free downloadable online tool allowing you to plan your group's Disney vacation, via computer, with other family (or friends), no matter where they live. You can plan itineraries, take group polls, list everyone's favorites, and even chat to come up with the perfect plan.

If you're looking to save a few dollars, try **Mousesavers** (**www.mouse savers.com**), which features information, insider Disney tips, and (the biggest perk) exclusive discounted deals for area hotels, resorts, and packages.

If a trip to one of Universal Orlando's theme parks or CityWalk is on your dance card, then stop at **www.universalorlando.com**. You can order tickets (including exclusive Internet-only deals), make resort reservations, and find out about special events, among other things on the site. Fish fans can get in the know about SeaWorld at **www.seaworld.com** and Discovery Cove at **www.discoverycove.com**.

If you're seeking general information about the city, accommodations, dining, nightlife, or special events, head over to the Orlando/Orange County Convention & Visitors Bureau site at **www.orlandoinfo.com**. *Orlando Weekly* (**www.orlandoweekly.com**) offers cutting-edge reviews and recommendations for arts, movies, music, restaurants, and much more. *The Orlando Sentinel* (**www.orlandosentinel.com**), along with all the local news and goings-on, features Go2Orlando, a section loaded with information on the area's dining, attractions, shopping, and more.

rollovers, and then drop deep below ground on this big, green, mean machine. (You might glow as green as the coaster when you're done.) See p. 278.

- **Rock 'n' Roller Coaster** (Disney–MGM Studios): You'll launch from 0 to 60 mph in 2.8 seconds, heading straight into the first of several inversions as 120 speakers in your "stretch limo" blast Aerosmith at (yeeeow!) 32,000 watts right into your ears. To add to the thrill of this indoor coaster, the entire experience takes place in the dark. See p. 237.

- **Dueling Dragons** (Islands of Adventure): Whether you choose the dragon of fire or of ice, your legs will dangle below as you sharply twist and turn through five inversions at speeds of 55 to 60 mph. The two intertwined coasters come within only inches (12 to be exact) of each other, only just missing a collision, not two, but three times. See p. 281.

- **Summit Plummet** (Disney's Blizzard Beach): This one starts slow, with a lift ride (even in Florida's 100°F/38°C dog days) to the 120-foot summit. But it finishes with the (self-proclaimed) world's fastest body slide, a test of your courage and swimsuit as it virtually goes straight down and has you moving sans vehicle at 60 mph by the end. See p. 253.

- **Twilight Zone Tower of Terror** (Disney–MGM Studios): The name says it all. The ride transports guests into the Twilight Zone as a haunted hotel's service elevator slowly rises— only to plummet 13 stories, terrifying those inside. But the freefall fun doesn't end there. The tower now

features a new twist—a computer program randomly alternates drop sequences to make sure you never experience the same ride twice. When you get off and your legs finally stop shaking, *some of you* will want to ride again. See p. 238.

- **The Amazing Adventures of Spider-Man** (Islands of Adventure): Combining the best of all worlds—3-D movie effects, a moving simulator car, and live action—this is by far the best ride in Orlando. Your vehicle spins, twists, pitches, and dives through elaborate sets as Spiderman tries to save the world (and you) from total annihilation. The chase ends in a dramatic, simulated 400-foot drop that feels an awful lot like the real thing. It doesn't offer the same type of thrills as a coaster, but it's sure to get your Spidey senses tingling. See p. 277.

- **Kraken** (SeaWorld): Named for a mythological creature, this stomach-churning ride is a beast! This floorless, open-sided coaster reaches speeds of up to 65 mph as it combines steep climbs, deep drops, and seven tremendous loops reaching high above water before plunging below the ground, to make it one of the most aggressive and intense coasters anywhere. See p. 289.

3 The Best Water Rides

- **Splash Mountain** (Magic Kingdom): You'll follow the adventure of Brer Rabbit and his friends, based on the 1946 movie *The Song of the South,* before taking a 52-foot vertical plunge straight down to the water below. See p. 200.

- **Dudley Do-Right's Ripsaw Falls** (Islands of Adventure): Dudley Do-Right and Snidely Whiplash are once again at odds and you're caught right in the middle. This flume sends you plummeting not once but twice, and

that second drop sends you 15 feet below the surface of the water before you make your escape. See p. 279.

- **Jurassic Park River Adventure** (Islands of Adventure): A seemingly calm tour through the age of the dinosaur suddenly takes a turn for the worse. Before you know it, your only escape route involves a dramatic 85-foot drop almost straight down, that's touted as the "longest, steepest, fastest water descent ever built." You will get drenched. See p. 281.

- **Journey to Atlantis** (SeaWorld): This flume ride sends you careening around the sharpest of curves as the forces of good and evil battle to claim Atlantis for their own. Before you know it, you're being thrown into total darkness, emerging only to find yourself plummeting down several steep, watery drops. See p. 289.

4 The Best Romantic Hideaways

- **Courtyard at Lake Lucerne** (Downtown; ✆ **407/648-5188**): This charming little B&B is an eclectic mix of some of Orlando's oldest homes—each impeccably restored and meticulously furnished to period. Ask for the honeymoon suite for a really romantic getaway; just off the main room is a quaint little glass-enclosed porch—the perfect spot to watch the sunset or sip a glass of wine. See p. 123.

- **Disney's Wilderness Lodge** (Lake Buena Vista; ✆ **407/934-7639**): This grand resort is reminiscent of the lodge found at Yellowstone National Park. The spewing geyser out back, the mammoth stone hearth in the lobby, the Artist's Point 360-degree view of Bay Lake, and the towering forest sheltering the resort from the rest of the world are just a few of the reasons to stay here. Some guest rooms have patios or balconies overlooking the lake, woodlands, or the meadow. See p. 96.

- **Portofino Bay Hotel** (Universal Orlando; ✆ **888/322-5541** or 407/503-1000): This enchanting resort recreates the romantic atmosphere and architecture of its namesake town in Italy. Lounge in the ultracomfy rooms, the state-of-the-art spa, or at one of the three heated pools. And it's only a stroll away from both of Universal Orlando's theme parks. See p. 116.

- **Villas of Grand Cypress** (Orlando; ✆ **800/835-7377** or 407/239-4700): This luxury villa-style resort offers lush grounds dotted with bougainvillea and hibiscus, lakes fat with largemouth bass and bream, and grounds speckled with trumpeter swans, wood ducks, and the occasional fox or bobcat. It shares a golf academy, racquet club, and equestrian center with the Hyatt Regency Grand Cypress. Best of all, the woodsy grounds make you feel as if you're far, far from Disney, which is right next door. See p. 106.

5 The Best Luxury Resorts

- **Disney's Grand Floridian Resort & Spa** (Orlando; ✆ **407/934-7639**): This magnificent Victorian inn has an opulent five-story lobby complete with a Chinese Chippendale aviary. An orchestra plays big-band music every evening near Victoria & Albert's, the resort's five-star restaurant. See p. 92.

- **Gaylord Palms** (Lake Buena Vista; ✆ **877/677-9352** or 407/586-0000): This destination resort features impeccable service; themed guest rooms (the Emerald Bay rooms are the best) with luxe amenities; a lush, 4½-acre glass-topped atrium; and (best of all) a branch of the renowned Canyon Ranch Spa. See p. 105.

- **Hyatt Regency Grand Cypress Resort** (Orlando; ✆ **800/233-1234** or 407/239-1234): This standout has some impressive treats, including a half-acre pool with a dozen waterfalls and three spas, 12 tennis courts, four Jack Nicklaus–designed golf courses, and a 45-acre nature walk. All that adds up to luxury. See p. 106.

- **Ritz-Carlton Orlando** (Grande Lakes; ⓒ **800/241-3333** or 407/ 529-2255). Perks at this posh getaway include luxurious rooms with first-class amenities, a 40,000-square-foot spa, a championship golf course, top-notch child-care facilities, and a lazy river pool. See p. 120.

6 The Best Moderately Priced Accommodations

- **Disney's Port Orleans Resort** (Lake Buena Vista; ⓒ **407/934-7639** or 407/934-5000): Here's a good value by Disney standards. It has dual Southern charm in its French Quarter and Riverside areas, and the pool has a water slide curving from the mouth of a colorful dragon. See p. 98.
- **Hilton in the Walt Disney World Resort** (Lake Buena Vista; ⓒ **407/ 827-4000**): It's the only official resort on Hotel Plaza Boulevard to offer Disney's Extra Magic Hour option. Other pluses include a huge variety of services, two pools, and spacious junior suites. And it has a great location next to Downtown Disney. See p. 104.
- **Staybridge Suites Lake Buena Vista** (Lake Buena Vista; ⓒ **800/866-4549** or 407/238-0777): Close to the action of Downtown Disney and the theme parks, this resort's one- and two-bedroom suites have full kitchens and are larger and more comfortable than most of the competition. And to help you relax, the resort will do your grocery shopping for you, so you don't have to deal with the hassle. See p. 109.

7 The Best Theme Restaurants

Orlando has elevated themed dining to an art form. The food at these restaurants may not be the best in town (though it won't be terrible either), but you can't beat the atmosphere.

- **World Showcase restaurants** (Epcot; ⓒ **407/939-3463**): Epcot's World Showcase is home to Orlando's best collection of theme restaurants in one setting. Dine in Italy, chow down in China, or watch a belly dancer do her thing as you eat couscous in Morocco. You'll have a blast no matter which dining spot you choose. See p. 132.
- **Sci-Fi Dine-In Theater Restaurant** (Disney–MGM Studios; ⓒ **407/939-3463**): Your table is set inside a 1950s-era convertible, your carhop (umm . . . waitress) serves you popcorn as an appetizer, and you can zone out on sci-fi flicks on a giant movie screen while you eat. It's an out-of-this-world experience. See p. 146.
- **50's Prime Time Café** (Disney–MGM Studios; ⓒ **407/939-3463**): Ozzie and Harriet would feel right at home inside this replica of mom's kitchen (ca. 1950), where classic TV shows play on black-and-white screens. Servers may threaten to withhold dessert (choices include s'mores!) if you don't finish your meatloaf, so clean that plate! See p. 145.
- **Enchanted Oak Tavern** (Islands of Adventure; no phone): Merlin himself would feel right at home at this dimly lit dining hall, set inside a hollowed-out "tree." The evocative decor looks even better after you've imbibed 1 of the 45 different beers on tap at the restaurant's Alchemy Bar. See p. 284.

8 The Best Places for Adults

Let's face it: Orlando and the theme park zones usually crawl with kids. That's fine if you have your own in tow, but if you're looking for some quality adult time (or at least a place not necessarily swarming with children), you do have some options. Some people are incredulous when informed that Orlando is the Honeymoon Capital of the United States, but it happens to be true; so be assured that there are activities, hotels, and so on that are geared to adults here (though, admittedly, avoiding kids altogether is tough). Aside from the romantic hideaways discussed above, here are some good bets for adults:

- **Visit Epcot.** Of all the major theme parks in Orlando, this one, thanks to its scientific and cultural themes, is the most adult-oriented of the bunch. Shop, stroll, and dine your way through the nations of the World Showcase; take a behind-the-scenes tour of the park's horticulture or architecture; or explore the technological- and scientific-themed attractions of Future World. Just be sure to break in your walking shoes before you arrive! See p. 212.

- **Swim with Dolphins at Discovery Cove.** It's popular with families, but thanks to the park's limit on guest entry (a mere 1,000 people per day), adults won't get overwhelmed by kids at SeaWorld's sister park. There are plenty of places to catch rays in relative serenity, and the dolphin swim's a thrill at any age. See p. 293.

- **Have a meal in an upscale restaurant.** Though it's not a firm rule (especially inside the theme parks), generally speaking, the more you pay for dinner, the more likely it is that you won't encounter children at your meal. So if you're looking for a romantic meal, save up and splurge (and we mean splurge). Great options in town for a special dinner include **Victoria &**

Albert's (p. 148), **Emeril's** (p. 160), **California Grill** (p. 150), and **Dux** (p. 164). For a great brunch, head to **Atlantis** (p. 162). For other options, check out chapter 5, "Where to Dine."

- **Explore Winter Park.** This upscale town north of Orlando oozes old-money Southern charm. And the pace here is decidedly slower than the mad rush of the theme parks (adults usually love it, kids get bored). Stroll Park Avenue's shops and restaurants, or take a boat tour along the lake. See p. 65.

- **Party the Night Away at Disney's Pleasure Island and Universal City-Walk.** Both nighttime entertainment districts offer adult atmospheres and have clubs where kids are *verboten*. **Pleasure Island** (p. 324) is a tad more family-friendly than **CityWalk** (p. 328), but its 21-and-over (and the staff is very serious about keeping out those who don't make the age grade) **Mannequins** is arguably the hottest dance club in town. At CityWalk, the best bets for grown-ups are Pat O'Brien's and CityJazz.

- **Head for the Circus.** Cirque du Soleil, that is. Forget about finding any animals, though. Cirque's stylish *La Nouba* combines theatrics, acrobatics, and the incredible style that the Montreal-based troupe is known for. It's an incredible (albeit pricey) way to spend an evening in Orlando. See p. 327.

- **Rev your Engines at the Richard Petty Driving Experience.** If you've ever watched the Daytona 500 race and imagined yourself at the wheel, this attraction is for you. Ride shotgun in a real NASCAR race car, or take a course and learn how to drive the thing yourself. It's an adrenaline-pumper you won't find in a theme park, and nobody under 18's allowed. See p. 370.

2

Planning Your Trip to Walt Disney World & Orlando

Winging it once you get there simply won't do when your destination is Walt Disney World. Without some pre-trip preparation, you will likely find yourself so overwhelmed upon arriving in Orlando that you will miss out on exactly what it was you came for in the first place—fun. In this chapter you'll find just about everything you need to know before you go, including tons of helpful information to get you started. In addition to the information contained in the following pages, you'll find more useful tips and information in chapters 5 through 8—those covering the area's best hotels, restaurants, theme parks, and smaller attractions.

1 Visitor Information

The best place to find information on Orlando and Central Florida is the **Orlando/Orange County Convention & Visitors Bureau,** 8723 International Dr., Suite 101, Orlando, FL 32819 (© **407/ 363-5872;** www.orlandoinfo.com). Staffers can answer questions, assist you with reservations, help you find discounts, and send maps and brochures, such as the *Official Destination Guide, the Fun Guide,* and *Unexpected Orlando.* The free packet should arrive in about 3 weeks and includes the Orlando "Magicard," which is good for over $500 in discounts on hotel rooms, car rentals, attractions, and more—the website also details all of the latest discounts. *Tip:* Keep the card handy so you won't lose out on any available discounts once you get into town. You can stop by once you've arrived and pick up additional brochures, maps, and other information, too.

If you don't mind talking to a machine, you can get all of the above by calling © **800/643-9492** or 800/551-0181.

Another good site worth checking out is **www.flausa.com,** which includes plenty of useful information on the entire Central Florida region.

For information specific to **Walt Disney World,** including vacation brochures and videos or to ask questions, you can write to Walt Disney World, Box 10000, Lake Buena Vista, FL 32830-1000; or call © **407/934-7639,** 407/824-4321, or 407/824-2222. On the Internet, visit **www.disneyworld.com.**

For information about **Universal Studios Florida, CityWalk,** and **Islands of Adventure,** call © **407/363-8000,** or write to **Universal Orlando,** 1000 Universal Studios Plaza, Orlando, FL 32819. On the Internet, visit **www.universal orlando.com.**

For information about **SeaWorld,** call © 407/351-3600 or visit online at **www. seaworld.com.** For **Discovery Cove** information and reservations call © **877/ 4-DISCOVERY,** or 407/370-1280. For online information visit **www.discovery cove.com.**

You can also visit the **Kissimmee–St. Cloud Convention & Visitors Bureau,**

1925 E. Irlo Bronson Memorial Hwy. (U.S. 192), Kissimmee, FL 34744; or write to P.O. Box 422007, Kissimmee, FL 34742-2007 (© **800/327-9159** or 407/847-5000; www.floridakiss.com). The folks there will send a packet of maps, brochures, coupon books, and the *Kissimmee–St. Cloud Vacation Guide,* which details area accommodations and attractions.

For information on the **International Drive** area, call © **407/248-9590** or head online to **www.InternationalDrive-Orlando.com**. The staff can provide information on hotels, restaurants, attractions, shops, and the I-Ride Trolley. Be sure to request their detailed map of the I-Drive area—it's very useful.

For information about places to stay, eat, and visit north of the Orlando metro area, contact the **Winter Park Chamber of Commerce Welcome Center** at © **877/972-4262.**

ONLINE INFORMATION

The websites listed above also provide a great abundance of other helpful and necessary information. Disney's **www.disneyworld.com** has theme park maps; current ticket prices; driving directions; park hours for specific days; and information on attractions (including refurbishment schedules), special events, recreational activities, resorts (including pricing and photos), and dining. There's also Disney Cruise Line information, an online booking service, a new online tool for vacation planning, and much, much more.

Deb's Unofficial Walt Disney World Information Guide (www.allearsnet. com) is an excellent information source and arguably the best unofficial Disney guide on the Internet. While Disney doesn't own or operate it, it's run and written by true-blue fans of Mickey. Though not entirely objective, the site's information is almost always right on the mark.

There's even a section devoted to travelers with special needs.

Another good site that includes comprehensive insider information on everything Disney, including the parks, resorts, restaurants (including menus; many with prices), the Disney Cruise Line, and more is **Travel Insights (www.travel-insights. com**). The bonus: It's packed full of helpful (and practical) travel tips as well as a theme park survival guide.

The sites operated by Universal Orlando (**www.universalorlando.com**) and Sea-World (**www.seaworld.com**) have both been revamped (Universal's completely overhauled) in the last year (though they still lack the thoroughness of Deb's and the Disney sites). You'll now find maps, ride descriptions, ticket prices, restaurant descriptions, upcoming events, resort information (for Universal), available guest services, and photos galore. Be prepared, however, for a bumpy ride, as navigating the sites can still be challenging at best. You may have to dig pretty deep to find just exactly what it is you're looking for as neither site is as easy to maneuver as Disney's.

The city's newspaper, the *Orlando Sentinel,* produces an online site at **www. orlandosentinel.com**. It has a variety of entertainment information. If you go to another Sentinel-produced website, **www. go2orlando.com**, you'll find the focus on attractions, accommodations, restaurants, discounts, and other things important to visitors. Also visit **www.insidecentral florida.com** for information about dining, clubs, performances, theme parks, sports, and special events.

If you're looking for the best tips and insider information on saving some cash on your Disney vacation, go to **www. mousesavers.com**—the website includes a list of discount and reservation codes for the Disney resorts, as well as special discounts and offers of their own.

Destination Orlando: Pre-Departure Checklist

- Did you pack your sunscreen? Along with The Mouse, Orlando's biggest draw is its warm and sunny climate. The Florida sun is hotter and stronger than in many other parts of the country and can deliver a dangerous burn year-round—even on a seemingly cloudy day. One of the most important survival rules of an Orlando vacation: **Use sunscreen!** Buy one with an SPF rating of at least 30 or higher, especially for kids, who need protection even more than you do. Other useful protective items include wide-brimmed hats, airy clothes, and sunglasses. If you have a child in a stroller, a light blanket will help to protect infants or sleeping toddlers from the sun's rays. Last but certainly not least, don't forget to pack a pair of comfortable walking shoes for those days spent pounding the theme-park pavement.

- To avoid missing out on some of Disney's greatest dining experiences (including character meals), be sure to use Walt Disney World's **Advance Reservations** (✆ 407/939-3463), which lets you stake a claim to a table up to 180 days in advance. Call as soon as possible to make your Advance Reservation as some of the more popular restaurants and shows get booked within hours—sometimes even minutes—of the time they start booking seating times.

- Check your desired theme park's operating schedules either by phone or online before you leave home (and certainly before you promise your kids anything). Many visitors come with their hearts set on (and days planned around) seeing a specific attraction, staying at a particular hotel, or dining at a certain restaurant only to be disappointed if for some reason there is an interruption in its operation or a change in its schedule.

ORLANDO INFORMATION ABROAD

There are several **Orlando Tourism Offices** located outside the United States. Information is available from the following sources:

- **Argentina** ✆ 0800-999-1749; www.orlandoinfo.com/argentina
- **Belgium** ✆ 32-2/705-7897; www.orlandoinfo.com
- **Brazil** ✆ 0800/556652; www.orlandoinfo.com/brasil
- **Canada** ✆ 1-800-646-2079; www.orlandokissimmee.com/canada
- **Germany** ✆ 0800-100-7325; www.orlandoinfo.com/de
- **Japan** ✆ 3-3501-7245; www.orlandoinfo.com/japan
- **Latin America** ✆ 407/363-5872; www.orlandoinfo.com/latinoamerica
- **Mexico** ✆ 01-800/800-4636; www.orlandoinfo.com/mexico
- **Spain** ✆ 407/363-5872; www.orlandoinfo.com/espana
- **United Kingdom** ✆ 0800-018-6760; www.orlandoinfo.com/uk

All the parks have **reduced hours** at certain times of the year—even on certain days of the week—some shows are staged only occasionally, and rides can be temporarily closed. Also note that theme park rides can occasionally break down or have to be shut down due to weather conditions (though you won't get a break on ticket prices when your favorite rides or shows are dark). Some of the websites listed earlier in this chapter, including Deb's Unofficial Walt Disney World Information Guide, have "rehab" schedules and update them almost daily. The parks can change their hours not only seasonally, but weekly—even daily—so check the week's schedule when you arrive so you'll know if you have to adjust your itinerary because of a just-scheduled closing.

- If you purchased traveler's checks, make sure to record the check numbers and store the documentation separately from the checks.
- Bring along your ID cards, including AAA and AARP cards, student IDs, the Orlando "Magicard," and so on, as producing them will help save a few dollars along the way.
- Speaking of identification, did you bring a photo ID? That's a necessity at the airports, among other places, so keep it handy.
- Make sure to bring along emergency drug prescriptions, any prescription medicine you are currently using, and the phone number of your doctor, pediatrician, and insurance company (and your insurance card), along with an extra pair of glasses and/or contact lenses.
- Leave a copy of your itinerary with someone at home, and keep an extra copy yourself. Be sure it includes your hotel, car, and airplane information, as well as any reservation numbers for shows or restaurants.

2 Entry Requirements & Customs

ENTRY REQUIREMENTS
PASSPORTS
For information on how to get a passport, go to **"Passports"** in the **"Fast Facts"** section in chapter 3—the websites listed provide downloadable passport applications as well as the current fees for processing passport applications. For an up-to-date, country-by-country listing of passport requirements around the world, go to the "Foreign Entry Requirement" Web page of the U.S. State Department at **http://travel.state.gov**. International visitors can obtain a visa application at the same website.

VISAS
For information on how to get a visa, go to **"Visas"** in the **"Fast Facts"** section in chapter 3.

The U.S. State Department has a **Visa Waiver Program** allowing citizens of the following countries (at press time) to enter the United States without a visa for stays of up to 90 days: Andorra, Australia, Austria, Belgium, Brunei, Denmark, Finland, France, Germany, Iceland, Ireland, Italy, Japan, Liechtenstein, Luxembourg, Monaco, the Netherlands, New Zealand, Norway, Portugal, San Marino, Singapore, Slovenia, Spain, Sweden, Switzerland, and

---

(Fun Fact Laying Out the International Welcome Mat

Orlando welcomes an average of just over 2.5 million international visitors each year. Over 75% cross an ocean to get to see the Mouse, with the remaining 25% coming from America's neighbors to the north and south. The British lead the international brigade with an average 1,054,000 citizens of the U.K. making the trip annually. Canada (631,000), Brazil (74,000), Colombia (74,000), and Germany (73,000) round out the top five.

---

the United Kingdom. Citizens of these nations need only a valid passport and a round-trip air or cruise ticket upon arrival. If they first enter the United States, they may also visit Mexico, Canada, Bermuda, and/or the Caribbean islands and return to the United States without a visa. Further information is available from any U.S. embassy or consulate. Canadian citizens may enter the United States without visas; they need only proof of residence.

Citizens of all other countries must have (1) a valid passport that expires at least 6 months later than the scheduled end of their visit to the United States, and (2) a tourist visa, which may be obtained without charge from any U.S. consulate.

MEDICAL REQUIREMENTS

Unless you're arriving from an area known to be suffering from an epidemic (particularly cholera or yellow fever), inoculations or vaccinations are not required for entry into the United States. If you have a medical condition that requires **syringe-administered medications,** carry a valid signed prescription from your physician—the Federal Aviation Administration (FAA) no longer allows airline passengers to pack syringes in their carry-on baggage without documented proof of medical need. If you have a disease that requires treatment with **narcotics,** you should also carry documented proof with you—smuggling narcotics aboard a plane is a serious offense that carries severe penalties in the U.S.

For **HIV-positive visitors,** requirements for entering the United States are somewhat vague and change frequently. For up-to-the-minute information, contact **AIDSinfo** (© **800/448-0440** or 301/519-6616 outside the U.S.; www. aidsinfo.nih.gov) or the **Gay Men's Health Crisis** (© **212/367-1000;** www. gmhc.org).

CUSTOMS
WHAT YOU CAN BRING INTO ORLANDO

Every visitor more than 21 years of age may bring in, free of duty, the following: (1) 1 liter of wine or hard liquor; (2) 200 cigarettes, 100 cigars (but not from Cuba), or 3 pounds of smoking tobacco; and (3) $100 worth of gifts. These exemptions are offered to travelers who spend at least 72 hours in the United States and who have not claimed them within the preceding 6 months. It is altogether forbidden to bring into the country foodstuffs (particularly fruit, cooked meats, and canned goods) and plants (vegetables, seeds, tropical plants, and the like). Foreign tourists may carry in or out up to $10,000 in U.S. or foreign currency with no formalities; larger sums must be declared to U.S. Customs on entering or leaving, which includes filing form CM 4790. For details regarding U.S. Customs and Border Protection, consult your nearest U.S. embassy or consulate, or **U.S. Customs** (© **202/927-1770;** www.customs.ustreas.gov).

WHAT YOU CAN TAKE HOME FROM ORLANDO

Canadian Citizens

For a clear summary of Canadian rules, write for the booklet *I Declare,* issued by the **Canada Border Services Agency** (© **800/461-9999** in Canada, or 204/983-3500; **www.cbsa-asfc.gc.ca**).

U.K. Citizens

For information, contact **HM Customs & Excise** at © **0845/010-9000** (from outside the U.K., 020/8929-0152), or consult their website at **www.hmce.gov.uk**.

Australian Citizens

A helpful brochure available from Australian consulates or Customs offices is *Know Before You Go.* For more information, call the **Australian Customs Service** at © **1300/363-263,** or log on to **www.customs.gov.au**.

New Zealand Citizens

Most questions are answered in a free pamphlet available at New Zealand consulates and Customs offices: *New Zealand Customs Guide for Travellers, Notice no. 4.* For more information, contact **New Zealand Customs,** The Customhouse, 17–21 Whitmore St., Box 2218, Wellington (© **04/473-6099** or 0800/428-786; **www.customs.govt.nz**).

3 Money

ATMS

Nationwide, the easiest and best way to get cash away from home is from an ATM (automated teller machine), sometimes referred to as a "cash machine" or "cashpoint." The **Cirrus** (© **800/424-7787;** www.mastercard.com) and **PLUS** (© **800/843-7587;** www.visa.com) networks span the country; you can find them even in remote regions. Look at the back of your bank card to see which network you're on, then call or check online for ATM locations at your destination. Be sure you know your personal identification number (PIN) and daily withdrawal limit before you depart. ***Note:*** Remember that many banks impose a fee every time you use a card at another bank's ATM, and that fee can be higher for international transactions (up to $5 or more) than for domestic ones (where they're rarely more than $2). In addition, the bank from which you withdraw cash may charge its own fee. To compare banks' ATM fees within the U.S., use **www.bankrate.com**. For international withdrawal fees, ask your bank.

ATMs are located on Main Street in the Magic Kingdom and at the entrances to Epcot, Disney–MGM Studios, and Animal Kingdom (where you'll find another one located across from the

---

Tips Easy Money

You'll avoid lines at airport ATMs by exchanging at least some money—just enough to cover airport incidentals and transportation to your hotel—before you leave home.

When you change money, ask for some small bills or loose change. Petty cash will come in handy for tipping and public transportation. Consider keeping the change separate from your larger bills, so that it's readily accessible and you'll be less of a target for theft.

TriceraTop Spin in Dinoland). They're also at Pleasure Island, in Downtown Disney Marketplace, at Disney resorts, and in the Crossroads Shopping Center.

There also are ATMs near Guest Services at Universal Studios Florida, Islands of Adventure, and SeaWorld.

CREDIT CARDS

Credit cards are the most widely used form of payment in the United States: **Visa** (Barclaycard in Britain), **Master-Card** (EuroCard in Europe, Access in Britain, Chargex in Canada), **American Express, Diners Club,** and **Discover.** They also provide a convenient record of all your expenses, and they generally offer relatively good exchange rates. You can also withdraw cash advances from your credit cards at banks or ATMs, provided you know your PIN.

It's highly recommended that you travel with at least one major credit card. You must have one to rent a car, and hotels and airlines usually require a credit card imprint as a deposit against expenses.

Visitors from outside the U.S. should inquire whether their bank assesses a 1% to 3% fee on charges incurred abroad.

ATM cards with major credit card backing, known as **"debit cards,"** are now a commonly acceptable form of payment in most stores and restaurants. Debit cards draw money directly from your checking account. Some stores enable you to receive "cash back" on your debit-card purchases as well. The same is true at most U.S. post offices.

Disney parks, resorts, shops, and restaurants (but not most fast-food outlets) accept five major credit cards: American Express, Diners Club, Discover, MasterCard, and Visa. Additionally, the WDW and Universal resorts will let you charge purchases made in their respective park shops and restaurants to your hotel room, but you must settle up when you check out. Be sure, however, to keep track of your spending as you go along so you won't be surprised when you get the total bill.

Inside most of the theme park entrances, you'll find park maps showing the locations for all ATMs. If this isn't the case when you visit, look for the maps at Guest Relations or Guest Services desks near the entrances, or at most inside-the-park shops.

Outside the parks, most malls have at least one ATM and they're in some convenience stores, such as 7-Elevens and Circle Ks, as well as in grocery stores and drugstores. There are frequently extra charges for using nonbank ATMs or bank ATMs not affiliated with your home branch. Depending on your institution, those charges can range from $1 to $3.50 per transaction—the average is $2.75 across Florida.

Be *very* careful when using ATMs, especially at night and in areas that are not well lit and heavily traveled. Don't let the land of Mickey lull you into a false

---

Tips Dear Visa: I'm Off to Disney World!

Some banks and credit card companies recommend that you notify them of any impending trip so that they don't become suspicious of large transactions and block your charges. If you don't call your bank or credit card company in advance, you can still call the card's toll-free emergency number (see "Fast Facts," p. 70) if a charge is refused—provided you remember to carry the phone number with you. Perhaps the most important lesson here is to carry more than one card, so you have a backup.

What Things Cost in Orlando	US$	UK£
Taxi from airport to Walt Disney World (up to four people)	50.00	29.00
Shuttle from airport to Walt Disney World (two adults, two kids)	82.00–115.00	47.00–66.00
Double room at Disney's Grand Floridian Resort & Spa (very expensive)	359.00–890.00	206.00–510.00
Double room at Disney's Caribbean Beach Resort (moderate)	139.00–215.00	80.00–123.00
Double room at Staybridge Suites Lake Buena Vista (moderate)	149.00–269.00	85.00–152.00
Double room at Disney's All-Star Music Resort (inexpensive)	79.00–137.00	45.00–79.00
Six-course fixed-price dinner for one at Victoria & Albert's, not including tip or wine pairing (very expensive)	150.00–215.00	86.00–123.00
All-you-can-eat buffet dinner at the Disney theme park restaurants, not including tip or wine (moderate)	28.00	16.00
Roll of ASA 100 Kodak film, 36 exposures, purchased at Walt Disney World	12.00	7.00
Tube of sunblock in the theme parks	11.00	6.00
Evening movie tickets at AMC, Pleasure Island	6.00–9.00	3.00–5.00
Adult 4-Day + Park Hopper admission to Walt Disney World	235.00	135.00
Child 4-Day + Park Hopper admission to Walt Disney World	200.00	115.00
Adult 1-day, one-park admission to Walt Disney World	63.00	36.00
Child 1-day, one-park admission to Walt Disney World	52.00	30.00
Adult 1-day, one-park admission to Universal Orlando or SeaWorld	63.00	36.00
Child 1-day, one-park admission to Universal Orlando or SeaWorld	52.00	30.00
Adult 4-park, 14-day Orlando FlexTicket	189.95	109.00
Child 4-park 14-day Orlando FlexTicket	155.95	90.00
Admission to Discovery Cove with Dolphin Swim	249.00–279.00	143.00–160.00
Adult admission to Orlando Science Center	14.95	8.00
Child admission to Orlando Science Center	9.95	5.00
Adult admission to Gatorland	19.95	11.00
Child admission to Gatorland	12.95	5.00

Value Online Ticketing

The Orlando theme parks have jumped head first into the Internet discounting game. **Disney** (www.disneyworld.com), **Universal** (www.universalorlando.com), and **SeaWorld** (www.seaworld.com), along with many of the smaller attractions, offer price discounts for online ticket purchases. Another advantage to ordering online is that the parks often feature Web-only deals, such as free extra days at the parks. Note that you must purchase tickets from your home (not from a laptop or hotel business center once you have arrived). Tickets may also need to be ordered in time to arrive at your home via mail (though select attractions may offer the option to pick up your tickets upon arrival), so keep your timeline in mind when purchasing.

---

sense of security. Goofy and Pluto won't mug you, but some of their estranged neighbors might. Cuddly characters aside, this is a big city and the crime rate here is the same as in comparable locations. When entering your PIN at an ATM, make sure you shield the keyboard from others in line. And if you're using a drive-through, keep your doors locked.

In addition to getting cash out of an ATM, you can also buy **Disney dollars** (currency with the images of Mickey, Minnie, and so on) in $1, $5, and $10 denominations. They're good at WDW shops, restaurants, and resorts, as well as Disney stores everywhere. This is a great way to give a preset allowance to kids for their souvenirs. If you have any of these dollars leftover, you can exchange them for real currency upon leaving WDW, or keep them as a souvenir. *Note:* Pay close attention if you have a refund coming. Some items, such as strollers, wheelchairs, and lockers, require a deposit, and Disney staffers will frequently use Mickey money for refunds instead of the cash. If you don't want it, just let them know and they'll be happy to give you real cash.

TRAVELER'S CHECKS

Traveler's checks are widely accepted in the U.S., but foreign visitors should make sure that they're denominated in U.S.

dollars; foreign-currency checks are often difficult to exchange.

You can buy traveler's checks at most banks. Most are offered in denominations of $20, $50, $100, $500, and sometimes $1,000. Generally, you'll pay a service charge ranging from 1% to 4%.

The most popular traveler's checks are offered by **American Express** (© 800/807-6233; © 800/221-7282 for card holders—this number accepts collect calls, offers service in several foreign languages, and exempts Amex gold and platinum cardholders from the 1% fee); **Visa** (© 800/732-1322)—AAA members can obtain Visa checks for a $9.95 fee (for checks up to $1,500) at most AAA offices or by calling © 866/339-3378—and **MasterCard** (© 800/223-9920).

If you do choose to carry traveler's checks, keep a record of their serial numbers separate from your checks in the event that they are stolen or lost. You'll get a refund faster if you know the numbers.

You can cash traveler's or personal checks of $25 or less (drawn on U.S. banks, if you have a driver's license and major credit card), and exchange foreign currency at **SunTrust** Bank, 1675 Buena Vista Dr., across from Downtown Disney Marketplace. The bank also has an ATM. It's open weekdays from 9am to 4pm and until 6pm on Thursday (© 407/828-6106).

For tips and telephone numbers to call if your wallet is stolen or lost, go to "Lost & Found" in the Fast Facts section of chapter 3.

4 When to Go

Orlando is the theme-park capital of the world, and you could almost argue that there really is no off season here, though the busiest seasons are whenever kids are out of school. Late May to just past Labor Day, long holiday weekends, winter holidays (mid-Dec to early Jan), and most especially spring break (late Mar to Apr) are very busy. Do, however, keep in mind that kids in other hemispheres follow a completely different schedule altogether. Obviously, an Orlando vacation—and most especially a Disney vacation—is most enjoyed when the crowds are at the thinnest and the weather is the most temperate. Hotel rooms (likely the largest chunk of your vacation bill) are also priced lower (albeit slightly) during the off season, though don't expect that period to follow the traditional winter/summer patterns of most areas.

Peak-season rates can go into effect during large conventions and special events either of which may occur at any time of the year. Even something as remote as Bike Week in Daytona Beach (about an hour by car northeast) can raise prices. These kinds of events will especially impact the moderately priced hotels and resorts located off Walt Disney World.

Best times: The week after Labor Day until the week before Thanksgiving when the kids have just returned to school, the week after Thanksgiving until mid-December, and the 6 weeks before and after school spring vacations (which generally occur around Easter).

Worst times: The absolute worst time of year to visit is during spring break—usually the 2 weeks prior to and after Easter. The crowds are unbelievable, the

Tips Weather Wise

It's not uncommon for the skies to open up on Orlando, even when the day began with the sun ablaze. Florida is well known for its afternoon downpours, so don't be too concerned—storms don't usually last too long. Most people simply run for temporary cover and then resume their activities when the rain slows to a drizzle or stops altogether. It is wise, however, to bring along some type of rain gear as storms can spring up rather quickly. A small fold-up umbrella can protect you until you can get to shelter. If you forget your gear, rain ponchos can be purchased throughout the parks for about $6 for a child-size poncho, or $8 for an adult size. The child-size poncho also happens to cover the average stroller quite well, protecting camera equipment and souvenirs—not to mention the child sitting inside it.

Don't let a rainy afternoon spoil your fun. Crowds are dramatically thinner on these days and there are plenty of indoor attractions to enjoy, particularly at Epcot, Disney–MGM, Universal Studios Florida, and even SeaWorld, where many of the attractions are actually indoors. The flip side, of course, is that many of the outdoor rides at Disney, Universal, and Sea-World are temporarily closed during downpours and lightning storms.

lines are unbearable (my kids have waited upwards of 2 hr. to hop on some of the most popular attractions), waiting times at local restaurants can lead to starvation, and traffic—particularly on International Drive—will give you a headache. The December holidays and summer, when out-of-state visitors take advantage of school breaks and many locals bring their families to the parks (the latter also flock to the parks during Florida resident discount months, which usually fall in May and Nov) can also prove a challenge. Packed parking lots are the norm during the week before and after Christmas, and the summer brings with it oppressive heat and humidity. *Seriously consider pulling your kids out of school* for a few days around an off-season weekend to avoid the long lines. (You may be able to keep them in their schools' good graces by asking teachers to let them write a report on an educational element of the vacation. Epcot, SeaWorld, and the Orlando Museum of Science offer the most in the way of educational exhibits.) Even during these periods, though, the number of international visitors guarantees you won't be alone.

Note: If you're taking advantage of a land/cruise package (see "Disney Cruise Packages," later in this chapter), make sure you take into account hurricane season, which generally runs from around June 1 to November 30 (when the majority of Central Florida's afternoon downpours tend to occur). Inland, the worst is usually only sheets of rain and enough wind to wipe the smile right off your face. That said, the summer of 2004 (when three hurricanes passed through the area) was a noticeable reminder that worse can happen. And 2005 brought with it what seemed like an endless number of storms, extending the rainy season well beyond the normal timeline. If you are on the coastal areas or at sea, you will likely be at the point where the storms hit their hardest, making them extremely dangerous. Tornadoes and lightning—two particularly active summer curses—should also not to be taken too lightly.

Central Florida Average Temperatures

		Jan	Feb	Mar	Apr	May	June	July	Aug	Sept	Oct	Nov	Dec
High	°F	72	73	78	84	88	91	92	92	90	84	78	73
	°C	22	23	26	29	31	33	33	33	32	29	26	23
Low	°F	49	50	55	60	66	71	73	73	73	65	57	51
	°C	10	10	13	16	19	22	23	23	23	19	14	11

ORLANDO AREA CALENDAR OF EVENTS

January

Capital One Florida Citrus Bowl. New Year's Day kicks off with this football game in downtown Orlando. It pits the second-ranked teams from the Southeastern and Big Ten conferences against each other. Tickets are $55 before November 1 and $65 thereafter. Call ⓒ **800/297-2695** or 407/423-2476 for information or **Ticketmaster** at ⓒ **877/803-7073** or 407/839-3900 for tickets (on the Internet, visit **www.fcsports.com**). A free downtown parade is held a few days before the game and features marching bands and floats.

Walt Disney World Marathon. About 90% of the 16,000 runners finish this 26.2-mile "sprint" through the resort area and parks. It's open to anyone over 18 years of age, including runners with disabilities as long as they are able to maintain the 16-minute mile pacing requirements. If you are unable to do so, you'll be picked up and transported to the finish line. The registration fee is $100 and includes a medal, cap, and other extras for those who finish—along with souvenirs for all who enter. The registration deadline is usually in early November, and pre-registration is required. There's also a half-marathon ($90), Goofy's Race and a Half Challenge (includes registration for both marathons; $190), and a Family Fun Run that includes shorter races for adults and kids ($25, if postmarked by Dec 26, $30 after that; $5 per child for the kids' races). Call ℂ **407/939-7810** or go to **www.disneysports.com**. January 6 to January 8.

Zora Neale Hurston Festival. This 4-day celebration in Eatonville, the first incorporated African-American town in America, highlights the life and works of the author and is usually held the last weekend in January. Eatonville is 25 miles north of the theme parks. Admission is $5 to $18 for adults, $3 for kids under 17. Additional fees are charged for lectures or seminars. Call ℂ **407/647-3307** or check out **www. zoranealehurstonfestival.com**.

February

Atlanta Braves. The Braves have been holding spring training at Disney's Wide World of Sports Complex since 1998. There are 15 home games during the 1-month season. (The team arrives in mid-Feb; games begin in early Mar.) Tickets are $14 to $22. You can get more information at ℂ **407/ 939-GAME (4236)** or **www.disney sports.com**. To purchase tickets, call Ticketmaster at ℂ **877/803-7073** or 407/839-3900. You can also get online information at **www.atlantabraves. com** or **www.majorleaguebaseball. com**.

Houston Astros. The Astros train at Osceola County Stadium, 1000 Bill Beck Blvd., Kissimmee. Tickets are $15 to $18. Get them through Ticketmaster at ℂ **877/803-7073** or 407/ 839-3900. For information, check the Astros' website at **www.astros.com**.

Mardi Gras at Universal Orlando. Floats, stilt walkers, live entertainment, and beads thrown to the crowd add to the fun of this event. A party to rival the original held in New Orleans, it's definitely geared for an adult crowd with plenty of drinking and carousing. Special discounted tickets are available allowing entrance to the park only after 5pm ($42.95), otherwise it's included in regular park admission ($63 adult). The celebration runs 1 night a week (usually Sat) from mid-February to mid-April. For information, call ℂ **888/389-4783** or 407/ 363-8000, or go online to **www. universalorlando.com**.

Silver Spurs Rodeo. It features real yippee-I-O cowboys in calf roping, bull riding, barrel racing, and more. This rodeo is the largest in the eastern United States. It's held at the Silver Spurs Arena, 1875 E. Irlo Bronson Memorial Hwy. (U.S. 192), Kissimmee. It runs for 3 days in February (and again for 3 days in Oct). Call ℂ **407/847-4052** or visit **www.silver spursrodeo.com** for details. Tickets run from $10, $15, and $25 when purchased ahead of time, to $12, $18, and $30 at the gate.

March

Bay Hill Invitational. Hosted by Arnold Palmer and featuring Orlando-based golfers such as Tiger Woods, this PGA Tour event is held at the Bay Hill Club, 9000 Bay Hill Blvd. Daily admission is $35 to $45 for an adult, $15 ages 11 to 17. Call ℂ **866/764-4843** or 407/876-7774, or check out **www.bayhillinvitational.bizland. com**.

World's Fair for Kids

Entertainment and education will be rolled up into one spectacular and very family-friendly event when the World's Fair for Kids makes its debut in Orlando. Themed pavilions will highlight the latest developments in sports, health, science and technology, communications, travel, learning, toys and games, and entertainment. Events, activities, and entertainment will be geared to kids ranging from tots to teens. It's all part of the city's Family Spring Break event—a family-friendly version of spring break. Single-day tickets will reportedly run $30, 2-day $50, and event-long $60. Kids 3 and under go free. Call ℂ 407/363-5872 or go to www.wfkids.com for a definitive date (one hadn't been set at press time), information, and tickets.

Sidewalk Arts Festival. Held in Winter Park's Central Park, this 3-day exhibition draws artists from all over North America from March 16 to March 18. The festival is consistently named one of the best in the nation by *Sunshine Artist* magazine. Admission is free, though you may have to pay for parking. Call ℂ 407/672-6390 or 407/644-8281, or go to www.wpsaf.org for details.

Viva La Musica. This celebration of Latin culture and music is held annually at SeaWorld. Festivities include concerts, and crafts and food displays throughout the park. There is no extra charge to join in the fun, which happens every Saturday in March. For more information and exact dates, head online to www.seaworld.com.

April

Florida Film Festival. The Enzian Theater has been showcasing American independent and foreign films for more than a decade. This annual event was named one of the top 10 such events in the world by *The Ultimate Film Festival Survival Guide, 2nd Edition.* Call 407/629-1088 or 407/629-0054, or look up www.floridafilmfestival.com.

Epcot International Flower and Garden Festival. This 6-week-long event showcases gardens, topiary characters, floral displays, speakers, and seminars. The festival is free with regular park admission ($63 adults, $52 kids 3–9). For more information, call ℂ 407/934-7639 or visit www.disneyworld.com. The festival kicks off in late April and goes through early June.

May

Orlando International Fringe Festival. Over 100 diverse acts from around the world participate in this eclectic event, held for 10 days in May at various venues in downtown Orlando. Entertainers perform drama, comedy, political satire, and experimental theater. Everything performed on outdoor stages, from sword swallowing to *Hamlet,* is available free to Fringe attendees after they purchase a festival button for about $6. Tickets for indoor events vary, but most are under $10. Call ℂ 407/648-0077 or visit www.orlandofringe.org for details.

Star Wars Weekends. Every year, Disney features a fan-fest full of activities for *Star Wars* fanatics. Characters are on hand for up-close meet-and-greets, as well as a handful of *Star Wars* actors. Games, parades, and special entertainment top off the festivities. The celebrations run for five consecutive weekends beginning in May and are included in park admission ($63 adult, $52 child).

June

Gay Days. The first weekend in June attracts tens of thousands of gays and lesbians to Central Florida for what amounts, with add-ons, to a week of festivities. It grew out of "Gay Day," held unofficially at Disney World since the early 1990s and drawing some 100,000 people to the area. Special events at Disney, Universal, and Sea-World also cater to gays and lesbians. Look for online information on discounts, packages, hosts, and more at **www.gayday.com** or **www.gaydays. com**. Also, see "Gay & Lesbian Travel," later in this chapter.

Wet 'n Wild Summer Nights. During the months of June and July you can ride and slide until 11pm on Friday and Saturday nights at this excellent water park. Arrive after 5pm and you'll get a $10 discount off the regular admission price ($37 adult, $31 kids 3–9).

July

Independence Day. Disney's Star-Spangled Spectacular brings bands, singers, dancers, and unbelievable fireworks displays to all the Disney parks, which stay open later than normal. Call ℂ **407/934-7639** for details or surf over to **www.disneyworld.com**. **SeaWorld** (ℂ **407/351-3600;** www. seaworld.com) features a dazzling laser/fireworks spectacular. There's also a free fireworks display in downtown Orlando at Lake Eola Park. For information, call ℂ **407/246-2827.** Other fireworks events are listed in the local newspaper, the *Orlando Sentinel.*

Tampa Bay Bucs. The NFL Tampa Bay Buccaneers run their training camp at the Wide World of Sports Complex from late July through August. For information call ℂ **407/939-GAME (4236)** or go to **www.buccaneers.com** for more information.

September

Night of Joy. The first weekend (Thurs–Sun) in September, the Magic Kingdom hosts a festival of contemporary Christian music featuring top artists. This is a very popular event, so obtain tickets early. Performers also make an appearance at Long's Christian Bookstore in College Park, about 20 minutes north of Disney. Admission (if you buy in advance) to the concert is $39.95 for 1 night (7:30pm–12:30am), $67.95 for 2 nights; single-night admission at the gate is $44.95. Use of Magic Kingdom attractions is included. Call ℂ **407/934-7639** for concert details; for information about the free appearance at Long's, call ℂ **407/422-6934.** Universal has gone head-to-head with Disney on this one, scheduling its **Rock the Universe** concert the same weekend (ℂ **866/788-4636**). Big-name Christian bands and speakers headline the event. Tickets (which include admission to the parks after 4pm) cost $37 for 1 night or $60 for both nights of the event. A package including both nights of celebration, as well as 3 full days of admission to the parks (Fri–Sun), runs $91.

October

Orlando Magic Basketball. The NBA team plays half of its 82-game regular season between October and April at the TD Waterhouse Centre, 600 W. Amelia Street. Ticket prices range from

---

⸧ **Fun Fact** **It's A Small World—Or Is It?**

WDW covers more than 47 square miles, roughly the same size as the Island of Manhattan. Believe it or not, only one-fourth of the property has actually been developed. Makes you wonder what Disney will do next.

$10 to $110. A few tickets, usually single seats, are often available the day before games involving lesser-known NBA challengers. Call ✆ **407/896-2442** for details, 877/803-7073 or 407/839-3900 for tickets. Online go to **www.nba.com/magic**.

Halloween Horror Nights. Universal Orlando's Islands of Adventure (✆ **888/389-4783** or 407/363-8000; www.universalorlando.com) transforms its grounds on select nights during October and into November into haunted attractions. Live entertainment and special shows, hundreds of ghouls and goblins roaming the streets, along with specially designed haunted houses make for a truly terrifying experience. The park essentially closes at dusk, reopening in a new macabre form from 7pm to midnight or later. Full admission ($63 adults) is charged for this event, which is definitely geared to grown-ups (as the liquor flows freely and the frightfulness is *truly* that). In 2005, for the first time since the event's inception, guests were permitted to wear costumes (regulated) on some evenings (they were originally prohibited so that Universal employees could spot their peers). There's no word on whether this policy will remain in effect for future Horror Nights, so call and ask in advance if you plan to attend.

Mickey's Not-So-Scary Halloween Party. The Magic Kingdom (✆ **407/934-7639;** www.disneyworld.com) invites you to join Mickey and his pals for a far-from-frightening time. In this one, you can come in costume and trick-or-treat throughout the Magic Kingdom from 7pm to midnight on any of 10 or so nights. The alcohol-free party includes parades, live music, and storytelling. The climax is a bewitching fireworks spectacular. Unlike the celebration at Universal Studios, this one

is completely family-friendly. A separate admission fee is charged ($38 adults, $30 kids 3–9; add $5 if ticket purchased the day of the event), and you should get tickets well in advance.

The FUNAI Classic at Walt Disney World. Top PGA tour players compete at WDW golf courses during the month of October. Many tour professionals, including Tiger Woods, call Orlando home, so there's usually plenty of first-rate talent on display. Daily ticket prices range from $15 to $35. Tickets for the 4-day event run about $50. For information, contact Walt Disney World Golf Sales, P.O. Box 10000, Lake Buena Vista, FL 32830 (✆ **407/824-2250;** www.disneyworld.com). You also can get tickets through Ticketmaster (✆ **877/803-7073** or 407/839-3900).

Epcot International Food & Wine Festival. Here's your chance to sip and savor the food and beverages of 25 cultures. More than 60 wineries from across the United States participate. Events include wine tastings for adults, seminars, food, dinners, concerts, and celebrity-chef cooking demonstrations. Tickets for the dinner-and-concert series or wine tastings are $35 to $125 including gratuity; signature dinners and vertical wine tastings are $95 to $185. The event also features 25 food-and-wine marketplaces where appetizer-size portions of dishes ranging from pizza to octopus on purple potato salad sell for under $5 each. Entrance to the festival is included in park admission. Call ✆ **407/934-7639** for details or check out **www.disney world.com**. Early October to mid-November.

November

ABC Super Soap Weekend. If you're a fan of ABC's daytime soaps, this is one you won't want to miss. Soap celebs are on hand for parades, parties, Q and As,

(Fun Fact Disney in December

No snow? No problem. While there may be a lack of the white stuff in Orlando during the month of December (or any other month for that matter), WDW more that makes up for it by decking the halls as only Disney can do: 11 miles of garlands, 3,000 wreaths, and 1,500 Christmas trees in all, decorate Walt Disney World during the holiday season.

music, and more in this weekend catering to fans and fanatics alike. The events are included with Disney–MGM Studios admission ($63 adults, $52 kids 3–9). Call ℂ **407/397-6808** or check out **www.disneyworld.com** for details.

Walt Disney World Festival of the Masters. One of the largest art shows in the South takes place at Downtown Disney Marketplace for 3 days during the second weekend in November. The exhibition features over 150 top artists, photographers, and craftspeople, all winners of juried shows throughout the country. You can listen to the music of the jazz festival or enjoy one of the many family activities all for free. Call ℂ **407/934-7639** or visit **www.disneyworld.com**.

The Osborne Family Spectacle of Lights. This classic holiday attraction returned by popular demand after being closed down for renovations in 2004 and 2005. Lighting up the nights at the Disney–MGM Studios are millions of sparkling bulbs acquired from a family whose Christmas light collection got a bit too bright for their neighbors. The holiday display runs from November to early January.

December

Christmas at Walt Disney World. During the holiday festivities, Main Street in the Magic Kingdom is lavishly decked out with twinkling lights and Christmas holly, all the while carolers are greeting visitors throughout

the park. Epcot, Disney–MGM Studios, and Animal Kingdom also offer special embellishments and entertainment throughout the holiday season, and the Disney resorts are decked out with towering Christmas trees, wreaths, boughs, and bows.

Some holiday highlights include **Mickey's Very Merry Christmas Party,** an after-dark (7pm–midnight) ticketed event ($43.95 adults, $34.95 kids 3–9). This takes place on select nights at the Magic Kingdom and offers a festive parade, fireworks, special shows, and admission to a handful of rides. Also included are cookies, cocoa, and a souvenir photo.

Holidays Around the World and the **Candlelight Procession** at Epcot feature hundreds of carolers, storytellers from a host of international countries, celebrity narrators telling the Christmas story, a 450-voice choir, and a 50-piece orchestra in a very moving display. Fireworks are included. Regular admission ($63 adults, $52 kids 3–9) is required. Call ℂ **407/934-7639** for details on all of the above or go to **www.disneyworld.com**. The holiday fun lasts from mid-December to early January.

Macy's Holiday Parade. *That's not a typo!* Universal and Macy's (the latter a tenant at the Mall at Millenia, p. 315) teamed up for the first time in December 2002 to offer a smaller version of **Macy's Thanksgiving Day Parade** held at Universal Studios Florida. It runs from mid-December to early

January, featuring several of the floats and gigantic balloons from the original New York City parade (© **407/363-8000;** www.universalorlando.com). Park admission ($63 for adults, $52 for kids 3–9) is required. Over at Islands of Adventure, even the Grinch celebrates the holidays at Seuss Landing, which is decked out like Whoville for the holidays, including wintry decorations and "Whos" running all about to create a festive mood.

Walt Disney World New Year's Eve Celebration. For 1 night a year, the Magic Kingdom stays open until the wee hours for a massive fireworks explosion. Other New Year's festivities in WDW include a big (and pricey—$89 a pop) bash at Pleasure Island featuring major music headliners, a special Hoop-Dee-Doo Musical Revue at Fort Wilderness, and guest performances by well-known musical groups at Disney–MGM Studios and Epcot. Call © **407/934-7639** for details or visit **www.disneyworld.com**. December 31.

5 Travel Insurance

TRAVEL INSURANCE AT A GLANCE

The cost of travel insurance varies widely, depending on the cost and length of your trip, your age and health, and the type of trip you're taking, but expect to pay between 5% and 8% of the vacation itself. You can get estimates from various providers through **InsureMyTrip.com**. Enter your trip cost and dates, your age, and other information, for prices from more than a dozen companies.

TRIP-CANCELLATION INSURANCE

Trip-cancellation insurance will help retrieve your money if you have to back out of a trip or depart early, or if your travel supplier goes bankrupt. Permissible reasons for trip cancellation can range from sickness to natural disasters to the State Department declaring a destination unsafe for travel.

For more information, contact one of the following recommended insurers: **Access America** (© 866/807-3982; www.accessamerica.com); **Travel Guard International** (© 800/826-4919; www.travelguard.com); **Travel Insured International** (© 800/243-3174; www.travelinsured.com); and **Travelex Insurance Services** (© 888/457-4602; www.travelexinsurance.com).

MEDICAL INSURANCE

Although it's not required of travelers, health insurance is highly recommended. Most health insurance policies cover you

---

Travel in the Age of Bankruptcy

Airlines go bankrupt, so protect yourself by **buying your tickets with a credit card.** The Fair Credit Billing Act guarantees that you can get your money back from the credit card company if a travel supplier goes under (and if you request the refund within 60 days of the bankruptcy). **Travel insurance** can also help, but make sure it covers against "carrier default" for your specific travel provider. And be aware that if a U.S. airline goes bust mid-trip, a 2001 federal law requires other carriers to take you to your destination (albeit on a space-available basis) for a fee of no more than $25, provided you rebook within 60 days of the cancellation.

> ⓘ *Tips* **Quick ID**
>
> Tie a colorful ribbon or yarn around your luggage handle, opt for colorful luggage rather than the usual black, or use a distinctive luggage tag. This makes it much easier to identify yours among the many other practically identical suitcases circling the luggage belt. If your luggage gets lost, this will help to identify it as well.

---

if you get sick away from home—but verify that you're covered before you depart, particularly if you're insured by an HMO.

International visitors should note that unlike many European countries, the United States does not usually offer free or low-cost medical care to its citizens or visitors. Doctors and hospitals are expensive, and in most cases will require advance payment or proof of coverage before they render their services. Good policies will cover the costs of an accident, repatriation, or death. Packages such as **Europ Assistance's "Worldwide Healthcare Plan"** are sold by European automobile clubs and travel agencies at attractive rates. **Worldwide Assistance Services, Inc.** (ⓒ **800/777-8710;** www. worldwideassistance.com) is the agent for Europ Assistance in the United States.

Though lack of health insurance may prevent you from being admitted to a hospital in nonemergencies, don't worry about being left on a street corner to die: The American way is to fix you now and bill the living daylights out of you later.

INSURANCE FOR BRITISH TRAVELERS Most big travel agents offer their own insurance and will probably try to sell you their package when you book a holiday. Think before you sign. **Britain's Consumers' Association** recommends that you insist on seeing the policy and reading the fine print before buying travel insurance. **The Association of British Insurers** (ⓒ **020/7600-3333;** www.abi.org.uk) gives advice by phone

and publishes *Holiday Insurance,* a free guide to policy provisions and prices. You might also shop around for better deals: Try **Columbus Direct** (ⓒ **0870/033-9988;** www.columbusdirect.net).

INSURANCE FOR CANADIAN TRAVELERS Canadians should check with their provincial health plan offices or call **Health Canada** (ⓒ **866/225-0709;** www.hc-sc.gc.ca) to find out the extent of their coverage and what documentation and receipts they must take home in case they are treated in the United States.

LOST-LUGGAGE INSURANCE

On flights within the U.S., checked baggage is covered up to $2,500 per ticketed passenger. On flights outside the U.S. (and on U.S. portions of international trips), baggage coverage is limited to approximately $9.07 per pound, up to approximately $635 per checked bag. If you plan to check items more valuable than what's covered by the standard liability, see if your homeowner's policy covers your valuables, get baggage insurance as part of your comprehensive travel-insurance package, or buy Travel Guard's "BagTrak" product.

If your luggage is lost, immediately file a lost-luggage claim at the airport, detailing the luggage contents. Most airlines require that you report delayed, damaged, or lost baggage within 4 hours of arrival. The airlines are required to deliver luggage, once found, directly to your house or destination free of charge.

6 Health & Safety

STAYING HEALTHY

Limit your exposure to Florida's strong sun, especially during the first few days of your trip and, thereafter, during the hours of 11am to 2pm, when the sun is at its strongest. Use a sunscreen with the highest sun protection factor (SPF) available (especially for children) and apply it liberally. If you have children under a year old, check with your pediatrician before applying a sunscreen—some ingredients may not be appropriate for infants.

GENERAL AVAILABILITY OF HEALTHCARE

Contact the **International Association for Medical Assistance to Travelers (IAMAT;** © **716/754-4883,** or 416/652-0137 in Canada; **www.iamat.org)** for tips on travel and health concerns in the countries you're visiting, and for lists of local, English-speaking doctors. The United States **Centers for Disease Control and Prevention** (© **800/311-3435;** www.cdc.gov) provides up-to-date information on health hazards by region or country and offers tips on food safety. The website **www.tripprep.com**, sponsored by a consortium of travel medicine practitioners, may also offer helpful advice on traveling abroad. You can find listings of reliable clinics overseas at the **International Society of Travel Medicine** (www.istm.org).

WHAT TO DO IF YOU GET SICK AWAY FROM HOME

We list **hospitals** and **emergency numbers** under "Fast Facts," p. 70.

If you suffer from a chronic illness, consult your doctor before your departure. Pack **prescription medications** in your carry-on luggage, and carry prescription medications in their original containers, with pharmacy labels—otherwise they won't make it through airport security. Visitors from outside the U.S. should carry generic names of prescription drugs. For U.S. travelers, most reliable healthcare plans provide coverage if you get sick away from home. Foreign visitors may have to pay all medical costs upfront and be reimbursed later. See "Medical Insurance," under "Travel Insurance," above.

ECO-TOURISM

You can find eco-friendly travel tips, statistics, and touring companies and associations—listed by destination under "Travel Choice"—at the TIES website, www.ecotourism.org. **Ecotravel.com** is part online magazine and part ecodirectory that lets you search for touring companies in several categories (water-based,

---

Avoiding "Economy Class Syndrome"

Deep vein thrombosis, or as it's know in the world of flying, "economy-class syndrome," is a blood clot that develops in a deep vein. It's a potentially deadly condition that can be caused by sitting in cramped conditions—such as an airplane cabin—for too long. During a flight (especially a long-haul flight), get up, walk around, and stretch your legs every 60 to 90 minutes to keep your blood flowing. Other preventative measures include frequent flexing of the legs while sitting, drinking lots of water, and avoiding alcohol and sleeping pills. If you have a history of deep vein thrombosis, heart disease, or another condition that puts you at high risk, some experts recommend wearing compression stockings or taking anticoagulants when you fly; always ask your physician about the best course for you. Symptoms of deep vein thrombosis include leg pain or swelling, or even shortness of breath.

Healthy Travels to You

The following government websites offer up-to-date health-related travel advice.

- **Australia:** www.dfat.gov.au/travel
- **Canada:** www.hc-sc.gc.ca/index_e.html
- **U.K.:** www.dh.gov.uk/PolicyAndGuidance/HealthAdviceForTravellers/fs/en
- **U.S.:** www.cdc.gov/travel

land-based, spiritually oriented, and so on). Also check out **Conservation International** (www.conservation.org)— which, with *National Geographic Traveler,* annually presents **World Legacy Awards** (www.wlaward.org) to those travel tour operators, businesses, organizations, and

places that have made a significant contribution to sustainable tourism.

For information about the ethics of swimming with dolphins and other outdoor activities, visit the **Whale and Dolphin Conservation Society** (www.wdcs. org) and **Tread Lightly** (www.tread lightly.org).

7 Specialized Travel Resources

TRAVELERS WITH DISABILITIES

There's no reason for those of you with disabilities to miss most of the fun that Orlando and the theme parks have to offer. There are more options and resources out there than ever before.

ACCOMMODATIONS Every hotel and motel in Florida is required by law to have a special room or rooms equipped for wheelchairs. A few have wheel-in showers. Walt Disney World's **Coronado Springs Resort** (© **407/934-7639** or 407/939-1000; www.disneyworld.com) has 99 rooms designed to accommodate guests with disabilities. **Disney's Polynesian** and **Grand Floridian** resorts are both particularly well suited to guests who use wheelchairs, as the location of the resorts on the monorail system makes travel to the Magic Kingdom and Epcot a bit easier. Make your special needs known when making reservations. For other information about special Disney rooms, call © **407/939-7807.**

If you don't mind staying 15 minutes from Disney, **Yvonne's Property Management** (© **877/714-1144** or 863/ 424-0795; www.villasinorlando.com) is a

rental agent for, among other things, some handicapped-accessible homes that have multiple-bedrooms, multiple-bathrooms with accessible showers, full kitchens, and pools outfitted with lifts. Most cost less than $250 a night and are located in Davenport.

Medical Travel Inc. (© **800/778-7953;** www.medicaltravel.org) is another source of rentals, scooters and vans, and medical equipment, and can satisfy other needs of disabled travelers, including those with terminal illnesses, and their families.

TRANSPORTATION Public buses in Orlando have hydraulic lifts and restraining belts for wheelchairs. They serve Universal Orlando, SeaWorld, the shopping areas, and downtown Orlando. Disney shuttle buses all accommodate wheelchairs as does the monorail system and some of the watercraft that travel to the parks and resorts.

If you need to rent a wheelchair or electric scooter for your visit, **Walker Medical & Mobility Products** offers delivery to your room, and there's a model for guests who weigh up to 375 pounds. These products fit into Disney's transports and monorails as well as rental cars. Get more information by calling ⓒ 888/726-6837 or 407/331-9500, or on the Internet go to www.walkermobility. com. CARE Medical Equipment (ⓒ 800/741-2282 or 407/856-2273; www.caremedicalequipment.com) offers similar services.

Disney (ⓒ 407/934-7639; www. disneyworld.com) offers wheelchair rentals at the parks, Downtown Disney, and in more limited numbers, at the resorts. In addition, a very limited number of Electric Convenience Scooters are also available for rent at the parks. *Note:* Although the Segway is becoming increasingly popular as a mode of transportation for those with disabilities, neither Disney nor SeaWorld permit Segways to be brought inside their parks. Universal Orlando does allow them inside their parks. Segways can be rented at the Orange County Convention Center, 9800 International Dr. (ⓒ 407/685-1600).

Amtrak (ⓒ 800/872-7245; www. amtrak.com) provides redcap service, wheelchair assistance, and special seats if you give 72 hours notice. Travelers with disabilities are also entitled to a 15% discount off the lowest available adult coach fare (though they cannot book online). Documentation from a doctor or an ID card proving your disability is required. Amtrak also provides wheelchair-accessible sleeping accommodations on long-distance trains. Service dogs are permitted aboard and travel free. TDD/TTY service is also available at ⓒ 800/523-6590, or you can write to P.O. Box 7717, Itasca, IL 60143.

Greyhound (ⓒ 800/752-4841; www. greyhound.com) allows a passenger with disabilities to travel with a companion for a single fare, and if you call 48 hours in advance, they'll arrange help along the way. The bus line also allows service animals.

THEME PARKS   Many attractions at the parks, especially the newer ones, are designed to be accessible to a wide variety of guests. People with wheelchairs and their parties are often given preferential treatment so they can avoid lines.

The available assistance is outlined in the guide maps you get as you enter the parks. All of the theme parks offer some parking close to the entrances for those with disabilities. Let the parking booth attendant know your needs, and you'll be directed to the appropriate spot. Wheelchair and electric cart rentals are available at most major attractions, but you'll be most comfortable in your chair or cart from home if you can bring it. Keep in mind, however, that wheelchairs wider than 24½ inches may be difficult to navigate through some attractions. And crowds may make it tough for any guest.

At Walt Disney World   Disney's many services are detailed in each theme park's *Guidebook for Guests with Disabilities.* You can pick one up at Guest Relations near the front entrances to each of the parks. Also, you can call ⓒ 407/934-7639 or 407/824-2222 for answers to any questions regarding special needs. The guide is also available online at Disney's website, www.disneyworld.com (click through to the site map, then Web info, then ADA/Guests with Disabilities). Examples of services are as follows:

- Almost all Disney resorts have rooms for those with disabilities.
- Braille guidebooks, cassette tapes, and portable tape players are available at City Hall in the Magic Kingdom and Guest Relations in the other parks (a $25 refundable deposit is required).
- Service animals are allowed in all parks and on some rides.
- All parks have special parking lots near the entrances.
- Assisted listening devices are available to amplify the audio at selected

> **Tips** **Don't Forget the 407**
>
> **Local calls** in Orlando require that you dial the area code **(407)** followed by the 7-digit local number, even when calling just across the street.

attractions at WDW parks. Also, at some attractions, hearing-impaired guests can use hand-held wireless receivers that allow them to read captions about the attractions. Both services are free but require a $25 refundable deposit.

- Wheelchairs and electric carts can be rented at all of the parks.
- Downtown Disney West Side, with crowded shops and bars, may be a bit difficult to navigate in a wheelchair. The movie theater is, however, wheelchair accessible.
- For information about Telecommunications Devices for the Deaf (TDDs) or sign-language interpreters at Disney World live shows, call (C) **407/827-5141** (TDD/TTY). You can usually get an ASL interpreter at several events and attractions if you call no later than 2 weeks in advance.

At Universal Orlando parks Guests with disabilities should go to Guest Services, located just inside the main entrances, for the *Riders Guide for Rider Safety and Guests with Disabilities* booklet, a TDD, or other special assistance. Wheelchair and electric cart rentals are available in the concourse area of the parking garage. Universal also provides audio descriptions on cassette for visually impaired guests and has sign-language guides and scripts for its shows (advance notice of 1–2 weeks is required; call (C) **888/519-4899** [TTY] or 407/224-5929 [voice] for details). You can also get additional information online at **www.universalorlando.com**. From the main page, click either on Islands of Adventure or Universal Studios Florida,

and scroll down the left side to the "ADA page."

At SeaWorld The park has a guide for guests with disabilities, although most of its attractions are easily accessible to those in wheelchairs. SeaWorld also provides a Braille guide for the visually impaired and a very brief synopsis of its shows for the hearing impaired. Sign language interpreting services are available at no charge but must be reserved by calling (C) **407/363-2414** at least a week in advance of your visit. Assisted listening devices are available at select attractions for a $20 refundable deposit. For information, call (C) **407/351-3600** or check out the park's website at **www.seaworld.com**.

OTHER RESOURCES You can get information online at the **Orlando/Orange County Convention & Visitors Bureau's (CVB)** website, **www.orlandoinfo.com**.

WheelchairsOnTheGo.com is a comprehensive website that lists information on accessibility in Florida, from ground transportation to medical equipment rentals, accommodations, and attractions (and plenty more).

Many travel agencies offer customized tours and itineraries for travelers with disabilities. Among them are **Flying Wheels Travel** ((C) **507/451-5005;** www.flyingwheelstravel.com); **Access-Able Travel Source** ((C) **303/232-2979;** www.access-able.com); and **Accessible Journeys** ((C) **800/846-4537** or 610/521-0339; www.disabilitytravel.com). **Avis Rent a Car** has an "Avis Access" program that offers such services as a dedicated 24-hour toll-free number ((C) **888/879-4273**) for customers with special travel needs; special car features such as swivel seats, spinner knobs, and hand controls; and accessible bus service.

Organizations that offer assistance to travelers with disabilities include **Moss-Rehab** (www.mossresourcenet.org); the **American Foundation for the Blind** (AFB; ✆ 800/232-5463; www.afb.org); and **SATH** (Society for Accessible Travel & Hospitality; ✆ 212/447-7284; www.sath.org). **AirAmbulanceCard.com** is now partnered with SATH and allows you to preselect top-notch hospitals in case of an emergency.

If you plan on visiting the Cape Canaveral National Seashore (p. 362) as a side trip while in Orlando, know that the **Golden Access Passport** gives visually impaired or permanently disabled persons (regardless of age) free lifetime entrance to all properties administered by the National Park Service, the U.S. Fish and Wildlife Service, the U.S. Forest Service, the U.S. Army Corps of Engineers, the Bureau of Land Management, and the Tennessee Valley Authority.

You may pick up a Golden Access Passport at any NPS entrance fee area by showing proof of medically determined disability and eligibility for benefits under federal law. Besides free entry, the Golden Access Passport also offers a 50% discount on federal-use fees charged for such facilities as camping, swimming, parking, boat launching, and tours. For more information, go to **www.nps.gov/fees_passes.htm** or call ✆ 888/467-2757.

The community website **iCan** (www.icanonline.net/channels/travel) has destination guides and several regular columns on accessible travel. Also check out the quarterly magazine *Emerging Horizons* (www.emerginghorizons.com); and *Open World* magazine, published by SATH.

GAY & LESBIAN TRAVEL

The popularity of Orlando with gay and lesbian travelers is confirmed by the expansion of the June "Gay Day" celebration at Disney World into a weekend event that includes Universal Orlando and SeaWorld. Park-goers can wear red on Gay Day to signify their support of the gay and lesbian community. Additional information on the event can be found at **www.gayday.com** or **www.gaydays.com**.

For information about events for that weekend or throughout the year, contact **Gay, Lesbian & Bisexual Community Services of Central Florida,** 934 N. Mills Ave., Orlando, FL 32803 (✆ 407/228-8272; www.glbcc.org). Welcome packets usually include the latest issue of the *Triangle,* a quarterly newsletter dedicated to gay and lesbian issues, and a calendar of events pertaining to the gay and lesbian community. Though not a tourist-specific packet, it includes information and ads for local gay and lesbian clubs. **Gay Orlando Network** (www.gayorlando.com) is another planning resource for travelers. *Watermark* (✆ 407/481-2243; www.watermarkonline.com) is another gay-friendly publication; it can be found in many bookstores.

Orlando is a Southern town, but the entertainment industry and the theme parks have helped in the building of a strong gay and lesbian community. Same-sex dancing won't draw any unwelcome attention at most of the clubs at Pleasure Island, especially the large, crowded Mannequins. Many of Universal's City-Walk establishments are similarly gender blind. The tenor of crowds can change, however, depending on what tour is in town, so respect your own intuition.

The International Gay and Lesbian Travel Association (IGLTA; ✆ 800/448-8550 or 954/776-2626; www.iglta.org) is the trade association for the gay and lesbian travel industry, and offers an online directory of gay- and lesbian-friendly travel businesses; go to their website and click on "Members."

Many agencies offer tours and travel itineraries specifically for gay and lesbian travelers. Among them are **Above and Beyond Tours** (© 800/397-2681; www. abovebeyondtours.com); **Now, Voyager** (© 800/255-6951; www.nowvoyager. com); and **Olivia Cruises & Resorts** (© 800/631-6277; www.olivia.com).

Gay.com Travel (© 800/929-2268 or 415/644-8044; www.gay.com/travel or www.outandabout.com) is an excellent online successor to the popular *Out & About* print magazine. It provides regularly updated information about gay-owned, gay-oriented, and gay-friendly lodging, dining, sightseeing, nightlife, and shopping establishments in every important destination worldwide.

The following travel guides are available at many bookstores, or you can order them from any online bookseller: *Spartacus International Gay Guide* (Bruno Gmünder Verlag; www.spartacusworld. com/gayguide); *Odysseus: The International Gay Travel Planner* (Odysseus Enterprises Ltd.); and the *Damron* guides (www.damron.com), with separate, annual books for gay men and lesbians.

SENIOR TRAVEL

Mention the fact if you're a senior when you make your travel reservations. Many hotels, resorts, and restaurants offer discounts to seniors. In most cities, people over the age of 60 qualify for reduced admission to theaters, museums, and other attractions, as well as discounted fares on public transportation.

You can order a copy of the *Mature Traveler Guide,* which contains local discounts mainly on rooms but also on attractions and activities, from the **Orlando/Orange County Convention & Visitors Bureau,** 8723 International Dr., Suite 101, Orlando, FL 32819 (© 800/643-9492 or 800/551-0181; www.orlandoinfo.com). You can also find it online at the CVB's website (click the

"senior" link under "other areas" on the left side of the home page).

Members of **AARP** (formerly known as the American Association of Retired Persons), 601 E St. NW, Washington, DC 20049 (© 888/687-2277; www. aarp.org), get discounts on hotels, airfares, and car rentals. AARP offers members a wide range of benefits, including *AARP: The Magazine* and a monthly newsletter. Anyone over 50 can join.

The **U.S. National Park Service** offers a **Golden Age Passport** that gives seniors 62 years or older lifetime entrance to all properties administered by the National Park Service—national parks, monuments, historic sites, recreation areas, and national wildlife refuges—for a one-time processing fee of $10, which must be purchased in person at any NPS facility that charges an entrance fee. Besides free entry, a Golden Age Passport also offers a 50% discount on federal-use fees charged for such facilities as camping, swimming, parking, boat launching, and tours. For more information, go to www.nps.gov/ fees_passes.htm or call © 888/467-2757.

Many reliable agencies and organizations target the 50-plus market. **Elderhostel** (© 877/426-8056; www.elder hostel.org) arranges study programs for those aged 55 and over.

Recommended publications offering travel resources and discounts for seniors include the quarterly magazine *Travel 50 & Beyond* (www.travel50andbeyond. com); *Travel Unlimited: Uncommon Adventures for the Mature Traveler* (Avalon); *101 Tips for Mature Travelers,* available from Grand Circle Travel (© 800/221-2610 or 617/350-7500; www.gct.com); and *Unbelievably Good Deals and Great Adventures That You Absolutely Can't Get Unless You're Over 50* (McGraw-Hill), by Joann Rattner Heilman.

FAMILY TRAVEL

If you have enough trouble getting your kids out of the house in the morning, dragging them thousands of miles away may seem like an insurmountable challenge. But family travel can be immensely rewarding, giving you new ways of seeing the world through smaller pairs of eyes.

No city in the world is geared more to family travel than Orlando. In addition to its theme parks, Orlando's recreational facilities provide an abundance of opportunities for family fun. Most restaurants have lower-priced ($4–$9) children's menus (if not, the appetizer menu works just as well) and fun distractions such as place mats to color while younger diners wait for their food. Many of the hotels and resorts offer children's activity centers (see chapter 4, "Where to Stay," for details).

Keep an eye out for coupons discounting meals and attractions; they can be found practically everywhere. The Calendar section in Friday's *Orlando Sentinel* newspaper often contains coupons and good deals. Many restaurants, especially those in tourist areas, offer great discounts that are yours for the clipping. Check the information you receive from the Orlando/Orange County Convention & Visitors Bureau (see "Visitor Information" earlier in this chapter) including free or cheap things to do. Additionally, many hotel lobbies and attractions have free coupon books for the taking.

Some theme parks offer parent-swap programs in which one parent can ride without the children, then switch off and let the other parent ride without returning to the end of the line. Inquire at Guest Services or Guest Relations, near the park entrances for details on which rides are included.

To locate accommodations, restaurants, and attractions that are particularly kid-friendly, refer to the "Kids" icon throughout this guide.

Here are more suggestions for making traveling with children easier:

- **Are Your Kids Old Enough?** Do you really want to bring an infant or toddler to the parks? If you plan on visiting Disney several times as your children grow, then the best age for a first visit to Disney is just about 3 years old. Why? Because the kids are old enough to walk around, enjoy the sights and sounds, and a good deal of the rides and shows as well. The thrill rides would most likely frighten them, but most inappropriate rides for the tiny tot set have height restrictions that prevent any unfortunate mistakes. If, however, this trip is going to be a one-time trip, then I recommend waiting until your child is between 7 and 10. They'll still be able to appreciate the magic and wonder of the experience but won't have reached the stage where all they'll want is chills and thrills.

  Some of the characters walking about may make young kids a bit nervous, though most will run right up to Donald or Mickey and give them a big hug. Younger kids may need a nap just when you want to see a show or hop on an attraction, but if you have kids this is nothing new to you. When you plan your day's activities, be sure to account for necessary breaks and naps. Will your whole family be able to enjoy the experiences that Disney, along with the other parks, have to offer? This is something you will have to decide. My five kids range in age from 5 to 13, and we have traveled with just about every age combination you can think of. On our first family trip, my oldest (now 13) was 4, and his two younger siblings were ages 3 and 1. While the 1-year-old has absolutely no recollection of the trip, he was thoroughly amused by the sights and

Moments   Kid-Friendly Tours

SeaWorld earns its reputation as an education-friendly park with a variety of small-group tours. One of the most interesting is the **Polar Expedition Tour.** This hour-long trek gives kids a chance to come face-to-face with a penguin and get a behind-the-scenes look at polar bears and beluga whales. **Saving A Species Tour,** another hour-long tour, lets guests see some of the park's rescue and rehabilitation work with several species, including manatees and sea turtles. Both cost $16 per adult, $12 per child (ages 3–9), plus park admission (© **800/406-2244**; www.seaworld.com). Both tours are kid-friendly, though the latter may appeal more to the older ones. Both are on a first-come, first-served basis, so reserve your place at the Guided Tour Information Desk when you enter the park. In June, July, and August, **Adventure Camps** including resident camps, day camps, and sleepover programs (© **800/406-2244**; www.seaworld.com) are offered.

At Walt Disney World, the kid-friendliest tour is the **Family Magic Tour,** an interactive scavenger hunt that costs $25 per person, plus park admission (© **407/939-8687**; www.disneyworld.com).

sounds everywhere we went. The 3-year-old (now 11) still remembers plenty. You'll need to take into account your kids' stamina, interest, and tolerance levels before you decide whether to make the trip and when planning your daily itineraries. My kids could go well into the evening inside the parks, but many other children can't, so it may take you longer to cover a park (it took me 2–3 days to do Magic Kingdom when my youngest was 2). My 7-year-old nephew was petrified by some of the rides in the parks, and even my own kids, who'll try anything once and have never been wary of rides, freak out at attractions involving sensory effects. It may be repetitious, but I'll say it again: Know your own child before deciding whether he or she's ready for this sort of trip. Not every child will fall in love with Disney World at first sight, and it's a rather large expense to incur if junior's going to be frightened, sleepy, or cranky for the whole trip.

• **Planning Ahead** Make reservations for "character breakfasts" at Disney (see chapter 5, "Where to Dine") as soon as possible. Disney usually accepts them up to 180 days in advance, and many are booked minutes (we're not kidding!) after the 180-day window opens, so mark your calendar to call (and be sure you keep in mind that the line opens for calls at 7am EST). Also, in any park, check the daily schedule for character appearances (all of the major ones post them on maps or boards near the entrances) and make sure the kids know when they're going to get to meet their heroes. It's often the highlight of their day. (Be wary, however, of promising specific characters, as schedules and character lineups can change.) Advance planning will help you avoid running after every character you see. The "in" thing of late is getting character autographs. The lines can be quite long so you may want to pick and choose just a couple of favorite characters to do this with.

- **Packing**   Although your home may be toddler-proof, hotel accommodations aren't. Bring blank plugs to cover outlets and whatever else is necessary to prevent an accident from occurring in your room. Most hotels have some type of cribs available; however they are usually limited in number. Some hotels can also supply bedrails, though they are not as readily available as cribs are.

  Outside of hotel supplies, your biggest packing priority should be sunscreen. Locals can spot tourists by their bright red, just-toasted sunburn; both parents and children should heed this reminder: *Don't forget to bring and use sunscreen with an SPF rating of at least 30.* If you do forget it, it's available at convenience stores, drugstores, and some theme-park shops. Young children should be slathered, even if they're in a stroller, and be sure to pack a wide-brim hat for infants and toddlers. Adults and children alike should drink plenty of water to avoid dehydration.

- **Accommodations**   Kids under 12, and, in many cases, those as old as 17, stay free in their parent's room in most hotels, but to be certain, ask when you book your room. Most hotels have pools and other recreational facilities that will give you a little no-extra-cost downtime. If you want to skip a rental car and aren't staying at Disney, International Drive and Lake Buena Vista are the places to stay. Hotels often offer family discounts; some offer "kids eat free" programs, and some provide free or moderate-cost shuttle service to the major attractions. International drive also has the I-Drive Trolley, which travels the length of the road and makes numerous stops along the way.

- **Ground Rules**   Set firm rules before leaving home regarding things such

as bedtime and souvenirs. It's easy to get off track as you get caught up in the excitement of Orlando, but don't allow your vacation to seize control of your better judgment. Having the kids earn their own money or at least allotting a specific pre-arranged amount for them to spend works wonders. Making them part of your decisions also works wonders. They're far more accommodating and cooperative when they understand that everyone in the family gets a say in the plan for the day and that they will eventually get to do something or go somewhere that they want to.

- **At the Parks**   Getting lost is unfortunately all too easy in a place as strange and overwhelming as the theme parks. Toss in the crowds and it's amazing it doesn't happen more often. For adults (yes, they get lost too) and older kids, arrange a lost-and-found meeting place before you arrive in the parks, and if you become separated, head there immediately. Make sure your kids know to find a staff member (point out the special name-tags staff members wear) to help them. Attach a name-tag with the child's first name and your cellphone (or hotel) number to the inside of younger kids' T-shirts and tell them to find a park employee (and only a park employee) immediately and show them the tag if they become lost.

- **Read the Signs**   Most rides post signs that explain **height restrictions,** if any, or identify those that may unsettle youngsters. Save yourself and your kids some grief before you get in line and are disappointed. (The ride listings in chapter 6, "Exploring Walt Disney World," and chapter 7, "Exploring Beyond Disney: Universal Orlando, SeaWorld & Other Attractions," note any minimum heights, as do the guide maps you can get at the parks.) A bad experience, whether it be a dark, scary section of a ride, the loop-de-loop of a roller coaster, or too big of a drop, can cause your child long-lasting anxiety. It can also put a damper on things for the rest of your day (and possibly even your vacation).

I've explained to my older boys that if they hear adults screaming, that's a pretty good indication that a ride is not the best choice for them. With younger kids you have to be steadfast in your decisions, though most height restrictions will keep those who really shouldn't be riding at bay. With the older ones, well, you may have to indulge them a bit and let them ride just one—they likely won't make the same mistake twice. Note that once you get past the height restriction, age is not always as much of a deciding factor when it comes to rides as one might think. It really depends on your child's previous experiences and their personalities. I've seen 5-year-olds squeal with glee on rides that I can't even stomach; on the other hand, I've observed kids as old as 8 or 10 walk out of some of the attractions with "touchy feely" effects practically in tears.

- **Take a Break** The Disney parks, Universal Orlando, and SeaWorld have fabulous interactive play areas offering both parents and young kids a break. By all means take advantage of them. They allow kids to expend some of their pent-up energy after having to wait in lines and not wander far from mom and dad all day long. They offer a nice break for you, too (if you can sit down to watch them, that is). Note that many of these kid zones are filled with water squirters and shallow pools, and most of the parks feature a fair number of water-related attractions, so getting

wet is practically inevitable—at least for the kids. It's advisable to bring along a change of clothes or even a bathing suit. You can rent a locker ($10 or less) for storing the spares until you need them. During the summer, the Florida humidity is enough to keep you feeling soggy, so you may appreciate the change of clothing even if you don't go near any water.

- **Show Time** Schedule an inside air-conditioned show two or three times a day, especially midafternoons in the summer. You may even get your littlest tykes to nap in the darkened theater. For all shows, arrive at least 20 minutes early to get the better seats, but not so early that the kids are tired of waiting (most waits are outside in the heat at Disney, while Universal has covered queue areas at most attractions).

- **Snack Times** When dreaming of your vacation, you probably don't envision hours spent standing in lines, waiting and waiting (unless you have done this before, that is). It helps to store some lightweight snacks in a backpack, or in the stroller if you have one, especially when traveling with small children. This may save you some headaches, as kids get the hungriest just when you are the farthest from food. It will also be much healthier, and will certainly save you money, as the parks' prices are quite high.

- **Bring Your Own?** While you will have to haul it to and from the car and on and off trams, trains, or monorails at Disney, having your own stroller can be a tremendous help. It will be with you when you need it—say, back in the hotel room as a highchair, or for an infant in a restaurant when a highchair is inappropriate. Remember to bring the right stroller, too. It should be lightweight, easy to fold and unfold with one hand, have a canopy, be able to recline for naps, and have plenty of storage space. The parks offer stroller rentals for around $10 to $18; however these are often hard and uncomfortable. They do not recline and have little or no storage space for the gear that goes along with bringing the kids. They are good, however, if you have older kids who may just need an occasional break from walking. For infants and small toddlers, you may want to bring a snugly sling or backpack-type carrier for use in traveling to and from parking lots and while you're standing in line for attractions (where strollers are not allowed). And while many parks now have a small number of infant-friendly strollers on hand, I still recommend (and highly) bringing your own if your kids are under 3.

- **Recommended Reading** *The Unofficial Guide to Walt Disney World* is a good source of additional information, as is *Frommer's Walt Disney World with Kids.*

We've also listed some additional tips for tackling the theme parks in the section "Making Your Visit More Enjoyable," in chapter 7.

GENERAL INFORMATION RESOURCES

Familyhostel (© **800/733-9753;** www.learn.unh.edu/familyhostel) takes the whole family, including kids ages 8 to 15, on moderately priced U.S. and international learning vacations. Lectures, field trips, and sightseeing are guided by a team of academics.

Recommended family travel websites include **Family Travel Forum** (www.familytravelforum.com), a comprehensive site that offers customized trip planning; **Family Travel Network** (www.familytravelnetwork.com), an award-winning site that offers travel features, deals, and tips; **Traveling Internationally with Your Kids** (www.travelwithyourkids.com), a comprehensive site offering sound advice for long-distance and international travel with children; and **Family Travel Files** (www.thefamilytravelfiles.com), which offers an online magazine and a directory of off-the-beaten-path tours and tour operators for families.

TRAVELING WITH PETS

For those of us who wouldn't dream of going on vacation without our pets, more and more lodgings are going the pet-friendly route. Be aware, however, policies vary from property to property, so call ahead to find out the particulars of your hotel.

None of the Disney resorts allow animals (except service dogs) to stay on the premises or have their own kennels (the only exception being Disney's Fort Wilderness Resort and Campground, where you can have your pet at the full-hook-up campsites), but resort guests are

---

Tips The Peripatetic Pet

It is illegal in Florida to leave your pet inside a parked car, windows rolled down or not. The sweltering heat can easily kill an animal in only a few minutes. All of the major theme parks have kennel facilities available, so if you have brought your pet along, take advantage of them.

Make sure your pet is wearing a name-tag that includes your name and phone number, as well as the phone number of a contact person who can take the call if your pet gets lost while you're away from home.

welcome to board their animals overnight in kennel facilities at the Ticket & Transportation Center. If you only require boarding during the day, kennels are located at all four Disney parks. Universal Orlando & SeaWorld will board small animals during the day only.

Universal's three Loews-run resorts do allow pets on-site. In fact, "Loews Loves Pets" is a program that caters to pets and their families by offering such pet-friendly amenities as food, leashes, bedding, toys, and more. Pet walking, pet pagers, and door hangers to let the resort staff know that there is a pet in the room are also available.

An excellent resource is **www.pets welcome.com**, which dispenses medical tips, names of animal-friendly lodgings and campgrounds, and lists of kennels and veterinarians. Also check out **www. dogfriendly.com**, which features links to Orlando accommodations, eateries, attractions, and parks that welcome canine companions.

8 Planning Your Trip Online

SURFING FOR AIRFARE

The most popular websites for booking airline tickets online are **Travelocity** (**www.travelocity.com** or www.travelocity.co.uk); **Expedia** (**www.expedia.com** or www.expedia.co.uk); and **Orbitz** (**www.orbitz.com**).

In addition, most airlines now offer online-only fares that even their phone agents know nothing about. For the websites of airlines that fly to and from your destination, go to "Getting There," p. 48.

Other helpful websites for booking airline tickets online include:

- www.biddingfortravel.com
- www.cheapflights.com
- www.hotwire.com
- www.lastminutetravel.com
- www.priceline.com
- www.sidestep.com
- www.site59.com
- www.smartertravel.com

SURFING FOR HOTELS

In addition to **Travelocity, Expedia, Orbitz, Priceline,** and **Hotwire** (see above), the following websites will help you with booking hotel rooms online:

- www.hotels.com
- www.quickbook.com
- www.travelaxe.net
- www.travelweb.com
- www.tripadvisor.com

It's a good idea to **get a confirmation number** and **make a printout** of any online booking transaction.

Note: Though they can be good sources for discount hotel rooms in Orlando, you can forget about getting anything better than a WDW "value" resort on Priceline and Hotwire, with the possible exception of the Dolphin (p. 94) or Swan (p. 95). Disney doesn't discount its best digs unless it's the one raking in the dollars directly.

SURFING FOR RENTAL CARS

For booking rental cars online, the best deals are usually found at rental-car company websites, although all the major online travel agencies also offer rental-car reservations services. Priceline and Hotwire work well for rental cars, too; the only "mystery" is which major rental company you get, and for most travelers the difference between Hertz, Avis, and Budget is negligible.

TRAVEL BLOGS & TRAVELOGUES

Popular travel blogs that might feature Orlando include:

- www.gridskipper.com
- www.salon.com/wanderlust
- www.travelblog.com
- www.travelblog.org
- www.worldhum.com
- www.writtenroad.com

Frommers.com: The Complete Travel Resource

For an excellent travel-planning resource, we highly recommend **Frommers.com** (www.frommers.com), voted Best Travel Site by *PC Magazine*. We're a little biased, of course, but we guarantee that you'll find the travel tips, reviews, monthly vacation giveaways, bookstore, and online-booking capabilities thoroughly indispensable. Among the special features are our popular **Destinations** section, where you'll get expert travel tips, hotel and dining recommendations, and advice on the sights to see for more than 3,500 destinations around the globe; the **Frommers.com Newsletter**, with the latest deals, travel trends, and money-saving secrets; our **Community** area featuring **Message Boards**, where Frommer's readers post queries and share advice (sometimes even our authors show up to answer questions); and our **Photo Center**, where you can post and share vacation tips. When your research is finished, the **Online Reservations System** (www.frommers.com/book_a_trip) takes you to Frommer's preferred online partners for booking your vacation at affordable prices.

9 The 21st-Century Traveler

INTERNET ACCESS AWAY FROM HOME

WITHOUT YOUR OWN COMPUTER

If you don't have a computer, you can still access your e-mail from cybercafes. To find cybercafes in your destination check **www.cybercaptive.com** and **www.cybercafe.com**. For a start there's a small Internet cafe located inside the Lake Buena Vista Factory Outlets.

At Walt Disney World, there is an Internet cafe inside DisneyQuest (p. 255), and you can also send e-mail at Innoventions in Epcot (p. 218), though you have to pay the park admission fees to use the Web terminals. Payphones with touch-screen displays offering Internet access have been installed at locations throughout Walt Disney World; you can access your e-mail for 25¢ a minute with a 4-minute minimum.

Many hotels have either a business center with computers available, or in some instances there may be a computer located in the lobby for guest use. Some even have Web TV available in the guest rooms, where a keyboard works in conjunction with the television. In either case, there will likely be (often exorbitant) fees for using them, generally payable with your credit card or, in a few cases, cash only (much like a vending machine).

Most major airports now have **Internet kiosks** scattered throughout their gates. These give you basic Web access for a per-minute fee that's usually higher than cybercafe prices.

WITH YOUR OWN COMPUTER

Of course, using your own laptop gives you the most flexibility. More and more hotels, cafes, and retailers are also signing on as Wi-Fi (wireless fidelity) "hotspots." Mac owners have their own networking technology, Apple AirPort. **T-Mobile Hotspot** (www.t-mobile.com/hotspot) serves up wireless connections at more than 1,000 Starbucks coffee shops nationwide. **Boingo** (www.boingo.com) and **Wayport** (www.wayport.com) have set up networks in airports and high-class hotel lobbies. iPass providers (see below) also give you access to a few hundred wireless hotel lobby setups. To locate other hotspots that provide **free wireless networks** in cities around the world, go to **www.personaltelco.net/index.cgi/ WirelessCommunities**.

Many Orlando hotels offer Wi-Fi access in public areas, however only a few provide in-room access.

For dial-up access, most business-class hotels in Orlando offer dataports for laptop modems, and a number of them offer free high-speed Internet access. For a list of Orlando hotels wired for Internet access, check out **www.wiredhotels.com**. Disney offers high-speed and Wi-Fi access to guests at several of its resorts, and all of Universal Orlando's resorts offer high-speed Internet access.

Major Internet Service Providers (ISPs) have **local access numbers** around the world, allowing you to go online by placing a local call. The **iPass** network also has dial-up numbers around the world. You'll have to sign up with an iPass provider, who will then tell you how to set up your computer for Orlando. For a list of iPass providers, go to **www.ipass. com** and click on "Individuals Buy Now." One solid provider is **i2roam** (www.i2roam.com; ℂ **866/811-6209** or 920/235-0475).

Wherever you go, bring a **connection kit** of the right power and phone adapters, a spare phone cord, and a spare Ethernet network cable—or find out whether your hotel supplies them to guests.

For information on electrical currency conversions, see "Electricity," in the "Fast Facts" section in chapter 3.

CELLPHONE USE IN THE U.S.

It's a good bet that your phone will work in the Orlando area, but take a look at your wireless company's coverage map on its website before heading out; T-Mobile, Sprint, and Nextel are particularly weak in rural areas. If you need to stay in touch at a destination where you know your phone won't work, **rent** a phone that does from **InTouch USA** (ℂ **800/872-7626**; www.intouchglobal.com) or a rental car location, but beware that you'll pay $1 a minute or more for airtime.

Online Traveler's Toolbox

Veteran travelers usually carry some essential items to make their trips easier. Following is a selection of handy online tools to bookmark and use.

- **Airplane Seating** (www.seatguru.com and www.airlinequality.com)
- **Airplane Food** (www.airlinemeals.net)
- **Foreign Languages for Travelers** (www.travlang.com)
- **Weather** (www.intellicast.com and www.weather.com)
- **Maps** (www.mapquest.com)
- **Subway Navigator** (www.subwaynavigator.com)
- **Time and Date** (www.timeanddate.com)
- **Travel Warnings** (http://travel.state.gov, www.fco.gov.uk/travel, www. voyage.gc.ca, and www.dfat.gov.au/consular/advice)
- **Universal Currency Converter** (www.xe.com/ucc)
- **Visa ATM Locator** (www.visa.com), **MasterCard ATM Locator** (www. mastercard.com)

If you're venturing deep into national parks, you may want to consider renting a **satellite phone ("satphones")**. It's different from a cellphone in that it connects to satellites rather than ground-based towers. Unfortunately, you'll pay at least $2 per minute to use the phone, and it only works where you can see the horizon (that is, usually not indoors). In North America, you can rent Iridium satellite phones from **RoadPost** (www.roadpost.com; ℂ 888/290-1606 or 905/272-5665). InTouch USA (see above) offers a wider range of satphones but at higher rates.

If you're not from the U.S., you'll be appalled at the poor reach of our **GSM (Global System for Mobiles) wireless network,** which is used by much of the rest of the world. Your phone will probably work in most major U.S. cities; it definitely won't work in many rural areas. (To see where GSM phones work in the U.S., check out **www.t-mobile.com/coverage/ national_popup.asp.**) And you may or may not be able to send SMS (text messaging) home.

10 Getting There

BY PLANE

THE MAJOR AIRLINES There are over 37 scheduled airlines and several more charter companies serving the more than 33 million passengers who land in Orlando each year. **Delta** (ℂ 800/221-1212; www.delta.com) recently relinquished its nearly 20% share of Orlando-bound flights when they dramatically decreased the number of gates they hold from 24 to 8. **Southwest Airlines** (ℂ 800/435-9792; www.southwest.com) now holds the top spot with just over 16% of the flights in and out of the Orlando International Airport, offering service from roughly 63 cities.

Other carriers include **Air Canada** (ℂ 888/247-2262; www.aircanada.ca), **America West** (ℂ 800/235-9292; www.americawest.com), **American** (ℂ 800/433-7300; www.americanair.com), **British Airways** (ℂ 800/247-9297; www.british-airways.com), **Continental** (ℂ 800/525-0280; www.continental.com), **Northwest** (ℂ 800/225-2525; www.nwa.com), **United Airlines** (ℂ 800/241-6522; www.united.com), and **US Airways** (ℂ 800/428-4322; www.usairways.com), to name a few.

Several so-called no-frills airlines (those offering lower fares but providing few or no amenities) fly to Orlando, including **Spirit Air** (ℂ **800/772-7117;** www.spiritair.com). **JetBlue Airways** (ℂ **800/538-2583;** www.jetblue.com) is another low-cost carrier that operates out

---

(*Tips*) Prepare to Be Fingerprinted

As of January 2004, many international visitors traveling on visas to the United States will be photographed and fingerprinted at Customs in a new program created by the Department of Homeland Security called **US-VISIT.** Non-U.S. citizens arriving at airports and on cruise ships must undergo an instant background check as part of the government's efforts to deter terrorism by verifying the identity of incoming and outgoing visitors. Exempt from the extra scrutiny are visitors entering by land or those that don't require a visa for short-term visits (mostly in Europe; see p. 19). For more information, go to the Homeland Security website at **www.dhs.gov/dhspublic.**

Tips Coping with Jet Lag

Jet lag is a pitfall of traveling across time zones. If you're flying north–south and you feel sluggish when you touch down, your symptoms will be the result of dehydration and the general stress of air travel. When you travel east–west or vice versa, however, your body becomes thoroughly confused about what time it is, and everything from your digestive system to your brain is knocked for a loop. Traveling east, say from San Francisco to Boston, is more difficult on your internal clock than traveling west, say from Atlanta to Hawaii, because most peoples' bodies are more inclined to stay up late than fall asleep early.

Here are some tips for combating jet lag:

- **Reset your watch** to your destination time before you board the plane.
- **Drink lots of water** before, during, and after your flight. Avoid alcohol.
- **Exercise and sleep well** for a few days before your trip.
- If you have trouble sleeping on planes, **fly eastward on morning flights.**
- **Daylight** is the key to resetting your body clock. At the website for **Outside In** (www.bodyclock.com), you can get a customized plan of when to seek and avoid light.

---

of a number of U.S. cities, and offers direct flights to Orlando out of New York City. The latter has video screens offering 24 TV channels—a big plus for those traveling with kids—and is a huge favorite with Frommer's editors.

The newest low-fare airline is really the stepsister of Delta: **Song Airlines** (✆ **800/ 359-7664;** www.flysong.com). As of 2004, the airline had personal video monitors—for child-distracting satellite TV and video games—installed on all of its jets. **Ted** (✆ **800/225-5833;** www.fly ted.com), United's younger sibling, is another offshoot airline that frequents Orlando and Central Florida. Tedtunes and movies will entertain the troops.

IMMIGRATION & CUSTOMS CLEARANCE   Foreign visitors arriving by air, no matter what the port of entry, should cultivate patience and resignation before setting foot on U.S. soil. Clearing immigration control can take as long as 2 hours. This is especially true in the aftermath of the September 11, 2001, terrorist attacks, when U.S. airports considerably beefed up security clearances. People traveling by air from Canada, Bermuda, and certain Caribbean countries can sometimes clear Customs and Immigration at the point of departure, which is much faster.

ORLANDO'S AIRPORT

Orlando International Airport (✆ **407/ 825-2001;** www.state.fl.us/goaa) offers direct or nonstop service from 60 U.S. cities and two dozen international destinations. Rated one of the top airports in the country, it's a thoroughly modern and user-friendly facility with tons of restaurants, shops, a 446-room on-premises Hyatt Regency Hotel, and centrally located information kiosks. All major car-rental companies are located at or near the airport; see "Getting Around" in chapter 4 and appendix B ("Useful Toll-Free Numbers & Websites") for more information about car rentals.

AN ALTERNATIVE Orlando Sanford International Airport (✆ **407/ 585-4000;** www.orlandosanfordairport. com) is much smaller than the main airport, but it has grown a bit in recent years, thanks mainly to a small fleet of international carriers including Air 2000,

Flying with Film & Video

Never pack film—exposed or unexposed—in checked bags, because the new, more powerful scanners in U.S. airports can fog film. The film you carry with you can be damaged by scanners as well. X-ray damage is cumulative; the faster the film, and the more times you put it through a scanner, the more likely the damage. Film under 800 ASA is usually safe for up to five scans. If you're taking your film through additional scans, U.S. regulations permit you to demand hand inspections. In international airports, you're at the mercy of airport officials. On international flights, store your film in transparent baggies, so you can remove it easily before you go through scanners. Keep in mind that airports are not the only places where your camera may be scanned: Highly trafficked attractions are X-raying visitors' bags with increasing frequency.

Most photo supply stores sell protective pouches designed to block damaging X-rays. The pouches fit both film and loaded cameras. They should protect your film in checked baggage, but they also may raise alarms and result in a hand inspection.

You'll have little to worry about if you are traveling with **digital cameras.** Unlike film, which is sensitive to light, the digital camera and storage cards are not affected by airport X-rays, according to Nikon.

Carry-on scanners will not damage **videotape** in video cameras, but the magnetic fields emitted by the walk-through security gateways and hand-held inspection wands will. Always place your loaded camcorder on the screening conveyor belt or have it hand-inspected. Be sure your batteries are charged, as you may be required to turn the device on to ensure that it's what it appears to be.

Britannia, and Aeropostal. The airport has Avis, Alamo, Dollar, and Hertz rental-car desks on-site and shuttles to Budget and Enterprise. Mears Transportation shuttles (see below) also serve it.

GETTING INTO TOWN FROM THE AIRPORT

Orlando International is 25 miles east of Walt Disney World and 20 miles south of downtown. At rush hour (7–9am and 4–6pm), the drive can be torture and take up to an hour or more; at other times, it's about 30 to 40 minutes depending on your exact destination. **Mears Transportation Group** (© 407/423-5566; www.mearstransportation.com) has vans that shuttle passengers from the airport (you catch them at ground level) to the Disney resorts and official hotels, as well as most other Orlando properties. Their air-conditioned vehicles operate round-the-clock, departing every 15 to 25 minutes in either direction. Rates vary by destination. Round-trip fare for adults is $25 ($18 for kids 4–11) between the airport and downtown Orlando or International Drive; $29 ($21 for kids 4–11) for Walt Disney World/Lake Buena Vista or West U.S. 192. Children 3 and under ride free.

Quicksilver Tours and Transportation (© 888/468-6939 or 407/299-1434; www.quick-silvertours.com) is a bit more personal. Their folks greet you at baggage claim with a sign bearing your name—they'll even help with your luggage. The bonus is a 30-minute grocery stop and free phone call included in the price. While a bit more expensive than Mears, they're coming for you. And they're only going to *your* resort. This is a good option for four or more people. Rates run from $110 (up to 10 people, round-trip) to I-Drive/Universal Studios and $115 for the Disney empire.

Tiffany Towncar (© **888/838-2161** or 407/370-2196; www.tiffanytowncar. com) offers a $110 round-trip rate for up to seven people in a van or $110 from Orlando International to Universal and Disney.

DRIVING TO WALT DISNEY WORLD To get from the airport to the attractions, take the **North** exit out of the airport to **Highway 528 West.** Follow signs to **I-4;** it takes about 30 to 40 minutes to get to Walt Disney World if the traffic isn't too heavy (however you can double that if it is rush hour or if there's an accident). When you get to I-4, follow the signs **west** toward the attractions.

Note: It's always a good idea when you make reservations to ask about transportation options between the airport and your hotel. Also be sure to ask how far you have to travel to pick up and drop off a rental car. Some lots are miles from the airport, and you could potentially spend lots of time waiting in line and catching shuttles before you actually get to the airport on your day of departure.

FLYING FOR LESS: TIPS FOR GETTING THE BEST AIRFARE

There's no shortage of discounted and promotional fares to Orlando. November, December, and January (excluding holidays) often bring fare wars that can result in savings of 50% or more, but, in a slower economy, specials may be available more often. Watch for ads in your local newspaper and on TV, call the airlines, or check out their websites. Here

are some other ways to keep your airfare costs down:

- Passengers who can book their ticket either **long in advance or at the last minute,** or who **fly midweek** or **at less-trafficked hours** may pay a fraction of the full fare. If your schedule is flexible, say so, and ask if you can secure a cheaper fare by changing your flight plans.
- Search **the Internet** for cheap fares (see "Planning Your Trip Online," earlier in this chapter).
- No-frills airlines have reduced their price advantage, but some **charter** flights still go to Florida, especially during the winter season and particularly from Canada. They often cost less than regularly scheduled flights, but they tend to be very complicated. It's best to go to a good travel agent and ask them to find one for you.
- Try to book a ticket **in its country of origin.** If you're planning a one-way flight from England to Orlando, a British-based travel agent will probably have the lowest fares. For foreign travelers on multileg trips, book in the country of the first leg; for example, book New York–Orlando–Chicago–New York in the U.S.
- **Consolidators,** also known as bucket shops, are great sources for international tickets, although they usually can't beat Internet fares within North America. Start by looking in Sunday newspaper travel sections; U.S. travelers should focus on the *New York Times, Los Angeles Times,* and *Miami Herald.* U.K. travelers should search in the *Independent,* the *Guardian,* or the *Observer.* **Beware:** Bucket shop tickets are usually nonrefundable or rigged with stiff cancellation penalties, often as high as 50% to 75% of the ticket price, and some put you on charter airlines, which may leave at inconvenient times and experience

Tips Getting Through the Airport

- Arrive at the airport 1 hour before a domestic flight and 2 hours before an international flight; if you show up late, tell an airline employee and he or she will probably whisk you to the front of the line.

- Beat the ticket-counter lines by using airport electronic kiosks or even online check-in from your home computer, from where you can print out boarding passes in advance. Curbside check-in is also a good way to avoid lines.

- Bring a current, government-issued photo ID such as a driver's license or passport. Children under 18 do not need government-issued photo IDs for flights within the U.S., but they do for international flights to most countries.

- Speed up security by removing your jacket and shoes before you're screened. In addition, remove metal objects such as big belt buckles. If you've got metallic body parts, a note from your doctor can prevent a long chat with the security screeners.

- Ship it—don't stow it: Though pricey, it's sometimes worthwhile to travel luggage-free. Specialists in door-to-door luggage delivery include **Virtual Bellhop** (www.virtualbellhop.com), **SkyCap International** (wwww.skycap international.com), **Luggage Express** (www.usxpluggageexpress.com), and **Sports Express** (www.sportsexpress.com).

- Use a TSA-approved lock for your checked luggage. Look for Travel Sentry certified locks at luggage or travel shops and Brookstone stores (or online at www.brookstone.com).

delays. Several reliable consolidators are worldwide and available online. **STA Travel** has been the world's lead consolidator for students since purchasing Council Travel, but their fares are competitive for travelers of all ages. **ELTExpress** (**Flights.com;** ℂ **800/TRAV-800;** www.eltexpress. com) has excellent fares worldwide, particularly to Europe. They also have "local" websites in 12 countries. **FlyCheap** (ℂ **800/FLY-CHEAP;** www.1800flycheap.com) has especially good fares to sunny destinations. **Air Tickets Direct** (ℂ **800/ 778-3447;** www.airticketsdirect. com) is based in Montreal and leverages the currently weak Canadian dollar for low fares; they also book trips to places that U.S. travel agents won't touch, such as Cuba.

- Join **frequent-flier clubs.** Frequent-flier membership doesn't cost a cent, but it does entitle you to better seats, faster response to phone inquiries, and prompter service if your luggage is stolen or your flight is canceled or delayed, or if you want to change your seat. And you don't have to fly to earn points; **frequent-flier credit cards** can earn you thousands of miles for doing your everyday shopping. With more than 70 mileage awards programs on the market, consumers have never had more options. Investigate the program details of your favorite airlines before you sink points into any one. Consider which airlines have hubs in the airport nearest you, and, of those carriers, which have the most advantageous alliances, given your most common routes. To play the frequent-flier game to your best advantage, consult Randy Petersen's **Inside Flyer** (www.inside flyer.com). Petersen and friends review all the programs in detail and post regular updates on changes in policies and trends.

STAYING COMFORTABLE IN THE AIR

- Your choice of airline and airplane will definitely affect your legroom. Find more details about U.S. airlines at **www.seatguru.com**. For international airlines, the research firm Skytrax has posted a list of average seat pitches at **www.airlinequality.com**.

- Emergency exit seats and bulkhead seats typically have the most legroom. Emergency exit seats are usually left unassigned until the day of a flight (to ensure that someone able-bodied fills the seats); it's worth getting to the ticket counter early to snag one of these spots for a long flight. Many passengers find that bulkhead seating (the row facing the wall at the front of the cabin) offers more legroom, but keep in mind that bulkheads are where airlines often put baby bassinets, so you may be sitting next to an infant.

- To have two seats for yourself in a three-seat row, try for an aisle seat in a center section toward the back of coach. If you're traveling with a companion, book an aisle and a window seat. Middle seats are usually booked last, so chances are good you'll end up with three seats to yourselves. And in the event that a third passenger is assigned the middle seat, he or she will probably be more than happy to trade for a window or an aisle.

- Ask about entertainment options. Many airlines offer seatback video systems where you get to choose your movies or play video games—but only on some of their planes. (Boeing 777s are your best bet.)

- To sleep, avoid the last row of any section or the row in front of an emergency exit, as these seats are the least likely to recline. Avoid seats near highly trafficked toilet areas. Avoid seats in the back of many jets—these can be narrower than those in the rest of coach. You also may want to reserve a window seat so you can rest your head and avoid being bumped in the aisle.

- Get up, walk around, and stretch every 60 to 90 minutes to keep your blood flowing. This helps avoid **deep vein thrombosis,** or "economy-class syndrome." See the "Avoiding 'Economy Class Syndrome'" box under "Health & Safety," p. 34.

- Drink water before, during, and after your flight to combat the lack of humidity in airplane cabins. Avoid alcohol, which will dehydrate you.

- If you're flying with kids, don't forget to carry on toys, books, pacifiers, and chewing gum to help them relieve ear pressure buildup during ascent and descent.

BY CAR

For car-rental information, see "Getting Around," on p. 65. Contact information for all of the major rental agencies in the United States are available in appendix B, "Useful Toll-Free Numbers & Websites," in the back of this book.

Orlando is 436 miles from Atlanta; 1,312 miles from Boston; 1,120 miles from Chicago; 1,009 miles from Cleveland; 1,170 miles from Dallas; 1,114 miles from Detroit; 1,088 miles from New York City; and 1,282 miles from Toronto.

- From Atlanta, take I-75 south to the Florida Turnpike to I-4 west.
- From points northeast, take I-95 south to Daytona Beach and I-4 west.
- From Chicago, take I-65 south to Nashville, then I-24 south to I-75, then south on the Florida Turnpike to I-4 west.
- From Cleveland, take I-77 south to Columbia, S.C., and then I-26 east to I-95 south to I-4 west.
- From Dallas, take I-20 east to I-49, south to I-10, east to I-75, then south on the Florida Turnpike to I-4 west.
- From Detroit, take I-75 south to the Florida Turnpike, then exit on I-4 west.
- From Toronto, take Canadian Route 401 south to Queen Elizabeth Way, then south to I-90 (New York State Thruway), east to I-87 (New York State Thruway), south to I-95 over the George Washington Bridge, then south on I-95 to I-4 west.

AAA (℡ 800/222-1134; www.aaa.com) and other auto club members should call their local offices for maps and optimum driving directions.

BY TRAIN

Amtrak trains (℡ 800/872-7245; www.amtrak.com) pull into stations at 1400 Sligh Blvd. in downtown Orlando (23 miles from Walt Disney World), and 111 Dakin Ave. in Kissimmee (15 miles from WDW). There are also stops in Winter Park, 10 miles north of downtown Orlando at 150 W. Morse Blvd.; and in Sanford, 23 miles northeast of downtown Orlando, 800 Persimmon Ave., which is also the end terminal for the Auto Train (see below).

FARES As with airline fares, you can occasionally get discounts if you book far in advance. There may be some restrictions on travel dates for discounted fares, mostly around very busy holiday times. Amtrak also offers money-saving packages—including accommodations (some at WDW resorts), car rentals, tours, and train fare (℡ 800/321-8684).

AMTRAK'S AUTO TRAIN This option offers the convenience of bringing your car to Florida without having to drive it all the way. It begins in Lorton, Virginia—about a 4-hour drive from New York, 2 hours from Philadelphia—and ends at Sanford, 23 miles northeast of Orlando. (There are no stops in between.) Reserve early for the lowest prices. Fares average $690 ($1,400 with a berth) for two passengers and an auto. Call ℡ 800/872-7245 for details.

11 Packages for the Independent Traveler

The number and diversity of package tours to Orlando is staggering. But you can save money if you're willing to do the research. Start by looking in the travel section of your local Sunday newspaper and checking the ads in the back of travel magazines such as *Travel & Leisure* and *Condé Nast Traveler*. Also, stop at a sizable travel agency and pick up brochures from several companies. Go over them at home and compare the offerings to find the optimum package for your trip.

You should also obtain the *Walt Disney World Vacations* brochure (see "Visitor Information" at the beginning of this chapter), which lists WDW packages, or head to **www.disneyworld.com** (where you'll find loads of information and can book a package as well). Disney's array of choices can include airfare, accommodations on or off Disney property, theme-park passes, a rental car, meals, a Disney cruise, and/or a stay at Disney's beach resorts in Vero Beach or Hilton Head, South Carolina. Some packages are tied to a season while others are for special-interest vacationers, including golfers, honeymooners, or spa aficionados. For

Tips Package Deals

Just about everybody seems to be in the business of package deals these days. While Disney itself offers a handful of package options, the discounts aren't usually that considerable. Do, however, ask reservations clerks what the latest and greatest promotion is, or what may be running at the time you intend to visit. Promotions tend to run for a limited time so be sure to get all the details—when it runs, what it includes, what it doesn't, and so on. You should also search the Disney website (**www.disneyworld.com**) for special deals and promotions.

For up-to-date coverage of promotional offerings and discount codes good at Disney World, check out **www.mousesavers.com**. The site also offers its own slate of Disney specials.

more information, or to book a Disney vacation package, call © **407/939-6244.**

Bank One has teamed up with Disney to offer the Disney/VISA credit card that allows cardholders to accumulate points—or Dream Dollars, as they are called—for everyday purchases. Certain special purchases qualifying for double or even triple Dream Dollars can be redeemed or applied toward the purchase of Disney tickets, vacation packages, or purchases at the Disney Store, Disney catalog, and Disney online.

Although not on the same scale as Disney's options, Universal Orlando packages have improved greatly with the addition of the Islands of Adventure theme park, the CityWalk food-and-club district, and Universal's Loews-run hotels. The options include lodging, VIP access to Universal's theme parks, and discounts to other non-Disney attractions. Some include round-trip airfare. Contact **Universal Studios Vacations** at © **800/ 711-0080** or go online to **www.universal studiosvacations.com**.

SeaWorld also offers 2- and 3-night packages that include rooms from a choice of a handful of SeaWorld area hotels, car rental, and tickets to Sea- World. Call © **800/557-4268** or surf the Internet to **www.seaworldvacations. com**.

One good source of package deals is the airlines themselves. Most major airlines offer air/land packages, including **American Airlines Vacations** (© 800/ 321-2121; www.aavacations.com), **Delta Vacations** (© 800/221-6666; www.delta vacations.com), **Continental Airlines Vacations** (© 800/301-3800; www.co vacations.com), and **United Vacations** (© 888/854-3899; www.unitedvacations. com). Several big **online travel agencies**—Expedia, Travelocity, Orbitz, Site59, and Lastminute.com—also do a brisk business in packages. Packages can include round-trip airfare, accommodations, rental car or round-trip airport transfers, unlimited admission to Disney (or other) parks, and other special features. In packages utilizing WDW and Universal Studios resorts, you will receive all of the advantages given to guests of these properties (see chapter 4, "Where to Stay," for details). Prices vary widely depending on the resort you choose, your departure point, and the time of year.

Touraine Travel (© **800/967-5583;** www.tourainetravel.com) is a source of packages to Disney, Universal Orlando, and SeaWorld.

For linksters, **Golf Getaways** (© **800/ 800-4028;** www.golfgetaways.com) and **Golfpac Vacations** (© **800/327-0878;** www.golfpacinc.com) offer play-and-stay packages.

Moments   A Mickey Mouse Affair: Getting Married at Walt Disney World

Want to fly up the aisle on Aladdin's magic carpet? Arrive in a glass coach pulled by six white horses? Or take the plunge, literally and figuratively, on the Twilight Zone Tower of Terror?

If you've always dreamed of a fairy-tale wedding, Disney is happy to oblige for a price (though often a large one). Recognizing WDW's popularity as a honeymoon destination—each year, more honeymooners head here than to any other spot in America—Disney, in 1995, cut out the middleman and officially went into the wedding business. And, oh, what big business it is!

Disney's first step was building the multimillion-dollar nondenominational chapel in the middle of the Seven Seas Lagoon. The next step was letting the world know the Disney wedding chapel was open for business. The first nuptials were televised live on the Lifetime television network. (Construction was still in progress at the chapel, so the bride and groom wore white hard hats.) Since it opened, over 20,000 couples, hailing from every state and a number of foreign countries, have mixed matrimony with Disney magic at the chapel, which resembles a Victorian summerhouse. You'll have to cough up at least $2,200 just to have the ceremony here (not including the minimum expenditure of between $10,000–$20,000 required for a custom wedding).

An intimate wedding at WDW for two starts at about $3,000 including a 4-night honeymoon at one of Disney's moderate resorts, theme-park tickets, a daylight ceremony at one of several Disney resort locations, a wedding cake, bouquet for the bride, a marriage certificate signed by Mickey himself, and a host of other trimmings. Custom weddings for parties of more than eight start at $10,000. The average Disney wedding costs $20,000 and has 100 guests (Prince Charming not included). A la carte add-ons range from $250 for a white-dove fly-over and $2,200 to arrive in Cinderella's glass coach. It would cost $42,000 or more to rent the Magic Kingdom for a reception (not including ceremony, food, and other doodads). If you can imagine it, Disney can probably do it, as long as your wallet matches that imagination.

For details, call ✆ **321/939-4610** (800/370-6009 for honeymoons only) or go to **www.disneyweddings.com** on the Internet.

Travel packages are also listed in the travel section of your local Sunday newspaper. Or check ads in the national travel magazines such as *Arthur Frommer's* *Budget Travel Magazine, Travel & Leisure, National Geographic Traveler,* and *Condé Nast Traveler.*

12 Disney Cruise Packages

There's hardly a Florida tourist market that WDW hasn't successfully tapped. Ocean-going vacations are no exception. **Disney Cruise Line** (✆ **800/951-3532;** www.disneycruise.com) launched the *Magic* and *Wonder* in 1998 and 1999, respectively. It didn't take long before the line made it all the way to the top of the family cruising market.

The *Magic* is Art Deco in style, with Mickey in the three-level lobby and a *Beauty and the Beast* mural in its top restaurant, Lumiere's. The *Wonder*'s decor is Art Nouveau. Ariel commands its lobby, and its featured eatery, Triton's, sports a mural from *The Little Mermaid*.

Subtle differences aside, these are nearly identical twins. Both are 83,000 tons with 12 decks, 875 cabins, and room for 2,400 guests. There are some adults-only areas including **Palo,** an intimate and romantic Italian restaurant; however, both ships have extensive kids' and teens' programs that take up almost an entire deck. They're broken into four age groups: the **Flounder's Reef Nursery** for ages 3 months to 3 years; **Disney's Oceaneer Club** for ages 3 to 7; **Disney's Oceaneer Lab** for ages 8 to 12; and **Common Grounds** (on the *Wonder*) or **The Stack** (on the *Magic*) for ages 13 to 17.

Restaurants, shows, and other onboard activities are extremely family-oriented. One of the line's unique features is a dine-around option that lets you move among main restaurants (each ship has four) from night to night while keeping the same servers.

The 3-night voyages visit Nassau and Castaway Cay, Disney's own private island; 4-night voyages add Freeport.

There also are 7-night eastern Caribbean (St. Thomas, St. Maarten, St. John, and Castaway Cay) and 7-night western Caribbean (Key West, Grand Cayman, Cozumel, and Castaway Cay) itineraries. Special 10-day and 14-day Caribbean cruises are offered as well; call for details and rates.

Seven-night land-sea packages include 3 or 4 days afloat, with the rest of the week at a WDW resort. Prices at press time ranged from $799 to $5,199 adults, $399 to $2,199 kids 3 to 12, and $139 kids under 3 (*Note:* infants under 12 weeks are not allowed aboard ship), depending on your choice of stateroom and resort. Packages are available that add round-trip air and unlimited admission to the WDW parks, Pleasure Island, and other Disney attractions. Cruise-only options for 3 nights are $429 to $2,999 adults, $229 to $1,099 kids 3 to 12, and $149 those under 3; 4-night cruises are $499 to $3,999 adults, $329 to $1,199 kids 3 to 12, and $149 kids under 3. Disney's 7-night cruises sell for $859 to $5,399 adults, $399 to $2,199 kids 3 to 12, and $169 kids under 3.

All cruises depart from Port Canaveral, which is about an hour east of Orlando by car. If you buy a Land and Sea package, transportation to and from Orlando is included. You can get discounted fares if you book well in advance and go during

---

(*Tips* **Ask Before You Go**

Before you invest in a package deal or an escorted tour:

- Always ask about the **cancellation policy.** Can you get your money back? Is there a deposit required?
- Ask about the **accommodations choices and prices** for each. Then look up the hotels' reviews in a Frommer's guide and check their rates online for your specific dates of travel. Also find out what types of rooms are offered.
- Finally, look for **hidden expenses.** Ask whether airport departure fees and taxes, for example, are included in the total cost—they rarely are.

> **Tips   Avoid the Ups & Downs**
>
> Nothing spoils a cruise like a storm—or worse. In the first case, consider avoiding hurricane season altogether (June 1–Nov 30, though the peak is July to mid-Oct). These unpredictable storms can both spoil your fun and upset the strongest of stomachs. Avoiding the stormy seasons aside, pack a few motion-sickness pills or patches just in case.
>
> **Speaking of spoiling a cruise,** several cruise ships, including the Disney *Magic,* have had outbreaks of a virus that caused stomach flu–like symptoms in the past. This is no ill reflection on any one line: Cruise ships are closed environments, and sometimes a passenger brings the illness on board. For an Internet rating by the **Centers for Disease Control,** go to **www.cdc.gov/nceh/vsp/default.htm**. Note, however, that the site is often weeks out of date.

non-peak periods, and specials or "Magic Rates" run periodically. For more information, call Disney Cruise Line or check out its very informative website, which also allows you to plan and reserve shore excursions before you go.

Note: At press time Disney announced that its cruise line would begin offering its first ever Mediterranean cruises out of Barcelona, Spain, in 2007. The 11-night itineraries aboard the *Disney Magic* will feature stops in such ports of call as Naples, Italy, and Marseilles, France,

among others. Two 14-day transatlantic sailings are also being put on the schedule (to Barcelona from Cape Canaveral and vice versa). The sailings are limited and advance bookings are recommended. Rates will range from $2,399 to $3,499 per person base on double occupancy. For more information on the European sailings, call © **888/325-2500.** For more information on the Disney Cruise Line, check out *Frommer's Cruises & Ports of Call.*

13 Recommended Reading

The best Walt Disney World & Orlando guidebook on the planet (yes, this one) covers almost everything most travelers need and want to know. But there are a few areas where we bow to the expertise of less-than-mainstream or special-interest books. So here are a few additional books that may be available in your local library or bookstore.

- *Florida's Ghostly Legends and Haunted Folklore* (2005, Pineapple Press). Move over Haunted Mansion, this is the real deal. Strange tales of the supernatural reveal Florida's slightly spookier side. Ghost stories, legends, and accounts of strange

occurrences may make you think twice about turning out the lights.

- *National Audubon Society Field Guide to Florida* (second edition, Audubon Society) is a handy back-pocket guide that delivers a wonderful education on the state's flora and fauna, parks and preserves, land, weather, natural phenomena, and much more. Plus, it's dripping with pictures to help newcomers and natives alike tell a yellow-bellied slider from a cooter.

- *A Photo Journey to Central Florida* (1992, AAA Publications), though somewhat hard to find, features some rather nice photos of the area's architecture, historical sites, and scenic spots, along with pictures of the parks and attractions. It offers a brief glimpse into Florida and its natural beauty alongside the more commercial aspects of Orlando.

- *Vegetarian Walt Disney World and Greater Orlando, 2E* (2003, Vegetarian World Guides) is the most comprehensive and enterprising guide around for vegetarians, vegans, or mainstream diners looking for a break from carnivorous menus. Susan Shumaker and Than Saffel review 275 restaurants and hotels, more than half of which are on Disney soil. They also give tips about what to eat going to and from Orlando as well as the do's and don'ts of ethnic dining in Central Florida. There's also a section on kids' dining.

- *Mickey's Gourmet Cookbook* (1994, Disney Editions) is full of some of the most popular recipes from the House of Mouse—a few culinary secrets that Disney is willing to share. You can keep your vacation going even after you get home—providing you can cook. For a collection of the Mouse's most requested recipes try perusing the pages of *Cooking with Mickey* (2000, The Walt Disney Company). Do note that another way to take home some of the flavor of WDW is to simply ask for the recipe of a dish that you enjoyed. In most cases, Disney will be happy to e-mail the instructions and ingredients to you at home.

- Kids (and even adults) will enjoy *Popping Up Around Walt Disney World* (2004, Disney Editions). This colorful and detailed pop-up book offers an illustrative tour through the world of Disney. It takes readers through the parks, details some of the attractions, and tosses in a bit of trivia, too.

- *50 Hikes in Central Florida* (2002, Countryman Press) and *Hiking Florida* (2000, Falcon) feature a more natural approach to visiting Florida, showcasing its parks and hiking trails for those who prefer the great outdoors.

- *Hidden Mickeys: A Field Guide to Walt Disney World's Best Kept Secrets* (2003, The Intrepid Traveler) is filled with trivia, and, of course, those Hidden Mickeys—including tips on where and how to look for them.

3

Getting to Know Walt Disney World & Orlando

It's hard to believe that Walt Disney World first opened its gates to the public just over 36 years ago. I doubt anyone could have imagined the incredible transformation that followed in the wake of the Magic Kingdom's 1971 debut. Orlando has evolved from a relatively quiet southern farming community into an international vacation destination. An incredible array of recreational activities, shopping and dining experiences, as well as world-class accommodations await those who visit, and it's all set right in the middle of the natural beauty of Central Florida.

Walt Disney World (WDW) is now home to four major theme parks of its own, two water parks, an incredibly diverse complex full of shopping, dining, and entertainment venues, along with tens of thousands of hotel rooms, scores of restaurants, and to top it all off—two cruise ships.

But there's more to Orlando than Mickeyville. With over 95 attractions both big and small, the city features a practically endless array of options. You could spend weeks here and still not experience all of the exciting things that

Orlando has to offer. You can take in the action-packed thrills of **Universal Studios Florida, Islands of Adventure,** and the excitement of Universal's nightclub and restaurant district, **CityWalk.** If, however, you are in need of something with a bit less hustle and bustle, **SeaWorld** and its sister **Discovery Cove** feature a laid-back park experience and crowds that aren't so horrid. **Gatorland,** once the city's first tourist attraction (yes, there was life here before Mickey arrived), is a throwback attraction where you can walk about leisurely and enjoy natural surroundings, a lack of crowds and lines, and an admission price that won't break the bank.

One piece of advice: Yes, the theme parks are a central part of an Orlando vacation. But, even with all there is to do in the parks, everyone should spend at least a day away from the hubbub to regroup and revitalize; even just a night away will work wonders if you just can't seem to pull yourself away for an entire day. There's plenty of great ways to spend a day or evening off here, from shopping to swimming to minigolf, and more.

1 Orientation

VISITOR INFORMATION

Once you've arrived, you can stop in at the **Orlando/Orange County Convention & Visitors Bureau (Orlando CVB),** 8723 International Dr., Suite 101, Orlando; however, it's best to call ahead (© **407/363-5872;** www.orlandoinfo.com) for information on the area's offerings. Staffers at the CVB can help answer your questions, as well as send out maps, brochures, and coupons good for discounts or freebies. It's worth a

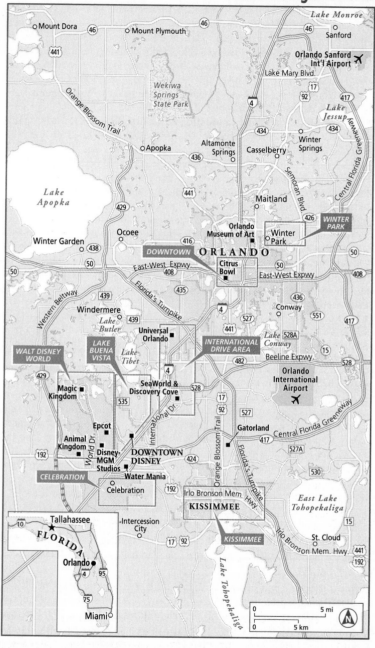

Lake Monroe

Mount Dora 46 Mount Plymouth 46 46 Sanford
441
Orlando Sanford
Int'l Airport ✈
Lake Mary Blvd.
17
4 92 417
Wekiwa
Springs
State Park Lake
Jessup
434 434
Altamonte
Apopka Springs Casselberry Winter
436 Springs
Maitland
Lake 441 426 WINTER
Apopka PARK
429 Orlando Winter
Museum of Art Park
Ocoee 50
Winter Garden 438 416 DOWNTOWN ORLANDO
50 Citrus 50 408
East-West Expwy. Bowl East-West Expwy.
408 435 436
Western Beltway 439 Conway 551 417
Windermere 439 527
Lake 4 441 Lake 528A
Butler Universal Conway 15
Orlando INTERNATIONAL
WALT DISNEY LAKE DRIVE AREA 482 528
WORLD BUENA Lake Beeline Expwy.
VISTA Tibet Orlando
429 International
Magic SeaWorld & Airport ✈
Kingdom Discovery Cove 528
535 17
Epcot 92 527
Animal Gatorland
Kingdom Disney- 417 527A
192 MGM DOWNTOWN Central Florida Greeneway
Studios DISNEY 424 530
CELEBRATION Water Mania
Celebration 192 East Lake
Irlo Bronson Mem. Hwy. Tohopekaliga
KISSIMMEE 15
Tallahassee Intercession
10 City St. Cloud 441
FLORIDA 17 92 KISSIMMEE 192
Orlando
4 95 Lake
75 Tohopekaliga
Miami

Orange Blossom Trail
Semoran Blvd.
Central Florida Greeneway
Florida's Turnpike
World Dr.
International Dr.
Orange Blossom Trail
Florida's Turnpike
Irlo Bronson Mem. Hwy.

0 ___ 5 mi
0 ___ 5 km
N

visit even if you take the advice in chapter 2, "Planning Your Trip to Walt Disney World & Orlando," and send for them before arriving. The CVB sells discount tickets to several attractions (savings on single-day passes to Universal and SeaWorld are $3 or less; only Disney's 3-day or longer passes are discounted with savings from $3–$27 depending on the ticket). The CVB's multilingual staff can make dinner reservations and hotel referrals for you. The CVB is open daily from 8am to 7pm, except Christmas. From I-4, take Exit 74A east 2 blocks, turn south on International Drive and continue 1 mile. The center is on the left, at the corner of I-Drive and Austrian Row.

The **Kissimmee–St. Cloud Convention & Visitors Bureau** is located at 1925 E. Irlo Bronson Memorial Hwy./U.S. 192, Kissimmee (© **800/327-9159** or 407/847-5000; www.floridakiss.com). It also offers maps, brochures, and discount coupons. From I-4, take Exit 64A/U.S. 192 east about 12 miles to Bill Beck Blvd., then go left into the CVB's parking lot. Again, you can call and have these items sent to you ahead of time so you can do some planning at home.

Five tourism centers around Florida have statewide information. They're located 4 miles north of Jennings on I-75 south; 3 miles north of Campbellton on Highway 231; 7 miles north of Yulee on I-95; 16 miles west of Pensacola on I-10 east; and at the capitol in Tallahassee.

Finally, nearly all hotel lobbies and many restaurants, highway rest stops, and attractions have racks brimming with brochures for area activities. Many are filled with dining discounts and cost-cutting coupons, so cover your bases and pick up a few of everything.

INFORMATION (& MORE) AT THE AIRPORT

Passengers arriving at or departing from Orlando International Airport can stroll over to one of two Disney shops. The **Magic of Disney** (© **407/825-2360**) is in the main terminal, third level, right behind the Northwest Airlines ticket desk. **Disney Earport** (© **407/825-2339**) is in the main terminal, across from the Hyatt Regency. They sell WDW multiday tickets, make dinner show and hotel reservations at Disney resorts, and provide brochures and assistance. They're open daily, usually from 7am to 10pm, but know that the airport stores are filled with a rather run-of-the-mill selection of Disney merchandise; unless you're on your way home and forgot to buy that must-have Mickey for Auntie Gertrude, you'll find a far better array of offerings elsewhere.

The **Universal Studios Stores** (© **407/825-2473**), usually open daily from 6am to 9pm, sell park tickets at two locations: Airside A, main terminal, and Airside B, Delta side before security, both on the third level. **SeaWorld** stores, at airsides A and B, are open from 7am to 10pm (© **407/825-2614**). **Kennedy Space Center** (© **407/445-1788**) has two locations at the airport, located in both the East and West halls, for space buffs coming through town. Even the **Ron Jon Surf Shop** (© **407/825-2217**) has an airport outpost.

CITY LAYOUT

Orlando's major artery is Interstate 4. Locals call it the **I-4** or that #@$*%^#!! It runs diagonally across the state from Tampa to Daytona Beach. The exits along this route will take you to Disney, Universal, SeaWorld, International Drive, U.S. 192, Kissimmee, Lake Buena Vista, and north to downtown Orlando and Winter Park. Most exits are well marked, but construction is common and exit numbers have been changed in the last few years. If you get directions by exit number, always ask the name of the road to help avoid getting lost. (Cellphone users can dial © **511** to get a report of I-4 delays.)

Fun Fact **Cars, Cars Everywhere**

If the traffic outside isn't enough for you, you can find cars inside as well. The rocking Race Rock Café located on International Drive is known for parking NASCAR racers in its lobby and having min-racers streaking across its ceiling. Another hot spot for car fans is the NASCAR Café at Universal's CityWalk (p. 328), which is loaded with racing memorabilia and driving-related video games.

The **Florida Turnpike,** a toll road, crosses I-4 and links with I-75 to the north and Miami to the south. **U.S. 192/Irlo Bronson Memorial Highway** is a major east–west artery that reaches from Kissimmee to U.S. 27, crossing I-4 near World Drive, the main Walt Disney World entrance road. Recent construction has widened this stretch of highway and made driving a bit easier while the addition of large numerical markers have made locating hotels, restaurants, and attractions much easier as well. The **B-Line Expressway** (Hwy. 528), also a toll road, goes east from I-4 past Orlando International Airport to Cape Canaveral and Kennedy Space Center. The **East–West Expressway** (also known as Hwy. 408) is a toll road that can be helpful in bypassing surface traffic in the downtown area. The **417,** also a toll road, runs from north of the Orlando International Airport to I-4 just below U.S. 192. This route is a good alternative to I-4 if you are staying on the lower end of International Drive, World Center Drive, or areas east of the I-4, as it is far less traveled than the main highway.

If you're jockeying between Disney and Universal, one of the lesser traffic evils is **Apopka–Vineland Road.** It tends to be less cluttered than I-4 or International Drive. Follow it north from Lake Buena Vista and the northeast side of Disney to Sand Lake Road, then go right/east to Turkey Lake Road, then left/north to Universal Orlando. Another way to avoid the highway when driving between Universal Orlando and Disney is to take the Palm Parkway (just off Apopka–Vineland Rd.) to Turkey Lake Road, which will take you right to Universal.

I-4 and Highway 535 roughly bound **Walt Disney World** to the east (the latter is also a northern boundary) and U.S. 192/Irlo Bronson Memorial Highway bounds it to the south. World Drive is WDW's main north–south artery. Epcot Center Drive (Hwy. 536/the south end of International Dr.) and Buena Vista Drive cut across the complex in a more or less east–west direction; the two roads cross at Bonnet Creek Parkway. Despite a reasonably good highway system and explicit signs, it's easy to get lost or miss a turn here. I've gotten lost or passed an exit on Disney property at least once or twice on every trip. Again, pay attention and drive carefully. Don't panic or pull across several lanes of traffic to make an exit, especially once you're on Disney property—there's always another exit just ahead where you can get turned around. All roads lead to the parks, and you'll soon find another sign directing you to the same place. It may take a bit longer, but Goofy will still be there. A big help to maneuvering the Disney property is the transportation map, as it has all of the roadways on property and it is easy to follow, even if the roads themselves may not be. Be sure to pick one up, either at the parks or at a Disney resort hotel—just ask the front desk or concierge for a copy.

Clever landscaping hides the fact that many parts of WDW are very close together. It took me several trips to discover that Disney–MGM Studios was just behind the BoardWalk, which is right next to the WDW Swan and the WDW Dolphin, which is across the lake from Disney's Yacht and Beach Club Resorts, which are next to

Epcot—you get the picture. Walking can occasionally be the most efficient way to get from one place to another; it's always worth looking at a map to check before you set out anywhere.

ORLANDO NEIGHBORHOODS IN BRIEF

Walt Disney World Though Walt Disney World and Orlando are often considered synonymous (surprise!), WDW isn't situated in Orlando. It's actually located southwest of the city in Lake Buena Vista. WDW encompasses over 47 square miles and claims four major theme parks, two smaller water parks, several smaller attractions, numerous themed resorts, a plethora of restaurants and shops, and an entertainment district.

Downtown Disney Though not actually a neighborhood, Downtown Disney is certainly large enough to be distinguished as such. It encompasses Disney's two nighttime entertainment districts—Pleasure Island and Downtown Disney West Side—as well as its shopping and dining complex, the Downtown Disney Marketplace. The area is filled with clubs, entertainment venues, unique restaurants, and shops. Here you can celebrate New Year's Eve every night, shop till you drop, or tempt your taste buds—all in the space of a single evening.

Lake Buena Vista Lake Buena Vista actually encompasses all of WDW but also includes much of the area bordering the resort. Here you can find the "official" (but not Disney-owned) hotels situated along Hotel Plaza Boulevard. The area along 535 (known locally as Apopka–Vineland), is home to its own share of resorts and restaurants. Though the region is bustling, many of its resorts, restaurants, and shops are set along alcoves and tree-lined side streets, far from the main thoroughfare, to maintain a quieter, more charming atmosphere.

Celebration As you drive through this quaint little town, full of beautiful homes trimmed in gingerbread, some of them with white picket fences, shade trees, and some of the loveliest landscaping around, you may find yourself musing about this 4,900-acre community's seeming perfection. The fact that Disney had a hand in its creation then should come as no great surprise—experts that they are at creating the perfect version of almost anything. The Market Street area's charming collection of shops, restaurants, even its own small hotel, is reminiscent of a bygone era—and a perfect upscale version at that.

Kissimmee Brought back to life by a multimillion-dollar "Rebeautivacation" project, U.S. 192, Kissimmee's main tourist strip, now sports extra wide sidewalks, colorful (and plentiful) streetlamps, landscaping, and location markers. Even the roadway itself has been improved to handle traffic more easily and safely. Kissimmee is lined practically end to end with a variety of budget and moderate resorts and hotels, most of which cater to families (though a few more upscale options have started to spring up), a plentitude of casual restaurants, and a handful of minor attractions.

International Drive Area (Hwy. 536) Known as **I-Drive,** this busy tourist zone is home to more than 100 resorts and hotels, countless restaurants, attractions both big and small, shopping, entertainment, and even its own transportation system—the I-Ride Trolley. There is literally something here for everybody. The areas north of

Sand Lake Road are by far the most congested, filled to capacity with T-shirt shops, tourist traps, resorts, restaurants, and attractions. If you head south, toward the intersection at S.R. 528 (aka the Beeline Expwy.), it's still chock-full of restaurants and hotels but the landscaping is far more appealing and tree-lined walkways offer a more pleasant place to walk. The driving, however, is still slow going at best.

Downtown Orlando Orlando is actually a lot smaller than most major U.S. cities but has a charm all its own. The downtown area is actually about 20 miles northeast of Walt Disney World, which ensures it's far less congested with tourists than the theme park zones. Here you'll find chic restaurants, trendy clubs, and upscale hotels, a cultural center that's filled with theaters, museums, the very visitor-friendly Orlando Science Center, and more. Shopping is plentiful as downtown streets are dotted with upscale boutiques and antiques shops (especially along "Antique Row" on Orange Ave. near Lake Ivanhoe).

Winter Park Those who make the effort to get up to Winter Park, located just north of downtown (Orlando, that is), will enjoy its upscale ambience and quaint southern charm. The town's biggest draw is Park Avenue, with its collection of upscale shops and restaurants set along tree-lined cobblestone streets. This part of the suburbs is a great adult getaway and a good place to relax and escape the WDW, Universal, and I-Drive crowds. It's not, however, a good place to take the kids.

2 Getting Around

In a city that thrives on its attractions, you won't find it difficult to get around—especially if you have a car. Don't count on the city bus system to get you where you want to go—not quickly or efficiently anyway. If you're traveling outside the tourist areas, avoid the 7 to 9am and 4 to 6pm rush if at all possible. Commuter traffic can be bad anywhere but here the complication of tourist traffic makes it even more of a headache. And don't expect weekends to be any better—the locals who run the hotels, restaurants, and attractions still have to get to work, making commuter traffic a 7-day-a-week problem. Most of the parks don't open until 9am or so, and they usually stay open at least until dusk; you won't miss much by leaving a little later. (The exception is Animal Kingdom, where the animals move around earliest in the day, then seek shelter and shade for the remainder of the day; see "Animal Kingdom" in chapter 6, "Exploring Walt Disney World.")

International Drive has two alternate means of transportation—pedestrian and the I-Drive Trolley. I don't recommend the former in the area around Sand Lake Road because, though there are plenty of sidewalks, you may be taking your life in your hands if you try to cross this extremely busy road. The farther south you move along I-Drive, the easier walking becomes. The **I-Ride Trolley** (© 407/248-9590; www. iridetrolley.com) is a safer bet. It makes 54 stops between the Belz Factory Outlets on the north end of the drive and SeaWorld to the south. The trolley runs every 20 minutes, from 8am to 10:30pm, and costs $1 for adults and 25¢ for seniors; kids under 12 ride free, and exact change is required. There's an unlimited 1-day pass available for $3 per person. Thanks to I-Drive's high traffic volume, the trolley offers a decent (and fun) alternative to the bumper-to-bumper traffic.

The good news, if you are driving, is that road signs throughout the area are more accurate than they were a few years back. But to make sure you're heading the right way, follow the directions supplied for the various attractions and hotels later in this book. Call ahead to your destination to check if there is any construction you should be aware of before heading out. Most attractions give directions as a voice-mail option when you call the main number, but you can also ask for an operator to get clarification.

Some hotels offer transportation to and from some theme parks and other tourist destinations; the service may or may not be free, however, so be sure to check with your individual hotel for details. It's not difficult getting around town, but it can get expensive, so know your options when you're deciding on your hotel.

BY DISNEY TRANSPORTATION SYSTEM

If you plan to stay at and spend most of your time at Disney, there's an extensive, free transportation system that runs throughout the entire WDW property.

Disney resorts and official hotels offer unlimited free transportation via bus, monorail, ferry, or water taxi to all WDW properties throughout the day, and at times, well into the evening. If, however, you want to venture elsewhere (say, to Universal or SeaWorld), you'll just have to pay extra to do so.

If you're staying at the Disney resorts, using the system can save you money on a rental car, insurance, and gas, as well as all those parking fees ($9 a day at the WDW theme parks). The drawback, however, is that you're at the mercy of Disney's schedules, which are often slow and, at times, *very* indirect; bus trips from the outlying resorts (especially Fort Wilderness) to the various parks (and vice versa) can take over an hour during peak times.

If you have time before locking in your trip, call (?) **407/934-7639** and ask the information specialist for Disney's new shopping and dining guide, which includes a copy of the **Disney World Transportation Guide Map.** (It shows where various resorts are in relation to the attractions you want to visit.) Along with the maps in this guide, pick up a guide map when you land at the Guest Services desks at any of the Disney resorts and theme parks, or view a more generic map and download it at **www.disneyworld.com** (you'll need Adobe Acrobat Reader).

The best rule when using Disney transportation: Ask the driver or someone at your hotel's front desk to help you take the most direct route. Keep asking questions along the way. Unlike missing a highway exit, missing a bus stop means you may reach your pension before you reach your destination.

BY CAR

Whether or not to rent a car while in Orlando is one of the most important decisions you will make when planning your trip (just behind selecting your hotel). First, think about your vacation plans. If you're planning on going beyond the boundaries of Disney to Universal, SeaWorld, or anywhere along I-Drive, a rental car may well be a necessity. If you want to head out in the evenings to smaller attractions, dinner shows, or other activities not located within the realm of Disney, a car will definitely allow you the most flexibility. If you plan to limit your vacation only to WDW, then a car may prove to be an extra and unnecessary expense.

If you've decided to stay right on Disney property, the question to ask yourself is how, exactly, will you get to the parks? If the Magic Kingdom is accessible only by taking a bus, switching to the monorail, and then catching a ferry, you may want to opt for a car. The least expensive properties, the All-Star resorts, are among the farthest from the Disney parks. Wait times between buses can be considerable—if not unendurable.

> **Tips** **Look Both Ways**
>
> Traveling on foot anywhere in Orlando, most especially on International Drive, can be tricky. If you have to walk across a parking lot or street, *be careful*. The Surface Transportation Policy Project's pedestrian safety report recently named Orlando the most dangerous city in the country for pedestrians. Drivers are paying far more attention to their maps and street signs, not the people running in front of them. Though walking up and down the sidewalks on International Drive or U.S. 192 can be an enjoyable way to get to a restaurant or minigolf course without having to pack up the car, you need to pay strict attention when it comes to crossing the street and should avoid crossing multiple lane roads altogether.

During peak hours in the busiest seasons, you may have trouble getting a seat on the bus, so keep that in mind if you're traveling with seniors or with companions with disabilities. Also, if you're bringing along children and strollers, consider the frustration factor of loading and unloading strollers and all of the paraphernalia that comes with them on and off buses, ferries, and trams.

A car may drastically cut the commute time between the parks and hotels not directly on the monorail routes, so decide how much your time is worth and how much the car will cost plus the $9 per day theme-park parking charge (Disney resort guests, however, are exempt from the parking fees) before making a decision about renting.

In general, if you're going to spend all of your time at Disney and you're ready, willing, and able to handle the transportation network's schedules, there's no sense renting a car that will sit in the parking lot. But if you're on an extended stay—a week or more—you'll probably want a car for at least a day or two to venture beyond the tourist areas. You can discover downtown Orlando, visit museums, or tour the Space Coast; it may be necessary for your sanity, not to mention your survival. After heading from park to park, day after day, a reality check may very well be in order, and there's no better way to come back down to earth than to enjoy some of Florida's more natural offerings.

If you are going to be spending the majority of your vacation outside the House of Mouse, a car is an absolute necessity (unless you plan on staying solely within the bounds of Universal Orlando for your entire trip). While there are plenty of transportation options such as shuttles, trolleys, and taxis, utilizing them every time you venture outside of your hotel can't be done without losing your sanity (and lots of cash)—don't even think of doing it!

All of the major car-rental companies are represented in Orlando and maintain desks at or near the airport. Many agencies provide discount coupons in publications targeted at tourists, though you should keep in mind that AAA discounts and online offers are often better. You may also want to ask your travel agent if he or she has a recommendation, or whether a discount is included in any vacation packages. Also, it never hurts to ask about specials. *Note:* Disney has an Alamo car-rental desk (© **800/ 327-2996**) right on property, so if you're interested in renting for only a few days instead of your entire vacation this may be a good option for you.

See appendix B, "Useful Toll-Free Numbers & Websites," in the back of this book for contact information.

CAR-RENTAL INSURANCE

Car-rental insurance costs around $25 a day. If you hold a private auto insurance policy, you are **probably** covered in the U.S. for loss or damage to the car, as well as liability in case a passenger is injured. The credit card you use to rent the car also may provide some coverage. Double-check with your insurance company as well as the car-rental company regarding what may or may not be covered on both ends. *Note:* Many car-rental companies now charge steep out-of-service fees, if the car is out of commission for any reason after its return.

Car-rental insurance probably does not cover liability if you caused the accident. Check your own auto insurance policy, the rental company policy, and your credit card coverage for the extent of coverage: Is your destination covered? Are other drivers covered? How much liability is covered if a passenger is injured? (If you rely on your credit card for coverage, you may want to bring a second credit card with you. Damages may be charged to your card, and you may find yourself stranded with no money.) You don't need any surprises spoiling your vacation, so look at your coverage before reaching the rental counter.

DRIVING IN TOWN

SPEED LIMITS   Obey posted speed limits. On highways and interstates, they're usually 55 or 65 mph but as high as 70 mph in some rural areas. In residential areas, 30 or 35 mph is usually the case. *Note:* The corridor between the attractions and downtown Orlando is a speed trap with fines for speeding starting at $157. Fines double in construction areas and school zones. It is best to stick to the speed limit for safety reasons as well, not just because of the threat of a monetary penalty. With so many tourists, most of them having no idea where they are going (and who are probably paying more attention to their maps than their driving), you will be able to react much more quickly if you are not speeding along.

SEAT BELTS   Seat belts are required for all passengers. Children under the age of 3 must be buckled into a car seat and those under 5 must be in a safety restraint. Police will issue tickets to parents who don't put their children in the proper restraints while driving. Many car-rental agencies offer car seat rentals, though if you will be here for more than just a few days you may want to consider bringing your own as the rental cost will almost add up to the price of a new car seat.

AIR BAG SAFETY   Children, in or out of car seats, should ride only in the back seats of cars that are equipped with air bags. Air bags have been linked to the deaths of several young passengers in the U.S. If you do not know if your car is equipped with passenger side air bags, you will need to ask the car-rental attendant; however, they are a standard feature on most new-model cars.

DRINKING & DRIVING   Don't. It's that simple. Florida's rules are strict and strictly enforced. If you're planning to drink (alcohol that is), especially after an exhausting day in the theme parks, designate a sober driver or find an alternative means of transportation (there are plenty of options). Some clubs even provide free soft drinks to designated drivers. If you don't obey the law, your accommodations may change from a four-star hotel room to a Florida jail cell in short order.

DEFENSIVE DRIVING   Drive with extra care in tourist-heavy areas. It's not uncommon for drivers to make sudden turns or to slow down unexpectedly when reading road signs. People often come to near stops on the highway while attempting to read their maps and decipher the Disney signs, which can be confusing. The tourist areas in Orlando are doubly difficult: The locals are in a hurry to get to their jobs, and tourists are scurrying to be the first to the fun. Assume all other drivers have no idea where they're going—which is often close to the truth—and you'll do fine. One of the best things to remember: Keep a safe distance between you and the car ahead of you. And, while it may sound like common sense, don't read a map while driving (you'd be surprised how many do). Get your copilot to do it, use this book to determine your exit in advance, or call ahead to your destination to find out which exit you should take. Stay in the far right lane, the slow lane, when you begin to get near your exit. If you miss your exit, don't panic—there are plenty others (especially around Disney) that can get you where you want to go.

DRIVING IN THE RAIN   Watch for a hazardous condition where oil on the road creates slick patches when the road gets wet. Rainstorms in Florida are intense and frequent; they're almost a daily occurrence in summer. Exercise extreme caution and drive in the far right lane when driving much slower than the speed limit. Don't pull off onto the shoulder of the road. If visibility is especially poor, pull off at the first exit and wait out the storm; they seldom last more than an hour. Florida law requires drivers to turn on their headlights whenever they turn on their windshield wipers.

IF YOU GET LOST   Exit numbers continue to change and signs continue to be confusing. On interstates or Orlando's toll roads, don't try a U-turn across the grassy median. Go to the next exit and reenter the highway by accessing the on-ramp near where you get off. Avoid pulling over to ask directions from people on the street. Instead, stop at a convenience store or gas station and ask the clerk. Don't forget, you can get maps ahead of time from the Orlando CVB. If you are renting a car, most agencies will provide a map (some even provide computer-generated directions). Some rental-car agencies offer GPS navigational systems with their rentals as an add-on; inquire when you rent your car. Most of the hotels have maps located in the racks with all of the brochures. They are usually inserts in the local tourist magazines.

SAFETY WHILE DRIVING   Question your rental agency about personal safety or ask for a brochure on traveler safety tips when you pick up your car. Obtain written directions from the agency or a map with the route marked in red, showing how to get to your destination. And, if possible, arrive and depart during daylight hours.

If you drive off a highway and end up in a dodgy-looking neighborhood, turn back around and leave the area as quickly as possible. If you have an accident, even on the highway, stay in your car with the doors locked until you assess the situation or until the police arrive. If you're bumped from behind on the street or are involved in a minor accident with no injuries, and the situation appears to be suspicious, motion to the other driver to follow you. Never open the window or get out of your car in such situations. Go directly to the nearest police station, well-lit service station, or 24-hour store. You may want to look into renting a cellphone on a short-term basis if you don't already have one. One recommended wireless rental company is **InTouch USA** (✆ **800/872-7626;** www.intouchusa.com).

If you see someone else on the road indicating a need for help, don't stop. Take note of the location, and call the police by dialing ✆ **911** to make them aware of the situation.

Park in well-lit, well-traveled areas whenever possible. Keep your doors locked, whether you're inside the car or not. Look around before you get out and never leave packages, pocketbooks, or any kind of valuables in sight. Although theme park lots are patrolled, it's best to secure your valuables at all times. For an added measure of security, you can always lock things in the lockers available near all of the park entrances. If it is an item you really don't need with you that day, use the hotel safe for storage and don't even bring it along.

If someone tries to rob you or steal your car, don't resist. Report the incident to the police immediately.

BY BUS

Stops for the **Lynx** bus system (© **407/841-5969;** www.golynx.com) are marked with a "paw" print. It will get you to Disney, Universal, and I-Drive (one-way fare is $1.50 adults, 75¢ kids in grades K–12 with valid school ID, kids 6 and under ride free; express passes and daylong passes are available as well), but it's generally not very tourist-friendly.

Mears Transportation (© **407/423-5566;** www.mearstransportation.com) operates buses to all the major attractions, including Kennedy Space Center, Universal Studios, SeaWorld, and Busch Gardens (yes, in Tampa), among others. Their service is the largest in the area, and with good reason. Rates will vary based on where you are going and where you are coming from, of course, so call ahead for the particulars. Many of the area hotels use Mears for their shuttle service to the parks and attractions.

BY MOTORCYCLE

The increasing popularity of Bike Week in nearby Daytona Beach and a growing number of weekend road warriors have sparked an increase in places specializing in motorcycle rental. The Harley Davidson, in all shapes and sizes, is the most popular. You must be at least 21 and sometimes 25 years of age, have a motorcycle license, and a major credit card. Rental fees start at about $750 for 1 week or $150 per day including helmets, locks, and a brief orientation. You can rent bikes at **American V Twin,** 5101 International Dr. (© **888/268-8946** or 407/903-0058; www.amvtwin.com). But plan ahead, months in advance if you're going to be here during Bike Week, late February to early March, or Biketoberfest (also in Daytona) in mid-October.

BY TAXI

Taxis will line up in front of major hotels in addition to a few smaller properties. The front desk will be more than happy to hail one down for you. If you wish, you can also call **Yellow Cab** (© **407/699-9999**) and **Ace Metro** (© **407/855-1111**) on your own. Both are good choices; however, rates can run as high as $3.25 for the first mile, $1.75 per mile thereafter, though occasionally you can get a flat rate if you ask. In general, cabs are economical only if you have four or five people aboard and aren't going very far or very many times. You could actually rent your own car (depending on the model) for the price of just a few taxi rides.

FAST FACTS: Walt Disney World & Orlando

Ambulances See "Emergencies," below.

American Express There's an American Express Travel Service Office located at 7618 W. Sand Lake Rd. (© **407/264-0104**).

ATM Networks See "Money," p. 21.

Automobile Organizations Auto clubs will supply maps, suggested routes, guidebooks, accident and bail-bond insurance, and emergency road service.

The **American Automobile Association (AAA)** is the major auto club in the United States. If you belong to an auto club in your home country, inquire about AAA reciprocity before you leave. You may be able to join AAA even if you're not a member of a reciprocal club; to inquire, call AAA (✆ **800/222-4357**). AAA is actually an organization of regional auto clubs, so look under "AAA Automobile Club" in the White Pages of the telephone directory. AAA has a nationwide emergency road service telephone number (✆ 800/AAA-HELP).

Babysitters Many Orlando hotels, including all of Disney's resorts, offer babysitting services, usually from an outside service such as **Kids Night Out** (✆ **800/696/8105** or 407/828-0920; www.kidsniteout.com), or **All About Kids** (✆ **800/728-6506** or 407/812-9300; www.all-about-kids.com). In-room rates usually run somewhere between $10 and $15 per hour for the first child and $1 to $3 per additional child, per hour. A transportation fee of $8 to $10 is charged as well. Several Orlando resorts have good child-care facilities with counselor-supervised activity programs right on the premises with rates that run per child per hour, or, in some cases, on a set schedule. The Disney resorts' programs—offered at its more expensive properties—generally run from 4:30pm to midnight and include activities, movies, and a meal. They're open to kids ages 4 to 12 (kids must be potty-trained); cost is $10 per child per hour. Reservations are a good idea; call ✆ **407/939-3463**.

Business Hours Theme park operating hours vary depending on the time of year, even on the day of the week. While most open at 8 or 9am and close at 6 or 7pm, you should call or check a park's website for its most current schedule before arriving. Other businesses are generally open from 9am to 5pm, Monday through Friday. Bars are usually open until 2am, with some after-hours clubs staying open into the wee hours of the morning (though the alcohol stops flowing at 2am).

Car Rentals See "Getting Around," p. 65, and appendix B, "Useful Toll-Free Numbers & Websites."

Cashpoints See "Money," p. 21.

Currency The most common bills are the $1 (a "buck"), $5, $10, and $20 denominations. There are also $2 bills (seldom encountered), $50 bills, and $100 bills (the last two are usually not welcome as payment for small purchases).

Coins come in seven denominations: 1¢ (1 cent, or a penny); 5¢ (5 cents, or a nickel); 10¢ (10 cents, or a dime); 25¢ (25 cents, or a quarter); 50¢ (50 cents, or a half dollar); the gold-colored Sacagawea coin, worth $1; and the rare silver dollar.

For additional information see "Money," p. 21.

Doctors & Dentists There are basic first-aid centers in all of the theme parks. There's also a 24-hour, toll-free number for the **Poison Control Center** (✆ 800/282-3171). To find a dentist, call the **Dental Referral Service** at ✆ 800/235-4111 or go online to **www.dentalreferral.com**.

Doctors on Call Service (✆ 407/399-3627) makes house and room calls in most of the Orlando area (including the Disney resorts). **Centra Care** has several walk-in clinics listed in the Yellow Pages, including ones on Turkey Lake Road, near Universal (© 407/351-6682); at Lake Buena Vista, near Disney (© 407/934-2273); and on U.S. 192 (W. Irlo Bronson Hwy.) in the Formosa Gardens shopping center (© 407/397-7032).

Drinking Laws The legal age for buying and consuming alcoholic beverages in Florida is 21; proof of age is required and often requested at bars, nightclubs, and restaurants, so it's always a good idea to bring a photo ID when you go out. Beer and wine often can be purchased in supermarkets. No liquor is served in the Magic Kingdom at Walt Disney World. Alcoholic drinks are available, however, at the other Disney parks and are quite evident at Universal Orlando's parks (even more so at its seasonal celebrations).

Do not carry open containers of alcohol in your car or any public area that isn't zoned for alcohol consumption. The police can and will fine you. Nothing will ruin your trip (not to mention your life and possibly the lives of others) faster than getting a citation for DUI ("driving under the influence"), so just don't do it.

Electricity Like Canada, the United States uses 110–120 volts AC (60 cycles), compared to 220–240 volts AC (50 cycles) in most of Europe, Australia, and New Zealand. Downward converters that change 220–240 volts to 110–120 volts are difficult to find in the United States, so bring one with you.

Embassies & Consulates All embassies are located in the nation's capital, Washington, D.C. Some consulates are located in major U.S. cities, and most nations have a mission to the United Nations in New York City. If your country isn't listed below, call for directory information in Washington, D.C. (© 202/555-1212) or log on to **www.embassy.org/embassies**.

The embassy of **Australia** is at 1601 Massachusetts Ave. NW, Washington, DC 20036 (© **202/797-3000**; www.austemb.org). There are consulates in New York, Honolulu, Houston, Los Angeles, and San Francisco.

The embassy of **Canada** is at 501 Pennsylvania Ave. NW, Washington, DC 20001 (© **202/682-1740**; www.canadianembassy.org). Other Canadian consulates are in Buffalo (New York), Detroit, Los Angeles, New York, and Seattle.

The embassy of **Ireland** is at 2234 Massachusetts Ave. NW, Washington, DC 20008 (© **202/462-3939**; www.irelandemb.org). Irish consulates are in Boston, Chicago, New York, San Francisco, and other cities. See website for complete listing.

The embassy of **New Zealand** is at 37 Observatory Circle NW, Washington, DC 20008 (© **202/328-4800**; www.nzemb.org). New Zealand consulates are in Los Angeles, Salt Lake City, San Francisco, and Seattle.

The embassy of the **United Kingdom** is at 3100 Massachusetts Ave. NW, Washington, DC 20008 (© **202/588-7800**; www.britainusa.com). Other British consulates are in Atlanta, Boston, Chicago, Cleveland, Houston, Los Angeles, New York, San Francisco, and Seattle.

Emergencies Call © **911** to report a fire, contact the police, or get an ambulance. This call is free from all public telephones and should be the first call made in case of any serious medical emergency or accident.

The Florida Tourism Industry Marketing Corporation, the state tourism promotions board, sponsors a **help line** (© 800/647-9284). With operators speaking over 100 languages, it can provide general directions and can help with lost travel papers and credit cards, minor medical emergencies, accidents, money transfer, airline confirmation, and much more.

Gasoline (Petrol) Petrol is known as gasoline (or "gas") in the U.S. and is sold at service stations and convenience stores. One U.S. gallon equals 3.8 liters or .85 imperial gallons. Fill-up locations are known as gas or service stations. There usually are three grades (and price levels) of gasoline available at most gas stations; the ones with the highest octane are the most expensive. If you have a rental car, use the least expensive, "regular" unleaded gas. Gas prices average $2.75 a gallon, but can be 20¢ or 30¢ a gallon higher in the main tourist areas.

Holidays Banks, government offices, post offices, and many stores, restaurants, and museums are closed on the following legal national holidays: January 1 (New Year's Day), the third Monday in January (Martin Luther King, Jr., Day), the third Monday in February (Presidents' Day), the last Monday in May (Memorial Day), July 4 (Independence Day), the first Monday in September (Labor Day), the second Monday in October (Columbus Day), November 11 (Veterans Day/Armistice Day), the fourth Thursday in November (Thanksgiving Day), and December 25 (Christmas). The Tuesday after the first Monday in November is Election Day, a federal government holiday in presidential-election years (held every 4 years, and next in 2008). However, you will find theme parks, accommodations, and most restaurants open on these days.

For more information on holidays see "Calendar of Events," on p. 26.

Hospitals **Sand Lake Hospital,** 9400 Turkey Lake Rd. (© 407/351-8550), is about 2 miles south of Sand Lake Road. From the WDW area, take I-4 east to the Sand Lake Road exit and make a left on Turkey Lake Road. The hospital is 2 miles up on your right. To avoid the highway, take Palm Parkway (off of Apopka–Vineland near Hotel Plaza Blvd.); it turns into Turkey Lake Road. The hospital is 2 miles up on your left. **Celebration Health** (© 407/303-4000), located in the near-Disney town of Celebration, is at 400 Celebration Place. From I-4, take the U.S. 192 exit. At the first traffic light, turn right onto Celebration Avenue. At the first stop sign, take another right. *Note:* Be sure to check with your healthcare provider or insurance carrier regarding regulations for medical care outside your home area.

Kennels The major theme parks offer animal boarding usually for about $6 per day. For information on Disney's kennel facilities, call © 407/824-6568. Resort guests can board their pets overnight for $9 ($11 for those not staying at Disney) at the Transportation and Ticket Center's kennel on Seven Seas Drive near the Polynesian Resort. SeaWorld and Universal Orlando also offer kennels, but overnight boarding is not available (though all Universal Orlando resorts welcome pets). A current vaccine record is a must at all kennels. *Note:* For more information on traveling with your pet in Orlando, see "Traveling with Pets," on p. 44.

Legal Aid If you are "pulled over" for a minor infraction (such as speeding), never attempt to pay the fine directly to a police officer; this could be construed as attempted bribery, a much more serious crime. Pay fines by mail, or directly into the hands of the clerk of the court. If accused of a more serious offense, say and do nothing before consulting a lawyer. Here the burden is on the state to prove a person's guilt beyond a reasonable doubt, and everyone has the right to remain silent, whether he or she is suspected of a crime or actually arrested. Once arrested, a person can make one telephone call to a party of his or her choice. International visitors should call your embassy or consulate.

Lost & Found Be sure to tell all of your credit card companies the minute you discover your wallet has been lost or stolen and file a report at the nearest police precinct. Your credit card company or insurer may require a police report number or record of the loss. Most credit card companies have an emergency toll-free number to call if your card is lost or stolen; they may be able to wire you a cash advance immediately or deliver an emergency credit card in a day or two. Visa's U.S. emergency number is ℂ **800/847-2911** or 410/581-9994. American Express cardholders and traveler's check holders should call ℂ **800/ 221-7282.** MasterCard holders should call ℂ **800/307-7309** or 636/722-7111. For other credit cards, call the toll-free number directory at ℂ **800/555-1212.**

If you need emergency cash over the weekend when all banks and American Express offices are closed, you can have money wired to you via **Western Union** (ℂ **800/325-6000;** www.westernunion.com).

Lost Children Every theme park has a designated spot for adults to be reunited with lost children (or lost spouses). Ask where it is when you enter any park (or consult the free park guide maps) and instruct your children to ask park personnel (not a stranger) to take them there if they get separated from you. Point out what park personnel look like so they will know who to go to. Children 7 and under should wear name-tags.

Mail At press time, domestic postage rates were 24¢ for a postcard and 39¢ for a letter. For international mail, a first-class letter of up to 1 ounce costs 84¢ (63¢ to Canada and Mexico); a first-class postcard costs 75¢ (55¢ to Canada and Mexico); and a preprinted postal aerogramme costs 75¢. For more information go to **www.usps.com** and click on "Calculate Postage."

If you aren't sure what your address will be in the United States, mail can be sent to you, in your name, c/o General Delivery at the main post office of the city or region where you expect to be. (Call ℂ **800/275-8777** for information on the nearest post office.) The addressee must pick up mail in person and must produce proof of identity (driver's license, passport, and so forth). Most post offices will hold your mail for up to 1 month, and are open Monday to Friday from 8am to 6pm, and Saturday from 9am to 3pm.

The post office most convenient to Disney and Universal is at 10450 Turkey Lake Rd. (ℂ **800/275-8777**). It's open Monday through Friday from 9am to 5pm, Saturday from 9am to noon. A smaller location, closer to Disney, is at 12133 Apopka–Vineland (S.R. 535) in Lake Buena Vista, just up the road from Hotel Plaza Boulevard (ℂ **800/275-8777**). If all you need is to buy stamps and mail letters, you can do that at most hotels.

Always include zip codes when mailing items in the U.S. If you don't know your zip code, visit **www.usps.com/zip4**.

Measurements See the chart on the inside front cover of this book for details on converting metric measurements to U.S. equivalents.

Newspapers & Magazines The *Orlando Sentinel* is the major local newspaper, but you can also purchase the Sunday editions of other papers (most notably, the *New York Times*) in some hotel gift shops or bookstores such as Barnes & Noble or Borders. Don't count on finding daily editions of West Coast papers, such as the *Los Angeles Times,* without making special arrangements. The Friday edition of the *Sentinel* includes extensive entertainment and dining listings, as does the *Sentinel*'s website, **www.orlandosentinel.com**. *Orlando Weekly* is a free, alternative paper that has a lot of entertainment and art listings focused on events outside tourist areas.

Passports **For Residents of Australia:** You can pick up an application from your local post office or any branch of Passports Australia, but you must schedule an interview at the passport office to present your application materials. Call the **Australian Passport Information Service** at © **131-232,** or visit the government website at **www.passports.gov.au**.

For Residents of Canada: Passport applications are available at travel agencies throughout Canada or from the central **Passport Office,** Department of Foreign Affairs and International Trade, Ottawa, ON K1A 0G3 (© **800/567-6868**; www.ppt.gc.ca). *Note:* Canadian children who travel must have their own passport. However, if you hold a valid Canadian passport issued before December 11, 2001, that bears the name of your child, the passport remains valid for you and your child until it expires.

For Residents of Ireland: You can apply for a 10-year passport at the **Passport Office,** Setanta Centre, Molesworth Street, Dublin 2 (© **01/671-1633**; www.irl gov.ie/iveagh). Those under age 18 and over 65 must apply for a €12, 3-year passport. You can also apply at 1A South Mall, Cork (© **021/272-525**), or at most main post offices.

For Residents of New Zealand: You can pick up a passport application at any New Zealand Passports Office or download it from their website. Contact the **Passports Office** at © **0800/225-050** in New Zealand or 04/474-8100, or log on to **www.passports.govt.nz**.

For Residents of the United Kingdom: To pick up an application for a standard 10-year passport (5-year passport for children under 16), visit your nearest passport office, major post office, or travel agency, or contact the **United Kingdom Passport Service** at © **0870/521-0410** or search its website at **www.ukpa.gov.uk**.

Pharmacies There's a **Walgreens** 24-hour pharmacy at 7650 W. Sand Lake Rd. (© **407/345-9497**). Other 24-hour locations can be found near Universal Orlando and Kissimmee by logging on to **www.walgreens.com**. Numerous other pharmacies in and around the Orlando area are listed inside the Yellow Pages.

Photography Two-hour film processing is available at all major parks. Look for the PHOTO EXPRESS sign. You can buy film, batteries, and disposable cameras in all of the theme parks, but you'll save money on almost everything if you shop at drugstores such as Walgreens or local grocery stores. These places often run specials for discounted processing or free double-prints, saving you a significant amount of money. They're listed in the Yellow Pages under "Photo Finishing."

The parks carry only a small selection of memory chips for digital cameras; if you need rechargeable batteries, you will have to go to one of the many camera shops found just off of park property.

Safety Just because Minnie, Mickey, Donald, and Goofy all live here doesn't mean that a few more seedy characters aren't lurking about as well. Even in the most magical place on earth you shouldn't let your guard down; Orlando has a crime rate that's comparable to that of other large U.S. cities. Stay alert and remain aware of your surroundings. It's best to keep your valuables in a safe. Most hotels today are equipped with in-room safes or offer the use of a safety deposit box at the front desk, just for that purpose. Keep a close eye on your valuables when you're in public places—restaurants, theaters, and even airport terminals. Renting a locker is always preferable to leaving your valuables in the trunk of your car, even in the theme-park lots. Be cautious, even when in the parks, and avoid carrying large amounts of cash in a backpack or fanny pack, which could be easily accessed while you're standing in line for a ride or show. And don't leave valuables unattended under a stroller—that's pretty much asking for them to be stolen.

If you're renting a car, carefully read the safety instructions that the rental company provides. Never stop for any reason in a suspicious, poorly lit, or unpopulated area, and remember that children should never ride in the front seat of a car equipped with air bags.

Smoking If you're a smoker, light up where and when you can. Smoking is prohibited in many of Florida's public places. While some bars have smoking areas and most hotels have smoking rooms, many are eliminating them. You're still permitted to inhale in most outdoor areas, but the Disney parks restrict where. *Note:* Don't expect to light up over dinner. In 2002, Florida voters approved a constitutional amendment that bans smoking in public work places, including restaurants and bars that serve food. Stand-alone bars that serve virtually no food and designated smoking rooms in hotels are exempt.

Special Diets Kosher, salt-free, and other dietary needs can be arranged at sit-down restaurants inside the Disney parks and resorts with 24-hour or longer notice. Call ⓒ **407/939-3463.**

Taxes A 6.5% to 7% sales tax (depends on the local county you happen to be in) is charged on all goods with the exception of most edible grocery-store items and medicines. Hotels add another 2% to 5% in resort taxes to your bill, so the total tax on accommodations can run you up to 12%.

The United States has no value-added tax (VAT) or other indirect tax at the national level. Every state, county, and city may levy its own local tax on all purchases, including hotel and restaurant checks and airline tickets. These taxes will not appear on price tags.

Telephone, Telegraph, Telex & Fax Generally, hotel surcharges on long-distance and local calls are astronomical, so you're better off using your **cellphone** or a **public pay telephone.** Many convenience groceries and packaging services sell **prepaid calling cards** in denominations up to $50; for international visitors these can be the least expensive way to call home. Many public phones at airports now accept American Express, MasterCard, and Visa credit cards. **Local calls** made from public pay phones in most locales cost either 25¢ or 35¢. Pay phones do not accept pennies, and few will take anything larger than a quarter.

Most long-distance and international calls can be dialed directly from any phone. **For calls within the United States and to Canada,** dial 1 followed by the area code and the seven-digit number. **For other international calls,** dial 011 followed by the country code, city code, and the number you are calling.

Calls to area codes **800, 888, 877,** and **866** are toll-free. However, calls to area codes **700** and **900** (chat lines, bulletin boards, "dating" services, and so on) can be very expensive—usually a charge of 95¢ to $3 or more per minute, and they sometimes have minimum charges that can run as high as $15 or more.

For **reversed-charge or collect calls,** and for person-to-person calls, dial the number 0, then the area code and number; an operator will come on the line, and you should specify whether you are calling collect, person-to-person, or both. If your operator-assisted call is international, ask for the overseas operator.

For **local directory assistance** ("information"), dial 411; for long-distance information, dial 1, then the appropriate area code and 555-1212.

Telegraph and telex services are provided primarily by Western Union. You can telegraph money, or have it telegraphed to you, very quickly over the Western Union system, but this service can cost as much as 15% to 20% of the amount sent.

Most hotels have **fax machines** available for guest use (be sure to ask about the charge to use it). Many hotel rooms are even wired for guests' fax machines. A less expensive way to send and receive faxes may be at stores such as **The UPS Store** (formerly Mail Boxes Etc.).

Note: Because of its growth spurt, Orlando has had to go to 10-digit dialing. If you're making a local call in Orlando's 407 area code region, even across the street, *you must dial the 407 area code followed by the number you wish to call,* for a total of 10 digits.

Time Orlando is in the **Eastern Standard Time (EST)** zone, which is 1 hour later than Chicago, 3 hours later than Los Angeles, 5 hours earlier than London, and 12 hours earlier than Sydney. Call ✆ **407/646-3131** for the correct time and temperature.

Daylight saving time takes effect at 2am the first Sunday in April until 2am the last Sunday in October, except in Arizona, Hawaii, the U.S. Virgin Islands, and Puerto Rico. Daylight saving moves the clock 1 hour ahead of standard time. (A new law will extend daylight saving in 2007; clocks will change the second Sun in Mar and the first Sun in Nov.)

Tipping Tips are a very important part of certain workers' income, and gratuities are the standard way of showing appreciation for services provided. (Tipping is certainly not compulsory if the service is poor!) In hotels, tip **bellhops** at least $1 per bag ($2–$3 if you have a lot of luggage) and tip the **chamber staff** $1 to $2 per day (more if you've left a disaster area for him or her to clean up). Tip the **doorman** or **concierge** only if he or she has provided you with some specific service (for example, calling a cab for you or obtaining difficult-to-get theater tickets). Tip the **valet-parking attendant** $1 every time you get your car.

In restaurants, bars, and nightclubs, tip **service staff** 15% to 20% of the check, tip **bartenders** 10% to 15%, tip **checkroom attendants** $1 per garment, and tip **valet-parking attendants** $1 per vehicle.

As for other service personnel, tip **cabdrivers** 15% of the fare; tip **skycaps** at airports at least $1 per bag ($2–$3 if you have a lot of luggage); and tip **hairdressers** and **barbers** 15% to 20%.

Toilets You won't find public toilets or "restrooms" on the streets in most U.S. cities, but they can be found in hotel lobbies, bars, restaurants, museums, department stores, railway and bus stations, and service stations. Large hotels and fast-food restaurants are probably the best bet for good, clean facilities. If possible, avoid the toilets at parks and beaches, which tend to be dirty; some may be unsafe. Restaurants and bars in resorts or heavily visited areas may reserve their restrooms for patrons. Some establishments display a notice indicating this. You can ignore this sign or, better yet, avoid arguments by paying for a cup of coffee or a soft drink, which will qualify you as a patron. Within the theme parks, restrooms will be clearly marked on the park maps.

Visas For information about U.S. visas go to **http://travel.state.gov** and click on "Visas." Or go to one of the following websites:

Australian citizens can obtain up-to-date visa information from the **U.S. Embassy Canberra,** Moonah Place, Yarralumla, ACT 2600 (© **02/6214-5600**), or by checking the U.S. Diplomatic Mission's website at **http://usembassy-australia. state.gov/consular**.

British subjects can obtain up-to-date visa information by calling the **U.S. Embassy Visa Information Line** (© **0891/200-290**) or by visiting the "Visas to the U.S." section of the American Embassy London's website at **www.usembassy. org.uk**.

Irish citizens can obtain up-to-date visa information through the **Embassy of the USA Dublin,** 42 Elgin Rd., Dublin 4, Ireland (© **353/1-668-8777**), or by checking the "Consular Services" section of the website at **http://dublin.us embassy.gov**.

Citizens of **New Zealand** can obtain up-to-date visa information by contacting the **U.S. Embassy New Zealand,** 29 Fitzherbert Terrace, Thorndon, Wellington (© **644/472-2068**), or get the information directly from the "For New Zealanders" section of the website at **http://usembassy.org.nz**.

Weather Call © **321/255-0212** for the local weather forecast (they answer as National Weather Service in Melbourne, FL, but after that you get an option to punch in 412 from a touch-tone phone, which plugs you into the Orlando forecast). A local 24-hour news station, Channel 13, offers weather forecasts several times an hour. You can also check out the Weather Channel on your hotel TV or at **www.weather.com** for the most up-to-date information.

4

Where to Stay

There seemed to be no end to Orlando's hotel boom a few years ago. About 4,000 new rooms were added every year through 2000, and then things began to slow down. The good news (though maybe not for your pocketbook) is that tourism numbers (and hotels) are rising once more, with roughly 3,400 rooms added to the city in 2006.

The Shingle Creek Resort, a 1,500-room full-service convention resort, opened near the Orlando Orange County Convention Center just as this book hit the shelves. The Four Seasons group, world renowned for the highest standards in hospitality, is opening its newest resort (and fourth in Florida) in the picture-perfect town of Celebration sometime in 2007. And they're not the only new kids on the block—more large-scale destination resorts are slated to open over the next few years. The Orlando area now has more than 115,000 rooms, including scores of places located in or near the major-league tourist draws: Walt Disney World, Universal Orlando, SeaWorld, and the rest of International Drive.

Disney alone has 31 resorts (two of them added within the last few years), time-shares, and "official" hotels.

Beautifully landscaped grounds are the rule at properties in WDW, neighboring Lake Buena Vista, Universal Orlando, and on the mid- and southern portions of I-Drive. But the beauty of the area is often offset by the beast of heavier traffic and, at times, higher prices. No matter what your budget or crowd tolerance, there is something for everyone. If you're looking for an inexpensive or moderately priced motel, check out the options in Kissimmee (though that area is no longer limited only to the budget conscious) and, to a lesser degree, on the northern end of International Drive.

Once you have decided on your vacation dates, book your accommodations as soon as possible, especially if you want to stay on Disney or Universal property. Advance reservations are an absolute necessity if you're planning on staying at any of the preferred resorts in town, whether on theme park property or in Orlando proper.

HOW TO CHOOSE A HOTEL & SAVE MONEY

All of the rates cited in the following pages are what are called "rack rates." That means they're typical prices listed in the hotel brochures or the ones that hotel clerks give over the telephone. You can almost always negotiate a better price by purchasing package deals, by assuring the clerks they can do better, or by mentioning to the clerk that you belong to one of several organizations that receive a discount (such as AARP, AAA, the armed services, or a labor union). The Orlando Magicard can save you plenty of cash as well (see p. 16 for more on this cost-saving option). Even the type of credit card you use could get you a **5% to 10% discount** at some of the larger chains. Any discount you get will help ease the impact of local resort taxes, which aren't included in the quoted rates. *These taxes will add 11% to 12% to your bill depending on where you're staying.*

Value Staying for Less

Although many people participate in the airlines' frequent-flier programs, not many take advantage of the major hotel chains' frequent-stay clubs. Even if you don't stay in a hotel for more than your yearly vacation, you may be able to realize real savings by joining its program.

Like the airlines, many hotels will let you build points for staying at a participating property, dining in its restaurant, or using another service they include as a partner. Although programs vary, points can generally be traded for free nights, discounted rates, special perks, or, in some cases, frequent-flier miles. And the price to join is right—it's free. Simply joining a hotel club may make you immediately eligible for discounts, give you express check-in and checkout privileges, and provide free breakfast, local calls, or a morning newspaper. And there's no reason you can't join more than one.

Here are a few frequent-stay programs that offer perks to travelers:

- **Six Continents Hotels Priority Club** (✆ 800/272-9273; www.priorityclub. com) covers the Inter-Continental Resorts, Crowne Plaza hotels and resorts, Holiday Inns, and Staybridge Suites. Priority Club members get express check-in, access to discounted rates at select hotels, and other perks. The perks vary according to hotel but often include breakfast, local phone calls, late checkout, and/or parking.

- **Choice Hotels International Guest Privileges** program (✆ 888/770-6800; www.guestprivileges.com) covers Sleep, Quality, Comfort, and Clarion properties. Participants receive perks such as express check-in, special rates, room upgrades based on availability, extended checkout times, and free local calls and newspapers.

- **Hyatt Hotel's Gold Passport** program (✆ 800/304-9288; www.gold passport.com) gives members a private reservation phone number and express check-in, complimentary newspapers, and access to the hotel's fitness center. You'll also receive special offers and discounted rates from select Hyatt properties.

- **Hilton Honors Worldwide** program (✆ 800/548-8690; www.hiltonhhonors. com) covers Hilton, Conrad, DoubleTree, Embassy Suites, Hampton Inn, and Homewood Suites properties. It offers expedited check-in, a dedicated reservation line, late checkout, and a free daily newspaper.

Other frequent-stay programs include **Starwood Hotels Preferred Guest** (✆ 888/625-4988; www.starwood.com), **Marriott Rewards** (✆ 801/468-4000; www.marriottrewards.com), and **Loews First** (✆ 800/563-9712; www. loewshotels.com).

The **average, undiscounted hotel rate** for the Orlando area is currently about $88 per night double, and that rate in good times climbs about 5% a year. The lowest rates at WDW are at the Pop Century and three All-Star resorts, which, depending on the season, can run from $79 to $137. They're pricier than comparable rooms in the outside world, but though they are small and basic, they are still Disney-owned and offer the same on-property advantages as Disney's more expensive resorts.

WDW's 2006 value seasons or lowest rates are generally available from January 1 to February 15, August 27 to October 4 (except Labor Day weekend), and November 26 to December 19. Regular season rates are available from April 23 to August 26 and October 5 to November 25. Peak rates apply from February 16 to April 22, and holiday rates from December 20 through December 31. While the actual dates will shift a little (and will also change depending on the level of hotel you choose), the same periods should apply in 2007.

If you're not renting a car or staying at a Walt Disney World or Universal resort, be sure to ask when booking your room if the hotel or motel offers **transportation to the theme parks** and, if so, whether there's a charge and exactly what it is if they do. Some hotels and motels offer free service with their own shuttles (listed in the reviews in this chapter). Others use Mears Transportation (see "Getting Around" in chapter 3), and rates can be as high as $15 per person round-trip (some hotels make these arrangements for you; others require you to do it). On the other hand, if you have a vehicle, expect to pay $9 a day to park it at Disney, SeaWorld, and Universal.

If you stay at a WDW resort or one of Disney's "official" hotels, transportation is complimentary within WDW. For more information on this and the other advantages of staying at Disney properties, see "The Perks of Staying with Mickey," below.

In or out of Walt Disney World, if you book your hotel as part of a **package** (see "Packages for the Independent Traveler" in chapter 2 for more details), you'll likely enjoy some type of savings. The **Walt Disney Travel Company** (✆ **407/934-7806**) offers a number of Disney resort packages.

Outside Disney, you'll probably be quoted a rate better than the rack rates contained in the following listings, but you should try to bargain even further to ensure you get the best rates possible. Ask about discounts for students, government employees, seniors, military, firefighters, police, AFL–CIO, corporate clients, and, again, AARP or AAA, holders of the Orlando Magicard, even frequent traveler programs (whether you have hotel or airline membership). Special Internet-only discounts and packages may also be featured on hotel websites, especially those of the larger chains. No matter where you end up staying, always ask again when you arrive if there are any additional discounts or promotions available. But never come to Orlando without a reservation: Taking chances on your negotiating skills is one thing, taking chances on room availability is quite another. Orlando is a year-round destination, with a heavy convention and business trade, and international vacationers flock here during periods when domestic travelers aren't. If you come without a reservation, you may find yourself extremely disappointed—or completely out of luck.

In the "Amenities" section of the accommodations descriptions that follow, we mention **concierge levels** where available. In these hotels within a hotel, guests pay more to enjoy a luxurious private lounge (sometimes with great views), free continental or full breakfast, hot and cold hors d'oeuvres served at cocktail hour, and/or late-night cordials and pastries. Rooms are usually on higher floors, and guests are pampered with additional special services (including private registration and check-out, a personal concierge, and nightly bed turndown) and amenities (such as upgraded toiletries, bathroom scales, terry robes, hair dryers, and more). Ask for the specifics when you reserve a room.

You'll also find counselor-supervised **child care** or **activity centers** at some hotels. Very popular in Orlando, these can be marvelous, creatively run facilities that might

---

> ⌒*Tips* **Tight Squeeze**
>
> An average hotel or motel room in the Orlando area has about 325 to 400 square feet and beds for four; while hardly a castle, most travelers find it adequate for a short stay. We've made a special note in the listings of properties where the rooms are substantially larger or smaller than the average.

---

offer movies, video games, arts and crafts, storytelling, puppet shows, indoor and outdoor activities, and more. Some provide meals and/or have beds where a child can sleep while you're out on the town. Check individual hotel listings for these facilities.

RESERVATION SERVICES

Many of the Kissimmee hotels listed under "Places to Stay in the Kissimmee Area," found later in this chapter, can be booked through the **Kissimmee–St. Cloud Convention & Visitors Bureau** (© 800/333-5477; www.floridakiss.com). The same goes for Orlando and the **Orlando/Orange County Convention & Visitors Bureau** (© 800/643-9492; www.orlandoinfo.com).

   Florida Hotel Network (© 800/293-2419; www.floridahotels.com), **Central Reservation Service** (© 800/555-7555 or 407/740-6442; www.crshotels.com), and **Hotels.com** (© 800/246-8357; www.hotels.com) are three other services that can help with room reservations and other kinds of reservations in Central Florida. **HotelKingdom.com** (© 877/766-6787 or 407/294-9600; www.hotelkingdom.com) is also a good source of room or vacation rental bargains. You can also book Disney World hotels directly by calling © 407/934-7639 or visiting **www.disneyworld.com**; Universal Orlando properties can be booked by calling © 800/837-2273 or 877/801-9720, or by visiting **www.universalorlando.com**.

HOW TO USE THIS CHAPTER

The hotels listed in this chapter are divided by location and price category. As you might expect, many of the inexpensive properties are the farthest from the action and/or have the most spartan, unimaginative accommodations.

   Keep in mind, however, that this isn't one of the world's best bargain destinations. Unlike other Florida tourist areas, there are few under-$60 motels that meet the standards demanded for listing in this book. That's why we've raised the price bar. The ones in our **inexpensive** category charge an average of less than $90 per night for a double room. Those offering $90 to $180 rooms make up the **moderate** category; $180 to $250 rooms are listed as **expensive,** and anything over $250 is listed as **very expensive.** Any included extras (such as breakfast) are listed for each property. Orlando's peak and off seasons are often complicated as the peak times are sporadically disbursed throughout the calendar. Even remote things such as the International Sweet Potato Growers convention in Orlando can raise off-season prices. These events especially impact moderately priced properties outside WDW.

   Keep in mind that rates are per night double unless otherwise noted, and they don't include hotel taxes of 11% to 12%. Also, most Orlando hotels and motels let **kids under 12 (and usually under 18) stay free** with a parent or guardian if you don't exceed maximum room occupancy. But to be safe, ask for details when booking your room.

1 The Best Hotel Bets

For more of our favorite Central Florida hotels and motels see chapter 1, "The Best of Walt Disney World & Orlando."

- **Best for Families:** Every Disney resort caters to families, with special menus for kids, video-game arcades, free transportation to the parks, extensive recreational facilities, and, in some cases, character meals. Some, however, stand out in particular among the others. **Disney's Old Key West Resort** (℃ **407/934-7639** or 407/827-7700) offers the relaxed laid-back charm of the Florida Keys and some of the best rooms on Disney property for families. Camping at the remote and wooded campgrounds of **Disney's Fort Wilderness Resort & Campground** (℃ **407/934-7639** or 407/824-2900) makes for a more down-to-earth family experience. To enjoy wilderness of a different kind try **Disney's Animal Kingdom** (℃ **407/934-7639** or 407/938-3000), where the animals of the African savanna seemingly come right to your doorstep. If you prefer the rustic and woodsy feel of the Pacific Northwest's national parks, head to **The Wilderness Lodge** (℃ **407/ 934-7639** or 407/824-3200).

  Outside the House of Mouse, **Nickelodeon Family Suites by Holiday Inn** (℃ **877/387-5437** or 407/387-5437) features 2- and 3-bedroom Kid Suites, multilevel water slides and extensive play areas, and an all-new Nickelodeon decor. The **Best Western Lakeside** (℃ **407/396-2222**) features plenty of casual dining, playgrounds, pools, and lots of recreational activities. At the **Holiday Inn Nikki Bird** (℃ **407/396-7300**), you'll find playgrounds, pools, a kids' club, and casual dining—all minutes from Disney.

- **Best Inexpensive Hotels:** That's easy: If you're going to stay on WDW property, you can't beat the prices at **Disney's All-Star Movies Resort, Disney's All-Star Music Resort, Disney's All-Star Sports Resort,** and the new **Disney's Pop Century Resort.** To book a room at any of Disney's inexpensive resorts, call ℃ **407/ 934-7639.** The **Comfort Suites Maingate Resort** (℃ **888/390-9888** or 407/ 390-9888) offers spacious rooms and plenty of amenities at reasonable rates. It's one of the nicest inexpensive properties in the Kissimmee area and is only 1½ miles west of Disney.

- **Best Budget Motel:** The **Fairfield Inn International Drive** (℃ **800/228-2800** or 407/363-1944) has clean rooms, a quiet location close to Universal Orlando, and lots of restaurants within walking distance. If you want to stay closer to Mickey, the **Best Western Lakeside** (℃ **800/848-0801** or 407/396-2222) and the **Seralago Hotel & Suites Maingate East** (℃ **800/046-4329** or 407/396-4488) both offer tons of recreational activities for kids and adults, good rooms, a free shuttle service to the theme parks, and much more—all at bargain rates.

- **Best for Business Travelers:** The **Crowne Plaza Universal** (℃ **407/355-0550**), **Renaissance Orlando Resort at SeaWorld** (℃ **800/327-6677** or 407/351-5555), **Gaylord Palms** (℃ **877/677-9352** or 407/586-0000), **Marriott's Orlando World Center** (℃ **800/621-0638** or 407/239-4200), and the **Peabody Orlando** (℃ **800/732-2639** or 407/352-4000) offer full concierge service, excellent restaurants, spacious lounges, and an extensive array of business services.

- **Best Location:** **Disney's Grand Floridian Resort & Spa** (℃ **407/934-7639** or 407/824-3000), **Disney's Polynesian Resort** (℃ **407/939-6244** or 407/824-2000), and **Disney's Contemporary Resort** (℃ **407/939-6244** or

407/824-1000) are on the WDW monorail route, providing easy access to the parks. The **Portofino Bay Hotel** (© **888/322-5541** or 407/503-1000), **Hard Rock Hotel** (© **888/232-7827** or 407/363-8000), and **Royal Pacific Resort** (© **800/232-7827** or 407/503-3000) are within walking distance of both Universal Orlando parks, and there's also boat service to the dock at CityWalk.

- **Best Service:** The elegant **Peabody Orlando** (© **800/732-2639** or 407/352-4000) offers attentive pampering from one of the best staffs in the area. The staff at the **Gaylord Palms** (© **877/677-9352** or 407/586-0000) also makes it their business to treat you as if you were their only guest.

- **Best Pools:** All of the Walt Disney World resorts have wonderfully whimsical themed swimming pools, and usually of Olympic-size. Arguably, the best is shared by **Disney's Beach Club Resort** (© **407/934-7639** or 407/934-8000) and **Disney's Yacht Club Resort** (© **407/934-7639** or 407/934-7000). Storm Along Bay, a 3-acre, free-form pool and water park, stretches between them, including a shipwreck for exploring and sand bottom pools for a toe-tickling experience. Outside the Disney complex, the best resort pool in Orlando can be found at the **Hyatt Regency Grand Cypress Resort** (© **800/233-1234** or 407/239-1234). It's a half-acre, lagoonlike, water-world pool that flows through rock grottoes, is spanned by a rope bridge, and has 12 waterfalls and two steep water slides. The addition of the 24,000-square-foot lazy river pool shared by the **Ritz-Carlton** and **JW Marriott Orlando** at Grande Lakes (© **800/576-5760** or 407/576-5760), however, may give it some stiff competition. Not to be ignored is the rock-'n'-roll themed pool at Universal's **Hard Rock Hotel** (© **877/917-2682**) with its underwater sound system and fantastic landscaping, or the **Nickelodeon Family Suites** (© **866/422-6425** or 407/387-5437) with its super kid-friendly water park–style pools, with towers, slides, climbing nets, miniflumes, and more.

2 The Perks of Staying with Mickey

The decision on whether to bunk with the Mouse is one of the first you'll have to make when planning an Orlando vacation. In the sections "Places to Stay in Walt Disney World" and "'Official' Hotels in Lake Buena Vista" of this chapter, you'll find information on the 31 hotels, resorts, villas, timeshares, and campsites that are owned by Disney or are "official" hotels—those that are privately owned but have earned Disney's seal of approval. All 31, including the new Saratoga Springs Resort and Spa, are in WDW or Lake Buena Vista.

In addition to their proximity to the theme parks, there are other advantages to staying at a Disney property or one of the "official" hotels. The following amenities are included at all Disney resorts; **some** are offered by the "official" hotels, but be sure to ask when booking:

- Guests and their baggage get free transportation from Orlando International Airport via Disney transportation to their Disney resort using **Magical Express** (though originally slated to run only through 2006, Disney renewed this program through 2011). See p. 2 for more on this option.

- Unlimited **free transportation** on the **Walt Disney World Transportation System**'s buses, monorails, ferries, or water taxis to and from the four WDW parks, from 2 hours prior to opening until 2 hours after closing. Free transportation is also provided to and from Downtown Disney and Pleasure Island, Downtown Disney Marketplace, Typhoon Lagoon, Blizzard Beach, and the WDW resorts.

Three of them—the Polynesian, Grand Floridian, and Contemporary resorts—are located on the Disney monorail system. The transportation services offered can save money you might otherwise spend on a rental car, parking, and shuttles. It also means you're guaranteed admission to all of the parks, even during peak times when parking lots sometimes fill to capacity.

- Kids under 17 **stay free** in their parent's room, and reduced-price children's menus are available in most restaurants.
- Character breakfasts and/or dinners at select restaurants.
- The **Extra Magic Hour** (see the box "The Early Bird . . . ," below).
- TVs equipped with the Disney Channel, **nightly bedtime stories** (Channel 22, 7–10pm, audio only), and WDW information stations.
- A **Lobby Concierge** (replacing the old Guest Services desk) where you can buy tickets to all Disney parks and attractions without standing in long lines at the parks, and get information on dining, recreation, and everything Disney.
- Playing privileges, **preferred tee times,** and, in some cases, free transportation to one of the Disney golf courses. (See "Hitting the Links," in chapter 7.)
- WDW has some of the **best swimming pools** in Orlando and recently has built new ones or remodeled old ones as zero-entry or zero-grade pools, meaning there's a gradual slope into the water on at least one side rather than only a step down. These include pools at the Grand Floridian, Animal Kingdom, and Polynesian resorts and others.
- On-premises car rental is available at the Magic Kingdom Auto Plaza through Alamo (✆ **407/824-3470**). There are also car-rental desks at the Walt Disney World Swan and Dolphin.
- Extensive recreational options (not including the parks), including fishing, tennis, boating, surfing, parasailing, horseback riding, golf, and more. Though many activities may cost a few dollars extra, they're all right at your fingertips and offer experiences you won't find elsewhere.
- Disney's **refillable mug program** lets you buy—for around $12—a bottomless mug for soda, coffee, tea, and/or cocoa at its resorts. The offer is for the length of your stay, but it isn't transferable to the theme parks. You can use it only at the property at which it is bought, with two exceptions: Mugs are transferable between the Beach Club and Yacht Club resorts or among the three All-Star resorts. A similar program is available at Disney's two water parks, but again, they're not transferable beyond the park where they were purchased and aren't valid beyond the day they are purchased.
- Resort guests can charge most purchases (including meals) made anywhere inside WDW to their room. In most cases, purchases made inside the theme parks can be delivered to your room at no extra charge.

Tips **The Early Bird . . .**

Disney's **Extra Magic Hour** lets resort guests into the parks either an hour before other guests, or allows them to stay and play up to 3 hours after everyone else has to head home. Many of the more popular rides and attractions are operational (pick up the latest schedule for a complete listing), as are some shops and restaurants. For more information on this program, see p. 208.

But there are also **disadvantages** to staying with the Mouse:

• The complimentary Walt Disney World Transportation System can be *excruciatingly time-consuming*. There are times when you have to take a ferry to catch a bus to get on the monorail to reach your hotel. The system makes a circuit but may not necessarily take the most direct path for you. It can take up to an hour or more to get to a place that's right across the lagoon from you.

• Resort rates tend to be about **20% to 30% higher** than comparable hotels and motels away from the parks.

• Without a car or another means to get off the property, you'll either be resigned to paying Disney's higher prices or paying for shuttles to get to Orlando's other offerings.

• If you don't spend a little time away from the Disney parks, the all-Mickey, all-the-time atmosphere can get a little overwhelming, and you'll miss out on the real Florida and all the other great parks, restaurants, shops, and activities Orlando has to offer.

WALT DISNEY WORLD CENTRAL RESERVATIONS OFFICE (CRO) & WALT DISNEY TRAVEL COMPANY

To book a room or package at Disney's resorts, campgrounds, and "official" hotels through the **Walt Disney World Travel Company,** contact the **Central Reservations Office (CRO),** P.O. Box 10000, Lake Buena Vista, FL 32830-1000 (© **407/934-7639;** www.disneyworld.com).

CRO can recommend accommodations suited to your price range and specific needs, such as being near a particular park, facilities that offer supervised child-care centers, or a pool large enough to swim laps. But the staffers who answer the phones usually don't volunteer information about a better deal or a special *unless you ask.*

Be sure to inquire about Disney's numerous package plans, which can include meals, tickets, recreation, and other features. The right package can save you money and time; but having a comprehensive game plan first is helpful in computing the cost of your vacation in advance.

CRO can also give you information about various theme-park ticket options, the airlines, and car rentals. It can also make dinner-show reservations for you at the resort of your choice.

OTHER SOURCES FOR ORLANDO PACKAGES

In addition to the Disney sources above, there are several other travel companies that offer packages utilizing Disney resorts. In addition to **AAA** (© **800/732-1991;** www.aaa.com) and **American Express Vacations** (© **800/346-3607;** http://travel.americanexpress.com/travel/personal), almost all of the major airlines offer vacation packages to Orlando. See "Packages for the Independent Traveler" in chapter 2 for more options. Give each source a call, ask for brochures, and compare offerings to find the best package for you.

On a slightly smaller scale than Disney, **Universal Orlando** offers several travel packages that can include resort stays, VIP access to the parks, discounts to other Orlando attractions, and cruises. Airfare and car rentals are also available. You can book a package by calling © **800/711-0080** or 407/224-7000. On the Internet, visit **www.universalstudiosvacations.com. SeaWorld** also offers vacation packages that include stays at nearby resorts and park tickets. These can be booked by calling © **800/423-8368,** or visiting **www.seaworld.com.**

> ⌒ *Tips* **Special Treatment**
>
> **AAA** (© 800/732-1991; www.aaa.com) members can take advantage of special lodging programs at select WDW resorts and preferred parking at the theme parks if they purchase a AAA Disney vacation package or prepurchase their park tickets at participating AAA locations (these cannot be purchased at the parks!). A member's Hospitality Desk located right inside the Magic Kingdom's Town Square provides basic member services.

3 Places to Stay in Walt Disney World

The resorts in this section are either Disney-owned or "official" Disney hotels that offer many of the same perks. All are on the Disney Transportation System, which means those of you who don't want to venture too far will be able to do without a car.

If you do decide that Disney is your destination, come up with a short list of preferred places to stay, then call CRO (© **407/934-7639**) for up-to-the-minute rates. Web surfers can get information at **www.disneyworld.com**.

Those who come by auto will find large signs along all of the major roads on Disney property pointing the way to the various resorts. You'll find these hotels listed on the map, "Walt Disney World & Lake Buena Vista Accommodations," on p. 88.

Individual resorts don't have their own **golf courses,** but WDW has 99 holes situated along the northern end of the property (see "Hitting the Links" in chapter 7). The same goes for kennels; resort guests can board their pets overnight at the Transportation & Ticket Center on Seven Seas Drive, near Disney's Polynesian Resort.

Prices in the following listings reflect the range available at each resort when this guide was published. Rates vary depending on season and room location, but the numbers should help you determine which places fit your budget.

Note: Most hotels and resorts, Disney or otherwise, have cribs (or portable cribs) available (though limited in number) at no extra charge. Rollaways or cots are usually available as well; however, many resorts will charge around $10 per night to use them. Refrigerators (mini ones, anyway) are sometimes available, though some hotels may charge up to $10 per night for the privilege. All hotels also offer at least some non-smoking rooms.

VERY EXPENSIVE

Disney's Beach Club Resort ✶✶✶   This property re-creates the grand turn-of-the-20th-century Victorian seaside resorts of Cape Cod and has a more casual ambience than its sister, the Yacht Club (detailed later in this chapter), with which it shares restaurants, shops, and numerous recreational activities. Striped and floral wicker furnishings, seashells, and beach umbrellas adorn the hotel's casual interior. The Beach Club is close enough to Epcot to allow you to walk to the park, though most guests prefer to take the ferry (the parks are workout enough!). The shipwreck at Stormalong Bay (a huge free-form swimming pool and water park that sprawls over 3 acres) invites you to explore its decks, climb around, and slide into the water waiting below. It includes a stretch of sandy beach, sand-bottom pools, whirlpools, and water slides (including a toddler slide, so no one misses out). Room views range from the pool (more expensive) to the parking lot. Some rooms have balconies.

Walt Disney World & Lake Buena Vista Accommodations

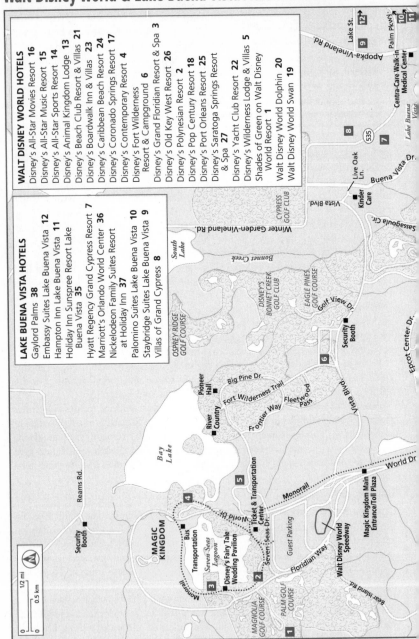

WALT DISNEY WORLD HOTELS

Disney's All-Star Movies Resort 16
Disney's All-Star Music Resort 15
Disney's All-Star Sports Resort 14
Disney's Animal Kingdom Lodge 13
Disney's Beach Club Resort & Villas 21
Disney's Boardwalk Inn & Villas 23
Disney's Caribbean Beach Resort 24
Disney's Coronado Springs Resort 17
Disney's Contemporary Resort 4
Disney's Fort Wilderness
   Resort & Campground 6
Disney's Grand Floridian Resort & Spa 3
Disney's Old Key West Resort 26
Disney's Polynesian Resort 2
Disney's Pop Century Resort 18
Disney's Port Orleans Resort 25
Disney's Saratoga Springs Resort
   & Spa 27
Disney's Yacht Club Resort 22
Disney's Wilderness Lodge & Villas 5
Shades of Green on Walt Disney
   World Resort 1
Walt Disney World Dolphin 20
Walt Disney World Swan 19

LAKE BUENA VISTA HOTELS

Gaylord Palms 38
Embassy Suites Lake Buena Vista 12
Hampton Inn Lake Buena Vista 11
Holiday Inn Sunspree Resort Lake
   Buena Vista 35
Hyatt Regency Grand Cypress Resort 7
Marriott's Orlando World Center 36
Nickelodeon Family Suites Resort
   at Holiday Inn 37
Palomino Suites Lake Buena Vista 10
Staybridge Suites Lake Buena Vista 9
Villas of Grand Cypress 8

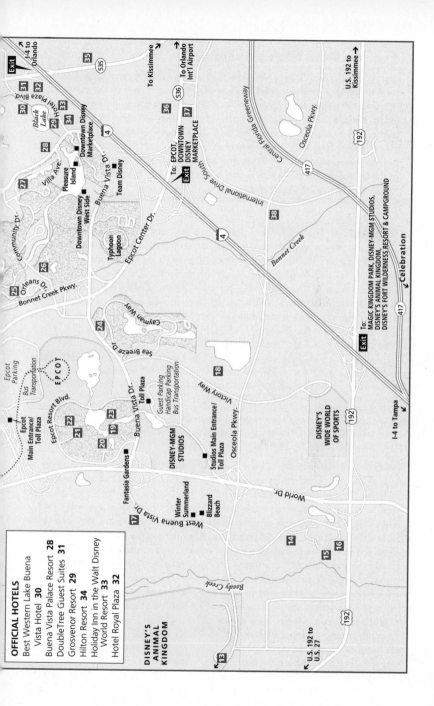

OFFICIAL HOTELS
Best Western Lake Buena
  Vista Hotel 30
Buena Vista Palace Resort 28
DoubleTree Guest Suites 31
Grosvenor Resort 29
Hilton Resort 34
Holiday Inn in the Walt Disney
  World Resort 33
Hotel Royal Plaza 32

(Tips) The Beach Club's Baby Sister

Disney's **Beach Club Villas** (© 407/934-7639 or 407/934-2175; www.disneyworld. com) make up a resort inspired by Cape May seaside homes of the early 20th century with clapboard exteriors and intricate white wood trim. The 280-room resort, opened in July 2002, is a member of the Disney Vacation Club that rents studios and 1- and 2-bedroom villas ($305–$475 studios, $410–$1,070 villas) to mainstream guests when their owners are not staying on the property. Amenities are shared with the Yacht Club and Beach Club resorts, with the exception of the Villa's quiet pool—which is only accessible to villa guests. It, too, is close to Epcot's International Gateway.

Note: Both the Beach Club and Yacht Club (see later in this chapter) offer the chance to charter a reproduction of a 1930s mahogany runabout to **cruise Crescent Lake** or see Epcot's IllumiNations fireworks display (from $179 plus tax for up to seven people for a 45-min. cruise to catch the fireworks). Daytime cruises ($80 for 30 min.) are available departing at 2:30pm and 5:30pm (© **407/824-2621**).

A kids' cruise, **Albatross Treasure,** for kids ages 4 to 10, sets sail to exotic ports of call on the high seas (Wed 9:30am and 11:30am) in search of pirate treasure. While on board, "the Legend of the Albatross" is read aloud and kids are treated to a PB&J lunch afterward. The cost is $28.17 per child (© **407/939-3463** to make reservations).

1800 Epcot Resorts Blvd. (off Buena Vista Dr.; P.O. Box 10000), Lake Buena Vista, FL 32830-0100. © **407/934-7639** or 407/934-8000. Fax 407/934-3850. www.disneyworld.com. 583 units. $305–$695 double; $525–$2,220 suite. Extra person $25. Children 17 and under stay free in parent's room. AE, DC, DISC, MC, V. Free self-parking; $7 valet. Pets $9 a night. **Amenities:** 2 restaurants; grill; 4 lounges; 3-acre pool and play area; 2 outdoor heated pools; kids' pool; 2 lighted tennis courts; health club; jogging trail; volleyball; croquet; Jacuzzi; watercraft rental; fishing; playground; supervised children's program; video arcade; WDW Transportation System; transportation to non-Disney theme parks for a fee; business center; salon; 24-hr. room service; babysitting; laundry service; valet. *In room:* A/C, TV, dataport, minibar, fridge and microwave (free, upon request), hair dryer, iron, safe.

Disney's BoardWalk Inn ✿✿✿   Disney's plush 1940s-style "seaside" resort is worth a visit even if you don't stay here. The grounds encompass 45 acres along Crescent Lake, and it's just a ferry ride across the lake from Epcot. It's a great place to recapture a little bit of yesteryear, whether that means relaxing in a wooden rocker overlooking the courtyard or strolling along the many shops, restaurants, and clubs that line the resort's quarter-mile boardwalk. After the sun goes down, the boardwalk springs to life with street performers, food vendors, and midway games, reminiscent of the hustle and bustle of the Atlantic City Boardwalk in its heyday. (*Note:* The activity on the boardwalk reaches well into the late evening hours, as does the noise, which carries to the rooms overlooking it.) Some of the Cape Cod–style rooms have balconies, and the corner units offer a bit more space. At night, the rooms overlooking the boardwalk, mostly those in the center, enjoy a view of Epcot's fireworks display. The more expensive rooms overlook the boardwalk or pool; the less expensive ones can't avoid a view of the parking lot but are sheltered from the boardwalk clamor. Hang on to your swimsuit if you hit the pool's famous—or infamous, depending on how you look at it—200-foot "keister coaster" water slide. See also the reviews for the **Flying Fish Café** (p. 151), **Spoodles** (p. 152), and **ESPN Club** (p. 154) restaurants.

2101 N. Epcot Resorts Blvd. (off Buena Vista Dr.; P.O. Box 10000), Lake Buena Vista, FL 32830-1000. ℂ **407/934-7639** or 407/939-5100. Fax 407/934-5150. www.disneyworld.com. 372 units, 520 villas. $305–$710 double; $575–$2,460 suites. Extra person $25. Children 17 and under stay free in parent's room. AE, DC, DISC, MC, V. Free self-parking; valet parking $7. Pets $9 per night. Take I-4 to the Hwy. 536/Epcot Center Dr. exit and follow the signs. **Amenities:** 4 restaurants; grill; 2 lounges; 3 clubs; 2 outdoor heated pools; kids' pool; 2 lighted tennis courts; health club; Jacuzzi; bike and sporting equipment rentals; playground; arcade; concierge; WDW Transportation System; transportation to non-Disney parks for a fee; business center; limited Wi-Fi access (fee); shopping arcade; 24-hr. room service; babysitting; guest laundry; concierge-level rooms. *In room:* A/C, TV, dataport, high-speed Internet (fee), fridge (free upon request), hair dryer, iron, safe.

Disney's BoardWalk Villas ✦✦✦
Located on the same site as the BoardWalk Inn, and sharing its amenities and ambience, the villas are a great option for those traveling in larger groups. Sold as timeshares, they're also rented to traditional tourists. Rooms range from standard-size studios (with separate sleeping and living quarters) and villas to 3-bedroom units with 2,100 square feet and beds for 12. Most have a balcony or patio and the same trimmings as the BoardWalk Inn. Studio rooms have kitchenettes while the larger suite-style villas have full kitchens. The service is impeccable, and the location near Epcot (plus Disney's MGM–Studios is just a hop, skip, and a jump behind it) is convenient as well. The spacious accommodations are great for families traveling together.

2101 N. Epcot Resorts Blvd. (off Buena Vista Dr.; P.O. Box 10000), Lake Buena Vista, FL 32830-1000. ℂ **407/934-7639** or 407/939-5100. Fax 407/934-5150. www.disneyworld.com. 520 units. $305–$2,020. Extra person $25. Children 17 and under stay free in parent's room. AE, DC, DISC, MC, V. Free self-parking; $7 valet. Pets $9 a night. **Amenities:** 4 restaurants; grill; 2 lounges; 3 clubs; 2 outdoor heated pools, kids' pool; 2 lighted tennis courts; health club; croquet; Jacuzzi; bike and sporting equipment rental; playground; supervised children's activity center; arcade; concierge; WDW Transportation System; transportation to non-Disney parks for a fee; business center; shopping arcade; 24-hr. room service; babysitting; laundry service; valet; concierge-level rooms; groceries. *In room:* A/C, TV, dataport, high-speed Internet access (fee), kitchenette, full kitchen with dishes (villas); fridge, coffeemaker, hair dryer, iron, safe, microwave, washer and dryer (villas).

Disney's Contemporary Resort ✦
If location is one of your priorities, it's hard to beat this Disney resort, which is right beside the Magic Kingdom, and one of only three resorts **on the monorail system** (the Grand Floridian and Polynesian are the others). The Contemporary offers great views of the Magic Kingdom and Seven Seas Lagoon from its west side and Bay Lake on its east. This 15-story concrete A-frame dates to WDW's infancy, and a complete renovation in 1999 was only the first phase of its restoration, a process that has once again resumed. The result will bring the resort in line with the others in the same class and category. Rooms will be completely redecorated to reflect an upscale Asian/Retro flair. It sounds complicated—it looks amazing! The decor will definitely appeal to adults (the flatscreen TVs are fabulous and the new color scheme is very appealing), and those with kids in tow will appreciate the rounded corners, kid-proof locks on the sliding doors (remember how high up you are here), and breakables placed high above a little one's reach. The pool is far less

---

⸜Tips Sink Space
Although Disney's resort rooms have notoriously cramped bathrooms, all but its inexpensive resorts sport double sinks, usually set in a small dressing area outside the bathroom. So while you may bang your shin on the shower, at least you won't have to wait in line to brush your teeth.

spectacular than most (it is, however, large and has a wading pool for toddlers with a small beach area off to the left). On the plus side, the rooms can fit up to five people instead of the usual four (though space will be tight). Kid-friendly facilities include a playground with a good-size sandbox and a pretty decent arcade. The best views are from upper floors, where the rooms are a tad quieter than those on the lower floors, which are exposed to noisy public areas and the monorail (which runs right through the hotel). Come here for dinner at **Chef Mickey's** (p. 175) or the **California Grill** (p. 150), but if you have very young kids you may be better off checking into accommodations elsewhere.

4600 N. World Dr. (P.O. Box 10000), Lake Buena Vista, FL 32830-1000. ✆ **407/939-6244** or 407/824-1000. Fax 407/824-3539. www.disneyworld.com. 1,008 units. $249–$725 double; $820–$1,220 suite; Concierge level $465–$2,530. Extra person $25. Children 17 and under stay free in parent's room. AE, DC, DISC, MC, V. Free self-parking; $7 valet. Pets $9 a night. **Amenities:** 3 restaurants; food court; 2 lounges; 2 outdoor heated pools, kids' pool; 6 lighted tennis courts; fitness center; Jacuzzi; watersports equipment; arcade; concierge; WDW Transportation System; transportation to non-Disney parks for a fee; business center; salon; 24-hr. room service; babysitting; laundry service; valet; concierge-level rooms. *In room:* A/C, TV, dataport, high-speed Internet access (fee), limited Wi-Fi access (fee), fridge (free upon request), hair dryer, iron, safe.

Disney's Grand Floridian Resort & Spa ★★★ *Moments*

From the moment you step into the opulent five-story domed lobby, you'll feel as if you've slipped back to an era that started with the late 19th century and lasted through the Roaring '20s, when a guy named Gatsby was at the top of his game. Expect tea to be served in the afternoon (4pm daily) while a piano runs the spectrum from lullabies to ragtime; then, as the evening arrives, a small, '40s-style band takes the helm upstairs. The Floridian has become the romantic choice for couples, especially honeymooners, who like luxuriating in the first-class spa and health club—the best in WDW. Families, however, will appreciate the extensive recreational facilities, including the large children's pool and play area, as well as the children's programs and character dining offered here. Virtually all of the inviting Victorian-style rooms overlook a garden, pool, courtyard, or the Seven Seas Lagoon; many have balconies, and the "dormer rooms" have vaulted ceilings (though they're smaller than standard rooms). It's one of three resorts located directly on the monorail system and near the Magic Kingdom.

Don't miss the reviews of its top-end restaurants, **Victoria & Albert's** (p. 148) and **Citricos** (p. 148), as well as some **special programs for young aspiring cooks** (p. 149).

4401 Floridian Way (P.O. Box 10000), Lake Buena Vista, FL 32830-1000. ✆ **407/934-7639** or 407/824-3000. Fax 407/824-3186. www.disneyworld.com. 900 units. $359–$890 double; $940–$2,600 suite. Extra person $25. Children 17 and under stay free in parent's room. AE, DC, DISC, MC, V. Self-parking free; valet parking $7. Pets $9 per night. Take I-4 to the Hwy. 536/Epcot Center Dr. exit and follow the signs. **Amenities:** 5 restaurants; grill; 3 lounges; character meals; heated outdoor pool; kids' pool; beach; 2 lighted tennis courts; health club; spa; watersports equipment; children's club; arcade; concierge; car-rental desk; WDW Transportation System; transportation to non-Disney parks for a fee; business center; limited Wi-Fi access (fee); shopping arcade; salon; 24-hr. room service; babysitting; guest laundry; concierge-level rooms; valet. *In room:* A/C, TV, dataport, high-speed Internet access (fee), minibar, fridge (free upon request), microwave (free upon request), hair dryer, iron, safe.

Disney's Old Key West Resort ★★★

Palms and pastels surround you with an understated theme (at least by Disney standards) at this beautiful resort, architecturally mirroring Key West at the turn of the 20th century. It's a good choice for those in search of a degree of separation from all the action. Located between Epcot and Downtown Disney West Side, it offers some of the quietest, homiest rooms on WDW property. Old Key West is affiliated with the Disney Vacation Club—a timeshare program—but many units are rented when not being used by owners. The 156-acre

---

(Moments   **A Piece of Yesterday, Today**

The *Grand 1*, the Grand Floridian's 44-foot yacht, is available for hire for groups of 2 to 13. It cruises Seven Seas Lagoon and Bay Lake, where in the evenings you can see the Magic Kingdom's Fantasy in the Sky fireworks or arrange a gourmet-dinner cruise. Voyages cost $400 per hour (dinner at an additional cost), including a captain and deck hand (**©** **407/824-2439** or 407/824-2682).

---

complex has tree-lined brick walkways edged by white picket fences. Two-bedroom villas have enough beds for eight; grand villas (2,202 sq. ft.) sleep 12. Villas have whirlpool tubs. All of the accommodations sport balconies or patios, and all have kitchens or kitchenettes.

1510 N. Cove Rd. (off Community Dr.; P.O. Box 10000), Lake Buena Vista, FL 32830-1000. **©** 407/934-7639 or 407/827-7700. Fax 407/827-7710. www.disneyworld.com. 761 units. $269–$389 studio; $360–$825 1- and 2-bedroom villas; $1,100–$1,545 grand villa. Children 17 and under stay free in parent's room. AE, DC, DISC, MC, V. Free self-parking. Pets $9 a night. **Amenities:** Restaurant; convenience store; 4 outdoor heated pools; kids' pool; 3 tennis courts (2 lighted); health club; basketball; volleyball; shuffleboard; Jacuzzi; sauna; watercraft rentals; bike rentals; playground; arcade game room; activity center with board games; WDW Transportation System; transportation to non-Disney parks for a fee; massage; babysitting; laundry service; groceries. *In room:* A/C, TV, dataport, high-speed Internet access (fee), kitchen or kitchenette, fridge, coffeemaker, hair dryer, microwave, washer and dryer (villas).

Disney's Polynesian Resort ☆☆ *(Kids*   One of only three resorts found **on the Disney monorail line**, the 25-acre Polynesian features extensive recreational areas, including a stretch of beach along a lagoon dotted with hammocks and palm trees, a volcano-themed swimming pool, and watercraft rentals. An on-site child-care facility makes it a good choice for those traveling with kids. Its landscaped and torch-lit walkways, along with its longhouse-style thatched-roof buildings, give the resort a South Pacific ambience. At press time the rooms were undergoing extensive renovations that include new space-conscious furnishings, a muted earth-toned color scheme, and upscale amenities such as flatscreen TVs and refrigerators. Rooms can accommodate up to five people. Many rooms have views of the grounds or Seven Seas Lagoon; some lagoon-view rooms offer great views of Cinderella Castle (at a higher price, of course), so request your desired view when making your reservation. See the review of the 'Ohana restaurant on p. 154 and its **Spirit of Aloha Dinner Show** on p. 321.

1600 Seven Seas Dr. (P.O. Box 10000), Lake Buena Vista, FL 32830-1000. **©** 407/939-6244 or 407/824-2000. Fax 407/824-3174. www.disneyworld.com. 853 units. $315–$600 double; $440–$780 concierge-level; $550–$2,640 suite. Extra person $25. Children 17 and under stay free in parent's room. AE, DC, DISC, MC, V. Self-parking free; valet parking $7. Take I-4 to the Hwy. 536/Epcot Center Dr. exit and follow the signs. Pets $9 per night. **Amenities:** Restaurant; cafe; 2 lounges; dinner show; character meals; 2 heated outdoor pools; kids' pool; watersports equipment; children's club; arcade; concierge; WDW Transportation System; transportation to non-Disney parks for a fee; shopping arcade; 24-hr. room service; babysitting; guest laundry; concierge-level rooms. *In room:* A/C, TV, dataport, high-speed Internet access (fee), fridge (free upon request), hair dryer, iron, safe.

Disney's Saratoga Springs Resort and Spa ☆   The first phase of the newest Disney Vacation Club resort opened in May 2004; construction is ongoing and the third phase is due to be completed in 2007. The resort transports guests back in time to the heyday of upstate New York's 19th-century resorts. It resembles the resort town of Saratoga Springs, and you'll find lavish gardens, Victorian architecture, and bubbling springs. The resort's main pool brings to mind its namesake's natural springs, with "healing" waters spilling over the rocky landscaping. The renowned spa offers an

> _**Tips**_ **Wired to the Rest of the World**
>
> By the end of 2006 all Disney resorts will be wired for high-speed Internet access. A fee of $9.95 per 24-hour period applies to use the service. Be sure to check if your resort has a pre-selected "start" time, often the mid-afternoon, or you may find yourself being charged twice in a single day, depending on when you sign up for the service. Select Disney resorts (mostly in the Very Expensive range) offer limited Wi-Fi access (in public areas only) for a 24-hour period at a rate of $9.95, or 60 minutes at $5.

array of services and treatments meant to invoke the healing powers of Saratoga's Springs themselves. Accommodations resemble those of the other Disney timeshare properties and range from studios that sleep four to grand villas that can sleep up to 12 people more than comfortably. Downtown Disney is a short ferry ride across the lake, but getting to the parks will require a bit more effort.

1960 Broadway St., Lake Buena Vista, FL 32830. (C) **407/827-1100** or 407/934-3400. Fax 407/827-1151. www.disney world.com. 828 units. $269–$389 studio; $360–$1,545 villa. Extra person no charge. Children 17 and under stay free in parent's room. AE, DC, DISC, MC, V. Self-parking free. **Amenities:** Restaurant; lounge; themed heated pool; kids' interactive pool area; golf; tennis; health club; spa; biking; boating; playground; arcade; free WDW transportation; limited room service; babysitting; guest laundry; barbecue areas; limited grocery delivery. *In room:* A/C, TV, dataport, high-speed Internet access (fee), VCR (villas), full kitchen (villas), kitchenette (studios), fridge, microwave, hair dryer, iron, safe, washer/dryer (villas).

Disney's Yacht Club Resort ⊛⊛   The Yacht Club has an atmosphere loaded with the posh elegance found in a turn-of-the-20th-century New England yacht club (as imagined by Disney). It is definitely more upscale than its sister resort, the Beach Club (see above), as the rooms, views, service, and atmosphere (nautically themed, of course) are a step or so better. Here you'll find fine leather furnishings, antique glass chandeliers, and brass accents adorning the lobby. It's geared more toward adults and families with older children, though young kids are certainly catered to (this is Disney, after all). The resort shares a 25-acre lake, a first-class swimming pool, and magnificent landscaping with the Beach Club, including a lighthouse to help you find your way back from the parks. Rooms have beds for up to five and most have balconies; views run from asphalt to Crescent Lake and the gardens; you would, however, have to be a contortionist to see the lake from some of the "water-view" rooms, so if this is a must, make sure that you request one with a direct view. Epcot is a 10- to 15-minute walk from the front door, but save your energy for the parks and use the Disney ferry.

1700 Epcot Resorts Blvd. (off Buena Vista Dr.; P.O. Box 10000), Lake Buena Vista, FL 32830-1000. (C) **407/934-7639** or 407/934-7000. Fax 407/924-3450. www.disneyworld.com. 630 units. $305–$545 double; $555–$2,440 suite; $435–$695 concierge-level. Extra person $25. Children 17 and under stay free in parent's room. AE, DC, DISC, MC, V. Self-parking free; valet parking $7. Take I-4 to the Hwy. 536/Epcot Center Dr. exit and follow the signs. Pets $9 per night. **Amenities:** 3 restaurants; grill; lounge; 2 heated outdoor pools; kids' pool; 2 lighted tennis courts; Jacuzzi; watersports equipment; children's club; arcade; concierge; WDW Transportation System; transportation to non-Disney parks for a fee; business center; limited Wi-Fi access (fee); shopping arcade; salon; 24-hr. room service; babysitting; guest laundry; concierge-level rooms. *In room:* A/C, TV, dataport, high-speed Internet (fee), minibar, fridge (free upon request), microwave (free upon request), coffeemaker, iron, safe.

Walt Disney World Dolphin ⊛   If Antonio Gaudí and Dr. Seuss had teamed up on an architectural design, they might have created something like this Starwood resort and its sister, the Walt Disney World Swan (see below). This hotel centers on a

27-story pyramid with two 11-story wings crowned by 56-foot twin dolphin sculptures. Because it isn't as theme-intensive as the other Disney resorts, it's popular with business travelers and those who prefer their accommodations a little less sugary. Rooms were recently renovated and now feature a more contemporary decor and additional amenities; all offer views of the grounds and other parts of Mickey's world. The resort shares a grotto pool with waterfalls, water slide, and whirlpools, as well as a Body by Jake health club (at an extra fee) with the Swan. The Mandara Spa opened a branch here in late 2005. Camp Dolphin is a supervised children's program for kids ages 4 to 12, offering a variety of activities to keep the little ones busy while mom and dad enjoy some time alone. Epcot is the nearest park, just a short water-taxi ride away, and the BoardWalk and Beach and Yacht Club resorts are within walking distance, greatly expanding the dining and entertainment options within reach of your own two feet; however, with the addition of **Todd English's bluezoo** (p. 152), you may not need to go too far for a really good meal.

1500 Epcot Resorts Blvd. (off Buena Vista Dr.; P.O. Box 22653), Lake Buena Vista, FL 32830-2653. © **800/227-1500** or 407/934-4000. Fax 407/934-4884. www.swandolphin.com. 1,509 units. $339–$499 double; $675–$4,300 suite. Extra person $25. Children 17 and under stay free in parent's room. AE, DC, DISC, MC, V. Self-parking $8; valet parking $14. Take I-4 to the Hwy. 536/Epcot Center Dr. exit and follow the signs. Pets $9 per night. **Amenities:** 4 restaurants; grill; 2 lounges; character meals; 4 heated outdoor pools; 4 lighted tennis courts; health club; spa; watersports equipment; children's club; 2 game rooms; concierge; car-rental desk; WDW Transportation System; transportation to non-Disney parks for a fee; business center; limited Wi-Fi access (fee); shopping arcade; salon; 24-hr. room service; massage; babysitting; guest laundry; concierge-level rooms. *In room:* A/C, TV, dataport, high-speed Internet access (fee), minibar, fridge, hair dryer, iron, safe, Nintendo.

Walt Disney World Swan ⚓   Not to be outdone by the huge dolphins at its sister property, this high-rise Starwood resort is topped with dual 45-foot swan statues and seashell fountains. It offers a good location as it is close to Epcot, Disney's MGM–Studios, Fantasia Gardens, and the nightlife of the BoardWalk. While the theme doesn't scream Mickey Mouse, the decor and atmosphere are colorful and inviting. It shares a beach, health club, children's program, a number of restaurants, and other trimmings with the Dolphin (see above). The best room views are from the 11th and 12th floors' Royal Beach Club, the hotel's concierge level; the beach next to the pool offers a great view of Epcot's IllumiNations fireworks. Guest rooms were last upgraded in 2003 (they now sport Westin's famous "Heavenly Beds") and are just a tad smaller than those at the Dolphin.

1200 Epcot Resorts Blvd. (off Buena Vista Dr.; P.O. Box 22653), Lake Buena Vista, FL 32830-2653. © **800/248-7926** or 407/934-3000. Fax 407/934-4499. www.swandolphin.com. 756 units. $339–$499 double; $675–$4,300 suite. Extra person $25. Children 17 and under stay free in parent's room. AE, DC, DISC, MC, V. Self-parking $8; valet parking $14. Take I-4 to the Hwy. 536/Epcot Center Dr. exit and follow the signs. Pets $9 per night. **Amenities:** 4 restaurants; grill; 2 lounges; character meals; 4 heated outdoor pools; 4 lighted tennis courts; health club; spa; watersports equipment; children's club; 2 game rooms; concierge; car-rental desk; WDW Transportation System; transportation to

---

Tips When a WDW Property Is Not a WDW Property

As mentioned earlier, there are nine "official" Disney hotels that aren't owned by Disney itself. That's true. But there are a couple of asterisks. The Walt Disney World Swan and the Walt Disney World Dolphin have the Walt Disney name and are located right on the WDW resort property, but they're not Disney-owned resorts, so they are considered "official" resorts.

non-Disney parks for a fee; business center; limited Wi-Fi access (fee); shopping arcade; salon; 24-hr. room service; massage; babysitting; guest laundry; valet; concierge-level rooms. *In room:* A/C, TV, dataport, high-speed Internet access (fee), minibar, fridge, hair dryer, iron, safe, Nintendo.

EXPENSIVE

Disney's Animal Kingdom Lodge ♕♕♕   The feel of an African game-reserve lodge immediately surrounds you upon entering the grand stories-high lobby, which features a thatched roof and ornate shield chandeliers. The resort's *kraal* design (a semi-circular layout) ensures most rooms overlook the 30-acre savanna, allowing guests an occasional view of the birds, giraffes, and array of other African animals that call the savanna home (rooms without the savanna view will save a few extra dollars; you can get the scenery for free through large picture windows in the lobby and from a nature trail set behind the pool area). Families will appreciate the array of unique activities including storytelling by the fire, singalongs, and more. Those in the mood for romance will appreciate the more remote and relaxed setting. Typical rooms are slightly smaller than those at Disney's other "Deluxe" resorts, but the distinctive theme and spectacular surroundings are unparalleled, making a stay here well worth the slightly tighter squeeze. "Mosquito netting" curtains, balconies, and other neat detailing in the decor continue the theme. The 9,000-square-foot pool has a water slide, a wading area for young children, and a good view of the savanna. The lodge is adjacent to Animal Kingdom, but most everything else on WDW property is quite a distance away. Families will appreciate the animals and array of activities for kids, not to mention the fabulous breakfast and dinner buffet at **Boma** (p. 150), while the more relaxed and sedate nature of the resort makes it a good spot for couples as well.

2901 Osceola Pkwy., Bay Lake, FL 32830. ℂ **407/934-7639** or 407/938-3000. Fax 407/939-4799. www.disneyworld. com. 1,293 units. $205–$525 double; $435–$625 concierge level; $655–$2,585 suite. Extra person $25. Children 17 and under stay free in parent's room. AE, DC, DISC, MC, V. Self-parking free; valet parking $7. Take I-4 to the Hwy. 536/Epcot Center Dr. exit and follow the signs. Pets $9 per night. **Amenities:** 2 restaurants; lounge; heated outdoor pool; kids' pool; health club; children's center; arcade; concierge; WDW Transportation System; transportation to non-Disney parks for a fee; shopping arcade; limited room service; babysitting; guest laundry; concierge-level rooms. *In room:* A/C, TV, dataport, fridge (free upon request), hair dryer, iron, safe.

Disney's Wilderness Lodge ♕♕♕   The geyser out back, the mammoth stone hearth in the lobby, and bunk beds for the kids are just a few reasons this resort is a favorite of families, though couples will find the surroundings to their liking as well. In keeping with the spirit of the Great American Northwest, the lodge has the feel of a rustic national park lodge, as it is patterned after one in Yellowstone National Park. Surrounded by 56 acres of oaks and pines, it offers a woodsy and remote setting. That geyser mentioned above "spouts off" periodically throughout the day just to add to the authenticity, and the nightly electric water pageants can be viewed from the shores of Bay Lake. The lodge also has an immense swimming area, fed by a thundering waterfall whose water flows in from the "hot springs" in the lobby. The nearest park is the Magic Kingdom, but because the resort is in a remote area, it can take some time to get there. The main drawback is the difficulty in accessing other areas via the WDW Transportation System. See the review of the **Artist Point** restaurant on p. 149. *Note:* The lodge offers a free tour touting its architecture, Wednesday through Saturday at 9am (kids will likely be bored), and each day a select family gets to traipse up to the roof to raise the resort's flag (if you're interested, ask at the front desk upon check-in).

The 181 units at the **Villas at Disney's Wilderness Lodge** were added in November 2000. This is another Disney Vacation Club timeshare property that rents vacant

> (*Tips* **A Night Out**
>
> Several of the higher-priced Disney resorts—including Animal Kingdom Lodge, Beach Club, Grand Floridian Resort & Spa, and Wilderness Lodge, as well as the Polynesian Resort—have supervised kid care, usually from 4 or 4:30pm to midnight daily ($10 per child 4–12, per hour, dinner and activities included; © **407/ 939-3463**). Disney also offers in-room sitters through **Kid's Night Out** (© **407/ 827-5444**). The Walt Disney World Dolphin, an "official" resort, also offers a supervised child-care program.

rooms. It offers a more upscale mountain retreat experience, and more room than accommodations at the Wilderness Lodge, though the properties share a grand lobby, amenities, and activities. The one- and two-bedroom villas have 727 and 1,080 square feet, respectively.

901 W. Timberline Dr. (on the southwest shore of Bay Lake just east of the Magic Kingdom; P.O. Box 10000), Lake Buena Vista, FL 32830-1000. © **407/934-7639** or 407/938-4300. Fax 407/824-3232. www.disneyworld.com. 909 units. $205–$575 lodge; $370–$500 concierge-level; $380–$1,250 suite; $295–$1,040 villa. Extra person $25. Children 17 and under stay free in parent's room. AE, DC, DISC, MC, V. Free self-parking; valet parking $7. Take I-4 to the Hwy. 536/Epcot Center Dr. exit and follow the signs. Pets $9 per night. **Amenities:** 3 restaurants; 2 lounges; heated outdoor pool; kids' pool; 2 Jacuzzis; watersports equipment; children's club; children's and family activities; arcade; WDW Transportation System; transportation to non-Disney parks for a fee; limited room service; babysitting; guest laundry; laundry service; concierge-level rooms. *In room:* A/C, TV, dataport, high-speed Internet access (fee), fridge (villas, free upon request at the lodge), microwave (villas), hair dryer, iron, safe.

MODERATE

Disney's Caribbean Beach Resort ⭐⭐ (Value) Thanks to its moderate pricing scheme and recreational activities, the Caribbean Beach is a great choice for families. The resort's rooms are spread across five villages (all Disney moderate resorts share a similar general layout) of pastel-colored buildings, each named for the islands of Aruba, Barbados, Jamaica, Martinique, and Trinidad (north and south). The lush tropical greenery adds a touch of island atmosphere. Parrot Cay, the resort's main pool area and playground, is themed to an old Spanish-style fort, complete with water cannons, water slides, and waterfalls. The closest park is Disney MGM–Studios, though it can take up to 45 minutes to get there using Disney transportation—it's best to rent a car if you stay here.

900 Cayman Way (off Buena Vista Dr.; P.O. Box 10000), Lake Buena Vista, FL 32830-1000. © **407/934-7639** or 407/934-3400. Fax 407/934-3288. www.disneyworld.com. 2,112 units. $139–$215 double. Extra person $15. Children 17 and under stay free in parent's room. AE, DC, DISC, MC, V. Free self-parking. Pets $9 a night. **Amenities:** Restaurant; food court; lounge; large outdoor heated pool; 6 smaller pools in the villages; kids' pool; beach; jogging trail; volleyball; Jacuzzi; watercraft rentals; multiple playgrounds; arcade; WDW Transportation System; transportation to non-Disney parks for a fee; limited room service; babysitting; laundry service. *In room:* A/C, TV, dataport, high-speed Internet access (fee), fridge (free upon request), hair dryer, iron, safe.

Disney's Coronado Springs Resort ⭐ An American Southwestern theme carries through four- and five-story grand hacienda–style buildings in shades of pink and desert-sand stucco, with terra-cotta tile roofs and shaded courtyards. The pool area, inspired by the Mayan ruins of Mexico, sports a tremendous Mayan temple with cascading water and a twisting water slide. (Watch out for the spitting jaguar—he will likely surprise you as you pass by!) The rooms are identical in layout to those in the Caribbean Beach Resort, including the small bathrooms. Those located nearest the

central public area, pool, and lobby tend to be a bit noisier. The nearest park is Animal Kingdom, but the Coronado is at the southwest corner of WDW and a good distance from most other areas in the park.

1000 Buena Vista Dr. (near All-Star resorts and Blizzard Beach), Lake Buena Vista, FL 32830. ✆ 407/934-7639 or 407/939-1000. Fax 407/939-1003. www.disneyworld.com. 1,921 units. $139–$215 double; $300–$1,170 suite. Extra person $15. Children 17 and under stay free in parent's room. AE, DC, DISC, MC, V. Free self-parking. Pets $9 a night. **Amenities:** Restaurant; grill/food court; 2 lounges; 4 outdoor heated pools; kids' pool; health club; volleyball; Jacuzzi; sauna; watercraft rentals; bike rentals; playground; 2 arcades; WDW Transportation System; transportation to non-Disney parks for a fee; business center; salon; limited room service; massage; babysitting; laundry service. *In room:* A/C, TV, dataport, high-speed Internet access (fee), limited Wi-Fi access (fee), fridge, hair dryer, iron, safe.

Disney's Port Orleans Resort ★★ *Value*
Port Orleans has the best location, landscaping, and, perhaps, the coziest atmosphere of the resorts in this class. This southern-style property is really a combination of two distinct resorts; the French Quarter and Riverside. The French Quarter offers magnolia trees, wrought-iron railings, cobblestone streets, and an idealistic vision of New Orleans's famous French Quarter. Riverside transports you back to Louisiana's Mississippi River towns, its rooms housed in buildings resembling grand plantation homes and the "rustic" wooden shacks of the bayou. Overall, this resort offers some romantic spots and is relatively quiet, making it popular with couples. The pools, playgrounds, and array of activities make it a favorite for families as well. The recently refurbished Doubloon Lagoon pool in the French Quarter is a family favorite, with a water slide that curves out of a Sea Serpent's mouth before entering the pool. The rooms and bathrooms (equivalent to all rooms at Disney's moderate resorts) are somewhat of a tight fit for four, though the Alligator Bayou rooms have a trundle bed that allows for an extra child, and the vanity areas now have privacy curtains. Port Orleans is just east of Epcot and Disney–MGM Studios. *Note:* All 1,080 rooms in the French Quarter side reopened in March 2004 after closing for a top-to-bottom refurbishment. The 2,048 rooms in Riverside were renovated in 2005.

2201 Orleans Dr. (off Bonnet Creek Pkwy.; P.O. Box 10000), Lake Buena Vista, FL 32830-1000. ✆ 407/934-7639 or 407/934-5000. Fax 407/934-5353. www.disneyworld.com. 3,056 units. $139–$215 double. Extra person $15. Children 17 and under stay free in parent's room. AE, DC, DISC, MC, V. Free parking. Take I-4 to the Hwy. 536/Epcot Center Dr. exit and follow the signs. Pets $9 per night. **Amenities:** 2 restaurants; grill/food court; 2 lounges; 6 heated outdoor pools; 2 kids' pools; Jacuzzi; watersports equipment rentals; playground; 2 arcades; WDW Transportation System; transportation to non-Disney parks for a fee; limited room service; babysitting; guest laundry. *In room:* A/C, TV, dataport, high-speed Internet access (Riverside, fee), fridge (free upon request), hair dryer, iron, safe, trundle bed (fee, upon request at the French Quarter).

Shades of Green on Walt Disney World Resort ★ *Value*
Shades of Green, nestled among three of Disney's golf courses near the Magic Kingdom, is open only to folks in the military and their spouses, military retirees and widows, 100% disabled veterans, and Medal of Honor recipients. If you qualify, don't think of staying anywhere else—it's

---

Tips Value in the Eyes of the Beholder

Disney's All-Star resorts charge a "preferred room" rate, but don't expect much for the top rate of $137. Guests who book it are paying for location: Preferred rooms are closer to the pools, food court, and/or transportation. If you've got a rental car or don't mind walking, don't bother paying extra; some of the quietest rooms at the All-Stars are the standard ones.

> **_Tips_ Getting Away**
>
> If you want to enjoy the amenities and service of a Disney resort but can't do without some beach time, the Disney Vacation Club offers visitors the option of renting a room just 2 hours south of WDW at its **Vero Beach Resort** (📞 **407/ 939-7775;** www.dvcresorts.com), directly on the Atlantic Ocean, with sand, surf, and all the Disney trimmings included. Studios, standard rooms, one- and two-bedroom villas, and three-bedroom cottages are all available ranging about $165 to $1,105 per night. You will need to arrange for your own transportation.

the best bargain on WDW soil. And it's even better now thanks to a $92-million renovation that was completed in 2004. The refit nearly doubled the room capacity of the resort and added fully ADA-compliant rooms with wide doorways and roll-in showers. In addition to the new rooms and suites (housing up to eight), existing rooms were completely overhauled. All the large rooms offer TVs with wireless keyboards (access to the Internet is offered for a fee), balconies or patios, and pool or golf-course views. Transportation—though slow—is available to all of the Disney parks and attractions.

1950 W. Magnolia Dr. (across from the Polynesian Resort). 📞 888/593-2242 or 407/824-3400. Fax 407/824-3665. www.shadesofgreen.org. 587 units. $76–$116 double (based on military rank), 6- to 8-person suites $225–$250 (regardless of rank). Extra person $15. Children 17 and under stay free in parent's room. Rollaway beds not available, cribs $5/night. AE, DC, DISC, MC, V. Take I-4 east to Exit 67, Hwy. 536/Epcot Center Dr. Follow signs to WDW, then to the resort. Pets $9 a night. **Amenities:** 2 restaurants (American, Italian); 2 lounges; 2 heated outdoor pools; kids' pool; 2 lighted tennis courts; arcade; playground; activities desk; WDW Transportation System; transportation to non-Disney parks for a fee; babysitting; guest laundry. *In room:* A/C, TV, fridge ($5 per day), coffeemaker, hair dryer, iron, safe ($1 per day).

INEXPENSIVE

Disney's All-Star Movies Resort   Most kids love the larger-than-life themes at the three All-Star resorts; however, it can be Disney overload for many adults. Movies such as *Toy Story, 101 Dalmatians,* and *Fantasia* live on in a very big (and we mean BIG) way at this family-friendly resort. Gigantic larger-than-life characters such as Buzz Lightyear, Pongo, and even Mickey himself mark this resort's buildings. They add the only Disney flair to what is essentially a no-frills, budget motel with basic, tiny (only 260 sq. ft.) rooms. Think old-school roadside motels, when all you expected was a clean bed and a bathroom (the ones here are positively Lilliputian). The soundproofing leaves something to be desired, especially with the number of children staying here. Like its two siblings (listed below), the All-Star Movies Resort is pretty isolated in WDW's southwest corner. If, like the White Rabbit, you're often "late for a very important date," renting a car is a far better choice than the Disney Transportation System.

1991 W. Buena Vista Dr., Lake Buena Vista, FL 32830-1000. 📞 407/934-7639 or 407/939-7000. Fax 407/939-7111. www.disneyworld.com. 1,900 units. $79–$137 double. Extra person $10. Children 17 and under stay free in parent's room. AE, DC, DISC, MC, V. Free self-parking. Pets $9 a night. **Amenities:** Food court; lounge; 2 outdoor heated pools; kids' pool; playground; arcade; WDW Transportation System; transportation to non-Disney parks for a fee; limited room service; babysitting; laundry services. *In room:* A/C, TV, dataport, fridge ($10 a night), safe.

Disney's All-Star Music Resort   Giant trombones and musical themes from jazz to calypso are the only things differentiating this from the other All-Star resorts (they're all clones of each other—including the microscopic bathrooms—except for the different themes). While the extra frills at the other Disney resorts won't be found

---

Fun Fact **Sizing Things Up**

Disney's Pop Century Resort sports a gigantic Big Wheel in its 1970s courtyard. If an actual child were to ride it, proportionally, he or she would have to weigh approximately 800 pounds.

---

at the All-Stars, the rooms do have a significant perk: They're the least expensive (by a large margin) of all the Disney resorts. Most people, however don't come to WDW to lounge in their rooms, so if you're only going to be here to sleep, the cramped quarters may not be so bad. The closest parks are the Blizzard Beach and Animal Kingdom, which you can reach (not necessarily in an expedient manner) via the Disney Transportation System.

Tip: Just as this book hits the shelves, Disney will open up new 550-square-foot family suites at this resort. Suites will sleep up to 6 and feature two bathrooms, a kitchenette, and a separate bedroom and living area. Prices for the suites are set to run from $169 to $259, depending on the time of year. If the suites prove popular, expect them to debut at other Disney value properties in the near future.

1801 W. Buena Vista Dr. (at World Dr. and Osceola Pkwy.; P.O. Box 10000), Lake Buena Vista, FL 32830-1000. © 407/ 934-7639 or 407/939-6000. Fax 407/939-7222. www.disneyworld.com. 1,920 units. $79–$137 double. Extra person $10. Children 17 and under stay free in parent's room. AE, DC, DISC, MC, V. Free self-parking. Pets $9 a night. **Amenities:** Food court; lounge; 2 outdoor heated pools; kids' pool; playground; arcade; WDW Transportation System; transportation to non-Disney parks for a fee; limited room service; babysitting; laundry service. *In room:* A/C, TV, dataport, fridge ($10 a night), safe.

Disney's All-Star Sports Resort   It's a replay of the other All-Star resorts, including the tight quarters (if you aren't a team player, the togetherness may cause frayed tempers after a while). The difference here is the theme, with buildings designed around football, baseball, basketball, tennis, and surfing themes. The turquoise surf buildings have huge waves along the roofs with colorful surfboards mounted on exterior walls and pink fish swimming along balcony railings. Again, if your threshold for visual overload is low, you may want to choose a different resort. As mentioned above, the rates and themes draw mostly families with little kids and the noise level can get quite high, so if you're looking for a quiet vacation or romantic getaway, these resorts are out of bounds.

1701 W. Buena Vista Dr. (at World Dr. and Osceola Pkwy.; P.O. Box 10000), Lake Buena Vista, FL 32830-1000. © 407/ 934-7639 or 407/939-5000. Fax 407/939-7333. www.disneyworld.com. 1,920 units. $79–$137 double. Extra person $10. Children 17 and under stay free in parent's room. AE, DC, DISC, MC, V. Free parking. Pets $9 a night. **Amenities:** Food court; lounge; 2 outdoor heated pools; kids' pool; playground; arcade; WDW Transportation System; transportation to non-Disney parks for a fee; limited room service; babysitting; laundry service. *In room:* A/C, TV, dataport, fridge ($10 a night), safe.

Disney's Pop Century Resort *Value*   After numerous delays, the first phase of Disney's latest inexpensive resort debuted in December 2003. Gigantic memorabilia representing the hottest fads of decades past—from Duncan Yo-Yos and the Rubik's Cube to flower power and 8-tracks—mark the exteriors of the Pop Century's buildings. Another clone of the All-Star school (though a slight step up because the rooms are newer and the furniture a tad nicer), you won't get a lot of frills, but the price is right for families on a budget. A family of four, could, with a bit of effort, squeeze into the small, basic rooms. The resort is divided into decades, starting with the Legendary

Years of the 1900s to 1940s (alas, there is no projected date for completion of this phase), and the Classic Years of the 1950s to 1990s (the only section currently operating). The resort is closest to the Wide World of Sports Complex but a bit of a ride (yes, you should definitely rent a car) from everything else.

1050 Century Drive Dr. (off the Osceola Pkwy; P.O. Box 10000), Lake Buena Vista, FL 32830-1000. ✆ **407/938-4000** or 407/939-6000. Fax 407/938-4040. www.disneyworld.com. 2,880 units. $79–$137 double. Extra person $10. Children 17 and under stay free in parent's room. AE, DC, DISC, MC, V. Free parking. Pets $9 a night. **Amenities:** Food court; lounge; 2 heated outdoor pools; kids' pool; arcade; WDW Transportation System; transportation to non-Disney parks for a fee; limited room service; babysitting; laundry service. *In room:* A/C, TV, dataport, fridge ($10 a night), safe.

A DISNEY CAMPGROUND
Disney's Fort Wilderness Resort & Campground 🌲   Pines, cypress trees, lakes, and streams surround this woodsy 780-acre resort. The only disadvantage of staying here is the distance from Epcot, Disney–MGM Studios, and Animal Kingdom (it is close to Magic Kingdom). But if you're a true outdoors type, you may appreciate the feeling of being more sheltered from some of the Mickey madness. There are 784 campsites for RVs, pull-behind campers, and tents (110/220-volt outlets, grills, and comfort areas with showers and restrooms).

Some sites are open to pets (the ones with full hook-ups)—at an additional cost of $3 per site, not per pet, which is less expensive than using the WDW resort kennel, where you pay $9 per pet. The 408 wilderness cabins (actually trailers made to look like cabins) offer 504 square feet, enough for six people once you pull down the Murphy beds, and they also feature kitchens and daily housekeeping service. Cabins also feature an outside deck with grill. Roughing it Disney style isn't so rough with all the comforts of home. Nearby Pioneer Hall is home to the popular **Hoop-Dee-Doo Musical Revue,** which I review on p. 321. In addition, there are plenty of outdoor recreational activities, including horseback riding, fishing, swimming, a petting farm, and playgrounds. The nightly campfire and marshmallow roast, followed by a Disney movie shown right in the great outdoors, is a big hit with families.

3520 N. Fort Wilderness Trail (P.O. Box 10000), Lake Buena Vista, FL 32830-1000. ✆ **407/934-7639** or 407/824-2900. Fax 407/824-3508. www.disneyworld.com. 784 campsites, 408 wilderness cabins. $39–$92 campsite double; $239–$349 wilderness cabin double. Extra person $2 campsites, $5 cabins. Children 17 and under stay free in parent's room. AE, DC, DISC, MC, V. Free self-parking. **Amenities:** 2 restaurants; grill; lounge; 2 outdoor heated pools; kids' pool; 2 lighted tennis courts; watercraft rentals; outdoor activities (fishing; horseback, pony, and carriage and hay rides; campfire programs); 2 game rooms; WDW Transportation System; transportation to non-Disney parks for a fee; babysitting; laundry services. *In room (cabins only):* A/C, TV/VCR, dataport, kitchen, fridge, coffeemaker, outdoor grill, hair dryer.

Tips Credit or Debit?

If you use your debit card (instead of a credit card) as collateral against any purchases you may make during your stay, your card may be charged anywhere from $50 to $250 (or more) *per day,* whether you actually charge anything to your room or not. This policy can seriously deplete your checking account, leaving you with far less funds than you realize or planned on—and you won't see a credit back to your account until *up to 10 days after* you have checked out of your resort. Though WDW does not (at least for now) follow this practice and no charges are applied to your account until you check out, other resorts in the area do. Be sure to ask exactly what your hotel's policy is regarding debit and credit charges the minute you check in (or before you arrive).

4 "Official" Hotels in Lake Buena Vista

These properties, designated "official" Walt Disney World hotels, are located on and around Hotel Plaza Boulevard, which puts them at the northeast corner of WDW. They're close to Downtown Disney Marketplace, Downtown Disney West Side, and Pleasure Island. The boulevard has been landscaped with enough greenery to make it a contestant for Main Street, U.S.A.

Guests at these hotels enjoy some WDW privileges (see "The Perks of Staying with Mickey," earlier in this chapter), including free bus service to the parks, but **be sure to ask when booking** which privileges you'll get because they do vary from hotel to hotel. Their locations put you close to the parks, and even closer to the action of Downtown Disney, but, unlike the resorts on WDW property, which occupy their own completely separate areas, the hotels here are set along the tree-lined boulevard. Traffic can be a frustration, as the boulevard is a main access route to Downtown Disney from the outside world. Also note that the Walt Disney World Dolphin and Walt Disney World Swan (listed in the previous section) should be considered the eighth and ninth of the "official" hotels because they're not Disney-owned. The difference is they're located directly on the WDW property.

Another perk of the "official" hotels is that they generally offer a less intense Mickey ambience, although some do offer character breakfasts a few days each week (ask the person answering the reservation line for details and schedules). Decide for yourself if that's a plus or a minus.

You can make reservations for all of the below-listed properties through the **CRO** (© **407/934-7639**) or through the direct hotel numbers included in the listings. To ensure you get the best rates, however, call the hotel or its parent chain directly to see if there are special rates or packages available.

You'll find all of these hotels located on the map "Walt Disney World & Lake Buena Vista Accommodations," earlier in this chapter.

EXPENSIVE

Buena Vista Palace Resort ★★   Previously known as the Wyndham Palace Resort & Spa, this hotel is still the most upscale of the Hotel Plaza Boulevard–area properties and is popular with leisure travelers, though business people still make up 75% of its guests. For that reason, some of the best rates are offered in July and August, contrary to the mainstream tourist resorts. Many of the upscale business-standard rooms have balconies or patios; ask for one above the fifth floor with a "recreation view." That's the side facing the pools on Recreation Island, Downtown Disney, and, in the distance, Disney–MGM Studios' Tower of Terror. The "Epcot view" offers views of the IllumiNations fireworks but little else. Allergy and asthma sufferers can take advantage of the Evergreen rooms, which offer individual air filtration systems and nonallergenic amenities. The best place to catch those fireworks is in the lounge on the 27th floor. The resort is known for its spacious fitness center and full-service European-style spa (massage, wraps, steam room, saunas, salon, fitness center, and more), which are open to the public. The recreational facilities are extensive and one of the resort's pools is situated partially indoors, providing cover from sun and rain.

1900 Buena Vista Dr. (just north of Hotel Plaza Blvd.; P.O. Box 22206), Lake Buena Vista, FL 32830. © **866/397-6516** or 407/827-3228. Fax 407/827-6034. www.buenavistapalace.com or www.downtowndisneyhotels.com. 1,012 units. $169–$219 double; $249–$389 suite. $12 daily resort fee. Extra person $10. Children 17 and under stay free in parent's room. AE, DC, DISC, MC, V. Self-parking free; valet parking $15. From I-4, take the Hwy. 535/Apopka–Vineland

> **Tips Added Extras**
>
> Several of the properties in this chapter add resort fees to their daily room rates. That's part of an unfortunate but growing hotel trend of charging for services that used to be included in the rates, such as use of the pool, admission to the health club, or in-room coffee or phones. If it's a concern, ask if your hotel charges such a fee when booking so you don't get blindsided at checkout.

Rd. exit north to Hotel Plaza Blvd. and go left. At 1st stoplight, turn right onto Buena Vista Dr. It's the 1st hotel on the right. **Amenities:** 3 restaurants; grill; 4 lounges; 3 heated outdoor pools; kids' pool; tennis; spa; Jacuzzi; sauna; arcade; playground; concierge; car-rental desk; complimentary bus service to WDW parks; transportation to non-Disney parks for a fee; business center; minimarket; salon; 24-hr. room service; massage; babysitting; guest laundry; concierge-level rooms; valet. *In room:* A/C, TV w/pay movies, dataport, high-speed and limited wireless Internet access (fee), minibar, fridge (suites), coffeemaker, hair dryer, iron, safe, PlayStation.

MODERATE

Best Western Lake Buena Vista Hotel ★ *Value*   This 12-acre lakefront hotel is reasonably modern, with nicer rooms and public areas than you might find in others within the chain. Rooms are located in an 18-story tower, and all have balconies. The views improve from the 8th floor and up, and those on the west side have a better chance of seeing something Disney. The hotel's 18th-floor lounge, Toppers, offers an excellent view of the Magic Kingdom's fireworks. Accommodations in this category are usually a step above the "moderates" inside WDW, and this one is not an exception. You can reserve an oversize room (about 20% larger) or WDW fireworks-view room for $15 more a night. You can also get the same rooms with full American breakfast for up to four people for $20 more per night. *Note:* It definitely pays to surf the corporate website at **www.bestwestern.com** if you plan to stay here. It sometimes offers great deals and special rates for this hotel.

2000 Hotel Plaza Blvd. (between Buena Vista Dr. and Apopka–Vineland Rd./Hwy. 535), Lake Buena Vista, FL 32830. ℂ 800/348-3765 or 407/828-2424. Fax 407/828-8933. www.orlandoresorthotel.com. 325 units. $79–$199 standard for 4; $299–$399 suite. Resort fee $6. 5th person $15. AE, DC, DISC, MC, V. Free self-parking. **Amenities:** Restaurant; grill; outdoor heated pool; kids' pool; tennis courts; playground; arcade; guest-services desk; complimentary bus service to WDW parks; transportation to non-Disney parks for a fee; limited room service; laundry service; valet. *In room:* A/C, TV w/pay movies, video games (fee), coffeemaker, hair dryer, iron, safe.

DoubleTree Guest Suites ★★   Children have their own check-in desk and theater, and they get a gift upon arrival at this hotel, the best of the "official" hotels for families traveling with little ones (how can you not love a hotel that gives you freshly baked chocolate chip cookies at check-in?). Adults may find some of the public areas lacking in personality, though the hand-painted mural that spans the lobby and large aviary is a nice touch. All of the accommodations in this seven-story hotel are two-room suites that offer 643 square feet—large by most standards—with space for up to six. This is the easternmost of the "official" resorts, which means it's farthest from the Disney action, but closest to (even within walking distance of) the shops, restaurants, and activities located in the Crossroads Shopping Center, or along Apopka–Vineland Road.

2305 Hotel Plaza Blvd. (just west of Hwy. 535/Apopka–Vineland Rd.), Lake Buena Vista, FL 32830. ℂ 800/222-8733 or 407/934-1000. Fax 407/934-1011. www.downtowndisneyhotels.com or www.doubletreeguestsuites.com. 229 units. $99–$299 double. Extra person $20. Children 17 and under stay free in parent's room. AE, DC, DISC, MC, V. Free parking. From I-4, take the Hwy. 535/Apopka–Vineland Rd. exit north to Hotel Plaza Blvd. and go left. It's the 1st hotel on the left. **Amenities:** Restaurant; 2 lounges; heated outdoor pool; kids' pool; 2 lighted tennis courts; fitness center; volleyball; playground; theater; game room; arcade; concierge; car-rental desk; complimentary bus service to WDW parks; transportation to non-Disney parks for a fee; Disney gift shop; minimarket; limited room service; guest laundry; valet. *In room:* A/C, 2 TVs w/pay movies and video games, dataport, fridge, microwave, coffeemaker, hair dryer, iron, safe.

Grosvenor Resort *Overrated*

This lakeside resort is within walking distance of Downtown Disney Marketplace's shops. The high-rise with low-rise wings has a British Colonial look and public areas. Unfortunately, time seems to be taking its toll on some of the rooms, which could definitely use a bit of refurbishing (so if you choose this hotel and are less than pleased with your room, we recommend you complain and ask for a new one). Nevertheless, its frequent package deals make it popular with budget travelers. Ask for a Tower Room on the west side (floors 9–19) for a limited view of Lake Buena Vista. A Saturday night mystery dinner theater ($40 adults, $11 kids 3–9) is held in the Baskerville's restaurant for an entertaining evening away from Disney. A character breakfast is also offered 3 mornings a week.

1850 Hotel Plaza Blvd. (just east of Buena Vista Dr.), Lake Buena Vista, FL 32830. Ⓒ **800/624-4109** or 407/828-4444. Fax 407/828-8192. www.grosvenorresort.com. 626 units. $89–$145 double. Extra person $18. Children 17 and under stay free in parent's room. AE, DC, DISC, MC, V. Free self-parking; valet parking $8. **Amenities:** 3 restaurants; 3 lounges; 2 outdoor heated pools; 2 lighted tennis courts; fitness center; sport court; shuffleboard; volleyball; Jacuzzi; playground; concierge; car-rental desk; business center; complimentary bus service to WDW parks; transportation to non-Disney parks for a fee; babysitting; laundry service; valet. *In room:* A/C, TV w/pay movies and VCR, dataport, coffeemaker, safe.

Hilton in the Walt Disney World Resort ★★

This upscale resort welcomes many a Disney vacationer, even though business travelers constitute the bulk of its clientele. Its major claim to fame: It's the only official resort on Hotel Plaza Boulevard to offer guests Disney's Extra Magic Hour option (see p. 208 for details). The lobby boasts a nautical flair and its public areas reflect a New England theme, sporting shingles, weathered-wood exteriors, and seafaring touches. The rooms have an upscale and contemporary Shaker-style decor and offer plenty of space in which you can relax and unwind. Rooms on the north and west sides of floors 6 though 10 offer a view of Downtown Disney (just a short walk away) and, in the distance, the Magic Kingdom fireworks. The resort offers a variety of recreational options, including a large pool area (with two pools and plenty of space to soak up the sun), and a game room for kids.

1751 Hotel Plaza Blvd., Lake Buena Vista, FL 32830. Ⓒ **407/827-4000.** Fax 407/827-6369. www.hilton.com. 814 units. $99–$345 double; $359–$1,500 suite. Resort fee $8.50 (only if you choose to use amenities covered by the fee; call for details). Extra person $20. Children 17 and under stay free in parent's room. AE, DC, DISC, MC, V. Self-parking free; valet parking $12. From I-4 take exit 68, turn right onto Hwy. 535/Apopka–Vineland Rd., then left onto Hotel Plaza Blvd. Follow the boulevard, and the resort is near the end on the left. **Amenities:** 4 restaurants; 3 lounges; 2 outdoor heated pools; whirlpool; game room; concierge; car rental; complimentary bus service to WDW parks; transportation to non-Disney parks for a fee; business center; shops; minimarket; salon; 24-hr. room service; babysitting; valet laundry; concierge-level rooms; in-house doctor. *In room:* A/C, TV w/pay movies and video games, dataport, high-speed Internet access (fee), fridge (fee), minibar, coffeemaker, hair dryer, iron, microwave (fee).

Holiday Inn in The Walt Disney Resort *Value*

This former Courtyard by Marriott suffered extensive damage during the summer hurricanes of 2004, an unfortunate happenstance given that the hotel had just undergone a $6-million face-lift prior to the storms. At press time the resort was closed while renovations were being carried out, and no specific reopening date was available; check the website for a progress report.

1805 Hotel Plaza Blvd. (between Lake Buena Vista Dr. and Apopka–Vineland Rd./Hwy. 535), Lake Buena Vista, FL 32830. Ⓒ **800/223-9930** or 407/828-8888. Fax 407/827-4623. www.downtowndisneyhotels.com or www.holiday innwdw.com or www.hiorlando.com.

Hotel Royal Plaza ★ᵣ The Plaza is one of the boulevard's originals, but renovations over its 25 years (including a recent multimillion-dollar makeover) have kept it in quite good shape. A favorite with the budget-minded, its hallmark is a friendly staff (some of whom have been there since the hotel opened) that provides excellent service. The rooms are oversize with enough space for five and are tastefully decorated. Poolside rooms have balconies and patios; the tower rooms have separate sitting areas, and some offer whirlpool tubs in the bathrooms. If you want a view from up high, ask for a room facing west and WDW; the south and east sides keep a watchful eye on I-4 traffic. The inner courtyard offers a quiet escape where you can sit by the pool and soak up the Florida sunshine surrounded by scattered palm trees.

1905 Hotel Plaza Blvd. (between Buena Vista Dr. and Hwy. 535/Apopka–Vineland Rd.), Lake Buena Vista, FL 32830. ℂ 800/248-7890 or 407/828-2828. Fax 407/827-6338. www.downtowndisneyhotels.com or www.royalplaza.com. 394 units. $160–$219 double; $180–$269 suite. $8 daily resort fee. No charge for extra person. Children 17 and under stay free in parent's room. AE, DC, DISC, MC, V. Self-parking free; valet parking $12. From I-4, take the Hwy. 535/Apopka–Vineland Rd. exit north to Hotel Plaza Blvd. and go left. It's the 2nd hotel on the left. **Amenities:** Restaurant; lounge; heated outdoor pool; 4 lighted tennis courts; fitness center; whirlpool; guest-services desk; children's activity program; complimentary bus service to WDW parks; transportation to non-Disney parks for a fee; Disney gift shop; limited room service; babysitting; guest laundry; valet. *In room:* A/C, TV w/pay movies, video games, dataport, high-speed Internet access (fee) minibar, coffeemaker, hair dryer, iron, safe.

5 Other Lake Buena Vista Area Hotels

The hotels in this section are within a few minutes' drive of the WDW parks. They offer a great location but not the Disney-related privileges given to guests in the "official" hotels, such as Disney bus service and character breakfasts. On the flip side, because you're not paying for those privileges, hotels in this category are generally a shade less expensive for comparable rooms and services.

Note: These hotels are also listed on the "Walt Disney World & Lake Buena Vista Accommodations" map, earlier in this chapter.

VERY EXPENSIVE

Gaylord Palms ★★★ It's a convention center in disguise, but the Gaylord Palms appeals to vacationers, too, and is not your run-of-the-mill resort. It could be considered a destination unto itself, offering its own entertainment, fabulous dining, shops, and recreational facilities. The 4½-acre octagonal Grand Atrium, topped by a glass dome, surrounds a miniature version of the Castillo de San Marcos, the old fort at St. Augustine. Waterfalls, lush foliage, live alligators, and a rocky landscape complete the feel.

The resort and its rooms are divided into themes: Emerald Bay, a 362-room hotel within the hotel, has an elegant air; St. Augustine captures the essence of America's oldest city; Key West delivers the laid-back ambience of Florida's southernmost city; and the Everglades uses a misty swamp, snarling faux gator, fiber-optic fireflies, and tin-roofed shanties to muster a wild-and-wooly air. The rooms are spacious, beautifully decorated, and well appointed (the soundproofing, though, could be a bit better); each has its own balcony. The kids' pool features a huge eight-legged octopus water slide, and cabanas at the adult pool have Internet access. And if you need to unwind further, try the 20,000-square-foot branch of the famous **Canyon Ranch SpaClub.** As is befitting a luxury resort, the service is impeccable; yet it's also extremely friendly and welcoming, not standoffish, as is the case at many other resorts of this class.

6000 Osceola Pkwy., Kissimmee, FL 34747. ℂ 877/677-9352 or 407/586-2000. Fax 407/239-4822. www.gaylord palms.com. 1,406 units. $199–$439 double; $635–$2,700 suite. $10 daily resort fee. Extra adult $20. Kids under 18 stay free in parent's room. AE, DC, DISC, MC, V. Self-parking $10; valet parking $12–$16. Take the I-4 Osceola Pkwy. exit east to the hotel. **Amenities:** 3 restaurants; 4 lounges; 2 outdoor heated pools; cabana rentals; fitness center; spa; children's center; concierge; tour desk; car-rental desk; free transportation to Disney parks; transportation to non-Disney parks for a fee; business center; shopping arcade; salon; 24-hr. room service; massage; babysitting; guest laundry; concierge-level rooms; valet. *In room:* A/C, TV w/pay movies, high-speed Internet access, dataport, coffeemaker, hair dryer, iron, safe, PlayStation.

Hyatt Regency Grand Cypress Resort ★★★ *Finds* A favorite of honeymooners and those seeking a luxurious adult oasis, yet there's plenty for families as well. This getaway's lobby has lush foliage from which macaws wave to passersby, with winding walkways and landscape lighting to add to the ambience. The 18-story atrium has inner and outer glass elevators (ride the outers to the roof for a panoramic rush). The rooms are beautifully decorated with a Laura Ashley flair and easily sleep four. If you find, however, you are in need of additional space, you can usually request a connecting room for a discounted price. The west-side rooms on floors seven and up have a distant view of Cinderella Castle and the Magic Kingdom's fireworks. (This vantage point also shows how much of WDW and the surrounding area still remain wooded.) The Hyatt shares a golf club and academy, racquet club, and equestrian center with its sister property, Villas of Grand Cypress (see below); both offer excellent packages aimed at the sports set. The Hyatt's half-acre, 800,000-gallon pool is one of the best in Orlando and features caves, grottoes, waterfalls, a rope bridge, and a 45-foot water slide. A very nice child-care facility is also available. **Hemingway's,** its signature restaurant (p. 158), has a Key West theme and a menu featuring seafood.

1 N. Jacaranda (off Hwy. 535/Apopka–Vineland Rd.), Orlando, FL 32836. © **800/233-1234** or 407/239-1234. Fax 407/239-3800. www.hyattgrandcypress.com. 750 units. $279–$585 double; $695–$5,750 suite. Optional $13 daily resort fee (includes health club, free local calls, daily newspaper, and in-room coffee). Extra person $25. Children 18 and under stay free in parent's room. AE, DC, DISC, MC, V. Free parking; valet $18. **Amenities:** 4 restaurants; 4 lounges; large heated outdoor pool; 45 holes of golf; 12 tennis courts (5 lighted); health club; 2 racquetball courts; spa; watersports equipment; children's center; arcade; concierge; car-rental desk; free Disney shuttle; transportation to non-Disney parks for a fee; store; salon; 24-hr. room service; in-room massage; babysitting; laundry service; valet; concierge-level rooms; equestrian center. *In room:* A/C, TV, dataport, high-speed Internet access (fee), minibar, hair dryer, iron, safe.

Villas of Grand Cypress ★★★ *Finds* This is an exceptional place to retreat to at the end of the day, though it's definitely a splurge in the budget department. At its "modest" end, this Mediterranean-inspired resort starts with standard-size rooms with Roman tubs and patios, many of them backing up to ponds whose inhabitants include mallards, soft-shelled turtles, and largemouth bass eager for bread crusts or whatever else you can spare. Floor plans progress to elegant one- to four-bedroom villas that reach about 1,100 square feet on the top end. Some include kitchens, dining rooms, and patios. The resort shares a golf club and academy, racquet club, and equestrian center with the Hyatt Regency Grand Cypress Resort (see above). Inside the resort, you're almost completely sheltered from Disney, which is situated only a few hundred yards away. Take some time to wander the lush grounds, which are dotted with lakes, bougainvillea, and hibiscus. There are also walking and jogging trails. Shuttle buses allow you to park your car and get around the resort and to the nearby theme parks without driving. Unlike its sister Hyatt property, this resort caters primarily to adults, though Villa guests with kids can use the Hyatt's child-care and other facilities—even the pool.

1 N. Jacaranda (off Hwy. 535/Apopka–Vineland Rd.), Orlando, FL 32836. © **800/835-7377** or 407/239-4700. Fax 407/239-7219. www.grandcypress.com. 146 villas. $215–$500 club suite; $315–$2,000 1- to 4-bedroom villa. Resort fee $12. 1 extra person over the room limit stays free. Children 17 and under stay free in parent's room. AE, DC, DISC,

(Tips) Marriott Montage

The December 2000 christening of **Marriott Village at Lake Buena Vista,** 8623 Vineland Ave., Orlando, FL 32821 (© **877/682-8552** or 407/938-9001; www. marriottvillage.com), brought together three of the flagship's properties in a cluster just east of Lake Buena Vista, 3 miles from WDW. The resort includes a 400-room SpringHill Suites ($79–$129 double; free continental breakfast), a 388-room Fairfield Inn ($65–$116 double; free continental breakfast), and a 312-room Courtyard by Marriott ($79–$129 double; free high-speed Internet). Children under 17 stay free in their parents' rooms, and an extra person costs an additional $10.

All rooms have fridges. Each property has adult and kids' pools, fitness centers, kids' clubs, whirlpools, and guest-services desks. All offer transportation for a fee ($5–$15 per person per day) to Disney parks and non-Disney parks. There are three restaurants within walking distance, as well as an array of snack-style eateries in the village. To get here, take I-4 Exit 68, Hwy. 535/Apopka–Vineland Rd., then head south to Vineland, and go left a half-mile to the village. There's free self-parking.

MC, V. Free self-parking. **Amenities:** 2 restaurants; 2 lounges; outdoor heated pool; 45 holes of golf; 12 tennis courts (5 lighted); health club; spa; 2 racquetball courts; watersports equipment; children's center (at the Hyatt); car-rental desk (Hyatt); arcade; concierge; free Disney shuttle; transportation to non-Disney parks for a fee; salon (Hyatt); 24-hr. room service; massage (in-room); babysitting; laundry service; valet; concierge-level rooms. *In room:* A/C, TV, dataport, high-speed Internet access (fee), full kitchens (some), minibar, hair dryer, iron, safe.

EXPENSIVE

Marriott's Orlando World Center ★★ (Finds)   An upscale resort that caters to both business and leisure travelers alike. Golf, tennis, and spa lovers will find plenty to do at this 230-acre resort, as will families. The lobby's centerpiece is a 28-story tower fronted by flowers and fountains. The large, comfortable, and beautifully decorated rooms sleep four, and the higher poolside floors offer views of Disney. For a large-scale resort, it is surprisingly easy to get around, as it is not spread out so much as up. The largest of its five pools has water slides and waterfalls surrounded by plenty of space to relax among the palm trees and tropical plants. There's plenty of on-site dining, ranging from counter service casual to gourmet cuisine; the **Mikado Japanese Steakhouse** (p. 170) headlines the hotel's four restaurants. The location, only 2 miles from the Disney parks, is a fabulous plus.

8701 World Center Dr. (on Hwy. 536 between I-4 and Hwy. 535/Apopka–Vineland Rd.), Orlando, FL 32821. © 800/ 621-0638 or 407/239-4200. Fax 407/238-8777. www.marriott.com. 2,111 units. $16–$329 for up to 5; $750–$1,600 suite. Children 17 and under stay free in parent's room. AE, DC, DISC, MC, V. Free self-parking; valet parking $16. **Amenities:** 4 restaurants; 2 lounges; 3 heated outdoor pools; heated indoor pool; kids' pool; 18-hole golf course; 8 lighted tennis courts; health club; spa; whirlpool; sauna; concierge; car-rental desk; transportation to all theme parks for a fee; business center; salon; 24-hr. room service; massage; babysitting; laundry service. *In room:* A/C, TV w/pay movies, dataport, high-speed Internet access (fee), limited Wi-Fi (fee), minibar, coffeemaker, hair dryer, iron, safe.

MODERATE

Embassy Suites Lake Buena Vista ★   Set near the end of Palm Parkway, just off Apopka–Vineland Road, this fun and welcoming all-suite resort is close to all the action of Downtown Disney and the surrounding area, yet still remains a quiet retreat.

Tips **Special Delivery**

Gooding's Supermarkets (© 407/827-1200; www.goodings.com) offers grocery delivery service to theme-park area hotels in Lake Buena Vista, Disney, Celebration, I-Drive, and Kissimmee. There is a $50 minimum, and a $10 service charge is added to all orders. You can order groceries (but no alcohol) online up to 48 hours before your requested delivery date (delivery hours are 9am–6pm). For details, see the website or call. This is a great service if you are staying in a hotel room with kitchen facilities, or if you have kids and want to stock your room with snacks and supplies.

Each suite sleeps five and includes a separate living area (with a pullout sofa) and sleeping quarters. The roomy accommodations make it a great choice for families. Some of the other perks here include a complimentary cooked-to-order breakfast, a daily manager's reception, and free transportation to Disney.

8100 Lake Avenue, Orlando, FL 32836. © 800/257-8483 or 407/239-1144. Fax 407/238-0230. www.embassysuites orlando.com. 333 units. $109–$229, extra person $15. Rates include full breakfast. AE, DC, DISC, MC, V. Free self-parking; valet parking $7. **Amenities:** Restaurant; cafe; lounge; indoor and outdoor heated pools; kids' pool and play area; whirlpool and sauna; fitness center; tennis court; basketball court; free shuttle to Disney parks; business center; high-speed Internet access; room service; laundry service. *In room:* A/C, TV w/pay movies, dataport, high-speed Internet access (fee), fridge, microwave, safe, hair dryer, iron.

Holiday Inn Sunspree Resort Lake Buena Vista ★ *Kids*   Just a mile from the Disney parks, this inn caters to kids in a big way. They can check in at their own check-in desk, watch a movie at the theater in the lobby area, or have fun at Camp Holiday, the supervised activity center (one of the best around). The hotel's 231 Kid Suites have beds for up to six and themes (an igloo, a space capsule, castle, and more); however, standard rooms are also available. If you like sleeping in, ask for a room that doesn't face the pool area. Kids under 12 eat free in their own restaurant, though fine dining it isn't (kids won't care about that anyway). The resort also offers plenty of other dining options. Recent renovations have spruced up appearances throughout.

13351 Apopka–Vineland Rd./Hwy. 535 (between Hwy. 536 and I-4), Lake Buena Vista, FL 32821. © 800/366-6299 or 407/239-4500. Fax 407/239-7713. www.kidsuites.com. 507 units. $99–$149 standard for up to 4; $119–$179 Kid Suite. AE, DISC, MC, V. Free self-parking. Pets under 25 pounds $25. **Amenities:** Restaurant; food court; minimart; outdoor heated pool; kids' pool; fitness center; Jacuzzi; playground; supervised children's center (fee); family activities; arcade; guest-services desk; free shuttle to Disney parks; transportation to non-Disney parks for a fee; limited room service; laundry service; valet; children's movie theater. *In room:* A/C, TV/VCR, fridge, microwave, coffeemaker, hair dryer, iron, safe.

Nickelodeon Family Suites Resort by Holiday Inn ★★ *Finds* *Kids*   This all-suite property, a former Holiday Inn transformed into the first ever Nickelodeon-branded resort, is one of the best properties in the Orlando area for families. Its two-bedroom Kid Suites feature a second bedroom for the kids with either bunk or twin beds, minikitchens, and a pullout sofa in the living area. Three-bedroom suites are also available and include more space, a second bathroom, and a full kitchen. The redecorated rooms are all themed with Nickelodeon colors and characters. An all-new lobby and mall area, filled with restaurants, an arcade, shops, and nightly entertainment (including Studio Nick), have been added. The resort's two pool areas (with lots of lifeguards) are veritable water parks, with extensive multilevel water slides, flumes, climbing nets, and water jets. Activities are scheduled poolside, and there are also a wide variety of recreational options, including a small minigolf course, playgrounds, and sand play areas. Required wristbands ensure that only resort guests can access the area. "Nick After Dark," an evening supervised activity program for kids ages 5 to 12, allows parents to take a night off. A daily character breakfast is offered in addition to the hotel's regular breakfast buffet (at the latter, kids eat free with paying adults).

14500 Continental Gateway (off Hwy. 536), Lake Buena Vista, FL 32821. © **877/387-5437**, 407/387-5437, or 866/ GO2-NICK. Fax 407/387-1489. www.hifamilysuites.com or www.nickhotel.com. 800 units. $160–$275 suite. AE, DC, DISC, MC, V. Free self-parking. **Amenities:** Restaurant; lounge; several fast-food counters; minimarket; 2 water park pools; minigolf course; fitness center; 2 Jacuzzis; 3 outdoor Ping-Pong tables; 2 shuffleboard courts; game room; complimentary recreation center for ages 4–12; tour desk; free shuttle to Disney and non-Disney parks; coin-op washers and dryers. *In room:* A/C, TV w/pay movies and VCR (some with Nintendo), dataport, free high-speed Internet access, full kitchen (select suites), fridge, microwave, coffeemaker, hair dryer, iron, safe.

Palomino Suites Lake Buena Vista ☆

These moderately priced family suites are less than 2 miles from Disney, located near Downtown Disney. This hotel is a good choice if you want a little home-style comfort and the chance to perform do-it-yourself stuff in the fully equipped kitchen. The hotel is only 7 years old, so everything is still in good shape. The two-bedroom suites sleep up to six and offer a decent amount of room. A complimentary hot buffet breakfast is offered daily.

8200 Palm Pkwy. (off S. Apopka–Vineland Rd./Hwy. 535), Orlando, FL 32836. © **800/225-5466** or 407/465-8200. Fax 407/465-0200. www.homewood-suites.com. 123 units. $109–$199 double. Extra person $15. Rates include continental breakfast. Children 18 and under stay free in parent's room. AE, DC, DISC, MC, V. Free self-parking. **Amenities:** Minigrocery; outdoor heated pool; exercise room; Jacuzzi; game room; concierge; car-rental desk; free shuttle to Disney parks; transportation to non-Disney parks for a fee; business center; babysitting; laundry service; valet; safe-deposit boxes; pizza delivery. *In room:* A/C, TV/VCR w/pay movies, dataport, fully equipped/stocked kitchen, fridge, microwave, coffeemaker, hair dryer, iron, daily newspaper.

Staybridge Suites Lake Buena Vista ☆☆

This chain hotel is ideally located just off of Apopka–Vineland Road, close to the action of Downtown Disney and the theme parks, as well as many restaurants. An excellent choice for families, the property's room sizes, price, and friendly staff are three more good reasons to stay here. Featured are one- and two-bedroom suites (which sleep up to eight), all with full kitchens; some two-bedroom suites have two bathrooms. The suites have large, comfortable separate living areas when compared to other all-suite hotels. A particularly unique plus to this property is the complimentary grocery-shopping service offered. You can check off items on the list, drop it off at the front desk, and your items will be delivered to you—even if you are not in your room. Prices run about 50¢ to $2.50 higher

---

Don't Worry, Dinners Delivered

For those of you who can't stand the thought of heading out to dinner after a long day at the parks, **Take Out Express** is a restaurant delivery service that will bring dinner to you from 4:30 to 11pm daily. Simply check out their list of participating restaurants in the area (and there are plenty of favorites to choose from), order from their menu, and your meal will be on its way. There is a charge of $5 per restaurant (you can order from more than just one) as well as the price of your order (and don't forget to tip). Call © **407/352–1170** to order or for more information.

---

than those you'll find at the supermarket, but the convenience factor often makes the expense worth it for time-strapped families.

8751 Suiteside Drive, Orlando, FL 32836. ℂ 800/866-4549 or 407/238-0777. Fax 407/238-2640. www.ichotelsgroup. com. 150 units. $149–$299. Rates include continental breakfast. Rollaway beds and cribs available at no charge. AE, DC, DISC, MC, V. **Amenities:** Deli; convenience store; outdoor heated pool; children's pool; 24-hr. exercise room; Jacuzzi; 24-hr. game room; free shuttle to Disney parks; guest-services desk; 24-hr. laundry service; accessible suites; complimentary grocery delivery service. *In room:* A/C, TV/VCR, dataport, free high-speed Internet access, kitchen, hair dryer, ironing board, iron, safe.

INEXPENSIVE

Hampton Inn Lake Buena Vista   Location rules at this modern property, which is only 1 mile from the entrance to Hotel Plaza Boulevard on the northeast corner of Disney. It's not fancy, but the price is right and there are lots of nearby places to eat, shop, and party.

150 Palm Pkwy., Orlando, FL 32836. ℂ 800/370-9259 or 407/465-8150. Fax 407/465-0150. www.hamptoninnlbv. com. 147 units. $59–$169 for up to 4. 5th person $10. Rates include continental breakfast. Children 17 and under stay free in parent's room. AE, DC, DISC, MC, V. Free self-parking. **Amenities:** Outdoor heated pool; Jacuzzi; guest-services desk; free shuttle to Disney parks; transportation to non-Disney parks for a fee. *In room:* A/C, TV w/pay movies, dataport, coffeemaker, hair dryer, iron, microwave and fridge available upon request, rollaways and cribs upon request.

6 Places to Stay in the Kissimmee Area

This stretch of highway (U.S. 192, also known as Irlo Bronson Memorial Hwy.) is within close proximity of the Disney parks. Over the last few years a revitalization of the area has added such features as extra wide sidewalks, streetlamps, highway markers, and widened roads to make it a more friendly and appealing area to stay and play. Traffic here can nevertheless be frustrating, especially when you are trying to cross the street. Budget hotels and restaurants abound, though a few higher-priced luxury resorts are starting to appear a bit off of the main drag. While Disney is close by, Universal and SeaWorld are not—the latter are a good 20-minute (or more) ride away. If you don't have a car, Mears Transportation (see "Getting Around" in chapter 3) is a good bet to take you there for about $13 to $15 per person per day, round-trip.

In addition to the hotels reviewed below, the **Double Tree Resort Orlando Villas At Maingate,** 4787 W. Irlo Bronson Hwy. (ℂ **407/397-0555;** www.doubletree.com), offers spacious one-, two-, and three-bedroom town house accommodations with kitchens that are great for families and larger groups. The **Quality Suites Maingate East,** 5876 W. Irlo Bronson Hwy. (ℂ **800/848-4148** or 407/396-8040; www.choice hotels.com), offers suites with separate bedroom and living areas, and fully stocked kitchens. And the **Radisson Resort Orlando-Celebration,** 2900 Parkway Blvd. (ℂ **800/833-3333** or 407/396-7000; www.Radisson.com), set back in off the main drag, has decent, but basic, rooms, a nice pool area with a water slide, and beautifully landscaped grounds.

Note: You'll find the hotels and motels described on the map "Kissimmee Accommodations" on p. 111.

EXPENSIVE

Celebration Hotel 🏠🏠   This hotel is as picture-perfect as the town that surrounds it. Its three-story, wood-frame design is straight out of 1920s Florida, as is its interior. A beautiful dark wooded bar is set just off to the right as you enter, and the lobby is filled with antiques and artwork, creating a warm inviting atmosphere. The beautifully

Kissimmee Accommodations

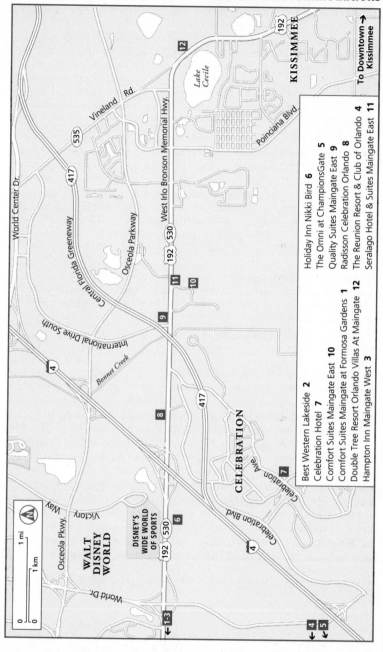

Best Western Lakeside **2**
Celebration Hotel **7**
Comfort Suites Maingate East **10**
Comfort Suites Maingate at Formosa Gardens **1**
Double Tree Resort Orlando Villas At Maingate **12**
Hampton Inn Maingate West **3**

Holiday Inn Nikki Bird **6**
The Omni at ChampionsGate **5**
Quality Suites Maingate East **9**
Radisson Celebration Orlando **8**
The Reunion Resort & Club of Orlando **4**
Seralago Hotel & Suites Maingate East **11**

decorated rooms have incredibly comfortable beds; to enjoy a soothing view, ask for a lakefront room. The upscale ambience caters to adults, especially those seeking a romantic getaway. The only drawback: You'll have to deal with the traffic on U.S. 192 to get anywhere.

700 Bloom St., Celebration, FL 34747. ℂ **888/499-3800** or 407/566-6000. Fax 407/566-6001. www.celebration hotel.com. 115 units. $215–$359 for up to 4; $299–$459 suite. $10 daily resort fee. AE, DC, DISC, MC, V. Free self-parking; valet parking $14. **Amenities:** Restaurant; lounge; outdoor heated pool; 18-hole golf course; state-of-the-art health-and-fitness center; spa; concierge; free shuttle to Disney parks; transportation to non-Disney parks for a fee; nearby shopping district. *In room:* A/C, TV/Nintendo, dataport, high-speed Internet access (fee), limited Wi-Fi access (fee), hair dryer, iron, safe.

The Omni at ChampionsGate 🐾🐾🐾
One of the newest luxury resorts to spring up just south of the Disney district in ChampionsGate, The Omni offers a comprehensive array of leisure facilities, including two championship golf courses designed by Greg Norman, a vast pool area with its very own lazy river, and a 10,000-square-foot spa. The beautifully decorated rooms feature 9-foot ceilings and are filled with plush amenities, including bathrobes and free Wi-Fi Internet access. The service is as impressive as the facility itself, and there's a program especially geared to youngsters so parents can get some relaxation time on their own.

1500 Masters Blvd., ChampionsGate FL 33896. ℂ **888/444-6664** or 407/390-6664. Fax 321/677-6600. www.omni hotels.com. 730 units. $199–$350 standard; $450–$2,500 suite. $10 daily resort fee. AE, DC, DISC, MC, V. Self-parking free; valet parking $12. Pets under 25 lb. ($50 fee). **Amenities:** 5 restaurants; grill; 3 lounges; 2 outdoor heated pools; 2 18-hole golf courses; tennis courts; volleyball; health and fitness center; spa; video arcade; Omni Kids Program; concierge; free shuttle to WDW parks; transportation to non-Disney parks for a fee; 24-hr. business center; retail gallery; salon; 24-hr. room service; laundry; valet; lazy river. *In room:* A/C, TV w/pay movies and Nintendo, free Wi-Fi Internet access, fridge and microwave (upon request, fee); minibar; hair dryer, iron/ironing board, safe, CD player, bathrobe.

The Reunion Resort & Club of Orlando 🐾🐾🐾
This luxury resort community is still in its early phases (with a completion date set for some 10 years into the future). Currently, several different villas and a variety of vacation homes (both available for rent to visitors) are open. The spectacular villas feature a rather unique layout. Bedrooms are located on the ground level, with the main living area and additional bedrooms on the second level (making it less likely you'll have to drag your luggage up a flight of stairs). Some of the villas have private patios or balconies; some of the vacation homes have their own private pools. Last summer saw the opening of the extensive on-site water park (in addition to other resort pools located throughout the property). Two championship golf courses are already operational. A kids' program offering a variety of supervised activities began in 2006. The downside: The property charges an exorbitantly high "gratuity" fee.

1000 Reunion Way, Reunion, FL 34747. ℂ **888/418-9611** or 407/662-1000. Fax 407/662-1111. www.reunionresort. com. Eventually 8,000 units. $295–$535 villas; $425–$945 homes. 9.6% gratuity fee assessed on total bill. Free self-parking. **Amenities:** Numerous pools; water park; 3 golf courses; kids' program. *In room:* A/C, TV w/pay movies, DVD/CD player, dataport, high-speed Internet access (fee), fully stocked kitchen, microwave, fridge, coffeemaker, hair dryer, iron/ironing board, safe, washer/dryer.

MODERATE

Comfort Suites Maingate East 🐾 *Value*
Set back from the main drag, this fairly new and welcoming hotel is one of the nicest in the area. The lobby and accommodations—consisting of studios and one-bedroom suites—are bright and inviting. The main pool and the children's pool, with an umbrella fountain to keep everyone cool,

Tips **Prime Real Estate**

The Four Seasons is scheduled to open a 425-room luxury resort in the pictur-esque community of Celebration, complete with its own 18-hole golf course, in 2007. Also opening in 2007 is the **Sonesta Orlando Tierra Del Sol,** a luxe resort community located just 10 minutes from Disney. And these are just the tip of the iceberg on the Orlando expansion front—several luxury properties and resort communities are scheduled to open around town in 2008. Stay tuned.

are open round-the-clock. For entertainment, Old Town (a small-scale shopping, din-ing, and entertainment complex) is next door, and a great miniature golf course is located just in front of the property.

2775 Florida Plaza Blvd., Kissimmee, FL 34746. ⓒ **888/782-9772** or 407/397-7848. Fax 407/396-7045. www. comfortsuitesfl.com. 198 units. $69–$175 double. Extra person $10. Rates include continental breakfast. Children 17 and under stay free in parent's room. AE, DC, DISC, MC, V. Free self-parking. **Amenities:** Outdoor heated pool; kids' pool; fitness center; game room; concierge; free shuttle to Disney, Universal, and SeaWorld parks; business center; laundry service. *In room:* A/C, TV, dataport, free high-speed Internet access, fridge, microwave, coffeemaker, hair dryer, iron, safe.

Holiday Inn Nikki Bird ★★ *(Value* *(Kids*   Spread out over 26 acres, this family-friendly resort has one of the most extensive arrays of recreational facilities in its class, including three pools and two toddler pools with squirting fountains, tennis courts, and more. And it's only a mile from the WDW entrance to boot. Thanks to the great landscaping, you'll never know its set along one of the busiest stretches of highway around (the location's a big plus, as the dining and entertainment choices in this area are practically countless). Kid Suite rooms offer a separate children's sleeping area, video games, and an additional TV. Kids can play at the supervised Camp Nikki while mom and dad relax and enjoy some adult time.

7300 West U.S. 192, Kissimmee, FL 34747. ⓒ **407/396-7300.** Fax 407/396-9196. www.hi-nikki.com. 530 units. $99–$149, extra person no charge. Children 17 and under stay free in parent's room. AE, DC, DISC, MC, V. Free self-parking. **Amenities:** 2 restaurants; 1 lounge; snack/convenience store; 3 heated pools; 2 children's pools; 3 lighted tennis courts; fitness center; basketball; volleyball; horseshoes; playground; supervised children's activity center; video game room; concierge; car-rental desk; free transportation to WDW parks; laundry service; valet; safe-deposit boxes. *In room:* A/C, TV w/pay movies, video games, dataport, minifridge, microwave, coffeemaker, hair dryer, iron/ironing board, safe, CD player (in some).

INEXPENSIVE

In addition to the accommodations described here, there are scores of other inexpen-sive but serviceable motels, including chains (see appendix B, "Useful Toll-Free Num-bers & Websites"). Most are within a few miles of Disney, have rooms in the 300-square-foot range, and arrange transportation to the parks. Many sell attractions tickets, but be careful. Many deeply discounted ticket offers are too good to be true. Some people land at the parks with *invalid tickets* or waste a half-day or more listen-ing to a timeshare pitch to get 30% to 40% off the regular price (single-day Disney park tickets are $63 for adults, $52 for kids 3–9). If a discount is more than $2 to $5 per ticket, it's probably too good to be true.

Stick to buying tickets through the parks or accept the modest discounts offered by such groups as AAA, AARP, and the visitor information centers listed in chapter 2, "Planning Your Trip to Walt Disney World & Orlando."

Best Western Lakeside 🎯🎯 *Kids* *Value*   The hand-painted exteriors, lobby, and common areas of this hotel give it a unique charm not found in its hotel brethren. Just up the road from the Disney entrance, this 24-acre resort looks deceptively small when you first pull up (most of the accommodations are hidden behind the lobby area), but amenities include numerous recreational options (pools, playgrounds, and so on), a food court, good-size convenience store, and bountiful free breakfast. Rooms are standard in size and offerings, but are nicely decorated and will comfortably sleep four. Other pluses include a child-care facility and free transport to *all* the major theme parks.

7769 Irlo Bronson Memorial Hwy. (U.S. 192), Kissimmee, FL 34747. © 800/848-0801 or 407/396-2222. Fax 407/396-7087. www.bestwesternlakeside.com. 651 units. $59–$129 double. Extra person $10. Rates include continental breakfast. Children 17 and under stay free in parent's room. Discount packages available. Small pets accepted ($25 fee). AE, DC, DISC, MC, V. Free self-parking. **Amenities:** 2 restaurants; food court; 3 outdoor heated pools; 2 kids' pools; small minigolf; 2 tennis courts; exercise room; Jacuzzi; playgrounds; kids' activities; guest-services desk; free bus to Disney, Universal, and SeaWorld parks; laundry service; valet. *In room:* A/C, TV w/pay movies and PlayStation, dataport, fridge, coffeemaker, hair dryer, iron, safe.

Comfort Suites Maingate Resort (at Formosa Gardens) *Value*   Just across the street from the Best Western Lakeside (see below) and up the road from WDW, this clean, comfortable place to stay has kept itself modern and in good shape. The "suites" have a small dividing wall slightly separating the living area from the sleeping quarters, but the illusion of privacy is there. Accommodations are a bit bigger than most and can squeeze in up to six. A bit of tropical landscaping gives it an inviting atmosphere and shelters guests from busy U.S. 192. At least 10 restaurants and a small shopping plaza are within walking distance, and there's a miniature golf course right across the street. A free expanded continental breakfast will start off your day. And there's free transportation to Disney, Universal, and SeaWorld to boot.

7888 W. Irlo Bronson Memorial Hwy. (U.S. 192), Kissimmee, FL 34747. © 888/390-9888 or 407/390-9888. Fax 407/390-09811607. www.kisscomfortsuite.com. 150 units. $59–$150. Rates include continental breakfast. Children 17 and under stay free in parent's room. AE, DC, DISC, MC, V. Free self-parking. **Amenities:** Bar; outdoor heated pool; kids' pool; Jacuzzi; arcade; car-rental/guest-services desk; free shuttle to Disney, Universal, SeaWorld, and Wet 'n Wild parks; laundry service. *In room:* A/C, TV, dataport, coffeemaker, fridge, microwave, hair dryer, iron, safe.

Hampton Inn Maingate West   Just 1½ miles west of WDW, this welcoming motel is a good choice for the budget-conscious vacationer. The rooms are nicely decorated, but are a bit on the small side, making them a snug fit for four. While there are not a lot of frills, the property is well maintained and provides the basics with good taste. There's no restaurant, but a free breakfast is served in the lobby, and there are more than enough dining choices just a minute or two away to keep you from going hungry.

3000 Maingate Lane, Kissimmee, FL 34747. © 800/936-9417 or 407/396-5457. Fax 407/396-8989. www.hampton innmaingatewest.com. 118 units. $69–$109 double. Extra person $10. Rates include continental breakfast. Children 17 and under stay free in parent's room. AE, DC, DISC, MC, V. Free self-parking. **Amenities:** Outdoor heated pool; guest-services desk; free shuttle to Disney, Universal, and SeaWorld parks. *In room:* A/C, TV w/pay movies, dataport, fridge, microwave, coffeemaker, iron.

Seralago Hotel & Suites Maingate East 🎯🎯 *Value* *Kids*   Location (it's just down the road from Disney) and price are just some of the perks at this former Holiday Inn. The revamped hotel sports new colors and a bright new look but still features themed Kid Suites with separate sleeping areas for your tots, as well as standard rooms and regular two-room suites. The rooms provide a reasonable amount of space for a family of five, with the two-room unit sleeping up to eight. There are plenty of family recreational activities, from swimming to tennis, and the hotel's movie theater shows

Tips   Homes Away from Home

Some travelers, especially those who like all the comforts of home or are traveling in groups of five or more, bypass motels in favor of rental condos or homes. Rates vary widely depending on quality and location; some may require at least a 2- or 3-night minimum. A lot of these properties are 5 to 15 miles from the theme parks and offer no transportation, so a car is a necessity.

On the plus side, most have two to six bedrooms and a convertible couch, two or more bathrooms, a full kitchen, multiple TVs and phones, and irons. Some have washers and dryers. Homes often have their own private screen-enclosed pool, while condos have a common one.

On the minus side, they can be lacking in services. Most don't have daily maid service, and restaurants can be as far away as the parks. (There's another reason you'll need a car.) And unless a condo or home is in a gated community, don't expect on-site security. Some properties offer dinnerware, utensils, and salt-and-pepper shakers—check when you book as amenities vary widely.

Rates range from about $79 to $475 per night ($350–$3,300 per week).

All Star Vacation Homes (© 888/249-1779 or 407/997-0733; www.allstar vacationhomes.com) is one of the area's best home and condo rental outfits, with a wide variety of properties to choose from—all of them within a 4-mile radius of Disney. Do check their website—you will be able to see the exact home you are renting, as opposed to a "typical" room. Other popular players include **Holiday Villas** (© 800/344-3959; www.holidayvillas.com); **Summer Bay Resort** (© 888/742-1100; www.summerbayresort.com); **LikiTiki Village** (© 407/239-5000); **Bahama Bay Resort** (© 888/782-9722); and **Cypress Point Orlando** (© 407/597-2700).

free family films nightly. There's a family-friendly food court, and kids 12 and under eat free (two kids per paying adult) in the hotel's cafe.

5678 Irlo Bronson Memorial Hwy. (U.S. 192), Kissimmee, FL 34746. © 800/366-5437 or 407/396-4488. Fax 407/396-8915. www.orlandofamilyfunhotel.com. 614 units. $59–$99 double. Extra person $10. Children 18 and under stay free in parent's room. AE, DC, DISC, MC, V. Free self-parking. **Amenities:** Restaurant; food court; convenience store; lounge; 2 outdoor heated pools; toddler pool; 2 tennis courts; exercise room; basketball; volleyball; Jacuzzi; playground; arcade; guest-services desk; free shuttle to Disney parks; transportation to non-Disney parks for a fee; limited room service; laundry service; small movie theater. *In room:* A/C, TV/VCR, video games, fridge, microwave, coffeemaker, hair dryer, iron, CD players (in some).

7 Places to Stay in the International Drive Area

The hotels and resorts listed here are 7 to 10 miles north of Walt Disney World (via I-4) and 1 to 5 miles from Universal Orlando and SeaWorld. The advantages of staying on I-Drive: It's a destination unto itself, filled with accommodations, restaurants, and small attractions; it has its own inexpensive trolley service (see "Getting Around" in chapter 3); and it's centrally located for those who want to visit Disney, Universal, SeaWorld, *and* the downtown area. The disadvantages: The north end of I-Drive is badly congested; the shops, motels, eateries, and attractions along this stretch can be tacky; and some of the motels and hotels don't offer free transportation to the parks (the going rate is $6–$15 round-trip).

You'll find these places located on the map "International Drive Area Accommodations" in this section.

VERY EXPENSIVE

Peabody Orlando ★★★ *(Moments*   The five mallards that march into a lobby fountain every morning at 11am and then back out at 5pm, accompanied by John Philip Sousa's *King Cotton March,* are just part of the appeal of this luxury hotel, famous for its friendly (and not stuffy) service. Primarily a business and convention destination, the Peabody also appeals to adults looking for a classy hotel that provides top-of-the-line service, amenities, and atmosphere. If your budget allows the splurge, you won't be disappointed. Rooms sleep up to five, and are tastefully decorated and well appointed. Those on the west side (sixth floor and higher) offer a distant view of Disney and its fireworks displays. The Peabody's signature restaurant, **Dux,** and the **B-Line Diner** are reviewed in chapter 5, "Where to Dine." *Tip:* Your best chance at getting bargain rates is in July and August; that's when the convention trade falls flat, and occupancy drops to as little as 20%.

9801 International Dr. (between Bee Line Expwy. and Sand Lake Rd.), Orlando, FL 32819. ✆ 800/732-2639 or 407/352-4000. Fax 407/354-1424. www.peabodyorlando.com. 891 units. $395–$490 standard room for up to 3; $550–$1,775 suite. Extra person $15. Children 17 and under stay free in parent's room. AE, DC, DISC, MC, V. Free self-parking; valet parking $14. **Amenities:** 3 restaurants; deli; 3 lounges; outdoor heated pool; kids' pool; 4 lighted tennis courts, instruction available (fee); fitness center; spa; Jacuzzi; game room; concierge; guest-services desk; shuttle to WDW and other parks for a fee; business center; shopping arcade; 24-hr. room service; valet; concierge-level rooms. *In room:* A/C, TV, dataport, high-speed Internet access (fee), Web TV (fee), minibar, hair dryer.

Portofino Bay Hotel ★★★ *(Finds*   Universal's first hotel is as grand as Disney's Grand Floridian and is a perfect getaway for couples and adults seeking a romantic, upscale atmosphere. This 6-year-old resort is a replica of the village of Portofino, Italy, complete with a harbor and canals on which boats travel to the theme parks. Old-world

---

(Tips Smaller Homes Away from Home

Several area timeshare resorts rent rooms or apartments to tourists when the owners aren't using them. The **Disney Vacation Club** (✆ 407/939-7775; www.dvcresorts.com) offers studios and one- to two-bedroom apartments at its timeshare resorts. Some have small fridges and microwaves; others have full kitchens. Rates start at about $250 per night and can run up to $1,550 per night. Outside Disney World, per-night rates begin at $200 to $250 per night for one- and two-bedroom apartments with kitchens. As with hotel rooms, you can get major discounts off the rack rates (as low as $70 a night) for these properties if you do your homework. An especially nice choice is **Sheraton's Vistana Resort** (✆ 866/208-0003; www.starwoodvo.com). Another good place to look is the **Marriott Vacation Club** (✆ 800/845-5279; www.vacationclub.com).

One minor caveat: Because each room and apartment that's rented is individually owned, quality can vary, so be sure to specify your exact requirements when booking.

International Drive Area Accommodations

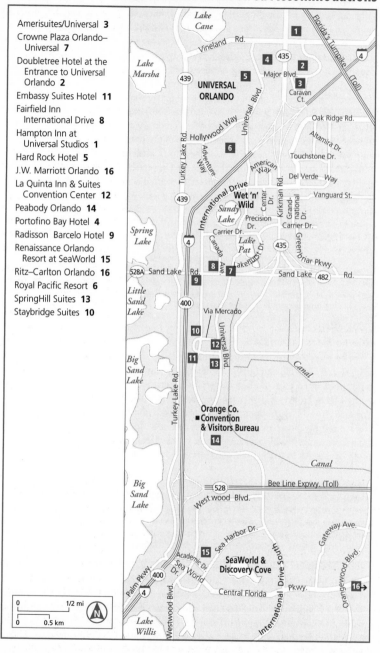

ambience is carried throughout the public areas, restaurants, and rooms. The luxurious rooms are large (with sleep space for five), and hypoallergenic rooms are available. The beds have Egyptian-woven sheets, and the pillows are so soft you'll want to take them home. Thanks to a recent multimillion-dollar renovation, rooms now feature additional amenities and a fresh new sophisticated decor; ask for a view overlooking the piazza and "bay" area. The Portofino doesn't just have swimming pools; its beach pool has a fort with a water slide, and the villa pool rents several private cabanas. The resort's privately run Mandara Spa (www.mandaraspa.com) features a state-of-the-art fitness center and full-service spa. The drawbacks: There are stairs everywhere you turn (be prepared for some exercise), and the sheer size of the resort can make it difficult to find your way around. Look for a review of the resort's premier restaurant, **Bice,** on p. 159.

Note: Guests enjoy special privileges at the Universal Orlando theme parks, including Express-line access to rides and preferred seating at shows and restaurants.

5601 Universal Blvd., Orlando, FL 32819. © **888/322-5541** or 407/503-1000. Fax 407/224-7118. www.loewshotels. com/hotels/Orlando, www.universalorlando.com. 750 units. $264–$488 double; $459–$2,400 suites and villas. Extra person $25. Children 17 and under stay free in parent's room. AE, DC, DISC, MC, V. Self-parking $10; valet parking $17. From I-4, take the Kirkman Rd./Hwy. 435 exit and follow the signs to Universal. Small pets stay free. **Amenities:** 4 restaurants; deli; 3 lounges; 3 outdoor heated pools (1 for concierge-level and suite guests only); kids' pool; fitness center; spa; watersports equipment; kids' club; playground; arcade; salon, concierge; tour desk; free water-taxi and bus transportation to Universal Studios, Islands of Adventure, and CityWalk; free shuttle to SeaWorld; transportation to WDW parks for a fee; business center; shopping arcade; 24-hr. room service; babysitting; guest laundry; concierge-level rooms; valet. *In room:* A/C, TV, high-speed Internet access (fee), fridge and microwave (suites), minibar, hair dryer, iron, safe, video games (fee), CD and DVD players.

EXPENSIVE

Crowne Plaza Universal ⓖ   This sleek, 15-story high-rise is conveniently located a block east of I-Drive and caters primarily to business travelers. Although it's closer to Universal Orlando and SeaWorld (about midway between them), getting to Disney is no problem because the hotel offers free shuttles to the major parks. It's also close to the I-Ride Trolley, which saves shoe leather for those interested in exploring International Drive. The subdued rooms (most inside the Crowne Wing, along with the hotel's meeting space) are well appointed and offer floor-to-ceiling windows. Some of the pricier rooms (with Jacuzzi tubs) are in the circular Atrium Tower, where you can climb to the top in high-speed glass elevators. Facilities include a state-of-the-art fitness center.

7800 Universal Blvd., Orlando, FL 32819. © **866/864-8627** or 407/355-0550. Fax 407/355-0504. www.crowneplaza universal.com. 400 units. $129–$679 double; presidential suites $450–$600. Extra person $20. Children 17 and under stay free in parent's room. AE, DISC, MC, V. Free self-parking; valet parking $8.55. **Amenities:** Restaurant; cafe; lounge; heated pool; fitness center; game room; concierge; tour desk; free transportation to Disney, Universal, and SeaWorld; business center; limited room service; babysitting; laundry service, valet. *In room:* A/C, TV w/video games and pay movies, dataport, high-speed Internet access (fee), coffeemaker, hair dryer, iron, safe, CD player.

Hard Rock Hotel ⓖⓖⓖ *Kids*   You can't get any closer than this to Universal Studios Florida. Opened in 2001, this California mission–style resort sports a rock-'n'-roll theme with rates a shade less expensive than the Portofino (see above). The atmosphere here is also more casual (though with an air of sophistication) and teen-friendly (thanks to its "coolness" quotient) than that of its Universal Orlando sisters. The collection of rock memorabilia found scattered throughout the public areas of the hotel is impressive. The pool area, however, takes center stage: A tremendous oasis of palm trees and rocky landscaping surround a large free-form pool whose most unique

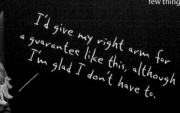

feature is a first-rate underwater sound system that makes sure you won't miss a beat. The rooms and amenities at the Hard Rock are a cut above some of Disney's comparable properties, even the Animal Kingdom Lodge (p. 96). Accommodations are very comfortable, with a sophisticated modern decor. Unfortunately, though the rooms are fairly soundproof, a few notes seep through the walls, so you may want to ask for one that's away from the lobby area. *Tip:* One of the biggest perks of staying on Universal property is that guests get Express-line access to almost every ride at Universal's theme parks, and preferred seating privileges for shows and restaurants.

5000 Universal Blvd., Orlando, FL 32819. © **800/232-7827** or 407/363-8000. Fax 407/224-7118. www.loewshotels. com/hotels/Orlando, www.universalorlando.com. 650 units. $229–$466 double; $409–$2,040 suite. Extra person $25. Children 17 and under stay free in parent's room. AE, DC, DISC, MC, V. Self-parking $10; valet parking $17. From I-4, take the Kirkman Rd./Hwy. 435 exit and follow the signs to Universal. Small pets stay free. **Amenities:** 3 restaurants; grill; 2 lounges; outdoor heated pool; kids' pool; fitness center; kids' club; arcade; playground; concierge; free water-taxi or bus transportation to Universal Studios, Islands of Adventure, and CityWalk; free shuttle to SeaWorld; transportation to WDW parks for a fee; shopping arcade; 24-hr. room service; babysitting; guest laundry; concierge level rooms, valet. *In room:* A/C, TV, high-speed Internet access (fee), minibar, fridge and microwave (suites), hair dryer, iron, safe, CD players, video games (fee).

Renaissance Orlando Resort at SeaWorld ★★

This resort just goes to show that you should never judge a book by its cover. What appears to be a rather blah-looking hotel from the exterior, is absolutely beautiful and inviting on the inside, with luxurious touches throughout. A glass-covered atrium rises high above a stunning indoor courtyard area that's filled with lush gardens, cascading waterfalls, and an elegant free-flight aviary. The tastefully decorated rooms are oversize, providing plenty of space to spread out and relax. Even after extensive renovations to the pool area, a $20-million makeover is currently underway; plans include the installation of an 8,000-square-foot full-service spa. You can't beat the location if you are a fan of SeaWorld—the park is just across from the hotel.

6677 Sea Harbour Dr., Orlando, FL 32821. © **800/327-6677** or 407/351-5555. Fax 407/351-1991. www.renaissance seaworld.com. 778 units. $119–$329 double. Extra person no charge. Children 17 and under stay free in parent's room. AE, DC, DISC, MC, V. Self-parking $7; valet parking $14. From I-4, take the Hwy. 528/Bee Line Expwy. exit east to International Dr., then go south to Sea Harbour Dr. and turn right. Small pets accepted. **Amenities:** 3 restaurants; grill; 3 lounges; outdoor heated pool; kids' pool; golf privileges (fee); 4 lighted tennis courts, tennis instruction (fee); basketball; volleyball; health club; spa; 2 Jacuzzis; sauna; arcade; playground; concierge; tour desk; car-rental desk; transportation to all the parks for a fee; business center; shopping arcade; salon; 24-hr. room service; massage; babysitting; guest laundry; valet. *In room:* A/C, TV w/pay movies, dataport, minibar, fridge (some rooms), hair dryer, safe, PlayStation.

Royal Pacific Resort ★★ (Kids)

The third of Universal Orlando's three resorts features a spectacular beachfront lagoon-style pool. It's lined with palm trees, winding walkways, waterfalls, and an exquisite orchid garden, all giving it a remote island feel (though admittedly the screams emanating from the nearby Islands of Adventure may remind you that you're not). The abandoned floatplane (a scene that reminds more than a few people of *Gilligan's Island*) makes a great backdrop. The rooms, smaller than those at other Universal resorts, are decorated with wood accents and intricate carvings, but are quite plain when lined up against those in comparable Disney resorts. The public areas (whether inside or out), however, are very impressive and well worth exploring. The addition of the Wantilan Luau Pavilion ensures that the resort's weekly luau is now held rain or shine. If you're traveling with young children (6 and under), the Royal Pacific is the best choice at Universal. The big plus: Guests get

---

Finds   Two Grand Hotels

Part of the 500-acre Grande Lakes Resort complex, the **Ritz-Carlton Orlando** 🦀🦀, 4012 Central Florida Pkwy. (📞 **800/682-3665** or 407/206-2400; www.ritzcarlton.com), debuted in July 2003 as the city's newest destination for deep-pocketed travelers. The posh 584-room luxury hotel ($269–$999 double; $499–$6,000 suites) features exquisitely manicured grounds, a lobby designed after an Italian Palazzo, and a 40,000-square-foot, three-level spa with 40 treatment rooms. The spacious rooms at this smoke-free hotel have balconies, flatscreen TVs, hand-painted Italian furniture, and lots of other luxury perks. The level of service is exceptional.

Sharing quarters (and most recreational facilities) with the Ritz at the Grande Lakes development is the less expensive 1,000-room **JW Marriott Orlando** 🦀, 4040 Central Florida Pkwy. (📞 **800/682-9956** or 407/206-2300; www.grandelakes. com). The smoke-free resort ($249–$649 for up to four people per room; $455–$5,999 for suites) has a fabulous 24,000-square-foot **Lazy River** pool that winds through rock formations and small waterfalls (depth 3–5 ft.). The tiptop rooms at the Moorish-themed resort are on par with those in Disney's moderate class. Ask for a west-facing room for the best views.

The major drawback: The hotels are outside of the main tourist areas, a 7- or 8-mile drive southeast of SeaWorld and about the same distance east of Walt Disney World. Free transportation is provided to Universal Orlando, but for the other parks, you're on your own.

Express-line access to almost every ride at Universal Studios Florida and Islands of Adventure, and preferred seating privileges for shows and restaurants.

6300 Hollywood Way, Orlando, FL 32819. 📞 **800/232-7827** or 407/503-3000. Fax 407/503-3202. www.loewshotels. com/hotels/Orlando, www.universalorlando.com. 1,000 units. $199–$428 double; $325–$1,875 suite. Extra person $25. Children 17 and under stay free in parent's room. AE, DC, DISC, MC, V. Self-parking $10; valet parking $17. From I-4, take Exit 75B, Kirkman Rd./Hwy. 435 and follow the signs to Universal. Small pets stay free. **Amenities:** 2 restaurants; 3 lounges; outdoor heated pool; kids' pool; sauna; Jacuzzi; kids' club; arcade; concierge; free water-taxi and bus transportation to Universal Studios, Islands of Adventure, and CityWalk, free shuttle to SeaWorld; transportation to WDW parks for a fee; babysitting; valet; concierge level rooms. *In room:* A/C, TV, dataport, high-speed Internet access (fee), fridge and microwave (suites), coffeemaker, hair dryer, iron, safe.

Staybridge Suites 🦀   Like its Lake Buena Vista cousin (reviewed on p. 109), this hotel is friendly, well run, and neat as a pin. Price and spacious one- and two-bedroom suites (the latter 550 sq. ft., with beds for eight) are two of its biggest pluses. The hotel attracts both leisure and business travelers. Courtyard rooms have balconies. The property is across the street from the Mercado shopping village and its restaurants, and just up the road from Pointe Orlando and its offerings.

8480 International Dr. (between Bee Line Expwy. and Sand Lake Rd.), Orlando, FL 32819. 📞 **800/866-4549** or 407/352-2400. Fax 407/352-4631. www.staybridgesuites.com. 146 units. $129–$269. Rates include continental breakfast. AE, DC, DISC, MC, V. Free self-parking. **Amenities:** Deli; outdoor heated pool; kids' pool; exercise room; Jacuzzi; arcade; guest-services desk; transportation to all theme parks for a fee; complimentary breakfast buffet, business center; laundry service; valet; ATM. *In room:* A/C, TV/VCR, dataport, free high-speed Internet access, pay movies, video library, kitchen, fridge, coffeemaker, iron, safe.

MODERATE

AmeriSuites Universal
It's tough to beat the value and roominess of these kitchenette-equipped suites, especially if your goal is to be very close to the Universal theme parks without having to pay the heftier rates that come with staying on park property. The modern, spacious rooms allow you to stretch out more than in standard hotel/motel accommodations, and the location is especially convenient if Universal Orlando is your target.

5895 Caravan Court, Orlando, FL 32819. ℂ 800/833-1516 or 407/351-0627. Fax 407/331-3317. www.amerisuites. com. 151 units. $139–$179 for up to 4. Rates include free full breakfast. Children 17 and under stay free in parent's room. AE, DC, DISC, MC, V. Free self-parking. **Amenities:** Outdoor heated pool; exercise room; tour desk; free transportation to all theme parks; laundry service; valet. *In room:* A/C, TV/VCR, dataport, high-speed Internet access (fee), kitchenette, coffeemaker, hair dryer, iron, safe.

DoubleTree Hotel at the Entrance to Universal Orlando ⋆
Location alone (right across the street from Universal Orlando) earns this hotel a star. Built for the convention trade, this former Radisson was recently renovated and features reasonably nice rooms. Rooms on the west side of floors 6 through 18 offer views of the Universal parks and CityWalk. DoubleTree's famous chocolate chip cookies are complimentary upon check in (though you may want to buy some to take home because they're *that* good).

5780 Major Blvd., Orlando, FL 32819. ℂ 800/333-3333 or 407/351-1000. Fax 407/363-0106. www.doubletree orlando.com. 742 units. $99–$209 double. Extra person $20. Children 17 and under stay free in parent's room. AE, DC, DISC, MC, V. Free self- or valet parking. **Amenities:** 3 restaurants; grill; lounge; outdoor heated pool; kids' pool; exercise room; Jacuzzi; arcade; free transportation to Universal and SeaWorld parks; transportation to Disney/airport for a fee; salon; limited room service. *In room:* A/C, TV w/pay movies, dataport, high-speed Internet access (fee), coffeemaker, hair dryer, iron.

Embassy Suites Hotel Orlando ⋆
This is another hotel with a run-of-the-mill exterior hiding an impressive interior atrium highlighted by brick and wrought-iron accents, palm trees, and lush foliage. Eight floors of suites surround the atrium, some with balconies overlooking the courtyard below. Suites are fairly spacious, with separate living and sleeping areas. This is one of the few hotels to offer both an indoor and outdoor pool. Another big advantage: the proximity to I-Drive's nightlife, restaurants, and shops. There's a complimentary reception in the evenings.

8978 International Dr., Orlando, FL 32819. ℂ 800/EMBASSY or 407/352-1400. Fax 407/363-1120. www.embassy suites.com. 244 units. $129–$289. Extra person $10. Rates include full breakfast. AE, DC, DISC, MC, V. Free self-parking; valet parking $8. **Amenities:** Restaurant; lounge; 2 heated pools (1 indoor, 1 outdoor); toddler pool; fitness center; game room; guest-services desk; free transportation to Disney; 24-hr. business center; room service; laundry service; valet. *In room:* A/C, TV w/pay movies, dataport, high-speed Internet access (fee), fridge, microwave, coffeemaker, hair dryer, iron.

Hampton Inn at Universal Studios
There's nothing fancy about this simple hotel, but it's in a good location if you plan to spend most of your time at Universal Orlando, which is only 2 blocks away. It's also relatively close to SeaWorld and Downtown Orlando and about 10 miles from Disney. Some rooms have microwaves and refrigerators. Although there's no restaurant on the premises, there are several within walking distance.

5621 Windhover Dr., Orlando, FL 32819. ℂ 800/426-7866, 800/231-8395, or 407/351-6716. Fax 407/363-1711. www.hamptoninn.com. 120 units. $79–$179 double. Extra person $10. Rates include free full breakfast. Children 17 and under stay free in parent's room. AE, DC, DISC, MC, V. Free self-parking. **Amenities:** Outdoor heated pool; exercise room; free transportation to Universal and SeaWorld, transportation for a fee to Disney; laundry service; valet. *In room:* A/C, TV w/pay movies, dataport, high-speed Internet access (fee), coffeemaker, iron.

I-Drive Alternatives

If you're coming into town during peak season and you're having trouble finding a room, the 1,052-room **Wyndham Orlando Resort**, 8001 International Dr. (© **800/WYNDHAM** or 407/351-2420; www.wyndham.com), is an impeccably landscaped property that's good for families and features numerous pools, playgrounds and a kids club for children ages 4 to 12. The 1,338-room **Caribe Royale**, 8101 World Center Dr. (© **800/823-8300** or 407/238-8000; www.caribe royale.com), offers spacious and newly remodeled one-bedroom suites (kitchenettes) and two-bedroom villas (Jacuzzis and full kitchens). The grounds are beautifully landscaped, the pool has cascading waterfalls and a 75-foot water slide, there is a playground nearby, and the service is tops.

La Quinta Inn & Suites Convention Center ⚐   Opened in 1998, this is one of a handful of upscale, moderately priced motels on Universal Boulevard, which runs parallel to (but isn't as congested as) I-Drive. The hotel is aimed at business travelers, but this is Orlando, so families traveling with kids are welcomed with open arms. King rooms are designed for extended stays and have a fridge and microwave. A limited number of two-room suites offering separate living and sleeping areas are available.

8504 Universal Blvd., Orlando, FL 32819. © **800/531-5900** or 407/345-1365. Fax 407/345-5586. www.laquinta. com. 184 units. $75–$125 double. Extra person $7. Rates include continental breakfast. Children 18 and under stay free in parent's room. AE, DC, DISC, MC, V. Free self-parking. Take I-4 to the Sand Lake Rd./Hwy. 482 exit, go east toward Universal, then right. Small pets accepted. **Amenities:** Outdoor heated pool; exercise room; Jacuzzi; transportation to all theme parks for a fee; guest laundry. *In room:* A/C, TV w/pay movies, dataport, free high-speed Internet access, fridge (some rooms), microwave (some rooms), coffeemaker, hair dryer, iron, Nintendo.

Radisson Barcelo Hotel   Like many I-Drive properties, the Radisson offers a good location for people whose vacations center on Universal Orlando or SeaWorld, and a central location for travelers who plan to visit Disney and downtown, too. Rooms are brightly decorated (the Deluxe towers rooms are larger and worth the extra dough) and have refrigerators, but views are basic. Otherwise, you'll be watching traffic on I-4 or I-Drive. As a plus, kids 10 and under eat free with a paying adult at breakfast. Guests may also use the YMCA aquatic facility nearby.

8444 International Dr., Orlando, FL 32819. © **888/380-9696** or 407/345-0505. Fax 407/352-5894. www.radisson-orlando.com. 520 units. $69–$139 double. Extra person $15. Children 17 and under stay free in parent's room. AE, DC, DISC, MC, V. Free self-parking. **Amenities:** Restaurant; grill; lounge; outdoor heated pool; lighted tennis court; bocce court; guest-services desk; free shuttle to Universal Orlando and SeaWorld; transportation to Disney parks for a fee; laundry service; valet. *In room:* A/C, TV w/pay movies and video games, dataport, fridge, microwave, coffeemaker, hair dryer, iron, safe.

SpringHill Suites Orlando Convention Center ⟨Value⟩   This property offers guests a chance to stay near but not in the middle of the I-Drive crowds and traffic. Clean, very spacious suites (about 700 sq. ft., with beds for five and a separate living area) and reasonable rates make this all-suite property worth considering, though you'll have to pay to get to all of the theme parks.

8840 Universal Blvd., Orlando, FL 32819. © **888/287-9400** or 407/345-9073. Fax 407/345-9075. www.springhill suites.com. 167 units. $79–$139 double. Extra person $10. Rates include continental breakfast. Children 17 and under stay free in parent's room. AE, DC, DISC, MC, V. Free self-parking. **Amenities:** Outdoor heated pool; exercise room; Jacuzzi; concierge; transportation to the theme parks for a fee; business center; laundry service; valet. *In room:* A/C, TV w/pay movies, dataport, high-speed Internet access (fee), minifridge, microwave, coffeemaker, hair dryer, iron.

INEXPENSIVE

Fairfield Inn International Drive ★ *Value* If you're looking for I-Drive's best value, it's hard to beat this one. This Fairfield combines a quiet location off the main drag, down-to-earth rates, and a clean, modern motel in one package. It's not only the best in this category, but is arguably a half step ahead of the Hampton in the previous one. The rooms are very comfortable, the staff is friendly, and there are a number of restaurants within walking distance of the hotel.

7495 Canada Ave. (off International Dr. near Sand Lake Rd.), Orlando, FL 32819. (*) **407/351-7000.** Fax 407/351-0052. www.fairfieldinn.com. 200 units. $77–$119 for up to 4. Rates include continental breakfast. AE, DC, DISC, MC, V. Free self-parking. From I-4, take the Sand Lake Rd./Hwy. 482 exit east, then turn east onto Canada Ave. **Amenities:** Outdoor heated pool; game room; guest-services desk; transportation to the parks for a fee; guest laundry; valet. *In room:* A/C, TV w/pay movies, dataport, fridge (some rooms), microwave (some rooms), hair dryer, iron/ironing board, safe.

8 Orlando Bed & Breakfasts

Although most of the properties in Orlando are resorts or chains, there are a few good bed-and-breakfast options. These properties offer a respite from the crowded, run-and-gun world of the theme parks, and they're ideal for couples looking for a little quiet time or romance. Note that most of the inns and B&Bs in Orlando do not accept children—a major selling point for some visitors. If you choose to stay at one of these properties, you'll need a car or some other kind of transportation, because these inns do not provide it. Unless otherwise noted, all B&Bs in this section can be found on the "Accommodations & Dining Elsewhere in Orlando" map on p. 171. You can find other options in the area through **Florida Bed and Breakfast Inns** (© **800/524-1880;** www.florida-inns.com).

EXPENSIVE

Courtyard at Lake Lucerne ★ *Finds* Speaking of romance, you might feel the sting of Cupid's arrows in this downtown hideaway. Each of the Courtyard's buildings is historic. The Art Deco Wellborn, a late-bloomer that arrived in 1946, offers 14 one-bedroom apartments and a honeymoon suite (styles range from Thai to the Fab '50s). The Norment–Parry Inn is an 1883 Victorian-style home with six rooms decorated with English and American antiques; four have sitting rooms, all have private bathrooms. It, too, has a honeymoon suite highlighted by a walnut bed and a Victorian fireplace. The I. W. Phillips House, built in 1919, is reminiscent of old Southern homes with large verandas. Upstairs, there are three suites, one with a whirlpool, all with verandas overlooking the gardens and fountain. Finally, the Dr. Phillips House, built in 1893, made its bed-and-breakfast debut on Valentine's Day 1999 with six impeccably furnished and antique-laden rooms.

211 N. Lucerne Circle E., Orlando, FL 32801. (*) **800/444-5289** or 407/648-5188. Fax 407/246-1368. www.orlando historicinn.com. 30 units. $89–$225 double. Rates include continental breakfast. AE, DC, MC, V. Free self-parking. Take Orange Ave. south; immediately following City Hall (dome building with fountains and glass sculpture), turn left onto Anderson. After 2 lights, at Delaney Ave., turn right. Take first right onto Lucerne Circle. Be aware of one-way streets. Follow the brown "historic inn" signs. Children are permitted. *In room:* A/C, TV.

MODERATE

Veranda Bed & Breakfast *Finds* Located in Thornton Park, this inn near scenic Lake Eola is another option if you want to stay near downtown. Its four buildings date back to the early 1900s. All units (studios to suites) include private bathrooms and entrances; some have garden tubs, balconies, kitchenettes, and four-poster beds. A few of the nicer options include the Washington Suite, which sports a four-poster bed and a Jacuzzi, and the romantic Carriage Suite, which has a four-poster bed and antique claw-foot tub. The two-bedroom, two-bathroom Keylime Cottage ($210) sleeps four and has a full kitchen.

115 N. Summerlin Ave., Orlando, FL 32801. © 800/420-6822 or 407/849-0321. Fax 407/849-0321, ext. 24. www. theverandabandb.com. 12 units. $99–$115 double; $209 cottage. Rates include continental breakfast. AE, DC, DISC, MC, V. From I-4, take Exit 84, Hwy. 50/Colonial Dr., left 1 mile to Summerlin, turn right, and go 1 mile, crossing Robinson St. The inn is 1 block on the left. Children are not permitted. **Amenities:** Outdoor pool; Jacuzzi; laundry service; dry cleaning. *In room:* A/C, TV, dataport, fridge, hair dryer, iron on request.

9 Downtown Orlando

The major reason travelers usually give for staying in downtown Orlando is to avoid the hustle and bustle (and crowds) of the theme park zone. One other plus: Those traveling without children may greatly appreciate the lack of them in the downtown hotels, which generally cater to business travelers.

But if you're traveling in the middle of the peak season, including summer or around the December holidays, you'll likely find yourself bumping into other people no matter where you go. And if you plan to spend most of your days in the theme parks, and nights at Pleasure Island or CityWalk, then you're better off staying in the thick of things. Unless you avoid driving during rush hour from 7 to 9am and 4 to 6pm, you'll likely spend a lot more vacation time on I-4 and its traffic than you'd like. It will also be harder to escape back to your hotel for an afternoon swim or a nap.

In our opinion, unless you're getting a really fabulous discount at one of downtown's many business hotels, there's only one property that really stands out in the area and is worth the schlep.

EXPENSIVE
Westin Grand Bohemian 🌟🌟 *Finds*   Downtown Orlando's jewel opened in spring 2001 with an early-20th-century Euro-Bohemian theme. It caters almost exclusively to the business and romance crowds, which means—much to the satisfaction of the adult guests here—you'll find almost no children on the premises. The comfortable and plush rooms have an Art Deco look with plenty of chrome and reds or purples. The "Heavenly Beds" (firm mattresses, down blankets and comforters, and five pillows) are among the best in Orlando. (You can buy one for $2,200!) The upper floors on the east side overlook the pool; those on the north side face downtown. The classy hotel, which is entirely smoke-free, has more than 100 pieces of 19th- and 20th-century American fine art, and its lounge features a rare Imperial Grand Bösendorfer Piano—one of only two in the world and valued at a cool quarter of a million. The downside: You'll have to pay for transportation to all of the theme parks.

Check out the hotel's location on "Accommodations & Dining Elsewhere in Orlando" map on p. 171.

325 S. Orange Ave. (across from City Hall). © 866/663-0024 or 407/313-9000. Fax 407/313-6001. www.grand bohemianhotel.com. 250 units. $239–$439 for up to 4; extra person $25; $349–$549 suite. AE, DC, DISC, MC, V. Valet parking $19. Take I-4 to the Washington St. exit, merge with W. Robinson/Hwy. 526, then head south on Orange St. The garage is 2 blocks west on Jackson St. **Amenities:** Restaurant; lounge; coffee shop; heated outdoor pool and spa; fitness center; concierge; shuttle to the theme parks for a fee; business center; 24-hr. room service; guest laundry and dry cleaning; concierge-level rooms. *In room:* A/C, TV w/pay movies, dataport, high-speed Internet access (fee), minibar, coffeemaker, hair dryer, iron, safe, CD player, Nintendo (fee).

5

Where to Dine

It should come as no surprise that Orlando has something for everybody when it comes to pleasing your palate, ranging from fast food to five-star restaurants and everything in between. The city overflows with over 5,000 dining options, though it's usually noted for its many theme and chain restaurants. The arrival of the Mouse in Orlando launched an invasion of the area by fast-food joints, mostly in response to the number of families now flocking to see Mickey. Theme restaurants, focusing on everything from race cars and rainforests to superheroes and sporting goods, weren't far behind.

The local dining scene doesn't compare to that found in such metropolitan foodie hot spots as New York, San Francisco, or Las Vegas, but there are certainly more than a few places here that could easily hold their own against the competition (disbelievers can grab a chair at **Emeril's** at CityWalk, or **Victoria & Albert's** at Disney's Grand Floridian Resort & Spa, among others). That said, keep in mind that Orlando is the undisputed king of U.S. family destinations, and restaurants generally do their darnedest to cater to their target audience.

As so many of Central Florida visitors spend the biggest chunk of their time at Disney, a good deal of this chapter deals with the restaurants and eateries at Disney. For those of you who find yourselves beyond the boundaries of Mickey's doorstep, there's no need to worry: I also cover what's cooking at Universal Orlando's best restaurants, the hottest dining spots on International Drive, and a fair share of other area dining rooms.

Note to parents: Keep in mind that most moderate to inexpensive restaurants have kids' menus ($4–$9), and many offer distractions, such as coloring books and crayons, in the hopes it will keep your little ones otherwise occupied until their dinner arrives. If you go to a place catering to children, expect the noise level to be high. They don't take a vacation from squeals of joy or fits of temper, so you shouldn't expect to either. On the plus side, if it's your kids who tend to turn up the volume, it's far more likely that their antics will go unnoticed when there are others around doing the very same things.

If dining with kids isn't your cup of tea, steer clear of any restaurant where Mickey and Minnie stop by to say "hi" during dinner. Character meals, no matter what restaurant they are in, are guaranteed to be filled with families, making them, at times, excruciatingly loud and almost unnerving to those not used to dining in a room full of children. As a general rule, the more expensive your meal, the less likely you'll be dining with a lot of little ones around. So if you prefer to dine in peace—and can afford it—consider a meal at some of the more expensive restaurants in the resorts, on International Drive, or around Orlando proper. *Tip:* Parents in need of a night off from the kids can arrange for in-room babysitting or supervised child care (p. 71) so they too can indulge in one of the area's finer dining options.

For additional online information about area restaurants, visit **www.orlando info.com**, **www.go2orlando.com**, or the websites in the listings that follow.

ADVANCE RESERVATIONS AT WDW RESTAURANTS

Walt Disney World's Advance Reservations (previously Priority Seating) system, while similar to a reservation, is not nearly as rigid. Essentially, the system guarantees that you will get the next available table that will accommodate your party *after* you've arrived at a restaurant (which should be 5–10 min. prior to the time you've reserved). In other words, a table isn't kept empty while the eatery waits for you. As such, it's likely that you'll end up waiting anywhere from 15 to 30 minutes, even if you arrive at the time you scheduled your meal. You can arrange Advance Reservations 180 days in advance at most full-service restaurants in the Magic Kingdom, Epcot, Disney–MGM Studios, Animal Kingdom, Disney resorts, and Downtown Disney. Advance Reservations can also be made for character meals (p. 174) and dinner shows throughout the World. To make arrangements, call ✆ **407/939-3463;** groups of eight or more can also call ✆ **407/939-7707.**

Nighttime dinner-theater shows (see chapter 9, "Walt Disney World & Orlando After Dark") can be booked up to 180 days in advance as well, a notable change from the previous time frame of 2 years. Be aware, however, that these dinner shows require full payment in advance and that cancellations must be made at least 48 hours prior to the time of the show to avoid penalties. *Note:* Since the Advance Reservations phone number was instituted in 1994, it has become much more difficult to obtain a table as a walk-in for the resorts' more popular restaurants. We *strongly* advise you to call as far ahead as possible, especially if you're traveling during the peak seasons. It wouldn't hurt to mark your calendar and enter the phone number into your speed dial either. Amazingly, some restaurants, especially the dinner shows and character meals, can book up quite literally within only a minute or two of the phone lines opening (7am EST) on that 180th day out.

If you don't make your dining plans in advance, you can take your chances by making your Advance Reservations once you have arrived in the parks. In addition to the places listed below, you can always head directly to your desired restaurant to see what's available.

- **In Epcot** at Guest Relations on the East side of Spaceship Earth.
- **In the Magic Kingdom** via the telephones at several locations including the Walt Disney World Railroad station just inside the entrance, and at City Hall near the front of Main Street U.S.A.
- **In Disney–MGM Studios** via the telephones just inside the entrance or at Guest Relations near Hollywood Junction.
- **In Animal Kingdom** at Guest Relations on the left near the entrance. (Note that Rainforest Cafe here is a *verrry* popular place, so the sooner you call for Advance Reservations, the better.)
- In **Downtown Disney** at Guest Services in the Marketplace and at West Side.

Also, keep these restaurant facts in mind:

- *All Florida restaurants* and bars that serve food are **smoke free.**
- The Magic Kingdom (including its restaurants) serves no alcoholic beverages, but liquor is available at Animal Kingdom, Epcot, and Disney–MGM Studios

restaurants and elsewhere in the WDW complex. And the selection of liquors and wines available at many of the hotels is both varied and extensive; Disney World, the largest single-site purveyor of wine in the world, employs more sommeliers than any other organization on the planet—over 500 of them, including one advanced and one master sommelier.

- All sit-down restaurants in Walt Disney World take American Express, Diners Club, Discover, MasterCard, Visa, and the Disney Visa Card.
- Unless otherwise noted, restaurants in the parks **require park admission.**
- Guests staying at Disney resorts and official properties can make restaurant reservations through Guest Services or the concierge.
- Nearly all WDW restaurants with sit-down or counter service offer children's menus with items ranging from $4 to $7, though in a few cases they're $9 to $12. Some include beverages and fries.

1 The Best Dining Bets

It may not have the caliber of restaurants of say, a New York or San Francisco, but Orlando has a few premier offerings that would make any foodie's best list. That said, keep in mind that for the most part Orlando is a family destination first and foremost—and therefore caters mostly to the masses. Here are our picks for the best eating in town.

- **Best for Kids:** Kids adore the meals served up with Disney characters bounding about and there are plenty to choose from throughout the **Walt Disney World** resorts and theme parks. (For the scoop, see "Only in Orlando: Dining with Disney Characters," p. 174.) They also love the eclectic atmosphere, sounds, and visuals of the jungle-themed **Rainforest Cafe** at Downtown Disney Marketplace (© **407/827-8500**) and Animal Kingdom (© **407/938-9100**). Monkey business is strongly encouraged there. If horsing around is more your style, try dining at the **Whispering Canyon Café** (© **407/939-3463**) inside Disney's Wilderness Lodge for some foot-stomping fun.
- **Best Character Meal:** It doesn't get any better than **Chef Mickey's** breakfasts and dinners at the Contemporary Resort (© **407/939-3463**). These "events" have their respective namesake and other characters, but a word of warning: They also attract *up to 1,600 guests* each morning. A close second is a meal at the **Crystal Palace Buffet** (© **407/939-3463**), located in the Magic Kingdom. You will not see Mickey and Minnie, but your kids will be greeted at your table by Winnie the Pooh, Tigger, and some of their pals.
- **Best Spot for a Romantic Dinner: Victoria & Albert's** (© **407/939-3463**) will spoil you with superior service and stylish surroundings. Dinner is an intimate seven-course meal offering some of the finest food around.
- **Best View: Manuel's on the 28th** (© **407/246-6580**), so named because it's on the 28th floor of a downtown bank building, has equally gorgeous views of the setting sun and the downtown skyline. The **California Grill** (© **407/939-3463**), high atop Disney's Contemporary Resort, offers a spectacular view of the Magic Kingdom, as well as a front row seat for the park's nightly fireworks display through its immense floor-to-ceiling windows.
- **Best Wine List:** For something a bit out of the ordinary try **Jiko** (© **407/939-3463**) at Disney's Animal Kingdom Lodge; it features one of the most extensive collections (65 vintages) of South African wines in the country.

- **Best Value:** At **Romano's Macaroni Grill** (© 407/239-6676), the casual yet lively ambience and the northern Italian cuisine score very high, and prices are low, low, low.
- **Best Oriental Cuisine:** The **Mikado Japanese Steakhouse** (© 407/239-4200) in Marriott's Orlando World Center offers a tastier meal, and a more intimate atmosphere than the other Japanese Steakhouses in the area. For Chinese cuisine, head to **Ming Court** (© 407/351-9988), which offers a menu as impressive as its elaborate surroundings. **Emeril's Tchop Chop** (© 407/503-2467) takes your taste buds on a tour of the Pacific Rim islands while its chic and trendy decor is among the most inviting around.
- **Best Barbecue:** Follow your nose to **Bubbalou's Bodacious BBQ** (© 407/628-1212) after catching a whiff of the tangy hickory smoke. It tastes as good as it smells.
- **Best Italian Cuisine:** It's a tossup between **Bice** (© 407/503-1000) at Universal's Portofino Bay Hotel, with its chic yet elegant atmosphere, and the more casual **Pacino's Italian Ristorante** in Kissimmee (© 407/396-8022).
- **Best Seafood:** Of the area's many seafood restaurants, the best around is: **Fulton's Crab House** (© 407/934-2628), which offers a creative menu and a rich wine list. **Todd English's bluezoo** (© 407/934-4644) blends a unique atmosphere with creative seafood dishes to great success.
- **Best Tapas:** **Cafe Tu Tu Tango** (© 407/248-2222) takes the tapas concept to another dimension, serving items ranging from Cajun egg rolls with blackened chicken to alligator bites in a fabulous artist-loft atmosphere.
- **Best Steakhouse:** The steaks, seafood, and poultry served at **Charley's Steakhouse** (© 407/363-0228) are prepared to perfection over a specially designed wood pit, ensuring a delicious dining experience.
- **Best Late-Night Dining:** The trendy **B-Line Diner** (© 407/345-4460) at the Peabody Orlando is open round-the-clock for eclectic fare ranging from steaks to falafel sandwiches to grits and eggs. You won't be able to pass up one of their decadent desserts.
- **Best Spot for Celebrating:** **Emeril's** at Universal's CityWalk (© 407/224-2424) and **Tchop Chop** at Universal's Royal Pacific Resort (© 407/503-2467) are great choices for a high-end special occasion. For the pure party factor, you can't beat **Jimmy Buffett's Margaritaville** (© 407/224-2155) at CityWalk.
- **Best Outdoor Dining:** The terrace at **Artist Point** (© 407/939-3463), the premier restaurant at Disney's Wilderness Lodge, overlooks a lake, waterfall, and scenery evocative of America's national parks. The **Rose & Crown Pub & Dining Room** at Epcot (© 407/939-3463) delivers a front-row seat for the IllumiNations fireworks display.
- **Best Sunday Brunch:** **Atlantis** at the Renaissance Orlando Resort at SeaWorld (© 407/351-5555) serves a champagne brunch in its sun-drenched atrium. Themes change monthly, but the menu usually features such treats as quail, duck, lamb chops, Cornish hen, clams, mussels, snapper, sea bass, sushi, and more. For a themed brunch, the **House of Blues** (© 407/934-2583), at Disney's West Side, has a down-home gospel brunch featuring live foot-stomping music and an array of Southern/Creole vittles. The food is so-so—the same quality of a dinner show, which this is, morning-style. But the entertainment makes it a certifiable winner.

2 Restaurants by Cuisine

AFRICAN

Boma ✦✦✦ (Animal Kingdom Lodge, $$$, p. 150)

Jiko—The Cooking Place ✦✦ (Animal Kingdom Lodge, $$$, p. 151)

AMERICAN

B-Line Diner (International Drive Area, $$, p. 165)

Cinderella's Royal Table ✦ (Magic Kingdom, $$$, p. 140)

Columbia Harbour House ✦ (Magic Kingdom, $, p. 141)

Cosmic Ray's Starlight Café (Magic Kingdom, $, p. 141)

ESPN Club ✦ (Disney's BoardWalk, $$, p. 154)

50's Prime Time Café (Disney–MGM Studios, $$, p. 145)

Hard Rock Cafe (Universal Orlando, $$, p. 161)

Hollywood Brown Derby (Disney–MGM Studios, $$$, p. 144)

Liberty Tree Tavern (Magic Kingdom, $$, p. 141)

Mythos ✦ (Islands of Adventure, $$$, p. 161)

Panera Bread ✦ (Downtown and elsewhere, $$, p. 172)

Pecos Bills ✦ (Magic Kingdom, $, p. 141)

Planet Hollywood (Pleasure Island, $$, p. 155)

Plaza Restaurant (Magic Kingdom, $, p. 144)

Sci-Fi Dine-In Theater Restaurant (Disney–MGM Studios, $$, p. 146)

Toy Story Pizza Planet (Disney–MGM Studios, $, p. 146)

Tusker House (Animal Kingdom, $, p. 147)

BARBECUE

Bubbalou's Bodacious BBQ ✦ (Winter Park, $, p. 173)

Wild Jacks (International Drive, $$, p. 169)

BRITISH

Rose & Crown Pub & Dining Room (Epcot, $$, p. 137)

CALIFORNIA

California Grill ✦✦✦ (Disney's Contemporary Resort, $$$, p. 150)

Pebbles ✦✦ (Lake Buena Vista, $$, p. 158)

Rainforest Cafe ✦ (Downtown Disney Marketplace & Animal Kingdom, $$, p. 147 and p. 156)

Wolfgang Puck Grand Café ✦ (Disney's West Side, $$, p. 157)

CANADIAN

Le Cellier Steakhouse (Epcot, $$, p. 137)

CARIBBEAN

Bahama Breeze ✦ (Lake Buena Vista, International Drive, $$, p. 167)

Jimmy Buffett's Margaritaville (Universal's CityWalk, $$, p. 162)

CHARACTER MEALS

Cape May Café (Disney's Beach Club Resort, $$, p. 175)

Chef Mickey's ✦✦ (Disney's Contemporary Resort, $$, p. 175)

Cinderella's Royal Table ✦ (Magic Kingdom, $$, p. 175)

Crystal Palace Buffet ✦ (Magic Kingdom, $$, p. 176)

Donald's Prehistoric Breakfastosaurus ✦ (Animal Kingdom, $$, p. 176)

Garden Grill ✦ (Epcot, $$, p. 176)

Liberty Tree Tavern (Magic Kingdom, $$, p. 176)

1900 Park Fare ✦ (Disney's Grand Floridian Resort & Spa, $$, p. 176)

'Ohana Character Breakfast (Disney Polynesian Resort, $$, p. 176)

Princess Storybook Dining (Epcot, $$, p. 177)

Key to Abbreviations: $$$$ = Very Expensive $$$ = Expensive $$ = Moderate $ = Inexpensive

CHINESE

Lotus Blossom Café (Epcot, $, p. 139)

Ming Court ✿ (International Drive, $$, p. 168)

Nine Dragons (Epcot, $$, p. 137)

CUBAN

Bongo's Cuban Cafe (Disney's West Side, $$, p. 156)

Colombia Restaurant (Celebration, $$, p. 173)

Rolando's ✿ (Casselberry, $$, p. 172)

The Samba Room ✿ (International Drive, $$, p 168)

FOOD COURT

Sunshine Seasons in the Land (Epcot, $, p. 139)

FRENCH

Citricos ✿ (Disney's Grand Floridian Resort & Spa, $$$$, p. 148)

Les Chefs de France (Epcot, $$$, p. 134)

GERMAN

Biergarten (Epcot, $$, p. 136)

Sommerfest (Epcot, $, p. 139)

INTERNATIONAL

Anaelle & Hugo ✿ (Sand Lake Road, $$$, p. 166)

Café Tu Tu Tango ✿✿ (International Drive, $$, p. 167)

Dux ✿✿ (International Drive, $$$$, p. 164)

Hue—A Restaurant ✿✿ (Downtown, $$$, p. 170)

La Coquina ✿ (Lake Buena Vista, $$$$, p. 157)

Manuel's on the 28th ✿✿✿ (Downtown Orlando, $$$$, p. 169)

The Plantation Room (Celebration, $$$, p. 173)

Seasons 52 ✿ (Sand Lake Road, $$$, p. 166)

Victoria & Albert's ✿✿✿ (Disney's Grand Floridian Resort & Spa, $$$$, p. 148)

ITALIAN

Bice ✿ (Universal's Portofino Bay Hotel, $$$$, p. 159)

Carrabbas ✿ (Kissimmee, $$, p. 170)

L'Originale Alfredo di Roma (Epcot, $$$, p. 135)

Mama Melrose's Ristorante Italiano (Disney–MGM Studios, $$, p. 145)

Pacino's Italian Ristorante ✿ (Kissimmee, $$, p. 170)

Pastamore Ristorante (Universal's CityWalk, $$, p. 162)

Portobello Yacht Club ✿ (Pleasure Island, $$$, p. 155)

Romano's Macaroni Grill ✿ (Lake Buena Vista, $, p. 158)

Tony's Town Square Restaurant (Magic Kingdom, $$$, p. 140)

JAPANESE

Mikado Japanese Steakhouse ✿✿ (Lake Buena Vista, $$$, p. 170)

Ran-Getsu of Tokyo (International Drive, $$$, p. 165)

Tempura Kiku (Epcot, $$$, p. 135)

Teppanyaki Dining Room (Epcot, $$$, p. 136)

Yakitori House (Epcot, $, p. 139)

MEDITERRANEAN

Portobello Yacht Club ✿ (Pleasure Island, $$$, p. 155)

Spoodles ✿ (Disney's BoardWalk, $$$, p. 152)

MEXICAN

Amigo's Original Tex-Mex (International Drive, $$, p. 164)

Cantina de San Angel (Epcot, $, p. 138)

San Angel Inn ✿ (Epcot, $$, p. 138)

MISSISSIPPI DELTA

House of Blues (Disney's West Side, $$, p. 156)

MOROCCAN

Marrakesh ✿ (Epcot, $$$, p. 135)

NEW ORLEANS

Boatwright's Dining Hall (Disney's Port Orleans Resort, $$, p. 153)

Emeril's ✸✸ (Universal's CityWalk, $$$$, p. 160)

NORWEGIAN

Akershus Royal Banquet Hall (Epcot, $$, p. 136)

Kringla Bakeri og Kafe (Epcot, $, p. 138)

PACIFIC RIM

Emeril's Tchoup Chop ✸✸✸ (Universal's Royal Pacific Resort, $$$, p. 160)

'Ohana ✸ (Disney's Polynesian Resort, $$, p. 154)

Roy's Restaurant ✸ (International Drive, $$$, p. 165)

SEAFOOD/STEAKS/CHOPS

Artist Point ✸✸ (Disney's Wilderness Lodge, $$$, p. 149)

Atlantis ✸ (International Drive Area, $$$$, p. 162)

Cape May Café (Disney's Beach Club Resort, $$, p. 153)

Celebration Town Tavern (Celebration, $$$, p. 173)

Columbia Harbour House ✸ (Magic Kingdom, $, p. 141)

Coral Reef (Epcot, $$$, p. 134)

The Crab House (Lake Buena Vista, $$, p. 158)

Fishbones (International Drive area, $$, p. 167)

Flying Fish Café ✸ (Disney's Board-Walk, $$$, p. 151)

Fulton's Crab House ✸✸ (Downtown Disney Marketplace, $$$$, p. 155)

Hemingway's (Lake Buena Vista, $$$, p. 158)

Kres Chophouse ✸ (Downtown, $$$, p. 170)

Mythos ✸ (Islands of Adventure, $$$, p. 161)

The Palm (Universal's Hard Rock Hotel, $$$$, p. 160)

Texas De Brazil (International Drive, $$$, p. 164)

Timpano Italian Chophouse ✸ (Sand Lake Road, $$$, p. 166)

Todd English's bluezoo ✸✸✸ (WDW Dolphin, $$$, p. 152)

Yachtsman Steakhouse ✸ (Disney's Yacht Club Resort, $$$$, p. 149)

Wild Jacks (International Drive, $$, p. 169)

TAPAS

Café Tu Tu Tango ✸✸ (International Drive, $$, p. 167)

Spoodles ✸ (Disney's BoardWalk, $$$, p. 152)

THAI

Siam Orchid ✸ (International Drive Area, $$, p. 169)

VIETNAMESE

Little Saigon ✸ (Downtown Orlando, $, p. 173)

---

3 Places to Dine in Walt Disney World

From fast food on the fly to fine dining establishments, there are literally hundreds of restaurants scattered throughout Walt Disney World, including those at the theme parks (Epcot, Magic Kingdom, Disney–MGM Studios, and Animal Kingdom), the Disney resorts, and the "official" hotels. And those totals don't include the eateries located throughout the Downtown Disney areas of Pleasure Island, West Side, and the Marketplace, some of which are listed in the Lake Buena Vista section later in this chapter. As a general rule, the food at Disney is decent enough, though only a small handful of the restaurants would truly qualify as gourmet. Portions are generally large, practically ensuring that you'll never walk away hungry, though prices match portion

Tips **Special Tastes**

When it comes to eating at Disney, just because something's not on the menu doesn't mean it's not available. Looking for kosher food? Worried WDW can't entertain your vegetarian taste buds? What about low sodium, low sugar, or fat-free diets? Disney can usually handle these and other lifestyle diets as well as other special dietary requirements (meals for those with allergies or a lactose intolerance) at any of their full-service restaurants as long as guests give Disney advance notice—3 days is suggested to accommodate special dietary needs, while at least 24 hours is necessary for lifestyle diets. This holds true for other dining requests, too. If you are headed to one of the resort's restaurants and know your kids may have a tough time with the menu, chicken nuggets and some other kid-friendly items can be requested in advance. It's easiest to make special requests when you make your Advance Reservations (© **407/939-3463**) or, if you're staying at a Disney resort, by stopping by the Lobby Concierge desk.

sizes accordingly. Be prepared to spend a rather hefty amount each day for just a few meals, a snack, and a drink (or two). If you have kids, sharing may be a good option, especially with very young children who tend not to eat so much when on the go. For those unwilling to share, sit-down and counter-service eateries, at least in the theme parks, do offer pint-size platters in the $4 to $9 range (though some may cost up to $12). Another option is to order a la carte, but don't expect to see this listed as an option on the restaurant menus—you have to ask.

The prices for meals at Orlando restaurants—except at theme parks and other attractions—are no more exorbitant than you'd find anywhere else. The better the restaurant, the higher the price you can expect to pay (though you shouldn't necessarily consider a restaurant's pricing a benchmark of its quality). To help you out a bit, the restaurants in this chapter have been categorized by **the price of an average entree** per person. In this chapter, restaurants in the Inexpensive category charge under $10 for an entree; those in the Moderate category charge anywhere from $11 to $20. Expensive restaurants will set you back $21 to $30, and Very Expensive restaurants will top that, sometimes by a rather large margin. Do note that when you toss in drinks, appetizers, side dishes, desserts, and the tip, the final tally at even a moderate restaurant can get rather high. Be sure to budget accordingly.

One last note: The restaurants we list in this chapter occasionally change menus (sometimes weekly, in some cases even daily). So items we feature here may not necessarily be on the menu when you visit. And, as entrees vary, so do prices.

That said, it's time to divide and conquer.

IN EPCOT

The world is at your feet at Epcot, quite literally, in fact. In addition to the eateries found at Future World, the World Showcase features several ethnic cuisines from around the globe, all served in some rather impressive settings. Though dining at one of the World Showcase pavilions is a traditional part of the Epcot experience, we remind you that many of the following establishments are rather overpriced when compared to an equivalent restaurant beyond the park's boundaries. Unless your budget is unlimited, you may want to consider the more casual counter-service eateries located

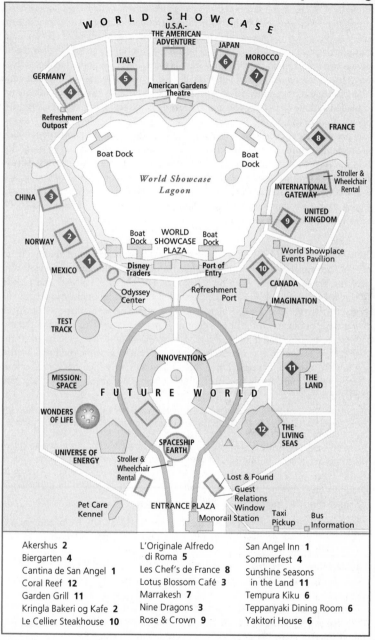

Akershus **2**	L'Originale Alfredo di Roma **5**	San Angel Inn **1**
Biergarten **4**		Sommerfest **4**
Cantina de San Angel **1**	Les Chef's de France **8**	Sunshine Seasons in the Land **11**
Coral Reef **12**	Lotus Blossom Café **3**	
Garden Grill **11**	Marrakesh **7**	Tempura Kiku **6**
Kringla Bakeri og Kafe **2**	Nine Dragons **3**	Teppanyaki Dining Room **6**
Le Cellier Steakhouse **10**	Rose & Crown **9**	Yakitori House **6**

throughout the park and save the sit-down service for somewhere else. These informal dining spots don't require Advance Reservations (for details, check the Epcot guide map that you picked up upon entering the park) and often go overlooked. If you simply can't resist a more formal meal (and it is difficult, at times), try eating lunch at the full-service restaurants when the price for a meal is much lower. Almost all of the establishments listed here serve lunch and dinner daily (hours vary with park hours), and, unless otherwise noted, they offer children's meals. All but one or two require theme-park admission and the $9 parking fee, too. These restaurants are located on the "Epcot Dining" map on p. 133.

Note: Because the clientele at even the fanciest Epcot World Showcase restaurant comes directly from the park, you don't have to dress up for dinner, but do bring along a sweater or sweatshirt to ward off the sometimes chilly indoor temperatures. **Advance Reservations,** which reserves your place but not a specific table, is available at all WDW sit-down restaurants and is strongly recommended. Otherwise, the chances of getting a table without a wait—often a long wait—are pretty slim. Call ℂ **407/939-3463** for Advance Reservations.

EXPENSIVE

Coral Reef SEAFOOD   All of the seating at this aptly named establishment surrounds a **5.6-million-gallon aquarium** filled with tropical fish and a coral reef. While some of Disney's denizens swim by, songs such as Debussy's "La Mer" and Handel's "Water Music" softly play in the background. Tiered seating, mainly in semicircular booths, allow everyone a good view. You'll be provided with pictorial fish listings so you can put names on the faces swimming by your table. This is one of the most popular restaurants in all of the parks, especially with kids—what could be better than a fish tank of tremendous proportions to entertain tinier tots while you eat? The menu primarily features fresh seafood and shellfish, including grilled mahimahi, Florida snapper, and salmon. A selection of landlubber fare is available as well. Wine is available by the glass.

Living Seas Pavilion, Future World. ℂ **407/939-3463.** www.disneyworld.com. Advance Reservations. Main courses $13–$22 lunch, $17–$31 dinner. AE, DC, DISC, MC, V. Daily 11:30am–3pm and 4:30pm–park closing. Parking $9.

Les Chefs de France TRADITIONAL FRENCH   Focusing on nouvelle cuisine, Les Chefs de France is one of the most expensive restaurants at Epcot, but not

---

Tips On a Budget?

Magic Kingdom: Try a turkey leg from a cart ($2.50–$4.50), fruits and snacks ($1–$3) at the Liberty Square Market, a hot dog at Casey's ($4), pastries at the Main Street Bakery ($2–$4), or a frozen fruity treat at Aloha Isle ($2–$4).

MGM Studios: Grab a burger and fries ($2–$7) at the Backlot Express, sweets ($2) at the Starring Rolls Bakery, or fruits and snacks ($2–$4) at Anaheim Produce.

Animal Kingdom: The stir-fry and pot stickers at the Chakranadi Chicken Shop ($4–$6) are a good bet, as are the pizzas at Pizzafari ($6) and sweet treats at the Kusafiri Coffee ($2–$4).

Epcot: Head to the Kringla Bakeri og Café for dessert ($3–$4), or snack on a bratwurst or apple strudel at Sommerfest ($4–$6).

without good reason. An eye-catching, domed-glass exterior hides an intimate Art Nouveau interior, filled with candelabras and glass-and-brass partitions. The addition of an outdoor dining area, previously the Au Petite Café, adds to the authentic Brasserie atmosphere. You can credit three internationally acclaimed chefs—Paul Bocuse, Roger Verge, and Gaston LeNotre—with the menu here, which combines fresh Florida ingredients with a good dose of French imports. Light sauces (when compared to more traditional French cooking, that is) complement such tasty entrees as sautéed chicken with wild mushrooms, and Mediterranean seafood casserole. A substantial wine list complements the menu, and the desserts and pastries are among the best in the World. The service, however, can get a bit lackluster when the restaurant is busy. If a slightly more formal setting (and a pricier dinner) is what you're seeking, try the **Bistro de Paris,** just upstairs.

France Pavilion, World Showcase. ⓒ 407/939-3463. www.disneyworld.com. Advance Reservations. Main courses $10–$18 lunch, $16–$28 dinner. AE, DC, DISC, MC, V. Daily noon–3pm and 5pm–1 hr. before park closes. Parking $9.

L'Originale Alfredo di Roma *(Overrated)* SOUTHERN ITALIAN   It may be the most popular restaurant in Epcot. L'Originale is actually L'Replica of Alfredo de Lelio's eatery in Rome, and the menu includes his celebrated fettuccine, which is dished out in an exhibition kitchen. Fresh pastas and traditional Italian favorites dominate the menu, though there are pork, veal, seafood, and chicken dishes available as well. The wine list is reasonably extensive. The dining room noise level can be quite high, so if you want a quieter meal, and a view of the fountains and statues, ask for a seat on the veranda. The restaurant itself is elegant yet welcoming, filled with tile accents, and rich warm earth tones; the music of strolling musicians also occasionally fills the air.

Italy Pavilion World Showcase. ⓒ **407/939-3463** or 407/827-8418. www.disneyworld.com. Advance Reservations. Main courses $11–$23 lunch, $19–$30 dinner. AE, DC, DISC, MC, V. Daily noon–park closing. Parking $9.

Marrakesh ★ *(Finds)* MOROCCAN   This unique dining spot exemplifies the spirit of Epcot more than any other restaurant. The restaurant's hand-set mosaic tiles, latticed shutters, and painted ceiling represent some 12 centuries of Arabic design. Exquisitely carved faux ivory archways frame the dining area. Unfortunately many guests shy away mistakenly thinking the cuisine's just too exotic—don't be put off. The menu features marinated beef shish kabob; braised chicken with green olives, garlic, and lemon; and a medley of seafood, chicken, and lamb. Most entrees come with the national dish, couscous (steamed semolina with veggies). If you can't decide what you want, sampler platters allowing you a taste of everything are available. Belly dancers and musicians entertain you while you dine. There's a small selection of wine and beer.

Morocco Pavilion, World Showcase. ⓒ **407/939-3463.** www.disneyworld.com. Advance Reservations. Main courses $15–$20 lunch, $18–$27 dinner; $32–$35 prix fixe. AE, DC, DISC, MC, V. Daily noon–park closing. Parking $9.

Tempura Kiku JAPANESE   Only 25 guests can sit around the central counter at this smallest of Japan's eateries, but if you get a seat, you will enjoy the tempura-battered shrimp, chicken, scallops, or beef. While the portions may be small, they are usually quite tasty. Tempura Kiku also serves sushi, sashimi, Kirin beer, plum wine, and sake, along with a handful of specialty drinks.

Japan Pavilion, World Showcase. ⓒ **407/939-3463.** www.disneyworld.com. Advance Reservations for teppanyaki; reservations not accepted at tempura counter. Main courses $9–$13 lunch, $13–$25 dinner. AE, DC, DISC, MC, V. Daily 11am–1 hr. before park closes. Parking $9.

Fun Fact **By the Numbers . . .**

Walt Disney World hosts millions of people each year, and those millions of people eat . . . a lot! Every year the Mouse serves up over 10,000 dessert souf-flés at Victoria and Albert's and 31,000 Cobb salads at the Hollywood Brown Derby. Each day 720 pounds of pasta is passed out at Mama Melrose's. Inside the theme parks, Disney annually dispenses 1.6 million turkey legs, 2.6 million chocolate-covered Mickey Mouse ice-cream bars, 322,000 pounds (or 5 million bags) of popcorn, and more than a million pounds of watermelon. Wow!

Teppanyaki Dining Room JAPANESE   If you've been to any of the Japanese steakhouse chains (teppanyakis), you know the drill: Diners sit around large grill tables while white-hatted chefs rapidly dice, slice, stir-fry, and occasionally launch a morsel or two onto your plate with amazing skill. Unfortunately, the culinary acrobat-ics here are better than the cuisine, which is rather average. (For a real treat, try the Mikado Japanese Steakhouse reviewed on p. 170.) Expect entrees to have chicken, steak, shrimp, scallops, lobster, or a combination. Miso soup, a small salad with gin-ger dressing, stir-fried veggies, and white rice accompany every meal, though you should opt for the fried rice—it's a much better choice—even if it does cost extra. Like Tempura Kiku (see above), Kirin beer, plum wine, and sake are served. Diners here sit at communal tables, making this a good bet for people traveling alone. It's also a lively and entertaining experience for kids. Even with five teppan rooms the restaurant is often filled to capacity, so be sure to make Advance Reservations if you plan on din-ing here for dinner.

Japan Pavilion, World Showcase. ✆ **407/939-3463**. www.disneyworld.com. Advance Reservations. Main courses $14–$35 lunch, $16–$35 dinner. AE, DC, DISC, MC, V. Daily 11am–1 hr. before park closes. Parking $9.

MODERATE

Akershus Royal Banquet Hall NORWEGIAN   This restaurant, set inside a re-cre-ated 14th century castle, now features Princess Storybook character meals for breakfast, lunch, and dinner. Here you can sample from an all-you-can eat feast of traditional Norwegian fare, making it a bargain for big eaters. It is also reasonably good food, though some diners will find it difficult to adapt to Scandinavian taste. An impressive smorgasbord of *smavarmt* (hot) and *koldtbord* (cold) dishes, including cured salmon with spicy mustard, poached cod, braised lamb and cabbage, and venison stew are among the choices at lunch and dinner. Kids can choose from more familiar options such as grilled chicken, pasta, hot dogs, and turkey sandwiches. The biggest draws are the Disney princesses (excluding Cinderella) that make their way around the hall, stop-ping at each table to say hello. The staff is friendly, and the white-stone interior, beamed ceilings, leaded-glass windows, and archways add to the authentic atmosphere. Norwegian beer and aquavit complement a list of French and California wines. *Note:* The popular Princess breakfast (p. 177) includes primarily American fare.

Norway Pavilion, World Showcase. ✆ **407/939-3463**. www.disneyworld.com. Advance Reservations. Character breakfast adult $23, child $13; character lunch adult $25, child $14; character dinner adult $29, child $14. AE, DC, DISC, MC, V. Daily 8:30–10am, 11:40am–3pm and 4:20–8:30pm. Parking $9.

Biergarten GERMAN   The Biergarten, with its festive atmosphere, feels like a Bavarian village at Oktoberfest. A working water wheel and geranium-filled flower boxes adorn the Tudor-style houses that line the dining area. An oompah band entertains with their accordions and cowbells, and guests are encouraged to dance and sing along. The all-you-can-eat buffet is filled with Bavarian fare (assorted sausages, pork schnitzel, sauerbraten, spaetzle, and sauerkraut), as well as rotisserie chicken, salmon, and trout. Beck's and Kirschwasser—served in immense steins—are both on tap for adults.

Germany Pavilion, World Showcase. ✆ 407/939-3463. www.disneyworld.com. Advance Reservations. Lunch buffet adult $16, child $8; dinner buffet adult $21, child $9. AE, DC, DISC, MC, V. Daily noon–3:45pm and 4pm–park closing. Parking $9.

Le Cellier Steakhouse CANADIAN   This restaurant's French Gothic facade and steeply pitched copper roofs lend it a castlelike ambience. The lantern-lit dining room resembles a wine cellar, and you'll sit in tapestry-upholstered chairs under vaulted stone arches. If you're in the mood for steak, this is the right place; offerings include the usual range of cuts. Options include a herb-crusted prime rib with a veal demi glace, and a seared king salmon with a maple and ginger glaze, among others. The lunch menu features lighter fare, including sandwiches and salads. Wash down your meal with a Canadian wine or choose from a selection of Canadian beers; for an after-dinner treat, try a Canadian ice wine.

Canadian Pavilion, World Showcase. ✆ 407/939-3463. www.disneyworld.com. Advance Reservations. Main courses $10–$22 lunch, $13–$41 dinner. AE, DC, DISC, MC, V. Daily 11:30am–3pm and 4pm–park closing. Parking $9.

Nine Dragons REGIONAL CHINESE   When it comes to decor, Nine Dragons shines with carved rosewood furnishings and inlaid ceilings. Some windows overlook a lagoon. But (is there an echo?) the food doesn't match its surroundings. Main courses feature Mandarin, Shanghai, Cantonese, and Szechuan cuisines, but portions are small and the prices are high, especially when compared to Chinese restaurants elsewhere. The dishes include spicy beef stir-fried with squash in *sha cha* sauce; lightly breaded lemon chicken; and a casserole of lobster, shrimp, and scallops sautéed with ginger and scallions. Groups that don't mind sharing can try the two-person and four-person sampler plates that offer a chance to try a bit of everything. Chinese and California wines are offered.

China Pavilion, World Showcase. ✆ 407/939-3463. www.disneyworld.com. Advance Reservations. Main courses $13–$20 lunch, $13–$39 dinner; $30–$44 sampler for 2, $60 sampler for 4. AE, DC, DISC, MC, V. Daily 11:30am–park closing. Parking $9.

Rose & Crown Pub & Dining Room BRITISH   Visitors from the U.K. flock to this spot, where English folk music and the occasionally saucy server entertain you as you feast your eyes and palate on a short but traditional menu. It beckons with cod and chips wrapped in newspaper, bangers and mash, prime rib with Yorkshire pudding, and, the best of the bunch, an English pie sampler (pork and cottage, and chicken and

---

Tips **Pint-Size & Picky?**

Traveling with less-than-adventurous eaters? WDW has plenty of familiar favorites for little ones more willing to ride the roller coasters than try any unfamiliar foods. Topping the menus are PB&J, pizza, chicken nuggets, grilled cheese sandwiches, burgers, hot dogs, and french fries. Even picky eaters will find plenty to please their palates.

leek). The interior has dark oak wainscoting, beamed Tudor ceilings, and a belly-up bar. Speaking of the bar, it features lighter fare such as sausage rolls, Cornish pasties, and a Stilton cheese and fruit plate. Wash it down with a pint of Irish lager, Bass Ale, or Guinness Stout (the pub has an ale warmer to make sure Guinness is served at 55°, just like its British guests prefer). If you only want to grab a pint or a snack at the bar, you don't need Advance Reservations.

Note: The outdoor tables, weather permitting, offer a fantastic view of IllumiNations (p. 229). These seats are first-come, first-served, so ask the hostess when you arrive if a patio table is available.

Tip: If you're in a hurry, you can grab some tasty fish (cod) and chips to go at Harry Ramsden's, a small quick-service kiosk adjoining the pub.

United Kingdom Pavilion, World Showcase. ② 407/939-3463. www.disneyworld.com. Advance Reservations for dining room, not for pub. Main courses $13–$16 lunch, $15–$27 dinner. AE, DC, DISC, MC, V. Daily 11am–1 hr. before park closes. Parking $9.

San Angel Inn ⓡ MEXICAN   It's always night at the San Angel, where you can dine under starry skies (a la Disney) and feast on some of the best south-of-the-border cuisine in all of the theme parks. The restaurant offers one of the best (and most romantic) atmospheres around. Against the backdrop of the marketplace, candlelit tables under star-lit skies set the mood, and the menu delivers reasonably authentic food—don't expect to find Americanized hard-shell tacos and nachos here. *Mole poblano* (chicken simmered in a combination of chile, green tomatoes, ground tortillas, 11 spices, and a hint of chocolate) is a popular choice. Another favorite: *filete motuleño* (grilled beef tenderloin served over black beans, melted cheese, pepper strips, and fried plantains—a sweet, banana-like fruit). The occasional rumble of a volcano and the sounds of the distant songbirds can be heard as you wait for your dinner— you may find yourself singing right along if you've tried too many margaritas or had more than your limit of Dos Equis.

Mexico Pavilion, World Showcase. ② 407/939-3463. www.disneyworld.com. Advance Reservations. Main courses $12–$19 lunch, $18–$24 dinner. AE, DC, DISC, MC, V. Daily 11:30am–park closing. Parking $9.

INEXPENSIVE

Cantina de San Angel MEXICAN   Counter-service eateries are the most common places to grab a bite in the parks, and this one's a good notch above Taco Bell. Come here for a decent burrito, taco, or churro on the fly. Located just across from the San Angel Inn, a seat at one of the umbrella-shaded tables offers a good view of the lagoon. You can also grab a Dos Equis or frozen margarita.

Mexico Pavilion, World Showcase. ② 407/939-3463. www.disneyworld.com. No Advance Reservations. Meals $7–$8. AE, DC, DISC, MC, V. Daily 11:30am–1 hr. before park closes. Parking $9.

Kringla Bakeri og Kafe NORWEGIAN   The lunch-pail crowd loves this combination cafe-bakery. Grab-and-go options include a plate of smoked salmon and scrambled eggs, and smoked ham and Jarlsberg cheese sandwiches, but it's the array of tempting pastries, cakes, cookies, and waffles with strawberry preserves that bring in the majority. Sit in the small, open-air seating area (just beyond the door, adjacent to the Stave Church) and let your kids work off excess energy at the Viking ship. Wine is sold by the glass.

Norway Pavilion, World Showcase. ② 407/939-3463. www.disneyworld.com. No Advance Reservations. Sandwiches and salads $4–$10. Treats $2–$6. AE, DC, DISC, MC, V. Daily 11am–park closing. Parking $9.

Tips Your Just Desserts

After a day of pounding theme park pavement, a sweet treat is just the ticket. Just some of Disney's bestsellers include a warm berry cobbler (Artist Point), Strawberry Napoleon (Flying Fish Café), old-fashioned s'mores (50's Prime Time Café), Jack Daniel's mousse cake (Yachtsman Café), Key lime pie (Olivia's Café), grapefruit cake (The Hollywood Brown Derby), and a satiny crème brûlée (Disney's Grand Floridian). In their efforts to satisfy your sweet tooth, Disney's pastry chefs used just over 700,000 pounds of sugar and 300,000 pounds of chocolate in a single year.

Lotus Blossom Café CHINESE   If you've in a hurry but still in the mood for some good Chinese, this counter-service stop offers fast-food favorites such as stir-fry, egg rolls, hot-and-sour soup, sweet and sour chicken, and fried rice. There's a small, covered outdoor patio, though the decor is not nearly as ornate as that of its neighbor, the Nine Dragons. Chinese beer and wine are available.

China Pavilion, World Showcase. ✆ 407/939-3463. www.disneyworld.com. No Advance Reservations. Meals $5–$7. AE, DC, DISC, MC, V. Daily 11am–park closing. Parking $9.

Sommerfest GERMAN   At the rear of the Germany pavilion, this outdoor eatery's quick-bite menu includes bratwurst and frankfurter sandwiches (one is still a hot dog) with sauerkraut. The black forest cake and apple strudel go nicely with a glass of German wine or a Beck's beer.

Germany Pavilion, World Showcase. ✆ 407/939-3463. No Advance Reservations. All meals under $6. AE, DC, DISC, MC, V. Daily 11am–park closing. Parking $9.

Sunshine Seasons in the Land *Value* FOOD COURT   This moderately upscale food court, thanks to a recent remodel, features a very contemporary earthy decor (continuing the look and feel of the intricate mosaic leading to its entrance). The large open seating area is separated into smaller sections by decorative partitions; open to the second story, it retains an airy feel. The food isn't gourmet, but of all the cafeterias and counter-service stops in the World, Sunshine Seasons has the most diversity because it is five walk-ups in one. It's especially good if you're traveling with kids who possess finicky (and varied) palates; it's often crowded with families for that very reason. There's an Asian Wok shop (stir-fry and barbecue), a wood-fired grill (Atlantic Salmon), a sandwich shop (black-forest ham, salami, Cuban), and a soup and salad counter (with veggies from the Land's own gardens). There's also a small bakery. An open kitchen allows everyone to watch the behind-the-scenes action. Wine by the glass, frosty drafts, and bottled beer are also available.

Land Pavilion, Future World. ✆ 407/939-3463. www.disneyworld.com. No Advance Reservations. Meals $6–$10. AE, DC, DISC, MC, V. 11am–park closing. Parking $9.

Yakitori House JAPANESE   Resembling the teahouse of the Imperial Summer Palace, this small eatery offers a menu of *yakitori* (skewered chicken with soy sauce and sesame), teriyaki chicken and beef, and a handful of other beef, chicken, and seafood items. The food is reasonably good though a little on the blah side, and portions are smaller than at many other Disney restaurants. There's seating both indoors and out, but no matter where you dine, you'll be overlooking tranquil Japanese gardens and a gentle waterfall.

Japan Pavilion, World Showcase. ℂ 407/939-3463. www.disneyworld.com. No Advance Reservations. Meals $5–$8. AE, DC, DISC, MC, V. 11am–park closing. Parking $9.

IN THE MAGIC KINGDOM

In addition to the restaurants mentioned below, there are plenty of fast-food outlets located throughout the park. You may find, however, that a quiet sit-down meal is an essential but all-too-brief way to get away from the day's activities. The restaurants listed below can all be found on the "Walt Disney World & Lake Buena Vista Dining" map on p. 142 and (more specifically) "The Magic Kingdom" map on p. 192. And remember—Magic Kingdom restaurants *don't serve alcohol.*

For information on Magic Kingdom's Crystal Palace restaurant, see "Only in Orlando: Dining with Disney Characters," at the end of this chapter.

EXPENSIVE

Cinderella's Royal Table ⭐ AMERICAN   You'll be greeted by handmaidens before making your way inside this royal restaurant—by far the most popular place to dine in the Magic Kingdom. Those who enter are usually swept off their feet as they're transported back to a time when medieval kings and queens reigned (a feeling that's helped along by the Gothic interior, which includes leaded-glass windows, stone floors, and high-beamed ceilings). The servers treat you like a lord or lady (we're not kidding, that's how they'll address you) and the menu has fetching names, but the fine print reveals traditional entrees. Pan-seared salmon, braised lamb, and roasted prime rib are just a sampling of the choices.

Upon your arrival the royal photographer will snap a few photos of your group to be delivered during your meal (and are included in the price). Dinner guests, in addition to the photos, receive a special Disney lithograph.

The restaurant recently expanded its character dining experience to include not only breakfast but lunch and dinner as well. Breakfast remains an all-you-can-eat buffet while lunch and dinner offer a selection of appetizers, entrees, and desserts to choose from (basic beverages are included, specialty coffees and smoothies will cost a bit extra). Cinderella and other Disney princesses are on hand during breakfast and lunch while the Fairy Godmother hosts the royal dinner.

Note: Because of its location and ambience, a meal here is sought by everyone from little girls who dream of Prince Charming to romantics seeking a more intimate meal. The problem: This is actually one of the smallest dining rooms in the World, making Advance Reservations a must. And you'll have your work cut out for you to get one—it may very well take several calls (and a lot of flexibility on your part) to ensure a spot.

Cinderella Castle, Fantasyland. ℂ 407/939-3463. www.disneyworld.com. Advance Reservations. Character breakfast adult $32, child $22; character lunch adult $34, child $23; character dinner adult $40, child $25. AE, DC, DISC, MC, V. Daily 8–11:15am, noon–3pm, and 4pm–1 hr. before park closing. Parking $9.

Tony's Town Square Restaurant ITALIAN   Inspired by the cafe in *Lady and the Tramp,* Tony's dishes up lunches and dinners of pastas and pizzas in a pleasant if somewhat harried dining room featuring etched glass and ornate gingerbread trim. The lunch menu includes sandwiches, salads, and pizzas, along with such entrees as pasta primavera, spaghetti and meatballs, and the catch of the day. Evening fare might include chicken Florentine, seafood pasta, or a NY strip steak. Kids will enjoy the pizzas and plainer pastas. Original cels from the movie (including the film's famous spaghetti smooch) line the walls. Additional seating is available in a sunny, plant-filled solarium. ***Tip:*** Dinner is by far the busiest time to dine here, but if you time it just right, you can see the Wishes fireworks display after your meal while remaining close enough to the park exit to make a quicker getaway than most.

Main Street. ✆ 407/939-3463. www.disneyworld.com. Advance Reservations. Main courses $11–$16 lunch, $19–$25 dinner. AE, DC, DISC, MC, V. Daily 8:30–10:45am, 11:30am–3pm, and 5pm–park closing. Parking $9.

MODERATE

Liberty Tree Tavern AMERICAN   Step into a replica of an 18th-century Colonial pub and its historic atmosphere, including oak-plank floors, pewterware-stocked hutches, and a big brick fireplace hung with copper pots. The background music suits the period. Lunch includes sandwiches, seafood (such as cured salmon and crab cakes), salads, soups, burgers, roast turkey, and pot roast. The nightly character dinner is a set family-style meal that includes roast turkey, carved beef, boneless ham with a mashed-potatoes stuffing, and macaroni and cheese—along with cherry cobbler and vanilla ice cream to top it off. While the fare's not all that interesting, it is appropriate to the early-American setting (see "Only in Orlando: Dining with Disney Characters," later in this chapter).

Note: If you're looking for a buffet with a bit more to offer than just the usual fare you could try Epcot's **Akershus Royal Banquet Hall** (p. 136) or Animal Kingdom Lodge's **Boma** (p. 150); if you don't want to venture outside of Magic Kingdom, this is your best option.

Liberty Square. ✆ 407/939-3463. www.disneyworld.com. Advance Reservations. Main courses $11–$16 lunch; character dinner buffet adult $28, child $13. AE, DC, DISC, MC, V. Daily 11:30am–3pm and 4pm–park closing. Parking $9.

INEXPENSIVE

Columbia Harbour House ✦ AMERICAN/SEAFOOD   This small eatery often goes overlooked because of its size—it features only a handful of cozy little rooms, all nautically themed—but it does offer some rather decent light fare. Battered fish and shrimp—far meatier than most—tasty sandwiches, clam chowder, and fruit are featured on the menu.

Liberty Square. ✆ 407/939-3643. www.disneyworld.com. All items $6–$7. AE, DC, DISC, MC, V. Daily 11am–park closing. Parking $9.

Cosmic Ray's Starlight Café AMERICAN   The largest of the park's fast-food spots, this cafe features an appropriately huge menu. Three separate counters, similar to a food court, serve a variety of chicken options (whole- or half-rotisserie, dark meat, white meat, fried or grilled), sandwiches, burgers, hot dogs, cheese steaks, soups, and salads. The combination of its casual atmosphere and varied menu makes Ray's a great choice for those with kids (who also enjoy the occasional mealtime entertainment by "alien" Sonny Eclipse). Do note, however, that you may have to wait in more than one line here, as each station offers a different selection. Other minuses: The large dining area fills up quickly at lunch and dinner, and the noise level is generally high. *Tip:* Kosher meals are available here for direct-purchase (though they're pricey and not particularly noteworthy in the taste department).

Main Street. ✆ 407/939-3463. www.disneyworld.com. All items $6–$14. AE, DC, DISC, MC, V. Daily 11am–park closing. Parking $9.

Pecos Bills ✦ AMERICAN   Set in an old-time saloon of sorts, with ornate wrought-iron accents, tile work scattered throughout, heavy flamelike chandeliers, and a golden stucco interior, this sit-and-go fast-food joint serves up burgers, hot dogs,

Walt Disney World & Lake Buena Vista Dining

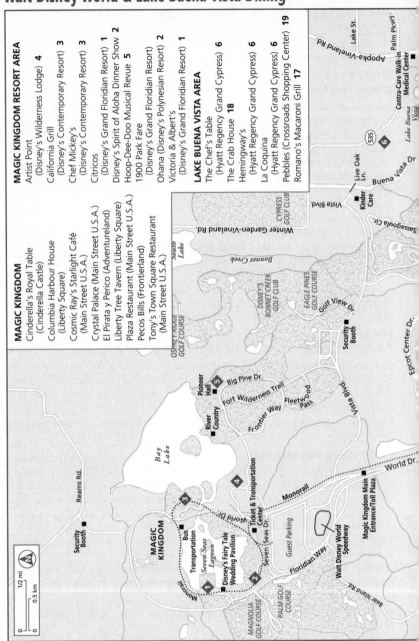

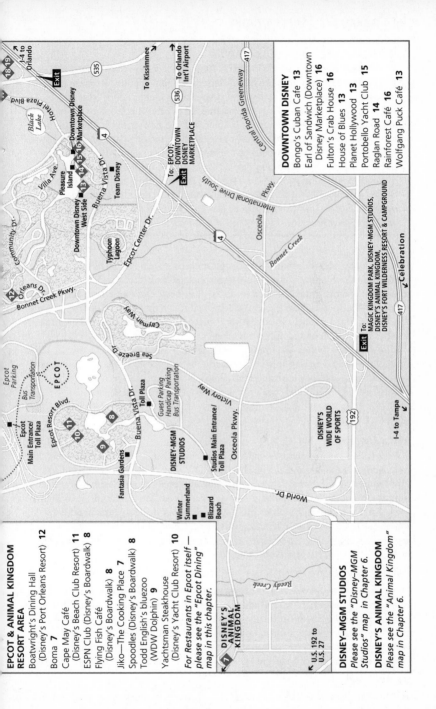

EPCOT & ANIMAL KINGDOM RESORT AREA

Boatwright's Dining Hall
(Disney's Port Orleans Resort) **12**

Boma **7**

Cape May Café
(Disney's Beach Club Resort) **11**

ESPN Club (Disney's Boardwalk) **8**

Flying Fish Café
(Disney's Boardwalk) **8**

Jiko—The Cooking Place **7**

Spoodles (Disney's Boardwalk) **8**

Todd English's bluezoo
(WDW Dolphin) **9**

Yachtsman Steakhouse
(Disney's Yacht Club Resort) **10**

For Restaurants in Epcot itself —
please see the "Epcot Dining"
map in this chapter.

DISNEY-MGM STUDIOS
Please see the "Disney-MGM
Studios" map in Chapter 6.

DISNEY'S ANIMAL KINGDOM
Please see the "Animal Kingdom"
map in Chapter 6.

DOWNTOWN DISNEY

Bongo's Cuban Cafe **13**

Earl of Sandwich (Downtown
Disney Marketplace) **16**

Fulton's Crab House **16**

House of Blues **13**

Planet Hollywood **13**

Portobello Yacht Club **15**

Raglan Road **14**

Rainforest Café **16**

Wolfgang Puck Café **13**

On Again, off Again . . . on Again

The Plaza Pavilion in Magic Kingdom's Tomorrowland was transformed in the spring of 2005 into **Tomorrowland Terrace Noodle Station.** Its new menu includes Oriental-style chicken and shrimp dishes, vegetarian noodles, stir-fry, egg rolls, pot stickers, and other Asian-themed cuisine. This is one of the nicest and largest outdoor seating areas in the park; you can eat out in the fresh air even as you get a respite from the hot Florida sun. And as an added bonus, you get a great view of the gardens, waterways, and Cinderella Castle. If you have picked up a sweet treat along one of Main Street's eateries and can't find a place to sit down (as is often the case), this is the perfect place to head as it's often overlooked by visitors. *Note:* Since its debut the Noodle Station has been open only sporadically, so be sure to check your Guide Map to see if it's open when you're visiting.

---

salads, a barbecue pork sandwich, and a great chicken wrap sandwich. There's also a fixin's bar full of extras. Portions are large, though, and like all other park dining options, so are the prices. Its good location—just between Frontierland and Adventureland—means that those traveling clockwise through the park will probably hit the area just in time for lunch. It can get very crowded at peak meal times, though there is quite a bit of indoor and outdoor seating.

Tip: If your cravings are running more toward Mexican than American, head through the indoor seating area in the back to the seasonal **El Pirata y Perico,** a covered outdoor snack spot featuring tacos, empanadas, chips, and taco salad (all under $6). It's located in Adventureland, just across from Pirates of the Caribbean.

Frontierland. ℂ **407/939-3643.** www.disneyworld.com. All items $5–$8. AE, DC, DISC, MC, V. Daily 11am–park closing. Parking $9.

Plaza Restaurant AMERICAN   It shouldn't be confused with the nearby Plaza Ice Cream Parlor, but the sundaes, banana splits, and other ice-cream creations at this popular dining spot are arguably the best in WDW. This 19th-century inspired restaurant features tasty if expensive sandwiches (turkey, Reuben, cheese steak, chicken, and burgers) that come with an order of fries or potato salad. You can eat inside in an intimate Art Nouveau dining room filled with glass and brass accents or outdoors at umbrella-shaded tables on a veranda overlooking Cinderella Castle.

Main Street. ℂ **407/939-3463.** www.disneyworld.com. Advance Reservations. Meals $10–$11; ice cream $3–$6. AE, DC, DISC, MC, V. Daily 11am–park closing. Parking $9.

AT DISNEY–MGM STUDIOS

Some of the most uniquely themed restaurants in all of WDW are set among the movie sets, action-packed shows, and wild rides of Disney–MGM studios. That fact, in turn, makes them some of the most difficult to get into. Be sure to make Advance Reservations if you want to eat at any full-service restaurant here. Listed below are the best of the bunch. They're located on the two maps, "Walt Disney World & Lake Buena Vista Dining" (p. 142) and "Disney–MGM Studios Theme Park" (p. 231).

EXPENSIVE

Hollywood Brown Derby AMERICAN   This elegant restaurant is modeled after the famed Los Angeles celebrity haunt where Louella Parsons and Hedda Hopper once held court. It features some of the finest food and the fanciest surroundings in the park—along with some of the highest prices. White linens top dark wood tables, chandeliers and amber lighting set the mood, and potted palms all add to the upscale atmosphere. Over 1,500 caricatures of its most famous patrons over the years line the walls, including those of Lucille Ball, Bette Davis, and Clark Gable. Owner Bob Cobb created the original restaurant's signature Cobb salad in the 1930's. (It's so popular that this Derby serves over 31,000 of them a year.) Dinner entrees at Disney's version include pan-fired grouper with balsamic roasted asparagus, sesame-seared Ahi tuna with wasabi whipped potatoes and ginger soy reduction, and pan-roasted pork tenderloin with smoked cheese tomato fondue. The Derby's signature dessert, grapefruit cake with cream-cheese icing, is the perfect way to end your meal. The Derby features a full bar and a modest selection of California wines.

Hollywood Blvd. ✆ **407/939-3463.** www.disneyworld.com. Advance Reservations. Main courses $14–$19 lunch, $18–$29 dinner. Fantasmic package adult $37, child $11. AE, DC, DISC, MC, V. Daily 11:30am–park closing. Parking $9.

MODERATE

50's Prime Time Café *Kids* AMERICAN   Did you ever want to go back to when life was simpler—well you can here, even if it's just for a meal. Several homey dining rooms, separated by knickknack-lined shelves and curtained windows, each look just like Mom's kitchen did back in the 1950s, complete with Formica countertops, a stove, fridge, and black-and-white TVs showing clips from classics such as *My Little Margie*. The servers add to the fun, greeting diners with lines like, "Hi Sis, I'll go tell Mom you're home," and they may threaten to withhold dessert if you don't eat all your food or catch you with your elbows on the table. Kids love it. The entrees—fried chicken, meatloaf (ask for extra catsup), pot roast, and open-faced sandwiches, among others— aren't quite as good as Mom used to make, but are decent nonetheless. The desserts, viewed via a View-Master, include s'mores, sundaes, and cakes; they're all definitely worth the wait. Beer and a varied list of specialty drinks (they make a mean margarita) are served. Kids will get a kick out of the glowing *electric* ice cubes in their drinks.

Near the Indiana Jones Stunt Spectacular. ✆ **407/939-3463.** www.disneyworld.com. Advance Reservations. Main courses $12–$17 lunch, $14–$20 dinner. AE, DC, DISC, MC, V. Daily 11am–park closing. Parking $9.

Mama Melrose's Ristorante Italiano ITALIAN   Found along the "movie" set of a New York street, this large, casual neighborhood eatery welcomes diners with red checkered table cloths, wood floors, and red vinyl booths. The best bets here are the

---

⟨Tips **A Royal Debut**

In the spring of 2004, **The Earl of Sandwich** (the famous edible was allegedly invented by said earl in 1762 when he was too busy playing cards to eat a real meal—and found that putting meat between two slices of bread allowed for both) made its debut in Downtown Disney. The casual eatery offers a great selection of hot and cold sandwiches, including French roasted beef with cheddar and horseradish sauce, turkey with apple bacon and Swiss cheese, and ham with brie and dijonaise. Cobb and Chinese chicken salads are available as well. There's a small amount of indoor seating though most diners head for the benches outside. If you're looking for a quick, light meal at a decent price (sandwiches and salads run $5–$6), this is the place to head.

> *Tips* **Disney–MGM Dining Alternative**
>
> If you forgot to make Advance Reservations or couldn't get a table at your cho-
> sen restaurant, try the **Sci-Fi Dine-In Theater Restaurant's** next-door neighbor,
> the **ABC Commissary.** While not a themed restaurant per se, it offers one of the
> most diverse menus in the park, featuring items such as Cuban sandwiches,
> vegetable noodle stir-fry, tabbouleh wraps, fish and chips, curry chicken, burg-
> ers, and more. They offer rather good desserts as well. Most items cost $6 or $7.
> Plainer than most Disney eateries, it really does resemble a commissary, and TVs
> lining the walls play commercials for the latest and greatest shows running on
> Disney-owned ABC.

---

wood-fired flatbreads (grilled pepperoni, four-cheese, vine ripened tomato, and others)
offered at both lunch and dinner. The dinner menu also includes seafood in a spicy
marinara sauce, veal *osso buco,* and oak-grilled salmon.

Near the Backlot Tour. © 407/939-3463. www.disneyworld.com. Advance Reservations. Main courses $12–$16
lunch, $12–$23 dinner. AE, DC, DISC, MC, V. Daily 11:30am–park closing. Parking $9.

Sci-Fi Dine-In Theater Restaurant *Kids* AMERICAN   This restaurant's simulated
nighttime sky is filled with fiber optic twinkling stars that look down on you as you
sit in a chrome "convertible" watching a giant screen showing '50s and '60s sci-fi
flicks, zany newsreels, cartoons, and B horror-movie clips, such as *Frankenstein Meets
the Space Monster.* Fun-loving carhops deliver free popcorn along with your meal.
We're disappointed that the menu, which was almost as fun to read as the movies are
to watch, is far less cosmic than it used to be. Entrees once listed as the Attack of the
Killer Club Sandwich, the Beach Party Panic, and the Red Planet now require little
translation as they sport names that are now far more down-to-earth (sure they're
more recognizable, but the fun factor ain't there). The menu includes a selection of
sandwiches, ribs, burgers, seafood, pasta, steak, and salads. Kids' meals are served on
souvenir glow-in-the-dark flyers. The food is average; it's the atmosphere that keeps
the crowds coming. Advance Reservations are highly recommended.

Near Indiana Jones Epic Stunt Spectacular. © 407/939-3463. www.disneyworld.com. Advance Reservations. Main
courses $12–$18 lunch, $12–$18 dinner. AE, DC, DISC, MC, V. Daily 11am–park closing. Parking $9.

INEXPENSIVE

Toy Story Pizza Planet AMERICAN   The menu here is far from original, but it
will satisfy some of the younger (and pickier) eaters in your family with pizza, salad,
drinks, and desserts. It's a big favorite of kids, thanks to the array of arcade games
located just next door—just remember to bring plenty of change.

In the Muppet's Courtyard. © 407/939-3463. www.disneyworld.com. No Advance Reservations. All meals $6–$9.
AE, DC, DISC, MC, V. Daily 10:30am–park closing. Parking $9.

IN THE ANIMAL KINGDOM

There are few restaurants in the newest of Disney's parks, and most that exist are
counter-service or grab-and-go places (of these, the Flame Tree Barbecue is the best
and the Chakranadi Chicken Shop the most unique). Nevertheless there are two
notable enough to list.

MODERATE

Rainforest Cafe ♿ *Kids* CALIFORNIA   Expect California fare with an island spin at this Rainforest, and its cousin (listed later in this chapter on p. 156). Menu offerings tend to be tasty and somewhat creative, with far more choices than most can contend with. That said, the cafe, like other Disney restaurants, tends to fall on the pricier side of dining. Fun dishes include Mogambo Shrimp (sautéed in olive oil and served with penne pasta), Rumble in the Jungle Turkey Wrap (with romaine, tomatoes, and bacon), and Maya's Mixed Grill (ribs, chicken breast, and shrimp). Tables situated among the dining room's dense vines and generally inanimate animals are usually packed; that's partially due to the lack of other full-service dining options at Animal Kingdom, but also due to the actual popularity of this loud (thanks in part to the cracks of thunder and chatter of animals) and lively establishment. Beer, wine, and other alcoholic concoctions are served.

Just outside Animal Kingdom entrance. *Park admission not required* (though there is an entrance from inside the park, too.). ✆ **407/938-9100.** www.rainforestcafe.com. Advance reservations strongly recommended. Main courses $10–$40 (most under $25) lunch and dinner. AE, DC, DISC, MC, V. Daily 8am–6pm. Parking $9.

INEXPENSIVE

Tusker House AMERICAN   The thatched-roof **Tusker House** in Harambe village features fast-food options that offer a bit of a culinary flair. Grilled chicken salad, rotisserie or fried chicken, a turkey wrap with corn chowder, roasted vegetable sandwiches, and grilled salmon are all on the menu here. The food is tasty enough; however, portions are small by Disney standards. A slightly shaded stone patio out back with a view over the trees allows you to relax and enjoy your meal tucked away from the crowds. Out front the pavilion offers shade, and if timed right a view of the live entertainment. Beer and wine are served.

In Africa, near entrance. ✆ **407/939-3463.** www.disneyworld.com. No Advance Reservations. Main courses $7–$8. AE, DC, DISC, MC, V. Daily 9:30am–10:30am and 11am–3pm. Parking $9.

IN THE WALT DISNEY WORLD RESORTS

Most restaurants listed in this category continue the Disney trend of being above market price. On the flip side, many offer food and atmospheres that far exceed what you'll find in the theme parks. The quality level means that even those not staying at Disney resorts like to dine at these restaurants, so Advance Reservations are a must if you don't want to miss out on a table. All of the restaurants in this section are located on the "Walt Disney World & Lake Buena Vista Dining" map on p. 142.

Tips Coming Attractions

At press time, Disney announced it would add two new themed restaurants to its already long list of interesting eateries. The first, an Asian restaurant slated to open sometime in 2007, will complement Animal Kingdom's Expedition Everest attraction and will have the look and feel of a Himalayan village. The second, scheduled to open in 2008 at the Downtown Disney Marketplace, will be similar to the Rainforest Cafe, but with a prehistoric twist. Instead of dense jungles and hanging vines, you'll find a paleontologist's paradise with animatronic dinosaurs. Both restaurants will be owned in part by Landry Restaurants, the people who run the Rainforest Cafe.

VERY EXPENSIVE

Citricos ⚜ NEW FRENCH   Located on the second floor of The Grand Floridian, Citricos offers a menu featuring a fusion of French and Mediterranean cuisine with a Florida twist. Items change regularly, but you might find yummy grilled lamb chops with crispy polenta and puttanesca sauce or sautéed salmon filet with roasted fennel and gold potatoes. The old-world decor featuring warm hues of yellows and oranges includes plenty of wrought-iron railings, mosaic-tile floors, flickering lights, a show kitchen, and a view of the Seven Seas Lagoon and Magic Kingdom fireworks. Add a three-course wine pairing for $26. The Chef's Domain offers an experience similar to the Chef's Table at Victoria & Albert's, *but beware:* Citricos won't piece together a group. You have to pay the full $650 sticker price (ouch!) for the table whether there are 2 or 12 in your party.

4401 Floridian Way, in Disney's Grand Floridian Resort & Spa. ℭ 407/939-3463. www.disneyworld.com. Advance Reservations. Main courses $25–$33. AE, DC, DISC, MC, V. Wed–Sun 5–10pm; Chef's Domain Tues–Sat 6 and 8:30pm. Valet or free self-parking.

Victoria & Albert's ⚜⚜⚜ *Finds* INTERNATIONAL   It's not often that we can describe dinner as "an event," but Disney's most elegant restaurant deserves that distinction. Dinner is next to perfect—if the portions seem small, they're designed that way to make sure you can get through all seven courses—and the setting is exceptionally romantic. The fare changes nightly, but expect a feast fit for royalty (and costing a royal fortune). You might begin with roasted duck with candy-striped and golden beets, followed by Monterey abalone with lemon and baby spinach. Then, pheasant consommé might precede an entree such as tamari-glazed bluefin tuna over bok choy stir-fry or veal tenderloin; pheasant with porcini pasta and truffle foam; or Australian Kobe Beef tenderloin. English Stilton served with a burgundy-poached pear sets up desserts such as vanilla bean crème brûlée and Kona chocolate soufflé. The intimate dining room (with seating for only 65) is crowned by a domed, chapel-style ceiling. Victorian lamps softly light 18 exquisitely appointed tables; a harp plays softly in the background, and your servers (always named Victoria and Albert) provide service that is unmatched anywhere else in Orlando. The luxurious experience ends as a personalized menu is presented to you and a rose given to all the ladies in your party. *Tip:*

Finds   The Chef's Table: The Best Seat in the World

There's a special dining option at **Victoria & Albert's**. Reserve the **Chef's Table** (far, far in advance) and dine in a charming alcove hung with copper pots and dried flower wreaths at an elegantly appointed candlelit table in the heart of the kitchen! Begin by sipping bubbly with the chef while discussing your food preferences for a menu (up to 13 courses) created especially for you. There's a cooking seminar element to this experience: Diners get to tour the kitchen and observe the artistry of the chefs at work. The Chef's Table can accommodate up to 10 people a night. It's a leisurely affair, lasting 3 or 4 hours. The price is $150 per person without wine, $215 including five wines. This is so popular that Disney takes Advance Reservations 180 days in advance, so reserve *early* by calling ℭ **407/939-3463.**

> (*Fun Fact*) **Cooking for Kids**
>
> Disney's Grand Floridian Resort & Spa offers two special cooking programs for children. **Grand Adventures in Cooking** invites up to 12 youngsters, 4 to 10 years old, to make dessert in a 2-hour decorating class ($29 per child). The **Wonderland Tea Party** gives kids the same age a 1-hour primer in cupcake decorating—with their fingers! They also feast on heart-shaped PB&Js and sip apple juice "tea" while they play with Alice and the Mad Hatter ($29 per child). Call (*C*) **407/824-3000** or 407/939-3463 for details on both programs.

Wine pairings, which provide a wine with most courses for an extra $55 per person, are a great way to enhance the dinner experience.

4401 Floridian Way, in Disney's Grand Floridian Resort & Spa. (*C*) **407/939-3463**. www.disneyworld.com. Advance Reservations required. Jackets required for men. Not recommended for children. Prix fixe $100 ($110 on holidays) per person, $155 with wine pairing; $150 Chef's Table, $215 with wine. AE, DC, DISC, MC, V. 2 dinner seatings daily Sept–June 5:45–6:30pm and 9–9:45pm; 1 dinner seating July–Aug 6:45–8pm. Chef's Table 6pm only. Free self- and validated valet parking.

Yachtsman Steakhouse 🕈 SEAFOOD/STEAKS/CHOPS   It is somewhat of a backhanded compliment to name this the best steakhouse in Disney—there are only two true steakhouses on property. Even so, when you compare it to similar spots in the outside world, the Yachtsman would still earn high grades. Its grain-fed Western beef is aged, cured, and cut here. You can see the cuts in a glass-enclosed aging room, and the exhibition kitchen provides a tantalizing glimpse of steaks, chops, and seafood being grilled over oak and hickory. Steak options range from an 8-ounce filet to a 12-ounce strip to a belly-busting 24-ounce T-bone. A filet and warm-water lobster tail combo tops the price chart. If you're not in the mood for beef, the Yachtsman also serves Chilean sea bass, scallops, and one daily vegetarian special. The decor includes knotty-pine beams, plank floors, and leather-and-oak chairs, though unlike most steakhouses it sports a lighter nautical New England feel. The staff is very cordial. The Yachtsman has an extensive wine list, though it's not in the same league as the other contestants in this category.

1700 Epcot Resorts Blvd., in Disney's Yacht Club Resort. (*C*) **407/939-3463**. Advance Reservations recommended. Main courses $21–$82. AE, DC, DISC, MC, V. Daily 5:30–10pm. Free self- and valet parking.

EXPENSIVE

Artist Point 🕈🕈 (*Finds*) SEAFOOD/STEAKS/CHOPS   Enjoy a grand view of Disney's Wilderness Lodge and tasty cuisine at this rustically elegant establishment. Hand-painted murals of Pacific Northwestern scenery adorn the impressive two-story center ceiling, and ornate iron lanterns hang from tremendous timber columns. Immense windows overlook the waterfalls, rocky landscaping, and the resort's own Fire Rock geyser. The menu changes seasonally and might feature grilled buffalo sirloin with sweet potato hazelnut gratin and sweet onion jam, but the restaurant's signature is the cedar plank–roasted king salmon with wild mushroom bread salad and béarnaise sauce. There's terrace seating for fair weather. Expect a reasonably extensive wine list now exclusively featuring wines from the Pacific Northwest. *Note:* Artist Point has a much more relaxed atmosphere than some of the busier WDW resort restaurants.

> *Tips* **For Smaller Stomachs**
>
> If your kids aren't satisfied with the offerings on the kids' menu, try the appe-
> tizer menu. They'll have more to choose from and the price is right. Also,
> always ask if half-portions are available; they are generally not advertised,
> though some restaurants offer them upon request. The same follows when
> requesting items a la carte. Disney's menus won't always reflect a la carte items
> though they are often available if you ask.

Tip: If you're looking for more family-oriented dining at the Wilderness Lodge, try
the **Whispering Canyon Café,** where a decor dedicated to cowboys and Indians is
warm and welcoming. Kids can horse-race on broomsticks, and everyone gets a
hoopin' and a hollerin' at dinner. Meals are served family style (though a la carte service is available if you so desire). They're open for breakfast, lunch, and dinner. Entrees
run from $9 to $13 at lunch, $16 to $23 at dinner.

901 W. Timberline Dr., in Disney's Wilderness Lodge. ✆ 407/939-3463. www.disneyworld.com. Advance Reservations recommended. Dinner $21–$49. AE, DC, DISC, MC, V. Daily 5:30–10pm. Free self- and valet parking.

Boma ✦✦✦ *Moments* AFRICAN Here's a truly unique and worthwhile dining
experience. This restaurant's warm welcoming atmosphere, similar to an African marketplace, is enhanced by colorful banners strewn from high above. An authentic
thatched roof and large wooden tabletops made from tremendous tree trunks add to
the impressive decor. In front of the open exhibition kitchen is an incredible buffet of
international cuisine featuring authentic African dishes from more than 50 African
nations. A wood-burning grill sends delicious aromas wafting throughout the room,
enticing diners to try some of the more diverse delicacies. Adventurous diners can
expect such treats as Moroccan seafood salad (mussels, scallops, shrimp, and couscous), curried coconut seafood stew, chicken pepper pot soup, and much more. The
watermelon rind salad is a specialty and is both delicious and refreshing–just don't forget to save room for the yummy desserts. Kids with less sophisticated taste buds can
dine on traditional American favorites. There's also a breakfast buffet (try the specialty
juices—they're delicious).

Tip 1: If there's something you particularly like, just ask for the recipe—Disney is
surprisingly good about sharing their culinary secrets. *Tip 2:* Most tables here seat
larger parties, so couples or single diners may end up waiting longer for a table.

2901 Osceola Pkwy., at Disney's Animal Kingdom Lodge. ✆ 407/939-3463. www.disneyworld.com. Advance Reservations. Breakfast buffet $17 adults, $10 kids 3–9; dinner buffet $26 adults, $12 kids. AE, DC, DISC, MC, V. Daily
7–11am and 5–10pm. Valet or free self-parking.

California Grill ✦✦✦ CALIFORNIA Located on the Contemporary Resort's
15th floor, this stunning restaurant offers views of the Magic Kingdom and lagoon
below while your eyes and mouth feast on an eclectic menu. A Wolfgang Puckish
interior incorporates Art Deco elements (curved pearwood walls, vivid splashes of
color, polished black granite surfaces) with a charged and upbeat atmosphere, but the
central focus is an exhibition kitchen with a wood-burning oven and rotisserie. The
menu's headliners change to take advantage of fresh market fare but may include
seared yellowfin tuna, black grouper with mushroom risotto, and soft-shell crabs with
corn salad. The Grill also has a nice sushi and sashimi menu (tuna, crab, and shrimp,

among others) ranging from appetizers to large platters. The servers are exceptionally attentive. This is one of the few spots in WDW that isn't inundated with kids. The list of California wines helps complement the meal and views.

Note: It can be tough to get a table at the Grill, especially on weekends and during Disney fireworks hours, so make a reservation as early as possible. Also be aware that a business casual dress code is required.

4600 N. World Dr., at Disney's Contemporary Resort. © 407/939-3463. www.disneyworld.com. Advance Reservations require a credit card guarantee. Main courses $21–$35; sushi and sashimi $13–$24. AE, DC, DISC, MC, V. Daily 5:30–10pm. Valet or free self-parking.

Flying Fish Café 🐟 SEAFOOD   Chefs at this upscale Coney Island–inspired restaurant take the stage in a show kitchen that turns out entrees such as potato-wrapped red snapper with a creamy leek fondue and coriander-crusted yellowfin tuna with Moroccan couscous. The food is better than what you'll find at the Coral Reef (p. 134) and Cape May Café (p. 153), but not quite in the same league as Artist Point (p. 149), or bluezoo (p. 152). Vibrantly colored tile floors, lily pads, and golden fish, along with delicate jellyfish-like lighting, hanging by fish hooks from high above, and accents of shimmering fish scales combine to create an undersea ambience. A whimsical Ferris wheel and hand-painted murals conjure thoughts of Coney Island. *Note:* If you can't get a table here, ask to sit at the counter—you'll get a great view of the exhibition kitchen.

2101 N. Epcot Resorts Blvd., at Disney's BoardWalk. © 407/939-3463. www.disneyworld.com. Advance Reservations. Main courses $23–$38. AE, DC, DISC, MC, V. Daily 5:30–10pm. Valet or free self-parking.

Jiko—The Cooking Place 🐟🐟 AFRICAN   The Animal Kingdom Lodge's signature restaurant offers a nice diversion from Disney's more conventional offerings and a complementary addition to the multicultural dining rooms at Epcot's World Showcase. Jiko's show kitchen, sporting two wood-burning ovens, turns out an innovative and creative menu of international cuisine with African overtones. Dishes, depending on the season, might include broiled buttermilk curry shrimp, pan-roasted monkfish, grilled salmon with heirloom potatoes and spinach in a horseradish vinaigrette, or roasted chicken with preserved lemons, olives, and garlic. An impressive wine list features South African vintages exclusively. Warm colors and diffuse lighting add to the sophisticated atmosphere.

Tips A Walk on the Wild Side

Disney's latest addition to its lineup of unique dining experiences is a **Lunch with Disney's Animal Program.** The weekly lunch series offers guests an opportunity to dine with, and learn from, Disney's animal experts. Each week a different presenter, ranging from trainers to veterinarians to curators, will share their experiences and expertise with guests as they dine on the innovative culinary creations of Chef Anette Gray-Grettchi. Guests will be treated to an impressive South African–inspired meal in the casual yet intimate setting of Jiko's Wine Room (at Disney's Animal Kingdom Lodge). The lunch program is offered every Tuesday from noon to 2pm at a cost of $65 per person ($80 with wine pairing). If you're staying at a WDW resort, your lobby concierge can make arrangements or you can call © **407/939-3463** to make reservations.

Tips **Pint-Size Portions**

If your kids are adventurous in the dining department but can't handle adult-size portions, several Disney restaurants allow kids to sample dishes geared to adult tastes that are served in portion sizes suited to smaller stomachs (and at smaller prices, too). Options include:

- **Coral Reef** (Epcot): Grilled mahimahi ($9)
- **Flying Fish Café** (BoardWalk): Lettuce Salad ($3), buttermilk fried flying fish ($8)
- **L'Originale Alfredo di Roma Ristorante** (Epcot): Fettuccine Alfredo ($7)
- **Artist Point** (Wilderness Lodge): Baked salmon with mashed potatoes and veggies ($9)
- **Citricos** (Grand Floridian): Chicken noodle soup ($2), oak-grilled filet of beef ($12)
- **California Grill** (Contemporary): Steak with mashed potatoes and veggies ($9)

2901 Osceola Pkwy., at Disney's Animal Kingdom Lodge. ✆ **407/939-3463**. www.disneyworld.com. Advance Reservations. Main courses $14–$34. AE, DC, DISC, MC, V. Daily 5:30–10pm. Valet or free self-parking.

Spoodles ✦ TAPAS/MEDITERRANEAN   Mediterranean flavor and old-world charm are vividly apparent upon entering this lively (read: noisy) family restaurant. Exposed brick, colorful tableware, high-beamed ceilings, and warm hues of deep red and golden yellow run throughout the sizeable open dining room. An eclectic mix of mismatched lighting and wooden farmhouse-style furnishings only add to the casual, comfortable feel. The large open kitchen raises the noise level a notch or two as does the pizza kitchen across the room, but that's all part of this restaurant's appeal. Start off with a sampling of Mediterranean dips with toasted pita, marinated olives, and almonds. Entrees might include oak-fired salmon with roasted vegetable stew or lemon chicken with toasted couscous, baby spinach, and vine-ripened tomatoes. A respectable wine list has recently been added, including tableside sangria presentations. *Note:* During the peak summer tourist season, thanks to Spoodles' location on the BoardWalk, the wait for a table can be long, even with Advance Reservations, so this may not be the best option for famished families. Though there's plenty of indoor seating, try for a table on the small patio outside, so you can take in all of the action on the BoardWalk. Breakfast is served daily.

2101 N. Epcot Resorts Blvd., at Disney's BoardWalk. ✆ **407/939-3463**. www.disneyworld.com. Advance Reservations. Breakfast $8–$15; dinner $17–$36. AE, DC, DISC, MC. V. Daily 7–11am and 5–9:30pm. Pizza Window 5pm–midnight. Valet or free self-parking.

Todd English's bluezoo ✦✦✦ SEAFOOD   Set inside the WDW Dolphin, this is the hippest, hottest, most happening place to dine in town. Internationally acclaimed chef Todd English has created an amazing menu of fresh seafood and coastal dishes that are served with creative flair in an artsy undersea setting. An exhibition kitchen showcases the chefs at work, and the dining areas feature a contemporary (and very blue) decor scheme designed to evoke the ocean, with lots of hip lighting and curved walls. Appetizers include the amazing "Olive's" classico flatbread, a roasted beet salad, and teppan-seared sea scallops. Melt-in-your-mouth entrees include lobster Bolognese, spit-roasted block of swordfish, and fresh grilled fish served in a choice of three unique sauces. Unlike those at many upscale restaurants of this caliber, the portions here are meal-worthy, not minuscule. That said, the prices here are hefty, and do not include side dishes (veggies, for example), which will run you an extra $5 to $7. Dress is casual (this is Disney), though the atmosphere is definitely adult and upscale.

Tip: The front of the restaurant has a bar and lounge where live music is often featured or a DJ spins a selection of today's hottest tunes.

1500 Epcot Resort Blvd., at the WDW Dolphin. © **407/934-1111.** www.disneyworld.com. Advance Reservations highly recommended. Main courses $18–$52. AE, DISC, MC, V. Daily 3:30–11pm. Free self-parking; free, validated valet parking (validate ticket on your way out).

MODERATE

Boatwright's Dining Hall *(Kids)* NEW ORLEANS   A family atmosphere (noisy), good food (by Disney standards), and reasonable prices (ditto) make Boatwright's a hit with Port Orleans Resort guests, if not outsiders. Most entrees have a Cajun/Creole spin. The jambalaya is sans seafood but is filled with vegetables, rice, chicken, and sausage—all rather spicy and giving it quite a kick. Vegetarians will appreciate the vegetable medley and the four-cheese ravioli. Other dinner items include bayou seafood stew, bourbon-glazed chicken, pork ribs, and pot roast. Boatwright's is modeled after a 19th-century boat factory, complete with the wooden hull of a Louisiana fishing boat suspended from its lofty beamed ceiling. Most kids like the wooden toolboxes on every table; each contains a saltshaker that doubles as a level, a wood-clamp sugar dispenser, a pepper-grinder-cum-ruler, a jar of unmatched utensils, shop rags (to be used as napkins), and a little metal pail of crayons.

2201 Orleans Dr., in Disney's Port Orleans Resort. © **407/939-3463.** www.disneyworld.com. Advance Reservations recommended. Main courses $7–$11 breakfast, $15–$21 dinner. AE, DC, DISC, MC, V. Daily 7–11:30am and 5–10pm. Free self-parking.

Cape May Café SEAFOOD   This New England–style clambake offers a selection of oysters, clams, mussels, baked fish, and small peel-and-eat shrimp. Accompaniments include corn on the cob, potatoes, and other assorted veggies. Landlubbers fear not; there is a selection of not-so-fishy fare including barbecued pork ribs, and prime rib. The casual nautical theme carries into the restaurant from the surrounding Beach

---

Tips Anyone Hungry?

There are plenty of places throughout the World to eat and eat and then eat some more, so plan on heading to these food-fests when you're plenty hungry. Disney boasts 11 **all-you-can-eat** restaurants, which is really Disney's polite way of saying feel free to eat absolutely everything in front of you.

Restaurants include: **'Ohana** at the Polynesian Resort, **Whispering Canyon Cafe** at the Wilderness Lodge, **Boma** at the Animal Kingdom Lodge, **Cape May Café** at the Beach Club Resort, **Crystal Palace** at the Magic Kingdom, **Liberty Tree Tavern** at the Magic Kingdom, **Garden Grill** at Epcot, **Akershus Royal Banquet Hall** (Norway) at Epcot, **Hollywood & Vine** at Disney–MGM Studios, **Chef Mickey's** at the Contemporary Resort, and **1900 Park Fare** at the Grand Floridian.

Fun Fact **Hidden Mickey?**

All over the Walt Disney World Resort you will find Mickey Mouse popping up in some rather interesting places. You had better take a good look at your food before you take a bite; you may be surprised to find it staring back at you. Mickey can be found in pancakes, waffles, muffins, pastas, and pats of butter. He can be seen in fruits and cheeses, sandwiches, and sundaes. There are Mickey mashed potatoes, ice-cream bars, cookies, and cakes. Even cucumbers are grown (with a little help from a plastic mold) to look like the famous mouse.

Club resort. The Cape May Café also offers a character breakfast buffet every morning (p. 175).

1800 Epcot Resorts Blvd., at Disney's Beach Club Resort. ✆ **407/939-3463**. www.disneyworld.com. Advance Reservations. Character breakfast $26 adults, $12 children 3–9; dinner buffet $24 adults, $10 children 3–9. AE, DC, DISC, MC, V. Daily 7:30–11am, 5:30–9:30pm. Free self- and valet parking.

ESPN Club ✿ AMERICAN   If you are a sports enthusiast, this is *the* place for you. Sports memorabilia hangs from every wall and television monitors (all 71 of them) surround you at every turn—ensuring you won't miss a minute of the big game. The all-American fare includes such choices as "Boo-Yeah" chili, hot wings, and burgers. Sandwiches and salads are available as well. The service is impeccable—never have we had a waiter so quick on his feet. While the food is quite good, it's the upbeat action-packed atmosphere that draws the crowds here.

2101 N. Epcot Resorts Blvd., at Disney's BoardWalk. ✆ **407/939-1177**. www.disneyworld.com. No Advance Reservations. $6–$17 lunch and dinner. AE, DC, MC, V. Mon–Thurs 11:30am–1am; Fri–Sat 11:30am–2am. Valet or free self-parking.

'Ohana ✿ *Kids* PACIFIC RIM   Its star is earned on the fun front, but the decibel level here can get a bit overwhelming, especially for those looking for a relaxing evening out. Inside, you're welcomed as a "cousin," which fits because *'Ohana* means "family" in Hawaiian. As your food is being prepared over an 18-foot fire pit, the staff keeps your eyes and ears filled with all sorts of shenanigans. The blowing of a conch shell summons a storyteller, coconut races get underway in the center aisle, and you can shed your inhibitions and shake it in the hula lessons. When it starts, the meal is served rapid fire (ask your waiter to slow the pace if it's too fast). The edibles include a variety of skewers (think shish kabob), including turkey, steak, and pork. Trimmings include assorted veggies, fried wontons, salad, shrimp, and chicken wings all served up family style. A full bar offers limited wine selections (tropical alcoholic drinks are available for an added fee). *Note:* Ask for a seat in the main dining room, or you won't get a good view of the entertainment.

1600 Seven Seas Dr., at Disney's Polynesian Resort. ✆ **407/939-3463**. www.disneyworld.com. Advance Reservations strongly encouraged. $26 adults, $12 children 3–9; character breakfast $19 adults, $11 kids 3–9 (p. 176). AE, DC, DISC, MC, V. Daily 7:30–11am and 5–10pm. Free self- and valet parking.

4 Places to Dine in Lake Buena Vista

In this section, we've listed restaurants located in Downtown Disney and the Lake Buena Vista area. Many eateries listed below can be found on the "Walt Disney World & Lake Buena Vista Dining" map on p. 142. Downtown Disney is located 2½ miles from Epcot off Buena Vista Drive. It encompasses the Downtown Disney Market-place, a complex chock-full of cedar-shingled shops and themed restaurants overlook-ing a scenic lagoon; the adjoining Pleasure Island, a lively nighttime entertainment venue full of clubs and a few restaurants of its own; and Downtown Disney West Side, a slightly more upscale collection of shops, restaurants, Cirque du Soleil (p. 327), and a multiplex. The restaurants below have kids' menus, usually in the $4 to $9 range, though sometimes higher.

Note: Pleasure Island's restaurants don't require an admission fee.

AT PLEASURE ISLAND
EXPENSIVE

Portobello Yacht Club ☞ SOUTHERN ITALIAN/MEDITERRANEAN   The pizzas here go beyond the routine to *quattro formaggi* (mozzarella, Gorgonzola, fontina, and Parmesan, with sun-dried tomatoes) and *margherita* (Italian sausage, plum tomatoes, and mozzarella). But it's the less casual entrees that pack people into this place. The menu changes from time to time. *Spaghettini alla portobello* (pasta with pieces of Alaskan king crab, scallops, shrimp, and clams in light olive oil, wine, and herbs) is the house specialty, though you'll find offerings such as wood-roasted Atlantic salmon, charcoal-grilled sea bass, as well as steaks and pastas. The Mediter-ranean-inspired decor is accented by vibrantly colored murals and contemporary Ital-ian artwork set against the warm earth tones and amber lighting. The Portobello's awning-covered patio overlooks Lake Buena Vista. Its cellar is small, but there's a nice selection of wine to match the meals.

1650 Buena Vista Dr., at Pleasure Island. ② 407/934-8888. www.levyrestaurants.com. Advance Reservations. Main courses $16–$47; pizzas $9–$11. AE, DC, DISC, MC, V. Daily 11:30am–3pm and 5–11pm. Free self-parking.

MODERATE

Planet Hollywood *Overrated* AMERICAN   Those who flock to this restaurant come for the unique surroundings, movie memorabilia, and scenery from some of Holly-wood's hottest hits, much like those who head to the Hard Rock (a far better choice) to check out their musical montage. Diners, however, are doomed to be disappointed. Though the atmosphere is fairly neat (including a planetarium-like ceiling), the Planet's servers can cop an attitude, and the food is at best blasé. If you must, you'll find the usual suspects: wings, sandwiches, big burgers, ribs, pasta, steaks, and seafood. Even with a less-than-stellar lineup on the menu, the lines to get in can at times be excruciatingly long.

1506 Buena Vista Dr., at Pleasure Island (look for the big globe). ② 407/827-7827. www.planethollywood.com. Limited Advance Reservations. Main courses $10–$29 (most under $18). AE, DC, DISC, MC, V. Daily 11am–1am. Free self-parking.

AT DOWNTOWN DISNEY MARKETPLACE
VERY EXPENSIVE

Fulton's Crab House ☞☞ SEAFOOD   Lobster (Maine and Australian) and crab (stone, king, and Dungeness) dominate the menu at this upscale eatery, which is housed in a replica of a (permanently moored) 19th-century Mississippi riverboat. It's one of the area's best seafood houses—and your bill will reflect that. The casual yet elegant decor is accented by folk art and seafaring paraphernalia scattered throughout its various rooms. The menu changes often, at times even daily, however with over 50 fresh seafood selections to choose from you won't be disappointed. The tuna mignon (served rare) and Dungeness crab cakes are delicious. And there's a scattering of Florida seafood, including black grouper and red snapper. In mild weather, consider dining on one of the three outdoor decks for a more panoramic view. Be prepared for a long wait (even with Advance Reservations); try having a late lunch to lessen your waiting time. Fulton's has one of Lake Buena Vista's better wine lists. And though you may not see many of them, kids are welcomed here.

1670 Buena Vista Dr., aboard the riverboat docked at Downtown Disney. ℭ **407/934-2628.** www.levyrestaurants. com. Advance Reservations. Main courses $10–$52 lunch, $26–$52 dinner. AE, DC, DISC, MC, V. Daily 11:30am–4pm and 5–11pm. Free self-parking.

MODERATE
Rainforest Cafe ★ Kids CALIFORNIA   Don't arrive starving unless you have Advance Reservations. Without them, waits average 2 hours, although even with them you'll wait longer here than at Animal Kingdom's Rainforest Cafe (p. 147). Expect fare with an island spin at this Rainforest. The menu can be tasty and creative, though somewhat overpriced. Fun dishes include Caribbean Coconut Shrimp (with a sweet mango sauce), and Maya's Mixed Grill (ribs, chicken breast, and shrimp), but the menu goes on and on (and on) with an extensive variety of salads, pastas, pizzas, burgers, sandwiches, seafood, beef, chicken, and pork. The setting is its biggest draw (though the food is pretty good), filled with jungles, waterfalls, and animatronic animals—with the occasional clap of thunder in the background, so don't expect a quiet evening out. Kids are thoroughly entertained by all the action; adults can calm their nerves with the beer, wine, and other alcoholic mixers.

Downtown Disney Marketplace; near the smoking volcano. ℭ **407/827-8500.** www.rainforest.com. Advance Reservations. Main courses $11–$40 lunch and dinner (most under $25). AE, DISC, MC, V. Sun–Thurs 10:30am–11pm; Fri–Sat 10:30am–midnight. Free self-parking.

DISNEY'S WEST SIDE
MODERATE
Bongo's Cuban Cafe Overrated CUBAN   Singer Gloria Estefan and her husband, Emilio, created this eatery with high expectations. Its exterior, with a giant pineapple standing tall against the Downtown Disney skyline, is hard to miss. The interior is Art Deco with a Havana flavor and includes colorful tile mosaics and hand-painted wall murals of Cuba in its heyday. A Desi Arnaz impersonator gets things going every night as the restaurant fills with loud Latin music. Alas, while visually appealing, the food isn't great, though the prices say it ought to be. The *palomilla* (a thin, tenderized steak) can't match what you find in Rolando's (p. 172). The *ropa vieja* (shredded beef) is tasty but dry, and the *arroz con pollo* (chicken with yellow rice) would be a highlight if the portion matched the price. The best bet: The Cuban sandwich—thinly toasted bread with ham, pork, and cheese—is safe and sanely priced. For a more relaxing experience, grab a drink at the bar (just know that the bongo-shaped barstools can be difficult to manage after more than a few drinks) or sit a spell out on the patio lounge upstairs.

1498 Buena Vista Dr., in Disney's West Side. ℭ **407/828-0999.** www.bongoscubancafe.com. Reservations not accepted. Lunch $8–$20; dinner $16–$29 (many under $20). AE, DC, DISC, MC, V. Daily 11am–2am. Free self-parking.

House of Blues MISSISSIPPI DELTA   Most folks come for the blues bands and Sunday's gospel brunch, a foot-tapping, thigh-slapping music affair worth high marks on the entertainment side. (The omelets are good, and there are enough fillers—bacon, salads, dessert, and bread—that few leave hungry.) The average food has a New Orleans flavor and includes such offerings as pan-seared voodoo shrimp; and gumbo with chicken, andouille sausage, and okra. The rustic backwater bayou interior has a Cajun Voodooish sort of feel and is by far the most interesting in Downtown Disney, filled (literally) with bottle caps and buttons, skeletal etchings, and hand-painted folk art. Do check out the restrooms; they're decorated with that diamond plating seen on the beds of some pickup trucks, especially in the South.

1490 Buena Vista Dr., at Disney's West Side, beneath water tower. ℂ **407/934-2583.** www.hob.com. Reservations not accepted (except brunch). Main courses $10–$27; pizza and sandwiches $9–$11; brunch $30 adults, $15 children 3–9. AE, DISC, MC, V. Daily 11am–2am; brunch 10:30am and 1pm. Free self-parking.

Wolfgang Puck Grand Café ℱ CALIFORNIA   The wait can be distressing but the energized atmosphere and eclectic mix of menu choices make it worth the effort. In the more casual downstairs cafe, colorful tiles accent practically everything and an eye-catching exhibition kitchen allows you to watch as your food is prepared. A favorite stop is the sushi bar, an artistic copper-and-terrazzo masterpiece that delivers some of the best sushi in Orlando. The upstairs, with tables that are available only with Advance Reservations, offers a more refined atmosphere and a separate menu to match. The seasonally changing menu might feature Szechuan beef and crimini satay with a spicy vegetable stir-fry and cilantro mint sauce; or pumpkin ravioli with sage, hazelnut butter, and Parmesan. Desserts include a crème brûlée sampler plate. Puck's is noisy, making conversation difficult no matter which level you choose. *Note:* If you're in a hurry or on the go you'll find a Wolfgang Puck Express, offering sandwiches, pizzas, desserts, and more, at both the Westside and Marketplace.

1482 Buena Vista Dr., at Disney's West Side. ℂ **407/938-9653.** www.wolfgangpuck.com/myrestaurants or www.levyrestaurants.com. Reservations not accepted on lower level; Advance Reservations for upstairs dining room. Main courses upstairs $22–$37; main courses cafe $11–$36; pizza and sushi $11–$27; Express $9–$15. AE, DC, DISC, MC, V. Daily 11am–1am. Free self-parking.

ELSEWHERE IN LAKE BUENA VISTA
VERY EXPENSIVE

La Coquina ℱ INTERNATIONAL   Expect an imaginative menu from the most acclaimed of the Hyatt Regency's five restaurants. La Coquina is an upscale but casual eatery that is well appointed with marine life and seashell themes and offers an intimate setting. Roasted veal tenderloin, seared ahi tuna with black pepper, roasted foie gras, buffalo tenderloin, and red pepper–marinated duck are just a sampling of what you will find on the menu.

The **Chef's Table** ℱℱℱ, available Thursday through Sunday evenings, allows guests the unique experience of dining right in the kitchen (completely transformed by ambient lighting and a chic contemporary decor into an intimate and upscale private dining room). Guests are invited and encouraged to come right into the exhibition kitchen as their dinner is prepared. Chef Orlando personally brings each of the five tantalizing courses to your table. A personalized menu signed by the chef and a Grand Cypress apron are given to each guest at the end of the experience. Even at $85 per person (or $135 with wine pairing), this unique dining experience is well worth the splurge. Make the very-hard-to-obtain reservations for this ultrapopular experience as far in advance as possible. The normal Sunday brunch also allows diners to try out the intimate setting of the kitchen, though most opt to sit in the main dining room.

1 Grand Cypress Blvd., in the Hyatt Regency Grand Cypress Resort. ℂ **407/239-1234.** www.grandcypress.com. Reservations recommended. Jackets suggested for men. Main courses $20–$45; chef's table $85; Sunday brunch $55 ($65 holidays), half price for children; no kids' menu. AE, DC, DISC, MC, V. Daily 6:30–10pm. Free self- and validated valet parking. Take I-4 Exit 68, Hwy. 535/Apopka–Vineland Rd., north to Winter Garden–Vineland Rd./Hwy. 535, then left.

EXPENSIVE

Hemingway's SEAFOOD The interior of Hemingway's has an upscale Key West air, and the walls are hung with sepia photos of the author and his fishing trophies. The restaurant has a romantic indoor dining room lit by hurricane lamps, and the wooden deck overlooks a waterfall. Several smaller rooms add to the intimate atmosphere, and the tall picture windows allow for plenty of natural light and some beautiful views. Several of the restaurant's dishes are displayed in a glass case near the entry, so if you have any questions the chefs are there to answer. Highlights include beer-battered coconut shrimp with horseradish sauce and orange marmalade, or the blackened mahimahi with Cajun tartar sauce. The wine list is decent, but to stay in the spirit of the experience order the *Papa Dobles,* a potent rum concoction invented by Hemingway, who, according to legend, once downed 16 at one sitting! It's usually pretty child-free here, though there is a kids' menu.

1 Grand Cypress Blvd., in the Hyatt Regency Grand Cypress Resort. ✆ **407/239-3854.** www.hyattgrandcypress.com. Reservations recommended. Main courses $25–$41. AE, DC, DISC, MC, V. Daily 6–10pm. Free self- and validated valet parking. Take I-4 Exit 68, Hwy. 535/Apopka–Vineland Rd., north to Winter Garden–Vineland Rd./Hwy. 535, then left.

MODERATE

The Crab House SEAFOOD Even if it is a chain, this casual restaurant offers a good variety of seafood (and a handful of options for landlubbers) at satisfactory prices. The all-you-can-eat seafood and salad bar is great for those who like variety and has lots of tasty dishes. The regular menu features a variety of fish dishes, seafood, Maine lobster, and, of course, crabs—from Alaskan and king to Maryland blue. The service is friendly and relatively prompt. Fishing gear and lobster traps are spread about the casual dining room, strands of lights are strewn across exposed ceilings, and brown paper (good for kids to draw on) lines the tables. *Note:* The chain has several other branches in the Orlando area.

8496 Palm Parkway, Orlando, FL. 32836 (just off Apopka–Vineland across and up from Hotel Plaza Blvd.). ✆ **407/ 239-1888.** www.crabhouseseafood.com. Reservations accepted. Main courses $10–$24; lobster varies according to market. AE, DC, DISC, MC, V. Daily 11:30am–11pm. Free self-parking. Take I-4 to exit 68 (Hwy. 535/Apopka–Vineland), turn right, follow past the Crossroads to Palm Pkwy., turn right. The restaurant is back a bit on the right.

Pebbles ★★ *Finds* CALIFORNIA If you want to dine like a gourmet without the hefty price, this is the restaurant for you. Pebbles is a locally owned chain that has a reputation for great food and creative appetizers. Its pleasant atmosphere is styled after Key West, casual and comfortable. Portions are generous and presented with an artistic flair. The Pebbles twin filets are seared, then bathed in a golden lager and delivered with caramelized onions and three-cheese mashed potatoes. The Mediterranean salmon is sprinkled with artichokes, capers, feta, polenta, and a balsamic demi-glaze. Some lighter bites include crab cakes with Key lime rémoulade, and baked chèvre coconut shrimp with sweet-and-sour sauce. *Note:* Pebbles also has a location in Winter Park, 2516 Aloma Ave. (✆ **407/678-7001**).

12551 Apopka–Vineland Rd., in the Crossroads Shopping Center. ✆ **407/827-1111.** www.pebblesworldwide.com. Reservations not accepted. Main courses $10–$28. AE, DC, DISC, MC, V. Sun–Thurs noon–11pm; Fri–Sat 11am–11pm. Free self-parking. Take the I-4 Hwy. 535/Apopka–Vineland Rd. exit north to the Crossroads Shopping Center on the right.

INEXPENSIVE

Romano's Macaroni Grill ★ *Value* NORTHERN ITALIAN Though it's part of a multistate chain, Romano's has the down-to-earth cheerfulness of a mom-and-pop joint. The laidback atmosphere makes it a good place for families or those looking for a casual dinner at a good price. The menu offers thin-crust pizzas made in a wood-burning oven and topped with such items as barbecued chicken. The grilled chicken portobello (simmering between smoked mozzarella and spinach orzo pasta) alone is worth a visit. Equally good is an entree of grilled salmon with a teriyaki glaze, also with spinach orzo pasta. Premium wines are served by the glass.

12148 Apopka–Vineland Rd. (just north of Hwy. 535/Palm Pkwy.). ✆ 407/239-6676. www.macaronigrill.com. Main courses $6–$15 at lunch, $8–$17 at dinner (most under $12). AE, DC, DISC, MC, V. Sun–Thurs 11am–10pm; Fri–Sat 11am–11pm. Free self-parking. Take I-4 Exit 68, Hwy. 535/Apopka–Vineland Rd. north and continue straight when Hwy. 535 goes to the right. Romano's is about 2 blocks on the left.

5 Places to Dine in Universal Orlando

Universal Orlando stormed onto the restaurant scene with the mid-1999 opening of its dining and entertainment venue, CityWalk, which is between and in front of its two parks, Universal Studios Florida and Islands of Adventure. But Universal's sudden entry onto the food front doesn't mean quality was lost in the rush. In fact some of the best dining options around can be found here—even inside the theme parks (and most especially at Islands of Adventure). Several of Universal's restaurants offer cuisine ranging from respectable light bites to dependable dinners (a few even border on fine dining!), with most offering unique and casual atmospheres. Do note, of course, that the better-than-average food and surroundings come with higher-than-average prices. Universal takes "Priority Seating" arrangements for its park and CityWalk restaurants, which can be made up to 30 days in advance by calling ✆ **407/224-3613** for USF restaurants, **407/224-4012** for IOA restaurants, and **407/224-3663** for CityWalk (except Margaritaville and NBA City) dining spots. Actual reservations are available only for **Mythos** (✆ **407/224-4534**) and **Emeril's** (✆ **407/503-2467**). For more information on dining at Universal, call ✆ **407/224-9255**.

Note: Most of the restaurants below can be found on the "CityWalk" map on p. 329. All of the hotel restaurants listed can be found on the "International Drive Area Dining" map on p. 163.

VERY EXPENSIVE

Bice ✿ ITALIAN   Universal Orlando's newest restaurant, appropriately located in the romantic and spectacular Italian setting of the Portofino Bay Hotel, replaced the old Delfino Riviera. The family-owned and -operated restaurant (part of a Milan-based international chain), features creative Italian cuisine served in a sophisticated and upscale atmosphere. The extensive menu includes items such as a Belgian endive salad in a light Dijon mustard dressing with Gorgonzola cheese and toasted walnuts; spaghetti with Maine lobster and cherry tomatoes in a tomato bisque; and veal chops with sautéed mushrooms, potatoes, and spinach. The dining room overlooks the waters along the piazza of the hotel, itself a beautiful and romantic setting—a table on the patio, if timed right, may allow you to enjoy the music of the strolling musicians performing just below along the piazza. The interior decor is elegant, accented by a beautiful muted fresco of the Italian countryside, soft subdued lighting setting the tone. The lounge has a more contemporary and chic feel about it (though the flatscreen TV above the bar detracts greatly from the otherwise exceptional ambience). If there's a disappointment to be found at this restaurant, it's the air of aloofness created by the servers and staff.

5601 Universal Studios Blvd., in the Portofino Bay Hotel. ☏ **407/503-3463** or 407/503-1415. Reservations recommended. Main courses $18–$44. AE, MC, V. Daily 5:30–10:30pm. Free 3-hr. validated self-parking; valet parking $17. From I-4, take Exit 75B, Kirkman Rd./Hwy. 435, and follow the signs to Universal.

Emeril's 🌟🌟 NEW ORLEANS   It's next to impossible to get short-term reservations for dinner (less than 3–4 weeks in advance) at Emeril's unless your stars are aligned or you come at the opening bell and take your chances with no-shows (highly unlikely). If you do get in, you'll find the dynamic cuisine is worth the struggle. The Creole-inspired (and seasonally changing) menu is varied and might include such dishes as a grilled double-cut pork chop with a cider pepper glaze or a roasted American rack of lamb with a Creole mustard crust. If you want some vino with your meals, the back half of the building houses a glass-walled, 12,000-bottle, aboveground wine cellar. The warehouse-style decor is casual and inviting yet still upscale; original artwork, much of it by New Orleans artists, lines the walls, and arched lighting spans the two-story ceilings. If you want a show, we highly recommend you try for one of eight counter seats where you can watch chefs working their magic, but to get one, reservations are required *excruciatingly* early (2–3 months in advance, especially during holidays, in summer, and on weekends).

Note: Lunch costs about half what you'll spend on dinner, and the menu has many of the same entrees. It's also easier to get a reservation, and the dress code is more casual—jackets are recommended for the guys at dinner, although that goes against the grain after a long day in the parks. No matter when you come, leave the kids at home—this restaurant caters to adults.

6000 Universal Studios Blvd., in CityWalk. ☏ **407/224-2424.** www.emerils.com/restaurants/orlando_emerils/. Reservations necessary. Main courses $18–$28 lunch, $31–$50 dinner. Daily 11:30am–2pm; Sun–Thurs 5:30–10pm; Fri–Sat 5:30–11pm. AE, DISC, MC, V. Parking $9 (free 2-hr. valet parking at lunch; free self-parking after 6pm). From I-4, take Exit 75B, Kirkman Rd./Hwy. 435, and follow the signs to Universal.

The Palm STEAKS/SEAFOOD   This upscale restaurant is the 23rd member of a chain started more than 75 years ago in New York. The food is good, although, as is the case with most Disney and Universal restaurants, somewhat overpriced for the value received. Beef and seafood rule a menu headlined by a 36-ounce New York strip steak for two ($73) and a 3-pound Nova Scotia lobster (market price). There are, however, plenty of steaks, pasta, seafood, and salads to please every palate. There are even a few options for those on smaller budgets. The decor leans toward the upscale supper club of the '30s and '40s, and the walls are lined with caricatures of celebrities and stars.

5800 Universal Blvd., in the Hard Rock Hotel. ☏ **407/503-7256.** www.thepalm.com. Reservations recommended. Main courses $9–$31 lunch, $17–$38 dinner. AE, DC, DISC, MC, V. Mon–Fri 11:30am–11pm; Sat 5–11pm; Sun 5–10pm. Free 3-hr. validated self-parking; valet parking $17. From I-4, take Exit 75B, Kirkman Rd./Hwy. 435, and follow the signs to Universal.

EXPENSIVE

Emeril's Tchoup Chop 🌟🌟🌟 PACIFIC RIM   Perfection is pronounced "chop chop." Emeril Lagasse's second restaurant in Orlando is named for the location of his original restaurant, Tchoupitoulas Street in New Orleans. Think bluezoo (p. 152) with an Asian Pacific twist—very chic, very contemporary, very cool. The upbeat yet relaxing atmosphere, visually stunning surroundings, and excellent food will ensure the experience is unmatched. The exotic decor features glass flower chandeliers and a grand stone wall that reaches high above an exhibition kitchen (a seat at the counter allows for quite an impressive show). Polynesian- and Asian-influenced dishes such as macadamia nut–encrusted Atlantic salmon, Polynesian crab cakes with mango habanero butter sauce and papaya salsa, and ahi tuna lettuce wraps are just a sampling of the tasty offerings found here. And not one but several waiters impeccably cater to your every need, serving meals as if they were in a perfectly choreographed production. *Note:* The dress code here is more casual than at Emeril's (listed earlier), but it's still pretty upscale, so leave the T-shirts and tanks at home.

6300 Hollywood Way, in Universal's Royal Pacific Hotel. (C) **407/503-2467.** www.emerils.com, www.universal orlando.com. Reservations strongly recommended. Main courses $13–$34. AE, DISC, MC, V. Daily 11:30am–2pm; Sun–Thurs 5:30–10pm; Fri–Sat 5:30–11pm. Valet parking (near the restaurant at the convention center entrance, not the hotel lot) $5. From I-4, take the Kirkman Rd./Hwy. 435 exit, and follow the signs to Universal.

Mythos ⚓ AMERICAN/SEAFOOD/STEAK   If you've ever wanted to dine inside a volcano covered in cascading waterfalls and images of Greek Titans, then here's the place for you. Actually, this upscale restaurant, which overlooks Islands of Adventure's Inland Sea, is quite classy. Diners are transported to a mythical underwater world upon entering the restaurant's cavernous interior, where low lighting and eerie music help set the atmosphere. The menu features wood-fired pizzas; salads, ranging from a simple bowl of greens to a full-fledged meal; and elaborate entrees of fish, seafood, and steaks. Simpler fare is available as well, including artistically presented burgers. *Tip:* You can actually dine here without paying for park admission, though you'll have to leave a credit card number at the gate and will be faced with a time limit. If you're running late, the restaurant can call the gate to let them know so you won't be charged.

1000 Universal Studios Plaza, in Islands of Adventure. (C) **407/224-9255** or 407/224-4534. www.universalorlando. com. Reservations recommended. Main courses $11–$19. AE, DISC, MC, V. Daily 11am–park closing. Parking $9 (free after 6pm). From I-4, take Exit 75B, Kirkman Rd./Hwy. 435, and follow the signs to Universal.

MODERATE

Hard Rock Cafe AMERICAN   The largest Hard Rock Cafe on the planet features a 1959 pink Cadillac spinning above the bar. With its size, however, comes that much more noise—and the sound levels are loud. Kids love it, but adults shouldn't even think about having a conversation here. The menu is the same found at Hard Rocks round the world and includes burgers, chicken, okay steaks, and fried this-and-that. And, of course, it has its very own souvenir shop, too. The food is average American fare; it's the experience that draws people in. *Note:* The adjacent Hard Rock Live! is a huge venue for concerts.

6000 Universal Studios Blvd., near Universal CityWalk. (C) **407/351-7625.** www.hardrock.com. Reservations not accepted. Main courses $8–$23. AE, MC, V. Daily 11am–1am. Parking $9 (free after 6pm). From I-4, take Exit 75B, Kirkman Rd./Hwy. 435, and follow the signs to Universal.

Tips Another Blockbuster

The **Bubba Gump Shrimp Co.** (www.bubbagump.com or www.universalor-lando.com) is the latest addition to Universal's CityWalk restaurant lineup. It takes the place of Decades Cafe near the CityWalk entrance (across from the Cineplex). This casual family-friendly eatery, based on the blockbuster film *Forrest Gump,* features a diverse menu likely to please almost every palate—don't let the name fool you, it's not just for seafood lovers. Spilling over with movie memorabilia, it's a perfect addition to a trip to Universal Studios Florida, a park where the movies come to life.

Jimmy Buffett's Margaritaville CARIBBEAN   The casual laid-back atmosphere may take you away to paradise, but the noise level after 4pm makes it futile for Parrot Heads and plain folk alike to try to talk with their table mates. But most people come to Margaritaville in the evenings to party, not to participate in a deep conversation. Come for lunch if you want to actually speak with your fellow diners during your meal. The back "Porch of Indecision" offers the quietest spot in the place to dine. Despite the cheeseburgers in paradise (yes, they're on the menu at $8–$9), the menu has Caribbean leanings and includes a Cuban meatloaf survival sandwich, Creole shrimp marinara, Jimmy's jammin' jambalaya, and corn and crab bisque. And, while it's not contending for a critic's choice award, it's fairly tasty grub. But watch the tab: At $6 to $8 a pop for margaritas, the bill can climb to $50 or more per person for a routine meal that includes even the jerk chicken or crab cakes. If you don't hanker for margaritas, the drink menu is almost as long as the main menu and features domestic and imported beer, as well as some unique tropical concoctions.

1000 Universal Studios Plaza, in CityWalk. ✆ 407/224-2155. www.margaritavilleorlando.com. Reservations not accepted. Main courses $9–$22 (most under $15). AE, DISC, MC, V. Daily 11am–2am. Parking $9 (free after 6pm). From I-4, take Exit 75B, Kirkman Rd./Hwy. 435, and follow the signs to Universal.

Pastamore Ristorante SOUTHERN ITALIAN   This family-style restaurant greets you with display cases brimming with mozzarella and other goodies lurking on the menu. The antipasto primo is a meal unto itself. The mound includes bruschetta, eggplant Caponata, melon con prosciutto, grilled portobello mushrooms, olives, a medley of Italian cold cuts, olives, plum tomatoes, fresh mozzarella, and more. The menu also features such traditional offerings as veal Marsala, chicken piccata, shrimp scampi, fettuccine Alfredo, lasagna, and pizza. The food is actually pretty interesting, and the presentation isn't bad either. There's an open kitchen that lets you see the chefs in action, and the atmosphere is pleasant and lively. Pastamore has a basic beer and wine menu. You can also eat in the Marketplace Café, where a lighter menu—breakfast fare and sandwiches—is served from 8am to 2am.

1000 Universal Studios Plaza, in CityWalk. ✆ 407/363-8000. www.universalorlando.com. Reservations accepted. Main courses $7–$18. AE, DISC, MC, V. Daily 5pm–midnight; the Marketplace Café 8am–2am. Parking $9 (free after 6pm). From I-4, take Exit 75B, Kirkman Rd./Hwy. 435, and follow the signs to Universal.

6 Places to Dine in the International Drive Area

International Drive has one of the area's larger collections of fast-food joints but mixed in around its midsection and southern end are some of the region's better restaurants. South I-Drive is 10 minutes by auto from the Walt Disney World parks. Restaurant Row, located in a small area just above I-Drive along Dr. Phillips Boulevard and Sand Lake Road, is currently the hottest dining area in Orlando. Most of the restaurants listed here are located on the "International Drive Area Dining" map on p. 162.

VERY EXPENSIVE

Atlantis ✿ SEAFOOD/STEAKS/CHOPS   This intimate dining room, adorned with hand-painted murals, has a rich, warm, elegant feel, especially in the booths separated by etched-glass panels. Chef's specials such as a Mediterranean seafood medley (Florida lobster, grouper, shrimp, and scallops) frequently complement menu standards such as grilled sea bass or pan-seared duck and rock shrimp. Sunday's champagne brunch is served in the beautifully landscaped atrium. Themes change monthly,

International Drive Area Dining

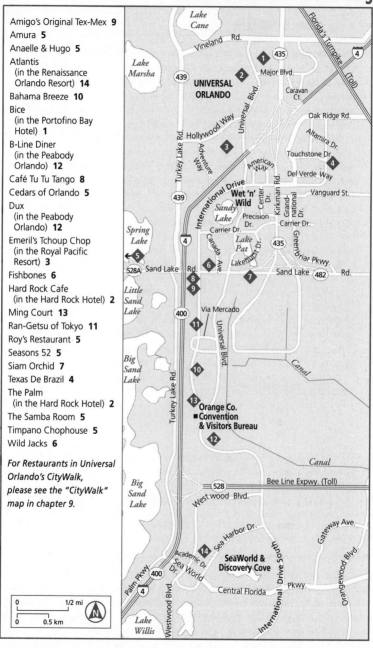

Amigo's Original Tex-Mex **9**

Amura **5**

Anaelle & Hugo **5**

Atlantis
(in the Renaissance
Orlando Resort) **14**

Bahama Breeze **10**

Bice
(in the Portofino Bay
Hotel) **1**

B-Line Diner
(in the Peabody
Orlando) **12**

Café Tu Tu Tango **8**

Cedars of Orlando **5**

Dux
(in the Peabody
Orlando) **12**

Emeril's Tchoup Chop
(in the Royal Pacific
Resort) **3**

Fishbones **6**

Hard Rock Cafe
(in the Hard Rock Hotel) **2**

Ming Court **13**

Ran-Getsu of Tokyo **11**

Roy's Restaurant **5**

Seasons 52 **5**

Siam Orchid **7**

Texas De Brazil **4**

The Palm
(in the Hard Rock Hotel) **2**

The Samba Room **5**

Timpano Chophouse **5**

Wild Jacks **6**

*For Restaurants in Universal
Orlando's CityWalk,
please see the "CityWalk"
map in chapter 9.*

0   1/2 mi
0   0.5 km

Tips **New & Notable**

Orlando restaurants come and go in what seems like the blink of an eye. There are, however, a handful of newcomers that (we hope) are here to stay. **Texas De Brazil**, 5259 International Dr. (© **407/355-0355;** www.texas debrazil.com), is one of them. After being seated you'll be directed to the extensive 40-item seasonal salad bar, filled with salads, roasted vegetables, and soups. After filling your plate head back to your seat, where you'll find a coasterlike disc—one side red, the other green. When you're ready for your main course just flip your disc to green. Immediately a troop of carvers will show up, offering a variety of grilled and roasted meats from their skewers. The filet is to die for—it simply melts in your mouth. When you've had your fill, just turn your disc back to red. Assorted side dishes (served tableside) are available to complement your meal (if you actually have any room for them). A handful of a la carte items, including Australian lobster tail and shrimp cocktail, are available as well (at an additional cost). Drinks and desserts are extra as well. Dinner is served up at a fixed price of $40; select a la carte items, beverages, and desserts are extra. Kids age 7 to 12 are charged half price, and kids under 6 can eat for free.

Another new eatery worth noting is **Amigo's Original Tex-Mex,** 8282 International Dr. (© **407/363-7708;** www.amigostex-mex.com). It's similar (architecturally anyway) to Pacino's Italian Ristorante in Kissimmee, with an open two-story interior filled with exposed brick, wrought-iron accents, and tremendous wood beams. Amigo's, however, looks and feels like a Mexican cantina. Colorful artwork and decorative accents, including a colorful group of oversize frogs strumming guitars, and lively music, create a festive, almost fiesta-like atmosphere. A varied menu of better-than-average Tex-Mex fare and the unique decor make this one a winner. Entrees run $7 to $11.

---

but the 100-item menu often has treats such as quail, duck, lamb chops, Cornish hen, clams, mussels, snapper, sea bass, sushi, and much more. Although pricey, it's one of Orlando's more popular brunches.

6677 Sea Harbour Dr., in the Renaissance Orlando Resort. © 407/351-5555. www.renaissancehotels.com. Reservations recommended. Main courses $27–$35; Sunday brunch $35 adults, $18 children. AE, DC, DISC, MC, V. Daily 6–10pm; Sun brunch 10:30am–2pm. Free self-parking, valet parking $14 (complimentary for brunch). From I-4, take Exit 71/Central Florida Pkwy. east and follow the signs to SeaWorld.

Dux ⭐⭐ *Finds* INTERNATIONAL   The name is a tribute to the Peabody Orlando's resident ducks, who parade ceremoniously along the red carpet in and out of the lobby every day (p. 116), while the food is a tribute to chefs who create a menu that changes weekly. It might include succulent Alaskan Halibut with lobster mashed potatoes and lobster reduction, or lemon grass skewered bluefin tuna. At other times, hope for a tender veal chop marinated in apple cider and honey and served medium rare; steamed red snapper in tomato fricassee and fennel; or sautéed salmon on a bed of couscous with black olives, tomatoes, and chives. A vegetarian entree is served each night. And don't skip dessert, especially if the hot chocolate mousse is on the menu.

Dux is best reserved for a very special night out or a meal on an expense account. Candlelit tables surround a large chandelier, and textured gold walls are hung with watercolors of the various duck species. (Speaking of ducks, you won't find any on the menu—staffers say that would be sacrilege.) The impeccable service that's a signature of the hotel carries into the restaurant, and Dux has one of the best wine lists in Orlando. *Note:* Because the convention trade slows in August, it's one of the best times to try Dux and avoid crowds. Early birds sometimes have the dining room to themselves.

9801 International Dr., in the Peabody Orlando. ✆ 407/345-4550. www.peabodyorlando.com. Reservations recommended. Main courses $30–$50. AE, DC, DISC, MC, V. Mon–Sat 6–10pm. Free self- and validated valet parking. From I-4, take Exit 74A, Sand Lake Rd./Hwy. 528, east to International Dr., then south. Hotel is on the left across from the Convention Center.

EXPENSIVE

Ran-Getsu of Tokyo JAPANESE   Authentic cuisine, including a sushi bar, has made Ran-Getsu a popular haunt for moneyed Asian tourists, though some travelers find its prices too high. *Tekka-don,* tender slices of tuna that are mild enough for first-timers, is a refreshing choice on the sushi side; so are platters, such as sashimi, maki rolls, and thinly sliced *chirashi* (rice topped with assorted seafood). *Yosenabe* is a bouillabaisse with an unconventional though savory twist—duck and chicken are added to the seafood mix; lobster is available at an added cost. Speaking of seafood, *una-ju* delights eel lovers; the filets are grilled in kabayaki sauce. Less adventurous palates may prefer shrimp tempura or a steak served in teriyaki sauce. A traditional Japanese drum show is performed in the evening, Thursday through Saturday. Ran-Getsu has a small wine list as well as sake and plum wine.

8400 International Dr., near Orlando Convention Center. ✆ 407/345-0044. www.rangetsu.com. Reservations recommended. Main courses $19–$50; sushi entrees $15–$45 (most under $25); fixed full-course menu $50–$70. AE, DC, DISC, MC, V. Daily 5–11pm. From I-4, take Exit 74A, Sand Lake Rd./Hwy. 528, east to International Dr., then south. Restaurant is on right.

Roy's Restaurant ✦ PACIFIC RIM   Created in Hawaii in 1988 by chef Roy Yamaguchi, this small chain made its Orlando debut in 2001. The restaurant has an island theme and, unlike the nearby Samba Room (see below), an atmosphere that allows for intimate conversation. The large main dining area has a large open exhibition kitchen, offering quite a show for those seated at the surrounding counter. The emphasis is on fresh seafood (though other items are offered as well), prepared with a variety of sauces and imaginatively garnished and presented with an Asian-style flair. Menus change weekly (classic dishes remain a constant), but entrees might include wood-roasted lemon grass shrimp with black-rice risotto; seared mahimahi with macadamia-lobster sauce; Korean-style barbecue beef with shiitake mushrooms; and Mongolian-style pork tenderloin in a sake, soy, and pineapple sauce. Roy's also has a reasonably deep wine list.

7760 W. Sand Lake Rd. ✆ 407/352-4844. www.roysrestaurant.com. Reservations suggested. Main courses $19–$38, fixed price menu $33. AE, DC, DISC, MC, V. Sun–Thurs 5:30–10pm; Fri–Sat until 10:30pm. Take I-4 Exit 74A, Sand Lake Rd./Hwy. 528, and go west 1 mile. Restaurant is on left.

MODERATE

B-Line Diner AMERICAN   You can sink into upholstered booths or belly up to the counter on a stool in this upscale '50s-style diner. The bold black and white decor has an Art Deco feel thanks to the pink and blue neon lighting accenting the chrome-lined ceiling. The round-the-clock menu features comfort foods such as a chicken pot-pie that's up to what mom made; a ham and cheese sandwich on a baguette; and roast

Dining on Restaurant Row

Over the past few years, just east of I-4 along a stretch of Sand Lake Road in the swanky suburb of Dr. Phillips, several very chic, very trendy, and very hip eateries have popped up. This high concentration of upscale (and, at times, ethnic) eateries, now known as **Restaurant Row,** is home to some of Orlando's best eating opportunities. In addition to the restaurants already listed in this guide (including **Roy's Restaurant** and **The Samba Room**), there are lots of others worth noting. A few of the best include:

- **Seasons 52** ⊛, 7700 Sand Lake Rd. (© **407/354-5212**; www.seasons52. com). Enter this combination grill and wine bar and you'll feel as if you've stepped onto the set of a Rock Hudson movie thanks to the '50s-style Art Deco architecture and an interior accented with stacked stone walls. The weekly changing menu is both sophisticated and designed to be healthy, so it's relatively easy on the waistline and the palate.

- **Cedars of Orlando,** 7732 W. Sand Lake Rd. (© **407/351-6000**; http://cedars oforlando.com). A simple yet elegant atmosphere featuring Ottoman arches and columns, white table linens, and a roof-topped terrace for outdoor dining combine with a selection of over 50 Lebanese specialties (and a bit of belly dancing) to make this Middle Eastern restaurant a very attractive package.

- **Amura** ⊛, 7786 Sand Lake Rd. (© **407/370-0007**). One of the city's best Asian restaurants features a contemporary decor that runs throughout its three unique dining areas, which include a sushi counter, performance grills, and a more intimate dining room. The main menu tilts toward a fusion of Japanese and European cuisines.

- **Anaelle & Hugo** ⊛, 7533 W. Sand Lake Rd. (© **407/996-9292**; www.anaelle andhugo.com). This award-winner is a great choice for Euro-American cuisine with a sophisticated flair. The warmly lit lounge offers a setting that's conducive to conversation. The dining area is contrastingly cool, filled with blue lights, white tablecloths, and live music on the weekends.

- **Timpano Chophouse** ⊛, 7488 W. Sand Lake Rd. (© **407/248-0249**; www. timpanochophouse.net). Classic, sophisticated styling (think old New York supper club) is the signature of this Italian steakhouse, which also features fabulous aged steaks and impeccable service. Large booths, chandeliers, an indoor fireplace, and baby grand piano add to the ambience, while the sounds of Sinatra, swing, and jazz play in the background.

To get to Restaurant Row: From I-4 East take exit 74A, turn left onto Sand Lake Road. From I-Drive turn left onto Sand Lake Road. Restaurants run along both sides of the road in the Fountains and the Venezia plazas, as well as The Marketplace.

pork with grilled apples, sun-dried cherry stuffing, and brandy-honey sauce. The portions are hearty but so are the prices. And although it is a diner-style restaurant, it is not particularly kid-friendly, unless your children are exceptionally well behaved.

9801 International Dr., in the Peabody Orlando. © 407/345-4460. www.peabodyorlando.com. Reservations not accepted. Main courses $4–$16 at breakfast, $11–$24 at lunch and dinner (most under $18). AE, DC, DISC, MC, V. Daily 24-hr. free self- and validated valet parking. From I-4, take Exit 74A, Sand Lake Rd./Hwy. 528, east to International Dr., then south. Hotel is on the left across from the Convention Center.

Bahama Breeze ☞ CARIBBEAN   This chain restaurant sports a creative menu that offers a variety of delicious sandwiches and chicken, fish, and pasta entrees with Caribbean twists. Try starting out with the Creole baked goat cheese before moving on to the Cuban sandwich, one of the most authentic around. If that is not to your liking, try the pan-seared pork, or Bahamian chicken kabobs. The atmosphere is island casual, with rich wood and wicker throughout. On a warm evening ask to eat outside. Once famous for its long waits, the restaurant now accepts call-ahead reservations—be sure and do so. *Note:* A second branch is located in Lake Buena Vista at 8735 Vineland Ave., near the I-4 intersection (© **407/938-9010**).

8849 International Drive, Orlando. © 407/248-2499. www.bahamabreeze.com. Call-ahead reservations available. Lunch and dinner $9–$25. AE, DISC, MC, V. Mon–Fri 4pm–1:30am; Sat noon–1:30am; Sun noon–1am. Free self-parking. From I-4, take exit 74A, follow I-Drive 1 mile south.

Café Tu Tu Tango ☞☞ *Finds* INTERNATIONAL/TAPAS   Authentic cuisine and the eclectic atmosphere of a Mediterranean artists' loft—complete with working artist—are the main draws at this interesting tapas bar. The portions are small, but the tastes are big. The roasted pears on pecan crisps—topped with Spanish bleu cheese and a balsamic reduction—are a must. The staff is fabulous and your server will be happy to educate you about the menu or make suggestions. Wine is available by the glass or bottle.

8625 International Drive. © 407/248-2222. www.cafetututango.com. Reservations accepted but not required. Tapas (small plates) $4–$20. AE, DC, DISC, MC, V. Sun–Thurs 11:30am–11pm; Fri–Sat 11:30am–2am. Free self-parking. From I-4, take exit 74A, Sand Lake Rd./Hwy 528, east to International Drive, then south. It is on the left.

Fishbones SEAFOOD   The fish at this Key West–themed restaurant is handpicked daily to ensure freshness and taste. You can create your own meal by mixing and matching sauces and salsas to enhance your selected fish (from which there are plenty of varieties to choose). If fish isn't your dish, other offerings include rack of lamb, prime rib, and duck. You can dine in one of two distinctive seating areas, one sporting a classic

---

(Value Self-Service Suppers

If you're on a tight budget and your room has a kitchen or a spot to sit and grab a bite, consider dining in a night or two and saving a few bucks. Area grocers, many with delis that turn out ready-to-eat treats, include **Albertson's** near I-Drive (7524 Dr. Phillips Blvd., © **407/352-1552**; www.albertsons.com), and **Gooding's** in Lake Buena Vista (Crossroads Shopping Plaza, 12521 Hwy. 535/Apopka–Vineland Ave.; © **407/827-1200**; www.goodings.com) and along I-Drive (8255 I-Drive; © **407/352-4215**). You can find more options in the Orlando Yellow Pages under "Grocers."

(Tips **Room Service**

For those of you who would rather take a break from eating out, there are several Orlando restaurants that are more than willing to come to you. A local delivery service, "Take Out Express," will deliver takeout from a number of area restaurants (even more than one at a time for an extra charge) right to your hotel room. The delivery cost is about $5 to order from one restaurant, with a separate (though lower) delivery charge for each additional restaurant you order from. Call ☏ **407/352-1170** for details or to order.

---

steakhouse decor, the other a more casual space that will have you feeling like you're dining on an outdoor porch.

6707 Sand Lake Rd., off of International Dr. Entrees run $13–$40 (most below $25). AE, MC, V. Sun–Thurs 5–10:30pm; Fri–Sat until 11pm. Free self-parking. From I-4 take exit 74A, go east on SR 482 (Sand Lake Rd.) .3 miles.

Ming Court ☘ CHINESE   Local patronage and a diverse menu make this one of Orlando's most popular Chinese eateries (recently named one of the top 100 Chinese restaurants in the country by a major restaurant trade publication). Start off with the duck lettuce cup before going on to the lightly battered, deep-fried chicken breast—it's got plenty of zip from a delicate lemon-tangerine sauce. If you're in the mood for beef, there's a grilled filet mignon that's seasoned Szechuan-style (the topping has toasted onions, garlic, and chile). The mildly innovative menu is extensive, featuring the freshest ingredients (there's not a freezer on-site). Portions are sufficient, there's a moderate wine list, and the service is quite good. The candlelit interior is decorated in soft earth tones and creates a romantic atmosphere. Glass-walled terrace rooms overlook lotus ponds filled with colorful koi, and a plant-filled area under a lofty skylight ceiling. A musician plays classical Chinese music on a *zheng* (a long zither) at dinner. The children's menu features a boxed meal featuring your choice of Oriental-style shrimp, pork, beef, or chicken (and french fries!), and comes with a story for kids to read along with their dinner. *Tip:* The restaurant's website is extensive and features lots of information on and photos of individual dishes.

9188 International Dr., between Sand Lake Rd. and Bee Line Expressway. ☏ 407/351-9988. www.ming-court.com. Reservations recommended. Main courses $7–$13 lunch, $13–$36 dinner; dim sum mostly $3–$5. AE, DC, DISC, MC, V. Daily 11am–2:30pm and 4:30–11:30pm. Free self-parking. From I-4, take Exit 74A, Sand Lake Rd./Hwy. 528, east to International Dr., then south. It's on the right.

The Samba Room ☘ CUBAN   Don't count on intimate conversation, because the Cuban and Brazilian music here is loud, Loud, LOUD (and the regulars like it that way). The atmosphere is upbeat and sophisticated, enhanced by contemporary artwork and vividly colorful murals. The kitchen turns out an enterprising menu that includes Rum teriyaki–glazed salmon with stir-fried veggies, soba noodles, and Kaffir lime sauce; Spanish paella (chicken, mussels, shrimp, calamari, and lobster over saffron rice); and pork barbacoa (marinated in beer and slow-roasted in banana leaves) with gringo rice and Asian barbecue sauce. And if you're worried that you won't be able to find room for dessert (portions are large)—the restaurant offers downsized versions of decadent desserts that won't bust your buttons. Alfresco dining is available on the patio and is especially enjoyable in the milder weather. *Tip:* Fridays feature late-night Samba lessons while live Latin bands play to the Saturday night crowds.

7468 W. Sand Lake Rd. © 407/226-0550. www.e-brands.net. Reservations recommended. Main courses $16–$30. AE, DC, DISC, MC, V. Mon–Fri 11:30am–4pm; Sun–Wed 4–10pm; Fri–Sat 4pm–midnight. Free self-parking. Take I-4 Exit 74A, Sand Lake Rd./Hwy. 528, west 1 mile. Restaurant is on left.

Siam Orchid ♠ *Finds* THAI   Owners Tim and Krissnee Martsching grow chiles, mint, cilantro, lemon grass, wild lime, and other ingredients in their garden, and the quality of their entrees is consistently high. Pad Thai (soft rice noodles tossed with ground pork, minced garlic, shrimp, crab claws, crabmeat, crushed peanuts, and bean sprouts in a tongue-twanging sweet sauce) is one of our favorites. Royal Thai (chicken chunks, potato, and onion in a yellow curry sauce) is another crowd pleaser. For intimate dining, request a *khun toke,* a private enclosure that's the Thai answer to Japanese *tatami* rooms. The split-level dining room has cushioned booths and banquettes and bamboo chairs; some tables overlook a lake. Siam Orchid serves sake and Thai beers from a full bar.

7575 Universal Dr. (between Sand Lake Rd. and Carrier Dr.). © 407/351-0821. Reservations recommended. Main courses $12–$24. AE, DC, DISC, MC, V. Mon–Fri 11am–2pm; daily 5–11pm. Free self-parking. From I-4, take Exit 74A, Sand Lake Rd./Hwy. 528, east to Universal, then go north to the restaurant (on the left).

Wild Jacks BARBECUE/STEAKS   Come hankering for red meat or don't come at all to this chuck wagon–style eatery. Jacks serves Texas-size (and sometimes Texas tough) hunks of cow grilled on an open pit and served with jalapeño smashed potatoes and corn on the cob. The ribs are generally moist and tender, but at crowded times, when the kitchen gets backed up, they may be dry and chewy. The menu also has chicken, salmon, and pork, but it's not a good idea to experiment in a beef house. To add to the mood, you'll be treated to mounted buffalo heads, long-stuffed jackalopes, and more dying-calf-in-a-hailstorm, twitch-and-twang country-western music than a city slicker can endure in a lifetime. Wash the meal down with an icy longneck (there is a wine list, but it's very basic).

7364 International Dr. (between Sand Lake Rd. and Carrier Dr.). © 407/352-4407. Reservations accepted. AE, DC, DISC, MC, V. Main courses $11–$21. Daily 4–10pm. Free self-parking. From I-4, take Exit 74A, Sand Lake Rd./Hwy. 528, east to International Dr., then go south. It's on the right.

7 Places to Dine Elsewhere in Orlando

There's life beyond the main tourist areas, as a lot of locals and some enterprising visitors discover. The restaurants in this part of the chapter are located on the map "Accommodations & Dining Elsewhere in Orlando" on p. 171.

VERY EXPENSIVE

Manuel's on the 28th ♠♠♠ *Moments* INTERNATIONAL   The 28th floor of a downtown bank provides part of the name and all of the view, which is no less than beautiful after dark. You can see the city and the distant theme parks (fireworks, too), and this is the rare case where the food actually matches the visuals. Despite a smallish kitchen, the chefs work wonders with a changing menu. When available, we can't resist the miso-marinated Chilean sea bass with seaweed salad. Seafood lovers also might encounter asparagus-seared ahi tuna with rice risotto and lump crab hollandaise. And the five peppercorn Angus filet with smoked Gouda potatoes wows the red-meat crowd. A four-course fixed price menu with optional wine pairing is available as well. To make sure you don't miss out on the view, the dining room has floor-to-ceiling windows. Expect very professional service and a far-above-par wine cellar.

390 N. Orange Ave., in the NationsBank Building. © 407/246-6580. www.manuelsonthe28th.com. Reservations required. Jackets suggested for men. Main courses $26–$45; fixed price menu $55, with wine pairing $75. AE, DC, DISC, MC, V. Tues–Sat 6–10pm. Free self-parking. From I-4 take Exit 82C/Anderson St. east to Orange Ave., then left/north to NationsBank Building.

EXPENSIVE

Mikado Japanese Steakhouse 🌟🌟 JAPANESE   This restaurant offers a tastier meal and a more intimate atmosphere than the other Japanese steakhouses in the area. The sushi menu is one of the area's best, as is its *teppanyaki*. Here the chefs slice, dice, and send the occasional piece of chicken, seafood, and beef from their grill to your plate, and the chef's addition of a few extra special spices make it the best *teppanyaki* in the area. Shoji screens lend intimacy to a dining area where windows overlook rock gardens, reflecting pools, and a palm-fringed pond. Sake, from the restaurant lounge, is the recommended mood enhancer.

8701 World Center Dr. (off Hwy. 536), in Marriott's Orlando World Center. © 407/239-4200. Reservations recommended. Main courses $16–$37. AE, DC, DISC, MC, V. Daily 6–10pm. Free self- and validated valet parking. Take I-4 Exit 67/Hwy. 536 east to the Marriott World Center.

MODERATE

Carrabbas 🌟 ITALIAN   Here's yet another chain, but one that is well run with above-average food. The menu features such specialties as *tagliarini picchi pacchiu* (a fine pasta with crushed tomatoes, garlic, olive oil, and basil served with either chicken or shrimp) and *pollo Rosa Maria* (fire-roasted chicken stuffed with fontina cheese and prosciutto, and topped with mushrooms and a basil lemon butter sauce). Also available are wood-fired pizzas, an array of soups and salads, pastas, and other favorite Italian classics. The atmosphere is casual but lively; the interior features a show kitchen and lots of exposed brick. Don't forget to save room for dessert—they're large enough to share (though you may not want to!).

7890 Irlo Bronson Memorial Hwy. (U.S. 192), in the Formosa Gardens Plaza, Kissimmee. © 407/390-9600. www. carrabbas.com. Main courses $10–$21 dinner only. AE, DC, DISC, MC, V. Sun–Thurs 4–10pm; Fri–Sat 4–11pm. Free self-parking. From I-4 take exit 64 for US 192, continue on and it is on the left in the Formosa Gardens Plaza.

Pacino's Italian Ristorante 🌟 NORTHERN ITALIAN   The house specialty, veal *osso buco*, is a delicious collision of veal shank, mushrooms, Barolo wine, herbs, and mushrooms. At 32 ounces, the porterhouse steak is a belly-buster, and the house's *frutti di mare* has shrimp, calamari, clams, and scallops sautéed with white wine and

---

Tips **Downtown Delights**

The revitalization of the downtown area has brought with it the addition of chic clubs and trendy upscale eateries well worth a second look—and the 20-minute drive. **Hue—A Restaurant** 🌟🌟, 629 E. Central Blvd. (© **407/849-1800;** www.huerestaurant.com), recognized in 2003 by *Condé Nast Traveler* as "one of the best new restaurants in the world," lives up to its reputation thanks to creative American cuisine and a sophisticated urban loft atmosphere. **Kres Chophouse** 🌟, 17 W. Church St. (© **407/447-7950;** www.kresrestaurant.com), a not-so-distant relative of Hue, offers an ever-changing menu of traditional yet exceptional steakhouse fare, as well as an extensive wine list.

Accommodations & Dining Elsewhere in Orlando

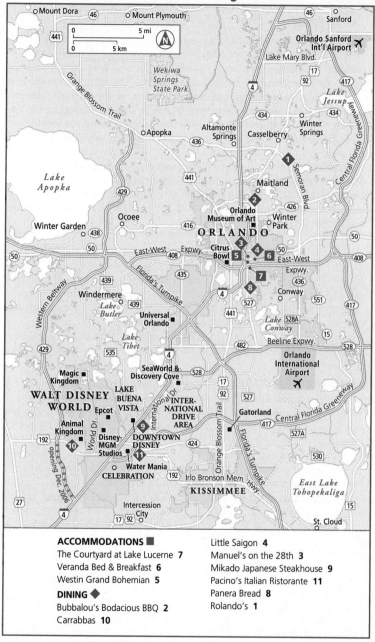

ACCOMMODATIONS ■
The Courtyard at Lake Lucerne **7**
Veranda Bed & Breakfast **6**
Westin Grand Bohemian **5**

DINING ◆
Bubbalou's Bodacious BBQ **2**
Carrabbas **10**

Little Saigon **4**
Manuel's on the 28th **3**
Mikado Japanese Steakhouse **9**
Pacino's Italian Ristorante **11**
Panera Bread **8**
Rolando's **1**

(Value) Bargain Buffets

We won't list them all, but if you spend time on International Drive or U.S. 192/Irlo Bronson Memorial Highway between Kissimmee and Disney, you'll see billboards peddling all-you-can-eat breakfast buffets for $5 to $8. This is a good way to fill your tanks early and skip or at least go easy on lunch, especially if your day is in the theme parks, where lunches are overpriced. Note that you won't find award-winning cuisine here, except perhaps for the highest concentration of grease! Those with kids will, however, appreciate the inexpensive and kid-friendly fare—especially over some of the high-priced restaurants at the resorts.

Breakfast buffets are served by **Golden Corral,** 8033 International Dr. (© **407/ 352-6606**); **Ponderosa Steak House,** 6362 International Dr. (© **407/352-9343**) and 7598 U.S. 192 W. (© 407/396-7721); and **Sizzler Restaurant,** 9142 International Dr. (© **407/351-5369**) and 7602 U.S. 192 W. (© **407/397-0997**). The latter two are the better bets.

---

herbs and heaped onto a mound of linguine. The open two-story interior is filled with exposed brick, wrought-iron accents, and a ceiling with fiber optics that creates the illusion of dining under the stars. The second story offers more intimate seating overlooking the interior courtyard below. Grape vines are strewn throughout for an authentic feel. Outdoor seating is available on the patio.

5795 W. Irlo Bronson Memorial Hwy./U.S. 192, Kissimmee. © **407/396-8022.** www.pacinos.com. Reservations accepted. Main courses $8–$32 (most under $20). AE, MC, V. Daily 4pm–midnight. Free self-parking. From I-4, take Exit 64A/U.S. 192 east 1 mile.

Panera Bread (Finds) AMERICAN This trendy cafe/bakery is a great place for a light meal, and its quick growth in the area (there are several locations) attests to its popularity among locals and tourists. The cafe menu offers a variety of delicious soups (broccoli cheddar, black bean, vegetable sirloin, and others) and salads (Asian sesame chicken, Caesar, and more). But the real main events are sandwiches such as turkey with chipotle mayonnaise, roast beef with creamy horseradish sauce, portobello and mozzarella panini, and a dozen others. The menu also includes an assortment of fresh bakery items (bagels, brownies, croissants, pastries, and such).

296 E. Michigan St., Orlando. © **407/481-9880.** www.panerabread.com. Reservations not accepted. Main courses $7–$14; baked goods $1–$5. AE, DISC, MC, V. Mon–Sat 6:30am–9:30pm; Sun 7am–8:30pm. Free self-parking. From I-4, take Exit 80B, U.S. 17/92, and go north to Michigan, then right 1½ miles.

Rolando's (Finds) CUBAN If you like neighborhood-style Cuban cuisine, you won't be disappointed here. This mom-and-pop restaurant serves large portions of traditional Cuban fare, such as *arroz con pollo* (chicken with yellow rice), *ropa vieja* (shredded beef), and, if you call a few hours or a day in advance, *paella* (fish and shellfish served on a bed of rice). Entrees are served with yucca (a chewy root) or plantains (a cooked banana-like fruit). The plain dining room has Formica tables, old photographs of Cuba, and potted philodendrons suspended from the ceiling. Soft lighting adds a smidgen of ambience, and there's a very limited beer and wine list.

870 E. Hwy. 436/Semoran Blvd., Casselberry. © **407/767-9677.** Reservations accepted. Main courses $4–$6 lunch, $8–$18 dinner. AE, DC, DISC, MC, V. Mon–Fri 11am–9:30pm; Sat noon–10pm; Sun noon–8:30pm. Free self-parking. From I-4, take Exit 82A, Hwy. 408/East–West Expwy., head east, and make a left on Hwy. 436.

INEXPENSIVE

Bubbalou's Bodacious BBQ *Value* BARBECUE   You can smell the hickory smoke emerging from this restaurant for blocks, the tangy scent cutting through the humid Florida air. This is, hands down, some of the best barbecue you'll find anywhere. And, if nothing else, you have to love the name. There are other things on the menu. If you can eat the night or day away, go for "The Big-Big Pig" platter (beef, sliced pork, and turkey with fixin's). There also are several barbecue baskets, combos, dinners, and sandwiches, as well as side orders ranging from fried pickles and okra to collard greens and black-eyed peas. The uninitiated should stay away from the "Killer" sauce, which can render your taste buds useless, likely for hours; you might even taste-test the mild before moving up to the hot. The beans are the perfect side dish. Only the sometimes-soggy garlic bread brings the meal down, but not too far. Beer is available.

5818 Conroy Rd. (near Universal Orlando). ℂ **407/423-1212.** www.bubbalous.com. Reservations not accepted. Main courses $4–$15, with larger sizes available for takeout up to $25. AE, MC, V. Mon–Thurs 10am–9:30pm; Fri–Sat 10am–10:30pm; Sun 11am–9pm. Free self-parking. Take I-4 Exit 75B, head East on Kirkman, and follow your nose; Bubbalou's is at the intersection of Kirkman and Conroy.

Little Saigon *Finds* VIETNAMESE   Asian immigrants created the demand for Vietnamese cuisine, and this noisy little eatery is one of the best. Better yet, it doesn't attract many tourists. Try the summer rolls—a soft wrap filled with rice, shrimp, and pork served with a delicious peanut sauce. Head next for the grilled pork and egg over rice and noodles or barbecued beef with fried egg and rice. If your appetite is larger than average, try one of the traditional soups with noodles, rice, vegetables, and either chicken, beef, or seafood. The numbered menu isn't translated well, so you may need to ask your server exactly what goes into No. 86. (Some don't speak English, so ask to speak to a manager.) As a testament to the restaurant's authenticity, tables here are usually filled with members of the local Vietnamese community. There are very limited wine and beer choices.

1106 E. Colonial Dr./Hwy. 50 (near downtown Orlando). ℂ **407/423-8539.** Reservations not accepted. Main courses under $5 lunch, $5–$10 dinner. AE, DISC, MC, V. Daily 10am–9pm. Free self-parking. Take Exit 83B, Colonial Dr./Hwy. 50, off I-4 and head east. Turn right on Thorton Ave. The parking lot is immediately to the left.

Tips **A Reason to Celebrate**

An eclectic array of upscale eateries lines the streets along Market Square in the Disney-built town of Celebration (www.celebrationfl.com). From the **Market Street Café** (ℂ 407/566-1144), an updated '50s-style diner, to the refined surroundings of **The Plantation Room** (ℂ 407/566-6000; www.celebration hotel.com; located within the Celebration Hotel), those in search of stylish surroundings and creative cuisine won't be disappointed. An ornate old-world Spanish decor and Cuban-influenced cuisine are the signature of the **Columbia Restaurant** (ℂ 407/566-1505; www.columbiarestaurant.com), while **Café D'Antonio** (ℂ 407/566-2233; www.antoniosonline.com) serves up tasty Italian cuisine in a warm and welcoming atmosphere. The **Seito Japanese Restaurant** (ℂ 407/566-1899; www.seitosushi.com) is known for its fresh sushi, fusion-style cuisine, and stylish atmosphere. And finally, **The Celebration Town Tavern** (ℂ 407/566-2526; http://thecelebrationtowntavern.com) is a more casual alternative that sports a nautical theme and fresh seafood.

Not Just Fries Anymore

Some of you may not be able to go your entire vacation without a trip to McDonald's for a Big Mac. If you just can't pass up a trip to Mickie D's for a fast-food fix, the good news is that Orlando has a handful of uniquely themed McDonald's unlike any you'll find in your neighborhood. All of them sport unique and eclectic menus, which, in addition to the usual fare, add (among other items) pizzas, portobello eggplant, turkey wraps, panini, and crème brûlée cheesecake.

The 24-hour McDonald's **European Café**, 7344 Sand Lake Road, Orlando (© 407/264-0776), boasts two levels with plenty of glass to allow sunlight to pour in. You won't mistake it for a European cafe (it's still a McDonald's, so don't get too carried away), but neat features include a pool table and arcade games on the second level, and fabulous views of the sand lakes.

The **Ancient Ruins** branch, located at 5401 Altamira Dr. (© 407/345-9477), is themed (wonder of wonders) to the ancient ruins of Greece, complete with broken columns, stone walls, and frieze-style moldings.

Moving on to Africa, the **Club Safari** location, 2944 S. Kirkman Rd. (© 407/296-6265), boasts an African Safari theme complete with rich wooden fixtures, African masks and artwork, crystal chandeliers, and animal prints galore. Animatronic toucan and Tiki figures sing jungle jingles, and you can't help but take note of the 13-foot bronze giraffe and two bronze tigers keeping watch.

Chrome shines everywhere you turn at the **Motorcycle McDonald's**, 5400 S. Kirkman Rd. (© 407/352-1526). Tail pipes, shocks, and various other bike parts adorn the restaurant's walls.

Finally, the **world's largest McDonald's** can also be found in Orlando, right on 6875 Sand Lake Rd. (© 407/351-2185). The location boasts a huge tubular maze with 25,000 feet of twists, turns, sliding, crawling, and jumping space for kids to play in. Another unique feature: You can book hotels, transportation, buy attraction tickets, and get daily park information, all while enjoying your fries and a Coke (or, in this case, maybe a gourmet coffee).

8 Only in Orlando: Dining with Disney Characters

Dining with your favorite costumed characters is a treat for many Disney fans, but it's a truly special occasion for those under 10. Some of the most beloved movie characters seemingly come to life: shaking hands, hugging, signing autographs, and posing for family photos (most never speak, with the exception of the princesses and a very small handful of others, so forget about conversation). These are huge events—it's not uncommon for Chef Mickey's, listed below, to have **1,600 or more guests on a weekend morning**—so make your Advance Reservations as far in advance as possible (when you book your room, if not earlier). Don't expect more than just a few moments of one-on-one, but what time there is, is sure to bring a big smile to your little ones' faces.

The prices for character meals are much the same, no matter where you're dining (with one exception; Cinderella's Royal Table). Breakfast (most serve it) runs $19 to $32 for adults and $11 to $22 for children 3 to 9; those that serve dinner charge $28 to $40 for adults and $13 to $25 for kids. The prices vary a bit, though, from location to location.

To make reservations for WDW character meals, call ✆ **407/939-3463.** American Express, Diners Club, Discover, MasterCard, Visa, and the Disney Visa Card are accepted at all character meals.

You'll find all of the restaurants mentioned in this section on the map, "Walt Disney World & Lake Buena Vista Dining," earlier in this chapter. For Internet information, go to **www.disneyworld.com**.

Note: Although the character appearances below were accurate when this book went to press, lineups and booking requirements change frequently (as do menus and prices). We strongly recommend against promising children they will meet a specific character at a meal. And you should never mention dining with the characters unless your Advance Reservations are confirmed first; character meals book up quickly and trying to make Advance Reservations too late in the game (or worse, attempting to walk in) will mostly likely result in disappointment. If you have your heart set on meeting a certain character, call to confirm his or her appearance when making your Advance Reservations.

Cape May Café   The Cape May Café, a delightful New England–themed dining room, serves lavish buffet breakfasts (eggs, pancakes, bacon, pastries) hosted by **Admiral Goofy** and his crew—**Chip 'n' Dale** and **Pluto** (characters may vary). Its location at the Beach Club Resort makes it a great way to start the day when you're on your way to nearby Epcot.

1800 Epcot Resorts Blvd., at Disney's Beach Club Resort. $19 adults, $11 children. Daily 7:30–11am.

Chef Mickey's 😊😊   The whimsical Chef Mickey's offers buffet breakfasts (eggs, bacon, sausage, pancakes, fruit) and dinners (entrees change daily; salad bar, soups, vegetables, ice cream with toppings). Aside from the characters, kids will also enjoy watching the monorail go by overhead as it passes through the Contemporary Resort. **Mickey and Minnie and various pals** make their way to every table while meeting and mingling with guests. While this is one of the largest restaurants offering character dining, if you plan on dining here during spring break and around the holidays, it's best to make Advance Reservations well ahead of time.

4600 N. World Dr., at Disney's Contemporary Resort. Breakfast $19 adults, $11 children; dinner $28 adults, $13 children. Daily 7–11:30am and 5–9:30pm.

Cinderella's Royal Table 😊   Cinderella Castle—the most recognized icon in all of the WDW resort, not to mention the center of the Magic Kingdom, serves character breakfast buffets daily (a variety of breakfast favorites including scrambled eggs, bacon, Danish), and recently began serving a character lunch and dinner (with a choice of appetizer, entree, salad, and dessert from a fixed menu) as well. Princess hosts vary, but **Cinderella** always puts in an appearance and the **Fairy Godmother** joins the celebration for dinner. This is one of the most popular character meals in the park and the hardest to get into, so **reserve far, far in advance** (reservations are taken 180 days in advance, and you must pay in full at the time you make your reservations). To have the best shot at getting in, be flexible about your seating arrangements and dining times, and call Disney exactly at 7am EST on your first date of reservations eligibility (if you aren't sure what date that is, call Disney and they'll help you figure it out). If you get through on your first try (lucky you!), tell the reservations clerk you want Cinderella's Table for whatever date you've picked. Don't even think about requesting a specific time—take whatever you can get (most reservations will be gone by 7:15am).

In Cinderella Castle, at the Magic Kingdom. Breakfast $22 adults, $12 children; lunch $34 adults, $23 children; dinner $40 adults, $25 children. Daily 8–10:20am, noon–3pm, and 4pm–park closing. Theme park admission required.

Crystal Palace Buffet ✿ The prettiest of the Magic Kingdom's restaurants, the Crystal Palace features a glass exterior that glimmers in sunlight. **Winnie the Pooh** and pals hold court here throughout the day. The restaurant serves breakfast (eggs, French toast, pancakes, bacon and more), lunch, and dinner. The latter features a long list of hot and cold entrees that usually include some type of poultry, beef, seafood, an array of veggies, salads, and kid-friendly favorites. The dessert buffet includes a make-your-own-sundae bar.

At Crystal Palace, in the Magic Kingdom. Breakfast $19 adults, $11 children; lunch $21 adults, $12 children; dinner $28 adults, $13 children. Daily 8–10:30am, 11:30am–3pm, and 4pm–park closing. Theme park admission required.

Donald's Prehistoric Breakfastosaurus ✿ **Donald, Goofy,** and **Pluto** host a buffet breakfast (eggs, bacon, French toast, and more) in Dinoland U.S.A.'s Restaurantosaurus.

In Dinoland U.S.A., at Disney's Animal Kingdom. $19 adults, $11 children. Daily park opening–10:30am. Theme park admission required.

Garden Grill ✿ There's a "Harvest Feast" theme at this revolving restaurant, where hearty, family-style meals are hosted by **Mickey** and **Chip 'n' Dale.** (Mickey sure gets around, eh?) Lunch and dinner (chicken, fish, steak, vegetables, potatoes) are served.

In the Land Pavilion at Epcot. Lunch $21 adults, $12 children; dinner $28 adults, $13 children. Daily 11am–3pm and 4:30–park closing. Theme park admission required.

Liberty Tree Tavern This Colonial-style 18th-century pub offers character dinners hosted by **Minnie, Goofy, Pluto,** and **Chip 'n' Dale.** The family-style meals include salad, roast turkey, ham, flank steak, cornbread, and apple crisp with vanilla ice cream.

In Liberty Square, in the Magic Kingdom. $28 adults, $13 children. Daily 4pm–park closing. Theme park admission required.

1900 Park Fare ✿ The elegant Grand Floridian offers breakfast (eggs, French toast, bacon, pancakes) and dinner buffets (steak, pork, fish) at the exposition-themed 1900 Park Fare. Big Bertha—a French band organ that plays pipes, drums, bells, cymbals, castanets, and xylophone—provides music. **Mary Poppins, Alice in Wonderland,** and friends appear at breakfast; **Cinderella** and friends show up for Cinderella's Gala Feast at dinner.

4401 Floridian Way, at Disney's Grand Floridian Resort & Spa. Breakfast $19 adults, $11 children; dinner $29 adults, $14 children. Daily 8–11:10am and 4:30–8:20pm.

'Ohana Character Breakfast Traditional breakfasts (eggs, pancakes, bacon) are prepared in an 18-foot fire pit and served family style. **Mickey, Stitch, Lilo,** and **Pluto** appear, and children are given the chance to parade around with Polynesian musical instruments.

1600 Seven Seas Dr., in 'Ohana at Disney's Polynesian Resort. $19 adults, $11 children. Daily 7:30–11am.

Other Casts of Characters

Not wanting to feel left out, Universal Orlando and SeaWorld have instituted their own character dining experiences. Like Disney's meals, these are very popular experiences, so be sure to reserve your spot as far in advance as possible.

At Islands of Adventure, the **Confisco Grill** is home to a character breakfast buffet where Spiderman, Captain America, the Cat in the Hat, and Thing 1 and Thing 2 all join in on the fun. It runs Thursday through Sunday, from park opening until 10:30am. The cost is $16 adults, $10 kids 3 to 9. Call ℂ 407/224-4012 for more information or to make reservations.

At SeaWorld, you can chow down on a buffet lunch right alongside the killer whales at the daily **Dine with Shamu,** at the Shamu Stadium. The cost is $37 adults, $19 children ages 3 to 9; park admission is required but not included in the cost. The **Shamu and Crew** character breakfast buffet, held at the Seafire Inn in the Waterfront district, is offered only seasonally and during the park's Halloween and Christmas celebrations. The action takes place 8:45 to 10:15am. The cost is $15 adults, $10 children ages 3 to 9; park admission is required but not included in the cost. For both character experiences, call ℂ 800/327-2420 or check out **www.seaworld.com** for more information or to make a reservation.

Princess Storybook Dining   Snow White, Jasmine, Ariel, Pocahontas, Belle, or Mary Poppins might show up at any of the character meals offered at Epcot's Norway pavilion. Breakfast features American fare (scrambled eggs, French toast, sausage, bacon, and potatoes), while lunch and dinner are served up family-style and offer Norwegian specialties in addition to traditional American fare for the kids.

At Akershus Royal Banquet Hall in Epcot's Norway Pavilion. Breakfast adults $23, children $13; lunch adults $25, children $14; dinner adults $29, children $14. Daily 8:30–10:10am, 11:40am–2:50pm, and 4:20–8:40pm. Theme park admission required.

6

Exploring Walt Disney World

The minute someone even mentions Walt Disney World, most people's minds immediately conjure up visions of Cinderella Castle and the Magic Kingdom. That's unsurprising when you take into account that the park that started it all—it opened in 1971—is still the most widely recognized and the most popular Disney destination in the United States.

Today, however, the Walt Disney World stable has grown to include an array of themed resorts, hundreds of restaurants and shops, nightclub venues, smaller attractions, and four major theme parks: the Magic Kingdom, Epcot, Disney–MGM Studios, and Animal Kingdom. And with the economy showing signs of recovery, park attendance is once again on the rise. WDW attracted nearly 43 million paying customers in 2005, according to estimates by *Amusement Business* magazine. All four Disney parks make the country's top five in attendance (the remaining park on the list is Disneyland in California). But that should hardly surprise you—they offer a fanciful, self-sufficient vacation where wonderment, human progress, and old-fashioned family fun are the key themes. The Disney Imagineers show off their creative capabilities through spectacular parades and fireworks displays, 3-D and CircleVision films, nerve-racking thrill rides, and adventurous journeys through time and space. Though still more expensive, you'll seldom hear people complain about failing to get their money's worth—at home, an evening out, including dinner, a movie, and a babysitter, can add up to a hefty amount without nearly the same return.

One reason people keep coming back for more is that rides and shows are periodically updated. And if something doesn't quite work, Disney usually fixes it. As part of this process, the company interviews some of its park-goers to decide how well, or poorly, things are working.

There have been changes and additions as Walt Disney World has matured, and new rides and attractions periodically enter the mix, including: Animal Kingdom's **Expedition Everest,** where an out-of-control train sends riders careening through the Himalayan Mountains only to end in a close encounter with the legendary Yeti; Epcot's **Soarin',** where guests fly over the landscapes of California while surrounded by a gigantic projection screen; and Disney–MGM Studios' **Lights, Motors, Action! Extreme Stunt Show,** featuring a behind-the-scenes look at stunts and special effects.

But before I dive into the action, giving you details of these and other exciting experiences, let me take care of some basic business.

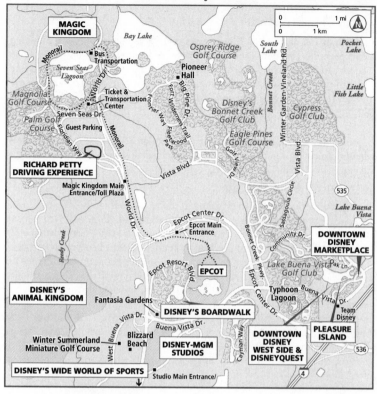

1 Essentials

GETTING INFORMATION IN ADVANCE

Before leaving home, call or write to the Walt Disney World Co., Box 10000, Lake Buena Vista, FL 32830-1000 (© **407/934-7639**), for a vacation CD and the *Walt Disney World Vacations* brochure; both are valuable planning aids. Both can also be ordered (and even viewed) online at **www.disneyworld.com**. When you call, also ask about special events that will be going on during your visit. While I list some of the annual events under "When to Go" in chapter 2, there are many other events that may be of interest to you.

Once you've arrived at your hotel, Guest Services and the concierge desks (especially at the Disney properties and "official" hotels) will have up-to-the-minute information about happenings in the parks. Stop by to ask questions and get literature, including a schedule of park hours and events. If you have questions your hotel's personnel can't answer, call Disney at © **407/824-4321.**

There are also information areas at City Hall in the Magic Kingdom and Guest Relations at Epcot, Disney–MGM Studios, and Animal Kingdom.

For Internet information, try **www.disneyworld.com**, which features extensive, entertaining, and regularly updated information on the parks.

> ⌜Tips⌟ **Tighter Security**
>
> Guards at the gates at all Disney parks check a variety of carry-ins, including backpacks, diaper bags, and pocketbooks and purses. They also have been known to check guests' IDs, so be sure to bring a government-issued photo identification card. All this, of course, means it may take a few minutes longer to get through the entrance and to your first ride of the day.

Also try the Orlando/Orange County Convention & Visitors Bureau site (**www.orlandoinfo.com**). Another good site, **www.floridakiss.com**, is sponsored by the Kissimmee–St. Cloud Convention & Visitors Bureau.

GETTING TO WDW BY CAR

The interstate exits to all Disney parks and resorts are well marked. Once you're off I-4, there are signs directing you to individual destinations. If you miss your exit, *don't panic.* Simply get off at the next one and turn around. It may take a little more time, but it's safer than cutting across five lanes of traffic to make the off ramp, or worse—to risk a fender bender. Drive with extra caution in the attractions area. Disney drivers are divided into two categories: workers in a hurry to make their shift and tourists in a hurry to get to the parks before anyone else (and trying to drive while looking at a map).

Upon entering WDW grounds, you can tune your radio to 1030 AM when you're approaching the Magic Kingdom, or 850 AM when approaching Epcot, for park information. Tune to 1200 AM when departing the Magic Kingdom, or 910 AM when departing Epcot. TVs in all Disney resorts and "official" hotels also have park information channels.

PARKING

All WDW lots are tightly controlled; the Disney folks have parking down to a science. You park where they tell you to park—and there's no room for discussion. *Remember to write your parking place (lot and row number) on something so you can find your vehicle later.* Parking attendants won't be there to direct you to it when you leave the park, and, at the end of the day, you'd be surprised how many cars look alike through tired eyes. And though you might think that catchy character name on the pole above your car will ring a bell when you return to your vehicle, what will really be ringing will be your ears with all of the names you've heard so many times throughout the day—was it Minnie . . . Donald . . . Goofy . . . Pluto?

Visitors should generally ride the free trams that travel the massive Magic Kingdom lots, but it's often easier to skip them and walk to the gates at Epcot, Disney–MGM Studios, and Animal Kingdom. You may not even have a choice. Disney has cut service to some parking areas near the entrances to its parks. Guests who can't make the hike have to park in special lots for travelers with disabilities (see below) or have a driver drop them at special unloading areas outside the entrances. If you're walking, *be careful!* These lots aren't designed for pedestrians, so if you hear a tram coming, move out of the way—and quickly.

Parking costs $9 at the four major WDW attractions ($10 for RVs). There are special lots for travelers with disabilities; a valid disabled parking permit is required (call

$\textcircled{C}$ **407/824-4321** for details). Those who have booked their Disney vacation through AAA can access a special lot close to the entrance.

TICKETS

In January 2005, Disney revamped its entire ticketing structure (now called **Magic Your Way**), giving visitors who stay here for a few days far better deals than those who come for just a day. Whereas before you had a limited number of ticket options (a 1-day/one-park ticket or a multiday/multipark pass), the new system allows guests to customize their tickets by first purchasing a Base Ticket for a set fee, and then allowing them to purchase add-ons, including a park-hopper option, a no-expiration option, and the option to include admission to some of Disney's smaller venues, such as Pleasure Island, the water parks, and DisneyQuest (the latter is known as the Water Park Fun & More option).

You can purchase your Base Tickets for durations running from a single day to several days, with the latter being the most cost effective; the longer you stay, the less you'll pay per day. If you crunch the numbers, tickets good for at least 4 days will cost almost $14 less per day than a single-day ticket would; buy a 6-day ticket and your per-day price drops by almost 50%. Do note, however, that under the new system, tickets now expire 14 days from the first day of use unless you add on a no-expiration feature (you don't, however, have to use the tickets on consecutive days within that 14-day period).

The following **don't** include *the 6 to 6.5% sales tax* (Disney actually falls in two different counties) unless noted. *Note:* Price hikes are frequent occurrences, so call ($\textcircled{C}$ **407/824-4321**) or visit WDW's website (**www.disneyworld.com**) for the most up-to-the-minute pricing.

Note: All tickets include unlimited use of the WDW transportation system. Bear in mind that Disney considers children 10 and older adults for pricing purposes, and children under 3 aren't charged admission.

One-day/one-park Base Tickets, for admission to the Magic Kingdom, Epcot, Animal Kingdom, or Disney–MGM Studios, are $63 for adults, $52 for children ages 3 to 9. Ouch! **Four-day Base Tickets** (one park per day) are $195 adults, $160 children ages 3 to 9. A **7-day Base Ticket** (one park per day) costs $204 for adults (about $29 a day), $165 for kids ages 3 to 9 (about $23 a day).

Adding on a **Park Hopper** option to your ticket allows you unlimited admission to the Magic Kingdom, Epcot, Animal Kingdom, and Disney–MGM Studios for the duration of your Base Ticket. Pricing for the Park Hopper is the same for adults and children and costs $40 above the price of your Base Ticket (no matter how many days that ticket is valid for). So if you purchase a single-day Base Ticket, adding the Park Hopper will cost an additional $40 (for a total of $103 for an adult—not cost effective), but if you

---

Tips Buy Ahead of Time

Purchasing multiday tickets (from 4 days and up) that include both the **Park Hopper** and **Water Park Fun & More** options ahead of time (through **www.disney world.com**) can result in substantial savings (up to $18 per adult and $12 per child ages 3–9). The savings for a family of four can add up to $60—that's worth a lunch (well, at least a snack in Mickeyville).

(Tips Shorter Days, Fewer Shows

They may have started to rebound, but the theme parks are still feeling a bit of the crunch as attendance slowly climbs back to where it once was a few years ago. If you haven't been to Disney in several years you may notice that, in many cases, the parks **close earlier** than at similar times in previous years, and some areas **open later**. Additionally, select shows and parades are offered less often or only on certain days. The hours and shows listed in this chapter generally apply, but in order to avoid being disappointed, call © **407/824-4321** or go to **www.disneyworld.com** for up-to-the-minute information.

---

purchase a 7-day Base Ticket, the option will still only cost you $40 (for a total of $244—a very good deal).

If you add a **Water Park Fun & More** option to your Base Ticket, you'll get several admissions to some of WDW's smaller attractions: Blizzard Beach, Typhoon Lagoon, DisneyQuest, Pleasure Island, and Disney's Wide World of Sports Complex. The number of visits allowed depends on the number of days your Base Ticket is good for (three visits for Base Tickets covering 1–3 days; four visits for 4- and 5-day tickets; five visits for 6-day tickets, and six visits for any Base Ticket 7 days or over). This option adds an additional $50 to the cost of your Base Ticket, and, like the Park Hopper, the longer you stay at Disney, the more cost-effective the option becomes. If you only plan on visiting one smaller attraction while at WDW, paying the separate admission fee is cheaper and smarter than opting for the add-on.

If you're adding both of these options to your Base Ticket, a way to save a bit more money is by buying your tickets in advance (see p. 181).

A **1-day ticket to Typhoon Lagoon, Blizzard Beach,** or **DisneyQuest** is $35 for adults, $29 for children.

A **1-day ticket to Pleasure Island** is $20.95. Because this is primarily an 18-and-over entertainment complex, there's no bargain price for children.

If you're planning an extended stay or going to visit Walt Disney World more than once during the year, **annual passes** ($415–$539 adults, $365–$475 children) are another great option.

OPERATING HOURS

Hours of operation vary throughout the year and are often influenced by special events, so it's a good idea to call to check opening/closing times.

The **Magic Kingdom** and **Disney–MGM Studios** are generally open from 9am to 6 or 7pm, with hours often extended to 9pm and sometimes as late as midnight during major holidays and summer. **Animal Kingdom** usually is open from 8 or 9am to 5 or 6pm but sometimes closes as late as 7pm.

Epcot's Future World is generally open from 9 or 10am to 7pm and occasionally later. **Epcot's World Showcase** usually opens at 11am or noon and closes at 9pm. Once again, there are extended holiday and summer hours.

Typhoon Lagoon and **Blizzard Beach** are open from 10am to 5pm most of the year (with slightly extended hours during summer and some holidays). Both are closed on a rotating basis during part of the winter for maintenance; be sure to check ahead if they're on your to-do list.

2 Making Your Visit More Enjoyable

HOW THIS CHAPTER IS USEFUL TO PARENTS

Before every listing in the major parks, you'll note the **"Recommended Ages"** entry that lists which ages will most appreciate that ride or show (though you should keep in mind your child's personality and maturity when evaluating these recommendations). Though most families want to do everything, these guidelines are helpful in planning your daily itinerary. In my ride ratings, I've indicated whether a ride will be more enjoyable for kids than for adults. Many, even a couple in the Magic Kingdom, are too intense for young kids; all it takes is one bad experience, and the rest of your day will be ruined. You'll also find any **height and health restrictions** noted in the listings.

BEST TIME OF YEAR TO VISIT

Because of the large number of international visitors, there's really no "off season" at Disney, but during the winter months, usually mid-January through March, crowds are smaller (except weekends), and the weather can be mild. The crowds also thin from mid-September until the week before Thanksgiving, and in May, before Memorial Day weekend. (Again, weekends tend to be clogged with locals.) Summer is when the masses throng to the parks. It's also humid and hot, *Hot,* **HOT.** If you can skip a summer visit, you also won't have to worry much about the possibility of a hurricane (admittedly rare, but as the summer of 2004 proved, not unheard of) or an electrical storm (an almost daily occurrence).

BEST DAYS TO VISIT

The busiest days at all parks are generally Saturday and Sunday. Seven-day guests usually arrive and depart on one of these days, so fewer of them turn the turnstiles; but weekends are when locals and Florida commuters come to play. Beyond that: Monday, Thursday, and Saturday are pretty frantic in the Magic Kingdom; Tuesday and Friday are hectic at Epcot; Sunday and Wednesday are crazy at Disney–MGM Studios; and Monday, Tuesday, and Wednesday are a zoo (forgive the pun) at the Animal Kingdom. Periods around major holidays also attract throngs—mid-December through the first weekend in January is busy beyond belief. Crowds tend to thin later in the day, so if you're going to visit during the busy season and have included the Park Hopper option on your ticket, you'll bump into fewer guests the later you visit. This also applies to the water parks.

The big attractions at Animal Kingdom are, obviously, the animals, and the best time to see them is early in the day or late in the afternoon or evening, when things are cooler. You'll also get a decent midday glimpse of some of them during the cooler months.

Tips Price Alert

Single-day and multiday admission prices don't include Florida's 6% to 6.5% sales tax and are subject to change. Annual price increases are normal, so, although the prices listed on these pages were accurate when this book went to press, they may be higher at the time you actually visit.

Tips FASTPASS

"Get a time—why wait in line . . ." says Disney. If lines aren't your thing—well . . . you had better turn back now. Lines are a part of the deal at Disney (and the other parks, too, for that matter). On the other hand, if you're savvy, you can usually avoid the worst of them if you take advantage of Disney's FASTPASS system. The free system allows you to wait on a far shorter line at some of the park's most popular attractions. Seems easy enough, right? Well, it is. There is, however, a small price to be paid for skipping the big lines. Here's the drill:

Hang onto your ticket stub when you enter and head to the hottest ride on your list. If it's a FASTPASS attraction (they're noted in the guide map you get when you enter), you'll see a sign marking the FASTPASS kiosk just near the entrance. Feed your ticket into the ticket taker. *Note:* Every member of your group must get an individual FASTPASS. Retrieve both your ticket and your FASTPASS slip. Printed on the slip are two times. You can return anytime during that 1-hour window and enter the ride (there's a much shorter and faster line for FASTPASS holders). Be sure to keep your slip handy as you'll need it to get in the right line.

Note II: Early in the day, your 1-hour window may begin as soon as 40 minutes after you feed the FASTPASS machine, but later in the day it may be hours later. Initially, Disney only allowed you to do this on one ride at a time. Now, your FASTPASS ticket has a time printed when you can get a second FASTPASS, usually about 2 hours after you got the first one, though it can sometimes be as soon as 45 minutes later, even if you haven't used the first pass yet.

Note III: Don't think you can fool Disney by feeding your ticket stub in multiple times, figuring you can hit the jackpot for multiple rides or help others in your group who lost their tickets. These "smart" stubs will reject your attempts by spitting out a coupon that says "Not A Valid FASTPASS."

Note IV: FASTPASS slips can run out. So if you have your heart set on a ride and it's the middle of the peak season, be sure to head to your chosen attraction's FASTPASS machine as soon as you can. Tickets for top rides often run out by the early afternoon, sometimes even earlier.

PLAN YOUR VISIT

How you plan your time at Walt Disney World will depend on a number of factors. These include the ages of any children in your party; what, if anything, you've seen on previous visits; your interests; and whether you're traveling at peak time or off season. Preplanning is always essential. So is choosing age-appropriate activities.

Nothing can spoil a day in the parks more than a child devastated because he or she can't do something that was promised. Before you get to the park, review this book and the suggested ages for children, including *height restrictions.* The WDW staff won't bend the rules despite the pitiful wails of your little ones. *Note:* Many rides that have minimum heights also have enough turbulence to make them unsuitable for folks with neck, back, or heart problems; those prone to motion sickness; or pregnant women.

Unless you're staying for more than a week or two, you won't be able to experience all of the rides, shows, or attractions included in this chapter. A ride may last only 5 minutes, but you may have to wait an hour or so, even with FASTPASS (detailed shortly). You'll wear yourself to a frazzle trying to hit everything. It's better to follow a relaxed itinerary, including leisurely meals and some recreational activities, than to make a demanding job out of trying to see everything. You vacation is supposed to be fun, not frenzied.

CREATE AN ITINERARY FOR EACH DAY

Read the previously mentioned *Walt Disney World Vacations* brochure and the detailed descriptions in this book, and then create your own "must see" list, including all the shows and attractions that you absolutely have to experience. After that, you can sort out just where to go, when to go, and what you would like to do while you're there.

At the same time, consider your loyalties. My kids could spend all day in Tomorrowland spinning around like space rangers with Woody and Buzz Lightyear, but touring Toontown is of far less interest to them. Put the ride featuring your favorite character, or theirs, at the top of your list. Sketch out a daily itinerary that includes your must-see attractions and shows; it's almost certain to change once you get to the parks, but will at least provide you with a good starting point. With a plan in mind and a map in hand (park maps can be found in this guide, but be sure to grab the free maps distributed as you enter each theme park), touring the parks will be that much easier. Understand that rides and exhibits nearest an entrance are usually the busiest when the gates open because a lot of people visit the first thing they see, even if the more popular attractions tend to be found deeper into the park.

I repeat this advice: Schedule sit-down shows, recreational activities (a boat ride or a refreshing swim late in the afternoon), and at least some unhurried meals where time permits. This will save you from exhaustion and aggravation. Our suggested itineraries (see below) allow you to see a great deal of the parks as efficiently as possible. If you have the luxury of a multiday pass, you can divide and conquer at a slower pace and can even repeat some favorites.

SUGGESTED ITINERARIES

Our suggested itineraries will allow you to cover most of the ground in each park in as efficient a manner as possible. Do note, though, that using FASTPASS may require you to double back to a land you've already covered.

There are a ton of ways to see the parks, and we feel, time and budget permitting, it's often better to do it in limited doses—where you spend 2 or more days in a park at a casual pace. We're offering suggested itineraries as options for those on a tighter schedule. The following itineraries are organized to get the most out of the least amount of time. Where appropriate, we break things into one game plan for families with kids and another for teenagers and adults. With few exceptions (I note them later), Disney World doesn't have enough true stomach-turning thrill rides to warrant a special itinerary for teens or take-no-prisoners adults. Frankly, the only Orlando park in that class is Universal's Islands of Adventure, which we tackle in chapter 7, "Exploring Beyond Disney: Universal Orlando, SeaWorld & Other Attractions."

A Day in the Magic Kingdom with Kids

Consider making Advance Reservations for dinner at **Cinderella's Royal Table** (✆ **407/939-3463**), located inside Cinderella Castle.

If you have preschoolers, go right to the **Walt Disney World Railroad** station on Main Street and take the next train. Get off at **Mickey's Toontown Fair,** where tots are wowed by Mickey, Minnie, and the gang. They can ride the **Barnstormer at Goofy's Wiseacre Farm,** a mini–roller coaster, and explore **Mickey's & Minnie's Country Houses.**

If your kids are 6 or older, start the day at **Tomorrowland** and brave **Buzz Lightyear's Space Ranger Spin,** and **Space Mountain.** (Little ones like the **Tomorrowland Indy Speedway,** but there's not much else for them here, so skip it if you don't have a lot of time.)

Most kids under 8 will find something that's fun in Fantasyland, including **Dumbo the Flying Elephant, Mickey's PhilharMagic, It's a Small World, Peter Pan's Flight, The Many Adventures of Winnie the Pooh,** and **Cinderella's Golden Carousel.** Toddlers will have fun crawling, climbing, sliding, and getting wet at **Pooh's Playful Spot.**

Grab lunch at Cosmic Ray's Starlight Café in **Tomorrowland** or the Columbia Harbour House in **Liberty Square.**

Next, head west to **Liberty Square.** Most kids 10 and older will like the animatronic history lesson in the **Hall of Presidents** show. Before leaving, visit the **Haunted Mansion,** and then move to **Frontierland. Splash Mountain** and **Big Thunder Mountain Railroad** are best suited for those 8 and older, while the **Country Bear Jamboree** and **Tom Sawyer Island** are fun for the younger set and parents looking to get off their feet.

Go to **Adventureland** next. Ride **The Magic Carpets of Aladdin, Pirates of the Caribbean,** and **Jungle Cruise,** and then let the kids burn some energy in the **Swiss Family Treehouse.** Younger kids (ages 4–8) will appreciate the **Enchanted Tiki Room.**

Consult the daily *Times Guide,* and if the **Wishes** fireworks display and **SpectroMagic** are scheduled, be sure to watch them.

A Day in the Magic Kingdom for Teenagers & Adults

Consider making Advance Reservations at **Cinderella's Royal Table** (✆ **407/ 939-3463**) if you want a sit-down dinner.

From Main Street, cut through the center of the park to Frontierland and challenge **Splash Mountain,** then ride **Big Thunder Mountain Railroad.** If you need to rest your feet or escape the heat, the **Country Bear Jamboree** is the place for it.

Next, go to Liberty Square and visit the **Haunted Mansion** and **Hall of Presidents,** then have lunch at the Liberty Tree Tavern.

Now cut diagonally through the park, past Cinderella Castle, and into Tomorrowland to **Space Mountain,** and **Buzz Lightyear's Space Ranger Spin.**

If time permits, head to Adventureland for the **Jungle Cruise** and **Pirates of the Caribbean,** then, if it's scheduled, end the day with the **Wishes** fireworks display.

If You Can Spend Only 1 Day at Epcot

Epcot deserves at least 2 days, so this is a barnstorming highlight tour. Remember to make **Advance Reservations** if you want to eat in the park (call ✆ **407/939-3463** before you arrive). We suggest the **Coral Reef** restaurant in the Living Seas or the **San Angel Inn** in the World Showcase's Mexico exhibit for lunch, and **Marrakech** in Morocco or **Akershus** in Norway for dinner. See other options in chapter 5, "Where to Dine."

This is the **least desirable of the parks for very young kids.** Even some older ones and teens may not enjoy the heavy educational and technology themes, but there are a few fun rides and other attractions that will entertain the young set.

As you enter, go to any of your favorite rides that have FASTPASS (they're noted in the handout guide map). If the lines are short, don't bother with the pass. If the fast track isn't in your itinerary, take the *other* strategic approach:

Future World, near the front of the park, is the first of Epcot's two areas to open, so start there. Skip **Spaceship Earth,** at least for now. It's nearest the entrance, and that big golf ball and its boring show attract most guests as they enter. Go straight to **Body Wars,** which is in the **Wonders of Life** pavilion to the left of Spaceship Earth. Next up is **Mission: Space,** where you can train as the astronauts do. Follow up with next-door-neighbor **Test Track.** Then cut to the west to Imagination! and its two great shows: **Journey into Imagination with Figment** and *Honey, I Shrunk the Audience.* Next up is the **Living Seas,** for a quick conversation with Crush, before heading on to **The Land** for the newest ride in the park, **Soarin'.**

If time permits before a late lunch, visit **Innoventions.** On its East Side, all but the smallest kids will like seeing some of today's and tomorrow's high-tech gadgets. Over on the West Side, kids and adults find it hard to leave **Video Games of Tomorrow.**

Unless you're eager for the **Spaceship Earth** snoozer, proceed to the **World Showcase** in midafternoon. For us, this is the best part of Epcot—the pavilions of 11 nations surround a big lagoon that you can cross by boat. But, again, kids (especially small ones) and teens may get the itch to leave.

Norway delivers a history lesson and boat ride called **Maelstrom, China** and **Canada** have fabulous 360-degree movies, and **France** has a magnificent large-screen production. Don't leave without taking in the show and concerts at **U.S.A.—The American Adventure.** And don't miss the Taiko drum show at **Japan.**

After dinner, be sure to watch **Illumi-Nations.**

If You Can Spend 2 Days at Epcot

Ignore the 1-day itinerary, but consider our earlier advice about Advance Reservations and choice of restaurants.

The basic plan of attack here is to hit Future World and all of its rides and exhibits on your first day, and then cruise the World Showcase the next day. (Because the showcase opens later, you can hit any missed areas or go back for seconds in Future World early on Day 2.) Remember to go straight to FASTPASS rides that appeal to you (check your guide map).

Day 1 If you want to eat in the park, book **Advance Reservations** for lunch and dinner if you haven't already. Skip **Spaceship Earth** because that's where a lot of the park's visitors go first. Instead, take a spin on **Test Track,** in the southeast corner of Future World. If it's crowded, use FASTPASS and come back later. Then blast off as the astronauts do on **Mission: Space.** Next, ride **Body Wars,** which is in the **Wonders of Life** pavilion to the left of Spaceship Earth, then visit the **Cranium Command** and **The Making of Me** shows in the same area. Then double back to **Ellen's Energy Adventure** in the Universe of Energy before grabbing lunch.

Next, spend time in **Innoventions East,** where most older kids and adults will love the household gizmos in the **House of Innoventions** and a look at tomorrow in **Future Cars.** At **Innoventions West,** try your luck at the **Video Games of Tomorrow** exhibit. Before you call it a day, enjoy the peaceful exhibits in the **Living Seas** and **The Land** (be sure to check out the new **Soarin'** attraction), then cut to **Imagination!** for the **Journey into Imagination with Figment** and *Honey, I Shrunk the Audience* shows.

Day 2 If you arrive when the park opens, go to any **Future World** rides or shows that you missed or want to repeat. Or sleep a little later and arrive for the opening of **World Showcase.**

Start in **Canada,** to the far right of the entrance. The movie there is uplifting and entertaining. Then continue counterclockwise to the **United Kingdom** for street shows, people-watching, and a real pub. **France** has a captivating film and a wonderful pastry shop; **Morocco** has a colorful casbah with merchants, Moorish tile and art, and little passages that put you in Bogartville. (For some, this is better than the real Casablanca, which is actually dirty and run-down.)

Japan has a store packed with enticements and grand architecture, but move quickly to **U.S.A.—The American Adventure,** a patriotic triumph of audio-animated characters. This is a large theater, so waits are rarely long. Next, head to **Italy** and St. Mark's Square, which comes complete with a 105-foot bell tower.

Germany's Biergarten has oompah bands, beer, and wursts. Don't miss the model railway and the Bavarian-looking shops. Then steer yourself to **China,** which offers food, bargain buys, gardens and ponds, and a 360-degree movie. Continuing counterclockwise, **Norway** features the **Maelstrom** ride. **Mexico** completes the World Showcase semicircle with a boat ride into its history.

End things with the **IllumiNations** fireworks display.

A Day at Disney–MGM Studios Theme Park

Here's a park that's easier to manage in 1 day.

Remember my advice on making **Advance Reservations** (© **407/939-3463**) if you want to eat in the park. The **Hollywood Brown Derby** is a decent sit-down option (see chapter 5, "Where to Dine," for more information on dining options in the park).

Head directly to the **Twilight Zone Tower of Terror.** The high-voltage ride is not for the young or faint of heart. The same goes for the **Rock 'n' Roller Coaster,** which blends incredible takeoff speed with three inversions.

The park is small, so backtracking isn't as much of a concern here. Consider passing up attractions that have long lines, or use FASTPASS where you can. Lines also can be long at **Star Tours,** the **Indiana Jones Epic Stunt Spectacular,** and the new **Lights, Motors, Action! Extreme Stunt Show.**

Voyage of the Little Mermaid is a must for the young (in years or yearnings); the same goes for **Jim Henson's Muppet*Vision 3-D,** a truly fun show for all ages.

With luck, you'll make it through most of the above before a late lunch at the **50's Prime Time Café,** where the food is so-so, but the experience is . . . well, surreal.

Afterward, watch (and maybe get lucky enough to win at) **Who Wants to Be a Millionaire—Play It!** before going on to the ton-of-fun **Backlot Tour.**

Check your show schedule for favorites such as **Playhouse Disney—Live on Stage!** (which is great for little kids) and **Beauty and the Beast,** and, at night, *don't miss* **Fantasmic!**

A Day at Animal Kingdom

Be here when the gates open, usually around 8 or 9am. (Call Disney information at © **407/824-4321** to check the time.) This will give you the best chance of seeing animals because they're most active in the morning air (the next best is late in the afternoon, although some can be seen throughout the day in cooler months). If you want to eat at the **Rainforest Cafe,** make Advance Reservations by calling © **407/939-3463.**

The size of the park (500 acres) means a lot of travel once you pass through the gates. Don't linger in the **Oasis** area or around the **Tree of Life;** instead, head directly to the back of the park, grab a FASTPASS for **Expedition Everest** (in Asia), then head immediately back to Africa to be first in line for **Kilimanjaro Safaris.** This will allow you to see animals before it gets hot and the lines become monstrous.

Work your way back through Africa, visiting **Pangani Forest Exploration Trail** and its lowland gorillas, and then head to the Flame Tree Barbecue for a bite to eat, though kids may prefer the Restaurantosaurus (sponsored by McDonald's) just inside Dinoland. After lunch, head to the **Tree of Life** on Discovery Island for **It's Tough to Be a Bug.** If you want a bird-show fix, see **Flights of Wonder,** then go on the **Maharajah Jungle Trek,** both in Asia. **Expedition Everest** will thrill older kids and teens (adults too), then it's off to tackle **Kali River Rapids,** a great way to cool off in the midday heat (you'll all get soaked).

Older kids, teens, and adults can also ride **Dinosaur** and **Primeval Whirl** in Dinoland U.S.A.; both are good choices if you get there before lines form or if you use FASTPASS. Younger kids deserve some time at the **Boneyard** and on **TriceraTop Spin** in Dinoland, as well as **Camp Minnie-Mickey,** on the other side of the park.

Be sure to make time in your day for **The Festival of the Lion King** over in Camp Minnie-Mickey; it's one of the best shows in all of WDW. Check the park's *Times Guide* to see which showing fits in best with your schedule.

SERVICES & FACILITIES IN THE PARKS

ATMs   Money machines are available near the entrances to all parks and usually at least one other place inside (see the guide map as you enter the park). They honor cards from banks using the Cirrus, Honor, and PLUS systems.

Baby Care   All parks have a Baby Care Center that's equipped with private breast-feeding rooms and sells baby-care basics, which are also available at Guest Relations. All women's restrooms, and some men's, are equipped with changing tables.

Cameras & Film   Film and Kodak disposable cameras are sold at various locations in all parks (at much higher prices than those in the free world).

Car Assistance   If you need a battery jump or other assistance, raise the hood of your vehicle and wait for security to arrive. When necessary, AAA provides free towing from the parks during park operating hours.

First Aid   All parks have stations marked on the handout guide maps.

Internet Access   Disney has installed phones with large touch-screens and Internet access capabilities at several locations in the theme parks, resorts, and other locations (locations are marked on park guide maps). For 25¢ a minute, with a 4-minute minimum, you can access the Internet or check your e-mail.

(*Tips*   **Smoking Alert**

Disney prohibits smoking in its shops, attractions, restaurants, and ride lines. There are a few designated outdoor smoking areas in the park if you feel the urge to light up.

Lost Children   Every park has a designated spot for lost children to be reunited with their families. In the Magic Kingdom, it's City Hall or the Baby Care Center; in Epcot, the Earth Center or the Baby Care Center; in Disney–MGM Studios, Guest Relations; and in Animal Kingdom, Discovery Island. *Children under 7 should wear name-tags inside their clothing; older children and adults should have a prearranged meeting place in case your group gets separated.* If someone gets lost, tell the first park employee you see—many wear the same type of clothing and all have special name-tags.

Package Pickup   Nearly all WDW stores can arrange for packages to be sent to the front of the park. Allow at least 3 hours for delivery. If you're staying at a Disney resort, you can also have all packages purchased by 7pm sent to your hotel (they will be delivered by noon the next day).

Parking   At press time, Disney charged $9 for car, light truck, and van parking, and $10 for RVs.

Pets   It's illegal to leave yours in a parked car, even with a window cracked open; cars become ovenlike death traps in Florida's sun. Only service animals are permitted in the parks, but there are five kennels at WDW (© **407/824-6568;** $6 per day, $9 overnight for resort guests; $11 overnight for those staying elsewhere). The ones at the Transportation and Ticket Center in the Magic Kingdom and near the entrance to Fort Wilderness board animals overnight. Day accommodations are offered at kennels just outside the Entrance Plaza at Epcot and at the entrances to Disney–MGM Studios and Animal Kingdom. *Proof of vaccination is required.* For more information, see "Fast Facts" in chapter 3.

Shops   In addition to the ones listed in the following pages, many of Disney's attractions feature small gift shops filled with merchandise and souvenirs based on that attraction's theme.

Stroller Rental   Strollers are available near all of the park entrances. The cost is $10 for a single and $18 for a double. Length-of-Stay rentals have been eliminated for 2007 (though they'll run through the end of 2006).

Tip Boards   Each park has a tip board that tells visitors the approximate waiting time at all of the major rides and attractions. In Magic Kingdom it's at the end of Main Street on the left as you face the castle; in Epcot, the digital board is in Innoventions Plaza; at MGM it's at the intersection of Hollywood and Sunset boulevards; inside Animal Kingdom, you'll find it just over the bridge to Discovery Island.

Wheelchair Rental   A wheelchair is $10 per day. Electric wheelchairs rent for $45, which includes a $5 refundable deposit.

FOR TRAVELERS WITH SPECIAL NEEDS

WDW does a lot to assist guests with disabilities. Its services are detailed in the *Guidebook for Guests with Disabilities.* You can get one from Guest Relations in the parks, other information areas, at Disney resorts, or online at **www.disneyworld.com** and **www.disney.go.com/disabilities**. You can also call © **407/824-4321** with questions regarding other special needs. Some examples of other services: Almost all Disney resorts have rooms for those with disabilities, and there are Braille director ies inside the Magic Kingdom: in the front of the Main Street train station, and in a gazebo in front of the Crystal Palace restaurant. There are special parking lots at all parks. Complimentary guided-tour audiocassette tapes and players are available at Guest Relations to

Moments **All Aboard**

If your kids appreciate experiences a bit out of the ordinary, ask if you can co-pilot the Disney monorail for a spin around the kingdom. Being a **monorail pilot** doesn't mean that you get to drive the train, but your family will get to ride upfront with the *real* pilot. It requires a little patience because no more than four or five people can do it per ride, so ask a cast member at the monorail stations at the Grand Floridian, Polynesian, or Contemporary resorts if there's room for you in the cockpit. You may not have much luck during peak seasons or busier times of the day (at park opening and closing), or if there's a pilot trainee on board. But at other times, especially if you're patient enough to wait for the next train, you may be treated to the best seats aboard. Best of all: It's free.

assist visually impaired guests, and personal translator units are available to amplify the audio at some Epcot Attractions (inquire at Earth Station). For hearing-impaired information call ✆ **407/939-7670** or for information regarding Telecommunications Devices for the Deaf (TDDs) call ✆ **407/827-5141 (TTY),** or the main number listed above.

3 The Magic Kingdom

The Magic Kingdom still attracts millions from around the world, drawn here by the opportunity to experience the fun and fantasy that only Disney can deliver. Attendance, once again on the rise at just over 16 million, makes this America's most popular theme park. The 107-acre Magic Kingdom is filled with over 40 attractions (with new experiences being added almost yearly), unique shops, and themed restaurants. Its most recognizable feature is Cinderella Castle, the park's icon and centerpiece. And surrounding the castle are the park's **seven themed lands,** stretching out like the spokes of a wheel.

ARRIVING   The parking lot here is huge—so big, in fact, that it's necessary to take a tram just to get to the **Transportation and Ticket Center** (more commonly known as the TTC), where you can buy your park tickets. Each of the parking lot's sections is named for Disney characters (Goofy, Pluto, Minnie, and so on), and aisles are numbered. We can't stress enough just how important it is *to write down where you left your vehicle—you would be amazed at how many white minivans look just like yours!* Once you have your tickets in hand (or if you've arrived with them—the best route), you'll need to make your first decision of the day—do you take the ferry or the monorail to the park from the TTC? The ferry offers a more leisurely (and windy) ride, while the monorail is the speedier of the two.

Upon arriving at the park entrance you will have to pass through security and have your bags inspected. All told, the time it takes to get from your car to Main Street U.S.A. is somewhere around **35 to 45 minutes,** sometimes longer. And that total doesn't include the time spent in lines if you have to stop at Guest Relations or rent a stroller. You'll face the same agony (complicated by escaping crowds) on the way out, so relax. This is one of the most crowded parks, so plan to arrive an hour before the opening bell or an hour or two after.

The Magic Kingdom

Frontierland Railroad Station

Caribbean Way

LIBERTY SQUARE

FRONTIERLAND

ADVENTURELAND

City Hall

MAGIC KINGDOM

MONORAIL

Disney's Contemporary Resort

Disney's Grand Floridian Beach Resort

FERRY

Seven Seas Lagoon

Disney's Polynesian Resort

Transportation and Ticket Center (Trams to parking areas)

Monorail Station

Boat Launch

MAIN STREET U.S.A
Main Street Vehicles **2**
Walt Disney World
   Railroad **1**

ADVENTURELAND
Enchanted Tiki Room **6**
Jungle Cruise **4**
Magic Carpets of Aladdin **7**
Pirates of the Caribbean **5**
Swiss Family Treehouse **3**

FRONTIERLAND
Big Thunder Mountain
   Railroad **13**
Country Bear Jamboree **8**
Frontierland Shootin'
   Arcade **9**
Splash Mountain **11**
Tom Sawyer Island **10**
Walt Disney World
   Railroad **12**

LIBERTY SQUARE
Hall of Presidents **15**
Haunted Mansion **16**
Liberty Square Riverboat **14**

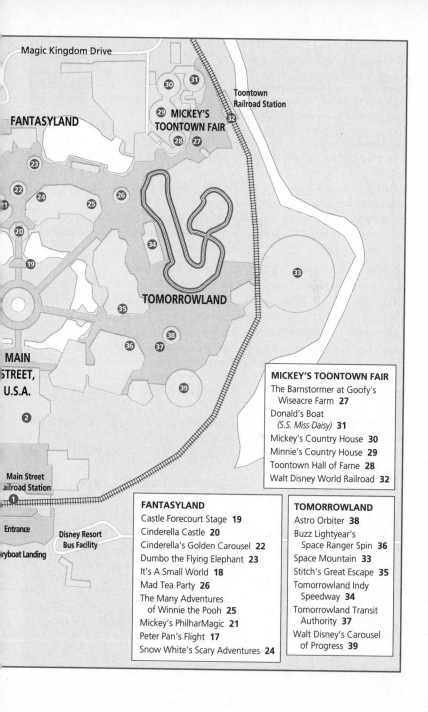

Magic Kingdom Drive

FANTASYLAND

Toontown
Railroad Station

MICKEY'S
TOONTOWN FAIR

TOMORROWLAND

MAIN
STREET,
U.S.A.

Main Street
Railroad Station

Entrance

Disney Resort
Bus Facility

Ferryboat Landing

MICKEY'S TOONTOWN FAIR
The Barnstormer at Goofy's
 Wiseacre Farm **27**
Donald's Boat
 (S.S. Miss Daisy) **31**
Mickey's Country House **30**
Minnie's Country House **29**
Toontown Hall of Fame **28**
Walt Disney World Railroad **32**

FANTASYLAND
Castle Forecourt Stage **19**
Cinderella Castle **20**
Cinderella's Golden Carousel **22**
Dumbo the Flying Elephant **23**
It's A Small World **18**
Mad Tea Party **26**
The Many Adventures
 of Winnie the Pooh **25**
Mickey's PhilharMagic **21**
Peter Pan's Flight **17**
Snow White's Scary Adventures **24**

TOMORROWLAND
Astro Orbiter **38**
Buzz Lightyear's
 Space Ranger Spin **36**
Space Mountain **33**
Stitch's Great Escape **35**
Tomorrowland Indy
 Speedway **34**
Tomorrowland Transit
 Authority **37**
Walt Disney's Carousel
 of Progress **39**

The most important thing you can do upon arriving at the park is to pick up a copy (or two) of the Magic Kingdom **guide map** (if you can't find one at the turnstiles, stop at City Hall or the nearest shop). It provides an array of detailed information about available guest services, restaurants, and attractions. The *Times Guide* (separate from the guide map) will be your key to the daily schedules for showtimes, parades, fireworks, character meet-and-greets, park and restaurant hours.

If you have questions, all park employees are very knowledgeable, and City Hall, on your left as you enter, is an information center—and, like Mickey's Toontown Fair, a great place to meet costumed characters. Character greeting places are also featured on the map.

HOURS   The park is usually open from at least 9am to 6 or 7pm, sometimes later—as late as midnight during major holidays and summer.

TICKET PRICES   Ticket prices for adults are $63, $52 for children 3 to 9. Kids under 3 get in free. See "Tickets," on p. 181, for information on the new Magic Your Way ticketing scheme.

SERVICES & FACILITIES IN THE MAGIC KINGDOM

Most of the following are noted on the handout guide maps in the park:

ATMs   Machines inside the park honor cards from banks using the Cirrus, Honor, and PLUS systems. They're near the main entrance; in Frontierland, near the Shootin' Gallery; and in Tomorrowland, next to Space Mountain.

Baby Care   Located next to the Crystal Palace at the end of Main Street, the Baby Care Center is furnished with a nursing room with rocking chairs and toddler-size toilets. Disposable diapers, formula, baby food, and pacifiers are sold at a premium (bring your own or pay the price). There are changing tables here as well as in all women's restrooms and some men's.

Cameras & Film   Film and Kodak disposable cameras are available throughout the park, but digital camera equipment is in far shorter supply.

First Aid   It's located beside the Crystal Palace next to the Baby Care Center and staffed by registered nurses.

Lockers   Lockers are located in the arcade below the Main Street Railroad Station. The cost is $7, which includes a $2 refundable deposit.

Lost Children   Lost children in the Magic Kingdom are usually taken to City Hall or the Baby Care Center. *Children under 7 should wear name-tags inside their clothing.*

Package Pickup   Any package can be sent by a shop clerk to Guest Relations in the Entrance Plaza; allow at least 3 hours for delivery. If you're staying overnight at a Disney resort, you can also have all packages purchased by 7pm sent to your hotel (they will be delivered by noon the next day).

Pet Care   Day boarding is available at the Transportation and Ticket Center for $6 (© 407/824-6568). The center also boards animals overnight ($9 for hotel guests, $11 for others). Proof of vaccination is required.

Strollers   They can be rented at the Stroller Shop near the entrance to the Magic Kingdom. The cost is $10 for a single and $18 for a double.

Wheelchair Rental   For wheelchairs, go to the gift shop to the left of the ticket booths at the Transportation and Ticket Center, or to the Stroller and Wheelchair

Frommer's Rates the Rides

Because there's so much to do, we're shifting from the star-rating system used for rooms and restaurants to one that has a bit more range. You'll notice most of the grades below are *As*, *Bs*, and *Cs*. That's because Disney designers have done a reasonably good job on the attractions front. But occasionally our ratings show *Ds* for Duds.

Here's what **Frommer's Ratings** mean:

A+	=	Your trip wouldn't be complete without it.
A	=	Put it at the top of your "to-do" list.
B+	=	Make a real effort to see or do it.
B	=	It's fun but not a "must see."
C+	=	A nice diversion; see it if you have time.
C	=	Go if there's no wait and you can walk right in.
D	=	Don't bother.

Shop inside the main entrance to your right. The cost is $10; $45, including a $5 deposit, for electric convenience vehicles.

MAIN STREET, U.S.A.

Designed to model a turn-of-the-20th-century American street (though it ends in a 13th-c. European castle), this is the gateway to the Kingdom. Don't dawdle on Main Street (it's filled mostly with shops and restaurants) when you enter; leave it for the end of the day when you're heading back to your hotel.

Main Street Vehicles

Frommer's Rating: C

Recommended Ages: Mainly nostalgic adults or toddlers

Ride a horse-drawn trolley, jitney, vintage fire engine, or horseless carriage *only* if you don't mind waiting around for a bit. While a nice little diversion, there are far more interesting things to see and do throughout the realm.

Walt Disney World Railroad

Frommer's Rating: B

Recommended Ages: All ages

Climb aboard an authentic 1928 steam-powered train for a relaxing, 15-minute tour of the perimeter of the park. This is a great way to entertain the younger kids in your family while the older ones are off taking in some of Disney's more thrilling attractions. It's also a good way for kids and adults alike to rest for a brief moment while taking in the surrounding sights. There are a total of three stations: at the park entrance, at Frontierland, and at Mickey's Toontown Fair.

And while you're cruising down Main Street, be on the lookout for **The Dapper Dans,** a lively barbershop quartet that harmonizes its way up and down the boulevard.

SHOPPING ON MAIN STREET

Shopping at Disney has almost become a pastime in and of itself, and the largest collection of shops in the Kingdom is located right along Main Street U.S.A. If you find you've forgotten something or just need a present for the neighbor who's taking care of your plants, you'll likely be able to find it here. The **Emporium,** in Town Square, has the park's largest selection of Disneyana, with everything from T-shirts and toys to picture frames and cookie jars. Stop by and pick up some of the more unique sweets and treats at the **Main Street Confectionary** or some shiny baubles at **Uptown Jewelers.** Many of the street's stores are interconnected, pretty much allowing you to shop from one end of Main Street to the other without ever having to walk outside.

ADVENTURELAND

Cross a bridge marked by Tikis and torches as the rhythm of beating drums sound in the distance. As you make your way through lush jungle foliage, trees hung with Spanish moss, dense vines, and stands of palm and bamboo, you are transported to an exotic locale where swashbuckling adventures await.

The Enchanted Tiki Room—Under New Management
Frommer's Rating: B for kids
Recommended Ages: 2–10 and older adults
The large, hexagonal Tiki Room serves up a Polynesian atmosphere, with its thatched roof, bamboo beams, tapa-bark murals, and torches. Inside guests are entertained by the likes of Iago (from *Aladdin*) and Zazu (from *The Lion King*), as well as an ensemble of boisterous tropical birds (over 200 of them, in fact), along with chanting totem poles and singing flowers that whistle, warble, and tweet. Overall, it's good family fun, but be aware that it's rather loud, and a brief simulated tropical storm, with crackling thunder and flashes of lightning, combined with the multitude of audio and visual effects may be a bit too overwhelming for very young children.

Jungle Cruise
Frommer's Rating: C+ (B for the foot-weary)
Recommended Ages: 4–adult
This 10-minute ride's slower pace is a yawner for many older kids and teens, but it's a nice break from the madness if the line isn't long or you use FASTPASS. You'll sail through the African veldt in the Congo, an Amazon rainforest, and along the Nile in Egypt as your boat captain offers somewhat corny but humorous commentary on your travels. You'll encounter dozens of exotic animatronic animals, ranging from playful elephants to lions and tigers, as you sail through dense tropical and subtropical foliage (most of it is real). You'll pass a Cambodian temple guarded by snakes, a rhino chasing terrified African beaters as they clamor up a totem pole for safety, and a jungle camp taken over by apes. While you're waiting to board, read the prop menu; it includes fricassee of giant stag beetle and barbecued three-toed skink.

Tips A Cut Above

The **Harmony Barber Shop** on Main Street, its entrance marked by signature candy-striped poles, is a real working barbershop. It's open daily from 9am to 5pm, and gives hundreds of haircuts each week. If your child gets his or her first cut here, Disney throws in several extras—bubbles, stickers, and a special set of mouse ears—to mark the occasion. Kids 12 and under can get a cut for about $14; cuts for adults cost around $17. To jazz up the experience, kids and adults can add some color to their coif (thanks to a special colored hair gel) for just $5.

Magic Carpets of Aladdin

Frommer's Rating: A for tykes and parents

Recommended Ages: 2–8

Younger kids will appreciate this ride's gentle ups and downs as they fly through the sky on the colorful magic carpets. The view of Agrabah from above is impressive, but be prepared as you make your way around the genie's giant bottle—the spitting camels have pretty good aim, making it likely that you'll get squirted with water (similar to One Fish, Two Fish, Red Fish, Blue Fish at Universal Orlando's Islands of Adventure; see p. 277). There are only 16 four-passenger fiberglass carpets on the ride, which can make for extremely long lines (though not nearly as unbearable as some you'll encounter in Fantasyland).

Pirates of the Caribbean

Frommer's Rating: A

Recommended Ages: 6–adult

The release of *Pirates of the Caribbean: The Curse of the Black Pearl* and its recent sequel, *Dead Man's Chest,* has revitalized the popularity of this oldie but goodie. They also inspired the recent renovations that now have Jack Sparrow and Barbossa joining the original set of swashbucklers. A tweak in the storyline to better mirror the movie, and a mix of new and updated special effects have been added, too. Still, the ride might be a bit scary for kids under 5 due to the unexpected yet small waterfalls and moments of darkness.

After making your way through dark and dank dungeons, guests board a boat and set sail for a small Caribbean town, its shores teeming with pillaging animatronic pirates who carouse, chase wenches, and wreak general havoc, all as Jack and Barbossa race to reach the pirates' treasure. There's plenty of gunfire and cannonballs flying through the air as the marauders battle each other, with you, of course, caught up in the middle. The effects are great, as is the yo-ho-ho music of "A Pirate's Life for Me" that plays in the background (you won't be able to stop yourself from humming along). The bonus here is an immense covered queue area that will protect you and your stroller-bound children from both sun and rain (this ride offers the only covered stroller parking in the park). *Tip:* Nod hello to the parrot (Peglegged Pete) above the entrance plaza and he may offer you his own greeting.

Swiss Family Treehouse

Frommer's Rating: C

Recommended Ages: 4–12

This attraction, based on the 1960 Disney movie version of *Swiss Family Robinson,* includes a few more comforts from home than did the original. After climbing its many, many steps, you'll finally reach the treehouse, its rooms filled with mahogany furnishings, decorative accents, and running water. If you're nervous about heights, this one's not for you—visitors will find themselves walking along a rope-suspended bridge high above the ground, not to mention the climbing that's required to make it up and down all the stairs that lead around this 50-foot banyan tree. The "tree," designed by Disney Imagineers, has 330,000 polyethylene leaves sprouting from a 90-foot span of branches; although it isn't real, it's draped with actual Spanish moss. It's a good place for kids to work off some excess energy, though things can get crowded up there. *Note:* People with limited mobility beware—this attraction requires a lot of climbing.

Tips A (Baker's) Dozen Suggestions for Fewer Headaches

1. **Be a Leader Not a Follower:** Try going against the grain and head left toward Adventureland to begin your day (most visitors sprint for Tomorrowland). If you have the time and aren't a slave to the compressed itinerary of a 1-day visit, make your way to one (maybe two) major attractions early on, then save the others for early on your second day when crowds are lightest. Pick up a FASTPASS when and wherever you can. And try and make mealtimes a bit earlier or later than usual—11am or 2pm for lunch and 4 or 7pm for dinner. Even a few minutes can make all the difference in the restaurant lines.

2. **Note Your Car's Location:** That big red Hummer in the next space may not be there when you get out. Write your lot and row number on something with ink that won't run if it gets wet.

3. **Avoid the Rush:** I-4 can get horribly crowded at times, so be ready for bumper-to-bumper traffic from 7 to 9am, 4 to 7pm, and often in between. Check your map for secondary roads and alternate routes, and try to leave the parks a half-hour before closing, when crowds disburse in droves.

4. **Be Realistic:** You aren't going to be able to do everything in every park (believe us, we've tried). As a group, list three or four "must-do" things each day. If you can, consider splitting up, with each adult taking one or more kids—one heading for the thrill rides, the other for the tamer, tot-friendly attractions. If time allows, you can always backtrack later, and this way no one really misses out on the fun.

5. **Timing Is Everything:** We often laugh when we see people racing to make a tram, and then gunning for the turnstiles. Relax—the park isn't going anywhere. And rushing just to wait in line seems rather silly, doesn't it? Once inside the park, mix it up a bit; stagger the attraction lines with indoor shows or even breaks on a shady bench.

6. **Call Ahead:** If a sit-down dinner in a special restaurant is important to you, make sure to make Advance Reservations (© **407/939-3463**) before your visit.

7. **Set a Spending Limit:** Kids should know they have a set amount to spend on take-home trinkets (if they do, they generally spend more wisely). You should, too. Sticking to your budget will be beneficial in

SHOPPING IN ADVENTURELAND

Located at the Pirates of the Caribbean exit, the **Pirates Bazaar** is filled with everything a child needs to play pirate, from hats to hooks and everything in between. There are also muskets, toy swords, and loads of other pirate booty, as well as a small selection of island wear and costume jewels.

FRONTIERLAND

From Adventureland you'll step into the wild and woolly past of the American frontier, where the sidewalks are wooden; rough-and-tumble architecture runs to log cabins and the end, but building in a small contingency "fun" fund for emergencies is still a good idea.

8. **Take a Break:** If you're staying at a WDW property, spend the midafternoon napping (don't laugh, you may need one) or unwinding in the pool. Return to the parks for a few more attractions and the closing shows. (Get your hand stamped when you leave, and you'll be readmitted without charge.)

9. **Dress Comfortably:** This may seem like common sense, but judging by the limping, blistered crowds trudging the parks, most people don't understand the immeasurable amount of walking they'll be doing. Wear comfortable, broken-in walking shoes or sneakers (you know, the ones that won't give you blisters because you just put them on) and skip the sandals and mules that can fall off or cause you to trip.

10. **Don't Skimp on the Sunscreen:** The Florida sun can be relentless, even in the shade, under the clouds, or in the cooler months. A bad first-day burn can ruin your trip, not to mention your skin. Dress appropriately—wear lightweight, light-colored clothing, and bring along hats (especially for toddlers and infants, even if they'll be in a stroller). If you must show off your skin, slather it in sunscreen (with at least a 30 SPF). This is especially important for children. Make sure that you and your kids drink plenty of water in summer to avoid dehydration. Bringing a pair of sunglasses is a smart move, too.

11. **Travel Light:** Don't carry large amounts of cash. The Pirates of the Caribbean aren't the only thieves in WDW. There are ATMs in the parks and most resorts if you run short.

12. **Get a Little Goofy:** Relax, put on those mouse ears, eat that extra piece of fudge, and sing along at the shows. Don't worry about what the staff thinks; they've seen it all (and they're dressed pretty goofy, too).

13. **Take Measure of your Kids:** This guide, park maps, and information boards outside the more adventurous rides list minimum heights. If you know the restrictions early, you can avoid disappointment in the parks. Trust us—WDW won't budge because of sad faces or temper tantrums when your safety is involved.

rustic saloons; and the landscape is Southwestern scrubby with mesquite, cactus, yucca, and prickly pear.

Big Thunder Mountain Railroad

Frommer's Rating: A

Recommended Ages: 8–adult

This roller coaster earns high marks for what it is—a ride designed for those not quite up to the lunch-losing thrills of the Rock 'n' Roller Coaster at Disney–MGM Studios (p. 237). Think of Big Thunder as *Roller Coasters 101*. (Survive and graduate to the

---

(Tips) Riding the Rails

Although it's an oldie, Big Thunder Mountain Railroad is still a magnet to the masses. If a FASTPASS isn't available (and that can happen), try riding it late in the day (coaster veterans swear the ride is even better after dark) or during one of the parades that draw visitors away from the attractions.

---

next level.) It sports fun hairpin turns and dark descents rather than sudden, steep drops and near collisions. Your runaway train covers 2,780 feet of track and careens through the ribs of a dinosaur, under a thundering waterfall, past spewing geysers, and over a bottomless volcanic pool. Animatronic characters (such as a long john–clad fellow in a bathtub) and critters (goats, chickens, donkeys) enhance the scenic backdrop, along with several hundred thousand dollars' worth of authentic antique mining equipment. *Note:* You must be at least 40 inches tall to ride, and Disney discourages expectant mothers and people prone to motion sickness or those with heart, neck, or back problems from riding.

Country Bear Jamboree *(Finds)*
Frommer's Rating: B+
Recommended Ages: 3–adult; though the younger the child, the better
This is a foot-stomping hoot! It opened as one of the park's original attractions way back when in 1971, a time when entertainment was more low-tech but fun just the same. The 15-minute show stars a backwoods troupe of fiddlin', strummin', harmonica-playin' bears (all audio-animatronic, of course) belting out lively tunes and woeful love songs. The chubby Trixie, decked out in a satiny skirt, laments lost love as she sings "Tears Will Be the Chaser for Your Wine." Teddi Barra descends from the ceiling in a swing to perform "Heart, We Did All That We Could." Big Al moans "Blood in the Saddle." In the finale, the cast joins in a rousing singalong. *Blue-light bonus:* The jamboree is a great summertime place to cool your heels in the A/C.

Frontierland Shootin' Arcade
Frommer's Rating: C
Recommended Ages: 8–adult
Combining state-of-the-art electronics with a traditional shooting-gallery format, this arcade presents an array of targets (slow-moving ore cars, buzzards, and gravediggers) in an 1850s boomtown scenario. Fog creeps across the graveyard, and the setting changes as a calm, starlit night turns stormy with flashes of lightning and claps of thunder. Coyotes howl, bridges creak, and skeletal arms reach out from the grave. If you hit a tombstone, it might spin around and mysteriously change its epitaph. To keep things authentic, newfangled electronic firing mechanisms loaded with infrared bullets are concealed in vintage buffalo rifles. Fifty cents buys you 25 shots. Though it's a pretty cool arcade, there are far better ways to spend your time in Magic Kingdom.

Splash Mountain
Frommer's Rating: A+
Recommended Ages: 8–adult
If you need a quick cooling off, this is the place to go—because you will get wet (soaked, is more like it)! Based on Disney's 1946 film *Song of the South,* Splash Mountain takes you flume-style down a flooded mountain, past 26 colorful scenes that

include backwoods swamps, bayous, spooky caves, and waterfalls. Riders are caught in the bumbling schemes of Brer Fox and Brer Bear as they chase the ever-wily Brer Rabbit, who, against the advice of Mr. Bluebird, leaves his briar-patch home in search of fortune and the "laughing place." The music from the film forms a delightful audio backdrop. Your hollow-log vehicle twists, turns, and splashes, sometimes plummeting in darkness as the ride leads to a 52-foot, 45-degree, 40-mph splashdown in a briar-filled pond (you'll feel the drop!). And that's not the end. The ride keeps going until it's a Zip-A-Dee-Do-Dah kind of day. *Note:* You must be at least 40 inches tall to ride. Also, expectant mothers and people prone to motion sickness or those with heart, neck, or back problems shouldn't climb aboard.

Tom Sawyer Island
Frommer's Rating: C for most, B+ for energetic kids who need a release
Recommended Ages: 4–12
Huck Finn's raft will take you on a 2-minute journey across the River of America to the densely forested Tom Sawyer Island, where kids can explore the narrow passages of Injun Joe's cave (complete with such scary sound effects as whistling wind), a walk-through windmill, a serpentine abandoned mine, and Fort Longhorn. The island's two bridges—one a suspension bridge, the other made of barrels floating on top of the water—create quite a challenge for anyone trying to cross. Maintaining your balance is difficult at best if (or should we say when) the other guests are jumping up and down—but that's half the fun. Narrow, winding dirt paths lined with oaks, pines, and sycamores create an authentic backwoods atmosphere. It's easy to get briefly lost and stumble upon some unexpected adventure, but for younger children, the woods and caves can pose a real problem—toddlers who can't easily find their way back to you or who may get scared by darkness and eerie noises should be watched very carefully. Aunt Polly's Dockside Inn, which serves up sandwiches and such, and has outdoor tables on a porch overlooking the river, is the perfect spot for a relaxing lunch after all that running around; as a bonus, it's generally not as crowded as eateries on the mainland.

SHOPPING IN FRONTIERLAND
Mosey into the **Frontier Trading Post** for the latest and greatest in cowboy wear. The **Prairie Outpost and Supply** is your best bet for sweets and treats.

LIBERTY SQUARE
Unlike the other lands in Magic Kingdom, Liberty Square doesn't have clearly delineated boundaries. Pass through Frontierland into this small area, and you'll suddenly find yourself in the middle of Colonial America. Before you can say "George Washington,"

Tips Parental Touring Tip

Many of the attractions at Walt Disney World offer a **Parent Switch program,** designed for parents traveling with small children. While one parent rides an attraction, the other stays with the kids not quite ready to handle the experience; then the adults switch places without having to stand in line again. The bonus (beyond the obvious) is that the kids able to ride the attraction will get to ride again, too. Notify a cast member if you wish to participate when you get in line. Most other Orlando theme parks offer this option, too.

Fun Fact **It's a Dirty Job . . .**

The Disney parks are usually fairly clean, but there's one notable spot in the Magic Kingdom that takes pride in its dreary image. In order to maintain the Haunted Mansion's weathered and worn appearance, employees spread large amounts of dust over the home's interior and also string up plenty of real-looking cobwebs. It takes a lot of effort to keep the place looking bedraggled, which may explain why your haunted hosts are only a handful of Disney cast members without smiles plastered on their faces.

---

you'll be standing in front of the Liberty Tree, an immense live oak decorated with 13 lanterns symbolizing the first 13 colonies. The entire area has an 18th-century, early American feel, complete with Federal and Georgian architecture, quaint shops, and flowerbeds bordering manicured lawns. You may even encounter a fife-and-drum corps marching along the cobblestone streets. The **Liberty Tree Tavern** (p. 141) is one of the better Magic Kingdom restaurants and offers a popular character meal.

Hall of Presidents
Frommer's Rating: B+ for school-age kids and adults
Recommended Ages: 8–adult
American presidents from George Washington to George W. Bush (who made his debut in the fall of 2001) are represented by lifelike audio-animatronic figures (arguably, the best in WDW). If you look closely, you'll see them fidget and whisper during the performance. The show begins with a film projected on a 180-degree, 70mm screen. It talks about the importance of the Constitution, then the curtain rises on America's leaders, and, as each comes into the spotlight, he nods or waves with presidential dignity. Lincoln then rises and speaks, occasionally referring to his notes. In a tribute to Disney thoroughness, painstaking research was done in creating the figures and scenery, with each president's costume reflecting period fashion, fabrics, and tailoring techniques.

Haunted Mansion
Frommer's Rating: A
Recommended Ages: 6–adult
What better way to show off Disney's eye for detailed special effects than through this oldie but goodie (Walt had an actual hand in its development), where "Grim Grinning Ghosts" come out to socialize—or so the ride's theme song goes. The queue here is one of the most amusing in the park as it winds through a graveyard filled with tombstones whose epitaphs are sure to make you chuckle. Upon entering you're greeted by a ghostly host, who encloses you in a windowless portrait gallery (are those eyes following you?) where the floor seems to descend (actually, it's the ceiling that's rising) and the room goes dark (the only truly scary moment). Darkness, spooky music, eerie howling, and mysterious screams and rappings enhance its ambience. Your vehicle, err . . . Doom Buggy takes you past a ghostly banquet and ball, a graveyard band, a suit of armor that comes alive, cobweb-draped chandeliers, a ghostly talking head in a crystal ball, and more. Keep your eyes on the mirror you pass at the end of your ride, as you'll find another passenger in your buggy . . . Boo! The experience is more amusing than terrifying; most children 6 and older will be fine, but those younger (and even some of the older ones) may not be so amused.

Liberty Square Riverboat *Overrated*

Frommer's Rating: C

Recommended Ages: All ages

The *Liberty Belle,* a grand steam-powered riverboat, offers lazy 17-minute cruises along the Rivers of America, allowing thrill-ride-weary passengers the chance to rest and relax. As you pass along the shores of Frontierland, the Indian camp, wildlife, and wilderness cabin will make it seem as if you're traveling through the wild and wooly West.

SHOPPING IN LIBERTY SQUARE

The **Heritage House** is filled with replicas of famous documents, including the Declaration of Independence; miniature models of the Statue of Liberty; and everything Americana, from souvenir spoons and campaign buttons to flags and red-white-and-blue T-shirts. **Ye Olde Christmas Shoppe,** filled with decorations and Disney ornaments galore, celebrates Christmas every day of the year.

FANTASYLAND

The most fanciful land in the park, Fantasyland features attractions that bring classic Disney characters to life. It is by far the most popular land in the park for young children, who can sail over Merry Ole' London and Never Never Land, ride in a honey pot through the Hundred-Acre Wood, and fly with Dumbo. If your kids are under 8, you'll find yourself spending a lot of your time here (and at Mickey's Toontown Fair, detailed later in this section).

Cinderella Castle *Moments*

Frommer's Rating: A (for visuals)

Recommended Ages: All ages

There's actually not a lot to do here, but it's the Magic Kingdom's most widely recognized symbol, and I guarantee that you won't be able to pass it by without a look. It's not as if you could miss it anyway. The fairy-tale castle looms over Main Street U.S.A., its 189-foot-high Gothic spires taking center stage from the minute you enter the park.

One of the most popular restaurants in the park is set inside the castle, **Cinderella's Royal Table** (p. 175), along with a shop or two. Elaborate mosaic murals depict the Cinderella story in the castle's archway, and Disney family coats of arms are displayed over a fireplace. An actress portraying Cinderella, dressed for the ball, often makes appearances in the lobby. The Castle Forecourt Stage features live shows daily so be sure to check the daily *Times Guide*'s schedule for **Cinderella's Surprise Celebration** and **Cinderellabration.** The latter, a new show imported from Tokyo Disneyland, continues the story of Cinderella with her coronation and stars Cinderella, the Fairy Godmother, and several other members of the royal court.

Cinderella's Golden Carousel *Moments*

Frommer's Rating: B+ for younger kids, A for carousel fans

Recommended Ages: All ages

One of the most beautiful attractions at Disney, the Golden Carousel is as enchanting to look at as it is to ride. Originally built by the Philadelphia Toboggan Co. in 1917, the carousel toured many an amusement park in the Midwest long before Walt Disney bought it and brought it to Orlando 5 years before the Magic Kingdom opened. Disney artisans meticulously refurbished it, adding 18 hand-painted scenes from Cinderella on a wooden canopy above the horses. Its organ plays Disney classics such as

"When You Wish Upon a Star." Adults and children alike adore riding the ornate horses round and round; there are even a few benches for the littlest tykes in the family. The ride is longer than you might expect, but the lines can get lengthy as well, so check back a bit later if your timing is off the first time around.

Dumbo the Flying Elephant

Frommer's Rating: B+ for younger kids and parents
Recommended Ages: 2–6

This is a favorite of the preschool set, a fact that will quickly become apparent when you see the line wrapping around, and around, and around. Much like Magic Carpets of Aladdin (p. 197), the Dumbo vehicles fly around in a circle, gently rising and dipping as you control them from inside the elephant. If you can stand the brutal lines—extending well beyond the barely covered queue and out in the blazing sun—this ride is almost sure to make your little one's day.

It's a Small World

Frommer's Rating: B+ for youngsters and first-timers
Recommended Ages: 2–8

Recently refurbished to spruce up some of its older displays, It's a Small World is one of those rides that you just have to do because it's been there since the beginning—it's a classic (built for the 1964 World's Fair before being transplanted to Disney), and in this day and age it's nice to see that some things don't change (or at least not too much). Besides, it's a big favorite of younger kids. And as much as some adults pooh-pooh it, we'd take bets they come out smiling and singing right along with their kids. If you don't know the song, you will by the end of the ride (and probably ever after), as the hard part is trying to get it *out* of your head. As you sail along you'll pass through the countries of the world, each filled with appropriately costumed audio-animatronic dolls greeting you by singing "It's a Small World" in tiny Munchkin voices. The cast of thousands includes Chinese acrobats, Russian kazachok dancers, Indian snake charmers, French cancan girls, and, well, you get the picture. To truly experience everything Disney, this one's a must.

Mad Tea Party

Frommer's Rating: C+
Recommended Ages: 4–adult

Traditional amusement park ride it may be, but it's still a family favorite—maybe because it is so simple. The mad tea party scene in Alice in Wonderland was the inspiration for this one, and riders sit in giant pastel-colored teacups set on saucers that careen around a circular platform while the cup, saucer, and platform all spin round and round. Occasionally, the woozy Dormouse mouse pops out of a big central teapot

---

(Fun Fact) Behind the Scenes

You'll never catch a glimpse of, say, Mickey relaxing with his head off, or Pluto taking a candy bar break—that would ruin the entire illusion (and this is a world built on fantasy). The people inside the characters, and other cast members, take breaks as well as travel around the park through an intricate system of underground tunnels that are off-limits to the public, unless you pay a premium for a behind-the-scenes tour that we tell you about on p. 217.

Tips **It Ain't Fair, But . . .**

Disney rides sometimes break down or need routine maintenance that can take them out of commission for a few hours, a day, a week, or sometimes months. Test Track at Epcot, for example, occasionally experiences technical difficulties. And Pirates of the Caribbean recently closed for a few months in 2006 for renovations.

Many, but not all, of the ride rehabs are listed on the Disney website **(www.disneyworld.com).** Deb's Unofficial Walt Disney World Information Guide site **(www.allearsnet.com)** and Travel Insights **(www.travel-insights. com)** list most ride rehabs as well. The moral of the story: Err on the side of caution and don't make promises to kids about specific rides just in case something happens. Note that refurbishments and technical difficulties are unfortunate but part of the deal—neither Disney nor Universal will discount or refund any tickets when rehabs occur.

---

to see just what's going on. Tame as it may appear, this can be a pretty active, even nauseating ride, depending on how much you spin your teacup's wheel. Adolescents seem to consider it a badge of honor if they can turn the unsuspecting adults in their cup green—you have been warned!

The Many Adventures of Winnie the Pooh
Frommer's Rating: B
Recommended Ages: 2–8 and their parents
When this replaced Mr. Toad's Wild Ride in 1999, it drew a small storm of protest from Toad lovers, but things have quieted since then. This fun ride features the cute and cuddly little fellow along with Eeyore, Piglet, and Tigger. You board a golden honey pot and ride through a storybook version of the Hundred-Acre Wood, keeping an eye out for Heffalumps, Woozles, Blustery Days, and the Floody Place. Young kids absolutely love it, but be prepared to brave some *very* long lines if you don't use FAST-PASS. *Tip:* Be sure to take your tinier tots across to Pooh's Thoughtful Spot, a small play area filled with places to crawl, slide, and occasionally get wet.

Mickey's PhilharMagic
Frommer's Rating: A+
Recommended Ages: All ages
This late 2003 arrival is by far the most amazing 3-D movie production we've ever laid eyes on and is a must-see for everyone. Popular Disney characters—including Ariel, Simba, and Aladdin—are brought to 3-D life on a 150-foot screen (the largest wrap-around screen on the planet) as they try to help (or in some cases hinder) the attempts of Donald Duck to retrieve Mickey's magical sorcerer's hat before the Mouse discovers it's missing. It's the first time the classic Disney characters have ever been rendered in 3-D. Even if you're not a big fan of shows, this is one you should see. Like (but far better than) the whimsical **Jim Henson's Muppet*Vision 3-D** (p. 235) at Disney–MGM Studios, the show combines music, animated film, puppetry, and special effects that tickle several of your senses. The kids will love the animation and effects, and parents will enjoy the nostalgia factor.

Peter Pan's Flight
Frommer's Rating: A for kids and parents

Recommended Ages: 3–8

Another of Disney's simple pleasures, this is a classic ride that's fun for the whole family. You'll fly through the sky in your very own ship (much like that of Captain Hook's), gliding over familiar scenes from the adventures of Peter Pan. Your adventure begins in the Darlings' nursery and includes a flight over an elaborate nighttime cityscape of Merry Ole' London, before you move on to Never Land. There you encounter mermaids, Indians, Tick Tock the Croc, the Lost Boys, Princess Tiger Lilly, Tinker Bell, Hook, and Smee, all while listening to the theme, "You Can Fly, You Can Fly, You Can Fly." It's *very* tame fun for the young and young at heart. It's also another one where the long lines could inspire the theme "you can wait, you can wait, you can wait."

Snow White's Scary Adventures

Frommer's Rating: C

Recommended Ages: 4–8

While Disney has changed this ride a bit since its debut, attempting to make it less scary for the small children that it was intended for, it still features the wicked witch rather predominantly (though Snow White appears far more often than before). Many of the scenes are now more pleasant, including such happier moments from the movie as the scenes at the wishing well and Snow White riding away with the prince to live happily ever after. There are new audio-animatronic dwarfs, and the colors have been brightened and made less menacing. Even so, this ride still has plenty of scary moments if your child is under 5 (and those much older likely won't even want to ride), so if the lines are long think about passing this one up.

SHOPPING IN FANTASYLAND

Fantasy Faire is filled with plenty of items for your little prince or princess to play with, including costumes, swords, and much more. Little girls adore **Tinker Bell's Treasures,** its wares comprising Peter Pan merchandise, costumes (Tinker Bell, Snow White, Cinderella, Pocahontas, and others), and collector dolls. **Pooh's Thotful Shop** is filled with T-shirts and toys featuring those cuddly characters from the Hundred-Acre Wood for kids and adults alike.

MICKEY'S TOONTOWN FAIR

Wondering where to find Mickey? Instead of walking about the park as he did many years ago, The Mouse now holds court in Toontown. The candy-striped **Judge's** and **Toontown Hall of Fame** tents inside this zone is where kids get a chance to meet many of their favorite Disney characters, including Mickey, Minnie, Donald, Goofy, and Pluto. The entire area (small as it may be) is filled with a whimsical collection of cartoonish attractions geared mostly to those under 6 (making it one of the more crowded spots in the park).

The Barnstormer at Goofy's Wiseacre Farm (Finds

Frommer's Rating: A for kids and parents

Recommended Ages: 4 and up

Designed to look and feel like a crop duster that flies slightly off course and right through the Goofmeister's barn, this mini–roller coaster is one of the more whimsically themed rides in the park. As coasters go, it offers very little in the dip-and-drop department, but there's plenty of zip on the spin-and-spiral front. It even gets squeals from some adults. The only ones likely to be disappointed are those who live for the thrills and spills of the bigger coasters. The Barnstormer is practically a twin of Woody

Woodpecker's Nuthouse Coaster (which it likely inspired) at Universal Studios Florida (p. 269). *Note:* The 60-second ride has a 35-inch height minimum, and expectant mothers are warned not to ride it.

Donald's Boat (S.S. *Miss Daisy*)

Frommer's Rating: B+ for kids
Recommended Ages: 2–10

The good ship *Miss Daisy* offers plenty of interactive fun for kids who enjoy getting wet. Watch out as you make your way around the surrounding "waters" as the leaks squirting from the boat are practically unavoidable—but that's half the fun (you can tell by the little squeals of joy heard from those who've been doused). *Tip:* The nearby Toon Park (a 40-in. height *maximum*) is a small covered playground with slides and a small playhouse for dryer adventures. There are also a handful of covered benches for weary parents in need of a momentary break.

Mickey's & Minnie's Country Houses

Frommer's Rating: B for younger kids
Recommended Ages: 2–8

These separate cottages offer a lot of visual fun and a small bit of interactive play for youngsters, but they're usually crowded—the lines flow like molasses. Mickey's place is more for looking than touching, though it does feature a small garden and garage playground. Minnie's lets kids play in her kitchen, where popcorn goes wild in a microwave, a cake bakes and then deflates in the oven, and the utensils strike up a symphony of their own.

SHOPPING IN MICKEY'S TOONTOWN FAIR

The **Toontown Hall of Fame Tent** has continuous meetings with Disney characters as well as a large assortment of Disney souvenirs.

TOMORROWLAND

This land was originally designed to focus on the future, but in 1994, the WDW folks decided Tomorrowland (originally designed in the 1970s) was beginning to look a lot like "Yesteryear." So it was revamped to show the future as envisioned in the '20s and '30s—a galactic, science fiction–inspired community inhabited by humans, aliens, and robots. A video-game arcade also was added.

Astro Orbiter

Frommer's Rating: C+
Recommended Ages: 4–10

Although touted as a tame ride much like the ones you might have ridden when you were a child and the carnivals came to town, it does offer a bit of unexpected uneasiness. Its "rockets" are on arms attached to "the center of the galaxy," and move up and down while orbiting the planets, but they also tilt to the side—and when you're on top of a two-story tower, looking down from your perch can make you rather anxious. Because of its limited capacity the line tends to move at a snail's pace, so unless it's short, skip this one.

Buzz Lightyear's Space Ranger Spin

Frommer's Rating: A+ for kids and parents
Recommended Ages: 3 and up

Recruits stand ready as Buzz Lightyear briefs you on your mission. The evil emperor Zurg is once again up to no good, and Buzz needs your to help save the Universe. As

Value   Extra Magic—Extra Time

The free **Extra Magic Hour** program allows Disney resort guests (as well as those staying at the WDW Swan, the WDW Dolphin, and the Hilton at the Walt Disney World Resort) some extra playtime in the parks (even the water parks). Under the program, a select number of attractions, shops, and restaurants at one of the four major Disney parks (or one of its two water parks) open an hour early on scheduled mornings, and those at another park remain open up to 3 hours after official closing on scheduled evenings. And because only resort guests can participate in the Extra Magic Hour, crowds are almost nonexistent, and lines are much shorter—not to mention that the temperatures are usually a lot more agreeable early in the morning and later in the evening.

To enter a park for the morning Extra Magic Hour, you must present your Disney resort room key and park ticket. For the evening Extra Magic Hour, your room key, park ticket, and a special wristband (for every member in your group) are required. You can obtain the wristband at the park scheduled to remain open that evening, but no earlier than 1 hour prior to park closing.

Warning: If you hold a ticket with a Park Hopper add-on (see p. 181 for information on Disney ticketing options), then you can attend any Extra Magic Hour at any park. But, if you hold a Base Ticket with no park-hopping privileges, then you can only attend the Extra Magic Hour at the park where you're spending your day. So, if you have only a Base Ticket and go to the morning Magic Hour at Epcot and spend the day there, you cannot head over to Magic Kingdom's evening Magic Hour on the same day. Call ⓒ 407/824-4321 or visit **www.disneyworld.com** for details.

you cruise through "space," you'll pass through scenes filled with brightly colored aliens, most of whom are marked with a big "Z," so you know where to shoot. Kids love using the dashboard-mounted laser cannons as they spin through the sky (filled with gigantic toys instead of stars). If they're good shots, they can set off sight and sound gags with a direct hit from their lasers (my 3-year-old, however, aims just about everywhere but at the target and still has loads of fun). A display in the car keeps score, so take multiple cars if you have more than one child. This ride uses the same technology as Universal Studios Florida's Men in Black Alien Attack (p. 267), but it's aimed at a younger audience, and therefore, it's far tamer.

Space Mountain
Frommer's Rating: B+
Recommended Ages: 10–adult

This cosmic roller coaster usually has *long* lines (but it has FASTPASS), and most guests find only marginal entertainment value in the pre-ride space-age music and exhibits (meteorites, shooting stars, and space debris whizzing past overhead). Once aboard your rocket, you'll climb and dive through the inky, starlit blackness of outer space. The hairpin turns and plunges make it seem as if you're going at breakneck speed, but your car doesn't go any faster than 28 mph. As on many coasters, the front seat of the train offers the biggest thrills and is the best place to maintain the illusion of flying through space. It's a bit outdated when compared to the newer rides out there but is a good coming-of-age test for future thrill-ride junkies; so if your kids are just starting out on the coasters, and don't mind a spin in the dark, this is a good place to begin. *Note:* Riders must be at least 44 inches tall. Also, expectant moms and people prone to motion sickness or those with heart, neck, or back problems shouldn't climb aboard.

Stitch's Great Escape

Frommer's Rating: D
Recommended Ages: 5–10

In 2003, the scarier **ExtraTERRORestrial Alien Encounter** was closed permanently to make way for this newer and (allegedly) more family-friendly attraction. Unfortunately, Disney missed the mark a bit on this one. Even though it features the mischievous experiment 626, otherwise known as Stitch—a favorite of many younger kids—the ride isn't really that child-friendly (at least not for the young set). It's not particularly exciting, either. Upon entering the attraction, guests are briefed on their responsibilities as newly recruited alien prison guards. Suddenly an alarm sounds—a new prisoner is arriving and the pandemonium begins. Stitch, after appearing by teleportation, is confined in the middle of the room, but only momentarily—the ride isn't called Stitch's Great Escape for nothing. Guests are seated around the center stage, overhead restraints on their shoulders (which are slightly uncomfortable unless you were sitting straight up when they are lowered) allowing them to "feel" special sensory effects. It's the attraction's long periods of darkness and silence that make this one inappropriate for younger children—a fact made apparent by some of the screams you'll hear from the audience. *Note:* There's a 38-inch height requirement to experience the attraction, though this may change—it's already been adjusted once since the ride first debuted.

Tomorrowland Indy Speedway

Frommer's Rating: B+ for kids, D for tweens, teens, and childless adults
Recommended Ages: 4–10

Younger kids love this ride, especially if they get the chance to drive one of the gas-powered, mini–sports cars—though they may need the help of a parent's foot to push down on the gas pedal—for a 4-minute spin around the track. Tweens and teens, however, hate it: Speeds reach a mere 7 mph, which for most is *incredibly* slow, and the steering is atrocious (we can't control the cars without bumping the rail that it follows). The slow speed seems to work well for young kids (who also think the bumping around is fun). The long lines move even slower than the ride does, so be prepared to wait this one out. There's a 52-inch height minimum to take a lap without an older

---

Tips Snacking in the Parks

For our money, you can't beat the smoked turkey drumsticks sold for just over $5 in WDW parks (they're called "Galactic Gobblers" at The Lunching Pad in Tomorrowland). How popular are they? Each year, Disney guests gobble-gobble 1.6 million of them.

Moments Where to Find Characters

Mickey's Toontown Fair was designed as a place where kids can meet and mingle with their favorite characters all day at the Judge's Tent and Toontown Hall of Fame Tent. Mickey, Minnie, and others can be found in residence. In **Fantasyland,** look for Ariel's Grotto and the Fantasyland Character Festival for daily greetings. **Main Street** (Town Square), **Adventureland** (at Pirates of the Caribbean and near Magic Carpets of Aladdin), **Frontierland** (The Diamond Horseshoe; Woody and Friends), and **Tomorrowland** (near the Space Ranger Spin) are other hot spots. Be sure to have your camera ready and waiting if you want to capture the moment before it's gone.

Tip: If you're willing to spend money to avoid waiting in a line, character meals at restaurants such as the **Crystal Palace, The Liberty Tree Tavern,** and **Cinderella's Royal Table** all offer the opportunity to meet your favorite characters. Just don't forget to make Advance Reservations if you go the dining route.

rider along with you. *Note:* It carries Disney's warning that expectant mothers and people with heart, neck, or back problems shouldn't climb aboard, likely because of the potential for getting bumped as you try to board or disembark.

Tomorrowland Transit Authority
Frommer's Rating: C, B+ for tired adults and toddlers
Recommended Ages: All ages
After making your way up a moving walkway, you'll spot the futuristic train cars that will take you on a tour of Tomorrowland from high above the ground. The engineless train runs on a track and is powered by electromagnets, creating no pollution, little noise, and using little power. Narrated by a computer guide named Horack I, TTA offers an overhead view of Tomorrowland, including a brief interior look at Space Mountain. Lines are often nonexistent as most riders are parents awaiting the return of their children from Space Mountain, or those with tired toddlers in need of a brief respite from the activity below.

Walt Disney's Carousel of Progress *(Overrated*
Frommer's Rating: C
Recommended Ages: 5–10
Only open seasonally, when crowds are at their peak, the Carousel of Progress offers more of a respite from the hustle and bustle of the crowds than it does an interesting experience. It first debuted at the 1964 World's Fair before Disney decided to include it in his collection. The ride emigrated from Disneyland to Disney World in 1975 and was refurbished to its original state just over 10 years ago. The entire show rotates through scenes illustrating the state of technology from the 1900s to the 1940s. Most adults find it rather boring, but kids willing to sit still for a few minutes may actually learn a thing or two.

SHOPPING IN TOMORROWLAND
Mickey's Star Traders is a large shop filled from top to bottom with Disneyana; it's probably the best place to shop in Magic Kingdom after Main Street.

PARADES, FIREWORKS & MORE

Pick up a guide map (or two) and a *Times Guide* (or three) when you enter the park. The information includes the day's **entertainment schedule**, listing all the special goings-on for the day. Included are concerts, encounters with characters, holiday events, parades, fireworks, restaurant hours, and the major happenings listed next. *Tip:* There's also an all-parks guide that includes much of the same information and is well worth picking up, too.

Wishes

Frommer's Rating: A+
Recommended Ages: All ages

Wishes, Disney's breathtaking 12-minute fireworks display, replaced the old **Fantasy in the Sky** fireworks in October 2003. The show, narrated by Jiminy Cricket and with background music from several Disney classics, is the story of a wish coming true, and it borrows one element from the old one—Tinker Bell still flies overhead. The fireworks go off nightly during summer and holidays, and on selected nights (usually Mon and Wed–Sat) the rest of the year. See your entertainment schedule for details. Numerous good views of the action are available, so long as you're standing on the front side of the castle—get too far off to the side or behind the display, and it loses much of its impressive and meticulously choreographed visual effect. Disney hotels close to the park (Grand Floridian, Polynesian, Contemporary, and Wilderness Lodge) also offer excellent views.

SpectroMagic *Moments*

Frommer's Rating: A
Recommended Ages: All ages

In April 2001, this after-dark display returned for a second engagement at WDW, replacing the **Main Street Electrical Parade,** a Disney classic that ran from 1976 to 1991, and again from 1996 to 2001 at the Magic Kingdom. *SpectroMagic is only held on a limited number of nights.* The 20-minute production combines fiber optics, holographic images, clouds of liquid nitrogen, old-fashioned twinkling lights, and a soundtrack featuring classic Disney tunes. Mickey, dressed in an amber and purple grand magician's cape, makes an appearance in a confetti of light. You'll also see the SpectroMen atop the title float, and Chernabog, *Fantasia's* monstrous demon, who unfolds his 38-foot wingspan. It takes the electrical equivalent of seven lightning bolts (enough to power a fleet of 2,000 over-the-road trucks) to bring the show to life. See your entertainment schedule for availability.

Share a Dream Come True Parade

Frommer's Rating: B
Recommended Ages: All ages

Replacing Magical Moments, this is the Magic Kingdom's newest parade. Floats topped by gigantic snow globes with Disney characters inside them make their way through the park and up Main Street on a daily basis. Each globe features a different theme; the Wish Upon A Star float features Pinocchio, Snow White, and their pals; the Face the Darkest Fears float is filled with some of Disney's more sinister characters, including the evil queen, Maleficent, and Cruella De Vil.

4 Epcot

Epcot is an acronym for *Experimental Prototype Community of Tomorrow,* and it was Walt Disney's dream for a planned city. (For an idea of what he wanted, visit **www. waltopia.com** on the Internet.) Alas, after his death, it became a theme park—Central Florida's second major one, which opened in 1982. Its aims are described in a dedication plaque: "May Epcot entertain, inform, and inspire. And, above all . . . instill a new sense of belief and pride in man's ability to shape a world that offers hope to people everywhere."

Ever growing and changing, Epcot occupies 300 vibrantly landscaped acres. If you can spare it, take a little time to stop and smell the roses on your way to and through the two major sections: **Future World** and **World Showcase.**

Epcot is so big that hiking the World Showcase end to end (1⅓ miles from the Canada pavilion on one side to Mexico on the other) can be an exhausting experience. That's why some folks are certain Epcot stands for "Every Person Comes Out Tired." Depending on how long you intend to linger at each country in World Showcase, this part of the park can be experienced in 1 day (though you can easily spend 2). Most visitors simply make a leisurely loop, working clockwise or counterclockwise from one side of the Showcase to the other.

Unlike Magic Kingdom, much of Epcot's parking lot is close to the gate. Parking sections are named for themes (Harvest, Energy, and so forth), and the aisles are numbered. While some guests are happy to walk to the gate from nearer areas, trams are available, but these days mainly to and from the outer areas.

Be sure to pick up a guide map and entertainment schedule as you enter the park. Folks with children can grab a copy of the *Epcot Kids' Guide.* The regular guide uses a yellow K in a red square to note "Kidcot" stops. These play and learning stations are for the younger set and allow them to stop at various World Showcase countries, do crafts, get autographs, have their Kidcot passports stamped (these are available for purchase in most Epcot stores and make a great souvenir), and chat with cast members native to those countries. They open at 1pm daily.

If you plan to eat lunch or dinner here and haven't already made Advance Reservations (© **407/939-3463**), you can make them at the restaurants themselves. Many Epcot restaurants are described in chapter 5, "Where to Dine."

Before you get underway, check the *Times Guide* for show schedules and incorporate any shows you want to see into your itinerary.

HOURS   Future World is usually open from 9 or 10am to 7pm but sometimes as late as midnight during major holidays and the summer. World Showcase doesn't open until 11am or noon, and it usually closes at 9pm but, like Future World, it sometimes has longer hours on holidays and in summer.

TICKET PRICES   Ticket prices are $63 for adults, $52 for children 3 to 9, free for children under 3. See "Tickets," earlier in this chapter, for the latest information on the new Magic Your Way ticketing system.

SERVICES & FACILITIES IN EPCOT

ATMs   The machines here accept cards issued by banks using the Cirrus, Honor, and PLUS systems and are located at the front of the park, in Italy, and near the bridge between World Showcase and Future World.

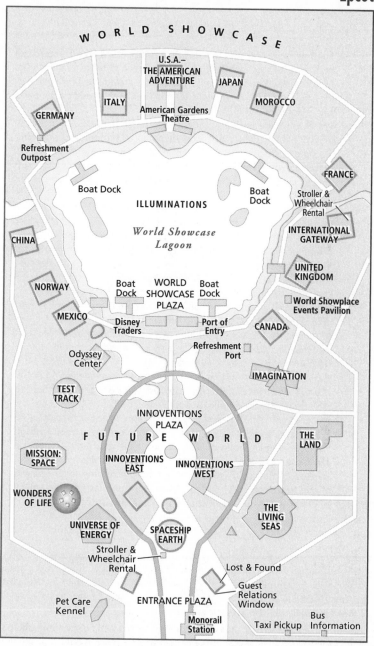

WORLD SHOWCASE

U.S.A.–
THE AMERICAN
ADVENTURE

JAPAN

ITALY

MOROCCO

GERMANY

American Gardens
Theatre

Refreshment
Outpost

FRANCE

Boat Dock

Boat
Dock

Stroller &
Wheelchair
Rental

ILLUMINATIONS

CHINA

*World Showcase
Lagoon*

INTERNATIONAL
GATEWAY

UNITED
KINGDOM

NORWAY

Boat
Dock

WORLD
SHOWCASE
PLAZA

Boat
Dock

World Showplace
Events Pavilion

MEXICO

Disney
Traders

Port of
Entry

CANADA

Odyssey
Center

Refreshment
Port

IMAGINATION

TEST
TRACK

INNOVENTIONS
PLAZA

FUTURE WORLD

THE
LAND

MISSION:
SPACE

INNOVENTIONS
EAST

INNOVENTIONS
WEST

WONDERS
OF LIFE

THE
LIVING
SEAS

UNIVERSE OF
ENERGY

SPACESHIP
EARTH

Stroller &
Wheelchair
Rental

Lost & Found

Guest
Relations
Window

Pet Care
Kennel

ENTRANCE PLAZA

Monorail
Station

Taxi Pickup

Bus
Information

Top 10 Orlando-Area Activities for Grown-Ups

1. **Spa Treatments**   First-rate spas such as those at Disney's Grand Floridian Resort & Spa, the WDW Dolphin, the Buena Vista Palace Resort, the Portofino Bay Hotel, and the Gaylord Palms provide heavenly pampering and relief for the sore muscles and tired feet caused by the parks (see chapters 1 and 4).

2. **World Showcase Pavilions**   Experience a 'round-the-world journey, visiting 11 "nations" with authentically reproduced architectural highlights, restaurants, shops, and cultural performances (see later in this chapter).

3. **Cirque du Soleil**   This no-animals circus (p. 327) is compelling for most anyone over the age of 6, but its intensity and choreography make it a real winner for adults.

4. **Pleasure Island and CityWalk**   These entertainment and restaurant districts are located at WDW and Universal Orlando, respectively (see chapter 9). They provide nonstop fun for the wine-dine-and-dance set.

5. **A Romantic Dinner at Victoria & Albert's**   Loving couples cherish the intimate evening and scrumptious seven-course dinner at the headline restaurant in Disney's Grand Floridian Resort & Spa (p. 148).

6. **Discovery Cove**   SeaWorld's sister park offers guests a chance to rest, relax, and swim with the dolphins in a remote island atmosphere. It's an expensive but ultimately satisfying retreat (see chapter 7).

7. **Richard Petty Driving Experience**   *Vrrrooooommmmmm!* If you're 18 or older and have the courage, try driving or at least riding in a real NASCAR rocket at speeds significantly above the legal limit (p. 254).

8. **The *Grand 1***   Take another break from the Mickey madness and cruise Disney's Seven Seas Lagoon (perhaps catching a glimpse of Wishes fireworks) aboard this vintage, 44-foot yacht (p. 93).

9. **Innoventions**   Epcot is generally geared more to adults than the other WDW parks, and this display of future technologies is especially intriguing, providing a preview of life well into the 21st century (p. 218).

10. **Tee Time**   Orlando is home to some of the country's best golf courses—Walt Disney World alone offers 99 holes, including one with a sand trap shaped like Mickey Mouse—so enthusiasts will find plenty of places to tee up (see "Hitting the Links," in chapter 7).

Baby Care   Epcot's Baby Care Center is by the First Aid station near the Odyssey Center in Future World. It's furnished with a nursing room with rocking chairs; disposable diapers, formula, baby food, and pacifiers are for sale. There are also changing tables in all women's restrooms as well as in some of the men's restrooms. Disposable diapers are also available at Guest Relations.

Cameras & Film   Kodak disposable cameras are available throughout the park, including at the Kodak Camera Center at the Entrance Plaza, though digital supplies are very limited.

First Aid The First Aid Center, staffed by registered nurses, is located near the Odyssey Center in Future World.

Lockers Attended lockers are to the west of Spaceship Earth as you enter the park; unattended lockers are located at the International Gateway. The cost is $7 a day, including a $2 deposit.

Lost Children Lost children in Epcot are usually taken to Earth Center or the Baby Care Center, where lost children logbooks are kept. *Children under 7 should wear name-tags inside their clothing.*

Package Pickup Any package you purchase can be sent by the shop clerk to Guest Relations in the Entrance Plaza. Allow at least 3 hours for delivery. There's also a package pickup location at the International Gateway entrance in the World Showcase. If you're staying overnight at a Disney resort, you can also have all packages purchased by 7pm sent to your hotel room (they will be delivered by noon the next day).

Parking It's $9 for cars, light trucks, and vans; $10 for RVs.

Pet Care Day accommodations are offered at kennels just outside the Entrance Plaza at Epcot for $6 (© **407/824-6568**). Proof of vaccination is required. This is the only kennel in WDW that features a dog walking service ($2.50 per walk). There are also four other kennels in the WDW complex. (See "Fast Facts" in chapter 3 for more details.)

Strollers These can be rented from special stands on the east side of the Entrance Plaza and at World Showcase's International Gateway. The cost is $10 for a single and $18 for a double. See p. 43 for tips on using a stroller at WDW.

Wheelchair Rental Rent wheelchairs inside the Entrance Plaza to your left, to the right of ticket booths at the Gift Shop, and at World Showcase's International Gateway. The cost for regular chairs is $10. Electric wheelchairs cost $45 a day, including a $5 refundable deposit.

FUTURE WORLD

Future World is in the northern section of Epcot, the first area mainstream guests see after entering the park. Its icon is a huge geosphere known as Spaceship Earth—aka, that giant golf ball. Major corporations sponsor Future World's 10 themed areas (that means they're making pricey investments, such as the $100 million that Hewlett Packard dropped on the Mission: Space ride you'll read about a little later in this chapter). The focus here is on discovery, scientific achievements, and tomorrow's technologies in areas running from energy to undersea exploration.

Tips A Cool Place to Cool Off

Club Cool, previously Ice Station Cool, may have a brand-new look but still offers complimentary Coke products to everyone who enters. Just don't expect to completely quench your thirst—drinks are served up in sampling sizes here. And don't expect to find the same flavors you would in your local grocery, either—the products served here come from all over the world and flavors are often unique. The club is located just outside Innoventions West, on your left as you exit the walkway heading to the plaza outside Mission: Space and Test Track.

Moments Behind the Scenes: Special Tours in Walt Disney World

In addition to the greenhouse tour in Epcot's The Land pavilion (p. 218), the Disney parks offer a number of walking tours and learning programs. The tours are subject to change. These tours represent a sampling of the most recent ones available at press time. Times, days, and prices also change. It's best to call ahead to Disney's tour line, © **407/939-8687,** to make reservations or get additional information. *Tip:* **Custom Guided Tours** (© **407/560-4033**) are available at $125 per hour ($95 per hour for WDW resort guests) with a 5-hour minimum.

- Epcot's **Aqua Seas Tour** lends you a wet suit and then takes you on a 2½-hour journey that includes a 30-minute swim in the 5.7-million gallon Living Seas Aquarium, home to some 65 marine species. The tour includes a souvenir T-shirt and group photo. The cost is $100, park admission is not required, and it's open to guests 8 and older (those under 16 must be accompanied by a participating adult). It's offered daily at 12:30pm.
- The **Family Magic Tour** explores the nooks and crannies of the Magic Kingdom in the form of a 2-hour scavenger hunt. You meet and greet characters at the end. Children (ages 3 and up) and adults are $25 per person. You must also buy admission tickets to the park and book in advance. If you have young kids and want to do a special tour, this is the one to take. It begins daily at 11:30am outside City Hall. It's sometimes held at 9:30am, too.
- The 3-hour **Magic Behind The Steam Trains** tour (ages 10 and up) is a fun one for locomotive buffs. A pair of veteran conductors gives you insight, which other guests don't get, into the history and present operations of the little engines that could. Monday, Tuesday, Thursday, and Saturday at 7:30am, $40 per person, plus park admission.

The following tours are for those 16 and older:

- The 3½-hour **Hidden Treasures of World Showcase** explores the architectural and entertainment offerings of Epcot's 11 "nations." The $59 tours (plus admission) are at 9:45am on Tuesday and Thursday.
- **Gardens of the World,** a 3-hour tour of the extraordinary landscaping at Epcot (with tips on improving your own), is held Tuesday and Thursday at

Here are the main attractions.

Imagination
Frommer's Rating: B+
Recommended Ages: 6–adult

In this pavilion, even the fountains are magical. "Water snakes" arc in the air, offering kids a chance to dare them to "bite." This pavilion was upgraded in 2001 to include more high-tech gadgets, and a year later Figment, the pavilion's much-loved mascot, returned (see below).

9:45am and is led by a Disney horticulturist ($59 per person, again, plus admission).

- The 4½-hour **Keys to the Kingdom** tour provides an orientation to the Magic Kingdom and a glimpse into the high-tech systems behind the magic. It's $58 (mandatory park admission not included) and is held daily at 8:30, 9:30, and 10am.

- At the top of the price chain ($199 per person, including lunch) is **Backstage Magic,** a 7-hour, self-propelled bus tour through areas of Epcot, the Magic Kingdom, and Disney–MGM Studios that aren't seen by mainstream guests. The 10am tour (Mon–Fri only) is limited to 20 adults, and you might have trouble getting a date unless you book early. Some will find this one isn't worth the price, but if you have a brain that must know how things work or simply want to know more than your family or friends, you might find it's worth the cost. You'll see WDW mechanics and engineers repairing and building animatronic beings from "It's a Small World" and other attractions. You'll peek over the shoulders of cast members who watch closed-circuit TVs to make sure other visitors are surviving the harrowing rides. And at the Magic Kingdom, you'll venture into the tunnels used for work areas as well as corridors for the cast to get from one area to the others without fighting tourist crowds. It's not unusual for tour takers to see Snow White enjoying a Snickers bar, find Cinderella having her locks touched up at an underground salon, or view woodworkers as they restore the hard maple muscles of the carousel horses. Park admission *isn't* required. Lunch is included.

- **Backstage Safari** at Animal Kingdom ($65 per person plus park admission) offers a 3-hour look at the park's veterinary hospital as well as lessons in conservation, animal nutrition, and medicine (Mon, Wed, Thurs, and Fri). *Note:* You won't see many animals.

- **Yuletide Fantasy,** available November 30 to December 24 each year, gives visitors a front-row look at how Disney creates a winter wonderland to get visitors in the holiday spirit. It costs $59 per person, and theme park admission *isn't* required.

The 3-D **Honey, I Shrunk the Audience** ride is the big attraction here, deserving of an **"A" rating** by itself. Based on the Disney hit *Honey, I Shrunk the Kids* film, you're terrorized by mice and, once you're shrunk, by a large cat; then you're given a good shaking by a gigantic 5-year-old. Vibrating seats and creepy tactile effects enhance dramatic 3-D action. Finally, everyone returns to proper size—except the family dog, which creates the final surprise.

Figment, the crazy-but-lovable dragon mascot of the park when it opened, was resurrected in a new **Journey into Your Imagination** ride in June 2002. Things begin with an open house at the Imagination Institute, with Dr. Nigel Channing taking you on a tour of labs that demonstrate how the five senses capture and control one's imagination, except you never get to touch and taste once Figment arrives to prove it's far, far better to set your imagination free. He invites you to his upside-down house, where a new perspective enhances your imagination. "One Little Spark," an upbeat ditty that debuted when the attraction opened in 1983, has also been brought back.

Once you disembark from the ride, head for the **"What If"** labs, where your kids can burn lots of energy while exercising their imaginations at a number of interactive stations that allow them to conduct music and experiment with video.

Innoventions East and West
Frommer's Rating: B+ for hungry minds and game junkies
Recommended Ages: 8–adult
Innoventions East, behind Spaceship Earth and to the left as you enter the park, features the **House of Innoventions.** It's a preview of tomorrow's smart house, but many of its products are already on the market (at astronomical prices). Its refrigerator has an Internet-savvy computer that can make a grocery list and place the order. A smart picture frame can store and send photos to other smart frames. And its toilet has a seat warmer, automatic lid opener and closer, and a sprayer and blow dryer that eliminate the need for toilet paper if you're worldly. The **Internet Zone** profiles tomorrow's online games for kids, including laser tag with Disney characters. **Opportunity City** is the latest addition and features an online game, Hot Shot Business. Across the plaza at **Innoventions West,** crowds flock to **Video Games of Tomorrow,** which has nearly three dozen game stations. **Where's the Fire,** geared to smaller kids, teaches the basics of fire safety and demonstrates how firefighters fight fires with the help of a pump truck.

Note: A new Underwriters Laboratories exhibit at Innoventions East, the **Test the Limits Lab,** has six kiosks that let kids and fun-loving adults try out a variety of products. In one, you can pull a rope attached to a hammer that crashes into a TV screen to see if it's shatter resistant. In another, you can push a button that releases a magnet that falls onto a firefighter's helmet.

The Land
Frommer's Rating: B+ for environmentalists, gardeners; C+ for others
Recommended Ages: 8–adult
The largest of Future World's pavilions highlights food and nature.

Living with the Land is a 13-minute boat ride through three ecological environments (a rainforest, an African desert, and the windswept American plains), each populated by appropriate audio-animatronic denizens. New farming methods and experiments ranging from hydroponics to plants growing in simulated Martian soil are showcased in real gardens. If you'd like a more serious overview, take the 45-minute **Behind the Seeds** guided walking tour of the growing areas, offered daily. Sign up at the Green Thumb Emporium shop on the ground floor near the Sunshine Season Food Festival. The cost is $12 for adults, $10 for children 3 to 9. *Note:* It's really geared to children.

Circle of Life combines spectacular live-action footage with animation in a 15-minute motion picture based on *The Lion King.* In this cautionary environmental tale, Timon and Pumbaa are building a monument to the good life called Hakuna Matata Lakeside Village, but their project, as Simba points out, is damaging the savanna for other animals. The message: Everything is connected in the great circle of life.

Soarin' is a copy of a popular attraction at Disney's California Adventure theme park. Guests are seated in giant hang gliders and surrounded by a tremendous projection-screen dome. After being lifted up over 40 feet into the air, you'll fly through the sky over the landscapes of California. This amazing adventure is enhanced by sensory effects as guests are treated to the sights, sounds . . . and smells (think orange blossoms and pine trees) of a dozen locations in California, including the Golden Gate Bridge, the redwood forests, Napa Valley, Yosemite, and more. You really will feel almost as if you're flying through the sky. The ride opened in spring 2005 and carries a 40-inch height minimum. For the best experience, try to get seated in the first row; if you're not sanguine about heights, the third row works best.

The Living Seas
Frommer's Rating: B+
Recommended Ages: 3–adult

This pavilion contains a 5.7-million-gallon saltwater aquarium including coral reefs inhabited by some 4,000 sharks, barracudas, parrotfish, rays, dolphins, and other critters. While waiting in line, visitors pass exhibits tracing the history of undersea exploration, including a diving barrel used by Alexander the Great in 332 B.C. and Sir Edmund Halley's first diving bell (1697).

A 2½-minute multimedia preshow about today's ocean technology is followed by a 7-minute film demonstrating the formation of the earth and seas as a means to support life.

After the films, you enter "hydrolators" for a hokey "descent" to the simulated ocean floor. Upon arrival, you can journey through rooms and more rooms for close-up views through acrylic windows of the denizens, including manatees and other marine life. Be sure to check out the adorable **Turtle Talk with Crush,** which debuted in late 2004. Crush (from *Finding Nemo*) chitchats with passersby from behind his undersea movie screen, engaging them in conversation and telling a joke or two. This is a first-of-its-kind attraction using digital projection and voice-activated animation to create a real-time experience. Your kids will get a huge kick out of it; you will, too.

Note: The **Epcot DiveQuest** enables certified divers (ages 10–14 must have an adult accompany them) to participate in a 3-hour program that includes a 40-minute dive in the Living Seas aquarium. The program costs $140. Call © **407/939-8687** for more information. Keep in mind, however, that you get far more for your money at Discovery Cove (p. 293) if you want to swim with the dolphins.

Mission: Space
Frommer's Rating: A+
Recommended Ages: 10–adult

Finding Nemo

The Living Seas will welcome a new arrival, **The Seas with Nemo & Friends,** sometime in the fall of 2006. Guests will board "clamobiles" for an undersea field trip led by Mr. Ray, who eventually discovers that Nemo's gone missing and it's up to everyone to find him. The attraction will use special technology that will allow the characters from *Finding Nemo* to swim amid the actual marine creatures that reside in the Living Seas saltwater aquarium (one of the world's largest). Naturally, you get a happy ending (did you think otherwise?).

This relatively new $100-million attraction, developed in partnership with Hewlett Packard and NASA, seats up to four riders at a time in a simulated flight to the Red Planet. You'll assume the role of commander, pilot, navigator, or engineer, depending on where you sit, and must complete related jobs vital to the mission (don't worry if you miss your cue, you won't crash). The ride uses a combination of visuals, sound, and centrifugal force to create the illusion of a launch and trip to Mars. Even veteran roller-coaster riders who tried the simulator said the sensation mimics a liftoff, as riders are pressed into their seats and the roar and vibration tricks the brain during the launch portion of the 4-minute adventure. As a new ride, this one is likely to have incredibly long lines, so get here early or FASTPASS it. **Note:** Riders must be at least 44 inches tall. If you're claustrophobic, have a low tolerance for loud noises, or have stuffy sinuses, then you should avoid the ride. If spinning causes you to get dizzy or motion sick, this isn't the ride for you either, though you can reduce the effects by focusing straight ahead. Speaking from experience, taller guests may have difficulties seeing the screen the way it was meant to be viewed—and shorter guests may have trouble reaching some of the gear.

Spaceship Earth *Overrated*
Frommer's Rating: C
Recommended Ages: All ages
This massive, silvery geosphere symbolizes Epcot, and is probably the most recognizable Disney icon next to Cinderella's Castle (and those mouse ears, of course). That makes it a must-do for many, though it's something of a yawner—another slow-track journey back in time to trace the progress of communications. Long lines can be avoided by saving it until late in the day when you might be able to just walk in. The 15-minute show/ride takes visitors to the distant past where an audio-animatronic Cro-Magnon shaman recounts the story of a hunt while others record it on cave walls. You advance thousands of years to ancient Egypt, where hieroglyphics adorn temple walls and writing is recorded on papyrus scrolls. You'll progress through the Phoenician and Greek alphabets, the Gutenberg printing press, and the Renaissance. Technologies develop at a rapid pace, through the telegraph, telephone, radio, movies, and TV. It's but a short step to the age of electronic communications. You're catapulted into outer space to see Spaceship Earth from a new perspective, returning for a finale that places the audience amid interactive global networks.

Test Track
Frommer's Rating: A+
Recommended Ages: 8–adult
Test Track is a $60-million (the figure once raised eyebrows but is considered mere peanuts next to HP's $100 million for Mission: Space) marvel that combines GM engineering and Disney Imagineering. Most of you will have a blast. The line can be more than an hour long in peak periods, so consider the FASTPASS option (but remember to get one early before they run out). The last part of the line snakes through displays about corrosion, crash tests, and other things from the GM proving grounds (you can linger long enough to see them even with FASTPASS). The 5-minute ride follows what looks to be an actual highway. It includes braking tests, a hill climb, and tight S-curves in a six-passenger convertible. The left front seat offers the most thrills as the vehicle moves through the curves. There's also a 12-second burst of speed that reaches 65 mph on the straightaway (no traffic!). **Note:** Riders must be at

---

Moments **Water Fountain Conversations**

Many an ordinary item at Disney World has hidden entertainment value. Take a drink at the water fountain in Innoventions Plaza (the one right next to MouseGear) and it may beg you not to drink it dry. No, you haven't gotten too much sun—the fountain actually talks (much to the delight of kids and the surprise of unsuspecting adults). A few more talking fountains are scattered around Epcot. The fountains aren't the only items at WDW that talk. We've kibitzed with a walking and talking garbage can (named PUSH) in Magic Kingdom, and a personable palm tree (who goes by Wes Palm) at Animal Kingdom. Ask a Disney employee to direct you if you want to meet one of these chatty contraptions.

---

least 40 inches tall. Also, expectant mothers and people prone to motion sickness or those with heart, neck, or back problems shouldn't test the track.

Note II: This is the only attraction in Epcot that has a single-rider line, which allows singles to fill in vacant spots in select cars. If you're part of a party that doesn't mind splitting up and riding in singles, you can shave off some serious waiting time by taking advantage of this option. FASTPASS offers the same time savings without the break up, but Test Track is often in such demand that the last FASTPASS for the *day* is often gone by 11am, so if you don't catch it early enough, the single rider line is the only option you'll have.

Note III: Test Track often experiences technical difficulties and, to add insult to injury, it's one of the few rides in Epcot that closes due to inclement weather. If you know a storm's brewing in the afternoon, be sure to head here early in the day.

Universe of Energy
Frommer's Rating: B+
Recommended Ages: 6–adult

Sponsored by Exxon, this pavilion has a roof full of solar panels and a goal of bettering your understanding of America's energy problems and potential solutions. Its 32-minute ride, **Ellen's Energy Adventure,** features comedian Ellen DeGeneres being tutored (by Bill Nye the Science Guy) to be a *Jeopardy!* contestant. On a massive screen in Theater I, an animated motion picture depicts the earth's molten beginnings, its cooling process, and the formation of fossil fuels. You move back in time 275 million years into an eerie, storm-wracked landscape of the Mesozoic Era, a time of violent geological activity. Here, giant audio-animatronic dragonflies, earthquakes, and streams of molten lava threaten you before you enter a steam-filled tunnel deep in the bowels of a volcano. When you emerge, you're in Theater II and the present. In this new setting, which looks like a NASA Mission Control room, a 70mm film projected on a massive 210-foot wraparound screen depicts the challenges of the world's increasing energy demands and the emerging technologies that will help meet them. Your moving seats now return to Theater I, where swirling special effects herald a film about how energy impacts our lives. It ends on an upbeat note, with a vision of an energy-abundant future, and Ellen as a new *Jeopardy!* champion. *Note:* I've taken kids as young as 2 on this ride with no problems, but recommend that children be at least 6 or they won't get much out of the experience beyond flashing lights and sounds.

Wonders of Life

Frommer's Rating: B
Recommended Ages: 10–adult

Housed in a vast geodesic dome fronted by a 75-foot replica of a DNA strand, this pavilion offers some of Future World's most engaging shows and attractions. *Note:* This pavilion operates seasonally, so call ahead to find out if it will be open when you're at the park.

The *Making of Me*, starring Martin Short, is a captivating 15-minute motion picture combining live action with animation and spectacular in utero photography to create a sweet introduction to the facts of life. It may, however, prompt a few questions from younger children, so unless you're prepared to answer, save this one for kids 10 and older. Short travels back in time to witness his parents as children, their meeting at a college dance, their wedding, and their decision to have a baby. Along with him, you'll view his development inside his mother's womb and witness his birth.

During the very popular **Body Wars** ride, you're reduced to the size of a cell for a medical rescue mission inside the immune system of a human body. Your objective: Save a miniaturized immunologist who has been accidentally swept into the bloodstream. This motion-simulator ride takes you on a wild journey through gale-force winds in the lungs and pounding heart chambers. Engineers designed this ride from the last row of the car, so that's where to sit to get the most bang for your buck. Although you know they're part of the Disney show, it's a little eerie passing through dermatopic purification stations in order to undergo miniaturization. It's not as good as the similarly built **Star Tours** at Disney–MGM studios, but it definitely has its moments. *Note:* Riders must be at least 40 inches tall. This one isn't a smart choice for those prone to motion sickness or who generally prefer to be stirred rather than shaken. Also, steer clear if you're an expectant mother, or have heart, neck, or back problems.

In the hilarious, multimedia **Cranium Command,** Buzzy, an audio-animatronic brain-pilot-in-training, is charged with the seemingly impossible task of controlling the brain of an average 12-year-old boy. The boy's body parts are played by Charles Grodin, Jon Lovitz, Bob Goldthwait, George Wendt, and Kevin Nealon and Dana Carvey (as Hans and Franz). It's another must-see attraction (recommended for ages 8 and up) and has a loyal following among Disney veterans. The audience is seemingly seated inside Bobby's head as Buzzy guides him through a day of typical preadolescent traumas such as running for the school bus, meeting a girl, fighting bullies, and a run-in with the school principal.

There are other large areas filled with fitness-related shows and participatory activities, including a film called *Goofy About Health,* and a hands-on exhibit that tests your senses.

SHOPPING IN FUTURE WORLD

Most of Epcot's more unique shopping lies just ahead in World Showcase, but there are a few places in this part of the park that offer special souvenirs. You can browse through cels and other collectibles at the **Art of Disney** in Innoventions West (how about an $8,800, 5-ft. wooden Mickey watch?), purchase almost anything imaginable at **MouseGear** (one of the best and most comprehensive shops in all of WDW) in Innoventions East, and find gardening and other gifts in **The Land.**

WORLD SHOWCASE

You can tour the world in a day at this community of 11 miniaturized nations, which line the 40-acre World Showcase Lagoon on the park's southern side. All of the showcase's countries have authentically indigenous architecture, landscaping, background music, restaurants, and shops. The nations' cultural facets are explored in art exhibits, song and dance performances, and innovative rides, films, and attractions. And all of the employees in each pavilion are natives of the country represented.

All pavilions offer some kind of live entertainment throughout the day. Times and performances change, but they're listed in the guide map and on the *Times Guide*. World Showcase opens between 11am and noon daily, so there's time for a Future World excursion if you arrive earlier. ***Note:*** There are **regular appearances by characters** at Showcase Plaza (consult the daily schedule for times).

Canada

Frommer's Rating: A
Recommended Ages: 8–adult

Our neighbors to the north are represented by architecture ranging from a mansard-roofed replica of Ottawa's 19th-century French–style Château Laurier (here called Hôtel du Canada) to a British-influenced stone building modeled after a famous landmark near Niagara Falls.

An Indian village, complete with a rough-hewn log trading post and 30-foot replicas of Ojibwa totem poles, signifies the culture of the Northwest. The Canadian wilderness is reflected by a rocky mountain; a waterfall cascading into a white-water stream; and a miniforest of evergreens, stately cedars, maples, and birch trees. Don't miss the stunning floral displays of azaleas, roses, zinnias, chrysanthemums, petunias, and patches of wildflowers inspired by the Butchart Gardens just outside of Victoria, British Columbia.

The pavilion's highlight attraction is **O Canada!**—a dazzling (though admittedly somewhat outdated) 18-minute, 360-degree CircleVision film that shows Canada's scenic splendor, from a dogsled race to the thundering flight of thousands of snow geese departing an autumn stopover near the St. Lawrence River. If you're looking for foot-tapping live entertainment, **Off Kilter** raises the roof with New Age Celtic music as well as some get-down country music. Days and times vary.

Fun Fact   Eat, Drink & Be Merry

In early October, Epcot's 6-week-long **International Food & Wine Festival** adds 25 booths to the park's 1⅓-mile World Showcase promenade. Here's your chance to walk off some calories while you sip and savor the food and beverages of several of the world's cultures. On the food front, the appetizer-size temptations might include burgundy escargot, seared alligator medallions, green mussels, shrimp on the barbie, octopus on purple potato salad, chicken sha cha, and much more ($1–$5). You can also sample wine and beer from more than 100 wineries and breweries. Tickets for the dinner-and-concert series or a special wine tasting are $75 to $185 including tip, but you can cruise the festival for standard park admission ($63 adults, $52 kids 3–9). Call (✆ 407/939-3378 for details or go to www.disneyworld.com.

Northwest Mercantile carries sandstone and soapstone carvings, fringed leather vests, duck decoys, moccasins, an array of stuffed animals, Native American dolls, Native American spirit stones, rabbit-skin caps, heavy knitted sweaters, and, of course, maple syrup.

China

Frommer's Rating: A

Recommended Ages: 10–adult

Bounded by a serpentine wall that snakes around its perimeter, the China pavilion is entered via a triple-arched ceremonial gate inspired by the Temple of Heaven in Beijing, a summer retreat for Chinese emperors. Passing through the gate, you'll see a half-size replica of this ornately embellished red-and-gold circular temple, built in 1420 during the Ming dynasty. Gardens simulate those in Suzhou, with miniature waterfalls, fragrant lotus ponds, and groves of bamboo, corkscrew willows, and weeping mulberry trees.

Reflections of China 𝖆𝖆 is a 20-minute movie that explores the culture and landscapes in and around seven Chinese cities. Shot over a 2-month period in 2002, it visits Hong Kong, Beijing, Shanghai, and the Great Wall (begun 24 c. ago!), among other places. **Land of Many Faces** is an exhibit that introduces China's ethnic peoples, and entertainment is provided daily by the amazing **Dragon Legend Acrobats** 𝖆𝖆.

The **Yong Feng Shangdian Shopping Gallery** features silk robes, lacquer and inlaid mother-of-pearl furniture, jade figures, cloisonné vases, Yixing teapots, brocade pajamas, silk rugs and embroideries, wind chimes, and Chinese clothing. Artisans occasionally demonstrate calligraphy.

France

Frommer's Rating: B

Recommended Ages: 8–adult

This pavilion focuses on La Belle Epoque, a period from 1870 to 1910 in which French art, literature, and architecture flourished. It's entered via a replica of the beautiful cast-iron Pont des Arts footbridge over the Seine. It leads to a park with bleached sycamores, Bradford pear trees, flowering crape myrtle, and sculptured parterre flower gardens inspired by Seurat's painting *A Sunday Afternoon on the Island of La Grande Jatte.* A one-tenth-scale replica of the Eiffel Tower constructed from Gustave Eiffel's original blueprints looms above *les grands boulevards.*

The highlight is **Impressions de France.** Shown in a palatial sit-down theater a la Fontainebleau, this 18-minute film is a scenic journey through diverse French landscapes projected on a vast 200-degree wraparound screen and enhanced by the music of French composers. The antics of **Serveur Amusant,** a comedic waiter, delights both children and adults, as do the yummy pastries at **Boulangerie Patisserie.**

The covered arcade has shops selling French prints and original art, cookbooks, wines (there's a tasting counter), French food, Babar books, perfumes, and original letters of famous Frenchmen ranging from Jean Cocteau to Napoleon. Another marketplace/tourism center revives the defunct Les Halles, where Parisians used to sip onion soup in the wee hours.

Germany

Frommer's Rating: B

Recommended Ages: 8–adult

Enclosed by castle walls and towers, this festive pavilion is centered on a cobblestone *platz* (square) with pots of colorful flowers girding a fountain statue of St. George and the Dragon. An adjacent clock tower is embellished with whimsical glockenspiel figures that herald each hour with quaint melodies. The pavilion's **Biergarten** (p. 136) was inspired by medieval Rothenberg and features a year-round Oktoberfest and its music. And 16th-century facades replicate a merchant's hall in the Black Forest and the town hall in Römerberg Square.

The shops here carry Hummel figurines, crystal, glassware, cookware, Anton Schneider cuckoos, cowbells, Alpine hats, German wines (there's a tasting counter), specialty foods, toys (German Disneyana, teddy bears, dolls, and puppets), and books. An artisan demonstrates molding and painting Hummel figures; another paints detailed scenes on eggs. Background music runs from oompah bands to Mozart symphonies.

Model train enthusiasts and kids enjoy the exquisitely detailed miniature version of a small Bavarian town, complete with working train station.

Italy

Frommer's Rating: B
Recommended Ages: 10–adult

One of the prettiest World Showcase pavilions, Italy lures visitors over an arched stone footbridge to a replica of Venice's intricately ornamented pink-and-white Doge's Palace. Other architectural highlights include the 83-foot Campanile (bell tower) of St. Mark's Square, Venetian bridges, and a piazza enclosing a version of Bernini's Neptune Fountain. A garden wall suggests a backdrop of provincial countryside, and citrus, cypress, pine, and olive trees frame a formal garden. Gondolas are moored on the lagoon.

Shops carry cameo and filigree jewelry, Armani figurines, kitchenware, Italian wines and foods, Murano and other Venetian glass, alabaster figurines, and inlaid wooden music boxes.

In the street entertainment department, Sergio, a talented juggler, performs in the pavilions courtyard.

Japan

Frommer's Rating: A
Recommended Ages: 8–adult

A flaming red *torii* (gate of honor) on the banks of the lagoon and the graceful blue-roofed Goju No To pagoda, inspired by a shrine built at Nara in A.D. 700, welcome you to this pavilion, which focuses on Japan's ancient culture. In a traditional Japanese garden, cedars, yews, bamboo, "cloud-pruned" evergreens, willows, and flowering shrubs frame a contemplative setting of pebbled footpaths, rustic bridges, waterfalls, exquisite rock landscaping, and a pond of golden koi. It's a haven of tranquillity in a park that's anything but. The **Yakitori House** is based on the renowned 16th-century Katsura Imperial Villa in Kyoto, designed as a royal summer residence and considered by many to be the crowning achievement of Japanese architecture. The moated **White Heron Castle** is a replica of the Shirasagi-Jo, a 17th-century fortress overlooking the city of Himeji. The **Bijutsu-kan Gallery** displays changing exhibits on various aspects of Japanese culture (at press time, it featured an exhibit focusing on Japanese tin toys).

The **Mitsukoshi Department Store** (Japan's answer to Macy's) is housed in a replica of the Shishinden (Hall of Ceremonies) of the Gosho Imperial Palace, built in Kyoto in A.D. 794. It sells lacquerware, kimonos, kites, fans, dolls in traditional costumes, origami books, samurai swords, Japanese Disneyana, bonsai trees, Japanese foods, Netsuke carvings, pottery, and modern electronics.

The drums of **Matsuriza**—one of the best performances in the World Showcase—entertain guests daily.

Finds   Great Things to Buy at Epcot

Sure, *you* want to be educated about the cultures of the world, but for most, the two big attractions at the World Showcase are eating and shopping. Dining options are explained in chapter 5. This list gives you an idea of additional items available for purchase.

If you'd like to check out the amazing scope of Disney merchandise at home, everything from furniture to bath toys, you can order a catalog by calling © **800/237-5751** or surfing the Web to **www.disneystore.com**.

- The silver jewelry at the Mexico pavilion is beautiful. Choose from a range of merchandise that goes from a simple flowered hair clip to a kidney-shaped stone and silver bracelet.
- There are lots of great sweaters available in the shops of Norway, and it's really tough to resist the Scandinavian trolls. They're so ugly, you have to love them.
- Forget about all those knockoff products stamped "Made in China." The merchandise in this country is among the more expensive to be found in Epcot, from jade teardrop earrings to multicolored bracelets to Disney art.
- Porcelain and cuckoo clocks are the things to look at in Germany. You might find a Goebel Collectible Winnie the Pooh or a handcrafted Pooh cuckoo clock. Of course, Hummel figurines are big sellers, too.
- In Italy, look for 100% silk scarves in a variety of patterns as well as fine silk ties and crystal.
- Your funky teenager might like the Taquia knit cap, a colorful fezlike chapeau, that's available in Morocco. There's also a variety of celestial-patterned pottery available in vases and platters.
- Tennis fans may be interested in the Wimbledon shirts, shorts, and skirts available in the United Kingdom. There's also a nice assortment of rose-patterned tea accessories, Shetland sweaters, tartans, pub accessories, and loads of other stuff from the U.K.

Mexico

Frommer's Rating: A

Recommended Ages: 8–adult

You'll hear the music of marimbas and mariachi bands as you approach the festive showcase of Mexico, fronted by a towering Mayan pyramid modeled on the Aztec temple of Quetzalcoatl (God of Life) and surrounded by dense Yucatán jungle landscaping. Upon entering the pavilion, you'll be in a museum of pre-Columbian art and artifacts.

Down a ramp, a small lagoon is the setting for **El Rio del Tiempo (River of Time),** where visitors board boats for an 8-minute cruise through Mexico's past and present. Passengers get a close-up look at the Mayan pyramid. **Mariachi Cobre,** a 12-piece band, plays Tuesday to Saturday.

Shops in and around the **Plaza de Los Amigos** (a "moonlit" Mexican *mercado* [market] with a tiered fountain and street lamps) display an array of leather goods, baskets, sombreros, piñatas, pottery, embroidered dresses and blouses, maracas, jewelry, serapes, colorful papier-mâché birds, and blown-glass objects (an artisan occasionally gives demonstrations). The Mexican Tourist Office also provides travel information.

Morocco

Frommer's Rating: A

Recommended Ages: 10–adult

This exotic pavilion has architecture embellished with geometrically patterned tile work, minarets, hand-painted wood ceilings, and brass lighting fixtures (the king of Morocco sent his own royal artisans to work on the pavilion). It's headlined by a replica of the Koutoubia Minaret, the prayer tower of a 12th-century mosque in Marrakech. Note the imperfections in each mosaic tile; they were put there on purpose in accordance with the Muslim belief that only Allah is perfect. The Medina (old city), entered via a replica of an arched gateway in Fez, leads to **Fez House** (a traditional Moroccan home) and the narrow, winding streets of the **souk,** a bustling marketplace where all manner of authentic handcrafted merchandise is on display. Here you can browse or purchase pottery, brassware, hand-knotted Berber or colorful Rabat carpets, ornate silver and camel-bone boxes, straw baskets, and prayer rugs. There are weaving demonstrations in the souk periodically during the day. The Medina's rectangular courtyard centers on a replica of the ornately tiled Najjarine Fountain in Fez, the setting for musical entertainment.

Treasures of Morocco is a three-times-per-day 45-minute guided tour (1–5pm) that highlights this country's culture, architecture, and history. The pavilion's **Gallery of Arts and History** contains an ever-changing exhibit of Moroccan art, and the Center of Tourism offers a continuous three-screen slide show. Morocco's landscaping includes a formal garden, citrus and olive trees, date palms, and banana plants. On the entertainment side, **Mo'Rockin'** plays Arabian rock music on traditional instruments Tuesday through Saturday.

Norway

Frommer's Rating: B+

Recommended Ages: 10–adult

This pavilion is centered on a picturesque cobblestone courtyard. A *stavekirke* (stave church), styled after the 13th-century Gol Church of Hallingdal, has changing exhibits. A replica of Oslo's 14th-century **Akershus Castle,** next to a cascading woodland waterfall, is the setting for the featured restaurant (p. 136). Other buildings simulate the red-roofed cottages of Bergen and the timber-sided farm buildings of the Nordic woodlands.

There's a two-part attraction here. **Maelstrom,** a boat ride in a dragon-headed Viking vessel, traverses Norway's fjords and mythical forests to the music of Peer Gynt. (It's the only attraction in World Showcase that offers FASTPASS.) Along the way, you'll see images of polar bears prowling the shore, then trolls cast a spell on the boat. The watercraft crashes through a narrow gorge and spins into the North Sea, where a storm is in progress. (This is a relatively calm ride, though it's not recommended for expectant mothers or folks with heart, neck, or back problems.) The storm abates, and passengers disembark safely to a 10th-century Viking village to view the 5-minute 70mm film *Norway,* which documents 1,000 years of history. **Spelmanns Gledje** entertains with Norwegian folk music.

Shops sell hand-knit wool hats and authentic (and expensive) Scandinavian sweaters, troll dolls, toys (there's a Lego table where kids can play), woodcarvings, Scandinavian foods, pewterware, and jewelry.

United Kingdom

Frommer's Rating: B

Recommended Ages: 8–adult

The U.K. pavilion takes you to Merry Olde England through **Britannia Square,** a formal London-style park complete with a copper-roof gazebo bandstand, a stereotypical red phone booth, and a statue of the Bard. Four centuries of architecture are represented along quaint cobblestone streets; there's a traditional British pub; and a formal garden with low box hedges in geometric patterns, flagstone paths, and a stone fountain that replicates the landscaping of 16th- and 17th-century palaces.

The **British Invasion,** a group that impersonates the Beatles daily except Sunday; pub pianist **Pam Brody** (Tues, Thurs, Fri, and Sun); and the comedic acting troupe, the **World Showcase Players** (daily), provide entertainment. High Street and Tudor Lane shops display a broad sampling of British merchandise, including toy soldiers, Paddington bears, personalized coats of arms, Scottish clothing (cashmere and Shetland sweaters, golf wear, tams, and tartans), English china, Waterford crystal, and pub items such as tankards, dartboards, and the like. A tea shop occupies a replica of Anne Hathaway's thatched-roof 16th-century cottage in Stratford-on-Avon. Other emporia represent the Georgian, Victorian, Queen Anne, and Tudor periods. Background music ranges from "Greensleeves" to the Beatles.

U.S.A.—The American Adventure

Frommer's Rating: A

Recommended Ages: 8–adult

Housed in a vast Georgian-style structure, **The American Adventure** is a 29-minute dramatization of U.S. history, utilizing a 72-foot rear-projection screen, rousing music, and a large cast of lifelike audio-animatronic figures, including narrators Mark Twain and Ben Franklin. The adventure begins with the voyage of the *Mayflower* and encompasses major historic events. You'll view Jefferson writing the Declaration of Independence, Matthew Brady photographing a family about to be divided by the Civil War, the stock market crash of 1929 (but not the crash of Disney stock in 1999 and 2000), Pearl Harbor, and the *Eagle* heading toward the moon. Teddy Roosevelt discusses the need for national parks. Susan B. Anthony speaks out on women's rights; Frederick Douglass, on slavery; and Chief Joseph, on the plight of Native Americans.

Tips Stay Tuned

Disney hasn't added a new "nation" to World Showcase since Norway became the 11th country in 1988. But the latest buzz has Spain possibly becoming the 12th, with a pavilion that would blend the city of Toledo with some architectural highlights of Madrid and Barcelona. It would be a great way to celebrate Epcot's 25th this year, wouldn't it? Call it another (potential) cash cow: Disney didn't pay to build the other countries (it charged the sponsoring companies and countries $50 million and up). Disney also doesn't pay any of the operating costs. But the Mouse collects the rent and a share of all merchandise sales.

Tips **Cruise Control**

Watching Epcot's IllumiNations fireworks display (below) from World Showcase Lagoon can make for a magical evening. You can charter the 1930s vintage speedboat *Breathless* ($180, up to seven people) or catch the show aboard a less romantic but also less expensive pontoon boat ($142, up to 12 people). Both last 45 to 50 minutes and you must rent the entire boat for your family or find your own boat mates. For information or to reserve a boat, call ✆ **407/ 939-7529.** You can make arrangements for snacks and beverages to be served on your cruise, though only through Disney, by calling ✆ **407/934-3160.**

It's one of Disney's best historical productions. Formal gardens shaded by live oaks, sycamores, elms, and holly complement the 18th-century architecture.

Entertainment includes the **Spirit of America Fife & Drum Corps; Voices of Liberty,** an a cappella group that sings patriotic songs; and **AMERICAN VYBE,** featuring the sounds of swing, jazz, and gospel.

The "Echoes of Africa" exhibit in the **American Heritage Gallery** showcases between 15 and 20 pieces of the Walt Disney–Tishman African Art collection, the largest privately owned significant collection of African art in the world. The pieces displayed rotate throughout the exhibit's 3-year run (ending this year).

Heritage Manor Gifts sells autographed presidential photographs, needlepoint samplers, quilts, pottery, candles, Davy Crockett hats, books on American history, historically costumed dolls, classic political campaign buttons, and vintage newspapers with banner headlines such as "Nixon Resigns!"

OTHER SHOWS
IllumiNations *Moments*
Frommer's Rating: A+
Recommended Ages: 3–adult
Little has changed since Epcot's millennium version of IllumiNations ended on January 1, 2001. This 13-minute grand nightcap continues to be a blend of fireworks, lasers, and fountains in a display that's signature Disney. The show is worth the crowds that flock to the parking lot when it's over (just be sure to keep a firm grip on young kids). *Tip:* Stake your claim to your favorite viewing area a half-hour before show time (listed in your entertainment schedule). The ones near Showcase Plaza have a head start for the exits. Another good place for viewing the show is the terrace at the Rose & Crown Pub in the United Kingdom (p. 137).

5 Disney–MGM Studios
You'll probably see the Tower of Terror and the Earrfel Tower, a water tank with mouse ears, even before you enter this park, which Disney bills as "the Hollywood that never was and always will be." Once inside, you'll find pulse-quickening rides such as **Rock 'n' Roller Coaster,** movie- and TV-themed shows such as **Who Wants to Be a Millionaire—Play It!,** and a spectacular laser-light show called **Fantasmic!** The main streets include Hollywood and Sunset boulevards, where Art Deco movie sets remember the golden age of Hollywood. The Streets of America sets include New York, lined with miniature renditions of Gotham's landmarks (the Empire State, Flatiron, and

Chrysler buildings); as well as San Francisco, Chicago, and others. You'll find some of the best street performing in the Disney parks here. More importantly, it's a working movie and TV studio where shows are occasionally in production.

Arrive at the park early. Unlike Epcot, MGM's 154 acres of attractions can pretty much be seen in a day. The parking lot reaches to the gate, but trams serve the outer-lying areas. Pay attention to your parking location; this lot isn't as well marked as the Magic Kingdom's. Again, write your lot and row number on something you'll be able to find at the end of the day.

If you don't get a *Disney–MGM Studios Guide Map* and entertainment schedule as you enter the park, you can pick one up at Guest Relations or most shops. First things first—check show times and then sketch out a plan for your day, because many of the of the park's best offerings are its shows. Schedule your rides around the shows that interest you most and go from there. Our favorite MGM restaurants are described in chapter 5, "Where to Dine."

There's a Tip Board listing the day's shows, ride closings, and other information at the corner of Hollywood and Sunset boulevards.

HOURS   The park is usually open from 9am to at least 6 or 7pm, with extended hours sometimes as late as midnight during holidays and summer.

TICKET PRICES   A 1-day park ticket is $63 for adults, $52 for children 3 to 9. Kids under 3 get in free.

SERVICES & FACILITIES IN DISNEY–MGM STUDIOS

ATMs   ATMs accepting cards from banks using the Cirrus, Honor, and PLUS systems are located on the right side of the main entrance and near Toy Story Pizza Planet.

Baby Care   MGM has a small Baby Care Center to the left of the main entrance where you'll find facilities for nursing and changing. Disposable diapers, formula, baby food, and pacifiers are for sale. Changing tables are also in all women's restrooms and some men's restrooms.

Cameras & Film   Film and Kodak disposable cameras are available throughout the park. Digital supplies, however, are very limited.

First Aid   The First Aid Center, staffed by registered nurses, is in the Entrance Plaza adjoining Guest Relations and the Baby Care Center.

Lockers   Lockers are located alongside Oscar's Classic Car Souvenirs, to the right of the Entrance Plaza after you pass through the turnstiles. The cost is $7, including a $2 deposit.

Lost Children   Lost children at Disney–MGM Studios are taken to Guest Relations, where lost children logbooks are kept. *Children under 7 should wear name-tags inside their clothes.*

Package Pickup   Any purchase can be sent to Guest Relations in the Entrance Plaza; allow at least 3 hours for delivery. If you're staying overnight at a Disney resort, you can also have all packages purchased by 7pm sent to your hotel (they will be delivered by noon the next day).

Parking   It's $9 a day for cars, light trucks, and vans; $10 for RVs.

Pet Care   Day accommodations for $6 are offered at kennels to the left and just out-side the entrance (© **407/824-6568**). There are also four other kennels in the WDW

Disney–MGM Studios Theme Park

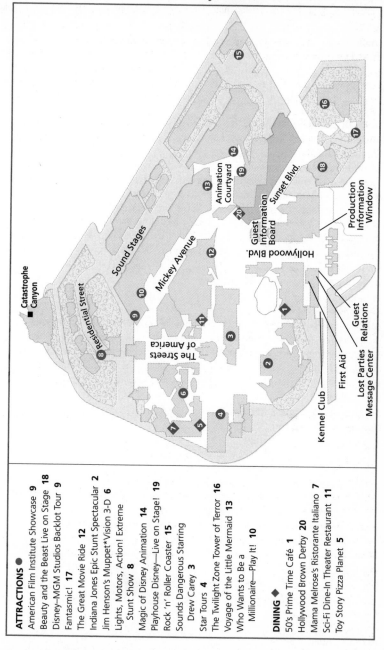

ATTRACTIONS ●

American Film Institute Showcase **9**
Beauty and the Beast Live on Stage **18**
Disney–MGM Studios Backlot Tour **9**
Fantasmic! **17**
The Great Movie Ride **12**
Indiana Jones Epic Stunt Spectacular **2**
Jim Henson's Muppet*Vision 3-D **6**
Lights, Motors, Action! Extreme
    Stunt Show **8**
Magic of Disney Animation **14**
Playhouse Disney—Live on Stage! **19**
Rock 'n' Roller Coaster **15**
Sounds Dangerous Starring
    Drew Carey **3**
Star Tours **4**
The Twilight Zone Tower of Terror **16**
Voyage of the Little Mermaid **13**
Who Wants to Be a
    Millionaire—Play It! **10**

DINING ◆

50's Prime Time Café **1**
Hollywood Brown Derby **20**
Mama Melrose's Ristorante Italiano **7**
Sci-Fi Dine-In Theater Restaurant **11**
Toy Story Pizza Planet **5**

complex. (See "Fast Facts" in chapter 3 for more details.) Proof of vaccinations is required.

Strollers   Strollers can be rented at Oscar's Super Service, inside the main entrance, for $10 for a single and $18 for a double.

Wheelchair Rental   Wheelchairs are rented at Oscar's Super Service inside the main entrance. The cost for regular chairs is $10 a day. Electric wheelchairs rent for $45, including a $5 refundable deposit.

MAJOR ATTRACTIONS & SHOWS
American Film Institute Showcase
Frommer's Rating: C
Recommended Ages: 10–adult
This shop and exhibit area is the final stop on the Backlot Tour (see below) and looks at the efforts of the editors, cinematographers, producers, and directors whose names roll by in the blur of credits. It also showcases the work of the American Film Institute's Lifetime Achievement Award winners, including Bette Davis, Jack Nicholson, and Elizabeth Taylor. A special exhibit here, **"Villains: Movie Characters You Love to Hate,"** features the costumes and props of several notable bad guys, including Darth Vader.

Beauty and the Beast Live on Stage
Frommer's Rating: B+
Recommended Ages: All ages
A 1,500-seat covered amphitheater is the home of this 30-minute live Broadway-style production of *Beauty and the Beast* that's adapted from the movie. Musical highlights from the show include the rousing "Be Our Guest" opening number and the poignant title song featured in the romantic waltz scene finale. The sets and costumes are lavish, and the production numbers are pretty spectacular. There are usually four or five shows a day.

Disney–MGM Studios Backlot Tour
Frommer's Rating: B+
Recommended Ages: 6–adult
This 35-minute tram tour takes you behind the scenes for a close-up look at the vehicles, props, costumes, sets, and special effects used in your favorite movies and TV shows. On many days, you'll see costume makers at work in the wardrobe department (Disney has around 2 million garments here). But the real fun begins when the tram heads for **Catastrophe Canyon,** where an earthquake in the heart of oil country causes canyon walls to rumble. A raging oil fire, massive explosions, torrents of rain, and flash floods threaten you and other riders before you're taken behind the scenes to see how filmmakers use special effects to make such disasters. The preshow is almost as interesting. While waiting in line, you can watch entertaining videos hosted by several TV and movie stars. The Backlot Tour is a solid ride that's of the same type as Universal Studios' Earthquake—The Big One (p. 266).

Fantasmic! *Moments*
Frommer's Rating: A+
Recommended Ages: All ages
Disney mixes heroes, villains, stunt performers, choreography, laser lights, and fireworks into a spectacular end-of-the-day extravaganza. This is a 25-minute visual feast

Tips Dinner & a Show

At press time, Disney was offering preferred seating at the end-of-the-day spectacular, **Fantasmic!**, along with a fixed-price dinner at one of Disney–MGM's sit-down restaurants. All you need to do is make Advance Reservations (© **407/939-3463**) and request the Fantasmic! package for the Hollywood Brown Derby ($36.99 adults, $10.99 kids 3–11), Mama Melrose's Ristorante Italiano ($28.99 adults, $10.99 kids 3–11), or Hollywood & Vine ($22.99 adults, $10.99 kids 3–11). You'll get your line pass at the restaurant and instructions on getting to the special entrance to the preferred seating area of the show.

Note: The prices above are for a fixed-price meal and do not include sales tax, tip, or alcoholic beverages; if you order off the menu, you'll pay more. The prices also don't include a reserved seat at Fantasmic!, only a pass that will get you into the preferred seating area (you must arrive at least 30 min. in advance—a much shorter wait than usual).

---

where the Magic Mickey comes to life in a show featuring shooting comets, great balls of fire (our apologies to Jerry Lee), and animated fountains that really charge the audience. The cast includes 50 performers, a giant dragon, a king cobra, and 1 million gallons of water, just about all of which are orchestrated by a sorcerer mouse that looks more than remotely familiar. You'll probably recognize other characters as well as musical scores from Disney movie classics such as *Fantasia, Pinocchio, Snow White and the Seven Dwarfs, The Little Mermaid,* and *The Lion King.* You'll also shudder at the animated villainy of Jafar, Cruella De Vil, and Maleficent in the battle of good vs. evil, part of which is projected onto huge, water-mist screens. The amphitheater holds 9,000 souls including standing room, and during busy periods (holidays and summers) it's often standing-room-only, so arrive early. (There is sometimes an additional show earlier in the evening.) *Note:* The show's loud pyrotechnics may frighten younger children, and earplugs aren't a bad idea for anyone with ears sensitive to very loud noises.

The Great Movie Ride
Frommer's Rating: C for most, B+ for adults who love classics
Recommended Ages: 8–adult
Film footage and 50 audio-animatronic replicas of movie stars are used to re-create some of the most famous scenes in filmdom on this 22-minute ride through movie history. You'll relive magic moments from the 1930s through the present: the classic airport farewell scene by Bergman and Bogart in *Casablanca;* Brando bellowing "Stellaaaaa"; Harrison Ford in full Indiana Jones mode while facing all of those snakes; Sigourney Weaver fending off slimy aliens; Gene Kelly singin' in the rain; and arguably the best Tarzan, Johnny Weissmuller, giving his trademark yell while swinging across the jungle. The action is enhanced by special effects, and outlaws hijack your tram en route. So pay attention when the conductor warns, "Fasten your seat belts. It's going to be a bumpy night." The setting is a full-scale reproduction of Hollywood's famous Mann's Chinese Theatre, complete with handprints of the stars out front. *Note:* Though it's a classic, the ride is somewhat dated, and is often the target of rumors claiming it will be replaced or upgraded (Disney remains closemouthed on the matter).

(Finds) Find the Hidden Mickeys

Hidden Mickeys started as an inside joke among early Disney Imagineers and soon became a park tradition (we're not kidding—the entire Disney–MGM Studios layout when viewed from the sky is one giant Hidden Mickey!). Today, dozens of subtle Mickey images—usually silhouettes of his world-famous ears, profile, or full figure—are hidden (more or less) in attractions and resorts throughout the Walt Disney empire. No one knows how many, because sometimes they exist only in the eye of the beholder. But there's a semiofficial, maybe-you-agree-maybe-you-don't list. See how many HMs (Hidden Mickeys) you can locate during your visit. And be sharp-eyed about it. Those bubbles on your souvenir mug might be forming one. Here are a few to get you started:

In the Magic Kingdom
- In the Haunted Mansion banquet scene, check out the arrangement of the plate and adjoining saucers on the table.
- In the Africa scene of It's a Small World, note the purple flowers on a vine on the elephant's left side.
- While riding Splash Mountain, look for Mickey lying on his back in the pink clouds to the right of the *Zip-A-Dee Lady* paddle-wheeler.

At Epcot
- In Imagination!, check out the little girl's dress in the lobby film of *Honey, I Shrunk the Audience*, one of five HMs in this pavilion.
- In The Land pavilion, don't miss the small stones in front of the Native American man on a horse and the baseball cap of the man driving a harvester in the *Circle of Life* film.
- As you cruise through the Mexico pavilion on El Rio del Tiempo, notice the arrangement of three clay pots in the marketplace scene.
- In Maelstrom in the Norway pavilion, a Viking wears Mickey ears in the wall mural facing the loading dock.

Indiana Jones Epic Stunt Spectacular
Frommer's Rating: A+
Recommended Ages: 6–adult

Visitors get a peek into the world of movie stunts in this dramatic 30-minute show, which re-creates major scenes from the Indiana Jones series. The show opens on an elaborate Mayan temple backdrop. Indy crashes onto the set via a rope, and, as he searches with a torch for the golden idol, he encounters booby traps, fire, and steam. Then a boulder straight out of *Raiders of the Lost Ark* chases him! The set is dismantled to reveal a colorful Cairo marketplace where a sword fight ensues, and the action includes virtuoso bullwhip maneuvers, gunfire, and a truck bursting into flames. An explosive finale takes place in a desert scenario. Theme music and an entertaining narrative enhance the action. Throughout this, guests get to see how elaborate stunts are pulled off. Arrive early and sit near the stage if you want a shot at being picked as an

- There are four HMs inside Spaceship Earth, one of them in the Renaissance scene, on the page of a book behind the sleeping monk. Try to find the other three.

At Disney–MGM Studios
- On the Great Movie Ride, there's an HM on the window above the bank in the gangster scene.
- At Jim Henson's Muppet*Vision 3-D, take a good look at the top of the sign listing five reasons for turning in your 3-D glasses, and note the balloons in the film's final scene.
- In the Twilight Zone Tower of Terror, note the bell for the elevator behind Rod Serling in the film. There are more than eight HMs in this attraction.
- Outside Rock 'n' Roller Coaster, look for two HMs in the rotunda area's tile floor. (Reportedly, the entire coaster is one giant HM.)
- By the way, the park's least Hidden Mickey is what's called the Earrfel Tower, Disney–MGM Studios' tall water tower, which is fitted with a huge pair of Mouseket-EARS.

In Animal Kingdom
- Look at The Boneyard in Dinoland U.S.A., where a fan and two hard hats form an HM.
- There are 25 Hidden Mickeys at Rafiki's Planet Watch, where Mickey lurks in the murals, tree trunks, and paintings of animals.

In the Resort Areas
- HMs are on the weather vane atop the Grand Floridian Resort & Spa's convention center, in the interactive fountains at the entrance to Downtown Disney Marketplace, and one forms a giant sand trap next to the green at the Magnolia Golf Course's 6th hole.

For more information on the plethora of HMs at WDW, check out **www. hiddenmickeys.org**.

audience participant. Alas, it's a job for adults only. Younger kids may prefer a seat a bit further away from all the action, and we've found that the mid- to upper rows offer the best views.

Jim Henson's Muppet*Vision 3-D
Frommer's Rating: A+
Recommended Ages: All ages
This must-see film stars Kermit and Miss Piggy in a delightful marriage of Jim Henson's puppets and Disney audio-animatronics, special-effects wizardry, 70mm film, and cutting-edge 3-D technology. The coming-right-at-you action includes flying Muppets, cream pies, and cannonballs, plus high winds, fiber-optic fireworks, bubble showers, even an actual spray of water. Kermit is the host; Miss Piggy sings "Dream a Little Dream of Me"; Statler and Waldorf critique the action (which includes numerous mishaps and disasters) from a balcony; and Nicki Napoleon and his Emperor Penguins

> (*Tips* **Out of the Warmth & into the Cold**
>
> Over at soundstage 4, on Mickey Avenue, the frozen world of Narnia comes alive. At **Journey Into Narnia: Creating the Lion, the Witch, and the Wardrobe,** guests can walk through a gigantic wardrobe and into an elaborate wintry landscape much like the set from the hit blockbuster movie. They'll be treated to a behind-the-scenes look at movie-making magic a la Disney. Filling the gallery just beyond the set are elaborate creatures, along with actual costumes, armory, and props used in the making of the film.

(a full Muppet orchestra) provide music from the pit. In the preshow area, guests view an entertaining Muppet video on overhead monitors. Note the cute Muppet fountain out front and the Muppet version of a Rousseau painting inside. The 25-minute show (including the 12-min. video preshow) runs continuously.

Tip: Sweetums, the giant but friendly Muppet monster, usually interacts with a few kids sitting in the front rows during the show.

Lights, Motors, Action! Extreme Stunt Show
Frommer's Rating: B+
Recommended Ages: 5–adult

MGM's newest addition debuted in mid-2005—and it's a biggie. Taking its cue from the original show at Disneyland Resort Paris, this stunt show features high-flying high-speed movie stunts full of pyrotechnic effects and more. Like the **Indiana Jones Stunt Spectacular** (p. 234), the storyline has the audience following the filming of an action-packed movie (in this case, a spy thriller set in a Mediterranean village). Over 40 vehicles are used in the show including cars, motorcycles, and watercraft—each modified to perform the rather spectacular stunts. It's entertaining and certainly offers its share of thrills, but it's not as engaging as the Indiana Jones production unless you're a car buff. Although the outdoor stadium seating is set back from the action, the noise level is extremely high—and completely unavoidable, no matter where you sit. Very young children may find it overwhelming. The show is part of the redevelopment of the MGM backlot area that's also seen the addition of new cityscapes of San Francisco and Chicago, among others. Check the entertainment schedule for show times.

Magic of Disney Animation
Frommer's Rating: B
Recommended Ages: 8–adult

Once hosted by Walter Cronkite and Robin Williams, the new version of **Magic of Disney Animation** features Mushu the dragon from Disney's *Mulan* as he co-hosts a theater presentation where some of Disney's animation secrets are revealed. The Q&A session that follows allows guests to ask questions about the animation process before attempting their own Disney character drawings while under the supervision of a working animator. Currently joining in on the fun for a meet-and-greet opportunity are the stars of *Chicken Little;* however, be aware that the lineup has changed several times in the past few years and will likely change again.

Playhouse Disney—Live on Stage!
Frommer's Rating: B
Recommended Ages: 2–5

Younger audiences love this 20-minute show where they meet characters from Bear in the Big Blue House, The Book of Pooh, and other kid-favorite cartoons. The show encourages preschoolers to dance, sing, and play along with the cast. The action happens several times a day. Check your show schedule.

Rock 'n' Roller Coaster ⸨Moments⸩

Frommer's Rating: A+
Recommended Ages: 10–adult

Some say this is one of Disney's attempts to go head-to-head with Universal Orlando's Islands of Adventure. True or not, this inverted roller coaster is one the best and definitely the hippest thrill rides at WDW. It's a fast-and-furious indoor ride in semidarkness. You sit in a 24-passenger "stretch limo" outfitted with 120 speakers that blare Aerosmith at 32,000 watts! Flashing lights deliver a variety of messages and warnings, including "prepare to merge as you've never merged before." Then, faster than you can scream "I want to live!" (around 2.8 sec., actually), you shoot from 0 to 60 mph and into the first gut-tightening inversion at 5Gs. It's a real launch (sometimes of lunch) followed by a wild ride through a make-believe California freeway system. One of three inversions cuts through an "O" in the Hollywood sign, but you don't feel you're going to be thrown out. It's too fast for that. So fast, the Disney hype says, it's similar to sitting atop an F-14 Tomcat. (We've never been in an F-14, so we can't argue.) The ride lasts 3 minutes, 12 seconds, the running time of Aerosmith's hit, "Sweet Emotion." Like Space Mountain, all of the ride action takes place indoors, but this one kicks it up a few notches. *Note:* Riders must be at least 48 inches tall, and expectant moms and people prone to motion sickness or those with heart, neck, or back problems shouldn't try to tackle this ride.

Sounds Dangerous Starring Drew Carey

Frommer's Rating: C+
Recommended Ages: 8-Adult

Drew Carey provides laughs while dual audio technology provides some hair-raising effects during this 12-minute show at ABC Sound Studios. You'll feel like you're right in the middle of the action of a TV pilot featuring undercover police work and plenty of mishaps. Even when the picture disappears and the theater is plunged into darkness (an effect that will likely turn off younger audience members), you continue on Detective Charlie Foster's chase via headphones that show off "3-D" sound effects.

Tip: After the show is over, check out **Sound Works,** which offers interactive activities that allow you to experiment with different sound effects.

Star Tours

Frommer's Rating: B+
Recommended Ages: 8–adult

Cutting-edge when it opened, **Star Tours,** based on the original *Star Wars* trilogy (George Lucas collaborated on the ride), is now a couple of rungs below the latest

---

⸨Fun Fact⸩ Water World

The large moat surrounding the "Fantasmic!" stage at Disney–MGM Studios contains 1.9 million gallons of water. More than 80,000 gallons of that is needed every minute to create the three mist screens used to project video portions of the show.

Tips **Tune Time**

Weekdays from noon to 4pm, you can watch BB Good broadcast her Radio Disney show live from a studio next to Sounds Dangerous Starring Drew Carey. You can tune into the show and others on Radio Disney at 990 on your AM dial.

---

technology but is still fun. The preshow has R2-D2 and C-3PO running an intergalactic travel agency (it offers some of the best detailing of any preshow at Disney World). After boarding a 40-seat "spacecraft," you're off with a whoosh on a journey that takes you through some of the more famous scenes from the movies, full of sudden drops, crashes, and oncoming laser blasts as you seemingly careen out of control. *Note:* The virtual-simulator may go nowhere at all, but it sure feels like you do. Riders must be at least 40 inches tall. Also, expectant mothers and people with neck, back, and heart problems or those prone to motion sickness shouldn't ride. There are, however, plenty of places to focus your vision other than the screen (unlike some of the newer simulator rides) if you begin to feel a bit green.

The Twilight Zone Tower of Terror *Moments*
Frommer's Rating: A+
Recommended Ages: 10–adult
This is a truly stomach-lifting (and dropping) ride, and Disney continues to fine-tune it to make it even better. The legend says that during a violent storm on Halloween night 1939, lightning struck the Hollywood Tower Hotel, causing an entire wing and an elevator full of people to disappear. And you're about to meet them as you become the star in a special episode of . . . *The Twilight Zone.* En route to this formerly grand hotel, guests walk past overgrown landscaping and faded signs that once pointed the way to stables and tennis courts; the vines over the entrance trellis are dead; and the hotel is a crumbling ruin. Eerie corridors lead to a dimly lit library, where you can hear a storm raging outside. After various spooky adventures, the ride ends in a dramatic climax: a 13-story free-fall in stages. The ride now features random drop sequences, allowing for a real sense of unknown (and a different experience every time you ride), and new visual, audio, and olfactory effects have also been added to make the experience even more frightening. Because it's a different experience every time you dare to ride, it's far better than any other ride of its kind. Some believe this rivals (even exceeds) Rock 'n' Roller Coaster in the thrill department (one of the Imagineers who designed the tower admitted to us that he's too scared to ride his own creation). At 199 feet, it's the tallest ride in WDW, and it's a grade above Dr. Doom's Fearfall at Islands of Adventure (and has far better atmosphere—it's one of Walt Disney World's best attractions in the theme department). *Note:* You must be at least 40 inches tall to ride, and expectant moms and people prone to motion sickness or those with heart, neck, or back problems shouldn't try to tackle it. Your stomach may need a few minutes to find its way back to where it belongs after it's all over.

Voyage of the Little Mermaid
Frommer's Rating: B+
Recommended Ages: 4–adult
Hazy lighting creates an underwater effect in a reef-walled theater and helps set the mood for this charming musical based on the Disney feature film. The show combines live performers with more than 100 puppets, movie clips, and innovative special

effects. Sebastian sings the movie's Academy Award–winning song, "Under the Sea"; the ethereal Ariel shares her dream of becoming human in a live performance of "Part of Your World"; and the evil Ursula, 12 feet tall and 10 feet wide, belts out "Poor Unfortunate Soul." It has a happy ending, as most of the young audience knows it will; they've seen the movie. This 17-minute show is a great place to rest your feet on a hot day, and you get misted inside the theater to further cool you off.

Who Wants to Be a Millionaire—Play It!

Frommer's Rating: B+

Recommended Ages: 8–adult

Contestants can't win $1 million, but they can win points used to buy prizes ranging from collectible pins to a leather jacket or a 3-night cruise on one of Disney's cruise ships. Based on Disney-owned ABC TV's game show, replicating even its dramatic music and lighting, the theme-park version has a few twists. Lifelines include asking the audience for help or calling a stranger on two phones set up in the park. Audience members play along on keypads, with the fastest to answer qualifying to become contestants in the hot seat themselves. It's amusing when you realize just how difficult it can be to try to answer when the pressure's on. Games run continuously, but the 600-seat studio fills up quickly, so be prepared for a wait.

PARADES, PLAYGROUNDS & MORE

Disney Stars and Motor Cars is MGM's parade celebrating the 100th anniversary of Uncle Walt's birth in Chicago. The motorcade includes a fun, highly recognizable procession of Disney characters and their chariots. The parade is popular enough that if you decide to skip it, you'll find shorter lines at the park's primo rides (check the parade schedule in your park map).

Discover the Stories Behind the Magic is an exhibit under the giant sorcerer's hat at the end of Hollywood Boulevard. Its interactive kiosks let you explore the magic inspirations of the chapters in Disney's life.

Aside from the parades, there are character-greeting hot spots at **Toy Story Friends,** near Mama Melrose's Ristorante Italiano; on **Commissary Lane;** on the north end of the **Streets of America;** on **Mickey Avenue** near the Backlot Tour; and at the **Magic of Disney Imagination.** See the handout *Times Guide* for the schedule.

SHOPPING AT DISNEY–MGM STUDIOS

With more that 20 shops we can't list them all, but some of MGM's more unique offerings include:

The **Animation Courtyard Shops** carry collectible cels, costumes from Disney classic films, and pins.

ⓘ *Tips* Call Ahead

Disney–MGM is home to some of Disney World's most unique restaurants (see chapter 5 for more details). If you plan to dine in any of them, be sure to make Advance Reservations (preferably before you arrive, but if not, then the minute you arrive at your hotel or in the park). Waiting until lunch or dinnertime will almost assure that you'll miss out, especially at the Sci-Fi Dinner Theater and 50's Prime Time Cafe.

Sid Cahuenga's One-of-a-Kind sells autographed photos of the stars, original movie posters, and star-touched items such as canceled checks signed by Judy Garland and others.

Celebrity 5 & 10, modeled after a 1940s Woolworth's, has movie-related merchandise: *Gone With the Wind* memorabilia, MGM Studios T-shirts, movie posters, Elvis mugs, and more.

The major park attractions also have their own shops selling Indiana Jones adventure clothing, Little Mermaid stuffed characters, *Star Wars* souvenirs, and so on.

6 Animal Kingdom

Disney's fourth major park opened in 1998 and combines exotic animals, the elaborate landscapes of Asia and Africa, and the prehistoric lands of the dinosaur. Animals, architecture, and lush surroundings take center stage here, with a handful of rides thrown in for good measure.

A conservation venue as much as an attraction ensures that you won't find the animals blatantly displayed throughout the 500-acre park; instead, naturalistic habitats blend seamlessly into the spectacular surroundings. This unfortunately means that, at times, you'll have to search a bit to find the inhabitants. Expect your experience here to be quite different from that at Disney's other parks. It's the spectacular surroundings, meticulously re-created architecture, and intricate detailing, not so much the attractions sprinkled throughout (even though **Expedition Everest** is pretty impressive), that make the park so unique and so interesting. The bonus: Because this is one of Disney's less ride-intensive parks, it's easily enjoyed in a single day, usually less, making it a good choice when you need to cut back and take it a bit slower and easier. Plus, one of the best shows in all of Disney can be found here, the **Festival of the Lion King,** so be sure to put it on your to-do list.

Animal Kingdom is divided into the **Oasis,** a shopping area near the entrance that offers limited animal viewing; **Discovery Island,** home of the Tree of Life, the park's very unique icon; **Camp Minnie-Mickey,** the Animal Kingdom equivalent of Mickey's Toontown Fair in the Magic Kingdom but without any of the fun little rides; **Africa,** where you can wander the village streets and head out on safari (you'll find the largest concentration of animals here); **Asia,** with Mt. Everest looming on the horizon (within it, the coolest thrill ride in the park), includes a raging river ride, exotic animal exhibits (including Bengal tigers and giant fruit bats), and a bird show; and **Dinoland U.S.A.,** filled with carnival-style rides and games, a large play area, and a herky-jerky thrill ride that transports you back in time.

Tips Dehydration Alert!

Animal Kingdom (and the other parks, too) can get very hot, especially during summer. Bring bottled water (freeze it the night before to keep it cold), refilling at the fountains inside the park. Remember to bring sunscreen and wide-brimmed hats *for the whole family,* and plan to ride Kali River Rapids during the hottest part of the day (be sure to bring a change of clothes—you will get soaked).

Animal Kingdom

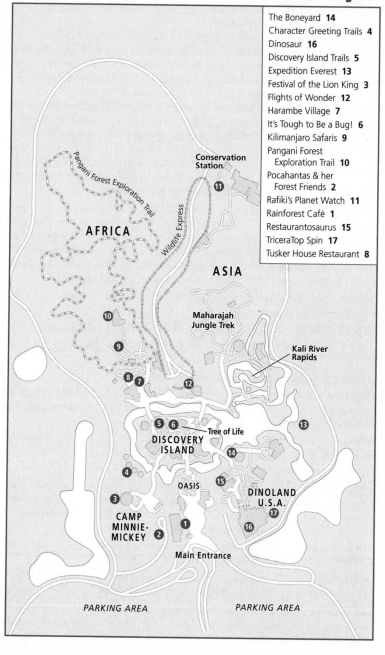

The Boneyard **14**
Character Greeting Trails **4**
Dinosaur **16**
Discovery Island Trails **5**
Expedition Everest **13**
Festival of the Lion King **3**
Flights of Wonder **12**
Harambe Village **7**
It's Tough to Be a Bug! **6**
Kilimanjaro Safaris **9**
Pangani Forest Exploration Trail **10**
Pocahontas & her Forest Friends **2**
Rafiki's Planet Watch **11**
Rainforest Café **1**
Restaurantosaurus **15**
TriceraTop Spin **17**
Tusker House Restaurant **8**

Pangani Forest Exploration Trail

Conservation Station

Wildlife Express

AFRICA

ASIA

Maharajah Jungle Trek

Kali River Rapids

Tree of Life

DISCOVERY ISLAND

OASIS

DINOLAND U.S.A.

CAMP MINNIE-MICKEY

Main Entrance

PARKING AREA

PARKING AREA

The park covers more than 500 acres, and your feet will tell you that you've covered the territory at the end of the day.

Most of the rides are accessible to guests with disabilities, but the hilly terrain, large crowds, narrow passages, and long hikes can make for a strenuous day if there's a wheelchair-bound person in your party. Anyone with neck or back problems, as well as pregnant women, may not be able to enjoy rides such as **Expedition Everest, Kali River Rapids,** and **Dinosaur.**

The 145-foot-tall **Tree of Life** is in the center of the park. It's an intricately carved free-form representation of animals, handcrafted by a team of artists over the period of a year. It's not nearly as tall or imposing as the silver golf ball–like dome, also known as Spaceship Earth, which has come to symbolize Epcot, or Cinderella Castle in the Magic Kingdom. The tree is impressive, though, with 8,000 limbs, 103,000 leaves, and 325 mammals, reptiles, bugs, birds, dinosaurs, and Mickeys in its trunk, limbs, and roots. For more on the tree, see "Discovery Island," below.

ARRIVING   From the parking lot, walk or (where available) ride one of the trams to the entrance. If you do walk, watch out for the trams and autos, because the lot isn't designed for pedestrians. Also, make certain to note where you parked (section and row). Lot signs aren't as prominent as in the Magic Kingdom, and the rows look alike when you come back out. Upon entering the park, consult the handout guide map for special events or entertainment. If you have questions, ask park staffers.

HOURS   Animal Kingdom is open at least from 8 or 9am to 5pm, but it sometimes stays open an hour or so later.

TICKET PRICES   The ticket prices are $63 for adults, $52 for children 3 to 9. See "Tickets," earlier in this chapter, for information on the new Magic Your Way ticketing system.

SERVICES & FACILITIES IN ANIMAL KINGDOM

ATMs   Animal Kingdom has an ATM near Garden Gate Gifts to the right of the entrance as well as in Dinoland across from the Primeval Whirl. It accepts cards from banks using the Cirrus, Honor, and PLUS systems.

Baby Care   The Baby Care Center is located near Creature Comforts gift shop on the west side of the Tree of Life, but as in the other Disney parks, you'll find changing tables in restrooms, and you can buy disposable diapers at Guest Relations.

Cameras & Film   You can drop film off for same-day developing at the Kodak Kiosk in Africa and Garden Gate Gifts near the park entrances. Cameras and film are available in Disney Outfitters in Safari Village; at the Kodak Kiosk in Africa, near the entrance to the Kilimanjaro Safari; and in Garden Gate Gifts.

First Aid   The First Aid Center, which is staffed by registered nurses, is located near Creature Comforts gift shop on the west side of the Tree of Life.

Lockers   Lockers ($7, including a $2 deposit) are located in Garden Gate Gifts to your right as you enter the park. They're also located to the left, near Rainforest Cafe.

Lost Children   A center for lost children is located near Creature Comforts at the Baby Care Center on the west side of the Tree of Life. This is also the site of same-day lost and found. At the risk of repeating myself, *make your younger kids wear name-tags inside their clothing.*

ⓘ Tips Animal Kingdom Tip Sheet

1. Arrive at opening or stay until near closing for the best view of the animals.
2. **Expedition Everest** offers the biggest thrills in the park, and a FAST-PASS may be your only ticket to avoiding the ride's excruciatingly long lines.
3. **Kilimanjaro Safaris** is one of the most popular rides and the best place to see a lot of animals in one sitting. But in summer, the animals can be scarce during the midday heat. If you can hoof it there first thing, do it. If not, try late in the day. The same applies to viewing the gorillas on the **Pangani Forest Exploration Trail.**
4. The **Festival of the Lion King** show is a must.
5. Looking for Disney characters? Go to the Character Greeting Trails in **Camp Minnie-Mickey.**

Package Pickup   Any packages can be sent to the front of the park at Garden Gate Gifts. Allow at least 3 hours for delivery. WDW resort guests can have their purchases delivered directly to their hotel; if purchased by 7pm, the item will be delivered by noon the next day.

Parking   The cost is $9 a day for cars, light trucks, and vans; $10 for RVs.

Pet Care   Pet facilities are located just outside the park entrance ($6 per day; ✆ **407/824-6568**). There are four other kennels located in the WDW complex. (See "Fast Facts" in chapter 3 for more information.) Proof of vaccinations is required.

Strollers   Stroller rentals are available at Garden Gate Gifts to the right as you enter the park ($10 for a single, $18 for a double). There are also satellite locations throughout the park. Ask a Disney employee to steer you.

Wheelchair Rental   You can rent wheelchairs at Garden Gate Gifts to the right as you enter the park. Rentals are $10 for a standard wheelchair; $45 for an electric wheelchair (includes a $5 refundable deposit). Ask Disney employees for other rental locations throughout the park.

THE OASIS

This painstakingly designed landscape of streams, grottoes, and miniwaterfalls sets the tone for the rest of the park. This is a good place to see wallabies, tiny deer, giant anteaters, sloths, iguanas, tree kangaroos, otters, and macaws (*if,* I remind you ad nauseum, you get here early or stay late). But thick cover provides a jungle tone and makes seeing the animals sometimes difficult. There are no rides in this area, and, aside from the animals, it's mainly a pass-through zone. Those guests traveling with eager children will probably have more time to enjoy these exhibits on the way out.

DISCOVERY ISLAND

Like Cinderella Castle in the Magic Kingdom and Spaceship Earth in Epcot, the 14-story **Tree of Life** located here has been designed to be the park's central landmark. The man-made tree and its carved animals are the work of Disney artists. Teams of them worked for 1 year creating the various sculptures, and it's worth a stroll on the walks around its roots, but most folks are smart to save it for the end of the day. (Much of it can be seen while you're in line for **It's Tough to Be a Bug!** or on the **Discovery Island Trails.**) The intricate design makes it seem as if a different animal appears from every angle. One of the creators says he expects it to become one of the most photographed works of art in the world. (He's probably a Disney shareholder.) There's a wading pond directly in front of the tree that often features flamingos.

Discovery Island Trails
Frommer's Rating: B
Recommended Ages: All ages
The old, pre-FASTPASS queue for It's Tough to Be a Bug! provides a leisurely path through the root system of the Tree of Life and a chance to see real, not-so-rare critters, such as axis deer, red kangaroos, otters, flamingos, lemurs, Galápagos tortoises, ducks, storks, and cockatoos. Again, the best viewing times are early or late in the day.

It's Tough to Be a Bug!
Frommer's Rating: A, C for young ones scared silly from sensory effects
Recommended Ages: 5–adult
This show's cuteness quotient is enough to earn it a B+. But it goes a rung higher thanks to the preshow: To get to the theater, you have to wind around the Tree of Life's 50-foot base, giving you a front-row look at this man-made marvel. After you've passed that, grab your 3-D glasses and settle into a sometimes creepy-crawly seat. Based on the film *A Bug's Life,* the special effects in this multimedia show are pretty impressive. It's not a good one for very young kids (it's dark and loud) or bug haters, but for others it's a fun, sometimes poignant look at life from a smaller perspective. Flick, Hopper, and the rest of the cast—ants, beetles, spiders, and, ugh, a stink bug—awaken your senses with, literally, some in-your-face action. And the show's finale always leaves the crowd buzzing.

DINOLAND U.S.A.
Enter by passing under Olden Gate Bridge, a 40-foot Brachiosaurus reassembled from excavated fossils. Speaking of which, until late summer 1999, this land had three paleontologists working on the very real skeleton of Sue, a monstrously big *Tyrannosaurus rex* unearthed 9 years earlier in the Black Hills of South Dakota. They patched and assembled the bones here because Disney helped pay for the work. Alas, Sue's permanent home is at Chicago's Field Museum, but Dinoland U.S.A. has a replica cast from her 67-million-year-old bones. It's marked as **Dino-Sue** on park guide maps.

The Boneyard
Frommer's Rating: B+ for children, B for parents who need to rest their feet
Recommended Ages: 3–12
Kids love the chance to slip, slither, slide, and slink through this giant playground and dig site where they can discover the real-looking remains of triceratops, *T. rex,* and

---

(*Fun Fact* **It Costs to Recycle**

The animals here deposit more than 1,600 tons of dung a year. Disney pays a company to haul it away and then buys some of it back as compost for landscaping.

Tips Pin Mania

Pin buying, collecting, and trading can reach frenzied proportions among Disney fans, including many cast members. All of the theme parks have special locations set aside for the fun, which are marked on the handout guide maps. There are, however, a few rules of pin-trading etiquette that must be followed. You can learn more about the madness on the Internet at **www.dizpins.com** and **www.officialdisneypintrading.com**.

---

other vanished giants. Contained within a latticework of metal bars and netting, this area is popular, but not as inviting as the *Honey, I Shrunk the Kids* play area in Disney–MGM Studios.

Dinosaur
Frommer's Rating: B
Recommended Ages: 8–adult
This ride hurls you through the darkness in CTX Rover "time machines" back to the time when dinosaurs ruled the Earth. The expedition takes you past an array of snarling and particularly ferocious looking dinosaurs, one of whom decides you would make a great munchie. What started out as a journey back through time becomes a race to escape the jaws of an irritated and rather ugly Carnotaurus. Young children may find the large lizards and the darkness a bit frightening, while everyone will find the ride a bit jarring. *Note:* You must be 40 inches or taller to climb aboard. Also, expectant mothers and people with neck, back, and heart problems or those prone to motion sickness shouldn't ride.

Primeval Whirl
Frommer's Rating: B+
Recommended Ages: 8–adult
Disney introduced this spinning, free-style twin roller coaster in 2002 in an effort to broaden the park's appeal to young kids (odd, as this ride has a pretty tall height minimum). You control the action through its wacky maze of curves, peaks, and dippity-do-dahs, encountering faux asteroids and hokey cutouts of dinosaurs. This is a cross between those old carnival coasters of the '50s and '60s and an expanded version of the Barnstormer at Goofy's Wiseacre Farm (p. 206). *Note:* The ride carries a 48-inch height minimum, and expectant moms as well as those with neck, back, or heart problems and folks prone to motion sickness should stay planted on firm ground.

TriceraTop Spin
Frommer's Rating: B+ for tykes and parents
Recommended Ages: 2–7
Cut from the same cloth as The Magic Carpets of Aladdin at WDW's Magic Kingdom, this is another minithrill for youngsters. In this case the cars look like cartoon dinosaurs. They circle the hub while gently moving up and down and all around. This ride, Primeval Whirl, and an arcade-game area make up the Dinoland U.S.A. mini-land called Chester & Hester's Dino-Rama.

CAMP MINNIE-MICKEY
Disney characters are the main attraction in this land designed in the same vein as an Adirondack resort. Aside from those characters, however, this zone for the younger set

isn't nearly as kid-friendly as rivals Mickey's Toontown Fair in the Magic Kingdom (reviewed earlier in this chapter) or Woody Woodpecker's KidZone in Universal Studios Florida (see "Universal Studios Florida," in chapter 7).

Character Greeting Trails (Moments

Frommer's Rating: A for kids, D for waiting parents
Recommended Ages: 2–12

Some say this is a must-do for people traveling with children; we say run the other way—quickly. If, however, your kids are hooked on getting every character autograph possible, this is the place to go. A variety of Disney characters, from Winnie the Pooh and Pocahontas to Timon and Baloo, have separate trails where you can meet and mingle, snap photos, and get those autographs. Mickey, Minnie, Goofy, and Pluto even make periodic appearances. Be aware, however, that the lines for these meet-and-greet opportunities are at times excruciatingly long, so unless your kids are really gung ho on collecting the characters' signatures, don't even think of coming here.

Festival of the Lion King (Finds

Frommer's Rating: A+
Recommended Ages: All ages

Almost everyone in the audience comes alive when the music starts in this rousing 28-minute show in the Lion King Theater. It's one of the top three theme-park shows in Central Florida. The production celebrates nature's diversity with a talented, colorfully attired cast of singers, dancers, and life-size critters leading the way to an inspiring sing-along that gets the entire audience caught up in the fun. Based loosely on the animated film, this stage show blends the pageantry of a parade with a tribal celebration. The action is on stage as well as moving around the audience. Even though the pavilion has 1,000 seats, it's best to arrive at least 20 minutes early.

Pocahontas and Her Forest Friends

Frommer's Rating: C
Recommended Ages: All ages

The wait can be nightmarish, and this 15-minute show isn't even remotely close to the caliber of Festival of the Lion King! In this one, Pocahontas, Grandmother Willow, and some friendly forest creatures relay the importance of treating nature with respect. If you must, go early. The theater only has 350 seats, but they allow standing-room crowds.

AFRICA

Enter through the town of Harambe, a worn and weathered African coastal village poised on the edge of the 21st century. (It actually took a great deal of effort to create the run-down appearance.) Costumed employees will greet you as you enter the buildings. The whitewashed structures, built of coral stone and thatched with reed by African craftspeople, surround a central marketplace rich with local wares and colors.

(Fun Fact Did You Know?

Tobacco products aren't the only things unavailable in the theme parks. You can't buy chewing or bubble gum either. It seems too many guests stuck it under tables, benches, and chairs—or tossed it on sidewalks, where it often hitched a ride on the soles of the unsuspecting.

(*Fun Fact* **Cool Trivia**

Two things you might hear during your day in the park: Bugs make up 80% of the real animal kingdom, and cheetahs are the only great cats that purr. Both are true.

Kilimanjaro Safaris

Frommer's Rating: A+ early or late, B+ other times
Recommended Ages: All ages

Animal Kingdom doesn't have many rides, but the animals you'll see on this one make it a winner as long as your timing is right. They're scarce at midday during most times of year (cooler months being the exception), so I recommend you ride it as close to park opening or closing as possible. If you don't make it in time for one of the first or last journeys, the lines can be horrific, so a FASTPASS may be in order.

A large rugged truck takes you through the African landscape (though just a few years ago it was a cow pasture). The animals usually seen along the way include giraffe, black rhinos, hippos, antelopes, Nile crocodiles, zebras, wildebeests, cheetahs, and a pair of lions that may offer half-hearted roars toward some gazelles that are safely out of reach. Early on, a shifting bridge gives riders a brief thrill; later, a bit of drama (a la Disney) as you help catch some poachers. While everyone has a good view, photographers may get a few more shots when sitting on the left side of their row.

Pangani Forest Exploration Trail *(Finds*

Frommer's Rating: B+, A if you're lucky enough to see the gorillas
Recommended Ages: All ages

The hippos put on quite a display (and draw a riotous crowd reaction) when they do what comes naturally and use their tails to scatter it over everything above and below the surface. There are other animals here, including ever-active mole rats, but the **lowland gorillas** are the main event. The trail has two gorilla-viewing areas: One sports a family, including a 500-pound silverback, his ladies, and his children; the other has bachelors. Guests who are unaware of the treasures that lie herein often skip or rush through it, missing a chance to see some magnificent creatures. That said, they're not always cooperative, especially in hot weather, when they spend most of the day in shady areas out of view. There's also an Endangered Animal Rehabilitation Centre with Colobus and Mona monkeys.

Rafiki's Planet Watch *(Overrated*

Frommer's Rating: C
Recommended Ages: All ages

Board an open-sided train (the Wildlife Express) near Pangani Forest Exploration Trail for a trip to the back edge of the park, which has three attractions. **Conservation Station** offers a behind-the-scenes look at how Disney cares for animals (and the entrance mural is loaded with Hidden Mickeys). You'll pass nurseries and veterinarian stations. But these facilities need to be staffed to be interesting, and that's not always the case. Older kids and adults will find the audio presentations at the sound booths pretty neat. **Habitat Habit!** is a trail with small animals such as cotton-top tamarins. The **Affection Section's** petting zoo has rare goats and potbelly pigs, but not much more.

ASIA

Disney's Imagineers have outdone themselves in creating the kingdom of **Anandapur.** The intricately painted artwork and detailed carvings are very appealing, and they even seem to make the lines move a tad faster.

Expedition Everest

Frommer's Rating: A+
Recommended Ages: 8–adult

If there's a knock against Animal Kingdom, it's that it doesn't pack a lot of punch in the adrenaline department due to its lack of thrill rides. But naysayers have been quieted by the 2006 debut of **Expedition Everest,** Animal Kingdom's first true thrill ride. Your journey begins in the small Himalayan village of Serka Zong, where guests board the Anadapur Rail Service for a seemingly casual trek to the snowcapped peak of Mount Everest. Upon departing, you'll pass through an Asian mountain range and dense bamboo forests, and then move past glacier fields and pounding waterfalls. But your journey will quickly get off track (almost literally) and become an out-of-control high-speed train ride that sends you careening along rough and rugged terrain, moving backward and forward along icy mountain ledges and through darkened caves— only to end up confronting the legendary Yeti. Our adrenaline is running already. The meticulous and painstaking detail is some of the most impressive in all of WDW. Prayer flags are strung across between the aged and distressed buildings, while intricately carved totems, stone carvings, and some 2,000 authentic handcrafted Asian objects are scattered throughout the village.

Flights of Wonder

Frommer's Rating: C+
Recommended Ages: All ages

This live-animal action show has undergone several transformations since the park opened. It's still a low-key break from the madness and has a few laughs, including Groucho the African yellow-nape, who entertains the audience with his op-*parrot*-ic a cappella solos. For thrills there's the just-above-your-head soaring of a Harris hawk and a Eurasian eagle owl. To entertain guests waiting in line for the show, trainers will often bring out an owl or hawk, allowing for an up-close look and the opportunity to learn some interesting facts about the stars of the show.

Finding Nemo, Take 2

Tarzan's taken his last swing, and his replacement is . . . a loveable clownfish. After *Tarzan Rocks!* closed in 2005 to make way for portions of Expedition Everest, Disney immediately began plans for another production, and making its debut sometime in late 2006 will be *Finding Nemo—The Musical.* The show will star Nemo, dad Marlin, and friend Dory, among others, and will feature original songs by the same composers who did the Tony Award–winning *Avenue Q.* Plans also include enclosing the formerly open Theater in the Wild to create an atmospheric undersea environment, and the use of puppetry and state-of-the-art special effects.

Kali River Rapids

Frommer's Rating: B+

Recommended Ages: 6–adult

Its churning water mimics real rapids, and the ride's optical illusions will have you wondering if you're about to go over churning falls. The ride begins with a peaceful tour of lush foliage, but soon you're dipping and dripping as your tiny craft is tossed and turned. The snowcapped peak of Expedition Everest makes a brief but impressive appearance along the way. If the rapids themselves don't drench you, the kids manning water cannons along the route will ensure you get soaked—hence the cart selling oversize towels just beyond the ride's exit. (Bring a plastic bag for your valuables. The rafts' center storage areas alone likely won't keep them dry.) The lines can be long, but keep your head up and enjoy the marvelous art overhead and on beautiful murals. It's not nearly as wild as the water rides at Universal Orlando, so even the younger kids will be able to handle this one. *Note:* There's a 38-inch height minimum, and expectant moms and people with neck, back, and heart problems or those prone to motion sickness shouldn't ride it.

Maharajah Jungle Trek

Frommer's Rating: B

Recommended Ages: 6–adult

Disney keeps its promise to provide up-close views of animals with this exhibit. If you don't show up in the midday heat, you may see Bengal tigers through a wall of thick glass, while nothing but air separates you from dozens of giant fruit bats hanging in what appears to be a courtyard. Some have wingspans of 6 feet. (If you have a phobia, you can bypass this, though the bats are harmless.) Guides are on hand to answer questions, and you can also check a brochure that lists the animals you may spot; it's available on your right as you enter. You'll be asked to "recycle" it as you exit.

PARADES

Mickey's Jammin' Jungle Parade at Animal Kingdom is an interactive street party featuring whimsical colorful animals and characters on expedition. The music and overall atmosphere are lively and the one-of-a-kind visuals are some of the best in all the parks.

7 Disney Water Parks

Note: All of the attractions mentioned in this section can be found on the "Walt Disney World Parks & Attractions" map on p. 179.

TYPHOON LAGOON

> *Ahoy swimmers, floaters, run-aground boaters!*
> *A furious storm once roared 'cross the sea*
> *Catching ships in its path, helpless to flee . . .*
> *Instead of a certain and watery doom*
> *The winds swept them here to TYPHOON LAGOON.*

Such is the Disney legend relating to **Typhoon Lagoon** ✪✪✪, which you'll see posted on consecutive signs as you enter the park. Located off Buena Vista Drive between the Downtown Disney Marketplace and Disney–MGM Studios, this is the ultimate in water-theme parks. Its fantasy setting is a palm-fringed island village of ramshackle, tin-roofed structures, strewn with cargo, surfboards, and other marine wreckage left

(Tips **Closed for the Winter**

Both Disney water parks are refurbished annually. That means if you're traveling in fall or winter, it is likely that one of the parks will be closed for a month
or more. So if a water park is on your itinerary, ask in advance about closings.

by the "great typhoon." A storm-stranded fishing boat (the *Miss Tilly*) dangles pre-
cariously atop 95-foot Mount Mayday, the steep setting for several attractions. Every
half-hour, the boat's smokestack erupts, shooting a 50-foot geyser of water into the air.

ESSENTIALS

HOURS   The park is open from at least 10am to 5pm, with extended hours during
some holiday periods and summer (© **407/560-4141;** www.disneyworld.com).

ENTRANCE FEES   A 1-day ticket (without 6.5% tax) to Typhoon Lagoon is $35
for adults, $29 for kids 3 to 9.

HELPFUL HINTS   In summer, arrive no later than 9am to avoid long lines. The
park is often filled to capacity by 10am and then closed to later arrivals. Beach towels
($2.50 per towel) and lockers ($5 and $7) can be rented, and beachwear can be pur-
chased at **Singapore Sal's.** Light fare is available at two eateries, **Leaning Palms** and
Typhoon Tillie's. A beach bar called **Let's Go Slurpin'** sells beer and soft drinks and
Lowtide Lou's sells ice cream and soft drinks. There are picnic tables (consider bringing picnic fare; you can keep it in your locker until lunch). Guests aren't permitted to
bring their own flotation devices, and glass bottles are prohibited.

ATTRACTIONS IN THE PARK
Castaway Creek
Hop onto a raft or an inner tube and meander along this 2,100-foot lazy river that circles most of the park. It tumbles through a misty rainforest, then by caves and secluded
grottoes and on into the sunshine, all the while passing along some of Disney's meticulously maintained tropical foliage. Tubes are included in the admission price.

Crush 'n' Gusher
The newest thrill to splash onto the scene is a first-of-its-kind water coaster featuring
three separate experiences to choose from. The **Banana Blaster, Coconut Crusher,**
and **Pineapple Plunger** each offer steep drops, twists, and turns of varying degrees as
you're sent careening through an old, rusted-out fruit factory. Intense jets of water
actually propel riders back uphill at one point.

Ketchakiddie Creek
Many of the park's other attractions require guests to be older children, teens, or
adults, but this section is a **kiddie area** exclusively for 2- to 5-year-olds. An innovative water playground, it has bubbling fountains to frolic in, mini–water slides, a pint-
size "white-water" tubing run, spouting whales and squirting seals, rubbery crocodiles
to climb on, grottoes to explore, and waterfalls to loll under. It's also small enough for
you to take good home videos or photographs.

Shark Reef
Guests are given free equipment (and instruction) for a 15-minute swim through this
very small snorkeling area that includes a simulated coral reef populated by about

4,000 parrotfish, angelfish, yellowtail damselfish, and other cuties including small rays and sharks. If you don't want to get in, you can observe the fish via portholes in a walk-through viewing area.

Typhoon Lagoon Surf Pool

This large (2.75 million gal.) and lovely lagoon is the size of two football fields and is surrounded by a white sandy beach. It's the park's main swimming area. The chlorinated water has a turquoise hue much like the Caribbean. **Large waves** roll through the deeper areas every 90 seconds. A foghorn sounds to warn you when one is coming. Young children can wade in the lagoon's more peaceful tidal pools—**Blustery Bay** or **Whitecap Cove.** The lagoon is also home to a **special weekly surfing program** (see "Staying Active," in chapter 7).

Water Slides

Humunga Kowabunga consists of three 214-foot Mount Mayday slides that propel you down the mountain on a serpentine route through waterfalls and bat caves and past nautical wreckage before depositing you into a bubbling catch pool; each offers slightly different views and 30-mph thrills. There's seating for non-Kowabunga folks whose kids have commissioned them to "watch me." Women should wear a one-piece swimsuit on the slides (except those who don't mind putting on a show for gawkers). *Note:* You must be 48 inches or taller to ride this. **Storm Slides** offer a tamer course through the park's man-made caves.

White-Water Rides

Mount Mayday is the setting for three white-water rafting adventures—**Keelhaul Falls, Mayday Falls,** and **Gangplank Falls**—all offering steep drops coursing through caves and passing lush scenery. Keelhaul Falls has the most winding route, Mayday

---

Tips Water Park Dos & Don'ts

1. Go in the afternoons, about 2pm, even in summer, if you can stand the heat that long and want to avoid crowds. The early birds usually are gone by then.

2. Go early in the week when most of the weeklong guests are filling the lines at the theme parks.

3. Kids can get lost just as easily at a water park as at the other parks, and the consequences can be tragic. All Disney parks have lifeguards, usually wearing bright red suits, but, to be safe, make yourself the first line of safety for the kids in your crew.

4. Women should remember the one-piece bathing suit rule we mentioned earlier under "Water Slides." And all bathers should remember the "wedgie" rule on the more extreme rides, such as Summit Plummet (at Blizzard Beach, below). What's the "wedgie" rule? It's a principle of physics that causes you to start out wearing baggies and end up in a thong.

5. Use a waterproof sunscreen with an SPF of at least 30 and drink plenty of fluids. Despite all that water, it's easy to get dehydrated in summer.

Fun Fact **Did You Know?**

- Walt Disney World sprawls across 47 square miles, which makes it the size of San Francisco or twice that of Manhattan.
- Mickey Mouse has more than 175 outfits, ranging from scuba gear to formal wear. But he's second banana to Minnie, who has a mere 200.
- The number of Disney T-shirts sold by the parks each year could plaster the image of Mickey Mouse on the chest of every Chicagoan.
- The DNA Tower at the entrance to the Epcot Wonders of Life pavilion is 5.5 billion times the actual size—just the right size for a human 6-million-miles tall.
- Mowing the lawn at WDW is no joke. The staff mows 450,000 miles each year—the equivalent of 18 trips around the earth's equator.
- The WDW Laundry handles 260,000 pounds of laundry *a day!* To get the equivalent, you'd have to wash and dry a load every day for 44 years.
- More than a million pounds of watermelon are served every year at Walt Disney World Resort (watch out for flying seeds!).
- Walt Disney World gift shops sell about 500,000 character watches annually. Not surprisingly, most of them are Mickeys.
- According to Kodak estimates, about 4% of the amateur photographs snapped in the U.S. are taken at Walt Disney World.

Falls has the steepest drops and fastest water, and the slightly tamer Gangplank Falls uses large tubes so that the whole family can pile on.

BLIZZARD BEACH

Blizzard Beach *✦✦✦* is the younger of Disney's water parks, a 66-acre "ski resort" in the midst of a tropical lagoon centering on the 90-foot, uh-oh, Mount Gushmore. There's a legend for this one as well. Apparently a freak snowstorm dumped tons of snow on Walt Disney World, leading to the creation of Florida's first—and, so far, only—mountain ski resort (complete with Ice Gator, the park's mascot). Naturally, when temperatures returned to their normal broiling range, the snow bunnies prepared to close up shop, when they realized—this is Disney, happy endings are a must—that what remained of their snow resort could be turned into a water park featuring the fastest and tallest waterlogged "ski" runs in the country. The base of Mount Gushmore has a sand beach with several other attractions, including a wave pool and a smaller version of the mount for younger children. The park is located off World Drive, just north of the All-Star Movie, Music, and Sports resorts.

ESSENTIALS

HOURS   It's open from at least 10am to 5pm, with extended hours during holiday periods and summer (© **407/560-3400;** www.disneyworld.com).

ENTRANCE FEES   A 1-day ticket to Blizzard Beach is $35 (without 6.5% tax) for adults, $29 for children 3 to 9.

HELPFUL HINTS   Arrive at or before opening to avoid long lines and to be sure you get in. Beach towels ($2.50 per towel) and lockers ($5 and $7) are available, and you can buy the beachwear you forgot to bring at the **Beach Haus.** You can grab something to eat at **Avalunch** and **The Warming Hut,** and **Lattawatta Lodge** (burgers, hot dogs, nachos, pizza, and sandwiches).

MAJOR ATTRACTIONS IN THE PARK
Cross Country Creek
Inner-tubers can float lazily along this park-circling 2,900-foot creek, but beware of the mysterious Polar Caves where you'll get splashed with melting ice.

Melt-Away Bay
This 1-acre bobbing wave pool is fed by waterfalls of melting "snow" and features relatively calm waves.

Runoff Rapids
Another tube job, this one lets you careen down any of three twisting-turning runs, one of which sends you through darkness.

Ski-Patrol Training Camp
Designed for 'tweens and teens, it features a rope swing, a T-bar drop over water, slides like the wet and slippery **Mogul Mania** from the Mount, and a challenging ice-floe walk along slippery floating icebergs.

Slush Gusher
This superspeed slide travels along a snow-banked gully. *Note:* It has a 48-inch height minimum.

Snow Stormers
These three flumes descend from the top of Mount Gushmore and follow a switchback course through ski-type slalom gates.

Summit Plummet
Read *every* speed, motion, vertical-dip, wedgie, and hold-onto-your-breast-plate warning in this guide. Then, test your bravado in a bullring, a space shuttle, or dozens of other death-defying hobbies as a warm-up. This puppy starts pretty slow, with a lift ride to the 120-foot summit. Then . . . well . . . kiss any kids or religious medal you may be carrying. Because, if you board, you *will enter* the self-proclaimed world's fastest body slide (we believe it!), a test of your courage and swimsuit that virtually goes straight down and has you moving *sans* vehicle at 60 mph by the catch pool (aka, stop zone). Even the hardiest rider may find this one hard to handle; a veteran thrill-seeker described the experience to us as "15 seconds of paralyzing fear." *Note:* It has a 48-inch height minimum. Also, expectant mothers and people with neck, back, and heart problems shouldn't ride.

Teamboat Springs
On the World's longest white-water raft ride, your six-passenger raft twists down a 1,200-foot series of rushing waterfalls.

Tike's Peak
This kid-size version of Mount Gushmore offers short water slides, rideable animals, a snow castle, a squirting ice pond, and a fountain play area for young guests.

Toboggan Racers
Here's an eight-lane slide that sends you racing head first over exhilarating dips into a "snowy slope." (If you've ever been on one of those tall super slides at amusement parks, imagine doing it headfirst, on your belly, on a raft. This baby can pack a lot of zip by the end.)

8 Other WDW Attractions

Note: All of the attractions mentioned in this section can be found on the "Walt Disney World Parks & Attractions" map on p. 179.

FANTASIA GARDENS & WINTER SUMMERLAND

Fantasia Gardens Miniature Golf ✿✿, located off Buena Vista Drive across from Disney–MGM Studios, offers two 18-hole miniature courses drawing inspiration from the Walt Disney classic cartoon of the same name. You'll find hippos, ostriches, and alligators on the **Fantasia Gardens** course, where the Sorcerer's Apprentice presides over the final hole. It's a good bet for beginners and kids. Seasoned minigolfers probably will prefer **Fantasia Fairways,** which is a scaled-down golf course complete with sand traps, water hazards, tricky putting greens, and holes ranging from 40 to 75 feet.

Santa Claus and his elves provide the theme for **Winter Summerland** ✿✿, which has two 18-hole miniature golf courses across from Blizzard Beach on Buena Vista Drive. The **Winter** course takes you from an ice castle to a snowman to the North Pole. The **Summer** course is pure Florida, from sandcastles to surfboards to a visit with Santa on the "Winternet."

Tickets at both venues are $11 for adults and $9 for children 3 to 9. Both are open from 10am to 10 or 11pm daily. For information about Fantasia Gardens, call ✆ **407/560-4582.** For information about Winter Summerland, call ✆ **407/560-3000.** You can find both on the Internet at **www.disneyworld.com**.

DISNEY'S WIDE WORLD OF SPORTS

The 200-acre Disney's Wide World of Sports complex has a 7,500-seat professional baseball stadium, 10 other baseball and softball fields, six basketball courts, 12 lighted tennis courts, a track-and-field complex, a golf driving range, and six sand volleyball courts. It's a haven for sports fans and wannabe athletes.

Note: The **Hess Sports Field North** opened in the spring of 2005, the first expansion of the Wide World of Sports venue since its opening in 1997. The addition features 20 acres of playing fields, with space for four football/soccer fields and four baseball-softball diamonds.

The complex is located on Victory Way, just north of U.S. 192 (west of I-4; ✆ **407/939-1500;** www.disneyworldsports.com). It's open daily from 10am to 5pm; the cost is $10.28 adults, $7.71 kids 3 to 9. Organized programs and events include:

- The **Multi-Sports Experience,** which challenges guests with a variety of activities, covering many sports: football, baseball, basketball, hockey, soccer, and volleyball. It's open on select days.
- The **Atlanta Braves** play 16 spring-training games during a 1-month season that begins in early March. Tickets cost $13.50 to $22. For tickets call Ticketmaster (✆ **407/939-4263**). In addition to the Braves, the facility also hosts the **Tampa Bay Buccaneers'** spring training camp.
- The **NFL, NBA, NCAA, PGA,** and **Harlem Globetrotters** also host events, sometimes annually and sometimes more frequently, at the complex. Admission varies by event.

RICHARD PETTY DRIVING EXPERIENCE

Test Track is for sissies. The **Richard Petty Driving Experience** at WDW gives you a chance to do the real thing in a 600-horsepower Winston Cup car. How real is it? Expect to sign a two-page waiver that features words like *DANGEROUS* and *CALCULATED*

Finds DisneyQuest

The reaction that visitors have upon experiencing this popular attraction is often the same. No matter if it's from kids just reaching the video-game age, teens who are firmly hooked, or adults who never outgrew *Pong,* they leave saying: "Awesome!"

Four separate zones—explore zone, a virtual adventureland; score zone, a superhero competition city; create zone, where imagination and invention rule; and replay zone, filled with classic games but in a futuristic setting—ensures that everybody will be entertained . . . and likely for hours.

This five-level virtual-video arcade has everything from nearly old-fashioned pinball to virtual games and rides. Want appetizers? **Aladdin's Magic Carpet Ride** puts you astride a motorcycle-like seat and flies through the 3-D Cave of Wonders. **Invasion! An ExtraTERRORestrial Alien Encounter** has the same kind of intensity. Your mission is to save colonists from intergalactic bad guys. One player flies the virtual module while others fire weapons.

Pirates of the Caribbean: Battle for Buccaneer Gold puts you and three mates in 3-D helmets so that you can battle pirate ships virtual-reality style. One plays captain, steering your ship, while the others assume positions behind cannons to blast the black hearts into oblivion. Each time you do, you're rewarded with some doubloons, but beware of the sea monsters that can gobble you and your treasure. In the final moments, you come face to face with a ghost ship, which can send you to Davy Jones's Locker.

Try the **Mighty Ducks Pinball Slam** if you're a pinball fan. It's an interactive life-size game where you ride platforms and use body English to score points.

If you have an inventive mind, stop in at **CyberSpace Mountain** ✦✦, where Bill Nye the Science-Turned-Roller-Coaster-Guy helps you create the ultimate loop-and-dipster, which you can then ride in a simulator. It's a major hit with the coaster-crazy crowd.

Finally, if you need some quiet time, sign up at **Animation Academy** for a minicourse in Disney cartooning. There are also snack and food areas for those who need something more tangible than virtual refreshment.

DisneyQuest (© **407/828-4600;** www.disneyquest.com) is located in Downtown Disney West Side on Buena Vista Drive. The admission ($35 for adults, $29 for kids 3–9; prices don't include 6% sales tax) allows you unlimited play from 11:30am to 11pm (until midnight Fri–Sat). Unfortunately, heavy crowds tend to gather here after 1pm, which can cut into your fun and patience.

RISK before you climb in. At one end of the spectrum, you can ride shotgun for a couple of laps at 145 mph ($105.44, including tax). At the other, spend from 3 hours to 2 days learning how to drive the car yourself and race fellow daredevils in 8 to 30 laps of excitement ($403.64–$1,330.19, including tax). *Note:* You must be 18 years old to do this. Hours and seasons vary. For reservations call © **800/237-3889,** or head on the Web to **www.1800bepetty.com.**

7

Exploring Beyond Disney: Universal Orlando, SeaWorld & Other Attractions

"**A**nything you can do, we can do better." This seems to be the Orlando motto. Every time one park adds an attraction, the next park feels the need to add two attractions (or at least one that's far more impressive), and so on, and so on, and so on. This has been going on since Mickey first arrived in town. The game of cat and mouse between Disney and its top-ranked challenger Universal Orlando, which each year since 1999 has chipped away at what was once WDW's virtual monopoly, however, is all good—at least for you and me. Each time one park tries to outdo the other, we reap the benefits of their additions. Still, make no mistake: Disney is king, leading in theme parks (4–2) and smaller attractions (9–1). It has a 2-to-1 edge in nightclub venues, a huge lead in restaurants, and, when it comes to hotel rooms, its lead is insurmountable.

Nevertheless, Universal is trying. It had a substantial growth spurt in 1999, bolstering its original park, **Universal Studios Florida,** with a second theme park, **Islands of Adventure;** a nightclub and restaurant complex, **CityWalk;** and its first resort, **Portofino Bay,** a 750-room Loews hotel. In January 2001, it opened a second resort, the **Hard Rock Hotel;** and, in 2002, it followed up with the **Royal Pacific Resort.** Universal Orlando still has plenty of room for expansion, and, while the company's lips are sealed,

it's known there are plans for at least two more hotels. A golf course and acres of additional rides and attractions are not inconceivable.

A few miles south, **SeaWorld** and its sister park, **Discovery Cove,** also grab a share of the Orlando action. In 2004, SeaWorld added a 5-acre shopping and dining area, appropriately named the Waterfront. Plans to add an eco-edutainment-themed water park are slated for 2008.

Aside from greater variety, these players mean more multiday packages and special deals for you. To compete with Disney, SeaWorld and Universal Orlando teamed up on multiday pass options a few years back. They offer a **FlexTicket** that also includes admission to **Wet 'n Wild** (a Universal-owned water park) and has an optional add-on that includes **Busch Gardens** in Tampa (p. 341).

While the wars rage on in the traditional tourist areas, it has finally dawned on the rest of Orlando that Central Florida is one of the world's favorite vacation destinations.

Since the early 1990s, and most notably in the past few years, downtown Orlando has undergone a transformation in hopes of wooing tourists to its own set of attractions, nightclubs, and restaurants. Expansions at the Orlando Museum of Art and the Orlando Science Center combined with an ever-increasing number of upscale dining options and trendy clubs springing up shows the city is trying to grab back a share of tourist dollars. This expansion means visitors can enjoy the spoils: more variety, greater opportunities, and a world beyond the theme parks.

THE FLEXTICKET The most economical way to see the various "other-than-Disney" parks is with these passes, which counter Disney's Park Hopper add-on. With the **FlexTicket,** you pay one price to visit any of the participating parks as many times as you want during a 14-day period. A four-park pass to Universal Studios Florida, Islands of Adventure, Wet 'n Wild, and SeaWorld is $189.95 for adults and $155.95 for children 3 to 9. A five-park pass, which adds Busch Gardens in Tampa, is $234.95 for adults and $199.95 for kids. Both passes also include entrance to Universal CityWalk. The **FlexTicket** can be ordered through Universal (© **407/363-8000;** www.universalorlando.com); SeaWorld (© **407/351-3600;** www.seaworld.com); or Wet 'n Wild (© **800/992-9453** or 407/351-1800; www.wetnwild.com). *Note:* There's a round-trip shuttle available to Busch Gardens (p. 341) that's free for FlexTicket buyers (it's $10 for other guests).

UNIVERSAL EXPRESS PLUS PASS This is Universal's answer to Disney's FASTPASS; however, at Universal, you'll pay a price (literally) to skip the long lines. Single-day and multiday ticket buyers not staying at a Universal resort can purchase an Express Plus Pass that's good for either 1 day at one park ($15) or 1 day at two parks ($25). The downside (other than having to fork out the extra cash): Express Plus Passes are only good on select dates (for a complete list see Universal's website) during the year, and they are only valid for a single entry to each ride featuring an express line. In other words, you can only wait in the express line for the Hulk once; if you want to ride a second (or third, or fourth) time, you'll have to head to the regular line with everyone else. And if you are a multiday ticket holder, the Express Pass is only good for a single day—you'll have to purchase an additional Express Pass if you want to skip the long lines for more than just a single day.

The plus in Express Plus: Waits are usually 15 minutes or less. Be aware, passes are not unlimited and can run out during busier times. If you're at the parks during peak season, really can't stand standing in line, and have plenty of cash to spare, the pass may be worth your while; otherwise, don't bother. A family of four would be far better off spending the extra bucks ($60–$100) to stay at one of Universal's resorts. Guests of the Portofino Bay, Hard Rock, and Royal Pacific hotels (see chapter 4, "Where to Stay") need only show their room key to skip the long lines. And the best part: Resort guests are allowed unlimited express line access for the length of time and number of parks that their park admission is valid for. Call © **407/363-8000,** or go to **www.universalorlando. com** for more information.

1 Universal Studios Florida

Even with fast-paced grown-up rides based on blockbusters such as *Twister, Terminator, The Mummy,* and *Men in Black,* Universal Studios Florida is a ton of fun for kids. And, as an added plus, it's a working motion picture and TV production studio, so occasionally there's even some live filming taking place. Even if there isn't a film or show in production, you can see reel history displayed in the form of some 40 actual sets exhibited along Hollywood Boulevard and Rodeo Drive. And there are plenty of action shows and rides including recent additions **Neutron's Nicktoon Blast, Shrek 4-D, Revenge of the Mummy,** and (the latest to debut, in 2005) **Fear Factor Live.**

ESSENTIALS

GETTING TO UNIVERSAL BY CAR   Universal Orlando is a half-mile north of I-4 Exit 75B, Kirkman Road/Highway 435. There may be construction in the area, so follow the signs directing you to the parks.

PARKING   If you park in the multilevel garages, remember the theme and row in your area to help you find your car later. Or, do it the old-fashioned way: Write it down. Parking costs $9 for cars, light trucks, and vans. Valet parking is $16. Universal's garages are connected to its parks and have moving sidewalks, but it's still a long walk.

TICKET PRICES   A **1-day ticket** costs $63 (plus 6.5% sales tax) for adults, $52 for children 3 to 9. At press time, Universal was also offering a **2-day/two-park** pass for $107.95 at the gate or $99.95 online that includes 3 days free (for a total of 5 days at the parks). Normally the price (a true bargain) is the same for both kids and adults and is good for consecutive days only. At press time, however, Universal was running a promotion allowing 1 child (ages 3–9) per paying adult (2-day/two-park tickets only) free admission. Note that these promotions often come and go, so be sure to check Universal's website (**www.universalorlando.com**) when planning your vacation.

All multiday passes let you move between Universal Studios Florida and Islands of Adventure. *Multiday passes also give you free access to the CityWalk clubs at night.* Because the parks are within walking distance of each other, you won't lose much time jockeying back and forth, which is not the case at Disney. Nevertheless, it's a long walk for tykes and people with limited mobility, so consider a stroller or wheelchair.

See the beginning of this chapter for information on the **FlexTicket,** which provides multiday admission to Universal Studios Florida, Islands of Adventure, SeaWorld, and Wet 'n Wild.

There are also 5-hour **VIP tours** at either Universal Studios Florida or Islands of Adventure, which include a guided tour, free valet parking, refreshments, and line-cutting privileges at a number of high-profile attractions among other perks, for $100 to $120 per person. A 7-hour, two-park VIP tour covers both parks and costs $125 to $150 per person. Prices for both tours do not include 6.5% tax and *do not cover admission to the parks!* For more information on the VIP tour, call © **407/363-8295** or send an e-mail to **viptours@universalorlando.com**. Tours start at 10am and noon daily. If you plan on visiting during peak season, money isn't an issue, and you aren't staying at one of the Universal resorts, this is a good way to experience the best of the park without having to spend most of your day in lines.

Tips **Shorter Days**

Like Disney, Universal juggles park hours to adjust for varying attendance due to seasonal shifts and holidays. The hours listed in this chapter are generally accurate, but sometimes the parks close earlier, or some rides or shows open later. To avoid disappointment, check the park's website at **www.universal orlando.com** or call © **407/363-8000** for up-to-the-minute schedules.

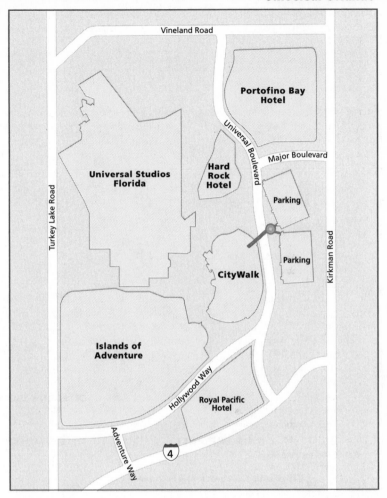

HOURS The park is open 365 days a year, usually at least from 9am to 6pm, though it's open as late as 8 or 9pm, sometimes later, in summer and around holidays. The best bet is to call before you go so that you're not caught by surprise.

MAKING YOUR VISIT MORE ENJOYABLE
PLANNING YOUR VISIT

You can get information before you leave home by calling **Universal Orlando Guest Services** at ℂ **800/224-4233** or 407/363-8000. Ask about travel packages as well as theme-park information. Universal sometimes offers a promotion that adds additional days free or at a deeply discounted price. You can also write to Guest Services, 1000 Universal Studios Plaza, Orlando, FL 32819-7601.

Universal Studios Florida

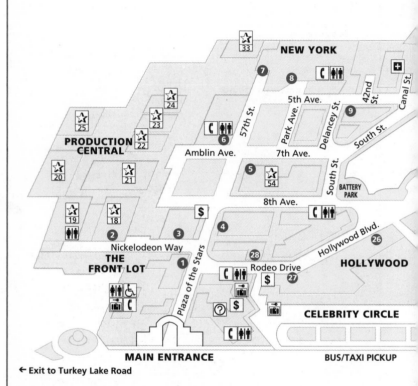

← Exit to Turkey Lake Road

CityWalk *See CityWalk Map in Chapter 9*

PRODUCTION CENTRAL
Classic Monster Cafe **5**
Jimmy Neutron's Nicktoon
  Blast **3**
Nickelodeon Studios **2**
Shrek 4-D **4**

NEW YORK
Blues Brothers **9**
Extreme Ghostbusters **7**
Revenge of the Mummy **8**
Twister...Ride it Out **6**

THE FRONT LOT
Universal Studios Store **1**

HOLLYWOOD
Lucy, A Tribute **28**
Terminator 2: 3-D Battle
  Across Time **27**
Universal Horror
  Make-Up Show **26**

WORLD EXPO
Back to the Future: The Ride **17**
International Food and Film
  Festival **18**
Men in Black Alien Attack **16**

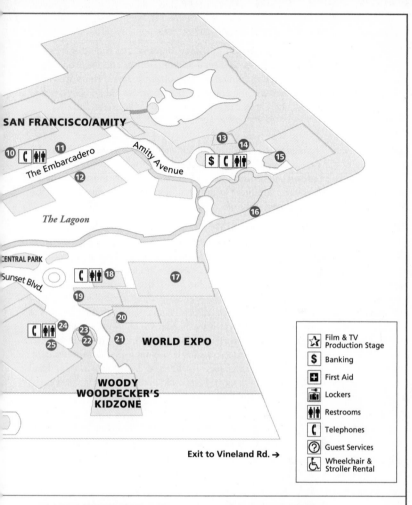

WOODY WOODPECKER'S KIDZONE
Animal Planet Live! **19**
Curious George Goes to Town **21**
A Day in the Park with Barney **20**
E.T. Adventure **25**
Fievel's Playland **23**
KidZone Characters Meet & Greet **24**
Woody Woodpecker's
    Nuthouse Coaster **22**

SAN FRANCISCO/AMITY
Beetlejuice's Rock 'n Roll
    Graveyard Revue **10**
Brody's Ice Cream Shoppe **14**
Earthquake—The Big One **11**
Fear Factor Live **15**
Jaws **13**
Lombard's Seafood Grille **12**

Moments **Universal Has a Few 'Toons, Too**

While the options pale in comparison to Disney, Universal has character meet-and-greets on a rotating basis. At **Universal Studios Florida,** you may run into Woody Woodpecker, SpongeBob SquarePants, Scooby Doo, Jimmy Neutron, and others. At **Islands of Adventure,** the cast may include Spider-Man, Popeye and Olive Oyl, Beetle Bailey, the Cat in the Hat, Betty Boop, or Boris and Natasha.

ONLINE   Find information about Universal Orlando at **www.universalorlando. com**. Orlando's daily newspaper, the *Orlando Sentinel,* also produces Orlando Sentinel Online at **www.orlandosentinel.com**. Additionally, there's a lot of information about the parks, hotels, restaurants, and more at the Orlando/Orange County Convention & Visitors Bureau site: **www.orlandoinfo.com**.

INFORMATION FOR VISITORS WITH SPECIAL NEEDS

Guests with disabilities should go to **Guest Services,** located just inside the main entrance, for a *Rider's Guide for Rider Safety & Guests with Disabilities,* a Telecommunications Device for the Deaf (TDD), or other special assistance. You can rent a standard wheelchair for $12 or an electric one for $40 (both require a signed rental agreement and a $50 deposit). You can reserve them a week or more in advance by calling ✆ **407/224-6350.** You can arrange for sign language interpreting services at no charge by calling ✆ **888/519-4899** (toll-free TDD), 407/224-4414 (local TDD), or 407/224-5929 (voice). Make arrangements for an appointment with an interpreter 1 to 2 weeks in advance. Information is also available at **www.universalorlando.com**.

Tip: The *Rider's Guide* is also a great tool for parents, as it describes in great detail the various rides' special effects, warnings, height requirements, and general guest services information at both Universal parks.

PETS   You can board your small animals at the shelter located inside the parking garages for $10 a day (no overnight stays), but you have to return to feed and walk Fido. Ask the attendant when you pay for parking to direct you to the kennel.

BEST TIME OF YEAR TO VISIT

As with Walt Disney World, there's really no off season for Universal, but the week after Labor Day until mid-December (excluding Thanksgiving week) and January to mid-May (excluding spring break) are known for smaller crowds, cooler weather, and less humid air. The summer months, when the masses throng to the parks, are the worst time for crowds and feature hot, sticky, humid days. During cooler months, you also won't have to worry about daily thunderstorms.

Some of the park's best rides are action-based thrill rides, so your options are limited if you're pregnant, are prone to motion sickness, or have heart, neck, or back problems. The same applies to smaller children. Review the rides and restrictions on the following pages or when you enter the park so that you don't stand in line for something you're unable to enjoy. (There are stationary areas available at some moving rides. Check your park guide under "expectant mothers," as well as the boards in front of each ride, and then ask the attendants for help as you enter.) A child-swap program (allowing parents to switch off on rides without having to stand in line twice) is available at the rides as well.

THE BEST DAYS TO VISIT

Go near the end of the week, on a Thursday or Friday. The pace is somewhat fast Monday through Wednesday, with the heaviest crowds on weekends and during summers and holidays. If you do end up visiting during peak seasons or on holidays (when the parks are open late), consider waiting until late afternoon and staying until closing time—after the dinner hour the parks are generally much less crowded.

CREATE AN ITINERARY

Pick three or four things that you must see or do and plan your day along a rough geographical guide. Universal Studios Florida and Islands of Adventure are both relatively small, so walking from one end of the park to the other isn't as daunting as it is at some of the Disney parks.

CHOOSE AGE-APPROPRIATE RIDES/SHOWS

Here, as in Walt Disney World, height and age restrictions aren't bent to accommodate a screaming child. Even where restrictions don't exist, some shows have loud music and pyrotechnics that can scare young kids. Check the attraction descriptions that follow to make sure your child won't be unduly disappointed or frightened.

Overall, Universal Studios does a much better job in the way of entertaining their guests while they wait in line for the attractions. Many have preshows or TV screens with previews or introductions to the attractions. They've also got it all over the House of Mouse when it comes to beating the sun—many of the attractions here have waiting areas under some sort of cover or, in some cases, indoors (unless the line is so long that it extends beyond these areas, which it sometimes does in the busiest seasons). It is also exponentially easier to get from your car (or resort) to the parks. From the parking lot, if you have kids and all of the gear that comes with them, pack your stroller and bring it along—you will be able to walk directly to the parks, but it can be a long haul for small feet (and there are no trams from the parking decks to the theme parks). Elevators, moving sidewalks, and covered walkways will take you up to the entrance of CityWalk. And, if you're staying at a Universal resort, you'll be glad to know that all three resorts are relatively close by and are serviced by a water taxi (and the Hard Rock is within walking distance) that'll drop you off in CityWalk. We're not saying that you will not have to wait at all—it can take several minutes—but not nearly as long as some trips at Disney can.

Tips Universal Characters & Shows, Too

Universal Studios Florida has a host of street characters and shows to entertain the crowds that flock here. The lineup includes: **Extreme Ghostbusters: The Great Fright Way,** a revised show that has Beetlejuice and The Ghostbusters singing and dancing to hits from the '60s through the '90s; **Lucy and Ricky,** in which Lucy pulls guests into an impromptu conga line; **Sarita and Rico,** two Latin characters who get guests singing and dancing to high-energy tunes such as "Hot, Hot, Hot" and "Mambo #5"; and the **Men in Black** show, in which the agents know there are a lot of aliens in the park, and they must put unsuspecting guests through a humorous screening test. *Note:* Characters rotate and often appear only seasonally.

⟨Value⟩ Money Saver

You can save 10% off your purchase at many Universal Orlando gift shops or eateries by showing your AAA (American Automobile Association) card. This discount isn't available at food and merchandise carts or on tobacco, candy, film, collectibles, and sundry items.

SUGGESTED ITINERARIES

A Suggested Itinerary for Families with Young Children

Waste no time: Hoof it to **Woody Woodpecker's KidZone,** where you and your kids can spend most of the day. If they're 36 inches or taller, don't miss multiple rides on **Woody Woodpecker's Nuthouse Coaster.** Try to make an early pit stop at **Fievel's Playland** (especially its water slide, which is slow-moving and has longer lines after 10:30am). Then adopt a leisurely pace to see **E.T. Adventure, A Day in the Park with Barney,** and **Animal Planet Live!**

Take a stroll down Hollywood Boulevard to **Mel's Diner** for a burger and a shake (and a brief reprieve from the chaos) before heading back and letting the kids loose at the wet-and-wild **Curious George Goes to Town.** After your kids have run down their batteries a bit, you can rest your feet at an afternoon showing of **Animal Planet Live!** before heading back to Production Central to blast off on **Jimmy Neutron's Nicktoon Blast.**

A Suggested Itinerary for Older Children, Teens & Adults

A single day is usually sufficient to see the park if you arrive early and keep a fairly brisk pace. Skip the city sidewalks of the main gate and **Terminator 2: 3-D Battle Across Time** until later. Go to the right and tackle **Men in Black Alien Attack** and **Back to the Future . . . The Ride.** Then make a counterclockwise loop, catch **Fear Factor Live,** visit **Jaws, Earthquake—The Big One, Revenge of the Mummy,** and **Twister . . . Ride It Out.** Break for lunch at some point in the midst of that quartet, then tackle the 'toons at **Jimmy Neutron's Nicktoon Blast** and the **Shrek 4-D** adventure, before catching the fun in **Terminator 2: 3-D Battle Across Time.**

A second day lets you revisit some of your favorites or see those you missed. With the pressure to hit all the major rides lessened, you can take on the park in a more leisurely fashion ensuring a more enjoyable experience. You can also visit the **Universal Horror Make-up Show** and **Beetlejuice's Rock 'n Roll Graveyard Revue.**

SERVICES & FACILITIES IN UNIVERSAL STUDIOS FLORIDA

ATMs   Machines accepting cards from banks using the Cirrus, Honor, and PLUS systems are to the right of the main entrance (outside and inside the park) and in San Francisco/Amity near Lombard's Landing restaurant.

Baby Care   Changing tables are in men's and women's restrooms; there are nursing facilities at Family Services, just inside the main entrance and to the right. A very limited amount of baby supplies are sold at select stores on the premises, so come prepared if you have little ones.

Cameras & Film   Film and disposable cameras are available at the On Location shop in the Front Lot, just inside the main entrance. One-hour photo developing is available, though we don't recommend paying park prices.

Car Assistance   Battery jumps are provided. If you need assistance with your car, raise the hood and use the call boxes located throughout the garage to call for security.

First Aid   The First Aid Center is located between New York and San Francisco, next to Louie's Italian Restaurant on Canal Street. There's also one just inside the main entrance next to Guest Services.

Lockers   Lockers are across from Guest Services near the main entrance and cost $8 and $10 a day, plus a $2 refundable deposit.

Lost Children   If you lose a child, go to Guest Services near the main entrance or contact any park employee for assistance. *Children under 7 should wear name-tags inside their clothing.*

Pet Care   A kennel is available ($10 a day) near the newest parking lot. Ask the parking attendant for directions upon entering the toll plaza. Overnight boarding is not permitted. Owners are responsible for walking and feeding their animals during their stay.

Stroller Rental   Strollers can be rented in Amity and at Guest Services just inside the entrance to the right. The cost (including tax) is $10 for a single, $16 for a double.

Wheelchair Rental   Regular wheelchairs can be rented for $12 in Amity and at Guest Services just inside the main gate. Electric wheelchairs are $40. Both require a $50 deposit and a signed rental contract.

MAJOR ATTRACTIONS AT UNIVERSAL STUDIOS FLORIDA

Rides and attractions use cutting-edge technology, including an OMNIMAX 70mm film projected on seven-story screens and a magnetic propulsion system to create terrific special effects. While waiting in line, you'll be entertained by excellent preshows—far better than those at the Disney parks (some are as entertaining as the attractions themselves). Universal, as a whole, takes itself less seriously than the Mouse, and the atmosphere is peppered by subtle reminders that in the competitive theme-park industry, it's really not such a small world after all.

Frommer's Rates the Rides

As we do for the Disney parks in chapter 6, "Exploring Walt Disney World," we're using a grading system to score the Universal Orlando and SeaWorld rides in this chapter. (We'll return to the star-rating system toward the end of the chapter, when we explore some of Orlando's smaller attractions.) Most of the grades below are *A*s, *B*s, and *C*s. That's because the major parks' designers have done a pretty good job on the attractions. But you'll also find a few *D*s for Duds. Here's what the Frommer's ratings mean:

A+ =	Your trip wouldn't be complete without it.
A =	Put it at the top of your "to-do" list.
B+ =	Make a real effort to see or do it.
B =	It's fun but not a "must see."
C+ =	A nice diversion; see it if you have time.
C =	Go if it appeals to you but not if there's a wait.
D =	Don't waste your time.

Animal Planet Live!

Frommer's Rating: B+ for young kids and parents
Recommended Ages: All ages

Get a behind-the-scenes look at the Animal Planet television network through a multimedia show that combines video clips and live action. The stars might include Meesha the fox, Sniffles the raccoon, and Spooner the Australian shepherd.

Back to the Future . . . The Ride

Frommer's Rating: A+
Recommended Ages: 8–adult

Blast through the space-time continuum in 1 of 24 flight simulators built to look like the movie's famous DeLorean. Along the way, you'll dive into blazing volcanic tunnels, collide with Ice Age glaciers, thunder through caves and canyons, and briefly get swallowed by a dinosaur in an eye-crossing multisensory adventure. You twist, you turn, you dip, you dive—all the while feeling like you're really flying. Sit in one of the car's back seats to avoid ruining the illusion (in the front seat you can lean forward and see your neighbors careening hydraulically in the next bay). This is similar to *but much more intense than* the Body Wars ride at Epcot (p. 222). It's bumpy and might not be a good idea if you're prone to dizziness or motion sickness. *Note:* Heed the health warnings displayed at the ride, which has a 40-inch height minimum. Also, Universal recommends that expectant mothers skip this ride.

Beetlejuice's Rock 'n Roll Graveyard Revue

Frommer's Rating: C+ for classic rock fans, C for others
Recommended Ages: 10–adult

A few years back, Universal added some new steps and tunes to this rock musical that stars Dracula, Wolfman, the Phantom of the Opera, Frankenstein and his bride, and Beetlejuice. The fun includes pyrotechnic special effects, some adult jokes, and MTV-style choreography. It's loud and lively enough to scare some small children and frazzle some older adults. It carries Universal's PG-13 rating, meaning it may not be suitable for preteens.

A Day in the Park with Barney

Frommer's Rating: A+ for tiny tots and parents, D for almost everyone else
Recommended Ages: 2–6

Set in a parklike theater-in-the-round, this 25-minute musical stars the Purple One, Baby Bop, and BJ. It uses song, dance, and interactive play to entertain the kids. This could be the highlight of the day for preschoolers (parents can console themselves with their kids' happiness). The playground adjacent to the theater has chimes to ring, treehouses to explore, and lots to intrigue wee ones. The theater is air-conditioned, so if you must endure this one, you'll at least be comfortable.

Earthquake—The Big One

Frommer's Rating: A
Recommended Ages: 6–adult

You climb on a BART train in San Francisco for a peaceful subway ride, but just as you pull into the Embarcadero Station, there's an earthquake—a big one, 8.3 on the Richter scale! As you sit helplessly trapped, slabs of concrete collapse around you, a propane truck bursts into flames, a runaway train hurtles your way, and the station floods (65,000 gal. of water cascade down the steps). *Note:* Universal says expectant moms should skip this one.

Tips **Quiet on the Set!**

The latest addition to USF's spectacular shows is **Fear Factor Live.** Having debuted in the spring of 2005, it's the first reality show (based on NBC's blockbuster hit *Fear Factor*) to become a theme park attraction. Audience members perform stunts that test their courage, strength, and at times their stomach—similar to the stuff seen on the hit TV show, but live in Orlando. You can catch the show in the venue set between Jaws and Men in Black, where the park's Wild Wild West Stunt Show once reigned supreme.

E.T. Adventure

Frommer's Rating: B for preteens and their families
Recommended Ages: All ages

You'll soar with E.T. on a mission to save his ailing planet, through the forest and into space aboard a bicycle. Along the way, you'll also meet some of the characters created by Steven Spielberg for the ride, including Botanicus, Tickli Moot Moot, Horn Flowers, and Tympani Tremblies. This family favorite is definitely a charmer. If there is a knock, it's that there are two waiting areas—inside and outside. And wait you will.

Jaws

Frommer's Rating: B+
Recommended Ages: 6–adult

As your boat heads into the 7-acre, 5-million-gallon lagoon, a dorsal fin appears on the surface. Then, what goes with the fin—a 3-ton, 32-foot, mechanical great white shark—tries to sink its urethane teeth into your hide (or at least your boat's). A 30-foot wall of flame that surrounds the vessel truly causes you to feel the heat in this $45-million attraction. We won't tell you exactly how it ends, but in spite of a captain who can't hit the broad side of a dock with his grenade launcher, some lucky Orlando restaurant will be serving blackened shark tonight. (*Tip:* The effects of this ride are far more spectacular after dark.) *Note:* While it lacks a height requirement, the shark may be too intense for some kids younger than 6, and Universal recommends that expectant mothers avoid it.

Jimmy Neutron's Nicktoon Blast

Frommer's Rating: A
Recommended Ages: 6–adult

Buckle up for one of the park's latest additions. In this one, you climb aboard Jimmy's Rocket Pod, which hurtles you through hyperspace thanks to a motion simulator, sophisticated computer graphics, state-of-the-art ride technology, animation, and programmable motion-based seats. Your task: Defeat the evil Yokians—egg-shaped aliens bent on taking over our world if you lose. The attraction also features Jimmy's robot dog, Goddard; his nemesis, Cindy Vortex; and popular characters from several other cartoons, including *SpongeBob SquarePants, Rugrats, Wild Thornberrys,* and *Fairly Odd Parents. Note:* Strange for a ride aimed at the kid set, this attraction carries a 40-inch height requirement.

Men in Black Alien Attack

Frommer's Rating: A+
Recommended Ages: 6–adult

Armageddon may be upon us unless you and your mates fly to the rescue and destroy the alien menace. Once on board your six-passenger cruiser, you'll buzz the streets of New York, using your "zapper" to splatter up to 120 bug-eyed targets. You have to contend with return fire and distractions such as light, noise, and clouds of liquid nitrogen (aka fog), any of which can spin you out of control. Your laser tag–style gun fires infrared bullets. Earn a bonus by hitting Frank the Pug (to the right, just past the alien shipwreck). The 4-minute ride relies on 360-degree spins rather than speed for its thrill factor. At the conclusion, you're swallowed by a giant roach (it's 30 ft. tall with 8-ft. fangs and 20-ft. claws) that explodes, spraying you with bug guts—okay, it's just warm water—as you blast your way to safety and into the pest-control hall of fame—maybe. When you exit, Will Smith rates you anywhere from galaxy defender to bug bait. (There are 38 possible scores; those assigned to less than full cars suffer the scoring consequences.) Guests must be at least 42 inches tall to climb aboard this $70-million ride.

Note: Men in Black often has a *much* shorter line for single riders. Even if you're not alone but are willing to be split up, get in this line and hop right on a vehicle that has less than six passengers.

Revenge of the Mummy
Frommer's Ratings: A+
Recommended Ages: 10 and up
Ten years in the making, the $40-million Revenge of the Mummy made its debut in 2004. The indoor roller coaster uses a sophisticated propulsion system to hurtle riders through the shadowy, darkened tombs of ancient Egypt (all spectacularly re-created) while trying to escape the curse of the Mummy. The sound system (enhanced by 200 speakers and surround-sound technology in the coaster cars) will spook you, too. Highly advanced robotics are used to bring to life some pretty scary-looking skeletal warriors, one of whom jumps aboard your car; even Imhotep himself makes an appearance. Overhead flames, fireballs, and creepy creatures all combine with surprising twists, turns, stops, and starts to make for a thrill like no other in the park. And just when you think it's over . . . well, we have to leave some surprises for you.

Shrek 4-D
Frommer's Rating: B+
Recommended Ages: All ages
Universal Studios' other (relatively) new ride is a 20-minute show that can be seen, heard, felt, and smelled thanks to film, motion simulators, OgreVision glasses, and other special effects, such as water spritzers. The attraction picks up where the movie left off—allowing you to join Shrek and Princess Fiona on their honeymoon (at least the G-rated portions of it). After one of the most amusing preshows in the park (featuring a ghostly Lord Farquaad, the Three Little Pigs, Pinocchio, and the Magic Mirror), you're settled into specially designed seats in the main auditorium and then transported to the fairy-tale realm of Duloc as the screen comes alive. The theater's seats are pneumatic air-propulsion nodules that are capable of turning and tilting (though not dramatically). Again, if your kids don't like touchy feely special effects, they may get upset at certain points while experiencing this attraction.

Terminator 2: 3-D Battle Across Time
Frommer's Rating: A
Recommended Ages: 10–adult
This is billed as "the quintessential sight and sound experience for the 21st century!" The same director who made the movie, Jim Cameron, supervised this $60-million

production. After a slow start, it builds into an impressive experience featuring the Governator (on film), along with other original cast members. It combines 70mm 3-D film (utilizing three 23×50-ft. screens) with thrilling technical effects and live stage action that includes a custom-built Harley Davidson "Fat Boy" and six 8-foot-tall cyberbots. *Note:* The crisp 3-D effects are among the best in any Orlando park, but Universal has given this show a PG-13 rating, meaning the violence and loud noise may be too intense for preteens. That may be a little too cautious, but some kids under 10 may be frightened.

Twister . . . Ride It Out
Frommer's Rating: B+
Recommended Ages: 10–adult
Visitors from the twister-prone Midwest may find this re-creation a little too close to the real thing. An ominous funnel cloud, five stories tall, is created by swirling 2 million cubic feet of air per minute (that's enough to fill four full-size blimps), and the sound of a freight train fills the theater at rock-concert level as cars, trucks, and a cow fly about while the audience stands just 20 feet away. It's the windy version of *Earthquake* and packs quite a wallop. Crowds have been known to applaud when it's over. *Note:* This show, too, comes with a PG-13 rating. Its loudness and intensity certainly can be too much for children under 8.

Woody Woodpecker's Nuthouse Coaster (Kids)
Frommer's Rating: A+ for kids and parents, B+ for others
Recommended Ages: 5–adult
This is the top attraction in Woody Woodpecker's KidZone, an 8-acre concession Universal Studios made a while back after being criticized for having too little for young visitors. This ride is a kiddie coaster that will thrill some moms and dads, too. While only 30 feet at its peak, it offers quick, spiraling turns while you sit in a miniature steam train. The ride lasts only 55 seconds and waits can be 30 minutes or more, but few kids will want to miss it. It's very much like the Barnstormer at Goofy's Wiseacre Farm in the Magic Kingdom (p. 206). *Note:* Its height minimum is 36 inches.

ADDITIONAL ATTRACTIONS
The somewhat corny **Universal Horror Make-Up Show** gives behind-the-scene looks at what goes into (and oozes out of) some of Hollywood's most frightening monsters (PG-13, shows from 11am). **Lucy, A Tribute** is a remembrance of America's queen of comedy, and the **Blues Brothers** launch their foot-stomping revue several times a day on Delancey Street.

Back at Woody Woodpecker's KidZone, **Fievel's Playland** is a wet, western-themed playground with a house to climb and a water slide for small fry. **Curious George Goes to Town** is filled with whimsical watery fun, from fountains to ball-shooting cannons—bring a change of clothes.

SHOPPING AT UNIVERSAL STUDIOS FLORIDA
Every major attraction has a theme store attached, many of them selling some rather unique merchandise. Although the prices are high when you consider you're just buying a souvenir, the **Hard Rock Cafe** shop in adjacent CityWalk is extremely popular and has a small but diverse selection of Hard Rock everything (including memorabilia with astronomical sticker prices). For just about everything else a la Universal, the **Universal Studios Store** carries a rather decent selection of toys, T-shirts, and souvenirs.

More than two dozen other shops in the park sell collectibles. Be warned, though, that unlike Walt Disney World, where Mickey is everywhere, Universal's shops are specific to individual attractions. If you see something you like, buy it; you probably won't find it in another store. If you did forget to pick something up, there's a shop-by-phone service—call ✆ **407/224-5800,** describe the item and where you think you saw it, and the likelihood is they'll be able to help you out. There is a Universal store at Orlando International Airport, but it mainly carries the usual souvenirs.

Note: Universal has a service similar to Disney's in which you can have your purchases delivered to the Universal Studios Store at the front of the park. Allow 3 hours.

GREAT BUYS AT UNIVERSAL STUDIOS FLORIDA

Here's a sampling of the more unusual gifts available at some of the Universal stores. Of course, in addition to these options, you can find the standard tourist fare with a staggering array of mugs, key chains, T-shirts, and the like. We've tried to include things you wouldn't find (or consider buying) anywhere else.

- **Back to the Future—The Store**   Real fans of the movie series will find lots of intriguing stuff here, but one of the more interesting items is a miniature version of a DeLorean.
- **E.T.'s Toy Closet and Photo Spot**   This is the place for plush stuffed animals including a replica of the alien namesake.
- **MIB Gear**   If you find yourself in need of a ray gun or alien blaster, this is the place to buy everything out of this world.
- **Quint's Surf Shack**   This is the place to go for a different kind of T-shirt. Tropical colors with subtle Universal logos and island wear are the thing here.

Universal Cuisine

The best restaurants here are just outside the main gates at CityWalk, Universal's restaurant and nightclub venue. But there are more than a dozen places to eat inside the park. Here are our favorites:

Best Sit-Down Meal: Lombard's Seafood Grille has a hearty fried clam basket, as well as lobster, fish, steak, pasta, and burgers ($10–$35). It's located across from Earthquake—The Big One.

Best Counter Service: Universal Studio's Classic Monster Cafe serves salads, pizza, pasta, and rotisserie chicken and ribs ($7–$12). It's off 7th Avenue near the Shrek 4-D.

Best Place for Hungry Families: Similar to a mall food court, the **International Food and Film Festival** offers a variety of food in one location. With options ranging from stir-fry to chicken Parmesan, it's a place where a family can split up and still eat under one roof. There are kids' meals for under $6 at most locations. The food is far from gourmet but a cut above regular fast food ($7–$10). It's located near the back of Animal Planet Live! and the entrance to Back to the Future . . . The Ride.

Best Snack: The floats ($3–$6) at **Brody's Ice Cream Shoppe** are just the thing to refresh you on a hot summer afternoon. Brody's is located near Jaws.

- **Silver Screen Collectibles**   Fans of *I Love Lucy* will adore the small variety of collectible dolls. There's also a Betty Boop line. For an interesting, practical, and inexpensive little something to take home, check out the Woody Woodpecker back-scratcher.
- **Universal Studios Store**   This store, near the entrance, sells just about everything when it comes to Universal apparel, and there are plenty of toys and trinkets as well.

2 Islands of Adventure

Universal's second theme park opened in 1999 with a vibrantly colored, cleverly themed collection of fast and sometimes furious rides. At 110 acres, it's the same size as its big brother, Universal Studios Florida, but it seems larger and it's definitely *the* Orlando park for thrill-ride junkies. Roller coasters roar above pedestrian walkways, and water rides slice through the park. The trade-off: Far fewer shows.

Expect total immersion in the park's various "island" sights, sounds, and surroundings. From the wobbly angles and Day-Glo colors in **Seuss Landing** to the lush foliage of **Jurassic Park,** Universal has done an amazing job of differentiating the various sections of this $1-billion park (unlike Universal Studios Florida, where you ease into the next area and all of a sudden you realize that you're in San Francisco, not New York any more). It's also done an outstanding job of differentiating Islands from Disney or any other Orlando park. The closest competitor (and that's a stretch) in Florida is Busch Gardens in Tampa, but this park clearly has the edge on the ride front—and most definitely in the atmosphere department.

The adventure is spread across six very different islands: the **Port of Entry,** a pass-through zone themed to resemble an exotic open-air bazaar and lined with a collection of shops and restaurants, and five themed islands—**Seuss Landing, The Lost Continent, Jurassic Park, Toon Lagoon,** and **Marvel Super Hero Island.** The park offers a concentration of thrill rides and coasters, but there are plenty of places to play for young kids, too.

ESSENTIALS

GETTING TO UNIVERSAL BY CAR   Universal Orlando is a half-mile north of I-4 Exit 75B, Kirkman Road/Highway 435. There may be construction in the area, so follow the signs directing you to the park.

PARKING   If you park in the multilevel garage, make a note of the row and theme in your area to help you find your car later. Parking costs $9 for cars, light trucks, and vans. Valet parking is available for $16.

TICKET PRICES   A **1-day ticket** costs $63 (plus 6.5% sales tax) for adults, $52 for children 3 to 9. A **2-day/two-park pass** is $107.95 for all ages at the gate, $99.95 online at **www.universalorlando.com**. Deals at press time included 3 days free and free kid's tickets (one child ages 3–9 gets in free per paying adult) with the purchase of a 2-day/two-park pass. All multiday passes let you move between Universal Studios Florida and Islands of Adventure. *Multiday passes also give you free access to the City-Walk clubs at night.* Because the parks are within walking distance of each other, you won't lose much time jockeying back and forth, unlike the situation at Disney. Nevertheless, it's a long walk for tykes and people with limited mobility, so consider a stroller or wheelchair.

Tips **Some Practical Advice for Island Adventurers**

1. **The Shorter They Are . . .**   Thirteen of the 14 major rides at Islands of Adventure have height restrictions. Dueling Dragons and the Incredible Hulk Coaster, for instance, deny access to anyone under 54 inches. For those who want to ride but come with kids, there's a baby or child swap at all of the major attractions, allowing one parent to ride while the other watches the tykes. But sitting in a waiting room isn't much fun for the little ones. So take your child's height into consideration before coming to the park or at least some of the islands. Think about splitting up for a while, then meeting up again a bit later.

2. **Cruising the Islands**   If you hauled your stroller with you on your vacation, bring it with you to the park. It's a very long walk from your car, through the massive parking garage and the nighttime entertainment district, CityWalk, before you get to the fun. (Universal, however, does a good job of disguising just how long it is with all of the covered walkways near the parking area, and the sights and sounds of CityWalk are entertaining in their own right.) Carrying a young child and the accompanying paraphernalia, even with a series of moving sidewalks, can make the long trek seem even longer—especially at the end of the day.

3. **The Faint of Heart**   Even if you don't have children, make sure you consider all of the ride restrictions. Expectant mothers; guests prone to motion sickness; and those with heart, neck, or back trouble will be discouraged—with good reason—from riding most primo attractions. There's still plenty to see and do, but without the roller coasters, Islands of Adventure is far less adventurous.

4. **Beat the Heat**   Some rides require that you wait outside without any cover to protect you from the sizzling Florida sun, so bring some bottled water (freeze it the night before) with you for the long waits (a 50¢ freeworld bottle costs $2.50 or more if you buy it here) or take a sip or two from the fountains placed in the waiting areas. Also, beer, wine, and liquor are more available at the Universal parks than the Disney ones, but booze, roller coasters, and hot weather can make for a messy mix.

5. **Cash in on Your Card**   You can save 10% on your purchases at any gift shop or on a meal at Islands of Adventure by showing your AAA (American Automobile Association) card. This discount isn't available at food or merchandise carts. And tobacco, candy, film, collectibles, and sundry items aren't included.

See the beginning of this chapter for information on the **FlexTicket,** which provides multiday admission to Universal Studios Florida, Islands of Adventure, SeaWorld, and Wet 'n Wild.

For details on VIP tours at Islands of Adventure, see "Ticket Prices" in the "Universal Studios Florida" section.

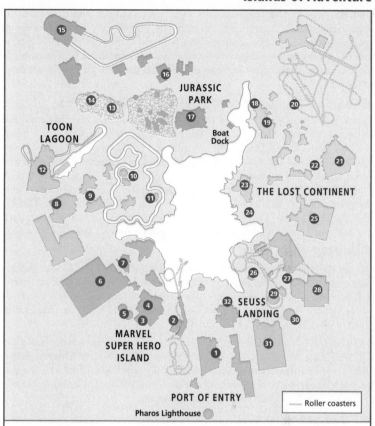

JURASSIC
PARK

Boat
Dock

TOON
LAGOON

THE LOST CONTINENT

SEUSS
LANDING

MARVEL
SUPER HERO
ISLAND

PORT OF ENTRY

Pharos Lighthouse

······ Roller coasters

PORT OF ENTRY
Confisco Grille **32**
Islands of Adventure
  Trading Company **1**

**MARVEL SUPER HERO
ISLAND**
The Amazing Adventures
  of Spider-Man **6**
Café 4 **4**
Captain America's Diner **7**
Doctor Doom's Fearfall **5**
Incredible Hulk Coaster **2**
Storm Force Accelatron **3**

TOON LAGOON
Comic Strip Café **8**
Dudley Do-Right's
  Ripsaw Falls **12**

Kings Row &
  Comic Strip Lane **9**
Me Ship, The Olive **11**
Popeye & Bluto's
  Bilge-Rat Barges **10**

JURASSIC PARK
Camp Jurassic **14**
Jurassic Park
  Discovery Center **17**
Jurassic Park
  River Adventure **15**
Pteranodon Flyers **13**
Thunder Falls Terrace **16**

THE LOST CONTINENT
Dueling Dragons **20**
Eighth Voyage
  of Sindbad **21**

Enchanted Oak Tavern
  (and Alchemy Bar) **19**
Fire-Eater's Grill **24**
Flying Unicorn **18**
Mystic Fountain **22**
Mythos **23**
Poseidon's Fury **25**

SEUSS LANDING
Caro-Seuss-El **29**
The Cat in the Hat **31**
Circus McGurkus
  Cafe Stoo-pendous **28**
Green Eggs and Ham
  Cafe **26**
If I Ran the Zoo **27**
One Fish, Two Fish,
  Red Fish, Blue Fish **30**

HOURS   The park is open 365 days a year, generally from 9am to 6pm, though often later, especially in summer and around holidays, when it's frequently open until 9pm, sometimes later. Also, during Mardi Gras and Halloween Horror Nights, the park closes around 5pm, reopens at 7pm (with a new admission), and remains open until at least midnight. The best bet is to call before you go so that you're not caught by surprise.

INFORMATION FOR VISITORS WITH SPECIAL NEEDS

Guests with disabilities should go to **Guest Services,** located just inside the main entrance, for a *Rider's Guide for Rider Safety & Guests with Disabilities,* a Telecommunications Device for the Deaf (TDD), or other special assistance. You can rent a standard wheelchair for $12 or an electric one for $40 (both require a $50 deposit and a signed rental contract). You can reserve them a week or more in advance by calling ✆ **407/224-6350.** You can arrange for sign language interpreting services at no charge by calling ✆ **888/519-4899** (toll-free TDD), 407/224-4414 (local TDD), or 407/224-5929 (voice). Make arrangements for an appointment with an interpreter 1 to 2 weeks in advance. Check **www.universalorlando.com** for more information.

PLANNING YOUR VISIT

You can get information before you leave by calling ✆ **407/224-4233,** or 407/363-8000. Ask for information about travel packages, as well as theme-park information and discounts (Universal sometimes offers additional days free or at a deeply discounted price). You can also write to Guest Services, 1000 Universal Studios Plaza, Orlando, FL 32819-7601.

ONLINE   Find information about Universal at **www.universalorlando.com.** Orlando's daily newspaper, the *Orlando Sentinel,* also produces Orlando Sentinel Online at **www.orlandosentinel.com**. Additionally, there's a lot of information about the parks, hotels, restaurants, and more at the Orlando/Orange County Convention & Visitors Bureau's website, **www.orlandoinfo.com**.

THE BEST DAYS TO VISIT

Like Universal Studios Florida, it's best to visit Islands near the end of the week, on a Thursday or Friday. The pace is somewhat fast Monday to Wednesday, with the heaviest crowds on weekends and during summer and holidays.

SERVICES & FACILITIES AT ISLANDS OF ADVENTURE

ATMs   Machines accepting cards from banks using the Cirrus, Honor, and PLUS systems are located outside and to the right of the main entrance and in the Lost Continent near the bridge to Jurassic Park.

Baby Care   There are baby-swap stations at all of the major attractions. This allows one parent to wait while the other rides. Nursing facilities are located at Family Services near the First Aid Station in the Port of Entry. Look for the FAMILY SERVICES sign. Changing tables are available in both the men's and women's restrooms throughout the park. Diapers and baby food are not sold in the park, so be sure to come prepared with a supply of diapers, food, and other necessities.

Cameras & Film   Film and disposable cameras are available at De Foto's Expedition Photography, to the right just inside the main entrance.

Car Assistance   Battery jumps are provided. If you need assistance with your car, raise the hood and use the call boxes located throughout the garage to call for security.

First Aid   There's one just inside and to the right of the main entrance and another in the Lost Continent, across from Oasis Coolers.

Lockers   Lockers are across from Guest Services near the main entrance and cost $8 a day (no oversize lockers here), plus a $2 refundable deposit. There are also lockers near the Incredible Hulk Coaster in Marvel Super Hero Island, the Jurassic Park River Adventure in Jurassic Park, and Dueling Dragons in the Lost Continent. The lockers at Dueling Dragons and the Incredible Hulk Coaster are free for the first 45 minutes. Thereafter, and at the Jurassic Park River Adventure, they're $2 per hour to a maximum of $14 per day. You're not supposed to—and shouldn't—take things on these rides, so put them in a locker or give them to a nonrider.

Lost Children   If you lose a child, go to Guest Services near the main entrance or go to the first park employee you see. *Children under 7 should wear name-tags inside their clothing.*

Pet Care   You can board your small animals at the shelter in the parking garages for $10 a day (no overnight stays), but you'll have to feed and walk them. Ask the attendant where you pay for parking to direct you to the kennel.

Ride Restrictions   Many of the park's attractions have minimum height requirements (see the listings that follow). Universal also recommends that expectant mothers steer clear of some rides (also noted in the listings).

Stroller Rental   Look to your left as you enter through the turnstiles. The cost (including tax) is $10 for a single, $16 for a double.

Wheelchair Rental   Regular wheelchairs can be rented for $12 in the center concourse of the parking garage or to your left as you enter the turnstiles of the main entrance. Electric wheelchairs are $40. Both require a $50 deposit and a rental contract.

SUGGESTED ITINERARIES
For Children & Families

If you have kids 8 and under, enter and go to the right to **Seuss Landing,** an island where everything is geared to the young and young at heart. You'll easily spend the morning or longer exploring real-life interpretations of the wacky, colorful world of Dr. Seuss. (The wild colors make for some good photographs.) Be sure to ride **The Cat in the Hat; One Fish, Two Fish, Red Fish, Blue Fish;** and **Caro-Seuss-El.** After all that waiting in line, let the little ones burn some energy playing in **If I Ran the Zoo.** Grab lunch at the **Green Eggs and Ham Café** or **Circus McGurkus Café Stoo-pendous** if you prefer to eat indoors. Next, head to the **Lost Continent** to ride the **Flying Unicorn** (36-in. height minimum) and talk to the **Mystic Fountain,** then let them play in **Camp Jurassic** (many could stay here for hours if you let them) or watch a "hatching" at the **Discovery Center** in **Jurassic Park.** They can have some more interactive fun in **Toon Lagoon** aboard **Me Ship, The Olive,** and grab autographs at the **King's Row and Comic Strip Lane.** Those 40 inches or taller—and a bit braver—can end the day in **Marvel Super Hero Island** by riding the **Amazing Adventures of Spider-Man.**

For Teens & Adults

Head left from Port of Entry to **Marvel Super Hero Island** and ride the **Incredible Hulk Coaster, The Amazing Adventures of Spider-Man,** and **Doctor Doom's Fearfall.** (If you arrive early, the line will be short for your first choice, but you'll have to wait—unless you have an Express Plus Pass for the others.) There should be time to squeeze in **Dudley Do-Right's Ripsaw Falls** in **Toon Lagoon** before you break for lunch (a full stomach isn't recommended) at **Comic Strip Café** or **Blondie's: Home of the Dagwood.** Now that you're fully refueled, ride **Popeye & Bluto's Bilge-Rat Barges,** then move to **Jurassic Park,** where you can ride **Jurassic Park River Adventure** and visit the **Discovery Center.** End your day in the **Lost Continent,** where you can catch the show in **Poseidon's Fury,** then test your courage aboard **Dueling Dragons.**

PORT OF ENTRY

This marketplace of sorts is filled with six shops and four different places to grab a bite, as well as many of the park's more mundane but necessary guest services (mostly near the very front of the Port). If you plan to save shopping for the end of the day, return to **Islands of Adventure Trading Company,** which offers a variety of merchandise linked to attractions throughout the park—from Jurassic T-shirts to stuffed Cat in the Hat dolls.

SEUSS LANDING

This 10-acre island, inspired by the works of the late Theodore Seuss Geisel, is awash in Day-Glo colors, whimsical architecture, and curved trees (the latter were downed and bent by Hurricane Andrew before the park acquired them). Needless to say, the main attractions here are aimed at the younger set, though anyone who loved the good Doctor as a child will enjoy some nostalgic fun on these rides. And those who aren't familiar with his work will enjoy the visuals—Seussian art is like Dalí for kids.

Caro-Seuss-El
Frommer's Rating: A+ for young kids, parents, and carousel lovers
Recommended Ages: All ages
Forget tradition. This not-so-average carousel gives you a chance to ride seven whimsical characters of Dr. Seuss (a total of 54 mounts), including cowfish, elephant birds, and mulligatawnies. They move up and down as well as in and out. Their eyes blink and heads bob as you twirl through the riot of color surrounding the ride. *Note:* A special ride platform lets guests in wheelchairs experience the up-and-down motion of the ride, making this a great stop for visitors with disabilities.

The Cat in the Hat
Frommer's Rating: A for the under 10 set, C+ for teens and adults
Recommended Ages: All ages
Any Seuss fan will recognize the giant candy-striped hat looming over the entrance to this ride and probably the chaotic journey. Comparable to, but spunkier than, It's a Small World at Magic Kingdom (p. 204), The Cat in the Hat is among the signature children's experiences at Islands of Adventure. Love or hate the idea, *do it* and earn your stripes. Your couch travels through 18 scenes retelling *The Cat in the Hat*'s tale of a day gone very much awry. You, meanwhile, spin about and meet Thing 1 and Thing 2 in addition to other characters. The highlight is a revolving 24-foot tunnel

---

Tips Finding Your Way

Other-than-English park maps are available at Guest Services in the Port of Entry in French, German, Japanese, Portuguese, and Spanish.

Tips **A Late Debut**

After 7 years of klonking, bonking, jerking, and berking, the minimonorail that hangs high over Seuss Landing (and has gone rider-less until now) is once again running—but this time with wee ones finally allowed aboard. Universal tweaked its design and twisted its name (not yet released at press time), and now guests can actually ride it.

---

that alters your perceptions and leaves your head with a feeling oddly reminiscent of a hangover. *Note:* Pop-up characters may be scary for riders under 5, and expectant moms are discouraged from riding The Cat.

If I Ran the Zoo *Kids*
Frommer's Rating: A for the very young
Recommended Ages: 2–6
This 19-station interactive play land features flying water snakes and a chance to tickle the toes of a Seussian animal. Kids can also spin wheels, explore caves, fire water cannons, climb, slide, and otherwise burn off some excited energy.

One Fish, Two Fish, Red Fish, Blue Fish
Frommer's Rating: B+ for kids and parents
Recommended Ages: 2–7
This kiddie charmer is similar to the Dumbo and Magic Carpets rides at Magic Kingdom (including the ridiculously long line, though this ride's waiting area is covered), although this one has a few added features. Your controls allow you to move your funky fish up or down 15 feet as you spin around on an arm attached to a hub. All the while, a song belts out rhyming flight instructions. Watch out for "squirt posts," which spray unsuspecting riders who don't follow the rhyme. Actually, even the most careful driver is likely to get wet.

MARVEL SUPER HERO ISLAND
Thrill junkies love the twisting, turning, stomach-churning rides on this island filled with building-tall murals of Marvel Super Heroes. Fans can **Meet the Marvel Super Heroes** in front of The Amazing Adventures of Spider-Man (check your adventure map, handed out when you enter, or grab a copy at Guest Services, for times). And the munch crowd can dig into sandwiches and burgers at **Captain America's Diner** (in the $7–$9 range) and **Café 4** for pizza, pasta, and sandwiches (around $4–$20, most under $9).

The Amazing Adventures of Spider-Man *Finds*
Frommer's Rating: A+
Recommended Ages: 8–adult
The original Web Master stars in this exceptional show/ride (arguably, the best in town), which features 3-D action and special effects. The story line: You're on a tour of the *Daily Bugle* when—yikes!—something goes horribly wrong. Peter Parker suddenly encounters evil villains and becomes Spider-Man. This high-tech ride isn't stationary like the Back to the Future ride at Universal Studios Florida (p. 266). Cars twist and spin, plunge and soar through a comic-book universe. Passengers wearing 3-D glasses squeal as computer-generated objects fly at their 12-person cars. There's a

simulated 400-foot drop that feels an awful lot like the real thing. If you want the biggest thrills, try to get a seat in the front row of your vehicle. *Note:* Expectant mothers or those with heart, neck, or back problems shouldn't ride. There's a 40-inch height minimum.

Tip: Waits can be 45 minutes or longer even on an off day. Unless you have an Express Plus Pass, heading to the single-rider line is the only way to drastically reduce your waiting time. So if it's an option on the day you're here and your party doesn't mind splitting up, take advantage of it.

Doctor Doom's Fearfall
Frommer's Rating: C+
Recommended Ages: 8–adult

Look! Up in the sky! It's a bird, it's a plane . . . uh, it's you falling 150 feet, if you're courageous enough to climb aboard this towering metal skeleton. The screams that can be heard at the ride's entrance add to the anticipation of a big plunge followed by smaller ones. The plot? You're touring a lab when—are you sensing a recurring theme here?—something goes wrong as Doctor Doom tries to cure you of fear. You're fired to the top, with feet dangling, and dropped in intervals, feet first, leaving your stomach at several levels. The thrills and the atmosphere aren't nearly as good as those of the Tower of Terror (p. 238), but it's still frightful (and you do get a neat view of the entire park). *Note:* Expectant mothers or those with heart, neck, or back problems shouldn't ride. Minimum height is 52 inches.

Incredible Hulk Coaster *Finds*
Frommer's Rating: A+
Recommended Ages: 10–adult

Bruce Banner is working in his lab when—yes, again—something goes wrong. But this rocking rocket of a ride makes everything oh, so right, except maybe your heartbeat and stomach. From a dark tunnel, you burst into the sunlight, while accelerating from 0 to 40 mph in 2 seconds. While that's only two-thirds the speed of Disney–MGM's Rock 'n' Roller Coaster (p. 237), this is in broad daylight, there's a lot more motion still to come, and you can *see* the asphalt! From there you spin upside down 128 feet from the ground, feel weightless, and careen through the center of the park over the heads of other visitors. Coaster-lovers will be pleased to know that this ride, which lasts 2 minutes and 15 seconds, includes seven inversions and two steep drops. The ride, however, is extremely smooth, making it one of the better coaster experiences for all types of riders. Sunglasses, change, and an occasional set of car keys lie in a mesh net beneath the ride—proof of its motion and the fact that most folks don't heed the warnings to stash their stuff in the nearby lockers (you should). As a nice touch, the 32-passenger metal coaster glows green at night (riders who ignore all the warnings occasionally turn green as well). *Note:* Expectant mothers or those with heart, neck, or back problems shouldn't ride it. Riders must be at least 54 inches tall.

Storm Force Accelatron
Frommer's Rating: C+
Recommended Ages: 4–adult

Despite the exotic name, this ride is little more than a spin-off of the Magic Kingdom's Mad Tea Party (p. 204)—spinning teacups that, in this case, have a 22nd-century design. While aboard, you and the X-Men's superheroine, Storm, try to defeat the evil Magneto by converting human energy into electrical forces. To do that, you need to spin faster and faster. In addition to some upset stomachs, the spiraling creates a thunderstorm of sound and light that gives Storm all the power she needs to blast Magneto into the ever-after (or until the next riders arrive). This ride is sometimes closed during off-peak periods. ***Note:*** Expectant moms are advised not to ride this ride.

TOON LAGOON

More than 150 life-size sculpted cartoon images—characters range from Betty Boop and Flash Gordon to Bullwinkle and Cathy—let you know you've entered an island dedicated to your favorites from the Sunday funnies.

Dudley Do-Right's Ripsaw Falls

Frommer's Rating: A

Recommended Ages: 8–adult

The setting and effects at WDW's Splash Mountain are better, but the adrenaline rush here is higher. The staid red hat of the heroic Dudley can be deceiving: The ride that lies under it has a lot more speed and drop than onlookers suspect. Six-passenger logs (they're pretty uncomfortable, especially if you have long legs) take you around a 400,000-gallon lagoon before launching you into a 75-foot drop at 50 mph. At one point, you're 15 feet below the surface. Though the water is contained on either side of you, you *will* get wet. ***Note:*** Once again, expectant mothers or folks with heart, neck, or back problems should do something else. Riders must be at least 44 inches tall.

Me Ship, The Olive

Frommer's Rating: B+

Recommended Ages: 4–adult

This three-story boat is a family-friendly play land with dozens of interactive activities from bow to stern. Kids can toot whistles, clang bells, or play the organ. Sweet Pea's Playpen is a favorite of younger guests. Kids 6 and up as well as adults will love Cargo Crane, where they can drench riders on Popeye & Bluto's Bilge-Rat Barges (see below). ***Tip:*** The second and third deck of the good ship offer great views and photo ops of the Incredible Hulk Coaster and some of the rest of Islands of Adventure.

Popeye & Bluto's Bilge-Rat Barges

Frommer's Rating: A

Recommended Ages: 6–adult

This is the same kind of ride with the same kind of raft as Kali River Rapids at WDW's Animal Kingdom, but it's a bit faster and bouncier. You'll be squirted by mechanical devices as well as the water cannons fired by guests at Me Ship, The Olive (see above), and the water is *c-c-cold,* a blessing on hot summer days but less so in January. The 12-passenger rafts bump, churn, and dip (14 ft. at one point) along a whitewater course lined with Bluto, Sea Hag, and other villains. You will get *s-s-soaked.*

Fun Fact Score One for the Park

Music at Universal's Islands of Adventure was composed specifically for the theme park, much like a score for a movie. It's the first time such a large-scale musical effort has been mounted for a theme park, and it truly adds to the feeling of total immersion in whatever land you happen to be in at the time.

⌒ Tips **Up, Up & Away**

Strength and fitness folks can get a little extra workout at the small rock-climbing venue ($5 per person) outside the Thunder Falls Terrace restaurant in Jurassic Park. If you or the kids are looking for a more economical and less strenuous option, try walking the elevated trails and climbing the net ladders beneath the Pteranodon Flyers attraction, also in Jurassic Park.

Note: Yes, once again, expectant mothers or people with heart, neck, or back problems shouldn't ride this one. Riders must be at least 42 inches tall.

Kings Row & Comic Strip Lane

Frommer's Rating: C+

Recommended Ages: All ages

Dudley Do-Right, Woody Woodpecker, Popeye and other favorites from the Sunday comics will have you rockin' and rollin' in the streets as they sing and make you laugh during this several-times-a-day show. It's one to skip if you're on a tight schedule, but it's a nice respite from the madness.

JURASSIC PARK

All of the basics and some of the high-tech wizardry from Steven Spielberg's wildly successful films are incorporated in this lushly landscaped tropical locale that includes a replica of the visitor center from the movie. Expect long lines at the River Adventure and pleasant surprises at the Discovery Center.

Camp Jurassic (Kids)

Frommer's Rating: A+ for young children

Recommended Ages: 2–12

This play area, similar in theme but even better than the Boneyard at Animal Kingdom (p. 244), has everything from lava pits with dinosaur bones to a rainforest. Watch out for the spitters that lurk in dark caves. The multilevel play area has plenty of places for kids to crawl, explore, and spend energy. Young kids need close supervision, though. It's easy to get turned around inside the caverns, and some of the areas enhanced with sound effects may be a bit too frightening for the very young. Be prepared for your kids to get soaked—you will be too if you have to retrieve them (very likely).

Jurassic Park Discovery Center

Frommer's Rating: B+

Recommended Ages: All ages

Here's an amusing, educational pit stop that has life-size dinosaur replicas and some interactive games, including a sequencer that pretends to combine your DNA with a dinosaur's. The "Beasaur" exhibit allows you to see and hear as the huge reptiles did. You can play the game show *You Bet Jurassic* (grin) and scan the walls for fossils. The highlight is watching a velociraptor "hatch" in the lab. Because there are a limited number of interactive stations, this can consume a lot of time on busy days. Be sure to enter from the lower level—the view is spectacular and there's an elaborate stone plaza—which is far more impressive than the doors upstairs.

Jurassic Park River Adventure
Frommer's Rating: A
Recommended Ages: 8–adult

A leisurely raft tour along a river is interrupted when some raptors, who could hop aboard your boat at any moment, escape. The ride lets you literally come face-to-face with "breathing" inhabitants of Jurassic Park. At one point, a *Tyrannosaurus rex* decides you look like a tasty morsel, and at another point, spitters launch venomous saliva your way. The only way out: an 85-foot plunge in your log-style life raft. It's steep and quick enough to lift your fanny out of the seat. (When Spielberg rode it, he made them stop the ride and let him out before the plunge.) Expect to get wet. If your stomach can take only one flume ride, this one's a lot more comfortable than Dudley Do-Right (see earlier), and the atmosphere is better. **Note:** Expectant mothers or those with heart, neck, or back problems shouldn't ride. Guests must be at least 42 inches tall.

Pteranodon Flyers (Kids
Frommer's Rating: C+
Recommended Ages: All ages

The 10-foot metal frames and simple seats are flimsy, but this quick spin around Jurassic Park offers a great bird's-eye view. The landing is bumpy and you'll swing side to side throughout, which makes some riders queasy. Unlike the traditional gondolas in the sky rides, on this one your feet hang free from the two-seat skeletal flyer, and there's little but a restraining belt between you and the ground. **Note:** That said, this is a child's ride—single passengers must be between 36 and 56 inches tall; adults can climb aboard *only* when accompanying someone that size. And, because this ride launches only two passengers every 30 to 40 seconds, it can consume an hour of your day, even in the off season. So, although it is nice, pass it up if you're pressed for time.

THE LOST CONTINENT

Although they've mixed their millennia—ancient Greece with a medieval forest—Universal has done a good job creating a foreboding mood in this section of the park, whose entrance is marked by menacing stone griffins.

Dueling Dragons (Finds
Frommer's Rating: A+
Recommended Ages: 10–adult

Maniacal minds created this thrill ride—sending two roller coasters right at each other at high speeds. True coaster crazies will love the intertwined set of leg-dangling racers that climb to 125 feet, invert five times, and three times come within 12 inches of each other as the two dragons battle, and you prove your bravery by tagging along. This coaster sports a tighter track with quick banking turns and sharp twists, making the ride somewhat jerky—far from the smooth and fluid experience of the Hulk. But the roughness may be part of its charm—a couple of thrill junkies (after riding this one for the third time in a day) revealed to us that this is where they head when they

---

Fun Fact Coaster Tidbit

One Dueling Dragon coaster seems to have an obvious advantage over the other. The Fire Dragon can reach speeds up to 60 mph, while the Ice Dragon tops out at only 55 mph.

(Fun Fact **Food for Thought**

Those green eggs at the Green Eggs and Ham Cafe get their color from a variety of spices, not food dye.

---

want the city's ultimate adrenaline rush. For the best ride, try to get one of the two outside seats in each of the eight rows. If you want to get into the front seat (for that extra jolt), there's a special (yes, longer!) line near the loading dock so that daredevils can claim the first car. *Note:* Expectant mothers or those with heart, neck, or back problems shouldn't ride. (Why aren't you surprised?) Riders must be at least 54 inches tall.

Eighth Voyage of Sindbad *(Overrated*
Frommer's Rating: C+
Recommended Ages: 6–adult
The mythical sailor is the star of a stunt demonstration that takes place in a 1,700-seat theater decorated with blue stalagmites and eerie, gloomy shipwrecks. The show has water explosions and dozens of pyrotechnic effects including a 10-foot circle of flames. Younger kids may find some of the characters too scary so a seat in the back may be in order if you have tots in tow. Although it offers a rest for park-weary feet, it doesn't come close to the quality of the Indiana Jones stunt show in Disney–MGM Studios (p. 234).

Flying Unicorn
Frommer's Rating: A for kids and parents
Recommended Ages: 6–adult
The Flying Unicorn is a small roller coaster that travels through a mythical forest on the Lost Continent, next to Dueling Dragons. It's very much like Woody Woodpecker's Nuthouse Coaster (p. 269) and the Barnstormer at Goofy's Wiseacre Farm (p. 206), but this is Universal so expect a bit more. That means a fast corkscrew run that is sure to earn squeals, but probably not at the risk of someone losing their lunch. *Note:* Here's another one expectant moms are warned not to ride. The Unicorn has a 36-inch height minimum.

Mystic Fountain *(Kids*
Frommer's Rating: B+ for kids
Recommended Ages: 3–8
Located just outside Sindbad's theater, this interactive "smart" fountain delights younger guests. It can see and hear, leading to a lot of kibitzing with those who stand before it. But if you want to stay dry, don't get too close when it starts "spouting" its wet wisdom. On the other hand, if you need a quick cool-off—go for it.

Poseidon's Fury
Frommer's Rating: B+
Recommended Ages: 6–adult
This is the park's best show—though with a lack of competition (there are only two productions at Islands), that's something of a backhanded compliment. The story line revolves around a battle between Poseidon, god of the sea, and the evil Darkenon. The highlight is when you pass through a small room with a 42-foot vortex where 17,500 gallons of water swirl around you, barrel-roll style. (If you wear glasses, note that they

will fog up completely when passing through the vortex—take them off if you can.) In the battle royale, the gods hurl 25-foot fireballs at each other. It's more interesting than frightening, but it's not worth the long lines that often plague it, so if you're on a tight schedule, use Universal Express or skip it. *Note:* The fireballs, explosive sounds, and rushing water (not to mention the dark and eerie passageways of the queue area) may be too intense for children under 6.

SHOPPING AT ISLANDS OF ADVENTURE

There are more than 20 shops within the park, offering a variety of theme merchandise. You may want to check out **Cats, Hats & Things** and the **Mulberry Street Store** for special Seussian souvenirs, books, and T-shirts. **Jurassic Outfitters** and **Dinostore** feature a variety of stuffed and plastic dinosaurs, plus safari-themed clothing. Superhero fans should check out **The Marvel Alterniverse Store** and the **Spider-Man Shop. Toon Extra** has the largest selection of souvenirs in Toon Lagoon. **Islands of Adventure Trading Company** is a good stop on the way out if you're still searching for something that will help you or the folks back home remember your visit.

Note: Universal has a service similar to Disney's in which you can have your purchases delivered to the front of the park. Allow 3 hours. Universal also has a shop by phone service—call © **407/224-5800,** describe the item and where you think you saw it, and the likelihood is they'll be able to help you out and have it shipped to you.

DINING AT ISLANDS OF ADVENTURE

The Islands offers some of the best theme park dining in town, with a number of stands where you can get a quick bite to eat, and a handful of full-service restaurants. The park's creators have taken some extra care to tie in restaurant offerings with the theme. The **Green Eggs and Ham Cafe** may be one of the few places on earth where you'd be willing to eat tinted huevos. (They sell as an egg-and-ham sandwich for about $7.) No matter which Island you're on, each offers a selection of sit-down restaurants, eateries, and snack carts. To save money, look for the kiddie menus, offering a children's meal

---

Tips **Great Things to Buy at Islands of Adventure**

Here's a sampling of some of the more unusual wares available at Islands of Adventure. It represents a cross section of tastes.

Jurassic Outfitters   There are plenty of T-shirts with slogans such as "I Survived (the whatever ride)."

Spider-Man Shop   This stop specializes in its namesake's paraphernalia, including red Spidey caps covered with black webs and denim jackets with logos.

Toon Extra   Where else can you buy a miniature stuffed Mr. Peanut beanbag, an Olive Oyl and Popeye frame, or a stuffed Beetle Bailey? Life doesn't get any better for some of us.

Treasures of Poseidon   Located in the Lost Continent, it carries an array of lovely blue glassware including tumblers, shot glasses, and oversize mugs, as well as brass sculptures.

and a small beverage for $6. Also consider combo meals (good for sharing), which usually offer a slight price break. **Thunder Falls Terrace** in Jurassic Park, for instance, offers a rib-and-chicken combo as well as other options in the $8 to $13 range.

Here are some of our other favorites at Islands:

- **Best Sit-Down Restaurant**   At **Mythos** (p. 161) on the Lost Continent, choose from selections such as cedar-planked salmon, lobster and corn bisque, a wrap of the day, or wood-fired pizzas. The atmospheric undersea cavelike setting is pleasant. This is a grown-up dining affair, best suited to adults and children over age 10. Entrees cost $11 to $20, and Mythos is usually open from 11:30am to 3:30pm and again at 5pm for dinner.

- **Best Atmosphere for Adults**   The **Enchanted Oak Tavern (and Alchemy Bar),** also in the Lost Continent, also has a cavelike interior, which from the outside looks like a mammoth tree, and is brightened by an azure blue skylight with a celestial theme. The tables and chairs are thick planks, and the servers are clad in "wench wear." Try the chicken/rib combo with waffle fries for around $13. The menu offers 45 types of beer.

- **Best Atmosphere for Kids**   The fun never stops under the big top at **Circus McGurkus Cafe Stoo-pendous** in Seuss Landing, where animated trapeze artists swing from the ceiling. Kids' meals, including a souvenir cup, are $6 to $8. The adult menu features fried chicken, lasagna, spaghetti, and pizza. Try the fried chicken platter for $8 or the lasagna for $7.

- **Best Vegetarian Fare**   **Fire-Eater's Grill,** located in the Lost Continent, is a fast-food stand that offers a tasty veggie falafel for $6. You can also get a tossed salad for around $3.

- **Best Diversity**   **Comic Strip Café,** located in Toon Lagoon, is a four-in-one counter service–style eatery offering burgers, Chinese food, Mexican food, and pizza and pasta (entrees run $6–$9).

There are also several restaurants (see chapter 5, "Where to Dine") and clubs (see chapter 9, "Walt Disney World & Orlando After Dark") that are just a short walk from the park in Universal's entertainment complex, CityWalk.

3 SeaWorld

Cleverly disguised as a theme park—or as SeaWorld likes to call it, an adventure park—this popular 200-acre marine park lets guests explore the mysteries of the deep and learn about the oceans and their inhabitants, all while having tons of fun. SeaWorld combines wildlife conservation awareness (otherwise known as edutainment), actual marine life care, along with plain old fun all in one fell swoop. While that's what Disney is attempting with its latest park, Animal Kingdom, the message here is subtle and a more inherent part of the experience.

SeaWorld's beautifully landscaped grounds center on a 17-acre lagoon and include flamingo and pelican ponds and a lush tropical rainforest. Shamu, a killer whale, is the star of the park along with his expanding family, which includes baby whales. The pace is much more laid-back than at either Universal or Disney, and it's a good way to break up a long week trudging through the other parks. Close encounters at feeding pools are among the real attractions (so be sure to budget a few extra dollars to buy fishy handouts for the sea lions and dolphins, which make begging an art form).

SeaWorld

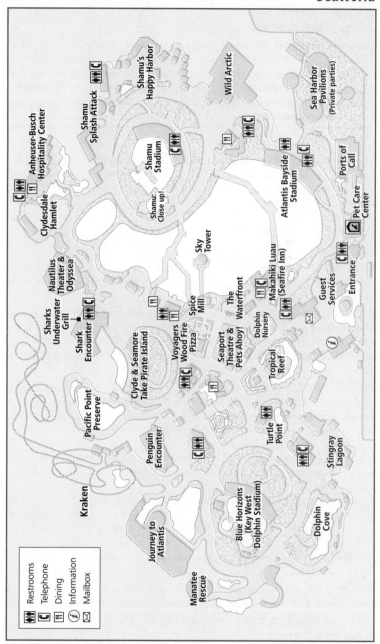

Shamu's Happy Harbor

Shamu Splash Attack

Wild Arctic

Sea Harbor Pavilions (Private parties)

Anheuser-Busch Hospitality Center

Shamu Stadium

Shamu: Close up!

Clydesdale Hamlet

Atlantis Bayside Stadium

Ports of Call

Pet Care Center

Nautilus Theater & Odyssea

Sky Tower

Entrance

Sharks Underwater Grill

Spice Mill

The Waterfront

Makahiki Luau (Seafire Inn)

Guest Services

Shark Encounter

Voyagers Wood Fire Pizza

Seaport Theatre & Pets Ahoy!

Dolphin Nursery

Clyde & Seamore Take Pirate Island

Tropical Reef

Pacific Point Preserve

Turtle Point

Kraken

Penguin Encounter

Stingray Lagoon

Journey to Atlantis

Blue Horizons (Key West Dolphin Stadium)

Dolphin Cove

Manatee Rescue

Restrooms
Telephone
Dining
Information
Mailbox

285

> ## *Tips* Shuttle Service
>
> SeaWorld and Busch Gardens in Tampa, both owned by Anheuser-Busch, have a shuttle service that offers $10 round-trip tickets to get you from Orlando to Tampa and back. The 1½- to 2-hour one-way shuttle runs daily and has five pickup locations in Orlando, including at Universal and on I-Drive (© **800/221-1339**). The schedule allows about 7 hours at Busch Gardens. The service is free if you have a FlexTicket.

SeaWorld manages a few thrills and chills. **Journey to Atlantis** is a high-tech water ride similar to Splash Mountain at Disney's Magic Kingdom. **Kraken** is a floorless roller coaster that sports seven inversions, much like coasters such as Montu and Kumba at SeaWorld's sister, Busch Gardens in Tampa (p. 341). But this park doesn't try to compete with the wonders of WDW or Universal. Instead it lets you discover the crushed-velvet texture of a stingray or the song of the seals.

ESSENTIALS

GETTING TO SEAWORLD BY CAR   The marine park is south of Orlando and Universal, north of Disney. From I-4, take Exit 72, Beeline Expressway/Highway 528, and follow the signs.

PARKING   Parking costs $9 for cars, light trucks, and vans; $12 for preferred parking closer to the park entrance. The lots aren't huge, and most folks can walk to the entrance. Trams also run. Note the location of your car. SeaWorld characters such as Wally Walrus mark sections, but at the end of a long day it's easy to forget where you parked.

TICKET PRICES   A **1-day ticket** costs $61.95 for adults, $49.95 for children 3 to 9, plus 6.5% sales tax. The park's new online ticketing system allows you to go to its website, **www.seaworld.com**, buy your ticket over the Internet, then print it out and take the printout right to the turnstiles. *Note:* SeaWorld sometimes offers a second day free as a promotion, so be sure to check online for the most up-to-date offers.

See the beginning of this chapter for information on the **FlexTicket,** a multiday ticket that provides admission to SeaWorld, Universal Orlando, Wet 'n Wild, and Busch Gardens.

SeaWorld's **Adventure Express Tour** ($89 adults, $79 kids 3–9, *plus mandatory park admission*) is a 6-hour guided excursion that includes front-of-the-line access to Journey to Atlantis, Kraken, and Wild Arctic; reserved seating at two animal shows; lunch; and a chance to touch or feed penguins, dolphins, stingrays, and sea lions (© **800/327-2424**). It's the only way to dodge park lines, which aren't as long as Disney's or Universal's.

HOURS   The park is usually open from 9am to 6pm and sometimes later, 365 days a year. Call © **800/327-2424** or 407/351-3600 for more information.

TIPS FOR MAKING YOUR VISIT MORE ENJOYABLE
PLAN YOUR VISIT

Get information before you leave by writing to **SeaWorld Guest Services** at 7007 SeaWorld Dr., Orlando, FL 32801, or call © **407/351-3600.**

ONLINE SeaWorld information is available at **www.seaworldorlando.com**. The *Orlando Sentinel* newspaper produces *Orlando Sentinel Online* at **www.orlando sentinel.com**. You can get a ton of information from the Orlando/Orange County Convention & Visitors Bureau website, **www.orlandoinfo.com**.

INFORMATION FOR VISITORS WITH SPECIAL NEEDS

The park publishes an accessibility guide for guests with disabilities, although most of its attractions are easily accessible to those in wheelchairs. SeaWorld also provides a Braille guide for the visually impaired. For the hearing impaired, there's a very brief synopsis of shows. Sign language interpreting services are available at no charge but must be reserved by calling © 407/363-2414 at least a week in advance of your visit. Assisted listening devices are available at select attractions for a $20 refundable deposit. For a complete rundown on all of your options, head to *Guest Services* when you enter the park; you can also call © 407/351-3600 for more information.

BEST TIME OF YEAR TO VISIT

Because this is a mostly outdoor, water-related park, you may want to keep in mind that even Florida gets a tad nippy during January and February. January through April are when crowds are smallest.

BEST DAYS TO VISIT

Weekends, Thursday, and Friday are busy days at this park. Monday through Wednesday are usually better days to visit because tourists coming for a week go to the Disney and Universal parks early in their stays, saving SeaWorld for the end, if at all.

CHOOSE AGE-APPROPRIATE ACTIVITIES

Because it has few thrill rides, SeaWorld has few restrictions, but you may want to check out the special tour programs offered through the education department. SeaWorld lives up to its reputation for making education fun. There are four 1-hour options: **Polar Expedition Tour** (touch a penguin), **Predators** (touch a shark), **Saving a Species** (see manatees and sea turtles), and the **Dolphin Nursery Close-Up**

Tips **New Dining Programs**

SeaWorld is diving deeper into the restaurant game with **Dine with Shamu** (© **800/327-2420** or 407/351-3600 for information and reservations; www. seaworldorlando.com), a reservations-only poolside dining experience with Shamu as a special guest. While eating, guests can mingle and question Sea-World trainers. The menu includes Cajun Creole, boeuf bourguignon, sides, rolls, and dessert. The cost is $37 for adults and $19 for kids 3 to 9, in addition to park admission. Reserving a spot 2 to 3 weeks in advance is usually more than enough unless you're coming in one of the crunch periods (summer, holidays). Last fall, the park also opened **Sharks Underwater Grill** (© **407/351-3600** for reservations), where diners can dig into Floridian and Caribbean treats while watching denizens swim by in the Terrors of the Deep exhibit. Menu prices run $20 to $29 for adults and $6 to $11 for kids 3 to 9 (pasta, hot dogs, chicken breast, steak, salmon, and popcorn shrimp), and theme-park admission is required.

(poolside interaction with young dolphins). All cost $16 for adults and $12 for children 3 to 9, plus park admission. Call ✆ **407/363-2380** for information or ✆ **800/406-2244** for reservations.

BUDGET YOUR TIME

SeaWorld has a leisurely pace, in part because its biggest attractions are up-close encounters with the animals. Don't be in a rush (you won't have to hurry everywhere for a change). This park can easily be enjoyed in a day. Its layout, lush landscaping, and many outdoor exhibits give it an open feel. Because of the large capacity and walk-through nature of many of the attractions, crowds generally aren't a concern except at Journey to Atlantis and Kraken. You also need to be in Shamu Stadium in plenty of time for the show. Wild Arctic can, at times, draw a sizable crowd, but the lines here don't come close to reaching Disney's proportions, so relax. Isn't that what a vacation is supposed to be about?

SERVICES & FACILITIES AT SEAWORLD

ATMs   An ATM is located at the front of the park. It accepts Cirrus-, Honor-, and PLUS-affiliated cards.

Baby Care   Changing tables are in or near most women's restrooms, and in the men's restroom at the front entrance near Shamu's Emporium. You can buy diapers in machines located near changing areas and at Shamu's Emporium. There's a special area for nursing mothers near the women's restroom at Friends of the Wild gift shop, near the center of the park.

Cameras & Film   Film and disposable cameras are available at stores throughout the park.

First Aid   First Aid Centers staffed with registered nurses are behind Stingray Lagoon and near Shamu's Happy Harbour.

Lockers   Lockers are located next to Shamu's Emporium, just inside the park entrance. The cost is $8 a day, plus a $2 deposit.

Lost Children   Lost children are taken to the Information Center. A park-wide paging system helps reunite guests. *Children under 7 should wear name-tags inside their clothing.*

Pet Care   A kennel is available between the parking lot and the main gate. The cost is $6 a day (no overnight stays). Owners are responsible for walking and feeding their pets.

Strollers   Fabric joggerlike strollers (replacing the old hard plastic dolphin-shaped ones) can be rented at the Information Center near the entrance. The cost is $10 for a single, $16 for a double. You can also purchase an umbrella stroller for $20.

Wheelchair Rental   Regular wheelchairs are available at the Information Center for $8; electric wheelchairs are $35.

MAJOR ATTRACTIONS
Blue Horizons
Frommer's Rating: A
Recommended Ages: All ages
At the partially covered, open-air Key West Dolphin Stadium, Blue Horizons combines elements of the sea and sky with a storyline that follows the dream of a young girl in this all-new dolphin spectacular. The show combines action both above and

below the water, featuring everything from divers to aerial acrobatics. Dolphins, whales, and exotic birds all star in the show, touted as a Broadway-style production filled with colorful costumes and performances.

Clyde & Seamore Take Pirate Island

Frommer's Rating: A

Recommended Ages: All ages

A lovable sea lion and otter, with a supporting cast of walruses and harbor seals, and a few quick-witted trainers appear in this fish-breath comedy with a swashbuckling conservation theme. It's corny, but don't hold it against the animal stars. With all those high-tech rides at the other parks, you need a break, and this one delivers some laughs. Watch out if you enter late—the mime entertaining the audience may make you part of the preshow.

Clydesdale Hamlet

Frommer's Rating: C+

Recommended Ages: All

Here is where you will find all of the famous Clydesdale Horses. Guests can walk through and see the grand beasts and in some instances watch them being hitched up for the occasional parade through the park. You can even have a photo taken with them (if you choose to keep the photo, there is a charge, of course). The **Anheuser-Busch Hospitality Center** is located just next door, offering beer samples, and a place to sit and have a light lunch or just relax for a bit.

Journey to Atlantis

Frommer's Rating: A

Recommended Ages: 8–adult

Taking a cue from Disney Imagineers, SeaWorld has created a story line to go with this $30-million water coaster. It has to do with a Greek fisherman and ancient Sirens in a battle between good and evil. But what really matters is the drop—a wild plunge from an altitude of 60 feet, in addition to lugelike curves and a shorter drop. Journey to Atlantis breaks from SeaWorld's edutainment formula and offers good old-fashioned fun. There's no hidden lesson, just a splashy thrill when you least expect it. It's nearly as good as Jurassic Park River Adventure at Islands of Adventure (p. 281). *Note:* Riders must be at least 42 inches tall. Expectant moms, as well as folks with heart, neck, or back problems, should find some other way to pass the time.

Key West at SeaWorld

Frommer's Rating: A+ for kids, B+ for adults

Recommended Ages: All ages

This Caribbean-style village has island food, entertainers, and street vendors. But the big attractions are the hands-on encounters with harmless Southern diamond and cownose rays at Stingray Lagoon; Sea Turtle Point, the home of threatened and endangered species; and Dolphin Cove, where you can feed smelt to the namesakes. *Warning:* If you have a soft heart, it's easy to spend $20 feeding them.

Kraken

Frommer's Rating: A+

Recommended Ages: 10–adult

SeaWorld's deepest venture onto the field of thrill-ride battle starts slow, like many coasters, but it ends with pure speed. Kraken is named for a massive, mythological,

Nighttime Fun

In addition to its regular productions, SeaWorld stages a few shows only sea-sonally, including *Mistify,* a nighttime spectacular combining fireworks and fountains on the lagoon. During summer months, guests are treated to the spe-cial-effects extravaganza nightly. If you're dining at the Spice Mill restaurant in the Waterfront, you can even enjoy dinner with the show.

underwater beast kept caged by Poseidon. This 21st-century version offers floorless and open-sided 32-passenger trains that plant you on a pedestal high above the track. When the monster breaks loose, you climb 151 feet, fall 144 feet, hit speeds of 65 mph, go underground three times (spraying bystanders with water), and make seven loops during a 4,177-foot course. It may be the longest 3 minutes, 39 seconds of your life. *Note:* Kraken carries a 54-inch height minimum. Expectant moms as well as folks with heart, neck, or back problems should skip this one.

Manatee Rescue

Frommer's Rating: B+
Recommended Ages: All ages

Today, the West Indian manatee is an endangered species. There are as few as 3,200 remaining in the wild. Underwater viewing stations, innovative cinema techniques, and interactive displays combine here for a tribute to these gentle marine mammals. While this isn't as good as seeing them in the great outdoors, it's as close as most folks get, and it's a much roomier habitat than the tight quarters their kin have at the Living Seas in Epcot.

Marine Mammal Keeper Experience

Frommer's Rating: A for trainer wannabes
Recommended Ages: 13–adult

This 9-hour program (starting bright and early at 6:30am) allows guests to work side by side with a trainer, preparing meals and feeding the animals, and learning how to care for and interact with dolphins, beluga whales, sea lions, and walruses. The cost is $399 (with tax), which includes 7 days of consecutive park admission, lunch, a career book, and a T-shirt. *Note:* You must be at least 13 years old and able to climb, as well as able to lift and carry 15 pounds of critter cuisine. Call © **800/432-1178** (hit "5," when prompted) for reservations.

Odyssea

Frommer's Rating: B+
Recommended Ages: All ages

This 30-minute, Cirque du Soleil–style stage show opened at SeaWorld's Nautilus Theater in July 2003. The show combines circus acrobatics, comedy, colorful cos-tumes, music, and special effects, to create a mythical underwater atmosphere. The special effects are good, and the aerial stunts even better.

Penguin Encounter *Overrated*

Frommer's Rating: C; B for young kids
Recommended Ages: All ages

Here you are transported by moving sidewalk through Arctic and Antarctic displays. You'll get a glimpse of penguins as they preen, socialize, and swim at bullet speed in their 22°F (–5°C) habitat. You'll also see puffins and murres in a similar, separate area. While it gives you a nice view of the penguins (and they are always a hit with the kids), the surroundings around the viewing area leave a bit to be desired, especially among so many other elaborate and well-done exhibits.

Pets Ahoy!
Frommer's Rating: B
Recommended Ages: All ages
Eighteen cats, 12 dogs, three pot-bellied pigs, and a horse are joined by birds and rats to perform comic relief in a 25-minute show held several times a day. Almost all of the stars were rescued from animal shelters.

Shamu's Happy Harbor (Kids)
Frommer's Rating: A for kids
Recommended Ages: 3–12
This 3-acre play area has a four-story net tower with a 35-foot crow's-nest lookout, water cannons, remote-controlled vehicles, nine slides, a submarine, and a water maze. It's one of the most extensive play areas at any park and a great place for kids to unwind. Bring extra clothes for the kids (and maybe for yourself, too) because it's not designed to keep you dry. Smaller kids will require close supervision, however, as they can easily get lost in all the action—and unlike many other play areas in other parks, there are several escape routes here. Recent additions that will assuredly entertain little ones include the **Shamu Express,** a kid-friendly coaster; the **Samba Tower,** that lifts and spins kids in jellyfish-like seats; and a **teacup**-style ride, where kids spin round and round in buckets that surround a gigantic sandcastle.

Shark Encounter
Frommer's Rating: A
Recommended Ages: 3–adult
SeaWorld has added other species to this formerly shark-exclusive attraction—about 220 specimens in all. Pools out front have small sharks and rays (feeding isn't allowed here). The interior aquariums have big eels, beautiful but poisonous lionfish, hauntingly still barracudas, and bug-eyed pufferfish. This isn't a tour for the claustrophobic because you have to walk through an acrylic tube, beneath hundreds of millions of gallons of water. Also, small fry may find the swimming sharks a little too much to handle.

A Whale of a Good Time
Debuting just as this book went to press, **Believe** is an all-new killer whale show (replacing the Shamu Adventure). Spectacular balletlike choreography, a new three-story high set design (featuring a gigantic whale tail, fountains, and video screens), and an exciting musical score, will all combine to create a rather impressive production.

   Shamu Underwater Viewing is an adjoining exhibit that lets you get close to killer whales and learn about breeding programs. The underwater viewing area allows a great close-up look at the tremendous creatures. You may even get to see a mother with her baby (the newest calf made his debut in Nov 2005).

Moments Swimming with the Sharks

In addition to the all-day (9-hr.) **Marine Mammal Keeper Experience** (see above), SeaWorld offers one other interactive program. **Sharks Deep Dive** gives guests a chance to have limited, hands-off contact with the 58 sharks, including a nearly 9-foot sand tiger, in the Shark Encounter area. Two at a time, guests don wet suits and a special underwater helmet (it lets you breathe and communicate with others) for a 30-minute encounter inside a cage that rides a 125-foot track. Part of the cage is above water, but participants can dive up to 8 feet underwater for a close-up look at the denizens. The cost is $150 (minimum age 10). The price includes a souvenir booklet, T-shirt, and a souvenir photo, but does not include the required park admission fee.

The program is not open to expectant mothers. Call © **800/432-1178,** 800/406-2244, or 407/363-2380, or visit **www.seaworldorlando.com** to make mandatory reservations or for more information.

Sizzlin' Pianos
Frommer's Rating: C
Recommended Ages: All
This amusing 25-minute show takes place several times a day at the Waterfront's Seafire Inn. Guests are entertained with many a merry musical tune, a dash of comedy, a tall tale or two, and a little interactive participation. Though you can see the show without eating at the inn, we think it makes for a very entertaining dining experience, especially with younger children, who at times require a diversion to make it through a meal.

Wild Arctic
Frommer's Rating: B+
Recommended Ages: All ages for exhibit; 6–adult for ride
Enveloping guests in the beauty, exhilaration, and danger of a polar expedition, Wild Arctic combines a high-definition adventure film with flight-simulator technology to display breathtaking Arctic panoramas. After a hazardous faux flight over the frozen north, you emerge into an exhibit where you can see a playful polar bear or two, beautiful beluga whales, and walruses performing aquatic ballets (on different levels, you can see them both above and below the surface). Kids and those prone to motion sickness may find the ride bumpy. There's a separate line if you want to skip the flight and just see the critters.

ADDITIONAL ATTRACTIONS
The park's other attractions include **Pacific Point Preserve,** a 2½-acre natural setting that duplicates the rocky home of California sea lions and harbor seals. Tropical fish and sea creatures at the **Tidepool** offer a hands-on experience for all ages. The **Tropical Reef** surrounds guests with aquariums filled with a variety of sea creatures to look at. Here you can touch the sea urchins, starfish, and anemones. **Tropical Rain Forest,** a bamboo and banyan tree habitat, is the home of cockatoos and other birds. And **Turtle Point** showcases sea turtles swimming in the lagoon or lounging on the beach

and sand dunes. **The Extreme Zone** tests your climbing and jumping skills with a rock wall and trampoline jump (both for an additional fee). A ride on the **Sky Tower,** open only seasonally and at an additional fee, lets you look out over the entire park.

The **Makahiki Luau** is a full-scale dinner show featuring South Seas–style food (fish, chicken, and pork) while you're entertained by music and dance of the Pacific Islands. It's hardly haute cuisine or Broadway but is very much on par with Disney's Spirit of Aloha Dinner Show (p. 321). It's held daily at 6:30pm. Park admission is not required. The cost is $45.95 for adults, $29.95 for children 3 to 9. Reservations are required and can be made by calling © **800/327-2420** or online at **www.seaworld orlando.com**.

SHOPPING AT SEAWORLD

SeaWorld doesn't have nearly as many shops as Walt Disney World and Universal Orlando, but with the opening of the Waterfront has added some rather unique boutiques, including **Allura's Treasure Trove** featuring fanciful dolls, mermaids, fairies, jewelry, and more. The **Tropical Trading Company** is filled with handcrafted gifts made by artisans from exotic ports all over the world. At **Oysters Secret,** guests can watch as pearl divers dive in search of just the right oyster, which will be pried open for the pearl inside. Guests can have the pearls made into jewelry. There are, of course, also lots of cuddly toys for sale around the park. Where else can you get a stuffed manatee but at **Manatee Gifts?** The **Friends of the Wild** gift shop (it's near Penguin Encounter) has one of the larger and more varied selections in the park. The shop attached to **Wild Arctic** is good for plush toys as well. **Shamu's Emporium** near the entrance is one of the largest stores in the park featuring an array of souvenirs, ranging from T-shirts to toys.

And, because of the Anheuser-Busch connection, the gift shop outside the entrance to the park offers a staggering array of Budweiser-related items.

DISCOVERY COVE: A DOLPHIN ENCOUNTER

Anheuser-Busch spent $100 million building SeaWorld's sister park, which debuted in 2000. Prices run from $249 to $279 per person (plus the 6.5% sales tax) for ages 6 and up if you want to swim with the dolphins. They run $149 to $179 if you just want to enjoy the fishes and other sea-life without having the dolphin experience. The prices vary seasonally so double-check when you make your reservations (which are a requirement to enter this park). In order to make the experience a bit more tolerable in the price department, admission includes a 7-day consecutive pass to either SeaWorld

---

Tips **On the Water**

SeaWorld's new 5-acre **Waterfront** area, which debuted in late spring 2003, added a seaport-themed village to the park's landscape. On High Street, look for a blend of shops; street shows; and the Seafire Inn restaurant, where lunch includes a musical revue. At Harbor Square, the funny Seaport Symphony orchestra has chefs making music with pots and pans. The park also is adding street performers, including a crusty old captain who tells fish tales and makes music with bottles and brandy glasses. Also at the Waterfront is an array of eateries, including the Spice Mill, Voyagers Wood Fire Pizza, and the Seafire Inn.

(which includes the Adventure Express tour) or Busch Gardens Tampa Bay. You can upgrade this feature to a 14-day combination pass for both parks for an additional $30.

If you've never gone for a dip with a dolphin, words hardly do it justice. It's exhilarating and exciting—exactly the kind of thing that can make for a most memorable vacation.

The actual dolphin encounter deserves an **"A+" rating.** It's open only to those ages 6 and older (younger guests or those who don't want to participate in the dolphin swim can take part in the other activities).

The park has a cast of more than two dozen dolphins, and each of them works from 2 to 4 hours a day. Many of them are mature critters that have spent their lives in captivity, around people. They love having their bellies, flukes, and backs rubbed. They also have an impressive bag of tricks. Given the proper hand signals, they can make sounds much like a human passing gas, chatter in dolphin talk, and do seemingly effortless 1½ gainers in 12 feet of water. They take willing guests for rides in the piggyback or missionary position. They also wave "hello" and "goodbye" with their flippers and take great pleasure in roaring by guests at top speed, creating waves that drench them.

The dolphin experience lasts 90 minutes, about 35 to 40 minutes of which is spent in the lagoon with one of them. Trainers use the rest of the time to teach visitors about these remarkable mammals.

The rest of the day isn't nearly as exciting, but it is wonderfully relaxing. Discovery Cove doesn't deliver thrill rides, water slides, or acrobatic animal shows; that's what SeaWorld, Disney, and Universal are for. This is where you come to get away from all that.

Here's what you get for your money, with or without the dolphin encounter:

- A limit of *no more than 1,000 other guests a day.* (The average daily attendance at Disney's Magic Kingdom is 41,000.) This ensures your experience will be more relaxing and private, which is really part of what you are paying for in the first place.
- A continental breakfast, lunch, snacks, and beverages (throughout the day), a towel, locker, sunscreen, snorkeling gear including a flotation vest, a souvenir photo, and free self-parking are also part of the deal.
- Other 9am-to-5:30pm activities include a chance to swim near (but on the other side of the Plexiglas from) **barracudas and black-tip sharks.** There are no barriers between you and the gentle rays (some of them 4 ft. in diameter) and brightly colored tropical fish in a new 12,000-square-foot lagoon. The 3,300-foot Tropical River is a great place to swim or float in a mild current—it goes through a cave, two waterfalls, and a large aviary where you can also take a stroll, becoming a human perch for some of the 30 exotic bird species. There are also beach areas for catching a tan.
- As mentioned above, 7 days of **unlimited consecutive admission** to SeaWorld and/or Busch Gardens Tampa Bay (park admission normally costs $61.95 a day for adults, $49.95 for children 3–9).

One other option is Discovery Cove's **Trainer For a Day Ticket,** which, for $419 to $479 (prices change seasonally), allows guests 6 and older to also have a dolphin training encounter, participate in guided snorkeling tours, feed fish, and interact with other critters, including rays. A paying adult must accompany guests ages 6 to 12. The ticket also includes a 14-consecutive-day admission to **both** SeaWorld and Busch Gardens.

For a more intimate experience try the **Twilight Discovery** program (only open to 150 guests; runs from 3–9pm), available mostly in summer. The program includes an upscale dinner, snacks and beverages, valet parking, a dolphin wade, snorkeling and gear, access to the various swim facilities, critter interaction, and a 7-day consecutive pass to SeaWorld or Busch Gardens. The cost is $279 if you want to wade with dolphins (and at least one person in your party must take this option), and $179 if you skip the dolphins.

You can drive to Discovery Cove by following the above directions to SeaWorld, then following the signs to the park. Unlike other parks, Discovery Cove doesn't have a parking charge. For up-to-the-minute information, call ℂ **877/434-7268,** or on the Internet go to **www.discoverycove.com**.

If you're headed for this adventure, we recommend making a reservation far, far in advance. With the limited number of guests admitted and the number of people who want a chance to swim with the fishes, this park gets booked very quickly. *Note:* There is an ever-so-small chance of getting in as a walk-up customer. The park reserves a small number of tickets daily for folks whose earlier dolphin sessions were canceled due to bad weather. The best chance for last-minute guests comes during any extended period of good weather.

4 Other Area Attractions

There are—surprise!—a number of cool things in Orlando that don't revolve around Mickey, the Hulk, or Shamu. Now that we've covered the monster parks, we're going to explore some of Central Florida's best smaller attractions.

IN KISSIMMEE

Kissimmee's main tourist strip is on Walt Disney World's southern border and extends about 2 miles west and 8 to 10 miles east. Irlo Bronson Memorial Highway/U.S. 192 is the highway that links the town to WDW and points west. Because it is so full of eateries and hotels, it can be hard to see some of the smaller destinations, though the roadway's guide markers can be quite helpful, as is the U.S. 192 map that you can pick up at any hotel lobby. Check with your hotel's front desk or the attractions for detailed directions or short cuts that might make finding them a little easier.

Note: The following prices don't include the 6.5% to 7% sales tax unless otherwise noted.

Gatorland ★★ *Finds*   Founded in 1949 with only a handful of alligators living in huts and pens, Gatorland now houses thousands of alligators (including a rare blue one) and crocodiles on its 70-acre spread. Breeding pens, nurseries, and rearing ponds are situated throughout the park, which also displays snakes, toads, insects, turtles, and a Galápagos tortoise. Its 2,000-foot boardwalk winds through a cypress swamp and breeding marsh. There are three shows. **Gator Wrestlin'** uses the old "put-them-to-sleep" trick, but it's more of an environmental awareness program. The **Gator Jumparoo** is a crowd-pleaser in which the big reptiles lunge 4 or 5 feet out of the water to snatch a hunk of meat from a trainer's hand. **Up Close Encounters** features a variety of wildlife, including some venomous snakes. Younger kids will enjoy the new **train ride** through the park; **Lilly's Pad,** a wet and dry play area; and **Allie's Barnyard,** a small petting zoo. While you're here, try the smoked gator ribs or nuggets in the open-air restaurant, or grab a gator-skin souvenir in the gift shop. Allow 4 to 5 hours. *Tip:* Look for additional parking, a refreshed facade, and additional landscaping renovations that have improved many areas throughout the park.

Note: Gatorland's **Trainer for a Day** program lets up to five guests get up close and personal with the gators for a day (or 2 hr., in this case). The $100, 2-hour experience puts you side by side with trainers and includes a chance to wrangle some alligators (minimum age 12). Advance reservations are required, and admission to the park is included (and a 20% discount off a regular admission ticket is extended to up to six members of your party). A 1-hour Night Shine tour is also available ($19 adults, $17 children), taking you on a tour along the wooden walkways with only a flashlight and a guide. Advanced reservations are required.

Tip: Printable discount coupons and special Internet ticket prices are available at the park's website. Be sure to check it out before you leave home.

14501 S. Orange Blossom Trail (U.S. 441; between Osceola Pkwy. and Hunter's Creek Blvd.). © **800/393-5297** or 407/855-5496. www.gatorland.com. Admission $20 adults, $13 children 3–12. Daily 9am–5pm, but closing times can vary by season. Free parking. From I-4, take Exit 65/Osceola Pkwy. east to U.S. 17/92/441 and go left/north. Gatorland is 1½ miles on the right.

INTERNATIONAL DRIVE AREA

These attractions are a 10- to 15-minute drive from the Disney area and 5 to 10 minutes from Universal Orlando. Most appeal to special interests, but one is free (the Peabody Ducks' show) and another, Wet 'n Wild, is in a class that includes WDW's top two water parks: Typhoon Lagoon and Blizzard Beach.

Holy Land Experience   Battles to get tax-exempt church status and smaller-than-expected attendance caused this tourist attraction to add a parking fee and boost rates by $13 in its first 2 years. But backers still believe Jesus Christ and John the Baptist can go head-to-head with (or at least play second harp to) Mickey Mouse and Woody Woodpecker. This $20-million, 15-acre attraction near Universal Orlando is trying to court more believers by offering exhibits focusing on Jerusalem between the years 1450 B.C. and A.D. 66. Instead of thrill rides, visitors get lessons about Noah's Ark, the limestone caves where the Dead Sea Scrolls were discovered, 1st-century Jerusalem, and Jesus's tomb. The trimmings include a display of old Bibles and manuscripts, a Bedouin tent where biblical personalities tell Old and New Testament stories, and a cafe serving Middle Eastern food. New additions include a multimedia production of music and art giving an overview of worship through the ages; a small play area for kids; and the Oasis Outpost, which features a rock wall and archaeological dig, misting station, and a small refreshment spot. The attraction has caused some controversy: Orlando-area rabbis, among others, say they believe it's a ploy to convert Jews to Christianity. I say, unless you're interested in a day dedicated to the history of the Bible, the high admission is pretty hard to swallow and this place is pretty skippable. Allow 3 to 4 hours.

4655 Vineland Rd. © **866/872-4659** or 407/367-2065. www.theholylandexperience.com. Admission $30 adults, $20 children 6–12. Mon–Sat 10am–5pm. Hours can vary by season, call before coming. Parking $5. From I-4, take Exit 78/Conroy Rd. west to Vineland Rd. It's on Vineland at Conroy.

Peabody Ducks ✦ *(Moments*   One of the best shows in town is short but sweet, and, more importantly, *free*. The Peabody Orlando's five mallards march into the lobby each morning, accompanied by John Philip Sousa's "King Cotton March" and their own red-coated duck master. They get to spend the day splashing in a marble fountain. Then, in the afternoon, they march back to the elevator and up to their 4th-floor "penthouse." Donald Duck never had it this good. Allow 1 hour.

Orlando Area Attractions

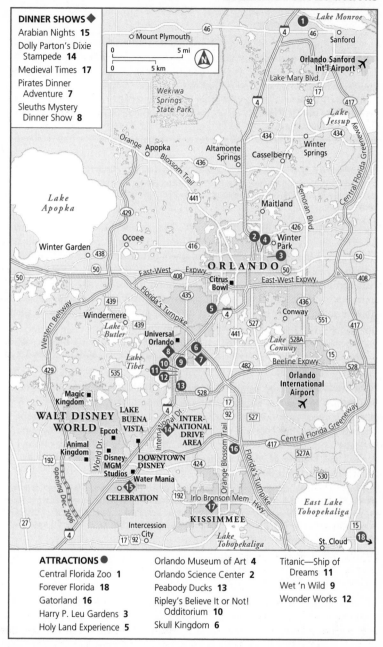

Mount Plymouth

0   5 mi
0   5 km

Lake Monroe

Sanford

Orlando Sanford
Int'l Airport

Lake Mary Blvd.

Wekiwa
Springs
State Park

Lake
Jessup

Orange Apopka

Altamonte
Springs

Casselberry

Winter
Springs

Central Florida Greeneway

Lake
Apopka

Maitland

Winter
Park

Ocoee

Winter Garden

O R L A N D O

East-West Expwy.

East-West Expwy.

Citrus
Bowl

Conway

Windermere

Lake
Butler

Universal
Orlando

Lake
Tibet

Lake
Conway

Beeline Expwy.

Orlando
International
Airport

Magic
Kingdom

LAKE
BUENA
VISTA

WALT DISNEY
WORLD

Epcot

INTER-
NATIONAL
DRIVE
AREA

International Dr.

Central Florida Greeneway

Animal
Kingdom

Disney-
MGM
Studios

DOWNTOWN
DISNEY

Water Mania

opening Dec 2006

Orange Blossom Trail

Florida's Turnpike

CELEBRATION

Irlo Bronson Mem. Hwy.

KISSIMMEE

East Lake
Tohopekaliga

Intercession
City

Lake
Tohopekaliga

St. Cloud

> **Tips Back in Action**
>
> After closing its doors in 2003, **Cypress Gardens Adventure Park** (© 863/324-2111; www.cypressgardens.com) has reopened and now features 38 thrill rides, an all-new water-ski show, and the beautiful botanical gardens that started it all. A water park has also opened just next door and features plenty of wild raft rides, a children's play area, and other aquatic fun. Call or visit the website for up-to-date details. The only downside is the hour-long drive to get to the park from the Disney area.

9801 International Dr. (between the Bee Line Expressway and Sand Lake Rd.). © **800/732-2639** or 407/352-4000. Free admission. Daily at 11am and 5pm. Free self-parking; valet parking $8 (day), $14 (overnight). From I-4, take Exit 74A, Sand Lake Rd./Hwy. 528, east to International Dr., then south. Hotel is on the left across from the Convention Center.

Ripley's Believe It or Not! Odditorium   Do you crave weird science? If you're a fan of the bizarre, here's where you'll find lots of oddities. Among the hundreds of exhibits: a two-headed kitten, a five-legged cow, a three-quarter–scale model of a 1907 Rolls-Royce made of 1 million matchsticks, a mosaic of the *Mona Lisa* created from toast, torture devices from the Spanish Inquisition, a Tibetan flute made of human bones, and Ubangi women with wooden plates in their lips. There are exhibits on Houdini and films of people swallowing coat hangers. Visitors are greeted by a holo-gram of Robert Ripley. Allow 2 hours.

8201 International Dr. (1½ blocks south of Sand Lake Rd.). © **407/345-0501**. www.ripleysorlando.com. Admission $17 adults, $12 children 4–12. Daily 9am–1am. Free parking. From I-4, take Exit 74A, Sand Lake Rd./Hwy. 528, and turn right on International Dr.

Skull Kingdom   As you wander the stone halls inside Skull Castle, you'll be taunted and terrified by a cast of ghoulish characters second in Central Florida only to the crew at Universal Orlando's Halloween Horror Nights, but this show runs year-round. The night show (after 5pm) on weekends is far more intense than the day show. In any case, it's not for children under 8. Allow about 30 minutes to walk through the castle. The **Chamber of Magic** dinner show (all-you-can-eat pizza and drinks) can also be combined with the haunted tour.

5933 American Way (just off the intersection of International Dr. and Universal Blvd., 3 blocks east of Universal Orlando). © **407/354-1564**. www.skullkingdom.com. Admission day show $9 per person, night show $14 per person; magic dinner show $20 adult, $16 kids under 7; magic show, dinner, and the haunted tour $28 adults, $24 kids under 7. Free parking. Mon–Fri 10am–5pm; Sat–Sun 6pm–midnight. From I-4, take Exit 75A/Hwy. 435 south to American Way and look for the giant skull castle.

Titanic—Ship of Dreams *Overrated*   If you didn't get enough of the movie, news clips, and expedition, you will get that *no more* feeling in this 25,000-square-foot attraction. It has some 200 artifacts (a deck chair, life jacket, stationery, and so on), movie memorabilia, actors, and even a replica of the great ship's grand staircase and re-created rooms. This one is strictly for ardent fans. Allow 1 to 2 hours.

8445 International Dr. (3 blocks south of Sand Lake Rd.). © **407/248-1166**. www.titanicshipofdreams.com. Admission $18 adults, $13 children 6–12. Free parking. Daily 10am–8pm. Take I-4 Exit 74A, Sand Lake Rd./Hwy. 528, turn left on International Dr., and go ¾ mile. It's in the Mercado.

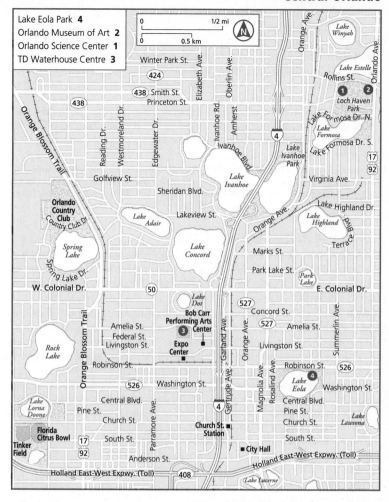

Lake Eola Park **4**
Orlando Museum of Art **2**
Orlando Science Center **1**
TD Waterhouse Centre **3**

Wet 'n Wild ★★ Who knew people came in so many shapes and sizes? Stacked or stubby, terribly tan or not, all kinds come here, so there's no reason to be bashful about squeezing into a bathing suit and going out in public. The 25-acre Wet 'n Wild is America's third most popular water park (behind Blizzard Beach and Typhoon Lagoon, respectively). **Disco H2O,** the park's newest addition, debuted in 2005; it's an enclosed flume ride where a four-passenger raft sends you flying through the sights and sounds of the '70s, complete with mirrored lights and disco tunes blasting in the background. Other options include **The Flyer,** a six-story four-passenger toboggan run through 450 feet of banked curves; the **Surge,** which is one of the longest (580 ft. of curves) and fastest multipassenger tube rides in the Southeast; and **Black Hole,** a two-person spaceship-style raft that makes a 500-foot twisting, turning voyage through darkness (all three rides require that children 36–48 in. be accompanied by an adult). You can also ride **Raging Rapids,** a simulated white-water run with a waterfall plunge; **Blue Niagara,** a 300-foot six-story loop-and-dipster that also has a plunge (48-in. height minimum); **Knee Ski,** a cable-operated half-mile knee-boarding course that's open in warm-weather months only (56-in. height minimum); **Der Stuka,** a six-story, free-fall speed slide; and **Mach 5,** which has a trio of twisting, turning flumes. The park also has a large kids' area with miniversions of the big rides. If you enjoy the water, plan on spending a full day here.

Note: In addition to the admission prices below, Wet 'n Wild is part of the multi-day **FlexTicket package** that includes admission to Universal Orlando (which owns this attraction), SeaWorld, and Busch Gardens in Tampa (see the beginning of this chapter for more information).

6200 International Dr. (at Universal Blvd.). ② 800/992-9453 or 407/351-1800. www.wetnwild.com. Admission $35 adults, $29 children 3–9. Hours vary seasonally, but the park usually is open at least 10am–5pm daily weather permitting (it's one of the few water parks open year-round). You can rent tubes ($4), towels ($2), and lockers ($5); each requires a $2 deposit, or rent them all ($9 plus $4 deposit). Parking is $7 for cars, light trucks, and vans. From I-4, take Exit 75A/Hwy. 435 South, and follow the signs.

ELSEWHERE IN CENTRAL FLORIDA

The listings that follow are out of the mainstream tourist areas, meaning you won't have to battle heavy crowds. The Central Florida Zoo, Orlando Museum of Art, and Orlando Science Center are close enough to incorporate a visit to Winter Park if you choose to make a day of it.

Central Florida Zoo *(Finds)*   This community zoo has come a long way since it was born in 1923 when a circus came to town, leaving a monkey and a goat behind. The monkey rode the goat in the earliest show. Today, the animal collection includes beautiful clouded leopards, cheetahs, and black-footed cats, all of which are endangered. You'll also meet a ham of a hippo named Geraldine as well as black howler monkeys, siamangs, American crocodiles, a banded Egyptian cobra, a Gila monster, barred owls, bald eagles, and dozens of other species. Recent additions include an insect zoo and a hyacinth macaw exhibit. The zoo has half-price admission for everyone Thursdays from 9 to 10am and all day Tuesdays for seniors 60 and over. Allow 2 to 3 hours. *Tip:* One-year memberships that include additional perks and free admission to this and 100 other participating zoos and aquariums across the country are available. A family membership is $55, which, depending on your family's size, may be more economical than purchasing individual tickets.

Have Some Extra Time?

Wonder Works is just the spot to spend a couple of hours (less than two) if you're in need of a less intense evening or rainy afternoon activity. This upside-down building's exterior catches the eye, and it's just as interesting on the inside, with an array of unique hands-on exhibits that include the bed of nails, the bridge of fire, the WonderCoaster, and more. There's plenty to do for kids ages 4 to 12, who (among other options) can stomp on giant piano keys to make music or create sheets of bubbles with bubble machines. Call ② **407/351-8800** or go to **www.wonderworksonline.com** for more information.

3755 NW U.S. 17/92, Sanford. ⓒ 407/323-4450. www.centralfloridazoo.org. Admission $8.95 adults, $6.95 seniors, $4.95 children 3–12. Daily 9am–5pm. Free parking. Take I-4 Exit 104 right onto Orange Ave., turn left at the traffic light on Lake Monroe Rd., then right on U.S. 17/92. The zoo is on the right.

Forever Florida   The 4,700-acre Crescent J Ranch is a nature preserve that offers a chance to see native wildlife, Florida flora, and a working cattle ranch by guided tour. Options include touring by horseback (must reserve at least 24 hr. in advance) or by Safari coach, a funky buggy that puts riders on a perch 10 feet above sea level. Allow a half-day or longer to get here, take the tour, and see the grounds, which also include a pony riding ring, hiking trails, and a petting zoo.

4755 N. Kenansville Rd., St. Cloud (southeast of Kissimmee). ⓒ 866/854-3837. www.floridaeco-safaris.com. Tours and rides from $25 adult, $20 kids (6–12) on up to $89 per person, higher for overnights. Daily tours at 10am and 1pm. Free parking. Take I-4 Exit 64A/U.S. 192 east about 15 miles to U.S. 441, then go south 7½ miles to Forever Florida on the left.

Harry P. Leu Gardens ⓖ 𝘝𝘢𝘭𝘶𝘦   This 50-acre botanical garden on the shores of Lake Rowena offers a serene respite from the theme-park razzle-dazzle. Paths lead through giant camphors, moss-draped oaks, palms, cicadas, and camellias—the latter represented by one of the world's largest collections: 50 species and some 2,000 plants that bloom from October through March. There are 75 varieties of roses in the site's formal gardens, as well as orchids, azaleas, desert plants, and colorful annuals and perennials. The attraction also has palm, bamboo, and butterfly gardens. Businessman Harry P. Leu, who donated his 49-acre estate to the city in the 1960s, created the gardens. There are $7 guided tours (a deposit of $25 is required) of his house and the gardens, built in 1888, on the hour and half-hour (at least 3 weeks advance registration required). The interior has Victorian, Chippendale, and Empire furnishings and pieces of art. Admission is free Mondays from 9am to noon. It takes about 2 hours to see the house and gardens.

1920 N. Forest Ave. (between Nebraska St. and Corrine Dr.). ⓒ 407/246-2620. www.leugardens.org. Admission $5 adults, $1 children grades K–12; Mon 9am–noon free. Gardens daily 9am–5pm; house daily 10am–4pm (closed during July). Free parking. Take I-4 Exit 85/Princeton St. and go east, then right on Mills Ave. and left on Virginia Dr. Look for the gardens on your left, just after you go around a curve.

Orlando Museum of Art ⓖ   This local heavyweight handles some of the most prestigious traveling exhibits in the nation. The museum, founded in 1924, hosts special exhibits throughout the year, but even if you miss one, it's worth a stop to see its rotating permanent collection of 19th- and 20th-century American art, pre-Columbian art dating from 1200 B.C. to A.D. 1500, and African art. Allow 2 to 3 hours.

2416 N. Mills Ave. (in Loch Haven Park). ⓒ 407/896-4231. www.omart.org. Admission $15 adults, $12 seniors and students, $5 children 6–18, local residents free Thurs 1–4pm. Mon–Thurs 10am–8pm; Fri–Sun 10am–5pm; closed on legal holidays. Free parking. Take I-4 Exit 85/Princeton St. east and follow signs to Loch Haven Park.

Orlando Science Center ⓖⓖ 𝘍𝘪𝘯𝘥𝘴   The four-story center, the largest of its kind in the Southeast, provides 10 exhibit halls that allow visitors to explore everything from Florida swamps to the arid plains of Mars to the human body. One of the big attractions is the **Dr. Phillips CineDome,** a 310-seat theater that presents large-format films, planetarium shows, and laser-light extravaganzas. Just a small sampling of what you can expect includes exhibits such as **KidsTown,** where little folks wander in exhibits representing a miniature version of the big world around them. In one section, there's a pint-size community that includes a construction site, park, and wellness center. **Science**

City, located nearby, includes physics lessons and a power plant, and **123 Math Avenue** uses puzzles and other things to make learning math fun. Dino Digs, the Body Zone, Measure Me, Weird Science, Touch the Sky, and Dr. Dare's Laboratory are some of the other exhibits that await you. Allow 3 to 4 hours, more if you have an inquiring mind.

777 E. Princeton St. (between Orange and Mills aves., in Loch Haven Park). © 888/672-4386 or 407/514-2000. www.osc.org. Admission (includes exhibits, CineDome film, and planetarium show) $15 adults, $14 seniors 55 and older, $10 children 3–11. Mon–Thurs 9am–5pm; Fri–Sat 9am–9pm; Sun noon–5pm. Parking available in a garage across the street for $3.50. Take I-4 Exit 85/Princeton St. east and cross Orange Ave.

5 Staying Active

You will most likely burn more calories than you ever thought possible by simply strolling through the theme parks. Nevertheless, if you want some exercise other than walking the parks, Walt Disney World and the surrounding areas have plenty of recreational options. Most of the following are open to everyone, no matter where you're staying (we note the exceptions below). For further information about WDW recreational facilities, call © **407/939-7529,** or on the Internet go to **www.disney world.com** and click the "recreation" link.

AIRBOATING

You can giddy-up-and-glide across the surface of local waters at **Boggy Creek Airboat Rides** in Kissimmee (© **407/344-9550;** www.bcairboats.com), where you'll pay $19 per adult and $15 per child for half-hour tours; night tours are available as well. Another choice is **Old Fashioned Airboat Rides** in Christmas, east of Orlando (© **407/ 568-4307;** www.airboatrides.com), which charges $37 per adult and $20 per child age 12 and under for 90 minutes.

BALLOONING   There are several places in the area to experience an early-morning hot-air balloon flight, including **Orange Blossom Balloons** in Lake Buena Vista (© **407/239-7677;** www.orangeblossomballoons.com) and **Blue Water Balloons** (© **800/586-1884** or 407/894-5040; www.bluewaterballoons.com). Sunrise flights are available daily, and all flights, which last approximately 1 hour, are followed by a champagne toast (sorry, kids) at the conclusion of the flight and a breakfast buffet or picnic afterward. Children who make the age grade will probably be delighted with the view and the unique sensation, unless they (or you) don't see eye-to-eye with heights. Blue Water offers hotel pickup at no extra charge. Rates run approximately $175 per adult and $95 per child ages 10 to 15.

BICYCLING   Bike rentals (single and multispeed adult bikes, tandems, baby seats, and children's bikes—including those with training wheels) are available from the **Bike Barn** (© 407/824-2742) at Fort Wilderness Resort and Campground on Walt Disney World. Rates for each bike are $8 per hour, $22 per day (surrey bikes run $18–$22 per half-hour) regardless of age. Fort Wilderness offers a lot of good bike trails. Many of the other Disney resorts also offer bicycle rentals at similar rates. Either call your hotel in advance or inquire upon check-in.

BOATING   With the many man-made lakes and lagoons dotting the WDW landscape, it's no surprise Disney owns a navy of pleasure boats. **Capt. Jack's** at Downtown Disney rents Water Sprites and canopy boats ($24–$26.50 per half-hour, including tax), pontoons ($42 per half-hour, tax included), and sailboats ($20–$30 per hour, tax included). For information call © **407/828-2204.**

The **Bike Barn** at Fort Wilderness (☎ **407/824-2742**) rents canoes and paddle boats ($6.50 per half-hour).

At both sites, kids must be at least 12 to rent a boat and those under 18 cannot rent without a signed parental waiver.

The **Winter Park Scenic Boat Tour** (☎ **407/644-4056**; www.scenicboattours.com) offers visitors another opportunity to see some of Orlando's sights, this time while sailing along the city's historic lakes and canals. Tickets cost $10 adults, $5 for kids ages 2 to 11.

FISHING There are several fishing excursions offered on Disney waterways, including Bay Lake and Seven Seas Lagoon. The lakes are stocked, so you may catch something, but true anglers probably won't find it much of a challenge. The excursions can be arranged 2 to 90 days in advance by calling ☎ **407/824-2621.** A license isn't required. The fee is $200 to $395 for up to five people for 2 hours ($90 for each additional hour), including refreshments, gear, guide, bait, and tax. Children above the toddler stage are permitted on these tours when accompanied by an adult; however, an hour-long excursion just for kids ages 6 to 12 is available for $30.

A less-expensive alternative: Rent fishing poles at the **Bike Barn** (☎ **407/824-2742**) to fish in the Fort Wilderness canals. Pole rentals cost $6 per hour, $10 per day (not including tax). Bait is $3.50 to $3.65. A license isn't necessary.

Outside the realm, **A Pro Bass Guide Service** (☎ **800/771-9676** or 407/877-9676; www.probassguideservice.com) offers guided bass fishing trips along some of Central Florida's most picturesque rivers and lakes. Hotel pickup is available; the cost is $260 for two people per half-day, $360 for a full day; a license is $17.

HANG GLIDING You'll get the chance to soar 2,000 feet in the air as you fly through the sky—with a little help from some instructors at the Wallaby Ranch (☎ **863/424-0070;** www.wallaby.com), located in Davenport, just south of Kissimmee. If you're a thrill-ride junkie, this is the real deal. The price depends on the number of lessons and type of flight you want; call or check the website for detailed information.

HAYRIDES A hay wagon departs **Pioneer Hall** at Disney's Fort Wilderness nightly at 7 and 9:30pm for 45-minute old-fashioned hayrides with singing, jokes, and games. Most kids will find it enjoyable, though some teens may think it corny. The cost is $8 for adults, $4 for children ages 3 to 9, and free for kids 2 and under. An adult must accompany children under 12. No reservations. Call ☎ **407/824-2832** for more information.

HIKING The **Nature Conservancy's Disney Wilderness Preserve** (☎ **407/682-3664;** www.nature.org/florida) is a 12,000-acre, little-discovered getaway from the theme-park madness. It has 7 miles of trails at the headwaters of the Everglades ecosystem, just south of Orlando. Self-guided trails range from a half-mile interpretive trail good for younger kids, to a 4.5-mile hiking trail for adults and teens. Picnic facilities are available along the trails. Admission costs $3 adults, and $2 for kids ages 6 to 17 and Nature Conservancy members. It's open Monday through Friday in summer from 9am to 5pm; it's open daily from 9am to 5pm the rest of the year. The preserve also features Sunday afternoon **buggy rides** ($12 adults, $6 kids).

HORSEBACK RIDING **Disney's Fort Wilderness Resort and Campground** offers 45-minute guided trail rides several times a day. The cost is $32 per person. Children must be at least 9 years old. Maximum rider weight is 250 pounds. If you

Tips Hitting the Links

Walt Disney World operates five 18-hole, par-72 golf courses and one 9-hole, par-36 walking course, so if you want to work on your putting and need some time away from the kids (who will most likely prefer an outing on one of Disney's minigolf courses—see p. 254), you'll have plenty of options. All are open to the public and offer pro shops, equipment rentals, and instruction. The rates are $99 to $159 per 18-hole round for resort guests ($10 more if you're not staying at a WDW property). Twilight specials are available for $60 to $80 per person. For tee times and information, call ℰ 407/939-4653 up to 7 days in advance (up to 30 days for Disney resort and "official" property guests). Call ℰ 407/934-7639 for information about golf packages.

Beyond Mickey's shadow, try **Celebration Golf Club** (ℰ 888/275-2918 or 407/566-4653; www.celebrationgolf.com), which has an 18-hole regulation course (greens fees $65–$129) that kids under 17 are eligible to play, and a 3-hole junior course for 5 to 9 year olds. Note that there is a dress code at the club, so be sure to ask ahead so that your kids are decked out in suitable attire. **Champions Gate** (ℰ 888/554-9301 or 407/787-4653; www.champions gategolf.com) offers 36 holes designed by Greg Norman, where greens fees will set you back $55 to $170, as well as the **David Leadbetter Golf Academy** (ℰ 407/787-3330; www.davidleadbetter.com). **Orange County National** (ℰ 407/656-2626; www.orangecountynationalgolf.com) has 36 Phil Ritson–designed holes; greens fees run $50 to $150.

Golf magazine recognized the 45 holes designed by Jack Nicklaus at the **Villas of Grand Cypress** ✦✦✦ resort (p. 106) as among the best in the

or your children have never ridden before, the tame horses and gentle terrain make this ride a good intro experience. For information and reservations up to 30 days in advance, call ℰ **407/824-2832.**

The **Villas of Grand Cypress** opens its equestrian center to outsiders and has programs and options for riders of all ages and all skill levels. You can go on a 45-minute walk-trot trail ride (offered four times daily) for $45, though your children must be at least 10 years of age to participate. A 30-minute private lesson is $55; an hour's lesson is $100. A private junior lesson (15 min.) is available for riders ages 2 to 9 for $25. A host of other package options are offered. For more information, call ℰ **800/835-7377** or 407/239-1938, or go online to **http://grandcypress.com.**

Another choice outside the world of Walt Disney is the **Horse World Riding Stables** (ℰ **407/847-4343;** www.horseworldstables.com) in Kissimmee. Trail rides range in price from $39 for an easy hour on a nature trail to $69 for a 1¼-hour advanced-level ride.

HORSE-DRAWN CARRIAGE RIDES   Disney offers evening carriage rides at two of its resort locations: **Fort Wilderness Resort and Campground** and the **Port Orleans Resort.** The 30-minute rides cost $30 for up to four people. Most kids will enjoy the ride and the sightseeing opportunity. For information, call ℰ **407/824-2832.**

nation. Tee times begin at 8am daily. Special rates are available for children under 17, and the resort even runs a 5-day summer golf program for kids interested in the game. For information call © **407/239-1909.** The course is generally restricted to guests or guests of guests (rates run approximately $120–$180 per round), but there's limited play available to those not staying at the resort. Fees run approximately $180 to $250.

With more than 150 courses located throughout the Orlando area, it's simply impossible to list them all. There are, however, several additional courses and academies worth noting: **Hawk's Landing Golf Club and Academy** (© 407/238-8660) at the World Center Marriott; and the **Legacy, Independence,** and soon-to-open **Tradition** golf courses, as well as the **National Golf School**—all located at Reunion Resort & Club of Orlando (© **888/418-9610** or 407/662-1000). The **Ritz Carlton Golf Club** and **Grande Pines Golf Club,** both located at the **Grande Lakes Orlando** (© 407/393-4814), offer the only golf caddie concierge program around to make your game all it can be; the program offers advice, helpful hints, caddie services, food and beverage service, and much more.

Also consider **Golfpac** (© **800/486-0948** or 407/260-2288; www.golfpac orlando.com), an organization that packages golf vacations with accommodations and other features and prearranges tee times at more than 40 Orlando-area courses. The earlier you call (months, if possible), the better your options. **Advanced Tee Times USA** (© 800/374-8633; www.teetimesusa.com) and **Golforlando** (© **800/981-8656;** www.golforlando.com) are two other reservation services that offer packages and course information.

JOGGING Many of the Disney resorts have scenic jogging trails. For instance, the **Yacht** and **Beach Club** resorts share a 2-mile trail; the **Caribbean Beach Resort's** 1.4-mile promenade circles a lake; **Port Orleans** has a 1.7-mile riverfront trail; and **Fort Wilderness's** tree-shaded 2.3-mile jogging path has exercise stations about every quarter-mile. Pick up a jogging trail map at any Disney property's Guest Services desk.

PARASAILING The **Sammy Duvall Watersports Centre** (© 407/939-0754; www.sammyduvall.com) at Disney's Contemporary Resort will take you up to 600 feet above Seven Seas Lagoon and Bay Lake on a flight that lasts 8 to 12 minutes. The cost runs approximately $90 for one rider, $140 for two riders. Kids over 2 are actually eligible if they fly in tandem with someone else (minimum weight of 115 lb.), though you'll have to judge whether your child is up to such an experience. While older kids and teens would probably fair well, younger children likely wouldn't. Everyone who goes up has to sign a waiver and parents have to sign off on their kids' participation. You can reserve a spot up to 90 days in advance.

SCUBA DIVING & SNORKELING Believe it or not, even in an inland location such as Orlando you can scuba and snorkel in the Florida waterways. **Fun 2 Dive Scuba and Snorkeling Tours** (© 407/322-9696; www.fun2dive.com) and **Orlando Dive and Snorkel Tours** (© 407/466-1668; www.floridamanateetours.com) both offer the chance to swim and snorkel with manatees (and other wildlife) as well as other eco-tour opportunities. Prices run approximately $85 per person (with a maximum of six) to swim and snorkel with Fun 2 Dive (which also offers scuba lessons and deep sea fishing excursions). Orlando Dive and Snorkel starts at $28 per person—rental gear is $10 extra.

SKATEBOARDING On the occasional rainy afternoon (or even on a good day) **Vans Skatepark** (© 407/351-3881; www.vans.com) offers skateboarders (beginners or advanced) the chance to ride the day away on ramps, bowls, street courses, and more. Safety equipment is required (and available for rent if you don't have your own) and those under 18 are required to have a parent or guardian sign a waiver (in front of a Vans employee or a notary). Rates run approximately $12 per session for non-members, $5 for members (requiring a 1-year commitment) on weekdays, $15 and $7 respectively on weekends and holidays. Sessions are 2 hours long and run at scheduled times. Equipment is available for rent, from boards to helmets and pads (prices run $2–$5, depending on what you rent). Private lessons, camps, and birthday parties are also offered. The park is located in the Festival Bay Mall at the far north end of International Drive.

SURFING It's true. The creative minds at Disney have added a way for you to learn how to catch a wave and "hang ten" at the Typhoon Lagoon water park (p. 249). Tuesdays and Fridays, instructors from **Carroll's Cocoa Beach Surfing School** show up for an early-bird session in the namesake lagoon, which has a wave machine capable of 8 footers. The 2½-hour sessions are held before the park opens to the general public and are limited to 14 people. Minimum age is 8. The $135 per person cost (including tax) doesn't include park admission, which you'll have to pay if you want to hang around after the lesson (© 407/939-7529). You'll also need alternative transportation to get here if you're staying in Walt's World because the Disney transportation system doesn't service Typhoon Lagoon until official park opening time.

The **Ron Jon Surf Park** (www.ronjons.com; www.surfparks.com), set to open in 2006 at the Festival Bay Mall, will feature three wave pools for surfers and bodyboarders of all abilities and experience. It will also sport a standing-wave and children's water-play area, and a restaurant. And the Ron Jon surf shop is right nearby in case you forgot any necessary surf or swim gear. Lessons are available at an extra cost (at press time, the park hadn't opened yet and prices were not yet available).

SWIMMING Almost all of Orlando's resorts have their own pools, some of which are rather unique, others rather extensive (and discussed in more detail in chapter 4). If you're not satisfied with the one at your hotel, the **YMCA Aquatic Center,** 8422 International Dr. (© 407/363-1911), has a full fitness center, racquetball courts, an indoor Olympic-size pool, and a heated 25m pool for kids. All pools have lifeguards. Admission is $10 per person, $25 for families.

TENNIS There are 26 lighted tennis courts scattered throughout the Disney properties and the Wide World of Sports Complex. Most are free and open to resort guests on a first-come, first-served basis. Call © 407/939-7529 for more information. The **Racquet Club at the Contemporary Resort,** with six clay courts, all lighted for evening play, will cost you $8 per hour to play and reservations are required. Private lessons are available for $40 to $50, depending on the duration. The courts at the Grand Floridian are for Grand Floridian guests only.

The **Grand Cypress Racquet Club** (© 407/239-1944; www.grandcypress.com) features 12 courts, 5 of which are lighted. Racquetball courts, a clubhouse, and pro shop are available as well. Clinics are offered daily, with private lessons ($70 per hour, $40 per half-hour) and semi-private ($85 per hour) lessons available as well.

WATER-SKIING & WAKEBOARDING Water-skiing trips (including boats, drivers, equipment, and instruction) can be arranged Tuesday through Saturday at **Walt Disney World** by calling the **Sammy Duvall Watersports Centre** at Disney's Contemporary Resort (© **407/939-0754;** www.sammyduvall.com). Make reservations up to 14 days in advance. The cost for skiing is $140 per hour for up to five people. You also can arrange for wakeboarding for up to four people; rates run $80 for a half-hour, $140 for an hour. There's no minimum age, though we wouldn't recommend this for children under 8, and definitely not for those at all uncomfortable in the water.

Outside Disney, you can get some time behind a boat or at the end of an overhead cable at the **Orlando Watersports Complex,** which has lights for nighttime thrill-seekers. Teens will likely think the nighttime option cool, but kids under 8 and those not completely comfortable in the water aren't the best candidates for this activity. The complex is located close to Orlando International Airport at 8615 Florida Rock Rd. Prices for skiing (including lessons) begin at about $21 an hour for a cable and $35 for a half-hour behind a boat. The complex offers a number of specials and discounts aimed at kids and families—call or check the website to see what's being offered during the time of your visit. For information call © **407/251-3100** or on the Internet go to **www.orlandowatersports.com.** Another good option is **Buena Vista Water Sports** (© **407/239-6939;** www.bvwatersports.com), located closer to all the action at Lake Bryan in Lake Buena Vista. It offers Sea-Doo rentals, water-ski and wakeboard lessons, and rides. Passes run in duration from 1 hour ($21) to all day ($39.50), to all week ($185.50). Cable lessons (lasting 1 hr.) run $65; those under the age of 10, and who pass their lesson, receive a 2-hour cable pass free of charge.

6 Spectator Sports

Disney doesn't want to give the competition a sporting chance. In May 1997, it branched out with the multimillion-dollar **Wide World of Sports Complex,** a 200-acre facility. The Mouse hit a home run with a 7,500-seat baseball stadium—dubbed Cracker Jack Stadium in 2002—that's the spring training home of the Atlanta Braves. In addition, there's a 5,000-seat field house featuring six basketball courts, a fitness center, and training rooms; major-league practice fields and pitching mounds; 4 softball fields; 12 tennis courts, including a 2,000-seat stadium center court; a track-and-field complex; a golf driving range; and more. The newest addition, the Hess Sports Fields, includes baseball, soccer, lacrosse, and football fields. A variety of events, from tennis tournaments to band competitions, have been held here since the center opened. For information about events taking place during your stay, call © **407/939-1500** or visit **www.disneyworldsports.com.**

So if you and your kids are sports nuts, you won't have to forgo your fix while in Orlando. Even taking the above into account, Disney isn't the only show in town.

ARENA FOOTBALL

The **Orlando Predators** play from February through mid-May. For the uninitiated, arena football is a wide-open sport played by eight-man teams on a much-abbreviated field. You don't necessarily need to know the rules to enjoy the up-close crunching and

---

⟨Moments⟩ The Multisports Experience

In 2002, Disney replaced its NFL Experience at the Wide World of Sports complex with an expanded multisports venue that not only lets you test your skills at football, but also at baseball, basketball, hockey, soccer, and volleyball. Admission is $11 for adults and $7.75 for kids 3 to 9. It's open on select days. For information call ℰ **407/939-1500.**

If you're a true sports fan, your best bet is to write in advance for a package of information about the facilities and a calendar of events at Wide World of Sports. Write to **Disney's Wide World of Sports,** P.O. Box 10,000, Lake Buena Vista, FL 32830-1000, or call ℰ **407/939-1500.**

---

beer-fest atmosphere. The Predators have a loyal and rowdy following, not to mention a few championships under their belts. Sold-out games are common, but single tickets ($6–$50) are often available the day of the game at the **TD Waterhouse Centre,** formerly the Orlando Arena. Call ℰ **407/447-7337** or surf the Web to **www.orlando predators.com.**

BASEBALL

The **Atlanta Braves** began spring training at Disney's Wide World of Sports (p. 254) in 1998. There are 18 games played during a 1-month season that begins in March. The smaller setting makes for a far more intimate experience for kids than a regular stadium game would and the atmosphere is usually a lot more relaxed. Tickets are $13 to $21. For information, call ℰ **407/828-3267.** You can get tickets through **Ticketmaster** (ℰ **407/839-3900**).

BASKETBALL

The 17,500-seat TD Waterhouse Centre—known in a prior life as the Orlando Arena—is the home court of the NBA's **Orlando Magic** (ℰ **407/896-2442;** www.nba.com/magic), which plays 41 of its regular-season games here from October to April. To get there, take I-4 east to Exit 83B, Highway 50/U.S. 17/92 (Amelia St.), turn left at the traffic light at the bottom of the off-ramp, and follow the signs. Single-game tickets ($25–$175) can be hard to get. The team schedules special theme nights and promotions throughout the season, many of them family-related, and mascot Stuff (that really is his name) the Dragon is a hit with kids. For up-to-the-minute parking information, turn your car radio to 1620 AM.

8

Shopping

Whether you're looking for mouse ears and souvenirs or the latest and greatest in designer labels, you'll find it in Orlando. Walt Disney World itself is home to an almost endless array of shops spread throughout its parks, resorts, and Downtown Disney. The House of Mouse, however, is not the only game in town. If you venture beyond its boundaries you'll discover first-rate shopping malls, outlet centers, and charming boutiques. There are two distinctively different options for shopping in Orlando: the local malls, which are home to an excellent and varied selection of retailers, and the outlet shopping centers.

But before you break out your credit cards, do remember to keep your shopping wits about you. The malls and their upscale stores can, at times, charge extremely outrageous prices that you'll easily better at home. And the outlets, once offering tremendous bargains, now

discount at times only marginally. The key to getting the best possible deals is to know what is *and isn't* a bargain.

And now, a note on souvenir shopping. If, after exercising your credit cards elsewhere, you've still got energy (and money) to burn, the parks and entertainment districts at Walt Disney World, Universal Orlando, and SeaWorld feature some of the most distinctive souvenir shopping you'll find anywhere. Sure, many of the stores are filled with trinkets and T-shirts, but some offer far more unique merchandise that you won't be able to find anywhere else—Orlando or otherwise. Besides the listings in this chapter, be sure to check out some unique shopping opportunities mentioned in Chapter 6, "Exploring Walt Disney World," and chapter 7, "Exploring Beyond Disney: Universal Orlando, SeaWorld & Other Attractions."

1 The Shopping Scene

The hottest spots for tourists to shop are at Downtown Disney, CityWalk, and the larger themed shopping centers scattered along International Drive. Kissimmee, though a very busy area, has little to offer shoppers other than seashells and T-shirts that, at 3 for $10, are a good example of the old saying "you get what you pay for." There are, of course, more than just a few of the same tourist traps located along I-Drive (mostly at the northern end) as well as along S.R. 535 in Lake Buena Vista. But don't despair; if you stick to the places listed in this chapter, you'll find plenty of quality merchandise.

If you're looking for a quieter, out-of-the-way shopping experience, the quaint tree-lined streets of Winter Park—Park Avenue in particular—are filled with one-of-a-kind boutiques, well-known shops, and antiques stores. Closer to the action, yet still far enough off the beaten path to remain quaint and quiet, is Market Street in Celebration,

---

(Tips Ship It

Because Orlando is geared to travelers, many retailers offer to ship packages home for a few dollars more (Disney definitely does). So, if you're pondering an extra-large purchase, or even just one you would rather not have to carry, ask. If a retailer doesn't offer such a service, check with your hotel. Many a concierge or business center staffer can arrange a pickup by United Parcel Service, the U.S. Postal Service, or another carrier. Anything's better than dragging that 6-foot stuffed Pluto through the friendly skies.

---

which is home to a small collection of tiny shops. Downtown Orlando has its own collection of unique shopping spots, with Antique Row (along Orange Ave.) and nearby Ivanhoe featuring antiques dealers, collectible shops, and better gift stores. If you're in search of a quiet retreat or an afternoon of simple indulgence, these shopping side trips should provide just the sort of peaceful experience you're seeking (you won't even mind coming away empty-handed).

Many Orlando area stores, particularly those in malls or other shopping centers, are usually open from 9 or 10am until 9 or 10pm Monday through Saturday, and from noon to 6pm on Sunday. It is always best to check before you go as hours, like those at the parks, can change during the holidays, as well as seasonally. Sales tax in Osceola County, which includes Kissimmee, the U.S. 192 corridor, and *all of Disney's All-Star resorts,* is 7%. In Orange County, which includes the International Drive area, SeaWorld, Universal Orlando, most (but not all) of Disney World, and most of the lesser attractions, it's 6.5%. In Seminole County, about 40 miles north of Walt Disney World, the rate is 7%. No matter where you are, plan on adding a few extra dollars in taxes to your bill when you get to the cash register.

One thing that's no different here than the rest of the country: If you arrive during the holiday season, from the end of November to January 1, it's best to avoid local shopping malls, especially on weekends. They're just as crazy and crowded as those back home—maybe even worse. And no matter what time of year it is, don't leave your good judgment at the door when you're shopping the outlet malls. Although there are some good bargains to be found, the prices on many items aren't really much better than you can find at home in many cases. The selection, however, may be much larger than you're used to—especially if you're from outside the United States. Remember, though, that you still have to get it home with you somehow, so if you can buy the same item at home, do you really want to have to carry it all the way from Florida?

GREAT SHOPPING AREAS

CELEBRATION   Though not the best place to head if you're the shop-'til-you-drop type, this is a rather pleasant spot to stroll leisurely along quaint streets filled with upscale shops, coffeehouses, and restaurants. Celebration, after all, is a Disney-designed community, making it practically the perfect little town. It's a throwback to mid-20th-century mainstream America, when main-street shopping was in style. Market Street and the area just surrounding it are home to a dozen or so shops, a couple of art galleries, a handful of restaurants, and a three-screen movie theater. The storefronts, especially the galleries and gift shops, offer interesting and unique merchandise, though

Shopping in Orlando

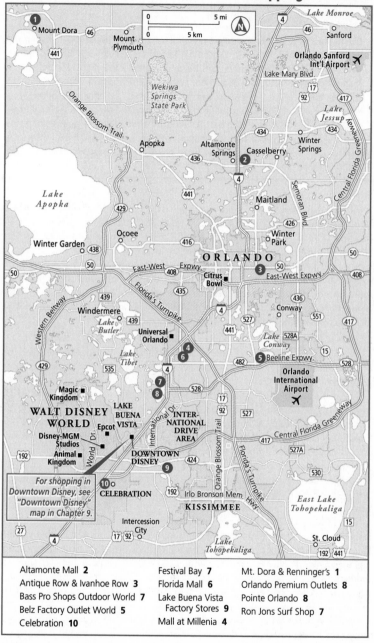

| | 0 _____ 5 mi | |
| 0 _____ 5 km | |

- ① Mount Dora
- Mount Plymouth
- Sanford
- Orlando Sanford Int'l Airport
- Lake Monroe
- Lake Mary Blvd.
- Wekiwa Springs State Park
- Lake Jessup
- Apopka
- Altamonte Springs
- ② Casselberry
- Winter Springs
- Lake Apopka
- Maitland
- Winter Garden
- Ocoee
- Winter Park
- **ORLANDO**
- ③
- East-West Expwy
- Citrus Bowl
- Conway
- Windermere
- Lake Butler
- Universal Orlando
- ④
- ⑥
- Lake Conway
- Orlando International Airport
- ⑤ Beeline Expwy.
- Lake Tibet
- ⑦
- ⑧
- Magic Kingdom
- **WALT DISNEY WORLD**
- LAKE BUENA VISTA
- Epcot
- **INTER-NATIONAL DRIVE AREA**
- Disney-MGM Studios
- Animal Kingdom
- **DOWNTOWN DISNEY**
- ⑨
- For shopping in Downtown Disney, see "Downtown Disney" map in Chapter 9.
- ⑩ **CELEBRATION**
- Intercession City
- **KISSIMMEE**
- Irlo Bronson Mem. Hwy.
- East Lake Tohopekaliga
- St. Cloud
- Lake Tohopekaliga

Altamonte Mall **2**	Festival Bay **7**	Mt. Dora & Renninger's **1**
Antique Row & Ivanhoe Row **3**	Florida Mall **6**	Orlando Premium Outlets **8**
Bass Pro Shops Outdoor World **7**	Lake Buena Vista	Pointe Orlando **8**
Belz Factory Outlet World **5**	Factory Stores **9**	Ron Jons Surf Shop **7**
Celebration **10**	Mall at Millenia **4**	

Tips Getting Your Fill

The neatest new way to buy toys at several Downtown Disney stores (especially Once Upon a Toy) is in bulk . . . sort of. Toys such as Lincoln Logs and Mr. Potato Head, as well as a few others, can be purchased by the piece. Here's how it works: You pick out a box (there are two sizes to choose from) and fill it up with as many (or few) pieces as you can fit inside. The only stipulation—you have to be able to close the lid properly. No matter how many pieces you've stuffed inside, the price of the box remains the same. If you've got good space-saving skills, buying your toys this way may net you a very good deal. (Here's a hint to get you started—Mr. Potato Head has a hole in his back, so fill it up and you'll fit more pieces in your box.)

---

you'll find that there's a price to pay for perfection. Stores here include the **Market Street Gallery** (Swarovski crystal, Disney collectibles, and more), **Sherlock's of Celebration** (a shop that sells wine and English tearoom goods), **DownEast** (an Orvis Shop filled with gifty items and resort wear), an art gallery, a grocer, a post office, a perfumery, and a jeweler, among others. The real attraction is the relaxing, picture-perfect atmosphere. The high prices, however, may make for more window-shopping than actual spending. If, by chance, Celebration reminds you of the movie *The Truman Show,* you're not alone. The movie was filmed in Seaside, a Florida panhandle community that inspired the builders of this burg.

DOWNTOWN DISNEY   With three distinct areas—West Side, Pleasure Island, and the Marketplace—**Downtown Disney** (© 407/939-2648; www.downtowndisney.com) is chock-full of some of the most unique shops in Orlando, as well as many restaurants and entertainment venues.

The best shops in the Marketplace include the 50,000-square-foot **World of Disney,** the largest store in Downtown Disney. There are rooms and more rooms filled with everything Disney, from toys and trading pins to clothes and collectibles—and everything (and we mean *everything*) in between. **Bibbiddi Bobbiddi Boutique** arrived in 2006 and is a place where little girls can have their hair styled, put on makeup, and have their nails done so they look like a princess when they emerge. In the princess room girls can play dress up, while the adventure room is geared more to boys—they can create their own pirate hat, play video games, and check out superhero, space explorer, and cowboy gear.

We always stop in at the **Lego Imagination Center** when we're in town. After extensive renovations it's now far easier to shop (in part due to the fact that it's much larger) and offers lots of play areas to entertain the kids (we'd hate to be the ones cleaning up at night). Shelves are filled with Lego blocks designed for everyone from toddlers to tweens, Bionicles, T-shirts, and trinkets. Check out the display behind the counter when you cash out—it's filled top to bottom with teeny tiny Lego people (visible thanks to a nifty magnifying glass that runs back and forth across their little faces). **Once Upon A Toy** is one of the best stores in the Marketplace, and the best toy store we've ever been in. It's stocked from floor to ceiling with games and toys, many of them classics—you know, the ones you played with while growing up. Its 16,000 square feet of space is divided into three separate sections: The first is filled with board games; the second is loaded with stuffed animals, building sets, and Playskool toys; the third features action figures, vehicles, and videos. **Team Mickey's Athletic Club** sells character clothing with a sporty spin. Other smaller, but similarly interesting shops include **Summer Sands,** featuring the hottest in beachwear from top names such as Quicksilver and Calvin Klein; and **The Art of Disney,** where you can buy limited edition animation cels and other Disney collectibles.

Pop Gallery, a high-end art gallery, features limited-edition, artist-signed original artwork (sculpture and paintings) along with an assortment of high-end gifts. There are also plenty of accessories, T-shirts, and trinkets for those of us not nearly as artistically (or financially) inclined. The 49,000-square-foot **Virgin Megastore** is the biggest store on the block, with two levels of music, videos, books, and more. You can preview your chosen song or movie before you purchase at 1 of the 300 audio and video stations. Other notable stores at West Side include **Magic Masters,** where you can load up on magic tricks for your budding Harry Houdini; **Magnetron,** which sells a huge variety of magnets (though, strangely enough, no Disney ones); and **Celebrity Eyeworks Studio,** where you can pick up a copy of those cool shades your favorite star was sporting in his or her last film.

INTERNATIONAL DRIVE AREA (*Note:* Locally, this road is almost always referred to as **I-Drive.**) Extending 8 or so miles northeast of Disney between Highway 535 and the Florida Turnpike, this busy thoroughfare is one of the most popular tourist districts in the area, in part because it is filled with so many restaurants, shops, hotels, and attractions. From indoor surfing and glow-in-the-dark golf to dozens of themed restaurants and shopping spots, this is *the* tourist strip in Central Florida. Its main shopping draw is the **Orlando Premium Outlets,** just off south I-Drive (see below). Another I-Drive shopping spot, **Pointe Orlando** (© 407/248-2838; www.pointeorlandofl.com), currently undergoing extensive renovations, features a collection of restaurants, clubs, and specialty shops. Upon completion additional retailers as well as brand-new landscaping and lighting will have been added in order to create a more inviting atmosphere. **The Mercado** (© 407/345-9337; www.themercado.com) is a Mediterranean-style marketplace on I-Drive that's filled with specialty shops, restaurants, and attractions; there's often live entertainment featured here in the evenings.

KISSIMMEE Skirting the south side of Walt Disney World, Kissimmee centers on U.S. 192/Irlo Bronson Memorial Highway, as archetypal of modern American cities as Disney's Main Street is of America's yesteryear. U.S. 192 is lined end to end with budget motels, smaller attractions, and almost every fast-food restaurant known to humankind (though a handful of good eateries can be found here as well). Kissimmee does not offer the fabulous array of shopping options found elsewhere in Orlando. The shopping here is notable for the quantity, not necessarily the quality, but it's a good place to pick up some knickknacks, white elephant gifts, or those seashells I mentioned earlier.

WINTER PARK Just north of downtown Orlando, Winter Park (© 407/644-8281) is the place many of Central Florida's old-money families call home. It began as a haven for Yankees trying to escape the cold. Today its centerpiece is Park Avenue, which has quite a collection of upscale retail shops—Ann Taylor, Restoration Hardware, Bath & Body Works, Crabtree & Evelyn, and Williams-Sonoma—along its cobblestone route. No matter which end of Park Avenue you start at, there are more shops than most can survive, but you're bound to find something here you'll not find anywhere else. Park

Value   **A Disney Bargain? The World's Best-Kept Secret**

From a pink Cadillac to a 4-foot beer stein, tons of wacky treasures are regularly put on the auction block at Walt Disney World.

In addition to castoffs from the theme parks and WDW resorts, there are more routine items available, from over-the-hill lawn maintenance gear to never-been-used stainless-steel pots and pans. If you're looking for a unique piece of Disney, the auctions are held six times a year. Some of the more unusual items sold in the past include furniture from Miss Piggy's dressing room and a motorized surfboard. The auction takes place on Disney's back lots. Call property control (© **407/824-6878**; www.auctionweb.com/disney) for information, dates, and directions.

Bigger yet are trinkets sold by gavel at **www.disneyauctions.com** on eBay. The mainstream includes stuffed animals, Winnie the Pooh watches, and other modest merchandise. But sometimes things go big time. A dress Glenn Close wore as Cruella De Vil in *102 Dalmatians* sold for $5,000, a Dumbo car from the ride at WDW earned $9,000, and the Porsche from the Disney movie *The Kid* fetched $77,100.

Avenue is also home to a handful of unique restaurants and art galleries. *Note:* Leave the kids with a sitter if you plan to shop (or dine) here. You'll both be happier for it. To get here, take I-4 Exit 87, Fairbanks Avenue/Highway 426, east past U.S. 17/92 to Park Avenue and turn left.

2 Orlando Area Outlets & Malls

FACTORY OUTLETS

Belz Factory Outlet World   This is the largest of the Orlando factory outlet centers. It has 170 stores in two enclosed malls and four shopping annexes. It offers a wide range of merchandise, and in a few cases the savings can be 75% off retail prices, but, as is the case with most outlets, *most buys here are no better than what you'll find in discount houses in your hometown.* There are more than a dozen shoe stores (Bass, Nike, Rockport, and so on); nearly as many housewares shops (Fitz & Floyd, Oneida, and more); a Universal Studios Outlet; and 60-some clothing shops for men, women, and children (Gap, Levi's, Van Heusen, OshKosh B'Gosh, Izod, Guess Jeans, and others). You can also shop for books, records, electronics, sporting goods, health and beauty aids, jewelry, toys, gifts, accessories, lingerie, and hosiery.

It goes on forever, but don't kill yourself trying to get to every building. Many of the manufacturers have more than one location here, with much the same selections. Also, unless you're from out of the country, most of the brand-name shoe stores don't offer much of a deal. The drawback here is the difficulty getting from building to building: Unless every store you are interested in is in only one of the many buildings, you have to get in and out of your car several times over just to shop here. It's also a bit off the beaten path unless you're staying closer to Universal Orlando, making some of the other outlet options a much better choice. 5401 W. Oak Ridge Rd. © **407/352-9611.** www.belz.com.

Lake Buena Vista Factory Stores   The three dozen or so outlets here include Big Dog Sportswear, Carters, Casuals (Ralph Lauren and Tommy Hilfiger), Liz Claiborne, Fossil, OshKosh, Reebok, Gap Outlet, and the only Old Navy Outlet in the area. Savings can reach 75%, but most deals are much more modest. The plaza itself is very tasteful and inviting, and the location, just between the I-Drive and U.S. 192 areas on the lower end of Apopka–Vineland, means you can easily get here without having to face too much traffic. This outlet center is a bit quieter and more relaxed than the Premium Outlets (see below), but its selection of shops is far smaller. It does, however, have a nicely done food court area for a quick bite, and even a salon if you are in need of a new do or a manicure. 15591 S. Apopka–Vineland Rd. ✆ 407/238-9301. www.lbvfs.com.

Orlando Premium Outlets 🌟🌟 *Finds*   Opened in June 2000, this 440,000-square-foot outlet center offers shoppers the atmosphere of a beautiful outdoor shopping mall filled with landscaping and natural lighting. It's inviting instead of outlet-ish. It's billed as Orlando's only upscale outlet and is by far the best choice for a great shopping experience in Orlando. It has 110 tenants, including Disney and Universal outlets, Coach, Donna Karan, Kenneth Cole, Nike, Polo/Ralph Lauren, Timberland, and Tommy Hilfiger. Others include DKNY, Fendi, Hugo Boss, Nautica, Salvatore Ferragamo, and Versace. Some of the best buys are at Banana Republic, and the selection at all the stores is fabulous. Set just between S.R. 535 and I-Drive, it's easily accessible from either location. 8200 Vineland Ave. ✆ 407/238-7787. www.PremiumOutlets.com.

> *Tips* **Homegrown Souvenirs**
>
> Oranges, grapefruit, and other citrus fruits rank high on the list of Florida's top local products. **Orange Blossom Indian River Citrus,** 5151 S. Orange Blossom Trail, Orlando (✆ **800/ 624-8835** or 407/855-2837; www. orange-blossom.com), is one of the top sellers during the late-fall-to-late-spring season.

THE MALLS

Altamonte Mall   As surely as Disney brought new life to Orlando, this mall—the second largest in the area behind the Florida Mall (see below)—brought new life (and a ton of traffic) to the then-one-stoplight town of Altamonte Springs, north of Orlando. A recent renovation added a food court, an indoor play area for kids, and an 18-screen AMC movie theater with stadium seating. The lineup features anchor stores Burdines, Dillard's, JCPenney, and Sears; and 175 other specialty stores, including The Body Shop, Foot Locker, Godiva, and Banana Republic. 451 E. Altamonte Dr. ✆ 407/830-4422. www.altamontemall.com.

The Florida Mall   Anchors at this popular shopping spot include Nordstrom, Burdines, Dillard's, JCPenney, Sears, and Saks, to go along with an Adam's Mark Hotel and more than 250 specialty stores, restaurants (Buca di Beppo, Le Jardin, and the Salsa Taqueria & Tequila Bar), a food court, and entertainment venues. 8001 S. Orange Blossom Trail. ✆ 407/851-6255. www.shopsimon.com.

Mall at Millenia   This 1.3-million-square-foot upscale center made quite a splash on the mall scene when it debuted in October 2002 with anchors that include Bloomingdale's, Macy's, and Neiman Marcus. In addition to the heavyweight anchors, Millenia offers 200 specialty stores that include Cartier, Chanel, Crabtree & Evelyn, Giorgio's of Palm Beach, Gucci, Louis Vuitton, Swarovski, and Tiffany & Co. It also features some of the better dining options around with restaurants ranging from fine dining to fast food; in January 2005, it opened the Blue Martini, an upscale martini lounge featuring regular live entertainment. The mall is 5 miles from downtown Orlando. 4200 Conroy Rd. (at I-4 near Universal Orlando). (℃ 407/363-3555. www.mallatmillenia.com.

3 Other Shopping in Orlando

IN DOWNTOWN ORLANDO

If you can think of nothing better than a relaxing afternoon of bargain hunting or scouring thrift and antiques shops, check out **Antique Row** and **Ivanhoe Row** on North Orange Avenue (stretching from Colonial Dr./Hwy. 50 to Lake Ivanhoe) in downtown Orlando. This collection is a long way from the manufactured fun of Disney. The shops are an interesting assortment of the old, the new, and the unusual. **Flo's Attic,** 1800 N. Orange Ave. (℃ 407/895-1800), and **A.J. Lillun,** 1913 N. Orange Ave. (℃ 407/895-6111), sell traditional antiques.

Down the road, a handful of places offer less conventional items. **Wildlife Gallery,** 1219 N. Orange Ave. (℃ 407/898-4544; www.fredlundwildlife.com), sells pricey, original works of wildlife art, including sculpture. And the **Fly Fisherman,** 1213 N. Orange Ave. (℃ 407/898-1989; www.flyfishermaninc.com), sells—no surprise here—fly-fishing gear. Sometimes you can spot people taking casting lessons in the park across the street.

Most of these downtown shops are open from 9 or 10am to 5pm, Monday to Saturday; the owners usually run them, so hours can vary. All are spread over 3 miles along Orange Avenue. The heaviest concentration of shops lies between Princeton Street and New Hampshire Avenue, although a few are scattered between New Hampshire and Virginia avenues. The more upscale shops extend a few blocks beyond Virginia. To get there, take I-4 Exit 85/Princeton St. and turn right on Orange Avenue. Parking is limited, so stop wherever you find a space along the street.

Additionally, you can shop for fresh produce, plants, baked goods, and crafts every Sunday from 9am to 2:30pm at the downtown **Sunday Eola Market.** It's located at the intersection of Osceola and East Central. Get more information at **www. downtownorlando.com.**

A HOMESPUN ALTERNATIVE

Mount Dora *(Finds* This haven for artists (and retirees) is also an enjoyable day trip, not to mention a wonderful alternative to all that is Disney. The town, established in 1874, has the genuine feel of old Florida, with an authentic Main Street, far less crowded than the one Disney has re-created. The 19th-century buildings lining the streets are picture-perfect, leading to the calm, dark green waters of Lake Dora. Unlike most of Florida, this town actually has rolling hills, adding to the charm. Highlights include **Renninger's Antique Center and Farmer's Market** (℃ 352/383-8393 for the antique center or 352/383-3141 for the farmer's market; www.renningers.com). The hundreds of shops and booths are open Saturday and Sunday. Up to 1,000 dealers attend Renninger's 3-day antique extravaganzas held the third weekends of January, February, and November. After you've worked up an appetite, take a lunch break at the Beauclaire Dining Room at the historic **Lakeside Inn,** 221 E. 4th Ave. (℃ 800/556-5016 or 352/383-4101; www.lakeside-inn.com). Enjoy lemonade and cookies while rocking on the front porch overlooking the lake. **Mount Dora.** © 352/383-2165. www.mountdora.com. Take I-4 Exit 92, Hwy. 436, go west to U.S. 441, then north and follow the signs to Mount Dora and its "business district."

SPECIALTY STORES

Bass Pro Shops Outdoor World   If you're looking for the retail version of fishing and hunting (including archery) heaven, schedule a visit to this store in Belz's Festival Bay shopping center. The store also features areas for watersports equipment, camping gear, and outdoor apparel, as well as a golf pro shop and an aquarium. The store is open daily, usually from 9am to 6pm (closed Christmas). 5156 International Dr. © 407/563-5200. www.basspro.com.

Ron Jons Surf Shop   This chain retailer opened in 2003 at Festival Bay on the upper north end of International Drive. The 15,000-square-foot beach shop sports an island flair and offers a huge selection of its world famous surfer wear and beach gear, among its other unique (and occasionally offbeat) surfing-themed merchandise. Complementing the store is the new indoor Ron Jon Surf Park, also at Festival Bay, which splashed onto the scene late in 2006. 5156 International Dr. © 407/481-2555. www.ronjons.com.

9

Walt Disney World & Orlando After Dark

For those of who you actually have the energy after a day at the parks, and simply can't call it quits, Orlando has plenty of after-dark venues suitable for a night out on the town. That said, even if you're Orlando veterans, and not first-timers (the ones most likely to overdo it), if you try to go-go-go from morning until night, you *will* be completely exhausted after only a few days, and will end up needing a vacation after your vacation.

Admit it, some of you know the feeling. You're hard-core partiers who aren't willing to give it up after a long day in the parks. You want the after-hours adventure as well. The good news: Orlando's certainly willing to accommodate you, offering a wide array of entertainment options to satisfy your cravings.

The success of Universal's **CityWalk,** a district filled with a variety of clubs, shops, and themed restaurants, shows that many visitors have the pizzazz to

withstand life after a day of schlepping around the House of Mouse. But don't think **Downtown Disney West Side** and **Pleasure Island** are hurting for business. The clubs, shops, and restaurants found there are typically filled to capacity as well.

Check the "Calendar" section of Friday's **Orlando Sentinel** for up-to-the-minute details on local clubs, visiting performers, concerts, and events. It has hundreds of listings, many of which are online at **www.orlandosentinel.com**. The **Orlando Weekly** is a free magazine found in red boxes throughout Central Florida. It highlights the more offbeat and often more spur-of-the-moment performances. You can see it online at **www.orlandoweekly.com**. Another good source on the Internet is **www.orlando info.com**, operated by the Orlando/Orange County Convention & Visitors Bureau.

1 The Performing Arts

While Disney occasionally hosts classical music acts, you'll usually have to go downtown to get a taste of the traditional arts.

CONCERT HALLS & AUDITORIUMS
The city continues to dream of getting financing for a multimillion-dollar world-class performing arts center. While you're holding your breath, there are two existing facilities, both of which fall under the wand of Orlando Centroplex.

Florida Citrus Bowl With 70,000 seats, the bowl is the largest venue in the area for rock concerts, which in the past has featured such heavyweights as Elton John and the Rolling Stones. 1610 W. Church St. (at Tampa St.). ℭ **407/849-2001** for event information,

407/849-2020 to get box office information; ℂ **877/803-7073** or 407/839-3900 to charge tickets via Ticketmaster. www.orlandocentroplex.com. Parking $10.

TD Waterhouse Centre   Formerly the Orlando Arena, this 17,500-seat venue has a resume that includes the NBA's Orlando Magic (see "Spectator Sports," in chapter 7), the Orlando Predators Arena Football, the Orlando Seals Atlantic Coast Hockey Team, as well as big-name concert performers such as Garth Brooks, Elton John, and Bruce Springsteen. It also features family-oriented entertainment, including the Ringling Bros. Barnum & Bailey Circus in January and a slate of cultural offerings such as Broadway-style shows, ballets, plays, and symphony performances. 600 W. Amelia St. (between I-4 and Parramore Ave.). ℂ **407/849-2001** for event information, 407/849-2020 to get box office information; ℂ **877/803-7073** or 407/839-3900 for tickets through Ticketmaster. www. orlandocentroplex.com. Parking $4–$8.

THEATER

Orlando–UCF Shakespeare Festival *(Finds*   The company is known for placing traditional plays in contemporary settings and offers special programs throughout the year geared toward students. Shows currently scheduled range from *A Twelfth Night* to *The Jungle Book.* Performances are held in three venues: the Ken and Trisha Margeson Theater, which has 300 seats wrapped around three sides of the stage; the Marilyn and Sig Goldman Theater, an intimate 120-seater; and the Lake Eola Amphitheater, where the 936 seats give a view of Shakespeare under the stars. 812 E. Rollins St. ℂ **407/447-1700.** www.shakespearefest.org. Tickets $10–$35. Call ahead for reservations. Free parking for indoor season; metered parking in fall.

Sun Trust Broadway In Orlando   Touring Broadway productions frequently play this venue, so if you missed *The Lion King, Les Misérables,* or *Mamma Mia* when it was playing in your local area (or if it didn't make it to you at all), you may be able to catch them here. 201 S. Orange Ave., ℂ **407/423-9999.** www.broadwayacrossamerica.com. Tickets $12–$70 depending on show and seating; parking $8–$40.

Theatre Downtown   These engaging local actors, some who've been working here since the group's formation in 1984, put on a range of Broadway-style plays, from *The Rocky Horror Show* to *Grease.* Performances are Thursday through Saturday nights and Sunday matinees. 2113 N. Orange Ave. ℂ **407/841-0083** for tickets. www.theatredowntown.net. Tickets $18, $15 for students and seniors.

OPERA

Orlando Opera Company   Local professionals, joined by guest artists from around the country, perform a repertoire of traditional fare. In 2006, its well-received productions included *The Marriage of Figaro* and *Tosca,* among others. Shows held in the October-to-May season seldom sell out. Performances are staged at the Bob Carr Performing Arts Centre. 401 W. Livingston St. ℂ **800/336-7372** or 407/426-1700. www.orlando opera.org. Tickets $25–$120. Parking $5–$8.

DANCE

Orlando Ballet   Formerly called Southern Ballet Theatre, and celebrating their 32nd year, this troupe stages traditional shows such as *The Nutcracker, Peter and the Wolf,* and *Camelot* among others, using guest artists to augment local talent. There has been a resurgence of interest in the ballet here in recent years, but performances rarely sell out. The season runs from October to May. Performances feature the Orlando

---

Tips **First-Run Films**

Orlando has a number of movie multiplexes in the mainstream tourist areas. Most theaters offer discounted ticket pricing for children under 12 and discounted matinees (though, really, who's going to sit in a movie theater instead of the theme parks?); some also offer discounts to students and seniors (bring ID).

Some of the top draws include: **AMC 24** at Pleasure Island (② **407/298-4488**); **Cinemark 16 Festival Bay** on North International Drive (② **407/351-3117;** www.cinemark.com); **Muvico Pointe 21 Theatres** at Pointe Orlando on International Drive (② **407/926-6843;** www.muvico.com), which also sports an IMAX screen; and **Universal Cineplex 16** (② **407/354-5998;** www.enjoytheshow.com) at CityWalk.

Philharmonic Orchestra (see below) and are staged at the Bob Carr Performing Arts Centre. 401 W. Livingston St. ② **407/426-1733** for information; ② **877/803-7073** or 407/839-3900 to get tickets via Ticketmaster. www.orlandoballet.org. Tickets $12–$65. Parking $5–$8.

FILM

Enzian Theater   This full-time, not-for-profit alternative cinema features first-run, first-rate independent films in a 250-seat theater outfitted with a 33-foot screen. The Enzian also hosts a variety of special events, including March's 10-day run of the Florida Film Festival. 1300 S. Orlando Ave., Maitland. ② **407/629-1088** or 407/629-0054 for tickets and show times. General admission is $8, matinees are $6, and film society members pay $5.50. Prices will vary for special events. www.enzian.org.

CLASSICAL MUSIC

Florida Symphony Youth Orchestra   Kids get in on the classical action in a program with roots reaching back to 1956. Its musicians, from a radius reaching 40 or so miles from Orlando, play at the Bob Carr Performing Arts Centre and include joint performances with the Orlando Philharmonic (see below), Orlando Opera (above), and Orlando Ballet (also above). 401 W. Livingston St. ② **407/999-7800.** www.fsyo.org. Tickets $8–$30. Parking $5–$8.

Orlando Philharmonic Orchestra   The orchestra offers a varied schedule of classics and pop-influenced concerts throughout the year at the Bob Carr Performing Arts Centre. The musicians also accompany the Orlando Ballet (see above). Some performances are aimed solely at families (a past program set classical music to a host of kids' cartoons). 401 W. Livingston St. ② **407/896-6700.** www.orlandophil.org. Tickets begin at $12 ($8–$13 for students) and climb to $60 or more depending on seating and the scheduled performance. Parking $5–$8.

2 Dinner Theater

IN WALT DISNEY WORLD

Disney's magic continues well into the evenings, offering plenty of nighttime entertainment, including laser-light shows, fireworks, IllumiNations (p. 229), and Fantasmic (p. 232). There are also two distinctly different dinner shows worthy of special note, the Hoop-Dee-Doo Musical Revue and Disney's Spirit of Aloha Dinner Show, and a third show that's an occasional player.

Note: While they offer family-friendly entertainment, don't expect haute cuisine. The food, though good, takes a back seat to the show.

Hoop-Dee-Doo Musical Revue ★★★ (Moments)   This is Disney's most popular show, so make reservations *early.* The reward: You feast on a down-home, all-you-can-eat barbecue (fried chicken, smoked ribs, salad, corn on the cob, baked beans, bread, salad, strawberry shortcake—all of it quite good, by the way—and your choice of coffee, tea, beer, wine, sangria, or soda). And while you stuff yourself silly in Pioneer Hall, performers in 1890s garb lead you in a foot-stomping, hand-clapping, high-energy show that includes a lot of jokes you haven't heard since second grade. *Note:* Be prepared to join in on the fun or the singers and dancers along with the rest of the crowd will humiliate you until you do. This is entertaining for the entire family. Even my husband gave it a good grade, which is really saying something.

Reservations should be made at least 90 if not the full 180 days in advance (at which time full payment is expected), especially during peak periods such as summer and holidays. Show times are 5, 7:15, and 9:30pm daily (the show lasts about 2 hr.). If you catch one of the early shows, consider sticking around for the Electrical Water Pageant at 9:45pm, which can be viewed from the Fort Wilderness Beach. 3520 N. Fort Wilderness Trail (at Fort Wilderness Resort and Campground). ☎ 407/939-3463. www.disneyworld.com. Reservations required. Adults $50.22, kids 3–9 $25.43, including tax and tip. Free parking.

Disney's Spirit of Aloha Dinner Show (Moments)   While not quite as much in demand as the Hoop-Dee-Doo, the Polynesian Resort's delightful (and new) 2-hour show is like a big neighborhood party. Disney's Spirit of Aloha Dinner Show features Tahitian, Samoan, Hawaiian, and Polynesian singers, drummers, and dancers who entertain you while you feast on a menu that includes tropical appetizers, lanai roasted chicken, Polynesian wild rice, South Seas vegetables, dessert, wine, beer, and other beverages. It all takes place 5 nights a week in an open-air theater (dress for nighttime weather and bring the sweaters) with candlelit tables, red-flame lanterns, and tapa-bark paintings on the walls. Reservations should be made 60 to 90 days in advance (but can be made up to 180 days in advance—full payment is expected when booking), especially during peak periods such as summer and holidays. Show times are 5:15 and 8pm Tuesday through Saturday. 1600 Seven Seas Dr. (at Disney's Polynesian Resort). ☎ 407/939-3463. www.disneyworld.com. Reservations required. Adults $50.22, kids 3–9 $25.43, including tax. Free parking.

(Tips **If You're Lucky . . .**

Mickey's Backyard BBQ (☎ 407/939-3463; www.disneyworld.com) is offered at Pioneer Hall at Fort Wilderness Resort & Campground, where Tom Sawyer and Huck Finn allow you onto their home turf to have a thigh-slapping time and a feast in a covered, outdoor pavilion. Expect Mickey and his pals to join you for a meal that includes barbecued pork ribs, baked chicken, hot dogs, corn on the cob, baked beans, macaroni and cheese, watermelon, beer, wine, lemonade, iced tea, and dessert. Meals are served at 6:30 and 9:30pm and cost $39.01 for adults, $25 for kids 3 to 9, including tax and tip. It happens only on Tuesdays and Thursdays, generally from March through December, but the weather plays a big factor and shows have been known to be canceled, so **call ahead.**

ELSEWHERE IN ORLANDO

Outside the Disney zone, Orlando has an active dinner-theater scene, but keep in mind that the city is a family destination—and the dinner shows are very reflective of that. You won't find sophisticated offerings like those in major cultural centers such as New York, London, or Paris. Most of the local dinner shows focus on pleasing the kids, so if you're looking for fun, you'll find it; but if you want critically acclaimed entertainment, look elsewhere. You also won't find four-star food; but dinners are certainly palatable enough, with some a bit better than others. Attending a show is considered by many to be a quintessential Orlando experience, and if you arrive with the right attitude, you'll most likely have an enjoyable evening. Your children certainly will.

Note: Discount coupons to the dinner shows below can often be found inside the tourist magazines that are distributed in gas stations and tourist information centers; you'll also find them in many non-Disney hotel lobbies and sometimes on the listed websites.

Arabian Nights   If you're a horse fancier, this one's a must. One of the classier dinner-show experiences, it stars many of the most popular breeds, from chiseled Arabians to hard-driving Andalusians to beefcake Belgians. They giddy-up through performances that include Wild West trick riding, chariot races, slapstick comedy, and bareback bravado. Locals rate it No. 1 among Orlando dinner shows; however, my kids much preferred the action of some of the other shows in town. On most nights, the performance opens with a ground trainer working one-on-one with a black stallion. The dinner, served during the 2-hour show, includes salad; a choice of prime rib, chop steak, chicken, or lasagna; vegetables; potatoes; dessert; wine; and beer. Special diets can be accommodated with advance notice. Show times vary, but there is at least one show nightly. *Tip:* Book your tickets online, and you'll save about $10 to $15 per person off the regular admission price. 6225 W. Irlo Bronson Memorial Hwy. (U.S. 192), Kissimmee. ✆ 800/553-6116 or 407/239-9223. www.arabian-nights.com. Reservations recommended. $46–$57 adults, $21–$31 children 3–11. Free parking.

Dolly Parton's Dixie Stampede   This fun show came to town in June of 2003, bringing with it the rivalry of the North and the South. The audience, split into the North and the South, participates in (or roots for competitors in) different competitions held throughout the show to determine a final winner. Elaborately costumed cowboys, settlers, Native Americans, and southern belles sing and dance; and you also get stampeding horses and buffalo, and ostrich racing. The stunt riders are duly amazing, and selected members of the audience will have you in stitches during audience-participation moments. The evening is capped off with a patriotic song from Dolly herself (on video, of course). While you watch the show, you'll chow down on a four-course dinner that includes rotisserie chicken, barbecue pork, vegetable soup, corn on the cob, a biscuit, an herb-basted potato, and an apple turnover for dessert (lasagna and fruit are available for vegetarians). *Note:* Alcoholic beverages are now available—utensils, however, are not, so if you aren't into messy eating, bring plastic utensils with you. Kids under 4 eat free if sitting on a parent's lap and eating off their plate; otherwise, a seat and a meal require a ticket. It is an entertaining evening, though if there's a knock against it, it's that it's really a bunch of jumbled individual performances rather than a continuous show that carries through a single theme. Show times vary, but there's usually at least one show nightly. 8251 Vineland Ave. ✆ 866/443-4943 or 407/238-4455. www.dixiestampede.com. Reservations recommended. $49 adult, $22 kids 4–11. Free parking.

Moments   Prime Rib & a Side of Murder

Ever dream about being Sherlock Holmes? **Sleuths Mystery Dinner Show** ✎✎, 8267 International Dr. (© **800/393-1985** or 407/363-1985; www. sleuths.com), is an interactive dinner show staged in an intimate theater setting where guests play detective and try to solve a whodunit murder mystery.

A roster of suspects and impending victims (okay, they're really actors) interact with guests throughout the experience, which includes a preshow where you're introduced to the characters and served appetizers and a salad. When the actual performance begins, the actors both entrance and, at times, reduce you to hysterical laughter. Then it's time for dinner, which includes a choice of a Cornish game hen, prime rib (for $3 more), or lasagna. While eating, you discuss clues with the other detectives at your table (the round tables seat eight). Each table is given the opportunity to interrogate the suspects (which can get quite hilarious, depending on the amount of alcohol—you get unlimited wine and beer—people have consumed before they get to ask their questions). The suspects duly questioned, a mystery dessert is served, and then the murderer is revealed. It makes for a very entertaining yet relaxing evening out.

Eleven different productions (each is about 2½ hr. long) are offered throughout the year so you can keep coming back for more. There are even two mystery shows designed specifically for kids. Admission costs $48 adults, $24 kids 3 to 11. For kids' performances, the cost is $28 adults, $16 kids 3 to 11. Reservations are recommended.

To get here, from I-4 West take exit 75A, go right onto Universal Blvd., and follow through two lights to the Republic Square Plaza. Parking is free.

Medieval Times   Orlando has one of the nine Medieval Times shows in North America, and this is the show my kids rate No. 1 in town. Inside, guests gorge themselves on barbecued spareribs, herb-roasted chicken, soup, appetizer, potatoes, dessert, and beverages including beer. But because this is the 11th century, you eat with your fingers from metal plates while knights mounted on Andalusian horses run around the arena, jousting and clanging to please the fair ladies. Arrive 90 minutes early for good seats and to see the Medieval Village, a re-created Middle Ages settlement. A new storyline, "Knights of the Realm," introduced in 2004, adds a touch of romance between one of the knights and the princess to the action. Show times vary, but there is at least one performance nightly (7:30pm), two during peak seasons (6:30 and 8:30pm). 4510 W. Irlo Bronson Memorial Hwy. (U.S. 192), Kissimmee. © **888/935-6878** or 407/396-1518. www.medievaltimes.com. Reservations recommended. $50 adults, $34 children under 12. Free parking.

Pirates Dinner Adventure   The special-effects show at this theater includes a full-size ship in a 300,000-gallon lagoon, circus-style aerial acts, a lot of music, and a little drama. Your kids may even get a chance to participate. Dinner includes an appetizer buffet with the preshow, followed by roast chicken and beef, rice, vegetables, dessert, and coffee. After the show, you're invited to the Buccaneer Bash dance party where you can mingle with cast members. This is a smaller production than the above-mentioned shows, but it is nicely done, and the stadium and crowds are not as large and overwhelming. Show times vary, but there is at least one show nightly. 6400 Carrier Dr. © 800/866-2469 or 407/248-0590. www.orlandopirates.com. Reservations recommended. $52 adults, $32 children 3–11. Free parking.

3 At Walt Disney World

The places described here can be located on the map "Downtown Disney" on p. 325. For information about nighttime activities throughout Downtown Disney, call © 407/939-2648.

PLEASURE ISLAND

This 6-acre complex of nightclubs, restaurants, and shops, not to mention a multi-screen movie-theater, will not disappoint those in search of an exciting night on the town. Guests can walk the grounds and enjoy the sights, sounds, and surroundings free of charge, but if you want to enter the clubs, admission is required. A single admission price, $20.95 plus tax, allows you to club hop and celebrate New Year's Eve into the wee hours every night of the week. If you prefer to head to a single club (though it may be difficult to stick to just one), admission is $10.60 (though the Comedy Club and the Adventurers Club don't offer single-club admission prices, so it's all or nothing if you want to hang at either of them). If you have a *Water Park Fun & More* admission ticket (see p. 182 for more on Disney's ticket options), you can use one of your options for a 1-night admission to all clubs on Pleasure Island. Pay special attention to **Mannequins** (listed a little later). This club is the cream of Pleasure Island's crop and fills quickly, so late arrivals may be left at the door.

Pleasure Island is designed to look like an abandoned waterfront industrial district with clubs in its lofts and warehouses. But the streets are decorated with brightly colored lights and balloons. Dozens of searchlights play overhead, and rock music emanates from the bushes. You'll be given a map and show schedule when you enter the park. Take a look at it and plan your evening around the shows that interest you. The mood is always festive, especially at midnight, which is celebrated with a high-energy street party, live entertainment, a barrage of fireworks, and showers of confetti.

Although this is Disney, it's essentially a bar district where liquor is served, so if you're sending your older children, use the same rules you use at home. Also note that they must be 18 to get in unless accompanied by a parent or legal guardian.

Pleasure Island has seven regular clubs, plus BET Soundstage, which is included in the ticket on nights it doesn't have a special concert going. In addition to the clubs, there are shops and eateries (some with outdoor umbrella tables) on the island. **Planet Hollywood** (p. 155) is adjacent. (You don't need an admission ticket to eat at any of the Pleasure Island restaurants.)

For more information on Pleasure Island's clubs and events, call © **407/939-2648** or surf over to **www.disneyworld.com**. Clubs are open daily from 7pm to 2am; shops open at 11am, and some are open till midnight or later. There's free self-parking, but as the night wears on spots can become very hard to find.

Here's the club lineup:

Adventurers Club   The most unique of Pleasure Island's clubs occupies a multi-story building that, according to legend, was designed to house the library and archae-ological trophy collection of island founder and compulsive explorer, Merriweather

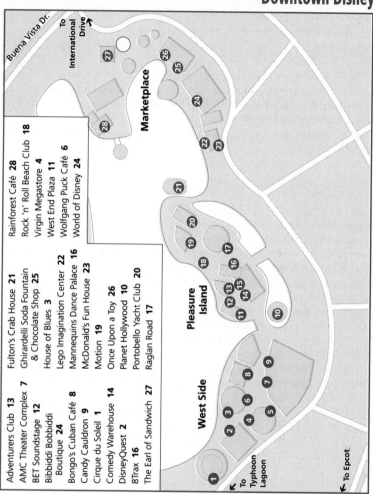

Downtown Disney

Marketplace

Pleasure Island

West Side

To Epcot

To Typhoon Lagoon

Buena Vista Dr.

To International Drive

Adventurers Club **13**
AMC Theater Complex **7**
BET Soundstage **12**
Bibbiddi Bobbiddi
  Boutique **24**
Bongo's Cuban Café **8**
Candy Cauldron **9**
Cirque du Soleil **1**
Comedy Warehouse **14**
DisneyQuest **2**
8Trax **16**
The Earl of Sandwich **27**

Fulton's Crab House **21**
Ghirardelli Soda Fountain
  & Chocolate Shop **25**
House of Blues **3**
Lego Imagination Center **22**
Mannequins Dance Palace **16**
McDonald's Fun House **23**
Motion **19**
Once Upon a Toy **26**
Planet Hollywood **10**
Portobello Yacht Club **20**
Raglan Road **17**

Rainforest Café **28**
Rock 'n' Roll Beach Club **18**
Virgin Megastore **4**
West End Plaza **11**
Wolfgang Puck Café **6**
World of Disney **24**

Adam Pleasure, a figment of Disney's imagination. It's also the global headquarters for the Adventurers Club, which Pleasure headed until he vanished at sea in 1941. The plush club is chock-full of artifacts: early aviation photos, hunting trophies, shrunken heads, Buddhas, goddesses, and a mounted "yakoose," a half yak, half moose that occasionally speaks, whether you've been drinking or not. In the eerie Mask Room, more strange sounds are heard, and the 100 or so masks move their eyes, jeer, and make odd pronouncements. Also on hand are Pleasure's zany band of globetrotting friends and servants, played by skilled actors who interact with guests while staying in character. Comedy, cabaret, and other shows run in various rooms within the club. We could easily hang out here all night, sipping potent tropical drinks in the library or the bar, where elephant-foot bar stools rise and sink mysteriously. This one's an especially good choice for those who may find dancing the night away at the other clubs a bit more than they bargained for.

BET Soundstage   This club grooves—loudly—to the sounds of reggae, the smooth moves of traditional R&B, and the rhyme of hip-hop. If you like the BET Cable Network, you'll love it. You can boogie on an expansive dance floor or kick back on an outdoor terrace. The club also serves Caribbean-style finger food and periodically has concerts for a separate charge (© **407/934-7666**). You must be 21 to enter Thursday through Saturday nights.

Comedy Warehouse   Housed in the island's former power plant, the Comedy Warehouse has a rustic interior with tiered seating. A troupe of comics—the Who, What, and Warehouse Players—perform 45-minute improvisational comedy shows based on audience suggestions. This is Disney, so the shows are neither as risqué as those at other improv clubs nor candidates for anyone's top 10 (though they do have their moments). There are several shows nightly and drinks are served. Arrive early.

8Trax   Disco and bell-bottoms rule in this 1970s-style club, where some 50 TV monitors air diverse shows and videos over the dance floor. A DJ plays everything from "YMCA" to "The Hustle" while the disco ball spins. All you need to bring is your polyester and patent leather.

Mannequins Dance Palace   Housed in a vast dance hall with a small-town, movie-house facade, Mannequins is supposed to be a converted mannequin warehouse (remember, you're still in Disney World). This high-energy club has a big rotating dance floor, and it's a local favorite—so much so that it's one of the toughest clubs in Orlando to get into—so arrive early, especially on weekends. Those who get in find three levels of bars and hangout space that are festooned with elaborately costumed mannequins and moving scenery suspended from the overhead rigging. A DJ plays contemporary tunes filtered through speakers powerful enough to wake Sleeping Beauty, and there are high-tech lighting effects. You must be 21 to get in, and they're very serious about it. Have your ID ready, even if you learned to dance to the Beatles.

Rock 'n' Roll Beach Club   Once the laboratory in which Pleasure developed a unique flying machine, this three-story structure today houses an always-crowded dance club where live bands play classic rock from the '60s through the '90s. There

---

Tips **The Luck of the Irish**

The Great Irish Pubs of Florida, Inc. (the company that created the Nine Fine Irishmen pub in Las Vegas's New York–New York Hotel & Casino) has brought the luck of the Irish to Downtown Disney. In October 2005, on the former site of the Pleasure Island Jazz Company, **Raglan Road** opened its doors to the public. The pub is an impressive and inviting addition to Disney's collection of unique eateries, immersing guests in a wholly Irish environment that includes custom-made furnishings direct from the Emerald Isles, incredibly high ceilings, rich woodwork, and leaded glass. The spirited atmosphere, where singing, dancing, and clapping are all encouraged, is enhanced by the live nightly entertainment. And the food's pretty good, too, thanks to the culinary creations of Kevin Dundon, one of Ireland's most celebrated chefs.

Finds Not Your Ordinary Circus

Lions and tigers and bears?

Oh, no. But you won't feel cheated.

This Disney partnership with the famed no-animals circus is located in Downtown Disney West Side. **Cirque du Soleil,** which translates to "circus of the sun" and flutters off the tongue as *"SAIRK doo so-LAY,"* is nonstop energy. At times it seems all 64 performers are on stage simultaneously, especially during the intricately choreographed trampoline routine. Trapeze artists, high-wire walkers, an airborne gymnast, a posing strong-man, mimes, and two zany clowns cement a show called *La Nouba* (it means "live it up") into a five-star performance.

Of all the Cirque du Soleil shows, I think this one may be second only to *Mystère* in Las Vegas. That said, though *La Nouba* is a ton of fun, it's also one of the priciest shows in town. If you're on a tight or even modest budget, it may be gut-check time: Can you blow your entertainment allowance for a day or two on 90 minutes of fun? There are three ticket categories that depend on seating location: $95 for adults and $76 for kids 3 to 9 (plus tax) for central seats; $77 and $62, respectively, for seats to the right and left of the stage; and $61 and $49 for the very upper levels. Shows are at 6 and 9pm, Tuesdays through Saturdays, though the show is dark 6 weeks each year. There are occasional matinees, so call ahead (© 407/939-7600) or check the show's website (www.cirquedusoleil.com) for information and tickets.

---

are bars on all three floors, including one that serves international brews. The first level contains the dance floor. The second and third levels offer air hockey, pool tables, basketball machines, pinball, video games, darts, and a pizza and beer stand.

Motion   Pleasure Island's newest dance club is a hyperactive joint that features Top-40 tunes appealing to younger or young-at-heart partiers. The club uses moody blue lighting to halfway convey the sensation that you're dancing the night away in space.

DISNEY'S WEST SIDE

This area adjoins Pleasure Island and offers additional shops, restaurants, and a 24-screen AMC Theater. But the two most popular entries are:

Bongo's Cuban Café *(Overrated*   Created by Cuban-American singer Gloria Estefan and her husband, Emilio, the cafe is Downtown Disney's version of old Havana. There are leopard spotted chairs and mosaic bar stools shaped like bongo drums. There's no dance floor to speak of, though you can cha-cha on the patio, an upstairs number that overlooks the rest of West Side. It's a great place to sit back and bask in the Latin rhythms and inviting surroundings. But, while the mood is good, the food, and at times the service, is a little lacking. Open daily from 11am to 2am, though it sometimes closes earlier. © 407/828-0999. www.bongoscubancafe.com. No cover charge. Free self-parking.

House of Blues Several well-known artists have performed here, including Jethro Tull, Blue Oyster Cult, Quiet Riot, Duran Duran, and others. The barnlike building, with three tiers, may be a little difficult for those with disabilities to maneuver in, but there really isn't a bad seat in the house. The atmosphere is dark and boozy, perfect for the bluesy sounds that raise the rafters. The dance floor is big enough to boogie on without doing the bump with a stranger. You can dine in the adjoining restaurant (p. 156) on baby back ribs, Louisiana crawfish, jambalaya, New Orleans–style shrimp, and Cajun meatloaf. There's also a Sunday gospel brunch (see p. 156 for more about the menu). ℂ **407/934-2583.** www.hob.com. Cover charges vary by event/artist. Free self-parking.

4 CityWalk

Located between the Islands of Adventure and Universal Studios Florida theme parks, this nightclub, restaurant, and shopping district had its coming-out party in 1999 and competes head-to-head with Disney's Pleasure Island. It opens daily at 11am, but the hours of many clubs and restaurants vary, so call in advance if you're interested in a specific venue. Most clubs stay open until 2am.

At 30 acres, CityWalk (ℂ **407/363-8000;** www.citywalk.com) is five times larger than Pleasure Island. Alcohol is prominently featured here as it's geared to an adult crowd; younger members of the family should always be accompanied by an adult if allowed to tag along. The nights can get pretty wild. (*Note:* Some clubs here won't allow anyone under 21 inside after a certain hour—see the listings below for details.)

> (Tips) **Chilling Out**
>
> You can grab a margarita to go and "chill" in the brightly colored wooden chairs (think of the Adirondacks) outside Jimmy Buffet's Margaritaville. It's a perfect spot to watch the crowds scurrying to and from the theme parks.

Just like Pleasure Island, you can walk this district for free at night or visit individual clubs and pay an individual cover charge. CityWalk also offers two **party passes.** A pass to all clubs costs $9.95 plus tax. For $13 plus tax, you get a club pass and a movie at Universal Cineplex (ℂ **407/354-5998**). Universal also offers free club access to those who buy select multiday theme-park tickets (see chapter 7, "Exploring Beyond Disney: Universal Orlando, SeaWorld & Other Attractions"). There's also a "Dinner and a Movie" option; for $19.95 you can get entrance to a movie at the Cineplex and dinner at one of the CityWalk restaurants (select menu items apply—see **www.universal orlando.com** for complete details).

Daytime parking in the Universal Orlando garages costs $9, but self-parking is free after 6pm. To get to CityWalk, take I-4 Exit 74B (westbound) or 75A (eastbound) and follow the signs to the parks.

Bob Marley—A Tribute to Freedom This hybrid bar/restaurant has a party atmosphere that will make the food more appealing as the night wears on. The clapboard building is said to be a replica of Marley's home in Kingston. Jamaican vittles—such as meat patties, jerk snapper, and, the brew of champions, Red Stripe Beer—are served under patio umbrellas amid portraits of the original Rastamon. If you try an

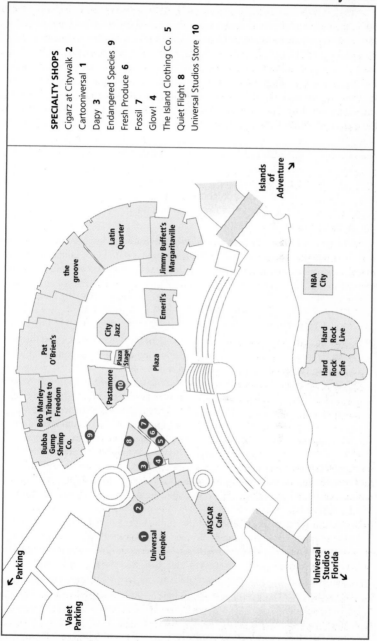

SPECIALTY SHOPS

Cigarz at Citywalk **2**
Cartooniversal **1**
Dapy **3**
Endangered Species **9**
Fresh Produce **6**
Fossil **7**
Glow! **4**
The Island Clothing Co. **5**
Quiet Flight **8**
Universal Studios Store **10**

Extreme Measure, have a designated driver. Local and national reggae bands perform on a microdot stage. Open daily 4pm to 2am. ✆ **407/224-3663**. Cover charge $7 after 8pm, more for special acts. Must be 21 or older after 9pm.

CityJazz   The cover charge at this club includes the **Downbeat Jazz Hall of Fame** (with memorabilia from Louis Armstrong, Ella Fitzgerald, and other greats) as well as the **Thelonious Monk Institute of Jazz,** a performance venue that's also the site of jazz workshops. The two-story, 10,500-square-foot building houses more than 500 pieces of memorabilia representing Dixieland, swing, bebop, and modern jazz. It also has a state-of-the-art sound system and stage. Graphic murals and oversize black-and-white photographs set the mood. Acts of national renown perform frequently. It's a real treat for true jazz fans, who can sip cocktails while browsing. On the food side of the equation, expect tapas, sushi, escargot, and such. Thursday through Saturday nights the theme gives way to comedy as BONKERZ Comedy Club invites you in for a good laugh with nationally recognized comics. Open Sunday through Thursday 8pm to 1am, Friday and Saturday from 7pm to 2am. ✆ **407/224-2189**. Cover charge $7 (more for special events). Must be 18 to enter.

the groove   This often-crowded multilevel club features a huge dance floor, a number of bars, and a handful of lounges for just hanging out. Three unique lounges are outfitted in blue, green, and red—each features its own decor, music, bar, and

---

Tips   **Lounging Around**

Some of Orlando's most unique nightlife is located in its hotels. Even locals head to some of these after dark. Consider any of the following and their parent hotels, all of which are listed in chapter 4:

   Todd English's bluezoo bar at the Walt Disney World Dolphin (✆ **407/ 934-1111**; www.thebluezoo.com) serves up classic cocktails in a hip and chic atmosphere. At Disney's Grand Floridian (✆ **407/824-3000**), a pianist and band alternate playing time from 3 to 9:45pm in the lobby. **Outer Rim** at the Contemporary Resort (✆ **407/824-1000**) is a trendy nightspot and close to the monorail. **Kimono's** sushi bar in the Walt Disney World Swan (✆ **407/ 934-3000**) offers karaoke after 8:30pm, while the entertainment is purely visual at the **Dolphin Lobby Bar** in the Renaissance Orlando Resort at Sea-World (✆ **407/351-5555**), which overlooks the huge atrium, glass elevators, and koi pond.

   The **Top of the Palace Lounge** at the Buena Vista Palace (✆ **407/397-6516**) has a great view of Disney's fireworks. **Baskerville's** in the Grosvenor (✆ **407/827-6534**) offers a solve-it-yourself mystery dinner show on Saturdays at 6 and 9pm ($40 adults, $11 kids 3–9). Nearby, **Moriarty's Pub** features English ales to go along with darts or billiards. And **Auggie's Jammin' Piano Bar** offers dueling pianos at 9pm nightly at the Gaylord Palms (✆ **407/586-0000**). Sit back and relax (in velvet chairs, we might add) at the **Velvet Lounge** at the Hard Rock Hotel (✆ **407/503-3700**), where you can down cocktails while surrounded by rock-'n'-roll memorabilia and music.

specialty drink. The high-tech sound system will blow your hair back; if you need a sound check try the upper level patio for a brief reprieve. A DJ plays tunes most nights, featuring the latest in hip-hop, retro hits, techno, and alternative music. Bands occasionally play the house, too. Open daily from 9pm to 2am. © **407/363-8000.** Cover charge $7. Must be 21 to get in.

Hard Rock Live   The first concert hall to bear the Hard Rock name is next door to the largest Hard Rock Cafe in the world (p. 161). This building, fashioned to look like an ancient coliseum, has a 2,500-seat concert venue. The sightlines and the sound system are great. Call ahead to find out what acts will be featured during your visit. Tickets for big-name performers sell fast. Concerts generally begin about 8pm. © **407/351-7655.** www.hardrocklive.com. Tickets $6–$150, depending on concert.

Jimmy Buffett's Margaritaville   Flip-flops and flowered shirts are the proper apparel here. Music from the maestro is piped throughout the building, with live music performed on a small stage inside later in the evening. A Jimmy sound-alike strums on the spacious back porch of indecision. True Parrot Heads know the lyrics at least as well as the singers. Bar-wise, there are three options. The Volcano erupts margarita mix; the Land Shark has fins hanging from the ceiling; and the 12 Volt, is, well, a little electrifying—we'll leave it at that. If you opt for dinner among the palm trees, go for the true Key West experience. Early in the day that means a cheeseburger (in paradise); later it's conch fritters, one of many kinds of fish (pompano, sea bass, dolphin fish), and Key lime pie. Open daily from 11am to 2am. (See p. 162 for more on the food here.) © **407/224-2155.** www.margaritavilleorlando.com. Cover $5 after 10pm (waived if you come only to dine on the deck).

Latin Quarter   This two-level restaurant/nightclub offers you a chance to absorb the salsa-and-samba culture of 21 Latin nations. It's filled with the music of the merengue, the mambo, and the tango, along with a bit of Latin rock thrown in for good measure—be prepared to move your hips. The surprisingly intimate atmosphere features mountainous architecture and waterfalls surrounding the dance floor; you'll feel like you're dancing in a Mayan temple. The sound system is loud enough to blow you into the next county, but before that happens you can check out the club's Latin American art gallery. Open Monday through Friday, 11:30am until 10pm, Saturday and Sunday noon to 2am. © **407/224-3663.**

NASCAR Café   This one-of-a-kind NASCAR-licensed eatery is a must for gearheads, though its basic vittles (so-so steaks, chicken, pork chops, shrimp, and sandwiches, most under $8) won't win any culinary awards. Race-related souvenirs and video games fill the first floor. Open daily from 11am to 11pm or later. © **407/224-3663.**

NBA City If you're a fan of the NBA, then this one's a must. Hoops and memorabilia hang from the walls, and TV monitors play seemingly every game on the airwaves. The mixed menu ($5–$20) ranges from steaks and chicken to fish, pasta, and sandwiches. Fans will love it, but if you're looking for better-than-average food and aren't a basketball junkie, look elsewhere. Open daily from 11am to midnight (last seating at 10:30pm), later on Friday and Saturday (last seating 11:30pm). ℭ **407/363-5919.**

Pat O'Brien's Just like the French Quarter, which is home to the original Patty O's, drinking, drinking, and more drinking are the highlights here. Creole treats and sandwiches (most $8–$10) take up only a page or two of the menu—the rest is filled with wild alcoholic libations. Enjoy the piano bar or the flame-throwing fountain while you suck down the drink of the Big Easy, a Hurricane. Although you can order a soft drink, Pat O'Brien's primarily promotes the hard stuff. If your plans for the evening fall anything short of full intoxication (unless you're the designated driver for the aforementioned planners), this may not be the place for you. Open daily from 3pm to 2am. ℭ **407/224-2106.** www.patobriens.com.

5 Hot Spots in Orlando

Pleasure Island, Downtown Disney, and CityWalk are the biggest nighttime draws for most tourists and some locals. However, the dozens of clubs and bars on International Drive, along Orange Avenue, and in the rest of downtown Orlando attract most homegrown night owls, business travelers who want to stay as far as possible from the Mickey madness, and a small number of enterprising tourists who venture north at night. These places can be located on the map "Downtown Orlando Nightlife" on p. 333.

Cricketers Arms Pub Regardless of whether you're British or just a sympathizer, this pub is a fun place to party. As the name implies, cricket (and soccer) matches are featured on the telly. Nightly entertainment ranges from karaoke to live bands (usually blues or soft rock). The revelry offers a good excuse to try a pint or two of any of the 17 beers and ales on tap, such as Boddingtons, Fullers ESB, and Old Speckled Hen. There's also a fun menu that offers English standards such as cottage pie and fish and chips, among others (main courses $4.50–$19, most under $10). Open daily from noon to 2am. 8445 International Dr. ℭ **407/354-0686.** www.cricketersarmspub.com. Free parking.

Sak Comedy Lab Locals perform at a 200-seat club that has performances several nights a week. Favorites include the Duel of Fools, where two teams face off in improvised scenes based on suggestions from the audience, and Lab Rats, where

---

Tips **Ghostly Experience**

Orlando Ghost Tours (ℭ **407/247-0452;** www.hauntedorlando.com) puts a different spin on the city's nightlife with 2-hour walking tours that explore the downtown's spookier side. The tours include narratives (some funnier than others) on Florida history and folklore followed by a chance to use "ghost-finding" equipment in a haunted building. It's good fun for those into the supernatural and ghost stories. The cost is $25 adults, $20 for seniors and college students, and $15 kids 7 to 12. Tours run Monday through Saturday at 8pm.

Downtown Orlando Nightlife

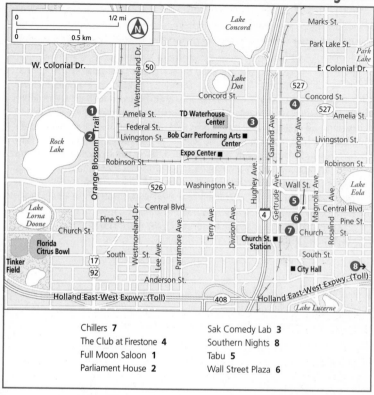

Chillers **7**
The Club at Firestone **4**
Full Moon Saloon **1**
Parliament House **2**

Sak Comedy Lab **3**
Southern Nights **8**
Tabu **5**
Wall Street Plaza **6**

students play in improv formats. Shows are usually Tuesday through Wednesday at 9pm, Thursday through Saturday at 8 and 10pm. 380 W. Amelia St. ✆ **407/648-0001.** www.sak.com. Admission $10–$13. Parking $5–$8.

Tabu   Inside a renovated theater, this downtown club holds a special appeal for members of the under-30 crowd who are on the prowl or older cruisers who want to relive their glory days. DJs spinning techno, top-40, hip-hop, dance, R&B, and Latin's hottest hits are the featured attraction on various theme nights. The club has a "stylish dress" requirement; leave the denim and tank tops at home. Open Tuesday through Sunday from 10pm to 2am. 46 N. Orange Ave., Orlando. ✆ **407/648-8363.** www.tabu nightclub.com. Cover $5–$12 most nights. Parking $5–$8, metered parking available. Must be 18 to enter.

6 Gay & Lesbian Nightspots

You can get all sorts of useful information on events from **Gay, Lesbian & Bisexual Community Services of Central Florida,** 946 N. Mills Ave., Orlando, FL 32803 (✆ **407/228-8272;** www.glbcc.org). **GayOrlando Network (www.gayorlando.com)** and the **Gay Guide to Florida (http://gay-guide.com)** also feature a lot of nightlife

Other Places to Party

In addition to the other clubs listed in this section, other Downtown hot spots include **Chillers, the Big Belly Brewery,** and **Lattitudes,** 33 W. Church St. (© 407/939-4270)—three separate clubs located in a single tri-level building that are all geared to the young-adult crowd with an atmosphere that's very casual. Another nighttime complex lined with clubs and bars is **Wall Street Plaza (www.wallstplaza.net),** a "meet market" on Wall Street that's home to **The Globe** (© 407/849-9904), a European patio cafe; **Slingapours** (© 407/849-9904), a dance club with an indoor and outdoor patio for relaxing; **Waitiki** (© 407/849-0471), a retro Tiki lounge and restaurant; the **Monkey Bar** (© 407/849-0471), a hip martini lounge and cocktail bar; **One Eyed Jacks** (© 407/648-2050) and the **Loaded Hog** (© 407/649-1918), both party bars; the **Tuk Tuk Room** (© 407/849-9904), a cocktail and sushi lounge; and the **Wall Street Cantina** (© 407/420-1515), a bar that serves mean margaritas.

entries. Travelers interested in sampling some of the city's gay and lesbian hot spots can check out the following places:

The Club at Firestone   Go-go boys and drag queens turn Saturday nights into a raucous party. The rest of the week, theme nights (Latin, hip-hop, and a crowd both gay and straight) and other shows keep the dance floor busy. This is a serious club with dark lighting, cavernous rooms, and a high-energy sound. Well-known DJs are sometimes featured. Upstairs, the View Bar offers a good look at the dance floor below. Open daily until 2am; show times vary. 578 N. Orange Ave. (at Concord St. in a converted garage that still bears a Firestone sign). © 407/872-0066. www.clubatfirestone.com. Cover charge varies, usually from $6–$10. Limited lot parking available for $3–$5.

Full Moon Saloon   DJs keep things hopping most nights, but the Moon sometimes offers live entertainment including bands. This club stakes a rightful claim to being Orlando's oldest gay bar. Expect a lot of leather and cowboy duds. The interior is big, but much of the fun happens on the patio and in the expanding backyard. Open daily from noon to 2am; show times vary. 500 N. Orange Blossom Trail (just west of downtown). © 407/648-8725. www.fullmoonsaloon.com. Open daily noon–2am. Free parking.

Parliament House   Now under new management, this is still one of Orlando's wilder, and most popular, gay spots. Not a fancy place, the Parliament House has had years of hard partying and shows it. This is a place to drink, dance, and watch shows that include female impersonators and male revues. There are also DJs. A relatively large dance floor tends to get small pretty quickly as the crowd swells. The Parliament has six bars scattered throughout the premises and a newly renovated 130-room hotel with a courtyard, small beach, and full-service restaurant. Open daily from 4pm to 2am; show times vary. 410 N. Orange Blossom Trail (just west of downtown). © 407/425-7571. www.parliamenthouse.com. Cover $2–$10. Free parking.

Southern Nights This perennial award-winner for Orlando's "Best Gay Bar" (according to the readers of a local alternative weekly paper) reopened in spring 2005 after undergoing a top-to-bottom makeover that added a new sound system, lighting, special effects, and a second lounge. It attracts a pretty diverse crowd. 375 S. Bumby Ave. (between Anderson St. and Colonial Dr.). *©* **407/898-0424.** www.southern-nights.com. Rendezvous opens at 5pm, Southern Nights at 10pm Mon–Sat. Free parking, valet $5, nearby lots $2.

7 Sports Bars

Champions The interior is chockablock with signed photos, posters, and artifacts. Entertainment includes pool tables, video games, Foosball, darts, and coin-op football and basketball. In addition, sporting events are aired on large-screen TVs and on smaller monitors around the room (a calendar at the entrance lists all game times). Champions offers a fairly extensive bar-food menu.

Note to single women: Men outnumber women about five to one, so this is a good place to meet guys if you don't mind the odds. Open Monday through Friday 4pm to 1am, Saturday and Sunday noon to 1am. In Marriott's Orlando World Center, 8701 World Center Dr. *©* **407/239-4200.** Free self-parking; valet parking $17.

ESPN Sports If you're dying for a sports fix, this is it. Ninety monitors—there are even a few in the bathrooms—broadcast sporting events from around the world. Need we say more? There's a full-service bar, but there's also a restaurant (p. 154) and a small arcade, so you have an excuse to drag your family along. Open daily from 11:30am to 1am. In Walt Disney World at Disney's BoardWalk Resort. *©* **407/939-3463.** www.disneyworld.com. Free parking.

⌒Tips Unsportsmanlike Options

Disney's BoardWalk has a few options for folks searching for off-the-field nightlife. Street performers sing, dance, and do a little juggling and magic most evenings on the outdoor promenade.

Atlantic Dance (*©* **407/939-2444** for limited recorded information) features top-40 and '80s dance hits Tuesday through Saturday. It's open to everyone 21 and over. Hours are from 9pm to 2am, and admission is free.

The rustic saloon-style **Jellyrolls** (*©* **407/939-5100**) offers dueling pianos and a boisterous crowd. Strictly for the over-21 set, it's open daily from 7pm to 2am. There's an $8 cover.

If you're looking to hoist a pint, the **Big River Grill & Brewing Works** (*©* **407/939-5100**) serves microbrewed beer as well as steaks, ribs, chicken, fish, sandwiches, and salads. Prices range from $9 to $25. It's open Monday through Thursday from 11:30am to 1am; Friday through Sunday from 11:30am to 2am. It's near Atlantic Dance.

Disney's BoardWalk can be a cheap night out if you enjoy strolling and people-watching (and if you stay out of the restaurants and clubs). It has something of a midway atmosphere reminiscent of Atlantic City's heyday.

Official All-Star Café This small chain entry opened at Disney in late 1998. It's just a line drive away from the entrance to the stadium where the Atlanta Braves play their spring training games (see "Spectator Sports," in chapter 7). The interior is dotted with sports memorabilia from Andre Agassi, Wayne Gretzky, Joe Montana, Shaquille O'Neal, and Tiger Woods. There are also a ton of televisions playing your favorite games. Open daily from 11:30am to 9pm (though hours can vary according to scheduled events at Wide World of Sports). At Walt Disney World's Wide World of Sports Complex. ℂ 407/939-3463. No cover. Free parking.

10

Side Trips from Orlando

Although many visitors to Orlando never venture outside the city while on vacation, an excursion away from the hubbub of the theme parks can allow you time to recharge your batteries, while still offering plenty of fun and enjoyment. One destination that many families will drive some distance to see is Busch Gardens Tampa Bay, another major area kiddie attraction an hour west of Orlando on I-4. But don't stop there: The city of Tampa is an exciting destination on its own.

Florida's very own city by the bay, Tampa is the commercial center of Florida's west coast—a major seaport and a center of banking, high-tech manufacturing, and cigar making (half a billion drugstore stogies a year). Downtown Tampa may roll up its sidewalks after dark, but a short ride will take you to Ybor City, the historic Cuban enclave, now an exciting entertainment and dining venue.

Visitors who opt to head southeast to the Space Coast may find themselves privy to the eye-popping spectacle of rockets blasting off from the Kennedy Space Center at Cape Canaveral. Nearby in Cocoa Beach, they can catch a wave with the surfing crowd.

Finally, you can catch both rays and races at Daytona Beach, though nowadays visitors seem to come more for the latter than the former. The city offers fabulous beaches, great nightlife, and lots of NASCAR excitement. It's also a mecca for motorcycle enthusiasts during its popular Bike Week (see "Calendar of Events," on p. 26).

1 Tampa

85 miles SW of Orlando

Even if you stay on the beaches 20 miles to the west, you should consider driving into Tampa for a mild taste of metropolis. If you have children in tow, they may *demand* that you go into the city so they can ride the rides and see the animals at Busch Gardens (and if you have purchased the FlexTicket, see p. 257, you'll get free admission and shuttle service from Orlando to the park). Once there, you can also educate them (and yourself) at the Florida Aquarium and the city's other fine museums. Additionally, historic Ybor City has the bay area's newest and most contemporary nightlife.

ESSENTIALS

GETTING THERE **Tampa International Airport** (© 813/870-8770; www.tampaairport.com), 5 miles northwest of downtown Tampa, is the major air gateway to this area. Most major and many no-frills airlines serve Tampa International, and all the major U.S. rental-car agencies have operations there (see appendix B, "Useful Toll-Free Numbers and Websites," for the major airlines' and car-rental agencies' contact details).

Tampa

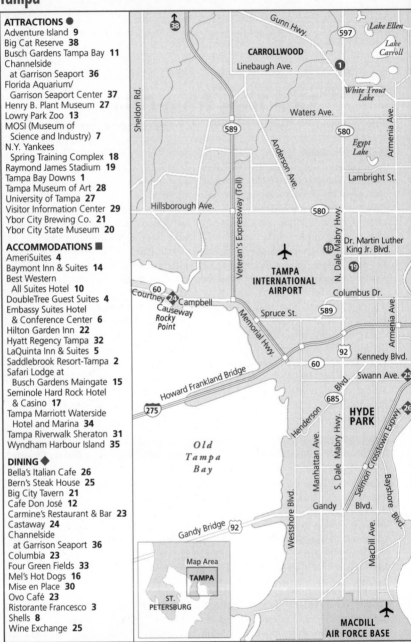

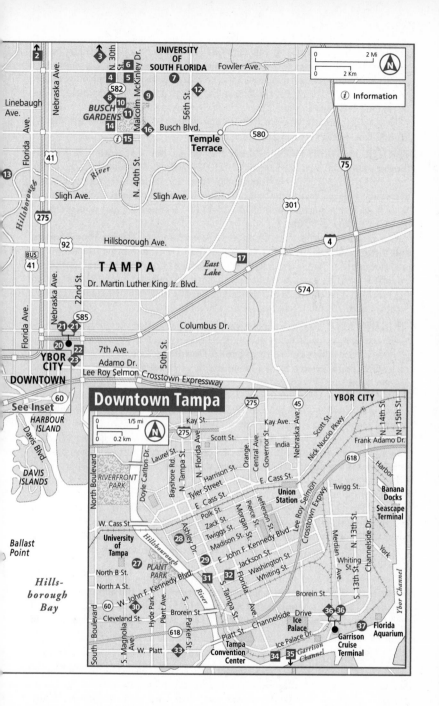

The **Limo/SuperShuttle** (© **800/282-6817** or 727/527-1111; www.supershuttle. com) operates van services between the airport and hotels throughout the Tampa Bay area. Fares for one person range from $35 to $48 round-trip, depending on your destination. **Taxis** are plentiful at the airport; the ride to downtown Tampa takes about 15 minutes and costs $15 to $20.

Amtrak trains arrive downtown at the **Tampa Amtrak Station,** 601 Nebraska Ave. N. (© **800/872-7245;** www.amtrak.com).

VISITOR INFORMATION   Contact the **Tampa Bay Convention & Visitors Bureau,** 400 N. Tampa St., Tampa, FL 33602-4706 (© **800/448-2672,** 800/368-2672, or 813/223-2752; www.visittampabay.com), for advance information. If you're downtown, you can head to the bureau's **visitor information center** at 400 N. Tampa St. (Channelside), Suite 2800 (© **813/223-1111**). It's open Monday through Saturday from 9:30am to 5:30pm.

Operated by the Ybor City Chamber of Commerce, the **Centro Ybor Museum and Visitor Information Center,** in Centro Ybor, 1514½ E. 8th Ave. (between 15th and 16th sts. E.), Tampa, FL 33605 (© **813/248-3712;** www.ybor.org), distributes information and has exhibits on the area's history. A 7-minute video will orient you to this area—an 8-block stretch of Seventh Avenue. The center is open Monday through Saturday from 10am to 6pm, Sunday from noon to 6pm.

GETTING AROUND   Like most other Florida destinations, it's virtually impossible to see Tampa's major sights and enjoy its best restaurants without a car. You can get around downtown via the free **Uptown-Downtown Connector Trolley,** which runs north–south between Harbor Island and the city's North Terminal bus station on Marion Street at I-275. The trolleys run every 10 minutes from 6am to 6pm Monday through Friday. Southbound, they follow Tampa Street between Tyler and Whiting streets, and Franklin Street between Whiting Street and Harbor Island. Northbound trolleys follow Florida Avenue from the St. Pete Times Forum to Cass Street. The trolleys are operated by the Hillsborough Area Regional Transit/HARTline (© **813/254-4278;** www.hartline.org), the area's transportation authority, which also provides scheduled **bus service** ($1.30–$3) between downtown Tampa and the suburbs. Pick up a route map at the visitor center (see above).

The transportation situation has gotten somewhat better, not to mention nostalgic, with the **TECO Line Street Car System,** a new but old-fashioned 2⅓-mile streetcar system, complete with overhead power lines, which hauls passengers between downtown and Ybor City via the St. Pete Times Forum, Channelside, Garrison Seaport, and the Florida Aquarium. The cars run every 30 minutes; one-way fares are $1.80. Check with the visitor center or call HARTline for schedules.

Taxis in Tampa don't normally cruise the streets for fares, but they do line up at public places, such as hotels, the performing-arts center, and bus and train depots. If you need a taxi, call **Tampa Bay Cab** (© **813/251-5555**), **Yellow Cab** (© **813/253-0121**), or **United Cab** (© **813/253-2424**). Fares are $1.75 at flag fall, plus $1.75 for each mile.

EXPLORING THE THEME & ANIMAL PARKS

Adventure Island *Kids*   If the summer heat gets to you before one of Tampa's famous thunderstorms brings late-afternoon relief, you can take a waterlogged break at this 25-acre outdoor water theme park near Busch Gardens Tampa Bay (see below). You can also frolic here during the cooler days of spring and fall, when the water is heated. The Key West Rapids, Tampa Typhoon, Gulf Scream, and other exciting water rides will drench the teens, while other, calmer rides are geared toward younger kids. Wahoo Run plunges up to five riders more than 15 feet per second as the half-enclosed tunnel corkscrews more than 600 feet to a waiting splash pool. There are also places to picnic and sunbathe, an arcade, a volleyball complex, and an outdoor cafe. Although some people tend to go barefoot here, I suggest you wear shoes at all times—it gets kind of nasty after a while.

10001 Malcolm McKinley Dr. (between Busch Blvd. and Bougainvillea Ave.). ℂ 813/987-5600. www.4adventure. com. Admission at least $33 adults, $31 children 3–9, plus tax; free for children 2 and under. Combination tickets with Busch Gardens Tampa Bay (1 day each) $100 adults, $90 children 3–9, free for children under 3. Website sometimes offers discounts. Parking $5. Mid-Mar to Labor Day daily 10am–5pm; Sept–Oct Fri–Sun 10am–5pm (extended hours in summer and on holidays). Closed Nov to late Feb. Take exit 50 off I-275 and go east on Busch Blvd. for 2 miles. Turn left onto McKinley Dr. (N. 40th St.); entry is on the right.

Big Cat Rescue *Kids*   Not your typical animal theme park, this one bills itself as an educational sanctuary in which visitors can get up close and "purrsonal" (groan) with over 150 big, wild cats. The world's largest accredited sanctuary for exotic cats, this one is definitely a unique experience for animal lovers because not only can you view and visit with bobcats and tigers but you can feed them, take photo safaris, or even spend a night in one of the sanctuary's cabins. Something different, for sure.

12802 Easy St. ℂ 813/920-4130. www.bigcatrescue.org. Day tours $20 per person ages 10 and over only Mon–Fri 9am–3pm; special kids tours for all ages, $10 Sat 9am; night tours $20 for ages 18 and over only, last Fri of the month at dusk; feeding tours $50 per person ages 18 and over only, reservations required; keeper-for-a-day tour $150 per person ages 18 and over only, reservations required. Call for directions.

Busch Gardens Tampa Bay *Kids*   Although its heart-stopping thrill rides get much of the ink, this venerable theme park (it predates Disney World) ranks among the largest zoos in the country. It's a don't-miss attraction for children and adults, who can see, in person, all those wild beasts they've watched on *Animal Planet*—and they'll get better views of them here than at Disney's Animal Kingdom in Orlando (p. 240). Busch Gardens has thousands of animals living in natural environments that help carry out the park's overall African theme. Most authentic is the 80-acre plain, reminiscent of the real Serengeti of Tanzania and Kenya, upon which zebras, giraffes, and other animals graze. Unlike the animals on the real Serengeti, however, these grazing creatures have nothing to fear from lions, hyenas, crocodiles, and other predators, which are confined to enclosures—as are the hippos and elephants. The park's sixth roller coaster, SheiKra, is the nation's first dive coaster that carries riders up 200 feet at 45 degrees and then hurtles them 70 mph back at a 45-degree angle. Yikes.

The park has eight areas, each with its own theme, animals, live entertainment, thrill rides, kiddie attractions, dining, and shopping. A Skyride cable car soars over the park, offering a bird's-eye view of it all. Turn left after the main gate and head to **Morocco,** a walled city with exotic architecture, crafts demonstrations, a sultan's tent with snake charmers, and an exhibit featuring alligators and turtles. The Moorish-style Moroccan Palace Theater features an ice show that many families consider to be the park's best entertainment for both adults and children. You can also attend a song-and-dance show in the Marrakech Theater. Overlooking it all is the Crown Colony Restaurant, the park's largest.

After watching the snake charmers, walk east past Anheuser-Busch's fabled Clydesdale horses to **Egypt,** where you can visit King Tut's tomb with its replicas of the real treasures and listen to comedian Martin Short narrate "Akbar's Adventure Tours," a wacky simulator that "transports" one and all across Egypt via camel, biplane, and mine car. The whole room moves on this ride, which lasts only 5 minutes—much less time than the usual wait to get inside. Youngsters can dig for their own ancient treasures in a sand area. Adults and kids 54 inches or taller can ride Montu, the tallest and longest inverted roller coaster in the world, with seven upside-down loops. Your feet dangle loose on Montu, so make sure your shoes are tied tightly and your lunch has had time to digest.

From Egypt, walk to the **Edge of Africa,** the most unique of the park's eight areas, and home of most of the large animals. Go immediately to the Expedition Africa Gift Shop and see if you can get on one of the park's zoologist-led wildlife tours (see the box, "How to See Busch Gardens," below).

Next stop is **Nairobi,** the most beautiful part of the park, where you can see gorillas and chimpanzees in their lush rainforest habitat in the Myombe Reserve. Nairobi also has a baby-animal nursery, a petting zoo, turtle and reptile displays, an elephant exhibit (alas, the magnificent creatures seem to be bored to the point of madness), and Curiosity Caverns, where bats, reptiles, and small mammals that are active in the dark are kept in cages (it's the most traditional zoolike area here). The entry to Rhino Rally, the park's safari adventure, is at the western end of Nairobi.

Now head to **The Congo,** where the highlights are the rare white Bengal tigers that live on Claw Island. The Congo is also home to two roller coasters: Kumba, the largest and fastest coaster in the southeastern United States (54-in. minimum height); and the Python (48-in. minimum), which twists and turns for 1,200 feet. You will get drenched—and refreshed on a hot day—by riding the Congo River Rapids, where you're turned loose in round boats that float down the swiftly flowing "river" (42-in. minimum). Bumper cars and kiddie rides can be found here, too.

From The Congo, walk south into **Stanleyville,** a prototypical African village, with a shopping bazaar, orangutans living on an island, and the Stanleyville Theater, featuring shows for children. Two more water rides here are the Tanganyika Tidal Wave (48-in. minimum height), where you'll come to a very damp end; and the Stanley Falls Flume (an aquatic version of a roller coaster). Also the picnic-style Stanleyville Smokehouse serves ribs and chicken that are among the best chow in the park.

Up next is **Land of the Dragons,** the most entertaining area for small children. They can spend the day enjoying a variety of elements in a fairy-tale setting, plus just-for-kids rides. The area is dominated by Dumphrey, a whimsical dragon who interacts with visitors and guides children around a three-story treehouse with winding stairways, tall towers, steppingstones, illuminated water geysers, and an echo chamber.

Tips **If You Need Another Day**

Once you're inside Busch Gardens Tampa Bay and decide you really need more time to see it all, check to see if the park has (frequently offered) **Next-Day Tickets,** which let you back in the next day for about $16 per person.

If you're going to Orlando as well, Busch Gardens Tampa Bay is included in the five-park version of the **FlexTicket,** a 14-day pass that also admits you to Universal Studios Florida, SeaWorld, Islands of Adventure, and Wet 'n Wild. For prices and more information on this pass, see p. 257.

Tips   How to See Busch Gardens

You can save a few dollars and avoid waiting in long lines by buying your tickets to Busch Gardens Tampa Bay at the privately owned **Tampa Bay Visitor Information Center,** opposite the park at 3601 E. Busch Blvd., at North Ednam Place (© **813/985-3601;** www.hometown.aol.com\tpabayinfoctr). Owner Jim Boggs worked for the park for 13 years and gives expert advice on how to get the most out of your visit. He sells slightly discounted tickets (buying here will also save you from the ticket line at the parks) to Busch Gardens, Adventure Island, and other attractions, and he will book hotel rooms and car rentals for you, often at a discount. The center is open Monday through Saturday from 10am to 5:30pm, Sunday from 10am to 2pm (closed Christmas).

Arrive early and allow at least a day to see the park. Try not to come when it's raining, since some rides may not be operating. Bring comfortable shoes; and, remember, you will get wet on some of the rides, so wear or bring appropriate clothing (shops near the rides sell plastic ponchos for $5 or $6, but they're cheaper in the outside world). There are lockers throughout the park where you can stash your gear.

As soon as you're through the turnstiles, pick up a map and the day's activity schedule, which tells you what's showing and when, at the 14 entertainment venues in the park. Then take a few minutes to carefully plan your time—it's a big park with lots to see and do.

Although you'll get close to Busch Garden's predators, hippos, and elephants in their glass-walled enclosures, the only way to mingle with the grazers is on a tour. The best is the **VIP Elite Adventure Tour,** which lets you roam the plains in the company of a zoologist. The 8-hour excursion costs $200 per person, free for children under 5 (in addition to the park's entry fee), and usually leaves at about 1:30pm daily. Note that kids under 5 (though free) aren't allowed on portions of the tour. You won't have to wait in line, and you'll receive a complimentary continental breakfast and lunch at the park's Crown Colony Restaurant. The tours can fill up fast, and you can't call ahead for reservations, so as soon as you enter the park, go to the Expedition Africa Gift Shop, opposite Crown Colony Restaurant in the Edge of Africa, to reserve a spot. Another option (though less attractive) is the 30-minute, zoologist-led **Serengeti Safari Special Tour,** in which you ride among the grazers on the back of a flatbed truck. This is worth the extra $34 per person. You can make reservations for the morning tour at the Expedition Africa Gift Shop, but the midday and afternoon tours are first-come, first-served. Note that children under 5 are not allowed on the Serengeti Safari, or on the Serengeti portion of the Elite Adventure Tour.

The next stop is **Bird Gardens,** the park's original core, offering rich foliage, lagoons, and a free-flight aviary for hundreds of exotic birds, including golden and American bald eagles. Be sure to see the Florida flamingos and Australian koalas while you're here.

Then you're off to take a break at the **Hospitality House,** which offers piano enter-tainment and free samples of Anheuser-Busch's famous beers. You must be 21 to imbibe (there's a limit of two free mugs per seating), but soft drinks are also available.

If your stomach can take another hair-raising ride, try **Gwazi** (48-in. minimum), an adrenaline-pumping attraction in which a pair of old-fashioned wooden roller coasters (named the Lion and the Tiger) start simultaneously and whiz within a few feet of each other six times as they roar along at 50 mph and rise to 90 feet. If you want to experience the park's fifth roller coaster, head to **Timbuktu** and climb aboard the **Scorpion,** a high-speed number with a 60-foot drop and 360-degree loop (42-in. height minimum).

Added attractions are a $350, 6-hour zookeeper-for-a-day program, and a 4-D mul-tisensory R. L. Stine film. You can exchange foreign currency in the park, and inter-preters are available. *Note:* You can get to Busch Gardens from Orlando via shuttle buses, which pick up at area hotels between 8 and 10:15am for the 1½- to 2-hour ride, with return trips starting at 5pm and continuing until the park closes. Round-trip fares are $5 per person. Call ℂ **800/511-2450** for schedules, pickup locations, and reservations.

3000 E. Busch Blvd. (at McKinley Dr./N. 40th St.). ℂ **888/800-5447** or 813/987-5283. www.buschgardens.com. **Note:** Admission and hours vary so call ahead, check website, or get brochure at visitor centers. Admission single-day ticket $58 adults, $48 children 3–9, plus tax; free for children 2 and under. Daily 10am–6pm (extended hours to 7 and 8pm in summer and on holidays). Parking $8 for cars; $9 for trucks and campers. Take I-275 north of down-town to Busch Blvd. (exit 50) and go east 2 miles. From I-75, take Fowler Ave. (exit 54) and follow the signs west.

Florida Aquarium ✸✸ 𝒦𝒾𝒹𝓈   See more than 5,000 aquatic animals and plants that call Florida home at this entertaining attraction. The exhibits follow a drop of water from the springs of the Florida Wetlands Gallery, through a mangrove forest in the Bays and Beaches Gallery, and out onto the Coral Reefs, where an impressive 43-foot-wide, 14-foot-tall panoramic window lets you look out at schools of fish and lots of sharks and stingrays. Also worth visiting are the educational "Explore a Shore" play-ground, a deepwater exhibit, and a tank housing moray eels. You can look for birds and sea life on 90-minute Eco Tour cruises in the *Bay Spirit,* a 64-foot catamaran. The aquarium also offers a **Dive with the Sharks** program (ℂ **813/367-4005**) that gives certified divers the chance to swim with blacktip reef, sand tiger, and nurse sharks for 30 minutes. The $150 price tag includes a souvenir photo and T-shirt.

701 Channelside Dr. ℂ **813/273-4000.** www.flaquarium.net. Admission $18 adults, $15 seniors, $12 children 3–11, free for children under 3. Eco Tour $19 adults, $18 seniors, $14 children 3–11, free for children under 3. Combination aquarium admission and Eco Tour $30 adults, $27 seniors, $20 children 3–11, free for children under 3. Website some-times offers discounts. Parking $5. Daily 9:30am–5pm. Dolphin Quest Mon–Fri 2pm; Sat–Sun 1 and 3pm. Eco Tour daily 2 and 4pm, plus Sat noon. Closed Thanksgiving and Christmas.

Lowry Park Zoo ✸ 𝒦𝒾𝒹𝓈   The opportunity to watch 3,000-pound manatees, Komodo dragons, Persian leopards, and rare red pandas makes this a worthwhile excursion after the kids have seen the plains of Africa at Busch Gardens. With lots of greenery, bubbling brooks, and waterfalls, this 24-acre zoo displays animals in settings similar to their natural habitats. Exhibits include the Florida wildlife display, Asian Domain, Primate World, Aquatic Center, free-flight aviary with a birds-of-prey show, hands-on Discovery Center, and endangered-species carousel ride. The Wallaroo Station has kids' rides, a small water park, a kangaroo walk-about, and a petting zoo. Lowry Park has one of Florida's three manatee hospital and rehabilitation centers. The Eco Tour is very popular, featuring a cruise on the Hillsborough River, where you'll

A Free Attraction

The Tampa Electric Company is a hot spot, not just because it provides the juice that makes the city tick, but also because the warm waters surrounding the plant are a haven for manatees—they need to be in temperatures of at least 68°F. The **Manatee Viewing Center** (© 813/228-4289; www.tampaelectric.com) is open November 1 to April 15 from 10am to 5pm.

see turtles, herons, and manatees. The cost is $10 for adults, $9 for seniors, and $7 for children 3 to 11. The zoo is also a sanctuary for Florida panthers and red wolves.

1101 W. Sligh Ave. © 813/935-8552, or 813/932-0245 for recorded information. www.lowryparkzoo.com. Admission $15 adults, $14 seniors, $11 children 3–11, free for children 2 and under. Daily 9:30am–5pm. Closed Thanksgiving and Christmas. Take I-275 to Sligh Ave. (exit 48) and follow the signs.

VISITING THE MUSEUMS

Henry B. Plant Museum   Originally built in 1891 by railroad tycoon Henry B. Plant as the super–chichi 511-room Tampa Bay Hotel, this ornate building is worth a short trip across the river from downtown to the University of Tampa campus. Its 13 silver minarets and distinctive Moorish architecture, modeled after the Alhambra in Spain, make this National Historic Landmark a focal point of the Tampa skyline. Although the building is the highlight of a visit, don't skip its contents: art and furnishings from Europe and Asia, plus exhibits that explain the history of the original railroad resort, Florida's early tourist industry, and the hotel's role as a staging point for Theodore Roosevelt's Rough Riders during the Spanish-American War.

401 W. Kennedy Blvd. (between Hyde Park and Magnolia aves.). © 813/254-1891. www.plantmuseum.com. Free admission; suggested donation $5 adults, $2 children 12 and under. Tues–Sat 10am–4pm; Sun noon–4pm. Closed Thanksgiving, Christmas Eve, and Christmas Day. Take Kennedy Blvd. (FL 60) across the Hillsborough River.

MOSI (Museum of Science and Industry) 🎔🎔 🄺ids   A great place to take the kids, MOSI is the largest science center in the Southeast, with more than 450 interactive exhibits. Step into the Gulf Hurricane to experience 74 mph winds, explore the human body in The Amazing You, and, if your heart is up to it, ride a bicycle across a 98-foot-long cable suspended 30 feet above the lobby (don't worry: You'll be harnessed to the bike). You can also watch stunning movies in Florida's first IMAX dome theater. Outside, trails wind through a nature preserve with a butterfly garden.

4801 E. Fowler Ave. (at N. 50th St.). © 813/987-6100. www.mosi.org. Admission $16 adults, $14 seniors, $12 children 2–12, free for children under 2. Admission includes IMAX movies. Daily 9am–5pm or later. From downtown, take I-275 N. to the Fowler Ave. E. exit (no. 51). Take this 2 miles east to museum on right.

Tampa Museum of Art   Located on the east bank of the Hillsborough River, next to the round Bank of America building (locals facetiously call it the "Beer Can"), this fine-arts complex offers eight galleries with changing exhibits ranging from classical antiquities to contemporary Floridian art. There's also a 7-acre riverfront park and sculpture garden. Call or check the website for the schedule of temporary exhibits. However, if you have time for only one art museum on your trip, skip this one and head to St. Petersburg for the more innovative Salvador Dalí Museum.

600 N. Ashley Dr. (at Twiggs St.), downtown. © 813/274-8130. www.tampamuseum.com. Admission $7 adults, $6 seniors, $3 children 6–18 and students with ID, free for children under 6, by donation Thurs 5–8pm and Sat 10am–noon. Tues–Sat 10am–5pm; Thurs 10am–8pm; Sun 11am–5pm. Parking 90¢ per hour. Take I-275 to exit 44 (Ashley Dr.).

YBOR CITY

Northeast of downtown, the city's historic Latin district takes its name from Don Vicente Martinez Ybor (*Eeee*-bore), a Spanish cigar maker who arrived here in 1886 via Cuba and Key West. Soon his and other Tampa factories were producing more than 300,000 hand-rolled stogies a day.

It may not be the cigar capital of the world anymore, but Ybor is still a smokin' part of Tampa, and it's one of the best places in Florida to buy hand-rolled cigars. It's not on a par with New Orleans's Bourbon Street, Washington's Georgetown, or Miami's South Beach, but good food and great music dominate the scene, especially on weekends when the streets bustle until 4am (note to claustrophobes: Avoid it at all costs then). Live-music offerings run the gamut from jazz and blues to rock.

At the heart of it all is **Centro Ybor**, a dining-shopping-entertainment complex that sprawls between 7th and 8th avenues and 16th and 17th streets (© **813/242-4660;** www.centroybor.com). Here you'll find a multiscreen cinema, a comedy club, several restaurants, and a large open-air bar. The Ybor City Chamber of Commerce has its visitor center here (see "Essentials," earlier in this chapter), and the Ybor City State Museum's gift shop is here as well (see below).

Check with the visitor center about walking tours of the historic district. **Ybor City Ghost Walks** (© **813/242-4660**) will take you to the spookier parts of the area. The tours cost $10 per person, last 75 minutes, and are by reservation only. For those who enjoy an even darker side, **Secret Ybor: Scandals, Crimes and Shady Ladies,** explores the more scandalous side of the city. Tours depart Saturdays at 6pm from **Gaspar's Grotto,** 1805 E. 7th Ave. (© **813/831-5214;** www.gasparsgrotto.com), a wacky, pirate-themed entertainment venue, bar, and restaurant. Cost is $10 per person.

Even if you're not a cigar smoker, you'll enjoy a stroll through the **Ybor City State Museum** ⊛, 1818 9th Ave., between 18th and 19th streets (© **813/247-6323;** www.ybormuseum.org), housed in the former Ferlita Bakery (1896–1973). You can take a self-guided tour to see the collection of cigar labels, cigar memorabilia, and works by local artisans. Admission is free. Walking tours of Ybor City are every Saturday morning at 10:30am, cost $6, and start at the Ybor City Museum State Park. Depending on the availability of volunteer docents, admission includes a 15-minute guided tour of **La Casita,** a renovated cigar worker's cottage adjacent to the museum; it's furnished as it was at the turn of the last century. The museum is open daily from 9am to 5pm, but you have the best chance for the guided tour if you visit between 11am and 3pm. Better yet, plan to catch a cigar-rolling demonstration (ongoing; no specific schedule), held Friday through Sunday from 10am to 3pm.

Housed in a 100-year-old, three-story former cigar factory, **Ybor City Brewing Company,** 2205 N. 20th St., facing Palm Avenue, produces Ybor Gold and other brews, none with preservatives.

Like any area with trendy bars and restaurants, things are always changing, opening, and going out of business, so you may want to check **www.ybortimes.com** for the latest in Ybor City.

ORGANIZED TOURS

Swiss Chalet Tours, 3601 E. Busch Blvd. (© **813/985-3601;** www.hometown.aol. com\tpabayinfoctr), opposite Busch Gardens in the privately run Tampa Bay Visitor Information Center (see the box, "How to See Busch Gardens," earlier in this chapter), operates guided bus tours of Tampa, Ybor City, and environs. The 4-hour tours of Tampa are given from 10am to 3pm daily, with a stop for lunch at the Columbia Restaurant in Ybor City. They cost $45 for adults and $40 for children 12 and under. The full-day tours (10am–5pm) of both Tampa and St. Petersburg give a good overview of the two cities and the beaches; these cost $70 for adults and $65 for children. Reservations are required at least 24 hours in advance; passengers are picked up at major hotels and various other points in the Tampa/St. Petersburg area. The company also books bus tours to Orlando, Sarasota, Bradenton, and other regional destinations (call for schedules, prices, and reservations).

OUTDOOR ACTIVITIES & SPECTATOR SPORTS

BIKING, IN-LINE SKATING & JOGGING Bayshore Boulevard, a 7-mile-long promenade, is famous for its sidewalk right on the shores of Hillsborough Bay and is a favorite with runners, walkers, and in-line skaters. The route goes from the western edge of downtown in a southward direction, passing stately old homes in Hyde Park, a few high-rise condominiums, retirement communities, and houses of worship, ending at Ballast Point Park. The view from the promenade across the bay to the downtown skyline is matchless. (Bayshore Blvd. is also great for a drive.)

> ### Cruise Control
> The **Port of Tampa** (© 800/741-2297 or 813/905-7678; www.tampaport. com) is home to four cruise lines and a changing cast of ships that travel the Caribbean and Latin America. At press time, the players were Celebrity Cruise Line, Royal Caribbean Cruise Lines, Holland America Cruise Lines, and Carnival Cruise Line.

FISHING For charters, try **Captain Jim's Inshore Sportfishing Charters,** 512 Palm Ave., Palm Harbor (© **727/439-9017;** www.captainhud.com), which offers private sport-fishing trips for tarpon, redfish, trout, and snook. Rates are $300 to $525 for two anglers. Call for schedule and reservations.

GOLF Tampa has three municipal golf courses where you can play for about $30 to $35, a relative pittance compared to fees at privately owned courses here and elsewhere in Florida. The **Babe Zaharias Municipal Golf Course,** 11412 Forest Hills Dr., north of Lowry Park (© 813/631-4374), is an 18-hole, par-70 course with a pro shop, putting greens, and a driving range. It is the shortest of the municipal courses, but its small greens and narrow fairways present ample challenges. Water provides obstacles on 12 of the 18 holes at **Rocky Point Golf Course,** 4151 Dana Shores Dr. (© 813/ 673-4316), located between the airport and the bay. It's a par-71 course with a pro shop, practice range, and putting greens. On the Hillsborough River in north Tampa, the **Rogers Park Golf Course,** 7910 N. 30th St. (© 813/673-4396), is an 18-hole, par-72 championship course with a lighted driving and practice range. All of the courses are open daily from 7am to dusk, and lessons and club rentals are available.

You can book starting times and get information about these and the area's other courses by calling **Tee Times USA** (© 800/374-8633; www.teetimesusa.com).

If you want to do some serious work on your game, the **Arnold Palmer Golf Academy World Headquarters** is at Saddlebrook Resort, 5700 Saddlebrook Way, Wesley Chapel, 12 miles north of Tampa (© **800/729-8383** or 813/973-1111; www. saddlebrookresort.com). Half-day and hourly instruction is available, as well as 2-, 3-, and 5-day programs for adults and juniors. You have to stay at the resort or enroll in the golf program to play at Saddlebrook. See p. 352 for more information.

For course information online, go to www.golf.com or www.floridagolfing.com; or call the **Florida Sports Foundation** (✆ 850/488-8347) or **Florida Golfing** (✆ 866/833-2663).

SPECTATOR SPORTS National Football League fans can catch the **Tampa Bay Buccaneers** at the modern, 66,000-seat Raymond James Stadium, 4201 N. Dale Mabry Hwy., at Dr. Martin Luther King, Jr., Boulevard (✆ 813/879-2827; www.buccaneers.com) August through December. Single-game tickets (starting at $30) are very hard to come by as they are usually sold out to the plethora of season-ticket owners. This is a huge football city!

The National Hockey League's **Tampa Bay Lightning,** winners of the 2004 Stanley Cup, play in the St. Pete Times Forum starting in October (✆ 813/301-6500; www.tampabaylightning.com). You can usually get single-game tickets ($8–$155) on game day.

New York Yankees fans can watch the Bronx Bombers during baseball's spring training, from mid-February to the end of March, at Legends Field (✆ 813/879-2244 or 813/875-7753; www.yankees.mlb.com), opposite Raymond James Stadium. This scaled-down replica of Yankee Stadium is the largest spring-training facility in Florida, with a 10,000-seat capacity. Tickets are $10 to $16. The club's minor-league team, the **Tampa Yankees** (same contact into), plays at Legends Field April through August.

The only thoroughbred racecourse on Florida's west coast is **Tampa Bay Downs,** 11225 Racetrack Rd., Oldsmar (✆ **800/200-4434** in Florida, or 813/855-4401; www.tampadowns.com), home of the Tampa Bay Derby. Races are held from December to May ($2 general admission, $3 clubhouse), and the track presents simulcasts year-round. Call for post times.

TENNIS Sharpen your game at the **Hopman Tennis Program,** at the Saddlebrook Resort (p. 352). You must be a member or a guest to play here.

SHOPPING

Hyde Park and Ybor City are two areas of Tampa worth some window-shopping, perhaps sandwiched around lunch at one of the fine restaurants (see "Where to Dine," later in this chapter).

On the mall front, there's the upscale **International Plaza** (✆ 813/342-3790; www.shopinternationalplaza.com) near Tampa International Airport, where the headliners include Neiman Marcus, Nordstrom, and Lord & Taylor.

CIGARS Ybor City is no longer a major producer of hand-rolled cigars, but you can still watch artisans making stogies at the **Gonzalez y Martinez Cigar Factory,** 2025 7th Ave., in the Columbia Restaurant building (✆ 813/247-2469). Gonzalez and Martinez are recent arrivals from Cuba and don't speak English, but the staff does at the adjoining **Columbia Cigar Store** (it's best to enter here). Rollers are on duty Monday through Saturday from 10am to 6pm. You can stock up on fine domestic and imported cigars at **El Sol,** 1728 E. 7th Ave. (✆ 813/247-5554), the city's oldest cigar store; **King Corona Cigar Factory,** 1523 E. 7th Ave. (✆ 813/241-9109); and **Metropolitan Cigars & Wine,** 2014 E. 7th Ave. (✆ 813/248-3304).

SHOPPING CENTERS **Old Hyde Park Village,** 1507 W. Swann Ave., at South Dakota Avenue (✆ 813/251-3500; www.oldhydeparkvillage.com), is a terrific alternative to cookie-cutter suburban malls. Walk around the little boutiques in the sunshine

> **Fun Fact   Did You Know?**
>
> Tampa used to be called Tanpa. No, this is not a spelling error. In the early days, when the place was an Indian fishing village, that's what it was called. Loosely translated, *Tanpa* means "land by the water." Early explorers had illegibly written Tanpa on the maps. It wasn't until 1539 that gold-searching explorers mistakenly changed the name to Tampa.

and simultaneously check out Hyde Park, one of the city's most historic neighborhoods. The cluster of 50 upscale shops is set in a village layout. The selection includes Williams-Sonoma, Pottery Barn, Restoration Hardware, Brooks Brothers, Crabtree & Evelyn, and Godiva, to name a few. There's a free parking garage on South Oregon Avenue behind Jacobson's department store. Most shops are open Monday through Saturday from 10am to 7pm and Sunday from noon to 5pm. A farmers' market (at Swan and Dakota aves.) is held every Saturday from 9am to 2pm, offering local produce, seafood, and assorted tchotchkes.

The centerpiece of the downtown seaport renovation is the massive mall known as **Channelside at Garrison Seaport,** on Channelside Drive between the Garrison Seaport and the Florida Aquarium (© **813/223-4250;** www.channelside.com). It has stores, restaurants, a dance club, and a multiscreen cinema with an IMAX screen.

In Ybor City, **Centro Ybor,** on 7th Avenue East at 16th Street (© **813/242-4660;** www.centroybor.com), is primarily a dining and entertainment complex, but you'll find a few chains here like American Eagle, Urban Outfitters, and Victoria's Secret.

WHERE TO STAY

The listings below are organized into three geographic areas: near Busch Gardens, downtown, and Ybor City. If you're going to Busch Gardens, Adventure Island, Lowry Park Zoo, or the Museum of Science and Industry (MOSI), the motels near Busch Gardens are much more convenient than those downtown, about 7 miles to the south. The downtown hotels are geared to business travelers, but staying there will put you near the Florida Aquarium, the Tampa Museum of Art, the Henry B. Plant Museum, the Tampa Bay Performing Arts Center, scenic Bayshore Boulevard, and the dining and shopping opportunities in the Channelside and Hyde Park districts. Staying in Ybor City will put you within walking distance of numerous restaurants and the city's hottest nightspots.

The Westshore area, near the bay, west of downtown and south of Tampa International Airport, is another commercial center, with a wide range of chain hotels catering to business travelers and conventioneers. It's not far from Raymond James Stadium and the New York Yankees' spring-training complex. Check with your favorite chain for a Westshore-Airport location.

Room rates at most hotels in Tampa vary little from season to season. This is especially true downtown, where the hotels do a brisk convention business year-round. Hillsborough County adds 12% tax to your hotel bill.

NEAR BUSCH GARDENS

The nearest chain motel to the park is a former Howard Johnson's that's now **Safari Lodge at Busch Gardens Maingate,** 4139 E. Busch Blvd. (© **813/988-9191**), a

---

⟨Tips⟩ Discount Packages

Many Tampa hotels combine tickets to major attractions such as Busch Gardens in their packages, so always ask about special deals.

---

motor lodge with very cheap rooms. It's 1½ blocks east of the main entrance. A bit farther away, the 500-room **Embassy Suites Hotel and Conference Center,** 3705 Spectrum Blvd., facing Fowler Avenue (© **800/362-2779** or 813/977-7066; fax 813/977-7933), is the plushest and most expensive establishment near the park. Almost across the avenue stands **LaQuinta Inn & Suites,** 3701 E. Fowler Ave. (© **800/687-6667** or 813/910-7500; fax 813/910-7600). Just south of Fowler Avenue are side-by-side branches of **AmeriSuites,** 11408 N. 30th St. (© **800/ 833-1516** or 813/979-1922; fax 813/979-1926), and **DoubleTree Guest Suites,** 11310 N. 30th St. (© **800/222-8733** or 813/971-7690; fax 813/972-5525).

Baymont Inn & Suites ⟨Value⟩   Fake banana trees and a parrot cage welcome guests to the terra-cotta-floored lobby of this comfortable and convenient member of the small chain of cost-conscious but amenity-rich motels. All rooms are spacious and have ceiling fans and desks. Rooms with king-size beds also have recliners, business rooms sport dataport phones, and suites have refrigerators and microwaves. Outside, a courtyard with an unheated pool has plenty of space for sunning. There's no restaurant on the premises, but many are within walking distance.

9202 N. 30th St. (at Busch Blvd.), Tampa, FL 33612. © **800/428-3438** or 813/930-6900. Fax 813/930-0563. www. baymontinns.com. 146 units. Winter $79–$149 double; off season $70–$134 double. Rates include continental breakfast and local phone calls. AE, DC, DISC, MC, V. **Amenities:** Outdoor pool; game room; coin-op washers and dryers. *In room:* A/C, TV, free high-speed Internet access in all rooms, fridge, coffeemaker, hair dryer, iron.

Best Western All Suites Hotel ⟨★ Value⟩   This three-story all-suite hotel is the most beachlike vacation venue you'll find close to the park. Whimsical signs lead you around a lush tropical courtyard with a heated pool, hot tub, and lively, sports-oriented Tiki bar. The place prides itself on being "so close" to Busch Gardens that "the parrots escape to our trees," hence the hotel's nickname: "that parrot place." The bar can get noisy before closing at 9pm, and ground-level units are musty, so ask for an upstairs suite away from the action. Suite living rooms are well equipped; the separate bedrooms have narrow screened patios or balconies. The 11 "family suites" with bunk beds are great for those with kids.

Behind Busch Gardens, 3001 University Center Dr. (faces N. 30th St. between Busch Blvd. and Fowler Ave.), Tampa, FL 33612. © **800/786-7446** or 813/971-8930. Fax 813/971-8935. www.thatparrotplace.com. 150 units. Winter $99–$159 suite for 2; off season $79–$99 suite for 2. Rates include hot and cold breakfast buffet. AE, DC, DISC, MC, V. **Amenities:** Restaurant (breakfast and dinner only); bar; heated outdoor pool; access to nearby health club; Jacuzzi; game room; limited room service; laundry service; coin-op washers and dryers. *In room:* A/C, TV, dataport, fridge, coffeemaker, hair dryer, iron.

DOWNTOWN TAMPA

Hyatt Regency Tampa ⟨★⟩   Just off the Franklin Street pedestrian mall, and in the heart of the business district, the Hyatt has lost its place as downtown's premier hotel to the newer Tampa Marriott Waterside (see below), but still attracts a corporate crowd. The spacious, recently renovated contemporary rooms lack balconies, and the higher office towers that now surround the hotel restrict views from the windows. Office workers congregate at the Avanzare restaurant for inexpensive light lunches.

2 Tampa City Center (corner of Tampa and E. Jackson sts.), Tampa, FL 33602. ℭ 813/225-1234. Fax 813/273-0234. www.tamparegency.hyatt.com. 521 units. $139–$359 double. Weekend packages available in summer. AE, DC, DISC, MC, V. Valet parking $12. **Amenities:** 2 restaurants; bar; heated outdoor pool; exercise room; Jacuzzi; concierge; business center; limited room service; laundry service; coin-op washers and dryers; concierge-level rooms. *In room:* A/C, TV, dataport/wireless Internet access, coffeemaker, hair dryer, iron.

Sheraton Tampa Riverwalk Hotel ☙

Set on the east bank of the Hillsborough River, this six-story hotel has gone through several chain-oriented hands, but no matter which parent company seems to own it, it remains one of Tampa's better stays. Half the rooms face west and have lovely views from their (unlighted) balconies of the Arabesque minarets atop the Henry B. Plant Museum and the University of Tampa across the river—quite a scene at sunset. These rooms cost more, but are preferable to units on the east side of the building, which face downtown's skyscrapers and lack balconies. Rooms here are clean and of moderate size, but are rather tired, impersonal, and decorated in Drexel Heritage furniture. Set beside the river, the Ashley Drive Grill serves indoor-outdoor breakfasts and lunches, then offers fine dining in the evenings. The Boulanger bakery and deli, open from 5am to midnight, purveys fresh pastries, soups, sandwiches, and snacks. Unless you're here on business, or are intent on staying downtown to be close to a specific attraction such as the performing-arts center, there's not much here to entice a mainstream traveler.

200 N. Ashley Dr. (at Jackson St.), Tampa, FL 33602. ℭ 800/333-3333 or 813/223-2222. Fax 813/221-5929. www.tampariverwalkhotel.com. 282 units. Winter $219–$235 double; off season $139–$179 double. AE, DC, DISC, MC, V. Valet parking $10; self-parking $7. **Amenities:** 2 restaurants; bar; heated outdoor pool; exercise room; access to nearby health club; sauna; concierge; limited room service; laundry service; coin-op washers and dryers; concierge-level rooms. *In room:* A/C, TV, dataport, coffeemaker, hair dryer, iron.

Tampa Marriott Waterside Hotel and Marina ☙☙

This luxurious 22-story hotel occupies downtown's most strategic location in the area's emerging Channel District—beside the river and between the Tampa Convention Center and the St. Pete Times Forum. Opening onto a riverfront promenade, the towering, three-story lobby is large enough to accommodate the many conventioneers drawn to the two neighboring venues and to the hotel's own 50,000 square feet of meeting space. The third floor has a fully equipped spa, modern exercise facility, and outdoor heated pool. About half of the guest quarters have balconies overlooking the bay or city (choice views are high up on the south side). Although spacious, the regular rooms are dwarfed by the 720-square-foot suites. For those interested in boating the bay, there's also a 32-slip marina.

700 S. Florida Ave. (at St. Pete Times Forum Dr.), Tampa, FL 33602. ℭ 800/228-9290 or 813/221-4900. Fax 813/221-0923. www.marriott.com. 717 units. Winter $239–$265 double, $379–$575 suite; off season $209–$239 double, $350–$500 suite. AE, DC, DISC, MC, V. Weekend rates available. Valet parking $14; no self-parking. **Amenities:** 3 restaurants; 3 bars; heated outdoor pool; health club; spa; Jacuzzi; concierge; activities desk; car-rental desk; business center; salon; limited room service; massage; babysitting; laundry service; coin-op washers and dryers; concierge-level rooms. *In room:* A/C, TV, fax, dataport (w/high-speed Internet), fridge, coffeemaker, hair dryer, iron.

Wyndham Harbour Island ☙☙☙

Close enough to downtown but still worlds away on its own 177-acre island, this tropical-flair Wyndham insists that you're here on vacation and not stuck in some insipid downtown convention hotel. Rooms overlook the harbor and are hyper-comfortable with pillow-top mattresses and large bathrooms with Golden Door products. Luna di Mare is the hotel's exquisite Italian restaurant, overlooking the water and offering an extensive wine list, seafood, and chops. Guest privileges at the Harbour Island Athletic Club include full workout facilities, tennis courts, racquetball courts, and full-service spa. Stroll the boardwalk to fully appreciate your surroundings.

725 S. Harbour Island Blvd., Tampa, FL 33602. © **877/999-3223** or 813/229-5000. Fax 813/229-5322. www. wyndham.com/hotels/TPAHI/main.wnt. 299 units. $199–$289 double; $495–$895 suite. Weekend rates available. AE, DC, DISC, MC, V. Valet parking $12; no self-parking. **Amenities:** Restaurant; 3 bars; heated outdoor pool; access to nearby health club; access to spa; Jacuzzi; concierge; activities desk; car-rental desk; business center; salon; limited room service; massage; babysitting; laundry service. *In room:* A/C, TV, fax, high-speed Internet, coffeemaker, hair dryer, iron.

YBOR CITY

Hilton Garden Inn ✿   This modern, four-story hotel stands just 2 blocks north of the heart of Ybor City's dining and entertainment district. A one-story brick structure in front houses the bright lobby, a comfy relaxation area with fireplace, a dining area providing cooked and continental breakfasts, and a small 24-hour pantry selling beer, wine, soft drinks, and frozen dinners. You can heat up the dinners in your comfortable guest room's microwave or store them in your fridge. Since Hilton's Garden hotels are aimed primarily at business travelers, your room will also have a large desk and two phones. If you opt for a suite, you'll get a separate living room and a larger bathroom.

1700 E. 9th Ave. (between 17th and 18th sts.), Tampa, FL 33605. © **800/445-8667** or 813/769-9267. Fax 813/769-3299. www.hiltongardeninn.com. 95 units. $119–$289 double. AE, DC, DISC, MC, V. **Amenities:** Restaurant (breakfast only); heated outdoor pool; exercise room; Jacuzzi; business center; laundry service; coin-op washers and dryers. *In room:* A/C, TV, dataport (w/high-speed Internet), fridge, coffeemaker, hair dryer, iron.

Seminole Hard Rock Hotel & Casino ✿✿   Not quite as flashy as its South Florida sibling, Tampa's Seminole Hard Rock Hotel & Casino is still full of nonstop action. The 12-story building has 250 rooms, all of which feature modern amenities such as a flatscreen TV, large bathroom with excellent lighting, and fully stocked minibar. The casino offers 90,000 square feet of video slots and poker—no Sin City gaming such as blackjack, roulette, or craps. Several restaurants and bars keep the non-gamblers entertained, especially when big-name talent performs here. The pool area is large, but not as nice as those at the Hard Rocks in Vegas or Hollywood, Florida. The fitness center is top-notch, and even does outdoor treatments in its Zen garden.

5223 Orient Rd., Tampa, FL 33605. © **866/502-PLAY** or 813/627-7625. Fax 813/623-6862. www.hardrockhotelcasino tampa.com. 250 units. Winter $179–$549 double; off season $169–$219 double. AE, DC, DISC, MC, V. **Amenities:** 10 restaurants and bars; heated outdoor pool; full-service spa; Jacuzzi. *In room:* A/C, TV, CD player; dataport (w/high-speed Internet), fridge, hair dryer, iron.

A NEARBY SPA & SPORTS RESORT

Saddlebrook Resort–Tampa ✿✿ (Kids)   Set on 480 rolling acres of priceless countryside, Saddlebrook is a landlocked condominium development off the beaten path (30 min. north of Tampa International Airport). But if you're interested in spas, tennis, or golf, we recommend this resort, which offers complete spa treatments, the Hopman Tennis Program (Jennifer Capriati pitches a tent here), and the Arnold Palmer Golf Academy (see "Outdoor Activities & Spectator Sports," earlier in this chapter). Guests are housed in hotel rooms (all renovated to the tune of $8.5 million in 2005) or one-, two-, or three-bedroom suites. Much more appealing than the rooms, the suites come with a kitchen and either patio or balcony overlooking lagoons, cypress and palm trees, and the resort's two 18-hole championship golf courses. There are shops, restaurants, a stunning pool, and a kids' club with supervised activities.

5700 Saddlebrook Way, Wesley Chapel, FL 33543. © **800/729-8383** or 813/973-1111. Fax 813/973-4504. www. saddlebrookresort.com. 800 units. Winter $242–$402 per person; off season $147–$234 per person. Rates include breakfast and dinner. Packages available. AE, DC, DISC, MC, V. Valet parking $10 overnight; free self-parking located

Amish Country South?

Twelve miles east of Tampa, you'll find **Behind the Fence**, 1400 Viola Dr., at Country Side Street (📞 **813/685-8201**), a fabulous and secluded country-style B&B in Brandon, Florida. Innkeeper Larry Yoss, raised in an Amish home in Ohio, brought his heritage to Florida by encouraging traveling artisans to frequent the inn's backyard, where they'd demonstrate their skills in soap making, candle dipping, basket weaving, looming, and open-hearth cooking. This became a yearly August-to-September weekend trip into the past, which is often carried over to Christmas, during which time Behind the Fence re-creates itself as an homage to Christmas in the 1800s. The inn itself is as charming as it sounds, with a porch overlooking a pool and breakfasts that include Amish sweet rolls. The three rooms in the main house are usually rented by friends or families traveling together because they share a single bathroom. The two cottage rooms by the pool are stunning and have their own facilities, including claw-foot tubs. Rates are Amishly reasonable, from $79 to $89.

1 mile east of I-75 at exit 279. **Amenities:** 3 restaurants; 2 bars; heated outdoor pool; 2 golf courses; 45 grass, clay, and hard tennis courts; health club; spa; Jacuzzi; sauna; bike rental; children's activities program; concierge; activities desk; car-rental desk; business center; limited room service; massage; laundry service; washers and dryers. *In room:* A/C, TV, dataport, kitchen, minibar, fridge, coffeemaker, hair dryer, iron.

WHERE TO DINE

The restaurants that follow are organized by geographic area: near Busch Gardens, in or near Hyde Park (across the Hillsborough River from downtown), and in Ybor City. Although Ybor City is better known, Tampa's trendiest dining scene is along South Howard Avenue—"SoHo" to the locals—between West Kennedy Boulevard and the bay in affluent Hyde Park.

NEAR BUSCH GARDENS

You'll find the national fast-food and family restaurants east of I-275 on Busch Boulevard and Fowler Avenue.

Moderate

Cafe Don José SPANISH/AMERICAN   It's not nearly on a par with the Columbia in Ybor City (see below), but this Spanish-themed restaurant is among the best there is within a short drive of Busch Gardens. High-back chairs, dark-wood floors, and Spanish posters and paintings set an appropriate scene for the house specialties of traditional *paella* (allow 30 min. for preparation) and Valencia-style rice dishes. Don José also offers non-Spanish fare such as red snapper baked in parchment.

11009 N. 56th St. (in Sherwood Forest Shopping Center, ¼ mile south of Fowler Ave.). 📞 **813/985-2392**. www.cafedonjose.com. Main courses $15–$59. AE, DC, MC, V. Mon–Fri 11:30am–4:30pm and 5–10pm; Sat 5–9pm.

Ristorante Francesco 📞 NORTHERN ITALIAN   This landmark Italian eatery has been kept just as it was, thanks to the fact that new owner Jay Lanier was original owner Frankie's right-hand man in the kitchen. The pasta remains homemade, and shows up in more traditional fare such as seafood over linguine with a choice of marinara or white-wine sauce. The Tris di Pasta is a carbo-loader's delight, offering homemade gnocchi, tortellini, and ravioli in three different sauces. Yum.

In La Place Village Shopping Center, 1441 E. Fletcher Ave. (between 14th and 15th sts.). ℂ **813/971-3649.** Reservations recommended. Main courses $11–$23. AE, DC, DISC, MC. V. Mon–Fri 11:30am–2:30pm and 5:30–10pm; Sat 5:30–10pm; Sun 5–9pm.

Shells 🖈 Ⓥalue SEAFOOD You'll see Shells restaurants in many parts of Florida, and with good reason, as this casual, award-winning chain consistently provides excellent value. Particularly good are the spicy Jack Daniel's buffalo shrimp and scallop appetizers. Main courses range from the fried seafood platters to pastas to grilled shrimp, fish, steaks, and chicken.

11010 N. 30th St. (between Busch Blvd. and Fowler Ave.). ℂ **813/977-8456.** Main courses $9–$20 (most $10–$12). AE, DISC, MC, V. Sun–Thurs 11:30am–10pm; Fri–Sat 11:30am–11pm.

Inexpensive

Mel's Hot Dogs Ⓚids AMERICAN Catering to everyone from businesspeople to hungry families craving all-beef hot dogs, Mel Lohn's red-and-white cottage offers everything from "bagel-dogs" to bacon/cheddar Reuben-style hot dogs. All choices are served on poppy-seed buns and can be ordered with fries and a choice of coleslaw or baked beans. Even the decor is dedicated to wieners: The walls and windows are lined with hot-dog memorabilia, and a wiener-mobile is usually parked out front. Mel's chili is outstanding, too. And just in case hot-dog mania hasn't won you over, there are a few alternatives (chicken, beef, and veggie burgers, and terrific onion rings).

4136 E. Busch Blvd., at 42nd St. ℂ **813/985-8000.** Most items $4–$9. No credit cards (but there's an ATM on the premises). Sun–Thurs 11am–8pm; Fri–Sat 11am–9pm.

HYDE PARK
Expensive

Bern's Steak House 🖈🖈 STEAKHOUSE The exterior of this famous steakhouse looks like a factory. Inside, however, some say it looks like a brothel containing eight ornate dining rooms with themes such as Rhône, Burgundy, and Irish Rebellion. However you perceive the decor, this is a carnivore's paradise, one to which I actually drove from Miami and back just for dinner. At Bern's, you order and pay for grilled steaks of perfectly aged beef according to the thickness and weight (the 60-oz., 3-in.-thick Porterhouse can feed four adults). The phone book–size wine list—one of the restaurant's most famous attributes—offers more than 7,000 selections, many available by the glass. Ask your server for a sampling before you purchase a bottle. Upstairs, the restaurant's other most famous attribute—the dessert quarters—has 50 romantic booths paneled in aged California redwood; each can privately seat from 2 to 12 guests. All of these little chambers are equipped with phones for placing your order and closed-circuit TVs for watching and listening to a resident pianist. The dessert menu offers almost 100 selections, plus some 1,400 after-dinner drinks. It's possible to reserve a booth for dessert only, but preference is given to those who dine.

The big secret here is that steak sandwiches are available at the bar but are not mentioned on the menu. Smaller versions of the chargrilled steaks served in the dining rooms, they come with a choice of french fries or crispy onion rings. Add a salad and you have a terrific meal for about half the price of the least-expensive main course.

Sidebern's, 2208 W. Morrison Ave., at South Howard Avenue (ℂ **813/258-2233**), is the restaurant's New American offshoot. It's also quite good, but choose the original:

Dining on the Bay

One of the newest additions to Tampa's dining scene is the 180-foot-long *StarShip* Dining Yacht (☎ **877/744-7999** or 813/223-7999; www.starship dining.com), which makes 2-hour lunch and dinner cruises from the Channelside out onto Tampa Bay. The ship's four dining rooms serve exceptional cruise fare. A house band plays during dinner and then moves to the top deck for dancing under the stars. Lunch cruises cost $40 per person with a meal, $16 for sightseers. Dinner cruises cost $70. There's also a Sunday brunch for $40. Call for the schedule.

Missing Bern's would be like watching the remake of *Psycho* without ever seeing the original.

1208 S. Howard Ave. (at Marjory Ave.). ☎ **813/251-2421.** www.bernssteakhouse.com. Reservations recommended. Main courses $17–$59; sandwiches $9–$12. AE, DC, DISC, MC, V. Daily 5–11pm. Closed Christmas. Valet parking $5.

Moderate
Castaway ☆ SEAFOOD   Gorgeous ocean views trump the inconsistent seafood at Castaway, where crab legs, coconut shrimp, and daily catches reel in a steady crowd of locals and visitors alike. Insist on sitting on the deck and time your meal around sundown; the vantage point for sunsets here is the kind that makes developers drool and diners delight in the fact that this Castaway isn't going anywhere anytime soon.

7720 Courtney Campbell Causeway. ☎ **813/281-0770.** Reservations recommended. Main courses $13–$40. AE, DC, DISC, MC, V. Mon–Sat 11:30am–10:30pm; Sun brunch 10:30am–2:30pm; Sun dinner 4–10pm.

Mise en Place ☆☆ ECLECTIC   Look around at all those happy, stylish people soaking up the trendy ambience, and you'll know why chef Marty Blitz and his wife, Maryann, have been among the culinary darlings of Tampa since 1986. They present the freshest of ingredients in a creative, award-winning menu that changes weekly. Main courses often include choices such as Creole-style mahimahi served with chili cheese grits and a ragout of black-eyed peas, andouille sausage, and rock shrimp.

In Grand Central Place, 442 W. Kennedy Blvd. (at S. Magnolia Ave., opposite the University of Tampa). ☎ **813/254-5373.** www.miseonline.com. Reservations recommended. Main courses $16–$35; tasting menu $53 with wine, $38 without. AE, DC, DISC, MC, V. Tues–Thurs 11:30am–2:30pm and 5:30–10pm; Fri 11:30am–2:30pm and 5:30–11pm; Sat 5–11pm.

Wine Exchange ☆☆ MEDITERRANEAN   This Tampa hot spot is an oenophile's dream come true, in which each dish is paired with a particular wine available by the bottle or the glass. The menu is rather simple, featuring pizzas, pastas, salads, and sandwiches, but daily specials are more elaborate, including grilled Delmonico steak, blackened pork tenderloin, or Dijon-crusted salmon. The outdoor patio is a great place to sit. There's almost always a wait at this buzzworthy eatery.

1611 W. Swan Ave. ☎ **813/254-9463.** Reservations not accepted. Main courses $10–$22. AE, DC, DISC, MC, V. Mon–Fri 11:30am–10pm; Sat 11am–11pm; Sun 11am–9pm; brunch Sat–Sun 11am–3pm.

Inexpensive
Bella's Italian Cafe ☆ *Value* ITALIAN   Creative dishes and very reasonable prices make this sophisticated yet informal cafe one of SoHo's most popular neighborhood

hangouts. Although you can go for wood-fired pizzas or homemade pasta under traditional Bolognese or Alfredo sauces, the stars here feature the tasty likes of blackened
chicken in a creamy tomato sauce over fettuccine, or shrimp and scallops in a roasted
tomato sauce over bow-tie pasta. Finish with the house version of tiramisu. Local professionals flock to the friendly bar during two-for-one happy hours, nightly from 4 to
7pm and from 11pm until closing. After 11pm, the open kitchen provides only appetizers, salads, pizzas, and desserts.

1413 S. Howard Ave. (at Mississippi Ave.). ☎ **813/254-3355.** www.bellasitaliancafe.com. Reservations not
accepted. Main courses $12–$20; pizza $7–$10. AE, DC, DISC, MC, V. Mon–Tues 11:30am–11:30pm; Wed–Thurs
11:30am–12:30am; Fri 11am–1:30am; Sat 4pm–1:30am; Sun 4–11:30pm.

Four Green Fields IRISH/AMERICAN   Just across the bridge from the downtown
convention center, this thatched-roof Irish pub may be surrounded by palm trees
instead of potato fields, but it still offers the ambience and tastes of Ireland. Staffed by
Irish immigrants, the large room with a square bar in the center smells of Bass and
Harp ales. The Gaelic stew is predictably bland, but the salads and sandwiches are
passable. The live Irish music Thursday through Saturday nights and Sunday afternoon draws a fun crowd, ranging from postcollege to early retirees.

205 W. Platt St. (between Parker St. and Plant Ave.). ☎ **813/254-4444.** www.fourgreenfields.com. Main courses
$9.50–$15; sandwiches $6–$7. AE, MC, V. Daily 11am–3am.

YBOR CITY
Moderate
Big City Tavern ⭑ NEW AMERICAN   Although this restaurant is a chain, with
additional locations in West Palm Beach and Fort Lauderdale, Ybor City's Big City
Tavern takes the prize for best decor: It's housed in a converted ballroom and features
columns, floor-to-ceiling windows, and wrought-iron balconies. The food's pretty
good, too, especially the roasted duck with mango and basil risotto. The bar scene is
a people-watching paradise in which a youngish, well-heeled, hip clientele gathers to
trade tales of life in the big city.

1600 E. 8th Ave. ☎ **813/247-3000.** Reservations recommended. Main courses $11–$20. AE, MC, V. Sun–Thurs
11:30am–1am; Fri–Sat 11:30am–2am.

Columbia ⭑⭑⭑ SPANISH   Celebrating 100 years in 2005, this tile building occupies an entire city block in the heart of Ybor City. Tourists flock here to soak up
the ambience, and so do the locals because it's so much fun to clap along during fire-
belching Spanish flamenco floor shows Monday through Saturday evenings ($6 per
person additional charge besides dinner charge). You can't help coming back time after
time for the famous Spanish bean soup and original "1905" salad. The *paella a la Valen-
ciana* is outstanding, with more than a dozen ingredients ranging from Gulf grouper
and Gulf pink shrimp to calamari, mussels, clams, chicken, and pork. Another favorite
is *boliche* (eye of round stuffed with chorizo), accompanied by plantains and black
beans and rice. Entrees come with a crispy hunk of Cuban bread with butter. Lighter
appetites can choose from a limited menu of tapas, including "Cuban caviar" (a spicy
black-bean dip). The decor throughout is graced with hand-painted tiles, wrought-iron
chandeliers, dark woods, rich red fabrics, and stained-glass windows.

2117 E. 7th Ave. (between 21st and 22nd sts.). ☎ **813/248-4961.** www.columbiarestaurant.com. Reservations recommended. Main courses $14–$28. AE, DC, DISC, MC, V. Mon–Thurs 11am–10pm; Fri–Sat 11am–11pm; Sun
noon–9pm.

Inexpensive

Carmine's Restaurant & Bar ★ CUBAN/ITALIAN/AMERICAN   Bright blue poles hold up an ancient pressed-tin ceiling above this noisy corner cafe. It's not the cleanest joint in town, but a great variety of loyal local patrons gather here for genuine Cuban sandwiches—smoked ham, roast pork, Genoa salami, Swiss cheese, pickles, salad dressing, mustard, lettuce, and tomato on crispy Cuban bread. There's a vegetarian version, too. The combination of a half-sandwich and choice of black beans and rice or a bowl of Spanish soup made with sausages, potatoes, and garbanzo beans makes a hearty meal for just $7 at lunch, $8 at dinner. Main courses are led by Cuban-style roast pork, thin-cut pork chops with mushroom sauce, spaghetti with a blue-crab tomato sauce, and a few seafood and chicken platters.

1802 E. 7th Ave. (at 18th St.). © 813/248-3834. Reservations not accepted. Main courses $7–$17; sandwiches $4–$8. No credit cards. Mon–Tues 11am–11pm; Wed–Thurs 11am–1am; Fri–Sat 11am–3am; Sun 11am–6pm.

TAMPA AFTER DARK

The Tampa/Hillsborough Arts Council maintains an **Artsline** (© **813/229-2787**), a 24-hour information service providing the latest on current and upcoming cultural events. Racks in many restaurants and bars have copies of *Weekly Planet* (**www.weekly planet.com**), *Focus,* and *Accent on Tampa Bay,* three free publications detailing what's going on in the entire bay area. You can also check the "BayLife" and "Friday Extra" sections of the *Tampa Tribune* (**www.tampatrib.com**), as well as the Thursday "Weekend" section of the *St. Petersburg Times* (**www.sptimes.com**). The visitor center usually has copies of the week's newspaper sections (see "Essentials," earlier in this chapter).

THE CLUB & MUSIC SCENE   Ybor City is Tampa's favorite nighttime venue. All you have to do is stroll along 7th Avenue East between 15th and 20th streets, and you'll hear music blaring from the clubs. On Friday and Saturday from 9pm to 3am, the avenue is packed with people, a majority high schoolers and early 20-somethings; but you'll also find something going on Tuesday through Thursday, and even on Sunday. The clubs change names frequently, so you don't need names, addresses, or phone numbers; your ears will guide you along 7th Avenue East. With all of the sidewalk seating, it's easy to judge what the clientele is like and make your choice from there.

The center of the action these days is **Centro Ybor,** on 7th Avenue East at 16th Street (© **813/242-4660;** www.centroybor.com), the district's large dining-and-entertainment complex. The restaurants and pubs in this family-oriented center tend to be tamer than many of those along 7th Avenue, at least on non-weekend nights. You don't have to pay to listen to live music in the center's patio on weekend afternoons.

THE PERFORMING ARTS   With a prime downtown location on 9 acres along the east bank of the Hillsborough River, the huge **Tampa Bay Performing Arts**

The Hub of Tampa's Bar Scene

Ybor City and Bern's Steak House are command central for the boozy sophisticates of Tampa, but if you go downtown, you'll find the true hub of Tampa's bar scene in the form of, well, **The Hub,** 719 N. Franklin St. (© **813/229-1553**). It's a classic dive bar in which judges, lawyers, and the over-21 set shake and stir over stiff libations and a fabulous jukebox.

(*Tips* **Careful Where You Park**

Parking can be scarce at night in Ybor City, and the area has seen an occasional robbery in the late hours. Play it safe and use the municipal parking lots behind the shops on 8th Avenue East or the new parking garages near Centro Ybor, on 7th Avenue East at 16th Street.

Center (*, 1010 N. MacInnes Place, next to the Tampa Museum of Art (© **800/ 955-1045** or 813/229-7827; www.tampacenter.com), is the largest performing-arts venue south of the Kennedy Center in Washington, D.C. Accordingly, this four-theater complex is the focal point of Tampa's performing-arts scene, presenting a wide range of Broadway plays, classical and pop concerts, operas, improv, and special events.

A sightseeing attraction in its own right, the restored **Tampa Theatre,** 711 Franklin St., between Zack and Polk streets (© **813/274-8286;** www.tampatheatre.org), dates from 1926 and is on the National Register of Historic Places. It presents a varied program of classic, foreign, and alternative films, as well as concerts and special events. (And it's said to be haunted!)

The 66,321-seat **Raymond James Stadium,** 4201 N. Dale Mabry Hwy. (© **813/ 673-4300;** www.raymondjames.com/stadium), is sometimes the site of headliner concerts. The **USF Sun Dome,** 4202 E. Fowler Ave. (© **813/974-3111;** www.sundome. org), on the University of South Florida campus, hosts major concerts by touring pop stars, rock bands, jazz groups, and other contemporary artists.

Bars featuring live music include **Whiskey Joe's,** 2500 N. Rocky Point Dr. (© **813/ 281-0557**), a bayfront shack with plenty of visual and audible color; Ybor City's **Twilight,** 1507 E. 7th Ave. (© **813/247-4225**), an industrial-chic soundstage for the likes of local bands and national acts such as Third Eye Blind; and **Skipper's Smokehouse,** 910 Skipper Rd. (© **813/971-0666**), a Key West–style former smokehouse turned blues, jazz, zydeco, ska, and reggae hot spot. **Ticketmaster** (© **813/287-8844**) sells tickets to most events and shows.

2 Cocoa Beach, Cape Canaveral & the Space Coast

46 miles SE of Orlando

The "Space Coast," the area around Cape Canaveral, was once a sleepy place where city dwellers escaped the crowds from the exploding urban centers of Miami and Jacksonville. But then came the NASA space program. Today, the region produces and accommodates its own crowds, particularly the hordes of tourists who come to visit the Kennedy Space Center and enjoy the area's 72 miles of beaches (this is, after all, the closest beach to Orlando's mega-attractions) and excellent fishing, surfing, and golfing.

Thanks to NASA, this is also a prime destination for nature lovers. The space agency originally took over much more land than it needed to launch rockets. Rather than sell off the unused portions, it turned them over to the Canaveral National Seashore and the Merritt Island National Wildlife Refuge (**www.nbbd.com/godo/minwr**), which have preserved these areas in their pristine natural states.

A handful of Caribbean-bound cruise ships depart from the man-made Port Canaveral. The south side of the port is lined with seafood restaurants and marinas,

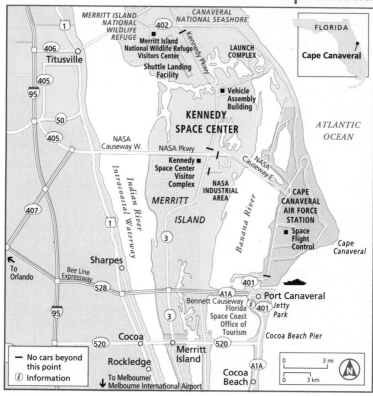

which serve as home base for gambling ships and the area's deep-sea charter and group fishing boats.

ESSENTIALS

GETTING THERE The nearest airport is **Melbourne International Airport** (© 321/723-6227; www.mlbair.com), 22 miles south of Cocoa Beach, which is served by **Continental** (© 800/525-0280; www.continental.com) and **Delta** (© 800/221-1212; www.delta.com). **Orlando International Airport** (p. 49), about 35 miles to the west, is a much larger hub with many more flight options and generally less expensive fares. It's an easy 45-minute drive from the Orlando Airport to the beaches via the Bee Line Expressway (FL 528, a toll road)—it can take almost that long from the Melbourne Airport, where **Avis, Budget, Hertz,** and **National** all have car-rental desks. The **Melbourne Airport Shuttle** (© 321/724-1600) will take you from the Melbourne Airport to most local destinations for about $10 to $20 per person.

VISITOR INFORMATION For information on the area, contact the **Florida Space Coast Office of Tourism/Brevard County Tourist Development Council,** 8810 Astronaut Blvd., Suite 102, Cape Canaveral, FL 32920 (© 800/872-1969 or 321/868-1126; www.space-coast.com). The office is in the Sheldon Cove building, on FL A1A a block north of Central Boulevard, and is open Monday through Friday from 8am to 5pm. It also operates an information booth at the Kennedy Space Center Visitor Complex (see below).

GETTING AROUND   A car is essential in this area. If you're not coming by car, you can rent one at the airport. **Space Coast Area Transit** (℃ **321/633-1878;** www.ridescat.com) operates buses ($1 adults, 50¢ seniors and students), but routes tend to be circuitous and therefore extremely time-consuming.

ATTRACTIONS

In addition to the two attractions below, Brevard College's **Astronaut Memorial Planetarium and Observatory,** 1519 Clearlake Rd., Cocoa Beach (℃ **321/634-3732;** www.brevardcc.edu/planet), south of FL 528, has its own International Hall of Space Explorers, but its big attractions are sound-and-light shows in the planetarium. Call or check the website for schedules and prices.

Brevard Zoo (Kids)   This delightful small-town zoo houses more than 500 animals, including white rhinos, red kangaroos, wallabies, crocodiles, howler monkeys, bald eagles, red wolves, and river otters. Enjoy a 10-minute train tour of the grounds ($2), a free-flight aviary, a cute and cuddly petting zoo, and alligator feedings usually 3 days a week. Check out the 10-acre Expedition Africa exhibit, where impala, gazelle, and Scimitar-Horned oryx chill out over the savanna. Don't miss the opportunity to kayak through the wetlands—this is the only zoo in the country that offers kayaking, and it's a bargain at only $3 per person. For an up close and personal view of the animals, take the behind-the-scenes tour with a zookeeper on Saturdays and Sundays at 1pm.

8225 N. Wickham Rd., Melbourne (just east of I-95 exit 73/Wickham Rd.). ℃ **321/254-9453.** www.brevardzoo.org. Admission $9 adults, $8 seniors, $6 children 3–12, free for kids under 3. Daily 10am–5pm.

John F. Kennedy Space Center (★★★)   Whether or not you're a space buff, you'll appreciate the sheer grandeur of the facilities and technological achievements displayed at NASA's primary space-launch facility. Astronauts departed earth at this site in 1969 en route to the most famous "small step" in history—the first moon walk—and today's space shuttles still lift off from here on their missions.

Since all roads other than FL 405 and FL 3 are closed to the public in the space center, you must begin your visit at the **Kennedy Space Center Visitor Complex.** A bit like a themed amusement park, this privately operated complex has received a $130-million renovation and expansion, so check beforehand to see if tours and exhibits have changed since press time. Call ahead to see what's happening on the day you intend to be here, and arrive early. You'll need at least 2 hours to see the space center's highlights on the bus tour, up to 5 hours if you linger at the stops along the way, and a full day to see and do everything here. Buy a copy of the *Official Tour Book;* it's easier to use than the rental cassette tapes, and you can take it home as a colorful souvenir (though some readers think you probably don't need the extra information, as the bus tours are narrated and the exhibits have good descriptions).

The visitor complex has real NASA rockets and the actual Mercury Mission Control Room from the 1960s. Exhibits look at early space exploration and where it's going in the new millennium. There are hands-on activities aimed at kids, a daily "Encounter" with a real astronaut, dining venues, and a shop selling space memorabilia. IMAX movies shown on 5½-story-high screens are both informative and entertaining.

Tips   Out to Launch

If you'd like to see a shuttle launch at the **Kennedy Space Center,** first call ℂ **321/867-5000** or check NASA's official website (www.ksc.nasa.gov) for a schedule of upcoming takeoffs. You can buy launch tickets at the Kennedy Space Center Visitor Complex (ℂ **321/449-4444**) or online at www.ksctickets. com. *A word of caution:* Shuttle launches are frequently delayed due to weather, equipment malfunctions, or other factors, so you might have to make multiple visits to see one. If you don't have that flexibility, the launch window may be delayed beyond your going-home date.

If you can't get into the space center, other good viewing spots are on the causeways leading to the islands and on U.S. 1 as it skirts the waterfront in Titusville. The **Holiday Inn Riverside–Kennedy Space Center,** on Washington Avenue (U.S. 1) in Titusville (ℂ **800/465-4329** or 321/269-2121; www.holiday innksc.com), has a clear view of the launchpads across the Indian River. Area motels raise their rates and often book up at launch periods.

While you could spend an entire day at the visitor complex, you must take a **KSC Tour** to see the actual space center where rockets and shuttles are prepared and launched. Take the bus tour early in your visit (the lines for these are brutal) and be sure to hit the restrooms before boarding—there's only one on the tour. Buses depart every 10 minutes or so, and you can reboard as you wish. They stop at the LC-39 Observation Gantry, with a dramatic 360-degree view over launchpads where shuttles blast off; the International Space Station Center, where scientists and engineers prepare additions to the space station now in orbit; and the Apollo/Saturn V Center, which includes artifacts, photos, films, interactive exhibits, and the 363-foot-tall Saturn V, the most powerful rocket ever launched by the United States. Unfortunately, the bus tour was the low point of my recent visit. Though the commentary on the bus was interesting, the stops were relatively dull, and waiting to board and reboard buses was more than frustrating (though touching a moon rock at the Apollo/Saturn V Center was pretty cool). If you're short on time, I suggest sticking around the visitor center.

Don't miss the Astronaut Memorial, a moving black-granite monument that bears the names of the U.S. astronauts who have died on missions or while in training. The 60-ton structure rotates on a track that follows the movement of the sun (on clear days, of course), causing the names to stand out against a brilliant reflection of the sky.

On launch days, the center is closed at least part of the day. These aren't good days to see the center, but they're great days to observe history in the making. For $37 per adult and $27 per child 3 through 11, you get a **combined ticket** that entitles you to admission to the center for the shortened operating hours, plus at least a 2-hour excursion to NASA Parkway to see the liftoff. You must pick up tickets, available 5 days before the launch, on-site.

For an out-of-this-world experience, do lunch with an astronaut, a once-in-a-lifetime opportunity available every day ($20 adults, $10 kids 3–11, in addition to space center admission). Astronauts who have participated in the past include some of the greatest, such as John Glenn, Jim Lovell, Walt Cunningham, Story Musgrave, and Jon McBride. Seating is limited; call ℂ **321/449-4400** to make a reservation.

Note: Kennedy Space Center acquired many of the exhibits from the **Astronaut Hall of Fame** and added them as a separate (and very worthwhile) attraction at the KSC visitor center ($17 adults, $13 kids 3–11; or $37 adults and $27 kids for a 2-day Maximum Access Admission to the Center and the Hall of Fame). The attraction includes exhibits and tributes to the heroes of the Mercury, Gemini, and Apollo space programs. There's also a collection of spacecraft, including a Mercury 7 capsule, a Gemini training capsule, and an Apollo 14 command module. In "Simulator Station," guests can experience four times the force of gravity, ride a Rover across Mars, and land a Space Shuttle.

NASA Pkwy. (FL 405), 6 miles east of Titusville, ½ mile west of FL 3. ℂ **321/449-4444** for general information, or 321/449-4444 for guided bus tours and launch reservations. www.kennedyspacecenter.com. Admission $30 adults, $20 children 3–11. Annual passes $48 adults, $32 children 3–11. Audio tours $5 per person. All tours and movies free for children under 3. Daily 9am–5:30pm. Shuttle-bus tours daily 9:45am–2:15pm. Closed Christmas and some launch days.

BEACHES & WILDLIFE REFUGES

To the north of the Kennedy Space Center, **Canaveral National Seashore** ✸✸✸ is a protected 13-mile stretch of barrier-island beach backed by cabbage palms, sea grapes, palmettos, marshes, and Mosquito Lagoon. This is a great area for watching herons, egrets, ibises, willets, sanderlings, turnstones, terns, and other birds. You might also glimpse dolphins and manatees in Mosquito Lagoon. Canoeists can paddle along a marked trail through the marshes of Shipyard Island, and backcountry camping is possible November through April (permits required; see below).

The main **visitor center** is at 7611 S. Atlantic Ave., New Smyrna Beach, FL 32169 (ℂ **321/867-4077,** or 321/867-0677 for recorded information; www.nps.gov/cana), on Apollo Beach, at the north end of the island. The southern access gate to the island is 8 miles east of Titusville on FL 402, just east of FL 3. A paved road leads from the gate to undeveloped **Playalinda Beach** ✸✸✸, one of Florida's most beautiful. Though illegal, nude sunbathing has long been a tradition here (at least for those willing to walk a few miles to the more deserted areas). The beach has toilets but no running water or other amenities, so bring everything you'll need. The seashore is open daily from 6am to 8pm during daylight saving time, daily from 6am to 6pm during standard time. Entry fees are $5 per motor vehicle, $3 per pedestrian or bicyclist. National Park Service passports are accepted. Backcountry camping permits cost $10 for up to six people and must be obtained from the New Smyrna Beach visitor center. For advance information, contact the seashore headquarters at 308 Julia St., Titusville, FL 32796 (ℂ **321/867-4077** or 321/267-1110; www.nps.gov/cana).

Canaveral National Seashore's neighbor to the south and west is the 140,000-acre **Merritt Island National Wildlife Refuge** ✸✸, home to hundreds of species of shorebirds, waterfowl, reptiles, alligators, and mammals, many of them endangered. Pick up a map and other information at the visitor center, on FL 402 about 4 miles east of Titusville (it's on the way to Playalinda Beach). The center has a ¼-mile boardwalk along the edge of the marsh. Displays show the animals you may spot from 6-mile Black Point Wildlife Drive or from one of the nature trails through the hammocks and marshes. The visitor center is open Monday through Friday from 8am to 4:30pm, Saturday and Sunday from 9am to 5pm (closed Sun Apr–Oct). Entry is free. For more information and a schedule of programs, contact the refuge at P.O. Box 6504, Titusville, FL 32782 (ℂ **321/861-0667;** www.nbbd.com/godo/minwr).

Note: Those parts of the national seashore near the Kennedy Space Center and all of the refuge close 4 days before a shuttle launch and usually reopen the day after a launch.

Another good beach area is **Lori Wilson Park,** on Atlantic Avenue at Antigua Drive in Cocoa Beach (© **321/868-1123**), which preserves a stretch of sand backed by a forest of live oaks. It's home to a small but interesting nature center, and restrooms are available. The park is open daily from sunrise to sunset; the nature center, Monday through Friday from 1 to 4pm.

The beach at **Cocoa Beach Pier,** on Meade Avenue east of FL A1A (© **321/783-7549**), is a popular spot with surfers, who consider it the East Coast's surfing capital. The rustic pier was built in 1962 and has 842 feet of fishing, shopping, and dining overlooking a wide, sandy beach (see "Where to Dine," below). Because this is not a public park, there are no restrooms other than the ones in restaurants on the pier.

Jetty Park, 400 E. Jetty Rd., at the south entry to Port Canaveral (© **321/783-7111;** www.portcanaveral.org/funport/parks.htm), has lifeguards, a fishing pier with bait shop, a playground, a volleyball court, a horseshoe pit, picnic tables, a snack bar, a grocery store, restrooms and changing facilities, and the area's only campground. From here, you can watch the big cruise ships as they enter and leave the port's narrow passage. The park is open daily from 7am to 10pm; the pier is open 24 hours for fishing. Admission is $5 per car, $7 per RV. The 150 tent and RV campsites (some of them shady, most with hookups) cost $18 to $31 a night, depending on location and time of year. No pets are allowed.

OUTDOOR ACTIVITIES & SPECTATOR SPORTS

BASEBALL   The **Washington Nationals** play spring-training games at **Space Coast Stadium,** 5800 Stadium Pkwy., Viera (© **321/633-4487**), located south of Cape Canaveral and north of Melbourne. Tickets are $5 to $18. The stadium also hosts minor-league action from the Brevard County Manatees, an affiliate of the Nationals.

ECO-TOURS   **Funday Discovery Tours** (© **321/725-0796;** www.fundaytours.com) offers a variety of day trips, including dinner and sunset cruises, airboat and swamp-buggy rides, dolphin-watching cruises, bird-watching expeditions, and personalized tours of the Kennedy Space Center and Merritt Island National Wildlife Refuge. Reservations are required.

FISHING   Head to Port Canaveral for catches such as snapper and grouper. **Jetty Park** (© **321/783-7111**), at the south entry to the port, has a fishing pier equipped with a bait shop (see "Beaches & Wildlife Refuges," above). The south bank of the port is lined with charter boats. Try deep-sea fishing on *Miss Cape Canaveral* (© **321/783-5274,** or 321/648-2211 in Orlando; www.misscape.com), one of the party boats based here. All-day voyages departing daily at 8am cost $50 to $65 for adults, $45 to $60 for seniors, $40 to $55 for students 11 to 17, and $30 to $45 for kids 6 to 10.

GOLF   You can read about Northeast Florida's best courses in the free *Golfer's Guide,* available at the tourist information offices and in many hotel lobbies.

The municipal **Cocoa Beach Country Club,** 500 Tom Warringer Blvd. (© **321/868-3351**), has 27 holes of golf and 10 lighted tennis courts set on acres of natural woodland, rivers, and lakes. Greens fees (including cart) are about $40 in winter, dropping to about $35 in summer.

On Merritt Island south of the Kennedy Space Center, the **Savannahs at Sykes Creek,** 3915 Savannahs Trail (℃ 321/455-1377), has 18 holes over 6,636 yards bordered by hardwood forests, lakes, and savannahs inhabited by a host of wildlife. You'll have to hit over a lake to reach the 7th hole. Fees with cart are about $40 in winter, lower in summer.

The best nearby course is the Gary Player–designed **Baytree National Golf Club,** 8010 N. Wickham Rd., ½ mile east of I-95 in Melbourne (℃ 321/259-9060), where challenging marshy holes are flanked by towering palms. This par-72 course has 7,043 yards with a unique red-shale waste area. Fees are about $90 in winter, dropping to about $50 in summer, including cart.

For course information, go to **www.golf.com** or **www.floridagolfing.com**; or call the **Florida Sports Foundation** (℃ 850/488-8347) or **Florida Golfing** (℃ 866/833-2663).

SURFING   Rip through some occasionally awesome waves (by Florida's standards, not California's or Hawaii's) at the **Cocoa Beach Pier** area or down south at **Sebastian Inlet.** Get outfitted at **Ron Jon Surf Shop,** 4151 N. Atlantic Ave. (℃ 321/799-8888; www.ronjons.com), or learn how to hang 5 or 10 with **Cocoa Beach Surfing School** ⟨★⟩, 150 E. Columbia Lane (℃ 321/868-1980; www.cocoabeachsurfing school.com). The school offers equipment and lessons for beginners and pros at area beaches. Be sure to bring along a towel, flip-flops, sunscreen, and a lot of nerve.

WHERE TO STAY

The hotels listed below are all in Cocoa Beach, the closest resort area to the Kennedy Space Center, about a 30-minute drive to the north. (For pop-culture junkies, Cocoa Beach was where the show *I Dream of Jeannie* took place.) Closest to the space center and Port Canaveral is the **Radisson Resort at the Port,** 8701 Astronaut Blvd. (FL A1A), in Cape Canaveral (℃ 800/333-3333 or 321/784-0000; www.radisson.com). It isn't on the beach, but you can relax in its landscaped courtyard, where a waterfall cascades over fake rocks into a heated pool. This well-equipped hotel caters to business travelers and passengers waiting to board cruise ships (with free transportation to the port and free parking while you cruise); it offers a great complimentary breakfast.

The newest chain motels in this area are the **Hampton Inn Cocoa Beach,** 3425 Atlantic Blvd. (℃ 877/492-3224 or 321/799-4099; www.hamptoninncocoabeach. com); and **Courtyard by Marriott,** 3435 Atlantic Blvd. (℃ 800/321-2211 or 321/784-4800; www.marriott.com). They stand side by side and access the beach via a pathway through a condominium complex.

The **Florida Space Coast Office of Tourism,** 8810 Astronaut Blvd. no. 102, Cape Canaveral, FL 32920 (℃ 800/93-OCEAN or 321/868-1126; www.space-coast.com), publishes a booklet of the area's "Superior Small Lodgings."

The area has a plethora of rental condominiums and cottages. **King Rentals Inc.,** 102 W. Central Blvd., Cape Canaveral, FL 32920 (℃ 888/295-0934 or 321/784-5046; www.kingrentals.com), has a wide selection in its inventory.

Given the proximity of Orlando, the generally warm weather year-round, and the business travelers visiting the space complex, there is little if any seasonal fluctuation in room rates here. They are highest on weekends, holidays, and during special events, such as space-shuttle launches.

Tent and RV camping are available at **Jetty Park,** in Port Canaveral (see "Beaches & Wildlife Refuges," above).

You'll pay a 4% hotel tax on top of the Florida 6% sales tax here.

DoubleTree Hotel Cocoa Beach Oceanfront ⟨ Although not as upscale as the Hilton Cocoa Beach Oceanfront (see below), this is the pick of the full-service beach-side hotels. All rooms have balconies with ocean views, and 10 suites have living rooms with sleeper sofas and separate bedrooms. A charming dining room serves decent Mediterranean fare; it faces the beach and opens onto a brick patio where water cascades between two heated pools. Conference facilities draw groups.

2080 N. Atlantic Ave., Cocoa Beach, FL 32931. ⟨ **800/552-3224** or 321/783-9222. Fax 321/799-3234. www.cocoa beachdoubletree.com. 148 units. $114–$179 double; $185–$294 suite. AE, DC, DISC, MC, V. **Amenities:** Restaurant; bar; 2 heated outdoor pools; exercise room; game room; limited room service; laundry service; coin-op washers and dryers; concierge-level rooms. *In room:* A/C, TV, dataport, coffeemaker, hair dryer, iron.

Hilton Cocoa Beach Oceanfront   Damaged by Hurricane Frances, the Hilton Cocoa Beach Oceanfront reopened in early 2005 after a $21-million renovation to guest rooms, pool area, restaurant, and lounge. The rooms at this seven-story Hilton lack balconies or patios; instead, they have small, sealed-shut windows, and only 16 of the rooms face the beach. These and other architectural features make this seem more like a downtown hotel transplanted to a beachside location. Nevertheless, it's one of the few upscale beachfront properties here. No doubt you'll run into a crew of name-tagged conventioneers, since it's especially popular with groups. Despite their lack of fresh air, the rooms are spacious and comfortable, especially since the renovations.

1550 N. Atlantic Ave., Cocoa Beach, FL 32931. ⟨ **800/445-8667** or 321/799-0003. Fax 321/799-0344. www.hilton. com. 296 units. $134–$294 double. AE, DC, DISC, MC, V. **Amenities:** Restaurant; 2 bars; heated outdoor pool; exercise room; game room; watersports equipment rentals; business center; limited room service; laundry service; coin-op washers and dryers; concierge-level rooms. *In room:* A/C, TV, dataport, coffeemaker, hair dryer, iron.

The Inn at Cocoa Beach ⟨⟨⟨   Despite having 50 units, this seaside inn has an intimate B&B ambience and is far and away the most romantic place in the area. Owner Karen Simpler, a skilled interior decorator, has furnished each unit with an elegant mix of pine, tropical, and French country pieces. Rooms in the three- and four-story buildings are much more spacious and have better sea views from their balconies than the "standard" units in the original two-story motel wing (all but six units here have balconies or patios). The older units open onto a courtyard with a pool tucked behind the dunes. Highest on the romance scale are the two rooms with Jacuzzi tubs and easy chairs facing gas fireplaces. Guests are treated to continental breakfast, afternoon tea, and evening wine and cheese. There's also an honor bar where you can pour your own drinks, and a library from which to feed your head.

4300 Ocean Blvd., Cocoa Beach, FL 32932. ⟨ **800/343-5307** or 321/799-3460. Fax 321/784-8632. www.theinnat cocoabeach.com. 50 units. $135–$325 double. Rates include continental breakfast and afternoon tea. AE, DISC, MC, V. No children under 12 accepted. **Amenities:** Bar (guests only); heated outdoor pool; sauna; massage; laundry service. *In room:* A/C, TV, dataport.

Riverview Hotel ⟨⟨⟨   Located right on the Intracoastal Waterway in New Smyrna Beach, the Riverview Hotel, a former fishing and hunting shack for sports-men scoping the Indian River Lagoon, is a spectacularly restored hotel featuring a 5,000-foot spa complete with mineral pool. There's jazz on the deck every night and a fabulous restaurant to boot (some consider Riverview Charlie's one of the state's best seafood spots). Owners Christa and Jim Kelsey used to work at the Faro Blanco Marina Resort in the Florida Keys, so they are well versed in the art of hospitality. Some rooms have private patios or porches; all are immaculate, charming, and stocked with modern amenities. If I had a choice, however, I'd go for the two-bedroom cottage or house with private pool, which are bargains at $175 to $210!

103 Flagler Ave., New Smyrna Beach 32169. ℂ **800/945-7416** or 386/428-5858. Fax 321/423-8927. www.riverview hotel.com. 18 units. $110–$125 double; $170 suite; private cottage $175 and 3-bedroom house for up to 4 people $225. Rates include expanded continental breakfast. AE, DISC, MC, V. **Amenities:** Restaurant; heated pool; spa; sauna; massage. *In room:* A/C, TV.

WHERE TO DINE

On the **Cocoa Beach Pier,** at the beach end of Meade Avenue, you'll get a fine view down the coast to accompany the seafood offerings at **Atlantic Ocean Grill** (ℂ 321/ 783-7549) and the mediocre pub fare at adjacent **Marlins Good Times Bar & Grill** (same phone). The restaurants may not justify spending an entire evening on the pier, but the outdoor, tin-roofed **Boardwalk Tiki Bar** ⚓, where live music plays most nights, is a prime spot to have a cold one while watching the surfers or a sunset.

Bernard's Surf/Fischer's Seafood Bar & Grill ⚓ SEAFOOD/STEAK Photos on the walls testify that many astronauts come to these adjoining establishments to celebrate their landings. It started as Bernard's Surf in 1948, serving standard steak-and-seafood fare in a nautical setting. The present Bernard's offers specials such as stone-crab claws, chargrilled red snapper, and a belly-busting platter of shrimp, scallops, grouper, crab cakes, lobster, and oysters. You can even get Russian beluga or Sevruga caviar if you so desire. The fresh seafood also finds its way into Fischer's Seafood Bar & Grill, a *Cheers*-like lounge popular with locals. The menu here features fried combo platters and mussels with a wine sauce over pasta, as well as burgers and other pub fare. It has the same 25¢ happy-hour oysters and spicy wings as a branch of **Rusty's Seafood & Oyster Bar** (see below), also part of this complex.

2 S. Atlantic Ave. (at Minuteman Causeway Rd.), Cocoa Beach. ℂ **321/783-2401.** Reservations recommended in Bernard's, not accepted in Fischer's. Bernard's main courses $14–$55. Fischer's main courses $9–$16; sandwiches and salads $4–$9. AE, DC, DISC, MC, V. Bernard's Mon–Fri 4–10pm; Sat 4–11pm. Fischer's Mon–Fri 11am–10pm; Sat 11am–11pm. Closed Christmas.

The Mango Tree ⚓⚓ CONTINENTAL Gourmet seafood, pastas, and chicken are served in a plantation-home atmosphere with elegant furnishings in this stucco house, the finest dining venue around. Although the ambience borders on Tavern on the Green tourist-tacky, the restaurant is rather picturesque. Indoor goldfish ponds and an outdoor waterfall splashing into a koi pond in the gardens provide pleasing backdrops. Start with Indian River crab cakes, then go on to the chef's expert spin on roast Long Island duckling, beef tips with peppercorn-mushroom sauce, or other excellent dishes drawing their inspiration from the Continent.

118 N. Atlantic Ave. (FL A1A, between N. 1st and N. 2nd sts.), Cocoa Beach. ℂ **321/799-0513.** Reservations recommended. Main courses $16–$40. AE, MC, V. Tues–Sun 6–10pm.

Rusty's Seafood & Oyster Bar ⟨Value⟩ SEAFOOD This lively sports bar beside Port Canaveral's man-made harbor offers inexpensive chow ranging from spicy seafood gumbo to a pot of seafood that will give two people their fill of steamed oysters, clams, shrimp, crab legs, potatoes, and corn on the cob. Raw or steamed fresh oysters and clams from the raw bar are first-rate and a good value, as is a weekday lunch buffet.

Seating is indoors or out, but the inside tables have the best view of the fishing boats and cruise liners going in and out of the port. Daily happy hour from 3 to 6pm sees beers drafted at 60¢ a mug, and tons of raw or steamed oysters and spicy Buffalo wings go for 25¢ each. The joint is busy and sometimes noisy, especially on weekend afternoons, but the clientele tends to be older and better behaved than those at other pubs along the banks of Port Canaveral. There's another **Rusty's** in the Bernard's Surf/Fischer's Seafood Bar & Grill restaurant complex in Cocoa Beach (see above).

628 Glen Cheek Dr. (south side of the harbor), Port Canaveral. ℂ **321/783-2033.** Main courses $7–$25; sandwiches and salads $4–$7; lunch buffet $6. AE, DC, DISC, MC, V. Sun–Thurs 11am–11:30pm; Fri–Sat 11am–12:30am (lunch buffet Mon–Fri 11am–2pm).

THE SPACE COAST AFTER DARK

For a rundown of current performances and exhibits, call the **Brevard Cultural Alliance's Arts Line** (ℂ **321/690-6819**). For live music, walk out on the **Cocoa Beach Pier,** on Meade Avenue at the beach, where **Oh Shuck's Seafood Bar & Grill** (ℂ **321/783-7549**), **Marlins Good Times Bar & Grill** (ℂ **321/783-7549**), and the alfresco **Boardwalk Tiki Bar** ✹ (same phone as Marlins) feature bands on weekends, more often during the summer season. The Tiki Bar is a great place to hang out over a cold beer all afternoon and evening.

3 Daytona Beach

54 miles NE of Orlando

Daytona Beach is a town with many personalities. It is at once the self-proclaimed "World's Most Famous Beach" and "World Center of Racing," a mecca for tattooed motorcyclists and pierced spring-breakers, *and* the home of a surprisingly good art museum. The city and developers spent millions of dollars to turn the somewhat seedy beachfront area (complete with the requisite T-shirt and souvenir shops) around the famous Main Street Pier into Ocean Walk Village, a redevelopment area of upscale shops, entertainment, and resort facilities.

Daytona Beach has been a destination for racing enthusiasts since the early 1900s, when "horseless carriages" raced on the hard-packed sand beach. One thing is for sure: Daytonans still love their cars. Recent debate over the environmental impact of unrestricted driving on the beach caused an uproar from citizens who couldn't imagine it any other way. As it worked out, they can still drive on the sand, but not everywhere, and especially not in areas where sea turtles are nesting.

Today, hundreds of thousands of race enthusiasts come to the home of the National Association for Stock Car Auto Racing (NASCAR) for the Daytona 500, the Pepsi 400, and other races throughout the year. The Speedway is also home to DAYTONA USA, a motor-sports entertainment attraction worth a visit even by nonracing fans.

Be sure to check the "Calendar of Events" (p. 26) to know when the town belongs to college students during spring break, thousands of leather-clad motorcycle buffs during Bike Week (Mar) and Biketoberfest (Oct), or racing enthusiasts for big competitions. You won't be able to find a hotel room, drive the highways, or enjoy a peaceful vacation when they're in town.

ESSENTIALS

GETTING THERE   Continental (ℂ **800/525-0280**) and **Delta** (ℂ **800/221-1212**) fly into the small, pleasant, and calm **Daytona Beach International Airport**

(© **386/248-8030;** http://flydaytonafirst.com), 4 miles inland from the beach on International Speedway Boulevard (U.S. 92), but you can usually find less expensive fares to **Orlando International Airport** (p. 49), about an hour's drive away (via I-4). **Daytona–Orlando Transit Service** (**DOTS;** © **800/231-1965** or 386/257-5411; www.dots-daytonabeach.com) provides van transportation to and from Orlando International Airport. One-way fares are about $28 for adults, $15 for children 11 and under. The service takes passengers to the company's terminal at 1034 N. Nova Rd., between 3rd and 4th streets, or to beach hotels for an additional fee.

If you fly into the Daytona Airport, rates for the **Daytona Shuttle** (© **386/255-2294**) run up to $12 per person, $14 per couple, or $6 per person for parties of three or more. The ride from the airport to most beach hotels via **Yellow Cab Co.** (© **386/255-5555**) is between $7 and $18.

Alamo (© 800/327-9622), **Avis** (© 800/831-2847), **Budget** (© 800/527-0700), **Dollar** (© 800/800-4000), **Enterprise** (© 800/325-8007), **Hertz** (© 800/654-3131), and **National** (© 800/227-7368) have booths at the airport. Or why not rent a Harley? This is Daytona, after all. Contact **Daytona Harley-Davidson** (© 800/307-4464 or 386/258-0638; www.daytonahd.com). Rates are $135 to $155 daily, $600 to $640 weekly. A special sunset rate of $75 is available from 4pm to 9am.

Amtrak (© **800/872-7245;** www.amtrak.com) trains stop at Deland, about 15 miles southwest of Daytona Beach, with bus service from Deland to the beach.

VISITOR INFORMATION   The **Daytona Beach Area Convention & Visitors Bureau,** 126 E. Orange Ave. (P.O. Box 910), Daytona Beach, FL 32115 (© **800/544-0415** or 386/255-0415; www.daytonabeach.com), can help you with information on attractions, accommodations, dining, and events. The office is on the mainland just west of the Memorial Bridge. The information area of the lobby is open daily from 9am to 5pm. The bureau also maintains a branch at DAYTONA USA, 1801 W. International Speedway Blvd. (daily 9am–7pm), as well as a kiosk at the airport.

GETTING AROUND   Although Daytona is primarily a driver's town, Volusia County's public transit system, **VOTRAN** (© **386/761-7700;** http://votran.org), runs a **free shuttle** in the Main Street Pier/Ocean Walk Village area and a pay **trolley** along Atlantic Avenue on the beach, Monday through Saturday from noon to midnight. Fares are $1 for adults, 50¢ for seniors and children 6 to 17, and free for kids under 6 riding with an adult. VOTRAN also runs **buses** through downtown and the beaches.

For a taxi, call **Yellow Cab** (© **386/255-5555**) or **Southern Komfort Cab** (© **386/252-2222**).

A VISIT TO THE WORLD CENTER OF RACING

Daytona International Speedway/DAYTONA USA ☆☆   You don't have to be a racing fan to enjoy a visit to the **Daytona International Speedway,** 4 miles west of the beach. Opened in 1959 with the first Daytona 500, this 480-acre complex is one of the key reasons for the city's fame. The track presents about nine weekends of major racing events annually, featuring stock cars, sports cars, motorcycles, and go-karts, and is used for automobile and motorbike testing and other events many other days of the year. Its grandstands can accommodate more than 150,000 fans. Big events sell out months in advance—tickets to the Daytona 500 in February can be gone a year ahead of time—so buy yours and make hotel reservations as early as possible.

Start your visit at the **World Center of Racing Visitor Center,** in the NASCAR office complex at the east end of the speedway. Admission to the center is free, and

Daytona Beach

Daytona Beach
Area

ACCOMMODATIONS ■
Old Salty's Inn **13**

The Plaza
Resort & Spa **4**

Shoreline All Suites Inn
& Cabana Colony
Cottages **14**

The Shores
Resort & Spa **15**

The Villa Bed
& Breakfast **3**

DINING ◆
The Avocado
Kingdom **6**

The Cellar **7**

Down the Hatch **16**

Frappes North **1**

Julian's Dining Room
& Lounge **2**

McK's Dublin Station **6**

Ocean Deck Restaurant
& Beach Club **5**

Rosario's Ristorante **9**

ATTRACTIONS ●
Daytona International
Speedway/
DAYTONA USA **11**

Daytona Flea and
Farmers' Market **12**

Halifax Historical
Museum **8**

Marine Science
Center **16**

Museum of Arts
and Sciences **10**

Ponce de León Inlet
Lighthouse
& Museum **16**

you can walk out and see the track during non-race days (there's a small admission to the track during qualifying races leading up to the main events). Entertaining 30-minute guided tram tours of the facility (garage area, pit road, and so on) depart from the visitor center and are well worth taking.

The visitor center houses a large souvenir shop, a snack bar, and the phenomenally popular **DAYTONA USA,** a 60,000-square-foot, state-of-the-art interactive motorsports attraction. Here you can learn about the history, color, and excitement of stock car, go-kart, and motorcycle racing in Daytona. In Daytona Dream Laps, you get the feel of what it's like to zoom around the track from a 32-seat motion simulator. If that doesn't get your stomach churning, hop inside your own 80%-scale NASCAR vehicle in Acceleration Alley, buckle up, and roar up to 200 mph in a spectacular simulator for the ultimate virtual-reality-like racing experience ($5 per ride). On the milder side, you can participate in a pit stop on a NASCAR Winston Cup stock car, see an actual winning Daytona 500 car still covered in track dust, talk via video with favorite competitors, and play radio or television announcer by calling the finish of a race. An action-packed IMAX film will put you in the winner's seat of a Daytona 500 race.

To really experience what it's like, you can make (for $134) three laps around the track in a stock car from May to October with the **Richard Petty Driving Experience Ride-Along Program** (© **800/237-3889;** www.1800bepetty.com). Professional drivers (sorry, none are named Petty) are at the wheel as you see and feel what it's like to travel an average of 115 mph.

Allow at least 4 hours to see everything, and bring your video camera.

1801 W. International Speedway Blvd. (U.S. 92, at Bill France Blvd.). © **386/253-7223** for race tickets, 386/253-7223 for information, or 386/947-6404 or 386/947-6800 for DAYTONA USA. www.daytonaintlspeedway.com and www.daytonausa.com. Speedway free admission except on race days; tram rides $7.50. DAYTONA USA admission $22 adults, $19 seniors, $16 children 6–12, free admission for children under 6. Speedway daily 9am–7pm; trams depart every 30 min. 9:30am–5pm except during races and special events. DAYTONA USA daily 9am–7pm (later during race events). Closed Christmas.

HITTING THE WORLD'S MOST FAMOUS BEACH

The beautiful and hard-packed beach here runs for 24 miles along a skinny peninsula separated from the mainland by the Halifax River. The bustling hub of activity is at the end of Main Street, where you'll find the **Main Street Pier** (also known as the Daytona Beach Pier or Ocean Pier), the longest wooden pier on the East Coast. Out here you'll find a restaurant, bar, bait shop, beach-toy concessions, a chairlift running its length, and views from the 180-foot-tall Space Needle. Admission as far out as the restaurant and bar is free (at about a third of the way, this is far enough for a good view down the beach), but you'll have to pay $1 to walk beyond that point, and more than that if you fish (see "Outdoor Activities," below). Beginning at the pier, the city's famous oceanside **Boardwalk** is lined with restaurants, bars, and T-shirt shops, as are the 4 blocks of Main Street nearest the beach. The city's $400-million **Ocean Walk Village** redevelopment project begins here and runs several blocks north featuring a movie theater, boutiques, restaurants, and even a 175-room hotel/condo, the **Ocean Walk Resort** (© **877/845-WALK**).

There's another busy beach area at the end of **Seabreeze Boulevard,** which has a multitude of restaurants, bars, and shops.

Couples seeking greater privacy usually prefer the northern or southern extremities of the beach. **Ponce Inlet,** at the very southern tip of the peninsula, is especially peaceful, since there is little commerce or traffic there to disturb the silence.

Tips **Driving on the Beach**

You can drive and park directly on sections of the sand along 18 miles of the beach during daylight hours and at low tide (Hurricane Floyd and other recent storms have greatly reduced the beach's width), but watch for signs warning of nesting sea turtles. There's a $5-per-vehicle access fee and 10-mph speed limit. *Watch out for the tides.* If you park on an incoming tide and lose track of time, your vehicle may become an inadvertent rust bucket or artificial reef!

OUTDOOR ACTIVITIES

CRUISES Take a leisurely cruise on the Halifax River aboard the 14-passenger, 25-foot *Fancy,* a replica of an 1890s-style fantail launch. It's operated by **A tiny Cruise Line River Excursions,** 425 S. Beach St., at Halifax Harbor Marina (© **386/ 226-2343**). Captain Jim regales passengers with river lore and points out dolphins (which are more commonly spotted in the mornings), manatees, herons, cormorants, pelicans, egrets, and osprey during his 2-hour midday cruise. In the afternoon, you can see the man-made estates along the river. Cruises range from $11 to $16 for adults, $6.50 to $9.50 for children 4 to 12. Weather permitting, the midday cruises depart year-round (with a brief hiatus during the holidays), Monday through Saturday at 11:30am. The 1-hour tour of riverfront homes is at 2pm, the tour of historic downtown at 3:30pm; there are no Monday cruises in winter months. Romantic sunset cruises are available; call for reservations. Rumor has it that Ponce de León discovered his Fountain of Youth along the St. Johns River in Volusia County. While you may not find it today, you will find a cool tour, the **Fountain of Youth Eco-History Tour,** which begins on the Spring Garden Run in the **De Leon Springs State Park,** 601 Ponce De Leon Blvd. (© **386/985-4212**). The 90-minute tour on a pontoon boat will give you great insight into the so-called healing waters of the springs in the 603-acre park. Tours cost $18 for adults, $16 for seniors, and $12 for kids. For more information, call (© **386/837-5537**) or go to **www.foytours.com**.

FISHING The easiest and least expensive way to fish offshore for marlin, sailfish, king mackerel, grouper, red snapper, and more is with the **Critter Fleet,** 4950 S. Peninsula Dr., just past the lighthouse in Ponce Inlet (© **800/338-0850** or 386/767-7676; www.critterfleet.com), which operates two party boats. One goes on all-day trips (about $60 adults, $35 kids under 12), while the other makes morning and afternoon voyages (about $40 adults, $25 kids under 12). The fares include rod, reel, and bait. Call for schedules, prices, and reservations.

Save the cost of a boat by fishing with the locals at **Main Street Pier,** at the ocean end of Main Street (© **386/253-1212**). Admission for anglers is $5 for adults, $3.50 for kids under 12. Bait and gear are available for $13, and no license is required.

GOLF There are more than 25 courses within 30 minutes of the beach, and most hotels can arrange starting times for you. **Golf Daytona Beach,** 126 E. Orange Ave., Daytona Beach, FL 32114 (© **800/881-7065** or 386/239-7065; fax 386/239-0064), publishes an annual brochure describing the major courses. It's available at the tourist information offices (see "Essentials," above).

For course information, go to www.golf.com or www.floridagolfing.com; or call the **Florida Sports Foundation** (© **850/488-8347**) or **Florida Golfing** (© **866/ 833-2663**).

Two of the nation's top-rated links for women golfers are at the **LPGA International** *★★*, 1000 Championship Dr. (© **386/274-5742;** www.lpgainternational. com): the Champions course, designed by Rees Jones; and the Legends course, designed by Arthur Hills. Each boasts 18 outstanding holes. LPGA International is a center offering workshops and teaching programs for professional and amateur women golfers, and the pro shop carries a great selection of ladies' equipment and clothing. Greens fees with a cart are usually about $75, lower in summer. *Pssst*—they let guys play here, too!

A Lloyd Clifton–designed course, the centrally located 18-hole, par-72 **Indigo Lakes Golf Course,** 2620 W. International Speedway Blvd. (© **386/254-3607;** www.indigolakesgolf.com), has flat fairways and large bunkered Bermuda greens. Fees here are about $40 in winter (including a cart), lower in summer.

The semi-private South Course at **Pelican Bay Country Club,** 550 Sea Duck Dr. (© **386/756-0034;** www.pelicanbaygolfclub.com), is one of the area's favorites, with fast greens to test your putting skills. Fees are about $45 with cart in winter, lower in summer (no walking allowed). The North Course is for members only.

The city's prime municipal course is the **Daytona Beach Country Club,** 600 Wilder Blvd. (© **386/258-3119**), which has 36 holes. Winter fees are about $20 to walk, $30 to share a cart. They drop $3 in summer.

HELICOPTER RIDES   Take a helicopter ride around the Daytona area to see the city from a different point of view. **Air Florida** (© **386/257-6993;** www.airflorida helicopters.com) offers rides starting at $20 (two-person minimum), leaving from the Daytona Flea and Farmers' Market (see below).

HORSEBACK RIDING   **Shenandoah Stables,** 1759 Tomoka Farms Rd., off U.S. 92 (© **386/257-1444**), offers daily trail rides and lessons. Call for prices and schedules.

SPECTATOR SPORTS   The **Daytona Cubs** (© **386/872-2827;** www.daytona cubs.com), a Class A minor-league affiliate of the Chicago Cubs, play April through August at Jackie Robinson Ballpark, on City Island downtown. A game here is a treat, since the park has been restored to its classic 1914 style by the designers of Baltimore's Camden Yards and Cleveland's Jacobs Field. Tickets are $6 to $9.

WATERSPORTS   Watersports equipment, bicycles, beach buggies, and mopeds can be rented along the Boardwalk, at the ocean end of Main Street (see "Hitting the World's Most Famous Beach," above), and in front of major beachfront hotels.

MUSEUMS & ATTRACTIONS

Halifax Historical Museum *★*   Located on Beach Street, Daytona's original riverfront commercial district on the mainland side of the Halifax River (see "Shopping," below), this local museum is worth a look just for the 1912 neoclassical architecture of its home, a former bank. A mural of Old Florida wildlife graces one wall, the stained-glass ceiling reflects sunlight, and across the room is an original teller's window. The eclectic collection includes tools and household items from the Spanish and British periods, thousands of historical photographs, possessions of past residents (even a ball gown worn at Lincoln's inauguration) and, of course, model cars. A race exhibit opens annually in mid-January as a stage-setter for Race Week.

252 S. Beach St. (just north of Orange Ave.). © 386/255-6976. www.halifaxhistorical.org. Admission $4 adults, $1 children 11 and under; free Sat for children. Tues–Sat 10am–4pm.

Marine Science Center *Kids*   This marine museum has interior displays (with exhibits on mangroves, mosquitoes, shells, artificial reefs, dune habitats, and pollution solutions), a 5,000-gallon aquarium, and educational programs and activities. Though the exhibit area is rather small, there's more than enough information for a child to digest at one time. Perhaps the most interesting part of the center is the space reserved for the rehabilitation of endangered and threatened sea turtles. You can watch them in any of seven turtle tanks—look for the ones who need life jackets to stay afloat!

100 Lighthouse Dr., Ponce Inlet. (C) 386/304-5545. www.marinesciencecenter.com. Admission $3 adults, $1 children 5–12, free for children under 5. Tues–Sat 10am–4pm; Sun noon–4pm. Closed Mon. See directions for Ponce de León Inlet Lighthouse & Museum (below).

Museum of Arts and Sciences 𝒸𝒸 An exceptional institution for a town of Daytona's size and reputation (as a culturally devoid, trashy, spring-break mecca), this museum is best known for its *Cuba: A History of Art* exhibit, with paintings acquired in 1956, when Cuban dictator Fulgencio Batista donated his private collection to the city. Among them is a portrait of Eva ("Evita") Perón, said to be the only existing painting completed while she was alive (it hangs near the lobby, not within the Cuban exhibit). The Dow Gallery displays American decorative arts; while the Bouchelle Study Center for the Decorative Arts contains American and European jewelry, furniture, mirrors, and more. Other rooms include the Schulte Gallery of Chinese Art; Africa: Life and Ritual, with the largest collection of Ashante gold ornaments in the U.S. (these are stunning); and the Center for Florida History, with the skeleton of a 13-foot-tall, 130,000-year-old giant ground sloth. Check out the unique collection of the late Chapman S. Root, a Daytona philanthropist and a founder of the Coca-Cola empire; among the memorabilia are the mold for the original Coke bottle and the Root family's two private railroad cars. The planetarium presents 30-minute shows of what the night sky will look like on the date of your visit. *Note:* Even though this is a first-class art museum, children are apt to be bored here.

1040 Museum Blvd. (off Nova Rd./FL 5A between International Speedway Blvd. and Bellevue Ave.). (C) 386/255-0285. www.moas.org. Museum $8 adults, $4 children and students with ID, free for children 5 and under. Planetarium shows $3 adults, $2 children and students. Tues–Fri 9am–4pm; Sat–Sun noon–5pm. Planetarium shows Tues–Fri 2pm; Sat–Sun 1 and 3pm. Closed Thanksgiving, Christmas Eve, and Christmas Day. Take International Speedway Blvd. west, make a left on Nova Rd. (FL 5A), and look for a sign on your right.

Ponce de León Inlet Lighthouse & Museum 𝒸𝒸 This National Historic Landmark is well worth a stop even if you're not a lighthouse enthusiast. The 175-foot brick-and-granite structure is the second-tallest lighthouse in the United States. Built in the 1880s, the lighthouse and the graceful Victorian brick buildings surrounding it have been restored. There are no guided tours, but you can walk through the 12 areas, which feature different exhibits (lighthouse lenses, historical artifacts, and a film of early car racing on the nearby beach), and around the tugboat *F. D. Russell,* now sitting high and dry in the sand. Use common sense if you climb the 203 steps to the top of the lighthouse; it's a grinding ascent, but the view from up there is spectacular.

4931 S. Peninsula Dr., Ponce Inlet. (C) 386/761-1821. www.ponceinlet.org. Admission $5 adults, $1.50 children under 12. Memorial Day to Labor Day daily 10am–9pm; rest of year daily 10am–5pm. Follow Atlantic Ave. south, make a right on Beach St., and follow the signs.

SHOPPING

On the mainland, Daytona Beach's main riverside drag, **Beach Street,** is one of the few areas in town where people actually stroll. The street is wide and inviting, with palms down its median, and decorative wrought-iron archways and fancy brickwork overlooking a branch of the Halifax River. Today, Beach Street between Bay Street and

Crossing Over into Cassadaga

If you're in the Daytona Beach/Orlando area, suspend your disbelief for a few hours and make a pit stop in Cassadaga, the tiny century-old community composed completely of psychics and mediums who will be happy to tell you your fortune or put you in touch with the deceased—for a price, of course.

Should you find the whole concept of psychics and talking to the dead completely kooky and out of whack, consider the history of Cassadaga, which is fascinating in its own right.

At the risk of sounding like the intro to the SciFi Channel show *Crossing Over with John Edward,* the story goes that as a young man from New York, George Colby was told during a séance that he would someday establish a spiritualist community in the South. In 1875, the prophecy came true when Colby was led through the wilderness of Central Florida by his spiritual guide to a 35-acre area that was to become the Cassadaga Spiritualist Camp.

Although it sounds like a bizarre cult, it's not. Consisting of about 57 acres and 55 no-nonsense clapboard houses, Cassadaga caters to those who have chosen to share in a community of like-minded people who happen to believe in the otherworldly. Yes, the people are eccentric, to say the least, but they're all very friendly. Designated a Historic District on the National Register of Historic Places, Cassadaga is the spiritualist version of Lourdes, to which skeptics and believers alike flock for answers, or at least kicks.

When you get to town, head straight for the information center (see below for directions), where you can find out which psychics and mediums are working that day, and make an appointment for a session, which ranges from $25 and up for a palm reading to $50 and up for a session with a medium. A general store, a restaurant, a hotel, and a few shops selling crystals and potions of sorts will keep you occupied while you wait for your appointment. Whether you're a believer or not, an hour or two in Cassadaga will make for interesting cocktail conversation.

From Daytona, take I-4 to exit 114. Turn right onto Highway 472 at the end of the exit ramp toward Orange City/Deland. At the traffic light, turn right onto Dr. Martin Luther King, Jr., Parkway. Turn right at the first light, which is Cassadaga Road. Continue 1½ miles to the intersection with Stevens Street. The information center is on the right. For more information, call ☎ 386/228-3171 or go to **www.cassadaga.org**.

Orange Avenue offers antiques and collectibles shops, galleries, clothiers, a magic shop, a historical museum (see "Museums & Attractions," above), and several good cafes. At 154 S. Beach St., you'll find the home of the **Angell & Phelps Chocolate Factory** (☎ 386/252-6531; www.angellandphelps.com), which has been making candy for more than 75 years. Watch the goodies being made (and get a free sample!).

"Hog" riders will find several shops to your liking along Beach Street, north of International Speedway Boulevard, including the **Harley-Davidson Store,** 290 N. Beach St., at Dr. Mary McLeod Bethune Boulevard (☎ 386/253-2453), a 20,000-square-foot retail outlet and diner serving breakfast and lunch. It's one of the nation's largest Harley dealerships. In addition to hundreds of gleaming new and used Hogs, you'll find as much fringed leather as you've ever seen in one place.

The **Daytona Flea and Farmers' Market,** on Tomoka Farms Road at the junction of I-95 and U.S. 92, a mile west of the Speedway (✆ **386/253-3330;** www.daytona fleamarket.com), is huge, with 1,000 covered outdoor booths plus 100 antiques and collectibles vendors in an air-conditioned building. Most of the booths feature new (though not necessarily first-rate) wares along the lines of socks, sunglasses, luggage, handbags, jewelry, tools, and the like. It's open year-round, Friday through Sunday from 8am to 5pm. Admission and parking are free.

Ocean Walk Shoppes, at Ocean Walk Village, 250 N. Atlantic Ave. (✆ **386/257-5077;** www.oceanwalkvillage.com), is a collection of upscale boutiques and restaurants and a 10-screen movie theater.

WHERE TO STAY

Room rates here are among the most affordable in Florida. Some properties have several rate periods during the year, but generally they are somewhat higher from the beginning of the races in February all the way to Labor Day. They skyrocket during major events at the Speedway, during bikers' gatherings, and during spring break (see the "Calendar of Events," beginning on p. 26), when hotels fill to the bursting point. Even if you can find a room then, there's often a minimum-stay requirement.

Hundreds of hotels and motels line Atlantic Avenue along the beach, many of them family owned and operated. The **Daytona Beach Area Convention & Visitors Bureau** (see "Essentials," earlier in this chapter) distributes a brochure that lists "Superior Small Lodgings" for Daytona Beach, Deland, and New Smyrna Beach. All of the small motels listed below are members.

If you're going to the races and don't care about staying on the beach, some upper-floor rooms at the **Hilton Garden Inn Daytona Beach Airport,** 189 Midway Ave. (✆ **877/944-4001** or 386/944-4000), overlook the international speedway track. Unlike most members of Hilton's Garden Inn chain, this one has a restaurant.

Thousands of rental condominiums line the beach. Among the most luxurious is the new, 150-unit condominium hotel **Ocean Walk Resort,** 300 N. Atlantic Ave., Daytona Beach, FL 32118 (✆ **800/649-3566** or 386/323-4800; www.oceanwalk resort.com), which is part of the Ocean Walk Village redevelopment. Near the Main Street Pier, it's in the center of the action and has one- and two-bedroom apartments with full kitchens, washers and dryers, and all of the usual hotel amenities, plus a wondrous computer-golf simulator, a "lazy river" in the outdoor pool, an island putting green, and much more—including the gaudiest lobby I've ever seen. One of the largest rental agents is **Peck Realty,** 2340 S. Atlantic Ave., Daytona Beach Shores, FL 32118 (✆ **800/447-3255** or 386/257-5000; www.peckrealty.com).

In addition to the 6% state sales tax, Volusia County levies a 4% tax on hotel bills.

Old Salty's Inn *Value*   The most unusual of the many mom-and-pop beachside motels here, Old Salty's is a lush tropical enclave with a *Gilligan's Island* theme, littered with old motors, rotting boats, life preservers, and a jeep. The TV series' main characters are depicted in murals painted on the buildings. The two-story wings flank a courtyard festooned with palms and banana trees (you can pick a banana for breakfast). Facing this vista, the bright rooms have microwaves, refrigerators, and front and back windows. The choice units have picture windows overlooking the beach. There are gas grills and rocking chairs under a gazebo by a heated beachside pool.

1921 S. Atlantic Ave. (FL A1A, at Flamingo Ave.), Daytona Beach Shores, FL 32118. ©️ **800/417-1466** or 386/252-8090. Fax 386/947-9980. www.visitdaytona.com/oldsaltys. 19 units. $53–$71 double; $63–$93 efficiency; $75–$121 suite. AE, DISC, MC, V. **Amenities:** Heated outdoor pool; free use of bikes; coin-op washers and dryers. *In room:* A/C, TV, kitchen, fridge, coffeemaker, hair dryer, iron.

The Plaza Resort & Spa ☆☆   These elegant adjoining 7- and 13-story buildings hold some of Daytona Beach's best rooms (in a much more tasteful atmosphere than many of the neighboring hotels)—provided you don't need a large bathroom. The best units are the corner suites, each with a sitting area and two balconies overlooking the Atlantic; some even have a Jacuzzi. All units have balconies and microwaves (an on-premises store sells frozen dinners). The full-service **Ocean Waters Spa** ☆☆ (©️ **386/267-1660;** www.oceanwatersspa.com) has 16 treatment rooms and a soothing menu of facials, massages, and wraps.

600 N. Atlantic Ave. (at Seabreeze Ave.), Daytona Beach, FL 32118. ©️ **800/874-7420** or 386/255-4471. Fax 386/238-7984. www.plazaresortandspa.com. 323 units. $139–$229 double; $189–$449 suite. AE, DC, DISC, MC, V. **Amenities:** Restaurant; bar; heated outdoor pool; exercise room; spa; Jacuzzi; watersports equipment rentals; game room; business center; limited room service; massage; babysitting; laundry service; coin-op washers and dryers; concierge-level rooms. *In room:* A/C, TV, dataport, fridge, microwave, coffeemaker, hair dryer, iron.

Shoreline All Suites Inn & Cabana Colony Cottages ☆ *Value*   The Shoreline All Suites Inn features one- and two-bedroom suites that occupy two buildings separated by a walkway leading to the beach. Most have small bathrooms with scant vanity space and—shall we say—intimate shower stalls. Every unit has a full kitchen, plus barbecue grills on the premises. For a change of scenery, consider the Shoreline's sister property, the **Cabana Colony Cottages** ☆☆. All 12 of the cottages were built in 1927 but have been upgraded. They aren't much bigger than a motel room with a kitchen, but they're light, airy, and attractively furnished. The cottages share a heated pool with the Shoreline.

2435 S. Atlantic Ave. (FL A1A, at Dundee Rd.), Daytona Beach Shores, FL 32118. ©️ **800/293-0653** or 386/252-1692. Fax 386/239-7068. www.daytonashoreline.com. 30 units, including 12 cottages. $79–$350 suites and cottages. Rates include continental breakfast. Golf packages available. AE, DISC, MC, V. **Amenities:** Heated outdoor pool; coin-op washers and dryers. *In room:* A/C, TV/VCR, kitchen, coffeemaker.

The Shores Resort & Spa ☆☆   Far enough south to escape the madding crowds of Main Street, and set in an upscale residential area directly on the beach, this hotel is the newest and most luxurious hotel here. It welcomes guests with an elegant terra-cotta-tiled lobby with a fountain and potted palms. The large guest rooms are grouped in pairs and can be joined to form suites; only one of each pair has a balcony. Oceanfront rooms are preferable; all have sea and/or river views. Baleen restaurant (with locations in Miami and Naples, too) is one of Daytona's most beautiful, offering stellar seafood with a gourmet and regional twist; patio dining overlooking the ocean is a fine option. The SpaTerre offers an Indonesian-inspired menu of treatments.

2637 S. Atlantic Ave. (FL A1A, between Florida Shores Blvd. and Richard's Lane), Daytona Beach Shores, FL 32118. ©️ **866/934-SHORES** or 386/767-7350. Fax 386/760-3651. www.shoresresort.com. 212 units. Winter $259–$489 double; $549–$1,129 suite; off season $179–$359 double, $509–$829 suite. AE, DC, DISC, MC, V. **Amenities:** Restaurant; bar; heated outdoor pool; exercise room; spa; salon; room service; babysitting; laundry service; dry cleaning. *In room:* A/C, TV, wireless Internet, dataport, kitchen, coffeemaker, hair dryer, iron.

The Villa Bed & Breakfast ☆☆☆   You'll think you're in Iberia upon entering this 70+-year-old Spanish mansion's great room with its fireplace, baby grand piano, and terra-cotta floors. A sunroom equipped with a TV and VCR, a formal dining room, and a breakfast nook are also located downstairs. The lush backyard surrounds a pool and a covered Jacuzzi. Upstairs, the nautically themed Christopher Columbus room has a vaulted ceiling and a small balcony overlooking the pool. The largest unit here is the King Carlos suite, once the original master bedroom, with a four-poster bed, entertainment system, fridge, rooftop deck, and bathroom equipped with four-head shower. The Queen Isabella room has a portrait of the queen over a queen-size bed, while the Marco Polo room features Chinese black-lacquer furniture and Oriental rugs.

801 N. Peninsula Dr. (at Riverview Blvd.), Daytona Beach, FL 32118. ©/fax **386/248-2020.** www.thevillabb.com. 4 units. $125–$400 double. Rates include continental breakfast. AE, MC, V. No children or pets accepted. **Amenities:** Heated outdoor pool; Jacuzzi. *In room:* A/C, TV, hair dryer, no phone.

WHERE TO DINE

Daytona Beach has a few interesting dining venues, but not many are likely to leave an indelible memory. A profusion of fast-food joints lines the major thoroughfares, especially along Atlantic Avenue on the beach and International Speedway Boulevard (U.S. 92) near the racetrack. Restaurants come and go in the Beach Street district on the mainland, and along Main Street and Seabreeze Boulevard on the beach. A casual restaurant out on the Main Street Pier serves burgers, chicken wings, and lots of suds.

In addition to the local **Shells** seafood restaurant, 200 S. Atlantic Ave. (© **386/258-0007;** www.shellsseafood.com), two other outlets of chain restaurants are worth a special mention here. **Buca di Beppo,** 2514 W. International Speedway Blvd. (© **386/253-6523;** www.bucadibeppo.com), a boisterous restaurant serving family-style Southern Italian specialties, is open for dinner only. Expect to take home leftovers, as the portions are huge and the food surprisingly good, especially for a "theme" restaurant. **Stonewood Tavern & Grill,** 100 S. Atlantic Ave., in Ormond Beach (© **386/671-1200;** www.stonewoodgrill.com), is a casual upscale restaurant with a nice but dark mahogany interior, good American food, and excellent service. Also open only for dinner, the restaurant won't disappoint with its menu of steaks, seafood, and the like.

AT THE BEACHES

Down the Hatch ⭐ *Value* SEAFOOD   Occupying a 1940s fish camp on the Halifax River, Down the Hatch serves big portions of fresh fish and seafood (note its shrimp boat docked outside). Inexpensive burgers and sandwiches are available, too. The scenic views include boats and shorebirds visible through the picture windows. At night, arrive early to catch the sunset over the river, and also to beat the crowd to this very popular place. In summer, light fare is served on a covered deck.

4894 Front St., Ponce Inlet. © **386/761-4831.** Call ahead for Priority Seating. Main courses $9–$25 (most $10–$16); breakfast $2–$5; burgers and sandwiches $3–$6.50; early bird menu (served 11am–5pm) $6–$8. AE, MC, V. Daily 8am–10pm. Closed 1st week in Dec. Take Atlantic Ave. south, make a right on Beach St., and follow the signs.

Julian's Dining Room & Lounge ⭐ AMERICAN   This family-owned restaurant has catered to locals and tourists since 1967, offering a casual atmosphere and friendly service. Unlike most eateries in this area, it specializes in prime Western beef (filet mignon, strip steak, and T-bone), but the seafood is far from second fiddle here. Good choices include broiled snapper, soft-shell crab, and king crab au gratin.

88 S. Atlantic Ave., Ormond Beach. © **386/677-6767.** www.juliansrest.com. Reservations suggested. Main courses $9–$26. AE, DC, MC, V. Daily 4–11pm. From Daytona Beach, take Atlantic Ave./FL A1A N. and look for the large A-frame on the left, 2 blocks before FL 40.

Ocean Deck Restaurant & Beach Club *Value* SEAFOOD/PUB FARE   Known by spring-breakers, bikers, and other beachgoers as Daytona's best "beach pub" since 1940, the three-story Ocean Deck is also the best restaurant in the busy area around the Main Street Pier. The downstairs reggae bar is as sweaty and packed as ever (a band plays nightly 9pm–2:30am). The upstairs dining room can be noisy, too, but come here for good food, reasonable prices, and great ocean views. You can choose from a wide range of seafood, chicken, sandwiches, and the best burgers on the beach, but don't pass up the mahimahi (look for "trophy" on the menu), a bargain at $9. There's valet parking after dark, or you can park free at the lot behind the Ocean Deck's Reggae Republic surf shop, a block away on Atlantic Avenue.

127 S. Ocean Ave. (at Kemp St.). ℂ 386/253-5224. www.oceandeck.com. Main courses $9–$18; salads and sandwiches $5–$8. AE, DISC, MC, V. Daily 11am–2am (bar to 3am).

ON THE MAINLAND

The Avocado Kingdom ⛄ VEGETARIAN   A healthy place to start your day or to have lunch while touring downtown, this establishment purveys a number of vegetarian omelets, burritos, salads, pizzas, and sandwiches such as an avocado Reuben. A few chicken and turkey items are on the menu, but the only red-meat selection is a burger. You can dine outside or inside the store, which has brick walls and ceiling fans suspended from black rafters.

110 S. Beach St. (between Magnolia St. and International Speedway Blvd.). ℂ 386/947-2022. Breakfast $2.50–$5; sandwiches, salads, and pizzas $4–$8. AE, DC, DISC, MC, V. Mon–Sat 8am–4pm.

The Cellar ⛄ AMERICAN   An excellent place for ladies who lunch, this tearoom occupies the basement of a 1907 Victorian built as Pres. Warren G. Harding's winter home and now listed on the National Register of Historic Places. The tearoom couldn't be more charming, with reproduction Tiffany windows, fresh flowers, linen tablecloths, china teacups, and a baby grand piano. A lunch menu offers the house signature chicken salad, quiche du jour, vegetarian lasagna, and chicken potpie. In warm months, there's outdoor seating on a covered patio.

220 Magnolia Ave. (between Palmetto and Ridgewood aves.). ℂ 386/258-0011. Soups, salads, and sandwiches $6–$9. AE, DISC, MC, V. Mon–Fri 11am–3pm.

Frappes North ⛄⛄ CREATIVE AMERICAN/FUSION   It's worth the 6-mile drive north to Bobby and Meryl Frappier's sophisticated, hip establishment, where they provide this area's most entertaining cuisine. Several chic dining rooms set the stage for an ever-changing "Menu of the Moment" fusing a multitude of styles. Ingredients are always fresh, and herbs come from the restaurant's garden. Bobby and Meryl offer at least one vegetarian main course. Lunch is a steal here. The restaurant is in a storefront on the mainland stretch of Granada Boulevard, Ormand Beach's main drag.

123 W. Granada Blvd. (FL 40; between Ridgewood Ave. and Washington St.), Ormand Beach. ℂ 386/615-4888. www.frappesnorth.com. Reservations recommended. Main courses $15–$26; lunch $7–$11. AE, MC, V. Mon–Fri 11:30am–2:30pm; Mon–Sat 5–10pm. From the beaches, drive 4 miles north on FL A1A and turn left on Granada Blvd. (FL 40); cross Halifax River to restaurant on right.

McK's Dublin Station AMERICAN/IRISH   Worth knowing about because it serves food in its bar after midnight, this upscale Irish pub has an eclectic menu. The fare includes club sandwiches, burgers, mahimahi wraps, and a few main courses of steak, fish, and chicken. The food isn't exceptional, but it's perfectly acceptable after a few Bass ales. The service is sometimes rushed, but usually pleasant.

218 S. Beach St. (between Magnolia St. and Ivy Lane). ℂ 386/238-3321. Reservations not accepted. Main courses $6–$15; salads and sandwiches $5–$8. AE, MC, V. Mon–Wed 11am–9pm; Thurs–Sat 11am–10pm (bar open later).

Rosario's Ristorante ✦ SOUTHERN ITALIAN/TUSCAN   A Victorian board-
inghouse with lace curtains makes an incongruous setting for this lively restaurant.
The menu delivers pastas with Bolognese and marinara sauces, but the nightly specials
are more intriguing, drawing inspiration from ancient Tuscan recipes. If the mixed
grill of squirrel, pheasant, rabbit, and quail in a hunter's sauce doesn't appeal to you,
opt for grouper Livornese. Many nights, there's music in the cozy bar.

In Live Oak Inn, 448 S. Beach St. (at Loomis Ave.). ⓒ **386/258-6066.** Reservations recommended. Main courses
$12–$24. MC, V. Tues–Sat 5–10pm.

DAYTONA BEACH AFTER DARK

Check the Friday edition of the Daytona Beach *News-Journal* (www.n-jcenter.com)
for its weekly "Go-Do," and the Sunday edition for the "Master Calendar" section,
which lists upcoming events. Other good sources listing nighttime entertainment are
Happenings Magazine and *Backstage Pass Magazine,* two tabloids available at the visitor center (see "Essentials," earlier in this chapter) and in many hotel lobbies.

Ghost tours are led by certified ghost hunters who merge legend with science.
You're guaranteed to have a spooky time (at least it's more interesting than most
touristy ghost tours). A portion of all proceeds goes to cemetery preservation and
restoration, so at least you can feel good about the fee. Tickets are $8 per person, free
for children under 6. Contact **Haunts of Daytona** (ⓒ **386/253-6034;** www.haunts
ofdaytona.com) for tours and times.

THE PERFORMING ARTS   The city-operated **Peabody Auditorium,** 600 Auditorium Blvd., between Noble Street and Wild Olive Avenue (box office ⓒ **386/254-
4545** or 386/671-3460), is Daytona's major venue for serious art, including concerts
by the local Symphony Society (ⓒ **386/253-2901**). Professional actors perform
Broadway musicals during winter and summer at the **Seaside Music Theater,** 176 N.
Beach St., downtown (ⓒ **800/854-5592** or 386/252-6200; www.seasidemusic
theater.org). The **Oceanfront Bandshell** (ⓒ **386/671-3400**), on the boardwalk,
hosts a series of free big-name concerts every Sunday night from early June to Labor
Day. It's also the scene of raucous spring-break concerts.

THE CLUB & BAR SCENE   **Main Street** and **Seabreeze Boulevard** on the beach
are happening areas where dozens of bars (and a few topless shows) cater to leather-
clad bikers.

The **Boot Hill Saloon,** 310 Main St. (ⓒ **386/258-9506**), is a bluesy, brew-sy
honky-tonk especially popular during race and bike weeks.

If line dancing is your thang, then scoot your boots over to the **Rockin' Ranch,** 801
S. Nova Rd. (ⓒ **386/947-0785**), an über-fun country-western bar with live music
and line-dancing lessons.

A popular beachfront bar for more than 40 years, the **Ocean Deck Restaurant &
Beach Club,** 127 S. Ocean Ave. (ⓒ **386/253-5224;** see "Where to Dine," above), is
packed with a mix of locals and tourists, young and old, who come for live music and
cheap drinks. Reggae or ska bands play after 9:30pm. There's valet parking after dark,
or leave your vehicle at Ocean Deck's Reggae Republic surf shop on Atlantic Avenue.

Appendix A:
Orlando in Depth

Orlando may have begun life as a sleepy little southern town, but it sure didn't stay that way for long. Over the years, the city has dramatically transformed itself into an international vacation destination and the theme park capital of the world. Orlando welcomes over 46 million visitors annually from all over the globe. What began with plantations, cattle ranches, and orange groves now boasts the world's greatest collection of thrill rides, fine dining, luxury accommodations, and superior shopping—not to mention an array of cultural and natural attractions. This, however, did not all happen overnight. Over the years, Orlando has felt its fair share of growing pains, even during its earliest days.

SETTLERS VS. SEMINOLES: THE ROAD TO STATEHOOD Florida history dates to 1513—more than a century before the Pilgrims landed at Plymouth Rock—when Ponce de León, a sometimes misguided explorer, spied the shoreline and lush greenery of Florida's Atlantic coast while he was looking for "the fountain of youth." He named it *La Florida*—"the place of flowers." After years of alternating Spanish, French, and British rule, the territory was ceded (by Spain) to the United States in 1821. Lost in the international shuffle were the Seminole Indians. After migrating from Georgia and the Carolinas in the late 18th century to some of Florida's richest farmlands, they were viewed by the *new* Americans as an obstacle to white settlement. A series of compromise treaties and violent clashes

between settlers and the Seminoles continued through 1832, when a young warrior named Osceola strode up to the bargaining table, slammed his knife into the papers on it, and, pointing to the quivering blade, proclaimed, "The only treaty I will ever make is this!"

With that dramatic statement, the hostilities worsened. The Seminoles' guerrilla-style warfare thwarted the U.S. Army's attempt to remove them for almost 8 years, during which time many of the resisters drifted south into the interior of Central Florida. In what is today the Orlando area, the white settlers built Fort Gatlin in 1838 to offer protection to pioneer homesteaders. The Seminoles kept up a fierce rebellion until 1842, when, undefeated, they accepted a treaty whereby their remaining numbers (about 300) were given land and promised peace. The same year, the Armed Occupation Act offered 160 acres to any pioneer willing to settle in the area for a minimum of 5 years. The land was fertile: Wild turkeys and deer abounded in the woods, grazing land for cattle was equally plentiful, and dozens of lakes provided fish for settlers and water for livestock. In 1843, what had been Mosquito County was more invitingly renamed Orange County. And with the Seminoles more or less out of the picture (though sporadic uprisings still occurred), the Territorial General Legislature petitioned Congress for statehood. On March 3, 1845, President John Tyler signed a bill making Florida the 27th state.

Settlements and statehood notwithstanding, at the middle of the 19th century, the Orlando area (then named Jernigan for one of its first settlers) consisted largely of pristine lakes and pine-forested wilderness. There were no roads, and you could ride all day (if you could find a trail) without meeting a soul. The Jernigans successfully raised cattle, and their homestead was given a post office in 1850. It became a way stop for travelers and the seat of future development. In 1856, the boundaries of Orange County were revised, and, thanks to the manipulations of resident James Gamble Speer, a member of the Indian Removal Commission, Fort Gatlin (Jernigan) became its official seat.

How the fledgling town came to be named Orlando is a matter of some speculation. Some say Speer renamed the town after a dearly loved friend, whereas other sources say it was named after a Shakespearean character in *As You Like It*. But the most accepted version is that the town was named for plantation owner Orlando Reeves (or Rees), whose homestead had been burned out in a skirmish. For years, it was thought a marker discovered near the shores of Lake Eola, in what is now downtown, marked his grave. But Reeves died later, in South Carolina. It's assumed the name carved in the tree was a marker for others who were on the Indians' trail.

Whatever the origin, Orlando was officially recognized by the U.S. Postmaster in 1857.

THE 1860s: CIVIL WAR/CATTLE WARS

Throughout the early 1860s, cotton plantations and cattle ranches became the hallmarks of Central Florida. A cotton empire ringed Orlando. Log cabins went up along the lakes and the pioneers eked out a somewhat lonely existence, separated from each other by miles of farmland. But there were troubles brewing in the 31-state nation that soon devastated Orlando's planters. By 1859, it was obvious that only a war would resolve the slavery issue. In 1861, Florida became the third state to secede from the Union, and the modest progress it had achieved came to a standstill. The Stars and Bars flew from every flagpole, and local men enlisted in the Confederate army, leaving the fledgling town in poverty. A federal blockade made it difficult to obtain necessities and many slaves fled. In 1866, the Confederate troops of Florida surrendered, the remaining slaves were freed, and a ragtag group of defeated soldiers returned to Orlando. They found a dying cotton industry, unable to function without slave labor. In 1868, Florida was readmitted to the Union.

Its untended cotton fields having gone to seed, Orlando concentrated on cattle ranching, a business heavily taxed by the

Dateline

- **1843** Mosquito County in Central Florida is renamed Orange County.
- **1856** Orlando becomes the seat of Orange County.
- **1875** Orlando is incorporated as a municipality.
- **1880** The South Florida Railroad paves the way for the expansion of Orlando's agricultural markets. Swamp

cabbage hits an all-time high on the commodities market.
- **1884** Fire destroys much of Orlando's fledgling business district.
- **1894–95** Freezing temperatures destroy the citrus crops, wreaking havoc on the groves and causing many growers to lose everything.
- **1910–25** A land boom hits Florida. Fortunes are made overnight.

- **1926** The land boom goes bust. Fortunes are lost overnight.
- **1929** An invasion of Mediterranean fruit flies devastates Orlando's citrus industry. But, who cares? Here comes the stock market crash.
- **1939–45** World War II revives Orlando's ailing economy.

continues

Fun Fact **A Fountain of Fruit**

Legend has it that Florida's citrus industry has its roots in seeds spit onto the ground by Ponce de León and his followers as they traversed the state searching for the fountain of youth. The seeds supposedly germinated in the rich Florida soil.

---

government, and one that ushered in an era of lawlessness and violence. A famous battle involving two families, the Barbers and the Mizells, left at least nine men dead in 2 months in a Florida version of the Hatfields and McCoys.

Like frontier cattle towns out West, post–Civil War Orlando was short on civilized behavior. Gunfights, brawls, and murders were commonplace. But as the 1860s came to an end, large-herd owners from other parts of the state moved into the area and began organizing the industry in a less chaotic fashion. Branding and penning greatly reduced rustling, though they didn't totally eliminate the problem. Even a century later—as recently as 1973—soaring beef prices caused a rash of cattle thievery. Some traditions die hard. Even today, there are a number of rustling complaints each year.

AN ORANGE TREE GROWS IN ORLANDO In the 1870s, articles in national magazines began luring large numbers of Americans to Central Florida with promises of fertile land and a warm climate. In Orlando, public roads, schools, and churches sprang up to serve the newcomers, many of whom replanted defunct cotton fields with citrus groves. Orlando was incorporated under state law in 1875, and boundaries and a city government were established.

New settlers poured in from all over the country, businesses flourished, and by the end of the year the town had its first newspaper, the *Orange County Reporter*. The first locomotive of the South Florida Railroad chugged into town in 1880, sparking a building and land boom—the first of many. Orlando got sidewalks and its first bank in 1883, the same year the town voted itself "dry" in hopes of averting the fist fights and brawls that ensued when cowboys crowded into local saloons every Saturday night for some rowdy R & R. For many years, the city continued to vote itself alternately wet and dry, but it made little difference. Legal or not, liquor was always readily available.

- **1964** Walt Disney begins surreptitiously buying Central Florida farmland, purchasing more than 28,000 acres for nearly $5.5 million.
- **1965** Disney announces his plan to build the world's most spectacular theme park, in Orlando.
- **1966** Walt Disney dies of lung cancer.
- **1971** The Magic Kingdom opens its gates for the first time.

- **1972** A new 1-day attendance mark is set December 27, when 72,328 people visit the Magic Kingdom. It will be broken almost every year thereafter.
- **1973** SeaWorld opens with a splash in Orlando.
- **1979** Mickey Mouse welcomes the Magic Kingdom's 100-millionth visitor, 8-year-old Kurt Miller from Kingsville, Maryland.

- **1982** Epcot opens with vast hoopla. Participating celebrities include former president Richard Nixon and New York Yankees president George Steinbrenner.
- **1989** WDW launches Disney–MGM Studios (offering a behind-the-scenes look at Tinseltown), Typhoon Lagoon (a 56-acre water theme park), and Pleasure Island (a nightclub district for adults).

FIRE & ICE In January 1884, a grocery fire that started at 4am wiped out blocks of businesses, including the *Orange County Reporter*. But 19th-century Orlando was a bit like a Frank Capra movie. The town rallied around, providing a new location for the paper and presenting its publisher, Mahlon Gore, with $1,200 in cash to help defray losses, and $300 in new subscriptions. The paper not only survived, it flourished. And the city, realizing the need, created its first fire brigade. By August 1884, a census revealed a population of 1,666. That same year, 600,000 boxes of oranges were shipped from Florida to points north—most of those boxes originating in Orlando. By 1885, Orlando was a viable town, boasting as many as 50 businesses. This isn't to say it was New York. Razorback hogs roamed the streets and alligator wrestling was major entertainment.

Disaster struck a week after Christmas in 1894, when the temperature plummeted to an unseasonable 24°F (–4°C). Water pipes burst and orange blossoms froze, blackened, and died. The freeze continued for 3 days, wrecking the citrus crop for the year.

Many grove owners went bust, and those who remained were hit with a second devastating freeze the following year. Tens of thousands of trees died in the killing frost. Small growers were wiped out, but large conglomerates that could afford to buy up the small growers' properties at bargain prices and wait for new groves to mature assured the survival of the industry.

SPECULATION FEVER: GOOD DEALS, BAD DEALS . . . As Orlando entered the 20th century, citrus and agriculture surpassed cattle ranching as the mainstays of the local economy. Stray cows no longer had to be shooed from the railway tracks. Streets were being paved and electricity and telephone service installed. The population at the turn of the 20th century was 2,481. In 1902, the city passed its first automobile laws, which included an in-town speed limit of 5 mph. In 1904, the city flooded. And in 1905, it suffered a drought that ended—miraculously or coincidentally—on a day when all faiths united at the local First Baptist Church to pray for rain. By 1910, prosperity returned, and Orlando, with a population of nearly 4,000, was in a small way becoming a tourism and convention center. World War I brought further industrial growth and a real-estate boom, not just to Orlando, but to all of Florida. Millions of immigrants, speculators, and builders descended on the state in search of a quick buck. As land speculation reached a fever pitch and property was bought and resold almost overnight, many citrus groves gave way to urbanization. Preeminent Orlando

- **1990** Universal Studios Florida opens, bringing the movies to life for all who enter its gates.
- **1993** SeaWorld expands, and Universal Studios unleashes the fearsome *Jaws*.
- **1998** Disney starts its own cruise line and opens most of Animal Kingdom. Universal opens CityWalk, a vast new entertainment complex. Disney's West Side, Pleasure Island, and Disney Village Marketplace become known as Downtown Disney.
- **1999** Islands of Adventure, Universal Orlando's second theme park, opens, featuring stomach-churning thrill rides. The final section of Animal Kingdom, Asia, opens. The Disney Cruise Line launches Good Ship No. 2, the *Wonder*.
- **2000** SeaWorld opens its second park, Discovery Cove, offering a chance to swim with the fishes, *er*, dolphins. SeaWorld also delivers its first roller coaster, Kraken. In December, Universal opens its second resort, the Hard Rock Hotel.
- **2001** Church Street Station closes its doors for good. The tourist industry takes a blow due to the September 11, 2001, terrorist attacks.

continues

Fun Fact   **Liquor Ain't Quicker**

The "Wet/Dry" battle in Orlando continued until 1998, when the city removed "Blue Laws" that restricted the sale of liquor on Sunday within the city limits.

---

builder and promoter Carl Dann described the action: "It finally became nothing more than a gambling machine, each man buying on a shoestring, betting dollars a bigger fool would come along and buy his option."

Quite suddenly, the bubble burst. A July 1926 issue of the *Nation* provided the obituary for the Florida land boom: "The world's greatest poker game, played with lots instead of chips, is over. And the players are now . . . paying up." Construction slowed to a trickle, and many newcomers who came to Florida to jump on the bandwagon fled to their homes in the North. Though Orlando wasn't quite as hard hit as Miami—scene of the greediest land grabs—some belt-tightening was in order. Nevertheless, the city managed to build a municipal airport in 1928. Then came a Mediterranean fruit-fly infestation that crippled the citrus industry. Hundreds of thousands of acres of land in quarantined areas had to be cleared of fruit, and vast quantities of boxed fruit were destroyed. The 1929 stock market crash that precipitated the

Great Depression added an exclamation point to Florida's ruined economy.

. . . & NEW DEALS President Franklin D. Roosevelt's New Deal helped the state climb back on its feet. The Works Progress Administration (WPA) put 40,000 unemployed Floridians back to work—work that included hundreds of public projects in Orlando. Of these, the most important was the expansion and resurfacing of the city's airport. By 1936, the tourist trade had revived somewhat, construction was up once again, and the state began attracting a broader range of visitors. But the event that finally lifted Florida—and the nation—out of the Depression was World War II.

Orlando had weathered the Great Depression. Now it prepared for war with the construction of army bases, housing for servicemen, and training facilities. Enlisted men poured into the city. The airport was again enlarged and equipped with barracks, a military hospital, administration buildings, and mess halls. By 1944, Orlando had a second airport and was known as "Florida's Air Capital,"

- **2002–03** Universal opens its third resort, the Royal Pacific.
- **2003** Disney's Pop Century Resort opens its first phase. The Waterfront entertainment district makes a splashy debut at SeaWorld.
- **2004** Cypress Gardens reopens as Cypress Gardens Adventure Park, featuring new thrill rides, water shows, concerts, and its famous botanical gardens.
- **2006** Expedition Everest becomes the first true thrill ride to debut at Animal Kingdom. The Ron Jon Surf Park opens, allowing surfers a chance to ride the waves indoors at Festival Bay. SeaWorld debuts a new Shamu whale show.

home to major aircraft and aviation-parts manufacturers. Thousands of servicemen did part of their hitch in Orlando, and, when the war ended, many returned to settle here.

POSTWAR PROSPERITY By 1950, Orlando, with a population of 51,826, was the financial and transportation hub of Central Florida. The city shared the bullish economy of the 1950s with the rest of the nation. In the face of the Cold War, the Orlando air base remained and grew, funneling millions of dollars into the local economy. Florida's population increased by a whopping 78.7% during the decade—making it America's 10th-most populated state—and tourists came in droves, nearly 4.5 million in 1950.

One reason for the influx was the advent of the air conditioner, which made life in Florida *infinitely* more pleasant. Also fueling Orlando's economy was a brand-new industry arriving in nearby Cape Canaveral in 1955—the government-run space program. Cape Canaveral became NASA's headquarters, including the Apollo rocket program that eventually blasted Neil Armstrong toward his "giant leap for mankind." During the same decade, the Glenn L. Martin Company (later Martin Marietta), builder of the Matador Missile, purchased 10 square miles for a plant 4 miles south of Orlando. Its advent sparked further industrial growth and property values soared. More than 60 new industries moved to the area in 1959. But even the most optimistic Orlando boosters couldn't foresee the glorious future that was the city's ultimate destiny.

THE DISNEY DECADES In 1964, Walt Disney began secretly buying millions of dollars worth of Central Florida farmland. As vast areas of land were purchased in lots of 5,000 acres here, 20,000 there—at remarkably high prices—rumors flew as to who needed so much land and had the money to acquire it. Some thought it was Howard Hughes; others, the space program. Speculation was rife almost to the very day, November 15, 1965 ("D" Day for Orlando), when Uncle Walt arrived in town and announced his plans to build the world's most spectacular theme park ("bigger and better than Disneyland"). In a 2-year construction effort, Disney employed 9,000 people. Land speculation reached unprecedented heights, as hotel chains and restaurateurs grabbed up property near the proposed park. Mere swampland sold for millions. The total cost of the project by its October 1971 opening was $400 million. Mickey Mouse escorted the first visitor into the Magic Kingdom, and numerous celebrities, from Bob Hope to Julie Andrews, took part in the opening ceremonies. In Walt Disney World's first 2 years, the attraction drew 20 million visitors and employed 13,000 people. The sleepy citrus-growing town of Orlando had become the "Action Center of Florida," and the fastest-growing city in the state.

Additional attractions multiplied faster than fruit flies, and hundreds of firms relocated their businesses to the area. SeaWorld, a major theme park, came to town in 1973. All the while, Walt Disney World continued to grow and expand, adding Epcot in 1982 and Disney–MGM Studios in 1989, along with water parks, more than a dozen

---

(*Fun Fact* **In the Words of Walt Disney**

Why be a governor or a senator when you can be king of Disneyland?
  You can dream, create, design, and build the most wonderful place in the world . . . but it requires people to make the dream a reality.

"official" resorts, a shopping/restaurant village, campgrounds, a vast array of recreational facilities, and several other adjuncts that are thoroughly described in this book. In 1998, Disney opened yet another theme park, this one dedicated to zoological entertainment and aptly called Animal Kingdom.

Universal Orlando, whose Universal Studios Florida park opened in 1990, continues to expand and keep the stakes high. In late 1998, it unveiled a new entertainment district, CityWalk, and in 1999, it opened Islands of Adventure, a second theme park including attractions dedicated to Dr. Seuss, Marvel Comics, and Jurassic Park. Also in 1999, it opened the Portofino Bay Hotel, a 750-room Loews property. In 2001, the curtain went up on the Hard Rock Hotel, and in summer 2002, the Royal Pacific resort opened as Universal announced plans to add two more hotels to the property in the next decade.

SeaWorld, too, got in on the action when it opened its $100-million sister park, Discovery Cove, in 2000. Now, visitors have the chance to swim with dolphins even in landlocked Orlando.

While the tourist economy suffered for almost 2 years after the September 11, 2001, terrorist attacks, the industry has regained much of its strength as the years have passed. Indeed, one unfortunate casualty of the economic slowdown following the attacks, Cypress Gardens, closed its doors in the spring of 2003, but has since reopened with a new name, Cypress Gardens Adventure Park, and a new lineup of attractions. Disney, Universal, and SeaWorld, are, as usual, in a building mode, albeit not as enthusiastically as they were during the late 1990s. All the parks have added new attractions, ranging from Soarin' at Epcot to Universal's Fear Factor Live, to SeaWorld's new entertainment and dining district, the Waterfront. In 2005, in honor of California sibling Disneyland's 50th anniversary, Disney World unveiled new shows, services, rides, and attractions. The year 2006 brought with it the addition of Expedition Everest, Animal Kingdom's first real thrill ride.

In the resort department, Disney opened up the first phase of its Pop Century Resort in 2003 and its new Saratoga Springs Resort in mid-2004, and construction continues on both resorts. And Disney's not the only one in a building frame of mind. Springing up and spreading out to untapped areas just south of Disney are new luxury destination resorts, further expanding the city's tourist district and Mickey's reach. Recent newcomers include the country's first ever Nickelodeon resort, as well as the multimillion-dollar Reunion Resort and Club. And those are just a taste of what will likely be many new debuts throughout the city over the next few years. Given the pace of progress in this ever-changing city, it's a sure bet they'll be joined by new resorts, rides, and shopping and dining experiences.

Appendix B:
Useful Toll-Free Numbers
& Websites

1 Airlines

Aer Lingus
☎ 800/474-7424 in the U.S.
☎ 01/886-8888 in Ireland
www.aerlingus.com

Aero Mexico
☎ 800/237-6639 in the U.S.
☎ 01/800-021-4010 in Mexico
www.aeromexico.com

Air Canada
☎ 888/247-2262
www.aircanada.ca

Air New Zealand
☎ 800/262-1234 or 800/262-2468 in
 the U.S.
☎ 800/663-5494 in Canada
☎ 0800/737-767 in New Zealand
www.airnewzealand.com

AirTran Airlines
☎ 800/247-8726
www.airtran.com

Alaska Airlines
☎ 800/426-0333
www.alaskaair.com

American Airlines
☎ 800/433-7300
www.aa.com

American Trans Air
☎ 800/225-2995
www.ata.com

America West Airlines
☎ 800/235-9292
www.americawest.com

British Airways
☎ 800/247-9297
☎ 0345/222-111 or 0845/77-333-77
 in Britain
www.british-airways.com

Continental Airlines
☎ 800/525-0280
www.continental.com

Delta Air Lines
☎ 800/221-1212
www.delta.com

Frontier Airlines
☎ 800/432-1359
www.frontierairlines.com

Hawaiian Airlines
☎ 800/367-5320
www.hawaiianair.com

JetBlue Airways
☎ 800/538-2583
www.jetblue.com

Midwest Express
☎ 800/452-2022
www.midwestexpress.com

Northwest Airlines
☎ 800/225-2525
www.nwa.com

Qantas
☎ 800/227-4500 in the U.S.
☎ 612/9691-3636 in Australia
www.qantas.com

Spirit Airlines
☎ 800/772-7117
www.spiritair.com

Southwest Airlines
© 800/435-9792
www.southwest.com

Song
© 800/359-7664
www.flysong.com

Ted
© 800/225-5833
www.flyted.com

United Airlines
© 800/241-6522
www.united.com

US Airways
© 800/428-4322
www.usairways.com

Virgin Atlantic Airways
© 800/862-8621 in continental U.S.
© 0293/747-747 in Britain
www.virgin-atlantic.com

2 Car-Rental Agencies

Alamo
© 800/327-9633
www.goalamo.com

Avis
© 800/331-1212 in continental U.S.
© 800/TRY-AVIS in Canada
www.avis.com

Budget
© 800/527-0700
www.budget.com

Dollar
© 800/800-4000
www.dollar.com

Enterprise
© 800/325-8007
www.enterprise.com

Hertz
© 800/654-3131
www.hertz.com

Luxury Rental Cars of Orlando
© 888/641-9211
www.luxrentals.com

National
© 800/CAR-RENT
www.nationalcar.com

Payless
© 800/PAYLESS
www.paylesscarrental.com

Thrifty
© 800/367-2277
www.thrifty.com

3 Major Hotel & Motel Chains

AmeriSuites
© 800/833-1516
www.amerisuites.com

Baymont Inns & Suites
© 800/301-0200
www.baymontinns.com

Best Western International
© 800/528-1234
www.bestwestern.com

Clarion Hotels
© 800/CLARION
www.clarionhotel.com or
www.hotelchoice.com

Comfort Inns
© 800/228-5150
www.hotelchoice.com

Country Inn and Suites
© 888/201-1746
www.countryinns.com

Courtyard by Marriott
© 800/321-2211
www.courtyard.com or
www.marriott.com

Crowne Plaza
© 877/239-1222
www.crowneplaza.com

Days Inn
📞 800/325-2525
www.daysinn.com

Doubletree Hotels
📞 800/222-TREE
www.doubletree.com

Econo Lodges
📞 800/55-ECONO
www.hotelchoice.com

Embassy Suites
📞 800/362-2779
www.embassy-suites.com

Fairfield Inn by Marriott
📞 800/228-2800
www.marriott.com

Hampton Inn
📞 800/HAMPTON
www.hampton-inn.com

Hawthorn Suites
📞 800/527-1133
www.hawthorn.com

Hilton Garden Inn
📞 800/774-1500
www.hiltongardeninn.com

Hilton Hotels
📞 800/HILTONS
www.hilton.com

Holiday Inn
📞 800/HOLIDAY
www.basshotels.com

Homewood Suites
📞 800/225-5466
www.Homewood-suites.com

Howard Johnson
📞 800/654-2000
www.hojo.com

Hyatt Hotels & Resorts
📞 800/228-9000
www.hyatt.com

Inter-Continental Hotels & Resorts
📞 888/567-8725
www.interconti.com

ITT Sheraton
📞 800/325-3535
www.starwood.com

Knights Inn
📞 800/843-5644
www.knightsinn.com

La Quinta Motor Inns
📞 800/531-5900
www.laquinta.com

Loews Hotels
📞 800/23-loews
www.loewshotels.com

Marriott Hotels
📞 800/228-9290
www.marriott.com

Motel 6
📞 800/4-MOTEL6 (800/466-8356)
www.motel6.com

Quality Inns
📞 800/228-5151
www.hotelchoice.com

Radisson Hotels International
📞 800/333-3333
www.radisson.com

Ramada Inns
📞 800/2-RAMADA
www.ramada.com

Red Carpet Inns
📞 800/251-1962
www.reservahost.com

Red Roof Inns
📞 800/843-7663
www.redroof.com

Renaissance Hotels
📞 800/228-9290
www.renaissancehotels.com

Residence Inn by Marriott
📞 800/331-3131
www.marriott.com

Ritz-Carlton
📞 800/241-3333
www.ritzcarlton.com

Rodeway Inns
Ⓒ 800/228-2000
www.hotelchoice.com

Sheraton Hotels & Resorts
Ⓒ 800/325-3535
www.sheraton.com

Sleep Inn
Ⓒ 800/753-3746
www.sleepinn.com

Springhill Suites
Ⓒ 888/287-9400
www.springhillsuites.com

Staybridge Suites
Ⓒ 800/238-8000
www.staybridge.com

Super 8 Motels
Ⓒ 800/800-8000
www.super8.com

Travelodge
Ⓒ 800/255-3050
www.travelodge.com

Westin Hotels & Resorts
Ⓒ 800/937-8461
www.westin.com

Wyndham Hotels and Resorts
Ⓒ 800/822-4200 in continental U.S.
and Canada
www.wyndham.com

Index

See also Accommodations and Restaurant indexes, below.

Frommer's® Complete Travel Guides

Alaska
Amalfi Coast
American Southwest
Amsterdam
Argentina & Chile
Arizona
Atlanta
Australia
Austria
Bahamas
Barcelona
Beijing
Belgium, Holland & Luxembourg
Belize
Bermuda
Boston
Brazil
British Columbia & the Canadian Rockies
Brussels & Bruges
Budapest & the Best of Hungary
Buenos Aires
Calgary
California
Canada
Cancún, Cozumel & the Yucatán
Cape Cod, Nantucket & Martha's Vineyard
Caribbean
Caribbean Ports of Call
Carolinas & Georgia
Chicago
China
Colorado
Costa Rica
Croatia
Cuba
Denmark
Denver, Boulder & Colorado Springs
Edinburgh & Glasgow
England
Europe
Europe by Rail

Florence, Tuscany & Umbria
Florida
France
Germany
Greece
Greek Islands
Hawaii
Hong Kong
Honolulu, Waikiki & Oahu
India
Ireland
Italy
Jamaica
Japan
Kauai
Las Vegas
London
Los Angeles
Los Cabos & Baja
Madrid
Maine Coast
Maryland & Delaware
Maui
Mexico
Montana & Wyoming
Montréal & Québec City
Moscow & St. Petersburg
Munich & the Bavarian Alps
Nashville & Memphis
New England
Newfoundland & Labrador
New Mexico
New Orleans
New York City
New York State
New Zealand
Northern Italy
Norway
Nova Scotia, New Brunswick & Prince Edward Island
Oregon
Paris
Peru

Philadelphia & the Amish Country
Portugal
Prague & the Best of the Czech Republic
Provence & the Riviera
Puerto Rico
Rome
San Antonio & Austin
San Diego
San Francisco
Santa Fe, Taos & Albuquerque
Scandinavia
Scotland
Seattle
Seville, Granada & the Best of Andalusia
Shanghai
Sicily
Singapore & Malaysia
South Africa
South America
South Florida
South Pacific
Southeast Asia
Spain
Sweden
Switzerland
Texas
Thailand
Tokyo
Toronto
Turkey
USA
Utah
Vancouver & Victoria
Vermont, New Hampshire & Maine
Vienna & the Danube Valley
Vietnam
Virgin Islands
Virginia
Walt Disney World® & Orlando
Washington, D.C.
Washington State

Frommer's® Dollar-a-Day Guides

Australia from $60 a Day
California from $70 a Day
England from $75 a Day
Europe from $85 a Day
Florida from $70 a Day

Hawaii from $80 a Day
Ireland from $90 a Day
Italy from $90 a Day
London from $95 a Day

New York City from $90 a Day
Paris from $95 a Day
San Francisco from $70 a Day
Washington, D.C. from $80 a Day

Frommer's® Portable Guides

Acapulco, Ixtapa & Zihuatanejo
Amsterdam
Aruba
Australia's Great Barrier Reef
Bahamas
Berlin
Big Island of Hawaii
Boston
California Wine Country
Cancún
Cayman Islands
Charleston
Chicago

Disneyland®
Dominican Republic
Dublin
Florence
Las Vegas
Las Vegas for Non-Gamblers
London
Los Angeles
Maui
Nantucket & Martha's Vineyard
New Orleans
New York City
Paris

Portland
Puerto Rico
Puerto Vallarta, Manzanillo & Guadalajara
Rio de Janeiro
San Diego
San Francisco
Savannah
Vancouver
Venice
Virgin Islands
Washington, D.C.
Whistler

Frommer's® Cruise Guides

Alaska Cruises & Ports of Call

Cruises & Ports of Call

European Cruises & Ports of Call

FROMMER'S® DAY BY DAY GUIDES

Amsterdam	London	Rome
Chicago	New York City	San Francisco
Florence & Tuscany	Paris	Venice

FROMMER'S® NATIONAL PARK GUIDES

Algonquin Provincial Park	National Parks of the American West	Yosemite and Sequoia & Kings
Banff & Jasper	Rocky Mountain	Canyon
Grand Canyon	Yellowstone & Grand Teton	Zion & Bryce Canyon

FROMMER'S® MEMORABLE WALKS

Chicago	New York	Rome
London	Paris	San Francisco

FROMMER'S® WITH KIDS GUIDES

Chicago	National Parks	Toronto
Hawaii	New York City	Walt Disney World® & Orlando
Las Vegas	San Francisco	Washington, D.C.
London		

SUZY GERSHMAN'S BORN TO SHOP GUIDES

Born to Shop: France	Born to Shop: Italy	Born to Shop: New York
Born to Shop: Hong Kong, Shanghai	Born to Shop: London	Born to Shop: Paris
& Beijing		

FROMMER'S® IRREVERENT GUIDES

Amsterdam	Los Angeles	Rome
Boston	Manhattan	San Francisco
Chicago	New Orleans	Walt Disney World®
Las Vegas	Paris	Washington, D.C.
London		

FROMMER'S® BEST-LOVED DRIVING TOURS

Austria	Germany	Northern Italy
Britain	Ireland	Scotland
California	Italy	Spain
France	New England	Tuscany & Umbria

THE UNOFFICIAL GUIDES®

Adventure Travel in Alaska	Hawaii	Paris
Beyond Disney	Ireland	San Francisco
California with Kids	Las Vegas	South Florida including Miami &
Central Italy	London	the Keys
Chicago	Maui	Walt Disney World®
Cruises	Mexico's Best Beach Resorts	Walt Disney World® for
Disneyland®	Mini Las Vegas	Grown-ups
England	Mini Mickey	Walt Disney World® with Kids
Florida	New Orleans	Washington, D.C.
Florida with Kids	New York City	

SPECIAL-INTEREST TITLES

Athens Past & Present	Frommer's Exploring America by RV
Cities Ranked & Rated	Frommer's NYC Free & Dirt Cheap
Frommer's Best Day Trips from London	Frommer's Road Atlas Europe
Frommer's Best RV & Tent Campgrounds	Frommer's Road Atlas Ireland
in the U.S.A.	Retirement Places Rated

FROMMER'S® PHRASEFINDER DICTIONARY GUIDES

French	Italian	Spanish